CARDIFF CITY FOOTBALL CLUB
The Official History of:
The Bluebirds
By John Crooks

Published by:

YORE PUBLICATIONS

12 The Furrows,
Harefield, Middx.
UB9 6AT.

Printed by:
THE BATH PRESS

ISBN 0 9513321 8 X

Acknowledgements:
(In random order)

Cardiff City Football Club: For their enthusiasm and interest in this project, and for allowing the Club crest, photographs and programmes to be reproduced.

Western Mail and Echo Ltd.: For allowing their photographs, where known, to be reproduced from Cardiff City programmes.

Members of the Association of Football Statisticians: Too many to mention individually, but all those who supplied information.

Richard Shepherd: B.B.C. Radio Wales football commentator and historian, who supplied a lot of the archive material reproduced in this book.

Ken Good: An exiled Cardiffian, who helped with the reproduction of many photographs.

To all the players who did not hesitate to talk about their careers and experiences, which form a cornerstone of this book.

Susan: A soccer widow whose support has been invaluable.

Yore Publications: For having the confidence in backing this book.

Dannie Abse: For his foreword.

Published by:
Yore Publications
12 The Furrows, Harefield,
Middx. UB9 6AT.

© John Crooks 1992

....

All rights reserved. No part of this publication may be reproduced or copied in any manner without the prior permission in writing of the copyright holder.

British Library Cataloguing-in-Publication Data.
A catalogue record for this book
is available from the British Library.

ISBN 0 9513321 8 X

- CONTENTS -

Chapter:
1. Riverside to Ninian Park — 5.
2. War, and the last days of non-League football — 12.
3. The League, Division 1 and the Bluebirds at Wembley — 14.
4. The pre-war slump years — 32.
5. Peacetime Promotions — 44.
6. The not so swinging Sixties — 74.
7. Not much respite in the Eighties — 112.
8. Bottom Basement .... But ready for a rise again — 131.
9. Ground - Works — 133.
10. The Men who kicked the Ball — 137.
11. Through the Players eyes — 150.

Appendix: Statistical Section - 1910/11 to 1990/91 — 169.

Subscribers List — 320.

- FOREWORD -

Those of us interested in the fortunes of Cardiff City A.F.C. who were lucky enough to read John Crooks's preliminary report, 'Cardiff City Chronology 1920-86', have been looking forward eagerly to the publication of the present volume. He hinted in the introduction to that Chronology that one day he might offer us a more authoritative history of the Bluebirds. And here it is, page after page of comment and facts that detonate old nostalgic remembrances.

I open up a page at random and I hear a military band playing "Happy Days Are Here Again" as the blue-shirted Division 3 (South) of pre-war days run out of the tunnel into pre-war winter sunlight. I turn another page and I recall how, as a small boy, I was handed down amongst a mass of friendly faces from the darkness at the back of the Grangetown Stand right to the front so that I could see my heroes display clearly their rare skills and their common blunders.

Look how, on another page, it's 1937 already and I can hear the crowd near me chanting:

> *A pint of beer, a pint of beer, a Woodbine and a match,*
> *a fourpenny halfpenny walking stick to see the football match.*
> *The ball was in the centre, the referee's whistle blew*
> *and Pugh had his temper and up the wing he flew.*
> *He passed the ball to Walton who didn't know what to do,*
> *he passed the ball to Collins and in the net it flew.*
> *Oh yes we can, we beat Gillingham.*
> *What was the score – four-nil, no more.*
> *Oh play up the boys in blue!*

Yes in those days they weren't shouting, 'kick his effing head in'. At least, not in English.

Only one disappointment about this official history of the Bluebirds. John Crooks hasn't told how Dannie Abse once played for Oswestry against Cardiff City reserves at Ninian Park – was it in 1944 or 1945? Cyril Spiers, the Cardiff manager, invited him to do so when Oswestry turned up with only ten men. In the second half, Abse suddenly found himself clear some thirty yards out, with only the advancing goalkeeper to beat. He heard Cyril Spiers shout hoarsely in the almost empty ground, 'Now's your chance, lad', but fool that he was Abse collided with the goalkeeper and the ball went the wrong side of the right hand post.

Each time I visit Ninian Park I look at that green bit of turf where I muffed it. What a shame. If I had scored, City might have signed me on and I would have appeared in John Crooks's splendid book.

I won't detain you any longer. Read on. Enjoy yourselves. Can you hear the distant roar of the crowd?

Dannie Abse
January 1992.

CHAPTER 1

RIVERSIDE TO NINIAN PARK

CARDIFF RIVERSIDE CRICKET CLUB MEMBERS.

(Left to right) Back Row: B.Hodson, J.Crabtree, W.Canter, P.Allen, W.Allen, W.Highway, A.Davey, J.Pearce, W.Rowley.
Middle Row: A.Sheen, T.Stringer, A.Shea, W.Edmunds, W.B.Wilson, E.W.Holder, C.Dring.
Front Row: G.Stephenson, D.McGregor, J.Redfern, G.Pearce, W.Jenkins, D.Jones.

An enthusiastic amateur cricket club from the Riverside district of Cardiff – in those far off days of gas street lamps, hackney carriages and heavily mustachioed men may seem a strange place to begin a journey that would eventually take in F.A. Cup Finals, competition in all divisions of the Football League, Welsh Cup triumphs and European adventures. But it was in those humble surroundings in 1899 that the seeds of Cardiff City Football Club were sown.

****

The camaraderie of Riverside's amateur cricketers, who played their summer game on the wide open spaces of Sophia Gardens, near Cardiff Castle, was such that meetings were organised to decide as to how the members could be kept together throughout the winter.

Despite the attraction of Rugby Union, the popular choice was to form an Association Football team. Mr Bartley Wilson, a Bristol-born lithographic artist, who despite being an invalid and needing the aid of walking sticks for mobility, was an active member of the cricket club and arranged an inaugural meeting for interested parties in his home at No.1 Coldstream Terrace. Only five people attended, and the project was almost aborted there and then, but a second meeting was proposed which received a better response. From those present the first committee of Riverside Football Club was elected.

The Committee consisted of:-

Messrs. Stanley Barrett, Frank Burfitt, William Canter, E.W. Holder, George Pearce, James Redfern, Andrew Sheen, A.J. Stone and Mr Bartley Wilson (Secretary).

Utilising the sparse facilities at the Sophia Gardens, where a shed had to serve as both a meeting place and dressing rooms, the newly formed team arranged local friendlies in the winter of 1899-1900. They suffered badly in their first fixture - a 1-9 beating by Barry West End. Enthusiasm knows no bounds however, and the club were accepted as members of the Cardiff and District League in 1900.

The first known colours of Riverside were chocolate and amber quartered shirts and black knickers. In the face of competitive local football, the playing strength within the club grew appreciably. This was a period when amateur players could be poached from other clubs, and many would join the organisation that could offer the best in terms of recreation. With their facilities needing to be improved, the Club acquired a disused stable, and the stalwarts successfully converted the building into acceptable premises which had gas and water installed.

An amalgamation with a rival club, Riverside Albion, was undertaken in 1902, and three years later Riverside A.F.C. gained their first recognised honour by winning the Bevan Shield, a local competition.

With the club now on a sound footing the committee felt that Riverside would benefit from a higher grade of football. They began to look at various options open to them, and when Cardiff was made a city in October 1905, they sought to change the club name to Cardiff City. This was refused by the authorities unless the club participated in the South Wales League, the strongest association at that time, which boasted such clubs as Aberdare, Barry District, Cwmparc, Maerdy, Merthyr Town and Ton Pentre, amongst others. Riverside A.F.C. applied for election, were accepted, and in 1908 they were allowed to change their name to Cardiff City.

Around this time the Southern League was in the process of forming a Second Division, and its representative - Mr H. Bradshaw - came to South Wales, where the Association game was beginning to boom, and approached Cardiff City and other Welsh clubs about possible membership, which would also mean adopting professional status. Unfortunately Cardiff City could not meet the standard requirements of an enclosed pitch, turnstiles and adequate spectator facilities, and so the proposal was held in abeyance.

The Club were receiving good support from the public in a traditional rugby stronghold, and when a friendly match was arranged with Crystal Palace of the Southern League, in October 1909, the fixture had to be staged at Cardiff Arms Park. The game resulted in a 3-3 draw, and the gate receipts of £33 delighted the committee so much that a month later Bristol City, then in the Football League First Division, were engaged in a friendly. The attendance was appreciably higher, but the receipts of £50 were swallowed up by Bristol City's guarantee, and the fledgling Cardiff City team received a 7-1 hiding in to the bargain!

Undaunted and determined to overcome such adversities another friendly was arranged, this time against First Division Middlesbrough, at the Harlequins Ground, Newport Road. Much to the delight of the Cardiff public, City defeated a team - which included stars such as Alf Common, the first £1,000 footballer, and England international Steve Bloomer - by 2-1 and the takings resulted in a £39 profit.

At this time the Cardiff City committee were negotiating with the Bute estate for land near Leckwith Common, but these were inconclusive. Instead they were offered an area of waste ground which had been used for refuse between Sloper Road and the railway sidings, land which belonged to the Cardiff Corporation. The club were quoted a seven year lease at £90 per annum for the site, and Mr Bartley Wilson conducted the arrangements with Councillors J. Mander and C. Wall. An agreement was reached when the Corporation gave an undertaking to offer every assistance in the preparation of the ground.

The Cardiff City club were now committed to professionalism, and when admission to the Second Division of the Southern League was accepted in 1910 a prospectus in the name of Cardiff City Association Football Club was issued. Lord Rhondda became the first shareholder and the club was floated, although it took some persuasion by the members to attract patrons.

A Board of Directors was elected which had Mr S.H. Nicholls as the first Chairman. Founder members of the old club Messrs. Charles Kyd, J. McGill, Ivor Parker, L.H. Nash, Frank Burfitt and P. Hansford were included, together with Messrs. J.H. Brain, Walter Empsall, John Pritchard, Walter Riden, David Robertson and Charles Wall. Mr Bartley Wilson continued as Secretary.

Jack Finn was appointed to prepare the new ground, and with the aid of a large number of voluntary helpers plus the promised assistance of Corporation workers, the refuse tips and allotments were levelled and an acceptable playing surface laid. The pitch was enclosed with white picket fencing and ash banking was raised on all four sides for spectators. A small wooden grandstand was built on the Sloper Road side of the ground, and the first changing rooms were erected to the left of the stand, which also incorporated the club offices. Although rather spartan the new ground met the requirements laid down by the Southern League.

When guarantors were needed, Lord Ninian Crichton-Stuart, the second son of the Marquis of Bute, consented his financial support, and in gratitude the Cardiff City club were unanimous in agreeing to call their new home Ninian Park - in preference to the intended title of 'Sloper Park'.

Mr Bartley Wilson assumed the responsibility for team building, and his first professional signing was Welsh-speaking outside-left Jack Evans, a printer born in Bala, North Wales, who was playing for Cwmparc, Near Aberdare. Evans had previously played for Wrexham before receiving a bad shoulder injury which forced him to quit the game when only 20 years of age. He came to Cwmparc in pursuit of his trade, resumed playing with the Valleys club without any ill-effects, and came to City's attention when playing against them in the South Wales League. Evans received a 6 shillings (30p) signing on fee which covered his railway and meal expenses.

Mr Bartley Wilson then appointed Davy McDougall, a left-half with Glasgow Rangers, as player-manager and captain. McDougall had experience of playing in Scotland and Ireland, and had also been with Bristol City. He recruited a number of players, mainly from the North and Scotland, of whom he had personal knowledge. They included:- Goalkeeper Ted Husbands (ex-Liverpool and Wrexham), full-backs John Duffy (ex Dundee) and James McKenzie (ex Millwall and Middlesbrough), right-half Bob Lawrie (ex Belfast Glentoran and Third Lanark), centre-half John Ramsey (ex Dundee and Brechin), outside-right James McDonald (ex QPR and Aberdeen), inside-right John Abley (ex Aston Villa and Treharris), centre-forward Jim Malloch (ex Dundee Centrals) and inside-forward Billy Watts (ex Dundee and Glossop).

One of the entrance paths to Sophia Gardens, where the early fixtures of the Club were played.

Obtaining these players and attracting them to Cardiff was expensive, but Davy McDougall knew that Cardiff City could not possibly progress in the Southern League with the home-spun players who had served the Club so admirably during their pioneering days. The Second Division of the Southern League consisted of only 12 clubs, which would provide only twenty-two games, so Cardiff City agreed to compete also in the Glamorgan League which would employ their players fully over the season.

Aston Villa, the Football League Champions, agreed to play a prestigious friendly match to open Ninian Park, and this took place on Thursday the 1st of September 1910, with the official kick-off being performed by Lord Ninian Crichton-Stuart at 5pm.

The teams were:–

Cardiff City: *Husbands, McKenzie, Duffy, Lawrie, Ramsay, McDougall, McDonald, Abley, Malloch, Watt, Evans.*
Aston Villa: *George, Layton, Kearns, Tranter, Buckley, Logan, Wallace, Gerrish, Reneville, Bache, Hall.*

In an exciting clash that enthraled an estimated crowd of 7,000, Aston Villa won 2-1, and to Jack Evans went the honour of scoring Cardiff City's first goal at Ninian Park. The team were now wearing blue shirts, white shorts and blue stockings which became their registered colours. In time, although exactly when is unknown, Cardiff City would be become nicknamed 'The Bluebirds', which has been part of their folk-lore ever since.

The man who gave his name to Ninian Park.

The programme cover of that first historic match.

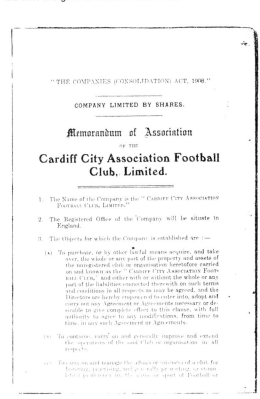

In 1910, Cardiff City became a Limited Company, with seven original shareholders.

THE SOUTHERN LEAGUE YEARS

1910-11 Season: Southern League – Division 2.

Following three matches in the Glamorgan League, in which centre-forward Bob Peake notched five goals, Cardiff City played their opening Southern League Second Division fixture at Ninian Park on the 24th of September 1910. The visitors were Ton Pentre, also making their Southern League bow, and before a crowd estimated at around 8,000, which included a large following from the Rhondda Valleys, City triumphed 4-1 with goals from Bob Peake (two), Billy Watt and Jack Evans.

The successful City line-up consisted of:- *Husbands, McKenzie, Duffy, Lawrie, Ramsay, McDougall, McDonald, Watt, Peake, Malloch, Evans.*

This victory set City on their way to a successful season, during which they spent most of the term up among the promotion contenders. The decision to bring in a large number of experienced professionals proved to be the correct one as City settled comfortably into their new surroundings. City's first defeat in the Southern League came in their sixth match, on the 7th of December, when Aberdare Athletic, as 2-1 victors, became the first team to win at Ninian Park in a League game. With crowds averaging between six and seven thousand, the spectators had to show their resilience against the elements, as the only cover at Ninian Park was the small wooden grandstand with its canvas roof which offered comfort to only 200 people, many of whom were patrons of the club.

City faced a difficult Yuletide on the road (or more correctly on the rail), for, after a sensational 7-4 victory at Kettering on Christmas Eve - Pinch (two), Evans, Peake (three) and McDonald were the scorers - they faced the leaders, Reading, at Elm Park on Boxing Day, and gained a creditable 0-0 draw. The following day City crashed to their heaviest defeat of the season, 0-5 to Stoke, where fatigue obviously paid its toll. After the game, Stoke's former Welsh international defender George Latham, in a chat with City's officials, hinted that he would be interested in a position at Cardiff City.

Player-manager Davy McDougall got his team back on song with four unbeaten matches in which Bob Peake scored seven goals. At lowly Chesham on the 14th of January, the diminutive Peake - who stood at barely 5'7", but had 'dynamite' in his boots - scored four times and Jack Evans blasted a hat-trick as City scorched to a runaway 7-1 win. Promotion looked to be beckoning, and on the 1st of March, George Latham was signed from Stoke as player-coach. But his debut at left-back coincided with City's first defeat in eight games - a 4-2 mauling at Ton Pentre on March the 11th - before a delighted 14,000 crowd. This was probably the turning point in the promotion chase, for the City's form in the final six matches hiccuped badly. Defeats at Ninian Park on successive days over Easter, by Reading and Stoke (both of whom were promoted), condemned City to fourth place in their debut season. Right-half Bob Lawrie was the only ever-present, and with 17 goals in 17 games Bob Peake was leading scorer whilst Jack Evans netted 11 times.

F.A. Cup:
Cardiff City met Bath City in the 4th preliminary round at Ninian Park, winning 3-1 with goals from Bob Peake (two) and Billy Watt. In the 3rd preliminary round City faced Southern League rivals Merthyr Town at Ninian Park but lost disappointingly 0-1, before a crowd of 12,000.

Welsh Cup:
Cardiff City won 1-0 at Maerdy in the first round at Ninian Park, and then swept Tredegar aside with a 4-1 victory. On the 10th of December, City and Ton Pentre fought out a 2-2 draw in the third round at Ninian Park, and the Valleys team won the replay 1-0 five days later.

Throughout that inaugural season the Cardiff players were instructed to report to Ninian Park in the early morning before all home games to assist with removing broken glass, shale and other small items of rubbish that worked its way to the playing surface. Quite often during games, the players wore knee and elbow padding to avoid cuts and grazes!

1911-12 Season: Southern League Division 2:

The Cardiff City Club made two major decisions at the end of the 1910-11 season. The board of directors saw the need for a full-time secretary-manager in order to advance their desire for a higher grade of football, and they advertised the position in the 'Athletic News', the magazine that was read nationwide by the football fraternity.

Of the applications received for the post one candidate stood out above all others – Stockport County secretary-manager Fred Stewart – a 38 year old who had been at Edgeley Park since 1893. Mr Stewart revealed that he had shown an interest in Cardiff City a year earlier when they had turned professional, believing it to be a club of rich potential in an area crying out for a successful football team. Stewart was initially secured on a three year agreement at £4 a week plus bonuses. The club also decided to withdraw from the Glamorgan League and to undertake regular friendly matches, which would maintain continuity for their professionals.

In a summer of hectic activity at Ninian Park, City turned down an attractive offer from Bradford City of £300 plus a friendly match, for outside-left Jack Evans, as the player had no desire to leave. Davy McDougall was retained as a player but clearly did not figure in Mr Stewart's plans, for one of the new secretary-manager's first signings was left half-back Billy Hardy from Heart of Midlothian, who had previously been with Mr Stewart at Stockport County. In fact it was rumoured that the City secretary-manager wanted Hardy so badly that he paid the £25 transfer fee out of his own pocket! In reality the club reimbursed Mr Stewart at a later date. Fred Stewart's knowledge of Scottish and Northern based players immediately bore fruit, as he recruited full-backs Arthur Waters from Stockport County and Bob Leah from Colne, half-back Eddie Thompson from Nelson, Harry Featherstone – a goal grabbing centre-forward from St. Mirren – Harry Tracey, a quicksilver outside-right (also from Colne), and Jack Burton, the stylish Nelson inside-forward.

Work continued throughout the summer on improving facilities at Ninian Park, and on the 15th of August, gas and water was connected to Mr Stewart's office and to the dressing rooms.

It was a vastly changed Cardiff City that opened their Southern League programme against Kettering Town at Ninian Park on September the 2nd. Only four players remained from the team that played regularly under Davy McDougall - goalkeeper Ted Husbands, half-back Bob Lawrie, and forwards Tom Abley and Jack Evans.

Over 6,000 saw City triumph with goals from Jack Burton, Tom Abley and Harry Tracey, and the happy crowd went away convinced that Fred Stewart's team had the makings of promotion contenders. On the 7th of October, Harry Featherstone struck four goals in a 5-1 home win over Cwm Albion.

Three weeks later, George Burton, a new signing from Middlesbrough who was paid £3 a week as against the normal £2, scored a debut goal as City completed the 'double' over the ill-fated mineworkers' team, with their 4-2 victory. Before the end of the season a coal strike prevented Cwm Albion from completing their fixtures, four games were left unplayed, but their results were allowed to stand, which suited City who had already gained the maximum four points.

The new look team settled down and remained largely unchanged, apart from reserve goalkeeper George Germaine filling in for the injured Ted Husbands in mid-season. They looked well set for a promotion place until losing two consecutive and vital games in February. On the 17th of the month, City travelled to Portsmouth, where Pompey were parading their new centre-forward from Barnsley, Harry Taylor, and the debutant delighted the 11,000 crowd at Fratton Park with a goal, as City went down narrowly with a 2-3 scoreline. A week later, 15,000 were at Ninian Park for the key clash with high-riding Merthyr Town, the eventual champions. Although Jack Evans scored for the City, it was the visitors that took the points, with a 2-1 victory, to repeat the scoreline of an F.A. Cup tie of four months earlier. There was much good natured rivalry between the supporters of both clubs, but now Merthyr could lay claim to being the best team in South Wales, something which the Cardiff club sportingly acknowledged. A good season saw the City end up in third place, seven points adrift of the Champions (Merthyr) and Portsmouth, who were both promoted.

F.A.Cup:
The City met local amateurs Cardiff Corinthians at home on the 16th of September, winning comfortably by 3-0, through goals from Harry Featherstone, George Latham and Tom Abley. A fortnight later Maerdy were the visitors and were defeated 2-0, with Featherstone and Abley again scoring. On the 14th of October, the City travelled to Merthyr, and in a 'ding-dong' match earned a replay through Jack Evans' goal in the 1-1 draw. Four days later, however, Merthyr proved the stronger outfit by winning 2-1 at Ninian Park, with Evans again scoring for the City.

Welsh Cup:
This was to prove to be an historic campaign for Cardiff City, for in only their second year in the competition (and as a professional club), they lifted the trophy and brought it to South Wales for the first time. On the 10th of January, a Featherstone goal defeated Treharris Athletic at Ninian Park, and three weeks later City travelled to Wrexham where they succeeded in defeating the North Wales team by 2-1, with goals from Featherstone and Jack Burton.

The City met Chester in the semi-final, on the 23rd of March, and following a 1-1 draw they triumphed 2-1 in the replay four days later, with Tracey and Burton goals. The stage was set for a titanic final against local rivals Pontypridd, who like the City, were in the Second Division of the Southern League, where they had finished in fifth position. A new record crowd of 18,000 at Ninian Park saw a dour 0-0 draw on the 8th of April, and ten days later almost 7,000 were at Pontypridd to witness a great performance by the fledgling City team, who won 3-0 in grand style, with goals from Featherstone and two from Tracey. Bob Lawrie had missed the replay through injury, his place being taken by player-coach George Latham who was only an occasional player. Latham demonstrated his great generosity and integrity, by afterwards making a gift of his winners' medal to Lawrie.

****

1912-13 season – Southern League Division 2:

The Cardiff City board of directors were unanimous in their decision to allow secretary-manager, Fred Stewart, extra financial licence, in order that further experienced players could be brought to the club. The board also sanctioned the club to join the Southern Alliance which would give their players good competition against English opposition, many of whom were in the First Division of the Southern League. Davy McDougall accepted an offer from Newport County to become their first player-manager, and one of his first signings for the Monmouthshire club was the City goalkeeper Ted Husbands. This proved to be the first of many transactions between the clubs, which lasted until the County's sad demise in 1989. Mr Stewart resolved his goalkeeping position by signing 29 year old Jack Kneeshaw from Colne, and in order to strengthen his defence, the City secretary-manager enlisted full-back Tommy Doncaster from Barnsley, wing-half Henry 'Kidder' Harvey from Wallsend, plus the big centre-half Pat Cassidy of Bradford City. Utility forward Harry Keggans was also obtained from Bradford City, and to complete another busy summer, full-back Reuben Croft came from Portsmouth plus local amateur Fred Keenor who was signed from Roath Wednesdays. Keenor in fact signed professional forms on the 28th of November 1912.

Kneeshaw, Croft, Harvey, Cassidy and Keggans were all in City's starting line-up that played in the opening fixture at Swansea on the 7th of September. It was Swansea's first Southern League match, and on a Vetch Field pitch of pressed clinker, the game ended 1-1 with Jack Burton scoring City's goal. Following a midweek 1-0 win at MidRhondda, where Harry Keggans scored and Tommy Doncaster made his debut, City played their first home match against Newport County on the 14th of September. Before a crowd of over 8,000, City's experience shone through, and both Harry Featherstone and Harry Tracey netted in a 2-0 victory. Mr Stewart signed centre-forward Billy Devlin from Stockport County on September the 23rd, and already there was healthy competition for places at the Club, as the City embarked upon an unbeaten run which included nine consecutive wins. This run did not end until Boxing Day when Luton Town won 2-0 at Kenilworth Road.

City bounced back on New Years' Day with a 5-0 home win over Llanelly; Devlin, Featherstone (two) and Jack Burton (two) where the scorers. A fortnight later they achieved a record-breaking 9-0 victory over Ton Pentre in which Devlin (three), Tracey (two), Cassidy (two), Jack Evans and Jack Burton shared the goals. The Ninian Park men swept all before them in no uncertain manner, and as they strode powerfully towards promotion, Fred Stewart paid Newport County £100 for winger Andy Holt, and signed both forward Jack Clarke and defender Colin McKechnie from Bradford City, as the home crowds increased and the revenue grew appreciably. Indeed there were over 20,000 packed into Ninian Park (a new ground record) on the 21st of March, for the table-topping game with Luton Town. The City exacted full revenge on the Hatters for their only defeat of the season, by winning handsomely 3-0.

Inside forwards Jack Burton (two) and George Burton were on target. This was the City's final home game of the season, and although they still had three away games to play, the Ninian Parkites celebrated both promotion and the championship.

Consistency had been a major factor in City's success, and centre-half Pat Cassidy had been ever-present. Billy Hardy, 'Kidder' Harvey, Jack Kneeshaw and Bob Leah all missed just one match each. The goals were evenly spread with Jack Burton scoring 11, Billy Devlin 9 and George Burton 8.

F.A. Cup:

Cardiff City had a marvellous win at Merthyr in the 1st preliminary round on the 12th of October, as Billy Devlin became the first City player to score a hat-trick in the competition, and both 'Kidder' Harvey and Jack Burton also netted in a runaway 5-1 victory. The next round saw City overcome Pontypridd 2-1 before a 12,000 crowd at Ninian Park, with Jack Burton and George Burton the marksmen. They followed this win with a 4-1 triumph at Llanelly, and on November the 30th, they met Exeter City in the 4th Qualifying round at Ninian Park. This was another high-class performance by City over a team from the First Division of the Southern League, and Devlin (two), George Burton, Jack Burton and 'Kidder' Harvey completed a 5-1 victory.

Hopes were high when Southend United visited Ninian Park, but the City gave a performance as drab as the weather and slumped to a disappointing 0-3 defeat.

Welsh Cup:

Cardiff City's defence of the trophy began with a 4-2 home win over Ton Pentre on the 4th of January, and three weeks later they swept to a 4-0 victory at Bangor City. On February the 15th, however, City crashed out of the competition when Swansea - in their first professional season - won 4-2 at Ninian Park which stunned the 12,000 crowd.

****

1913-14 Season – Southern League Division 1:

Fred Stewart returned to his favourite North Eastern-hunting grounds to search out new players during the close season, and he bought forward Jim Henderson from Scotswood, inside-forward George West plus full-back Tom Witts from Wallsend, goalkeeper John Stephenson from Jarrow Caledonians, forward Joe Clarke from Hebburn Argyle and halfback Billy Davidson from Wallsend Shipway.

When the new term in the higher division got underway Mr Stewart decided to stick with his championship winning players of the previous season. But much to the dismay of all concerned the opening five matches were all lost by a single goal, and this left the City anchored to the bottom of the table. On the 4th of October both Jim Henderson and Tom Robertson made their debuts at Coventry, replacing George Burton and Jack Burton. Robertson scored twice in a 2-2 draw and a week later both players were on the mark as City secured their first win in the Southern League First Division. Watford were beaten, with a 2-0 scoreline at Ninian Park, which lifted the City off the foot of the table.

Fred Stewart signed Len Hopkins from Brierley Hill, and the beefy centre-forward scored twice on his home debut as City enjoyed a 3-0 victory over Southend United on November the 7th. Following successive defeats at Brighton, and at home to Portsmouth, John Stephenson replaced Jack Kneeshaw in goal. Both Fred Keenor and George West made their debuts in a 1-1 home draw with Exeter City on the 6th of December, as City again languished in bottom place. Stephenson and West were to keep their places, but young Fred Keenor remained a reserve player – at least for the time being.

George West was to prove a great acquisition and had a ten year association with the club, a run broken only by World War One. West brought a new dimension to the City attack and formed a quite devastating partnership with outside-left Jack Evans, besides being a scorer of many a clever goal himself.

F. STEWART.
Secretary-Manager. Came to Cardiff from Stockport County, where he occupied a similar position.

B. WILSON.
Assistant Secretary. One of the founders of the club. Has charge of the Reserve team.

Perhaps one of Mr Stewart's most astute signings was completed on the 28th of November 1913, when Cardiff City agreed to pay Tottenham Hotspur £1,000 for their accomplished right-back Charlie Brittan, who had been unable to keep his place in the Spurs First Division side. This transfer was seen, by the football media, as a major step forward in Cardiff City's ambitions. An imposing figure and a natural leader, Brittan made his debut in City's first away win of the season - 2-1 at Swindon on the 20th of December - where Billy Devlin scored twice to shoot the Bluebirds off the bottom and up to 15th place. It was away from Ninian Park that caused the City most anguish, for their home form was now good enough for the Bluebirds to maintain a mid-table position. But on their travels it was another story, until Easter Saturday when a Billy Devlin goal earned the points at Exeter.

The City defence had improved with the arrival of Brittan, and they kept five clean sheets in the final six games of the season, which helped them end the term in a creditable 10th position. The step up in status had its obvious effect, and Stewart regarded the season as a watershed, which he used to sort out his playing staff and improve standards. The lack of a consistent goalscorer and the experience of being in the relegation places until Christmas had obviously caused anxiety, but the Bluebirds had come out of it and emerged as a useful side. Billy Hardy was ever present, and George West - with 10 goals in 25 appearances - was the leading scorer.

F.A.Cup:
Cardiff City were drawn at Swansea Town in the 4th qualifying round and in keeping with their miserable away League form, they lost 0-2. At left-back for the Bluebirds was Dr. J.L. McBean, an amateur signed from the Scottish club, Queen's Park, but this match was to be his only one in the first-team.

Welsh Cup:
On the 3rd of January 1914 Cardiff City were drawn to play at Oswestry Town, and on the same day had a Southern League fixture at Southampton. The City sent their reserve team to Oswestry and lost 1-2, Billy Goughan scoring the goal.

****

1914-15 Season - Southern League Division 1:

Fred Stewart brought in two experienced players during the summer - right wing George Beare, who had played 104 games in the First Division with Everton, and full-back Arthur Layton from Middlesbrough who had appeared in the Aston Villa team which opened Ninian Park in September 1910. Both men lined up for the City in the opening match at Watford, on the 2nd of September, but found themselves on the wrong end of a 2-1 defeat; centre-half Pat Cassidy scored City's goal.

A somewhat chequered start to the season, saw goals again in short supply and resulted in City dropping to 17th position. Mr. Stewart introduced Liverpool's Arthur Goddard - who had spent twelve years at Anfield (making 415 appearances during which he scored 80 goals) - to form a right wing pairing with the pacey George Beare. The goals began to flow, particularly at Ninian Park, where the City ran up seven consecutive victories. The most impressive of these being a 3-2 triumph over championship contenders Reading, on the 5th of December, two goals by Billy Devlin and a Crawford own goal deciding the outcome.

Bristol Rovers were swept away on the wrong end of a 7-0 drubbing, with Billy Devlin (three), George West, Arthur Goddard, George Beare and Jack Evans sharing the goals; every City forward was on the scoresheet. Billy Devlin was again to the fore with two goals in a 5-0 win over Northampton Town on 19th December, with Arthur Goddard (two) and George Beare also netting. City climbed into third place following a 2-0 win over Plymouth Argyle on Boxing Day, but they received a jolt at Ninian Park on New Year's Day, when the eventual champions, Watford, won by 3-2. Lack of transport and awful weather meant that less than 2,000 spectators were at the game. These numbers were in stark contrast to the regular attendances of around 10,000. This game was to be the last that the City would lose at home during this season, as they made a charge for the championship. But their away form let them down, and not even the introduction of inside-forward Albert Barnett from Glossop, at Brighton on the 23rd of January, could change the City's fortunes on their opponents' grounds.

Fred Keenor slipped in and out of the team, as something of a utility player, and he even had a brief run at centre-forward. With the half-back line of Harvey, Cassidy and Hardy being recognised as the finest in the Southern League, Keenor had to content himself with the role of replacement for injured players, but even so he still made 22 appearances.

On the 10th of April, the City won for the fifth time in six outings, and this result lifted them into second position. This latest victory came at Elm Park, where City's 2-1 success - George West and Jack Evans scoring - effectively ended Reading's hopes of winning the championship. The Berkshire club finished runners' up to Watford, and the City - on the strength of their home form where they won 16 and drew 1 of the 19 games played - ended the season in third position.

Billy Hardy, Jack Evans and George Beare missed just one match each, and George West, with 13 goals, was the top scorer.

F.A.Cup:
The City faced First Division Bristol City at Ashton Gate in the first round, and although they fought pluckily, two goals from Edwin Burton - who was to lose his life in the First World War - condemned City to defeat.

Welsh Cup:
Cardiff City withdrew from the competition.

E.E. (Bert Smith), considered by many as the club's greatest ever centre-half and George West, for a number of seasons City's inside-left.

CHAPTER 2
WAR, AND THE LAST DAYS OF NON-LEAGUE FOOTBALL

WAR-TIME FOOTBALL 1915-19:

Cardiff City had played throughout the 1914-15 season without feeling any effect of the conflict that had been going on in Belgium since August 1914. The summer of 1915 saw the recruitment drive intensified as it was realised that the War was going to continue for longer than first anticipated. The Football League answered the call for recruits by disbanding all fixtures, and thus enabling players to enlist. Almost 1,000,000 volunteers had already seen action at Mons and Ypres during that first year of conflict, and with the British and German armies now locked in trench warfare there seemed little likelihood of the hostilities coming to an early conclusion.

The Football League allowed its members to organise regional leagues, for morale purposes as much as anything else, and a number of local friendly games were played up to Christmas 1915. Cardiff City managed to participate in a South West Combination against Bristol City, Bristol Rovers, Newport County, Portsmouth, Southampton and Swindon Town, between January and April 1916. These games were little more than friendlies, and were not a success as travelling became arduous due to the railway network being used for the War effort. With very poor crowds, the drain on finances became a cause of concern.

Several players, such as Jack Kneeshaw, George Beare, Jack Evans and Billy Hardy (until he enlisted), continued in City's service, but Mr Stewart was left with selecting teams from virtually unknown amateurs, and players who were on leave. At the end of the 1915-16 season, Cardiff City withdrew from competitive fixtures for the duration of the War. In the 1916-17 season just seven friendly games were undertaken, and in 1917-18 only three games were played.

Following the signing of the Armistice on the 11th of November 1918, the slow demobilisation of the British Army resulted in players trickling back to their respective clubs. By Christmas 1918, Fred Stewart was fortunate to have enough of his playing staff back in training for a number of friendly matches to be organised. Some of these games were very well attended, as the country looked forward to the return of competitive football, in August 1919.

A RETURN TO COMPETITIVE FOOTBALL.

1919-20 Season – Southern League – Division 1:

The First World War over, saw the resumption of competitive football, and like most clubs Cardiff City had to regroup their staff, and wherever necessary strengthen positions by recruitment. Fortunately, the carnage of the Great War had not been too severe on Cardiff City, only one player - reserve full back Tom Witts - failing to return. There was one significant loss however, as Lord Ninian Crichton Stuart, one of Cardiff City's leading patrons, was reported killed in action.

Fred Stewart had remained in Cardiff, building up his corn and coal merchant business in Roath, while work had continued on improving spectator facilities at Ninian Park. Mr. Stewart was successful in re-engaging most of his team from 1915, and even though money was short and the board of directors had kept the club afloat from their own pockets, the secretary-manager was allowed to buy inside-forward Billy Grimshaw from Bradford City for £1,000 and the agreed payment of £3 per week in wages.

January 1920: Cardiff City directors C.B.Cox (left) and Dr.W.Nicholson survey the construction work in progress on the main Stand at Ninian Park.

Full-back Alex Stewart was recruited from Watford, and centrehalf E.E. 'Bert' Smith - an Irishman from Donegal - was given a trial on his demobilisation from the Army; the big pivot was eventually signed, on the recommendation of secretary Bartley Wilson. Mr Stewart took on Billy Williams and Tom Dalton, both of Pontypridd, plus local amateurs Eddie Jenkins and Len Davies, who would later be offered professional terms. Inside-forward Charlie Jones arrived from Troedyrhiw, and goalkeeper Charlie Hewitt was signed. Insideforward Harold Beadles - an amateur from Newtown - was released following a trial, and joined Liverpool. This move proved a costly decision as City would sign Beadles from the Anfield club in May 1924.

Billy Grimshaw and Charlie Jones were included in the City team that opened their fixtures at Reading on the 30th of August. They lost 0-2, and centre-half Pat Cassidy, a tower of strength before the War, was replaced by Bert Smith. The Irishman held the pivot's role for the remainder of the season, as the popular Cassidy faded from the scene. Fred Keenor, who had 'guested' for Brentford, as well as receiving wounds in the War, was now becoming a regular choice, and another local - Len Davies - made his City debut (and only appearance of the season) at Luton on September the 13th. Billy Grimshaw scored twice in a hard-fought 2-2 draw.

Billy Hardy was released from the Army, and returned to stake his claim for a regular berth, and in a flurry of transfer activity, Mr Stewart brought in utility forward Billy Cox from Clydebank. Cox marked his home debut with the only goal, in a 1-0 win over Exeter City on the 4th of October. The success of Cox allowed the City to accept an offer from Newport County for their popular forward Billy Devlin.

But surely the success story of the season began when Mr Stewart was allowed to sign centreforward Arthur Cashmore from Darleston, a player with previous experience at Oldham Athletic and Manchester United. The hard shooting Cashmore began to deliver the goods immediately, scoring one of the goals on his home debut that beat Crystal Palace 2-1, on the 6th of December, as City embarked upon an unbeaten run of 15 games. These successes saw Ninian Park attendances booming to around 20,000, in fact 23,000 witnessed City's narrow 1-0 win over rivals Swansea Town on February the 7th; George Beare scored the goal as the Bluebirds settled into third place.

News came through, that the Football League intended to extend its membership to a Third Division, and midway through the season the Cardiff City board of directors lodged an application for admission to the League. This request was held in abeyance until all proposals were finalised. Following an impressive 4-2 home win over Millwall on the 12th of March, the City's form suddenly dipped, and not only did fail to win for six matches, but they were also unable to score in five of them. It was this lapse that inevitably went a long way in preventing the Bluebirds from winning the Championship, and although they bounced back with a 6-1 thrashing of Northampton Town on the 10th of April, the City had to settle for a final fourth position.

Although the club had began the 1919-20 season with a substantial debt, by the end of the year they had wiped the slate clean, and had enough resources to undertake further ground improvements. These included the building of the all-seater Canton Stand, in order to raise the capacity at Ninian Park.

City were also able to present cheques to those players who had played without pay at the outbreak of the War, and this included the widow of the deceased Tom Witts.

The Football League revealed their plans for a Third Division, which would consist mainly of Southern League Division One clubs. However, on the 31st of May 1920, the League agreed to accept Leeds United - who polled 31 votes - and Cardiff City (with 23), into a reconstructed Second Division. It meant that the mid-season lobbying by Mr Stewart and his directors had paid handsome dividends, and Cardiff City, after only a decade as a professional club, became full members of the Football League.

Consistency had been a great factor in City's final season of Southern League Football, with Bert Smith, George Beare, Fred Keenor, Jack Kneeshaw, Jack Evans and Charlie Brittan missing few matches. Arthur Cashmore was top scorer with 14 goals from 22 games and Billy Grimshaw, Jack Evans and George West all reached double figures.

F.A.Cup:

Cardiff City met First Division Oldham Athletic at Ninian Park in the first round, and they overcame the Latics in a stirring performance which saw George West and Jack Evans scoring in a 2-0 win before 20,000 excited Ninian Parkites. Three weeks later City travelled to Second Division Wolves, and pulled off a staggering 2-1 win. A crowd of over 37,000 saw Bert Smith and George Beare score City's goals.

A large contingent of City supporters travelled to Ashton Gate by excursion trains for the third round tie with Bristol City, on the 21st of February. The Second Division side proved just too strong on the day, and although George Beare had a fine match and scored for the City, goals by Bert Neesam and Tommy Howarth took Bristol City through.

Welsh Cup:

Cardiff City were in irresistible form in their Welsh Cup matches, and despite fielding several reserves at home to Merthyr Town on January the 14th, they won comfortably by 5-0, with goals from Joe Clarke (three), 'Kidder' Harvey and Billy Cox. City then rattled up another five goals without reply against Chester in the 4th round at Ninian Park. When they played Swansea Town in the semi-final, on the 24th of March, they had full-back Arthur Layton playing in goal, yet still won by 2-1, with goals from Jack Evans - a penalty - and George West.

City faced Wrexham in the Final on the 21st of April, and two goals from George West brought the Welsh Cup to Ninian Park for the second time, as they triumphed by 2-1.

On the 27th of April, over 7,000 turned out at Ninian Park for Jack Evans' testimonial match against Bristol City, which the Second Division side won by 3-1. This began a series of games between the clubs, for various benefits, over the ensuing seasons.

CHAPTER 3

THE LEAGUE, DIVISION 1 AND THE BLUEBIRDS AT WEMBLEY

1920-21 season - Division 2:

Secretary-Manager Fred Stewart was a busy man during the summer months of 1920, before and after Cardiff City's successful application to the Second Division of the Football League on 31st May. Players signed before City's admission to Football League status were goalkeeper Ben Davies from Middlesbrough, defender Jack Page from Everton and Ernie Anderson from Belfast Distillery. Following the City's election, Mr Stewart completed the club's most expensive signing to date when he paid £750 to The Wednesday for inside-forward Jimmy Gill, who would prove to be a marvellous investment. Among a number of non-League players to be signed, Herbie Evans - an amateur from Cardiff Corinthians - would go on to bigger and better things whilst with the Club. Other signings included A. Andrews, Tommy Wilmott, Sid Evans, Jack Sayles and Billy Newton.

A major change at Ninian Park was the erection of the Canton Stand with its unique bench seating which offered cover and comfort for several thousand spectators.

Cardiff City's opening encounter was at Edgeley Park on the 28th August, when they faced Stockport County, ironically Fred Stewart's former employers. Stockport took an early lead, but the Bluebirds remained unruffled, and after a quarter of an hour they drew level when Jimmy Gill scored Cardiff City's first goal in League football. Within another 15 minutes, Gill had repeated the dose and City were on their way to their first League victory. Billy Grimshaw, Fred Keenor and Jack Evans took the score to five before Stockport managed a second consolation goal, to make the final result 5-2 to the Bluebirds. Two days later 25,000 were at the still primitive Ninian Park enclosure, to see City's first home League match, against Clapton Orient, but they went away a little disappointed as the game finished goalless. The following Saturday, the Bluebirds earned the plaudits of a 23,000 crowd when they completed the 'double' over Stockport County with a handsome 3-0 victory, and Arthur Cashmore scored the first League goal at Ninian Park. Two days later, on the 6th September, the Bluebirds had their first taste of defeat when they went down 0-2 at Clapton Orient. City then settled down with an unbeaten run of eight games, up to the end of October, which put them among the promotion contenders.

With attendances running at a healthy level the club directors allowed Fred Stewart to set the record fee for a full-back when he paid The Wednesday £3,500 for their unsettled 32 year old Scottish international Jimmy Blair. Within weeks the stylish Blair and his new team-mates completed the 'double' over *The Wednesday*, as they were then known, with George West the scorer in both single goal wins. Before Christmas Ernie Gault, Ernie Anderson and Arthur Layton, none of whom were first team regulars, all joined Stockport County.

Goalkeeper Ben Davies replaced Jack Kneeshaw on January 22nd as City defeated Bristol City by 1-0, with Albert Barnett's only goal of the season before, 43,000 - Ninian Park's highest crowd of the term. City kept well in the promotion frame throughout the winter months but, Jimmy Gill apart, goalscoring was causing concern. In order to remedy this situation, Fred Stewart made another signing, on the 8th February 1921, when he obtained inside-forward Harry Nash from Coventry City. The new man immediately responded with a debut goal at Barnsley in a 2-0 win, which saw Len Davies also make his League debut in City's front line.

Three weeks later a £1,500 cheque secured the signature of Arsenal centre-forward Fred Pagnam, to provide the goals in the Bluebird's final push towards the First Division. On his City debut at home to Barnsley, Pagnam repaid a large slice of his transfer fee by scoring in a dramatic 3-2 win, which put City into second place in the Division. There was a slight hiccup as City lost their next two League matches, 0-2 at Rotherham and 1-2 at home against Port Vale, but they recovered their poise and in the final eleven League matches they were absolutely magnificent, and miserly, for they conceded just four goals in those games. During this period, they also kept eight clean sheets, six of them in consecutive matches.

City powered towards promotion, and a 'double' over Wolves - who had beaten the Bluebirds in the semi-final of the F.A. Cup - in their final two League games gave the Ninian Park men the runners' up spot behind Birmingham City. In a 'mathematical' finish, City missed the championship of the Second Division by goal average only. Promotion to the First Division, after just one season, brought much-needed joy and excitement to City's growing support, many of whom were facing the despair and anguish of unemployment. Jimmy Gill was top scorer with 19 League goals and there was solid consistency from Bert Smith, Fred Keenor, Billy Hardy and Charlie Brittan, in a City defence which conceded only 32 goals, and who had Jack Kneeshaw and Ben Davies sharing the custodian duties. The public response to League football was excellent with attendances at Ninian Park running at an average of over 28,000.

Surrounded by Chelsea defenders, Cashmore (Cardiff's number nine) goes tumbling as 'keeper Molyneux punches the ball away.
5th March: F.A.Cup versus Chelsea.

F.A. Cup:

Not only did Cardiff City's performances in their first season of League football impress observers, but their exploits in the F.A. Cup caught the public's imagination. A tough first round encounter at Roker Park on 8th January 1921, before 41,923 committed Wearsiders, saw the City rise to the occasion and inflict a 1-0 defeat on Sunderland. George Beare scored the Bluebirds' winning goal, but the real hero was the Geordie, Billy Hardy, who totally negated the influence on the game of Sunderland's master craftsman Charlie Buchan.

On the 29th January City travelled to the Goldstone Ground for a second round tie against Brighton and Hove Albion. The game ended 0-0 and the midweek replay was another close affair, settled only by Arthur Cashmore's winning goal for the Bluebirds, before 31,000 delighted customers at Ninian Park. The third round on 19th February saw City return to the South Coast to face Southampton, and in a tight match, Jimmy Gill scored the only goal of a bruising affair that could have gone either way.

A record crowd of 50,000 thronged Ninian Park for the fourth round clash with Chelsea on the 5th March. Arthur Cashmore put the City into a 5th minute lead which they clung to in a match of titanic proportions. The scenes at the end as the Bluebirds reached the semi-final were some of the most ecstatic ever to be seen at Ninian Park.

Cardiff City faced fellow Second Division adversaries Wolverhampton Wanderers in the semi-final at Anfield, on the 19th March - a day when history was made for when King George V and Queen Mary took their seats after the interval it was the first time that reigning monarchs had attended a football match in Britain. Neither side could rise to this royal occasion, and a dour encounter ended goalless. The replay took place at Old Trafford four days later, and City's fate was decided by two glaring refereeing mistakes. Already without the potency of the injured Jimmy Gill, the Bluebirds were stunned when Brooks got away with a clear indiscretion to put Wolves ahead. Before half-time Edmunds, who looked well offside, scored Wolves' second, which put the men from Molineux in control of the match. City got a second-half lifeline through Fred Keenor's penalty, but it counted for nothing when Richards scored a third goal for Wolves, to put the Midlanders into the F.A. Cup final. The Wolves went on to lose the final to Tottenham Hotspur at Stamford Bridge, when Jimmy Dimmock scored the game's only goal - after 54 minutes - before 74,000 spectators.

Welsh Cup:

Cardiff City went out of the competition at the first time of asking. On the same day - the 22nd January - the Bluebirds had a Second Division fixture at Ashton Gate (which they drew 0-0 with Bristol City). Therefore a City reserve team travelled to Pontypridd and lost 1-3, with Len Davies, then a second string player, scoring Cardiff's lone goal.

1921-2 Season - Division 1:

Faced with First Division football after only one season in the Football League, Cardiff City Secretary-Manager Fred Stewart busily recruited players from various backgrounds, which included re-signing Ernie Anderson (again!) from Stockport County and Jack Rutherford of Brighton, who was contacted by wireless whilst crossing the Atlantic! Other players brought in were Jimmy Nelson from Belfast Crusaders, Frank Mason from Coventry City, Tommy Brown from Brighton, A. Melville from Partick Thistle, Hugh Ollershaw of Wombwell, H. Smith of Hebburn Colliery and Willie Page (brother of Jack) from Stoke.

Before a ball was kicked in the First Division Cardiff City were fined £50 for an alleged illegal approach to Waugh of Wolves. The Club directorate and management claimed innocence, and it was revealed that a 'follower' of the club had acted in Cardiff City's interest, and had 'fixed' the transaction which never took place.

Cardiff City made the worst possible start to their First Division career by not only losing the opening fixture, 0-1 to Tottenham Hotspur (the F.A. Cup holders), at Ninian Park, but going on to six successive defeats. During this run, Spurs, Aston Villa and Oldham Athletic all completed 'doubles' over the Bluebirds. In the 1-2 defeat at Villa Park, centre-half Bert Smith, scored City's first-ever goal in Division One. The attendance for the opening match against 'Spurs was 50,000, and a month later, on the 24th of September, there were only 10,000 fewer to see Cardiff City record their first win in the top flight, when they beat Middlesbrough 3-1. To Jimmy Gill, who netted twice, went the honour of scoring the first home goal in the First Division for the club, with Harry Nash scoring the other. Middlesbrough were League leaders before the game whereas City were rock-bottom!

A fortnight later City recorded their first victory in a First Division away match, when two goals from Jimmy Gill brought about a 2-0 win at Bolton Wanderers. A week later the directors agreed to Fred Stewart paying £1500 to Everton for their silky inside-forward Joe Clennell, and they recouped some of that outlay in the next fortnight when Arthur Cashmore was transferred to Notts County, and George Bears moved to Bristol City. Both players had given good service to the club. Jimmy Gill was consistent in his goalscoring but poor Fred Pagnam could do little right, and after 14 barren games he made way for Len Davies. Before Christmas, Pagnam was transferred to Watford, where he went on to a long and successful career.

Len Davies was immediately among the goals as City showed a marked improvement, hitting a rich vein of form through the darkest months, which sent them shooting up the table on a run of only one defeat in sixteen League matches, between the 12th of November and the 25th of February 1922. Their improvement and confidence was highlighted on the 2nd of January, at Ewood Park, when illness overnight ruled out both Jack Evans and Jimmy Gill for the match against Blackburn Rovers. Reserve Harry Nash stepped in and 42 years old trainer George Latham (once a Welsh international) became the oldest League debutant in Cardiff City's history. Billy Grimshaw moved inside to take Gill's place, and the portly figure of George Latham lined up at outside right. City won handsomely by 3-1, with Len Davies and Grimshaw (two) doing the scoring.

It is now well documented that with the game won, the City players had some fun at Latham's expense, by continually hitting long passes for him to chase - much to everybody's amusement. George later claimed an 'assist' for the final goal, as he admitted to sitting on the Blackburn goalkeeper, as the ball entered the net!

On the 21st January, the Bluebirds beat Bradford City 6-3 at Ninian Park, and Len Davies - now established as a firm favourite, - hit the Clubs' first hat-trick in the Football League, with Jimmy Gill (2) and Joe Clennell notching the other goals.

By the end of the season Fred Stewart had used no less than 30 players, seven of whom made only a single appearance. This measure was mainly due to reserve players coming in when established members of the team were called away on international duty. Jimmy Gill was top scorer with 20 League goals, Len Davies hit an impressive 17 from 24 appearances, and schemer Joe Clennell chipped in with 10 very useful successes. Wingers Billy Grimshaw and Jack Evans played consistently and goalkeeper Ben Davies, Jimmy Blair, Billy Hardy, Herbie Evans, Bert Smith, Charlie Brittan and Fred Keenor, all made solid contributions to the team effort.

Another link with Cardiff City's successful Southern League days was broken when George West joined Stockport County in March 1922. There was the first sighting of a football legend in City's last League game of the season, when Irishman Tom Farquharson, signed from Abertillery in February, made his League debut in goal against Manchester United - a match which the City won by 3-1. The Bluebirds ended their first season in Division One in a highly creditable 4th position, and had it not been for that disastrous beginning when 12 points were lost, one can only wonder what City's final position might have been. Although five home games were lost, City still attracted almost 32,000 on average for their games at Ninian Park.

F.A.Cup:

Cardiff City were in their best form of the season by the time they entered the 1921-2 F.A.Cup competition, and this was emphasised to the full in their first round match against Manchester United, at Old Trafford on the 7th January. The Bluebirds romped to a magnificent 4-2 victory, with Joe Clarke making a rare appearance in place of Jack Evans on the left wing. The goals came from Len Davies (2), Harry Nash, who played instead of the sick Jimmy Gill, and Joe Clennell. As in the 1920-21 season, City had to meet Southampton, but this time in the second round on the 28th of January.

Jimmy Gill, now well again, scored the goal that earned the Bluebirds a 1-1 draw, and a midweek replay at Ninian Park. Before an estimated 40,000 crowd, City made home advantage pay, and Jimmy Gill and Joe Clennell were the marksmen in a 2-0 win.

The third round brought Nottingham Forest to Ninian Park, and a packed crowd of 50,470 were enthraled as City swept to a scintillating 4-1 victory, with regular goalscorers Len Davies (2), Jimmy Gill, and Joe Clennell once again sharing the goals. On the 4th of March, the Bluebirds entertained Tottenham Hotspur, and over 51,000 squeezed into Ninian Park for a fourth round match, that ended 1-1. Len Davies scored the Bluebirds last minute goal, which equalised Jimmy Seed's earlier effort for the F.A. Cup holders. The replay, at White Hart Lane, five days later attracted 53,626, and some sources later stated that a further 20,000 had been locked out.

The lucky fans in the ground saw an exciting match in which Jimmy Gill gave City a first half lead. But the Bluebirds buckled in the final twenty minutes when Spurs scored twice to win the tie with goals from Wilson and Dimmock.

4th of March: F.A.Cup, Cardiff versus 'Spurs at Ninian Park. City's brilliant wing-half Hardy, heads clear.

Welsh Cup:
It was glory all the way for Cardiff City in the Welsh Cup. With no clash of fixtures they were able to field strong teams for every tie, and their undoubted class shone through. Len Davies helped himself to 4 goals in a 7-1 romp against Newport County on the 10th of January, with Billy Grimshaw (2) and Fred Keenor scoring the others.

Against Merthyr Town, on the 22nd of February, Len Davies weighed in with another hat-trick; Harry Nash, and an 'own goal' from Jackson, completed a 5-0 home win. In the semi-final, City met Pontypridd, who had put out a weakened City XI in the 1920-21 season, but this time the Bluebirds made no mistake with a 3-0 win. Evergreens, Fred Keenor and Jack Evans, got a goal apiece and Jimmy Gill completed the scoring.

City faced Ton Pentre of the Rhondda Valley, in the Final at Pontypridd, and a comfortable 2-0 win earned by goals from Len Davies and Jimmy Gill brought the Welsh Cup to Ninian Park.

There was delight in the Ninian Park camp when Englishman Billy Grimshaw was selected to play for the Football League in February 1922.

1922-23 Season – Division 1:

Once more the summer months of 1922 saw Cardiff City Secretary-manager Fred Stewart recruiting a number of non-League players to supplement the large playing staff at Ninian Park. Players signed included centre-forward Jimmy Jones from Ton Pentre, plus Jack Pugsley, George Whitcombe and Charley Evans, each of whom was from local football, Vince Jones from the Army and Billy Turnbull from West Stanley. The first-team virtually picked itself, having knitted together well in previous season.

With three wins and a draw from the first five games – which included a 'double' over Aston Villa – the Bluebirds could not have foreseen that they would lose their next six matches (shades of the 1921-22 season!). They won only once in eleven games, before steadying the tide following the signing of Walsall forward George Reid and Fergus Aitken from Blackburn Rovers, in December. Neither player made a great impact at Ninian Park, despite Reid making a goalscoring debut at the new Maine Road Ground, as Manchester City gave the Bluebirds a 5-1 walloping.

Reid then contributed to a 3-0 Boxing Day win over West Bromwich Albion and scored the only goal when City beat Bolton Wanderers in their next home match on 6th January.

Due to being 'Cup-tied' while at Walsall, Reid lost his place to the recalled Len Davies, who proceeded to recapture his best goalscoring form in no uncertain manner. In the six League matches, between 27th January and 10th March, Len hit nine goals including a hat-trick in a 6-1 home win over Chelsea. Jimmy Gill scored even more than Davies notching eleven goals in eight League games – his best performance being a hat-trick against Blackburn Rovers in a 5-0 win on 27th January. This victory began a run of five home games in which City hit nineteen goals without reply! Newcastle were also dispatched 5-0, on the 10th of February, and four weeks later the Bluebirds gained their best League win thus far, by beating Chelsea 6-1 with goals from Len Davies (3), Jimmy Gill (2) and Jack Evans. On Good Friday the Bluebirds cantered to their best away win since their League entry, with a 5-1 victory at Burnley. Joe Clennell bagged a hat-trick and Len Davies and Fred Keenor got the other goals.

City's depth of quality throughout their playing staff was no better illustrated than on 14th April 1923 when international calls robbed them of **six** players. Playing in the Wales versus Ireland game at Wrexham were Fred Keenor, Len Davies and Jack Evans for Wales, and Tom Farquharson and Bert Smith for Ireland; while at Hampden Park Jimmy Blair was left-back for Scotland against England. City had to release their Welsh players, and made it their policy not to stand in the way of other men selected for their countries. Incidentally, Bert Smith had dropped out of the Irish team two years previously, preferring to help City beat South Shields in a Second Division match! Without these six regulars Cardiff City took on– and beat – Sheffield United at Ninian Park, by Joe Clennell's goal after 58 minutes. Frank Mason and Vince Jones made their only appearances for the Club, and left winger Bill Taylor made his debut. For veteran Jack Kneeshaw, this was his only League appearance that season, and it was also the solitary game for Sid Evans, who took the place of Billy Grimshaw on the right wing, with the latter moving inside. Finally full-back Jack Page came in at centre-half, and this patchwork City team fully merited their 1-0 win, whilst setting a record for having six players on international duty and still winning a First Division match.

The Bluebirds ended the season in 9th position, which at one stage had looked highly unlikely, and their tally of 73 goals – with Len Davies notching 19 from 27 games, Jimmy Gill scoring 17 and Joe Clennell bagging 14 – made them one of the country's more attractive teams. Jack Evans missed only one match, playing for Wales prevented him being ever-present, and good contributions came from Fred Keenor, Billy Hardy, Bert Smith and Jimmy Blair. Home attendances averaged just below 30,000.

F.A. Cup:

The first round saw City paired with Watford, and it took three games before the Bluebirds progressed into the second round. The first game at Ninian Park ended 1-1, with Jack Evans netting a penalty, and the replay at Vicarage Road finished 2-2 after Len Davies and Joe Clennell had scored for the Bluebirds. The tie was settled a week later, when goals from Len Davies and Herbie Evans (playing in place of Billy Hardy), put an end to Watford's brave challenge. The 2-1 win was played at neutral Villa Park, on the 22nd January. The Bluebirds travelled to Leicester in the second round and Len Davies' goal was enough to ensure a 1-0 win, before 35,690 spectators, at Filbert Street.

The third round produced an epic tie at White Hart Lane with Tottenham Hotspur, who had beaten the City the previous season in the fourth round, once again proving to be something of a bogey team. Spurs sprinted into a three goal lead before half-time, and although City hit back with a Jack Evans penalty and a Jimmy Gill goal, the Londoners held on to win by 3-2, their goals having been scored by Seed, Lindsay and Handley.

Welsh Cup:

For the second successive season the Bluebirds sailed through the opening rounds with huge wins over Rhymney (7-0) and Oswestry (10-0). In the Oswestry match three players - Len Davies, Jimmy Gill and George Reid - each scored hat-tricks, with Fred Keenor making it ten.

In a hard-fought semi-final City defeated Swansea Town 3-2 with Joe Clennell (2) and Len Davies the scorers. The final against Aberdare Athletic was played at the Vetch Field, and the Bluebirds retained the trophy with Billy Grimshaw, Jimmy Gill and Len Davies the marksmen in a 3-2 victory.

Seven Cardiff City players were capped during 1922-3: Fred Keenor, Jack Evans, and Len Davies for Wales ; Bert Smith, Tom Farquharson, George Reid appeared for Ireland and Jimmy Blair represented Scotland.

1923-24 season – Division 1:

Fred Stewart, who liked to bring players from the North East to Ninian Park, reinforced his Geordie connections by signing Newcastle reserves Alfie Hagan and Harry Wake, plus Wallsend's William Robb. In a busy summer Mr Stewart also brought in Elvet Collins and A.James - from local football - plus Tom McGill, after a successful trial.

The Bluebirds embarked on their most successful campaign in the Football League with an unbeaten run of eleven matches, before slumping to their first defeat on the 27th of October, when Preston North End won 3-1 at Deepdale. Len Davies with eight goals in those eleven games, set a new individual scoring record when he netted all four goals in City's 4-2 win at West Bromwich Albion on the 10th of November. Mr Stewart signed Scottish winger Dennis Lawson from St. Mirren, and this allowed City to accept a £5000 fee from Sunderland for Billy Grimshaw, who had been a virtual ever-present for four years.

The Bluebirds marched on relentlessly at the top of the First Division completing League 'doubles' over West Bromwich Albion, Nottingham Forest and Liverpool, and it was not until the final match of 1923 that the City suffered another defeat, when they slipped by 1-2 at Aston Villa, before an estimated 70,000 crowd.

A week later, on January the 5th, at Ninian Park, Villa completed the 'double' over the Bluebirds. But the City responded by taking it out on Arsenal, who they beat twice in the League and also in the second round of the F.A. Cup, on three consecutive Saturdays. Jimmy Gill notching a hat-trick in the 4-0 home win over the Gunners, on the 26th of January.

City's challenge for the Football League Championship was severely dented by four consecutive defeats, in a run of seven matches without a win. On St. David's Day City crashed 0-2 at Leeds Road, to championship rivals Huddersfield Town, and as if that was not bad enough the Bluebirds lost twice within seven days to mid-table Notts County (when five players were on international duty). They also went down 1-2 at Blackburn Rovers, where Joe Clennell's effort was the only City goal in six games. Herbie Evans suffered a broken leg at Ewood Park, and with Len Davies missing several games through injury, the team struggled.

Harry Wake was called up as the replacement for Herbie Evans in the right-half berth. The damage had been done, and although the City remained unbeaten in their last eight games, the Championship decider boiled down to the final day of the season.

Cardiff City began the day, the 3rd of May, as undisputed First Division leaders, by one point over Herbert Chapman's Huddersfield Town. The Bluebirds had to travel to Birmingham City, whereas the Yorkshire team stayed at home, to face Nottingham Forest. The intriguing situation presented itself, that if City won by any score, then the Football League Championship pennant would fly in the Welsh capital, but if the Bluebirds only drew, then Huddersfield would need to win by at least 3-0.

In an afternoon of unprecedented drama, the latter situation eventuality happened, but not before City had rejected a golden opportunity to take the title. With a little over 20 minutes remaining at St. Andrews, Jimmy Gill's goal-bound header was fisted away by a Birmingham defender. With both Jack Evans and Jimmy Gill reluctant to accept the ultimate responsibility of taking the resultant penalty kick, it was 23 goal Len Davies who stepped forward, in a tension charged atmosphere. To the dismay of the many Welshmen in the 49,000 crowd the usually reliable Len shot straight at Tremelling in the Birmingham goal, and in that moment the championship was lost, as the game ended scoreless. At Leeds Road, Huddersfield were leading Nottingham Forest 1-0 at half-time, and when they heard that City were drawing 0-0 at Birmingham the Yorkshiremen attacked with renewed vigour, knowing that two further goals had to be netted if the score remained the same at St. Andrews. Huddersfield duly got their 3-0 win, not knowing at the time of Len Davies' missed penalty, to win the Football League Championship for the first time.

The final count was a goal average difference of 0.024 (the equivalent of less than a one goal margin), and no other team in League history has ever missed out on the Championship by such a small fraction. Poor Len Davies said in later years that the missed penalty haunted him, although he was to continue as one of Cardiff City's most loyal and best-known players. Huddersfield went on to complete a unique treble of First Division titles under Herbert Chapman in 1925 and 1926, and he then repeated this feat with Arsenal in the 1930's.

During the season several prominent players left the club. Billy Grimshaw was transferred to Sunderland for £5000, three week after Dennis Lawson had signed from St. Mirren. George Reid, unable to command a first team place, moved on to Fulham, and E.E. 'Bert' Smith joined Middlesbrough after losing the pivot position to Fred Keenor. During March, veteran campaigner Charlie Brittan retired to go into business in Birmingham. Smith and Brittan had contributed greatly to the rise of Cardiff City

(Left): The team and officials in Berlin on the end of season tour. (Right): A proud day for Cardiff City, as Jimmy Blair (on the left) and Fred Keenor, respectively, captain Scotland and Wales in the International match at Ninian Park.

F.A. Cup:

The first round saw Cardiff City paired with Gillingham, and after a shock 0-0 draw at Ninian Park, the Bluebirds triumphed in the replay (despite the atrocious conditions at Priestfield Stadium), when Jimmy Gill and Len Davies scored in a 2-0 win.

City met Arsenal at Ninian Park in the second round, after the Bluebirds had just completed a League 'double' over the Gunners. In their third meeting on successive Saturdays, the Bluebirds completed a hat-trick of victories, when Jimmy Gill's goal settled a hard-fought tie.

The third round produced another home tie for the Bluebirds, and they nonchalantly swept Bristol City aside with a 3-0 victory. Goals came from Jimmy Gill (two) and Joe Clennell, before a 50,000 crowd. City had to travel to Manchester City for their fourth round tie, and 76,166 (the biggest crowd to attend a Bluebirds match to that time), witnessed a dour encounter without goals. Four days later, on the 12th of March, the replay at Ninian Park attracted another 50,000 crowd. With the match locked in a goalless stalemate after 90 minutes, it took some wizardry in extra time by 50 year old Billy Meredith to turn the game. Recalled to the Manchester City team during February the magical Meredith, with over 100 F.A. Cup appearances to his credit, produced the run and cross from which Tommy Browell scored to put the Bluebirds out of the completion.

Welsh Cup:

Cardiff City travelled to Shrewsbury in the 4th round where they earned a 0-0 draw, and a fortnight later they won the reply 3-0 with two goals from Joe Clennell, and one from Billy Hardy. The next round saw City paired with neighbours Newport County, and the tie went to four titanic tussles, before the Monmouthshire Club triumphed 3-0 at Ninian Park. City fielded a number of their Championship chasing side and Newport's eventual victory was a major triumph for the Third Division (South) side.

At the end of the season Cardiff City embarked on their first overseas tour. They played two matches in Czechoslovakia, against Sparta Prague – losing 2-3 and winning 3-2, on successive days. Moving on to Austria, the City beat First Vienna 2-0 and then went onto Germany, where they played two further matches.

Six players were capped at international level during the season. Fred Keenor, Herbie Evans and Len Davies played for Wales: Tom Farquharson and E.E. 'Bert' Smith represented Ireland, whilst Jimmy Blair appeared for Scotland. On the 16th of February 1924, Fred Keenor and Jimmy Blair captained Wales and Scotland in the international match played at Ninian Park. On the same day Cardiff City played at Tottenham Hotspur and drew 1-1.

****

1924-25 Season – Division 1:

Fred Stewart signed Harold Beadles from Liverpool just before Cardiff City left for their overseas tour in May 1925, and the inside-forward made the trip with his new team-mates. Beadles, like the City trainer – Capt. Geo. Latham – hailed from Newtown. The inside-forward had in fact been previously associated with the Bluebirds for a short period after the Great War.

In a busy summer of transfer activity, Mr Stewart signed three Irishmen – Pat McIlvenny of Belfast Distillery, Tommy Sloan of Belfast Crusader and James McLean of Barn Athletic; the latter player was both deaf and dumb! A £2,500 cheque brought Welsh International winger Willie Davies from Swansea Town, thus allowing the Vetch Field club to avoid a cash crisis. Jack Nicholls, an amateur inside forward whose father was a Cardiff director, was signed from Newport County, and wing half Joe Nicholson was purchased from Clapton Orient. Goalkeeper Joe Hills of Northfleet was signed after a trial period and the City signed Alex McLachlan from local football. Winger Stan Smith of Cradley Heath, re-signed, after completing the previous season with his former club. Departing Ninian Park were Albert Barnett to Aberdare Athletic, and Billy Turnbull who went to Newport County. The League season was largely uninspiring as Mr Stewart rang the changes in an attempt to find a settled side. There was keen competition in a number of positions, as the Club boasted a very large staff with a number of international players on their books. On the 14th of February, five Cardiff City players were called up for International duty and on the same day, the Bluebirds drew 1-1 with Notts County. Two weeks later, City surrendered seven players to International calls, but still beat Newcastle United 3-0 in a First Division match at Ninian Park!

When injury robbed City of top scorer Len Davies, wing-half Joe Nicholson took over the attack leaders' role, and he secured some vital league and F.A. Cup goals. Cardiff City maintained a position between midway and the lower half of the table for much of the season, but they drew both games with League champions Huddersfield Town.

Len Davies again topped the club scorers with 20 goals in 30 games, three of which came in a 4-1 home win over Bury on November the 15th. Harold Beadles scored ten goals in 25 appearances, whilst Jimmy Gill managed nine.

In February 1925, Joe Clennell was transferred to Second Division Stoke, to assist in their relegation battle. Others to leave Ninian Park during the season were reserve forwards Jimmy Jones and Jack Nock, who both joined Wrexham in November 1924. Reserve winger Billy Taylor signed for Aberdare Athletic in February 1925, although he would eventually become a major capture for Hull City. The Bluebirds rather ordinary home form showed up in their home attendances which averaged over 22,000, a drop of almost 9,000 on the previous season.

F.A.Cup:
After reaching the semi-final stages in 1921 and the quarter finals in both 1922 and 1924, this was the season when Cardiff City would go all the way to the twin towers of Wembley.

It took three games for the Bluebirds to get past Darlington (the eventual champions of the Third Division North) in the first round. After two goalless draws, the City came through the second replay at neutral Anfield by 2-0, with Len Davies and Willie Davies scoring.

Fulham visited Ninian Park for the second round, and the City were unconvincing in their disposal of the Londoners with a single Len Davies goal.

The game was ruined by monsoon-like conditions which saw the unprecedented step of the game being suspended for ten minutes, before the teams agreed to carry on. The Bluebirds travelled to fellow First Division rivals Notts County in the third round, where they produced a fine performance – in front of 39,000 at Meadow Lane – to win 2-0. Joe Nicholson – who was switched from wing-half to replace the injured Len Davies in attack – and Jimmy Gill scored City's goals.

Leicester City were the fourth round opponents, at Ninian Park, and the Bluebirds edged out the eventual Second Division champions in sensational fashion. Harold Beadles put the Welsh club ahead, but Leicester hit back to equalise through Duncan. The magnificent crowd of 50,272 were enthraled at the struggle and there were some unbelievable scenes when, with the last kick of the match, Willie Davies scored the winning goal direct from a corner kick at the Grangetown end. Many of the crowd did not believe that City had won, until it was announced over the tannoy system.

The Bluebirds returned to Meadow Lane, scene of their third round win over Notts County five weeks earlier, to meet Blackburn Rovers in the semi-final. Pre-match forecasts pointed to an evenly contested game as both sides were around the middle of the First Division table. The Bluebirds rose to the occasion and in the opening twenty minutes booked their place in the Wembley final, by roaring into a virtually unassailable 3-0 lead, with goals from Nicholson, Gill and Beadles. Blackburn pulled one back, but the City won the match by 3-1.

Cardiff City were confident of beating Sheffield United in the F.A. Cup Final on 25th April 1925, but they fell short of their usual standards that day. Sheffield United, four times winners of the trophy in its 50 year existence, were inspired by the genius of bald-headed Billy Gillespie, and won the Jubilee Cup Final in the 32nd minute of a tedious game. A tragic mistake by Harry Wake, who was caught in possession by Tunstall, allowed the England international winger to run on and beat Tom Farquharson for the only goal of the game. In his post-match statement, a frank Fred Keenor apologised for the Bluebirds' disappointing performance; absolved Harry Wake of causing City's downfall and vowed the clubs' intention of returning to Wembley and winning the trophy. In many Bluebirds' supporters' minds however, was the loss of Len Davies and his goalscoring potential that probably cost City the chance of lifting the coveted English Cup.

A rare and faded newspaper photo' of the fateful only goal of the match: Tunstall turns away after shooting past Farquharson.

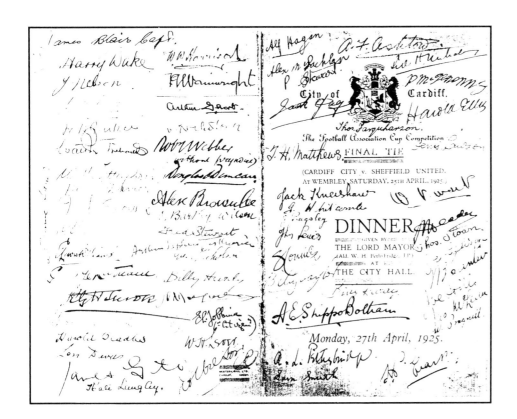

A menu – fully autographed – for the Dinner which was given at City Hall in recognition of Cardiff City's achievement in reaching the F.A. Cup Final – Two years later, there was to be cause for greater celebration!

Welsh Cup:
Cardiff City's exploits in the Welsh Cup were short and – not so sweet – to say the least, as they visited the Vetch Field, and slumped 0-4, their heaviest defeat in the Competition, to that time. City rested Blair, Keenor, Hardy and Gill, and paid the price to a Swansea side who were well on their way to the Third Division (South) championship.

At the end of the season, Cardiff City undertook a tour of Ireland, playing Belfast Crusaders and Portadown – in the North – plus Bohemians at Dalymount Park, in Dublin. Seven Cardiff City players earned International honours that season: Fred Keenor, Willie Davies, Len Davies, Jack Nicholls, Harold Beadles and amateur Edgar Thomas (who guested for City although registered with Cardiff Corinthians) who all played for Wales, plus Tom Farquharson (Ireland) and Jimmy Nelson (for Scotland).

••••••••••••••••••••••••••••••••••••

1925-26 Season – Division 1:

During Cardiff City's close-season tour of Ireland, Fred Stewart signed David Nelson (brother of Jimmy) and defender Tom Watson, who both came from Belfast Crusaders. Also recruited during the summer were, wing-half Ebor Reed, from Newcastle United, Billy Charlton from Newport County, full-back Jack Jennings from Wigan Borough and left-winger Percy Richards from Merthyr Vale. Changes at Boardroom level saw the popular 'Genial Sid' Nicholls take over the Chair from Dr. Nicholson.

The season began badly for Cardiff City and Jimmy Nelson in particular, for the Scottish International full back became the first City player to be sent off in a League match. Nelson was involved in a flare-up with Johnson, the Manchester City winger, in the last minute of the game at Maine Road – when the scores were level at 2-2. The City full back was dismissed, and Manchester scored the winning goal from the resultant penalty. To make matters worse, Nelson was banned for four weeks and missed seven matches.

On a different note, the Directors purchased an electric mower and roller, resulting in the redundancy – and advertisement for the sale of – the horse that had been used by the groundsman!

City won only three of their first thirteen games and after being beaten 3-6 at Blackburn, Mr Stewart took an active interest in the transfer market. On 21st October, Jimmy Gill was transferred to Blackpool for £3,200 – good business when one realised that Gill had cost City only £750, and they had five good seasons from him before making £2,500 profit. The club directors sanctioned the money be used to bring inside-forward Joe Cassidy from Bolton Wanderers, for a new club record fee of £3,800. Then, in the first week of November, Cardiff City shook the football world with a double swoop in Scotland. They paid Motherwell another new record fee of £5,000, for their prolific 28 year old centre-forward Hughie Ferguson, and also invested £2,000 in Clyde's 23 year old left-winger George McLachlan.

A 30,000 crowd saw Ferguson's and McLachlans' home baptisms, and were delighted as City swamped newly promoted Leicester City 5-2, with Ferguson contributing a debut goal. Willie Davies also scored but the real hero was Joe Cassidy who netted a hat-trick. Two weeks later, Harold Beadles and Pat McIlvenny were transferred to Sheffield Wednesday. City began to pull away from the lower reaches of the First Division, until Boxing Day, when they lost 0-3 at West Bromwich Albion.

At their next match, on New Year's Day, the club suffered their worst ever league defeat (a record which still stands today), when they lost 2-11 at Bramall Lane to their Cup Final conquerors Sheffield United.

Conditions on the day were described as:
" Wretched, with a persistent chilling rain turning the pitch into a quagmire ".
United mastermind Billy Gillespie, set the Blades on their way with a 13th minute goal and Boyle made it 2-0 seven minutes later. In the 28th minute, Willie Davies replied for the Bluebirds, but before half-time Harry Johnson and Dave Mercer (2) gave United a 5-1 interval lead. Billy Gillespie notched his second, and Sheffield's sixth, in the 53rd minute. Two minutes later Johnson scored his second goal to make it 7-1. At this juncture, City full-back Jimmy Blair, was forced to leave the game with an injured foot. The Blades showed no mercy, and further goals by Mercer – who completed his hat-trick in the 71st minute – and Boyle three minutes later, stretched the score to 9-1. The drenched spectators, delirious with excitement, forgot their own discomfort as Fred Tunstall – the scorer of the F.A. Cup winning goal against City – netted the best goal of the match when he completed a clever dribble with a blistering shot from an oblique angle, to score the Blades tenth after 76 minutes. Harry Johnson then went on to complete his hat-trick in the 81st minute, and there was a special cheer two minutes from time when Len Davies notched a second consolation for the Bluebirds to make the final score 11-2!

After this heavy reverse, City managed to steer clear of the relegation zone, and in nine games – during February and March – they lost just once. On the 17th of April, the Bluebirds won a vital match at Notts County, when Hughie Ferguson's hat-trick helped City to a 4-2 scoreline; Fred Keenor getting the other goal. This ensured City's safety and virtually condemned the Magpies to relegation. Hughie Ferguson's record of 19 goals in 26 matches fully justified his record fee, and without his contribution, Cardiff City would probably have been relegated.

In a troublesome season, Mr Stewart selected no fewer than 27 players. Home attendances dropped a little but still averaged a little over 20,000.

F.A.Cup:
The competition was revamped this season, for the First and Second Division clubs now entered at the third round stage. The City were drawn against fellow First Division strugglers Burnley, at Ninian Park, and the game ended 2-2 with Joe Cassidy and Len Davies scoring for the Bluebirds. The midweek replay produced a good performance by the City team which was climaxed by Hughie Ferguson's brace in a 2-0 win. The fourth round brought Newcastle United to Ninian Park and the Magpies won easily by 2-0. But the United were dumped out of the competition by Clapton Orient in the next round. Over 42,000 attended the Newcastle tie, Ninian Park's largest crowd of the season.

Welsh Cup:
Cardiff City paid the ultimate price for not fielding a full strength team when they entertained Merthyr Town, for the Third Division (South) side won 2-1, City's only consolation being a Ferrans own goal.

Between the 24th October 1925 and the 20th November 1925, there were a record number of 16 International players on the Cardiff City's staff. Harold Beadles, Len Davies, Willie Davies, Herbie Evans, Jack Evans, Fred Keenor, Jack 'Ginger' Lewis Jack Nicholls and Edgar Thomas, had all represented Wales. Jimmy Blair, Joe Cassidy, Dennis Lawson and Jimmy Nelson were the Scottish representatives, whilst Tom Farquharson, Pat McIllvenny and Tommy Sloan were Ireland's men. Tom Watson was capped by Ireland on 27th February 1926.

The City were elected to the London Combination League for the next season. The Directors announced that they would allow ladies to stand in the boys' enclosure at the Grangetown end, to avoid being crushed; they had, however, to occupy the back of the enclosure!

****

1926-27 Season – Division 1:

Jack Evans, Cardiff City's first professional player, signed for Bristol Rovers in the close-season, where he linked up once again with Joe Clennell. Jack's first appearance had been in 1910, and his last game was against Bolton Wanderers at Ninian Park on the 10th of April 1926. In sixteen years he had been a virtual ever-present, until the arrival of George McLachlan. He would become remembered as one of City's great pioneers. In the Boardroom, Councillor W.H.Parker took over the Chair.

Once again the summer months produced a flurry of transfer activity with Joe Nicholson being exchanged for ex-England International George Blackburn of Aston Villa. Leaving Ninian Park were Jack Page for Merthyr Town, and Alfie Hagan to Tranmere Rovers, where the latter player joined Herbie Evans and Jack Lewis, who had been transferred the previous March. Goalkeeper Joe Hills joined Swansea Town. Fred Stewart signed local amateur Ernie Curtis, plus Tom Pirie from Aberdeen, Tommy Wainwright from Bolton, G.F. Tysoe of the Birmingham Tramway Company, and James Baillie of Wishaw. A week before the start of the new season, former record signing Joe Cassidy was exchanged for utility player Sam Irving of Dundee.

Cassidy had not been the success hoped for. It was later revealed that during his time at Bolton he had lost 22lbs, due to severe influenza. Although his health improved during his time at Cardiff, he still lacked stamina, and had to be rested on several occasions.

Just as they had done in 1925-6, City made a poor start to their League Campaign. On this occasion they had only one win, 3-1 against Leeds, in the opening nine games. As Stewart tried to settle the team into a regular pattern he showed signs of desperation by giving debuts to Jim Baillie, Tom Pirie and Ernie Curtis, in the same home match against Manchester United, on the 25th of September, which City – not surprisingly – lost 0-2 .

Another worry for club officials was the effect that the General Strike was having on attendances. Although the Cardiff tramline system had by now been extended to Sloper Road, many supporters just could not afford a visit to Ninian Park. Gone for the time being were the gates of 30,000+ of previous seasons, for these were replaced by crowds that dipped as low as 8,000 – for the visit of West Ham United, in November.

The Bluebirds disappointing performances and injury problems meant that the amateur Frank Matson plus Fred Castle and Tom Hampson, all signed in the winter months, were given League baptisms. Also to make their debuts were, Percy Richards, who had signed the previous year, and G.F. Tysoe. To add to City's misery, Welsh international Willie Davies was confined to Talgarth Sanatorium after contracting pleurisy, an illness which kept him out for a year.

One notable departure from Ninian Park was veteran Scottish International full-back Jimmy Blair, who had been transfer-listed at the end of the 1925-6 season. The former City record buy finally, on Christmas Eve 1926, moved on to Bournemouth. Blair, now 38 years old, had given the defence class and poise in his 200 first-team games for the Bluebirds. It was reported that Bournemouth paid £3,900 for the defender, which meant that the City realised a profit of £400, which was quite remarkable.

City's much-needed change in fortune coincided with their successful F.A. Cup run which saw them reach Wembley for the second time in two years. Thankfully this Cup form transferred itself to League games as well, and between the 15th January, when they drew 0-0 at home with Burnley, and the end of March, the City lost only one League match in ten games. Hughie Ferguson was back in the goalscoring grooves, after being played on the right-wing, and the Bluebirds clawed themselves out of danger. The signing of flying winger Billy Thirlaway from Birmingham City allowed Ferguson to return to his customary centre-forward berth, and he responded with 11 goals in 12 League matches. Fulham visited Ninian Park for the second round, and the City were unconvincing in their disposal of the Londoners with a single Len Davies goal.

On April the 9th, the City had five players on International duty, yet still drew 2-2 at West Ham. But at Liverpool, on Good Friday, the Bluebirds' went down with a 0-5 defeat, after reserve goalkeeper Tom Hampson had been hurt and George McLachlan had taken over in goal. The following day, Cardiff beat Sheffield Wednesday 3-2, but had Harry Wake injured after he scored one of the City goals. On Easter Monday, only five days before their F.A. Cup Final appearance, the Bluebirds atoned for their 0-5 defeat at Anfield by beating Liverpool at Ninian Park 2-0 before 20,000 fans, their best League crowd of the season.

Hughie Ferguson was the campaign's top scorer with 25 League goals and, despite Fred Stewart using 26 players during the season, City were well served by regulars, Tom Farquharson, Billy Hardy, George McLachlan, Jimmy Nelson and Tom Watson. The depression in South Wales caused by the General Strike had an alarming effect on City's 'gates', which averaged only 14,000. Indeed it was reported that many poor supporters would walk from the Rhondda Valleys for some home games - dedication indeed!

F.A.Cup:

The most momentous run in the competition by Cardiff City saw the Bluebirds go all the way to Wembley and take the F.A. Cup out of England for the first time, when they defeated Arsenal 1-0 in the Final on the 23rd of April 1927.

City began their Cup trail on the 8th of January with a home tie against Aston Villa in the Third Round. The Bluebirds League form had been dismal, indeed they had won only twice in their previous nine League outings, and Mr Stewart had been shuffling the team about. With Fred Keenor absent through injury, Tom Sloan took over at pivot and Hughie Ferguson, normally at centre-forward, was switched to outside-right, with Harry Wake inside. On the left flank were two 19 year olds, Ernie Curtis plus Percy Richards who took the place of the demoted George McLachlan. This same team had beaten and lost to Arsenal over the Christmas/New Year period, and before a crowd of 31,000, they set about Villa in style. There was no doubting City's credentials as they cruised to a 2-0 lead, through Len Davies who was back at centre-forward, and Ernie Curtis, playing in only his 14th first team outing. A late goal for Villa, credited in some quarters as an 'own goal' by Tom Farquharson, made the final scoreline of 2-1 appear a much more tighter game than it really was.

City's fourth round tie was at Darlington, on the 29th of January, the team that had opposed the Bluebirds in their 1925 F.A.Cup run, when it had taken three games before the Welshmen could progress. There was no such scare this time, although Darlington did make City battle all the way to a flattering 2-0 victory, with goals from George McLachlan, recalled to the left wing, and Hughie Ferguson, still operating at outside-right.

Fred Keenor, free from injury and off the transfer list, had settled his differences with the club - which had occurred several months earlier - and was recalled for the fifth round tie at Bolton on February the 19th. The Wanderers, riding high in Division One, and formidable at Burden Park, were clear favourites, but on this day, and before a crowd of 49,465, Cardiff City pulled out all the stops and stunned the football world with a terrific performance. There was drama a-plenty as the City were denied a clear cut penalty appeal, following a handling offence by Cope, the Bolton defender. Midway through the first-half England forward David Jack was denied a goal for Bolton when his shot appeared to cross the line, after striking an upright, but in the midst of the crowds' baying and the protests of the Bolton players, the referee waved play on! Despite being pegged back for long periods the City defence, revolving around the inspirational figure of Fred Keenor, kept the Wanderers at bay. Cardiff got due reward for their dogged determination, ten minutes after half-time, when Bolton full-back Finney was spotted by the referee handling McLachlan's centre, inside his own penalty-area. Hughie Ferguson, keeping cool in the Burnden Park cauldron, slotted home the resultant spot-kick. The Bluebirds oozed class and confidence, whilst Bolton were a spent force, and with twenty minutes to go Len Davies put the result beyond doubt when he scored City's second goal following Ferguson's accurate centre from the right.

City's reward for their finest performance of the season was an away sixth round tie against Chelsea, promotion challengers in the Second Division. General strike or not, F.A. Cup fever had gripped South Wales, and it was estimated that 12,000 Cardiff City followers were in the mammoth crowd of 70,184. As so often happens the game failed to live up to expectations, with the muddy conditions hampering many of the constructive movements. The match ended scoreless, and for the midweek replay at Ninian Park another 47,853 turned up, to take the total attendance for the two games to 118,000. The Ninian Park crowd were not to be disappointed as the game turned out to be one of the most dramatic and controversial ever played at the ground.

Conditions were again heavy underfoot, and the Bluebirds', noted for their Scottish-style ground passing game, caught Chelsea on the hop by implementing long ball tactics which soon met with results. Only ten minutes had gone when Len Davies saw his shot rebound from the bar and Sammy Irving followed up to rifle the loose ball past Millington, to put City ahead. In the 20th minute, Millington was again picking the ball from the Chelsea net after Len Davies had hared past Wilding to score with an opportunist shot. Ten minutes before half-time there came an incident which was to have a bearing on the eventual outcome of the match, and have far-reaching consequences in the laws of the game. Chelsea's centre-forward Turnbull was fouled by Tommy Sloan at the Canton end and a penalty was awarded. As Andy Wilson prepared to take the kick, Tom Farquharson retreated to the back of the net. When the Chelsea inside-left ran up to the ball Farquharson advanced so quickly that he effected the save from inside the six yard box, having successfully narrowed the angle to minimal proportions! Two years later the laws were changed to ensure that a goalkeeper could not move, and be standing on the goal-line when the ball is kicked.

That was not the end of the controversy for on the stroke of half-time the Chelsea right-half, Priestley, put in a shot which appeared to have skimmed the far post and gone off for a goal kick. Mr Pennington, the referee, had a different view and awarded a goal. In the midst of the City protests, Mr Pennington pointed out that the net pegs behind the upright had been tugged free by the passage of the ball. A policeman confirmed that the ball had indeed gone through the netting, and the goal was allowed to stand! City were stunned by a Chelsea onslaught immediately after the break, and within five minutes of the restart the Londoners had equalised when Turnbull headed home Pearson's free-kick. The Bluebirds were tottering as Thain hit the crossbar, and they were reduced to ten men for a while when Ernie Curtis had to temporarily leave the field. The Cardiff teenager returned to play on the right-wing, and with only seven minutes remaining, he produced a teasing cross that tempted Wilding into using his hands as Hughie Ferguson lurked ominously behind him. Another penalty resulted, and Ferguson smote the winning goal from the 'spot' which heralded great scenes at the final whistle.

Second Division Reading were City's semi-final opponents, at Molineux, on the 26th of March 1927.

The Bluebirds had just completed three successive home wins, 2-0 over Derby County, 2-1 versus Bury and 2-0 against Huddersfield Town, with Ferguson responsible for five of the six goals scored. So City, with an improving League position, were in confident mood as they spent a week at Southport, their favourite retreat. With Thirlaway 'cup-tied', Wake took over at outside-right, Ferguson resumed at centre-forward and Davies played in the inside-left berth. Reading, who had beaten Swansea Town in the sixth round, fancied their chances of completing a Welsh 'double', but they never really got started, and once the irrepressible Ferguson had opened the scoring in the 25th minute, it was destination Wembley for the rampant Bluebirds.

McLachlan, tormenting the Reading defence, provided the perfect cross, and Ferguson steadied himself before netting with a low shot. Eight minutes later McLachlan powered to the bye-line and pulled back an inviting centre. Harry Wake converted the cross with a flying header, and the City never looked back. Reading battled to keep the score down in the second-half as the City, with eight International players in their line-up, teased them with their possession play. The Bluebirds scored another goal when Ferguson (who else?), linked again with George McLachlan and cut through the heart of the Reading defence to net his second goal, and City's third, with a firm drive.

For the second time in three years, Cardiff City had reached the F.A. Cup Final at Wembley.

F.A. Cup semi-final action at Molineux:
(Left) The first City goal from Fergusson - hidden by Reading defenders.
(Right) Ferguson (far left) watches in admiration as Wake (out of the picture) gets the second.

The 23rd of April 1927 remains the greatest day in Cardiff City's colourful and chequered history, as on that date they became the only team to take the F.A. Cup out of England. The fates must have laughingly decreed that the Welsh dragon would triumph on St. George's Day!

The City were forced to make one significant change in their line-up from their successful F.A. Cup semi-final team however. Wake, eager to atone for his costly mistake in the 1925 F.A. Cup Final, had the misfortune to be injured only a week before the Wembley showpiece, while helping City to a 3-2 home League win over Sheffield Wednesday, during which he had scored one of the Bluebirds' goals. Harry's injury required hospitalisation, and an over-zealous reporter with one of the leading newspapers went so far as to report Harry's demise! A City supporter, overcome with emotion, took flowers to Cardiff Royal Infirmary and must have had a great shock to see the City player sitting up in bed and tucking into a hearty meal! With Wake unavailable and Thirlaway 'cup-tied', Fred Stewart named Ernie Curtis at outside-right, making the teenager the youngest player to appear in an F.A. Cup Final up to that time. City stayed at Southport for their preparations, enjoying the hospitality of the Palace Hotel, before travelling to London by train on the Friday afternoon. Learning from their experience of two years earlier, when they had arrived at Wembley too early, the Bluebirds made sure they reached the stadium barely an hour before kick-off, much later in fact than many of their supporters.

It was the first occasion at Wembley for community singing, and the many Welshmen in the vast crowd gave two renditions of the Welsh National anthem. Keenor led his team out and kicked a ball on to the pitch so that the players could run after it whereas Arsenal, led by Charlie Buchan, marched out rather stiffly like a line of soldiers. The Bluebirds were relaxed, even when introduced to King George V, who, by coincidence, had been in Cardiff only two days earlier where he had opened the National Museum of Wales in Cathays Park. Back in the Welsh capital that Saturday afternoon thousands of people had gathered to listen to the match outside City Hall where specially mounted speakers would relay the first ever live commentary on an F.A. Cup Final. The match, refereed by Mr W.F. Bunnell, was never a classic, although the crowd made plenty of noise to create a good atmosphere. Both defences were on top with Hardy doing his usual reliable job on Charlie Buchan whereas Ferguson and Len Davies found openings difficult to come by.

Half time arrived with no goals and precious little to report, but the second-half did show some improvement as Farquharson sprung to City's rescue with several fisted clearances. The crowd, sensing that just one flash of inspiration, or one mistake, would probably settle the match, grew more subdued as there appeared to be little sign of the deadlock being broken. Sixteen minutes from time came the incident that provided the only memory and talking point of this dour encounter. From a throw-in on the left, and level with the Arsenal penalty-area McLachlan switched the ball infield to Ferguson. The Scot, whose main forte' was his shooting from the edge of the box, duly obliged. Arsenal's Welsh international goalkeeper, Dan Lewis, went down to his left and seemed to gather the ball in a sideways kneeling position. Len Davies was following up and the Arsenal 'keeper, who momentarily looked up, inadvertently knocked the ball behind himself with his left elbow. Mortified with his slip and the presence of Len Davies, Lewis spun around and in reaching for the loose ball only succeeded in helping it over the line as the City forward jumped over the Arsenal 'keeper to follow the ball into the net! Much has been spoken and written and about the goal:
Did Ferguson impart some sort of wicked spin on the ball? .... Did Lewis, a Welshman, deliberately concede the goal?
Did grease on Lewis's jersey cause him to mishandle? .... Did Davies get the final touch?

The goal was officially credited to ace marksman Hughie Ferguson and that is the way it has remained in the record books. But film taken from behind the goal shows conclusively that it was Lewis's elbow that finally propelled the ball over the line. Mr David Lloyd George led the Welsh rejoicing, as Fred Keenor accepted the F.A. Cup from King George V, and the scenes of joy were echoed by the listening thousands outside City Hall in Cardiff.

The team had a tumultuous reception on their return to the Welsh capital and by winning the F.A. Cup the Bluebirds had demonstrated what could be achieved in such a short time; after only seven years in the Football League with astute management, by Fred Stewart, the good training of George Latham M.C., and careful administration from the clubs' founder, Bartley Wilson.

Welsh Cup:

Cardiff City's opening match was against the Welsh Cup holders Ebbw Vale, and due to the mining disaster on St. David's Day at Marine Colliery, Cwm – in which 52 men had lost their lives – the City agreed to switch the game to Ebbw Vale and give their receipts to the disaster fund. The match ended 0-0 and the game was replayed, again at Ebbw Vale, the following week, when a City team showing several changes, won comfortably by 6-1. The goals came from Len Davies (2), reserve Fred Castle (2), George McLachlan and Ernie Curtis. On April the 28th, City entertained Barry Town and goals by George McLachlan and Len Davies gave the Bluebirds a 2-0 victory. There was great excitement when the semi-final was played at Wrexham on 2nd May, for by then the City had become the F.A. Cup winners, and they were greeted ecstatically by the North Walians.

Two goals by the popular Len Davies in a 2-1 win put the Bluebirds into the Welsh Cup Final. The Final, again at Wrexham, took place only three days after the semi, and City's opponents were Rhyl. The non-Leaguers weren't quite good enough to prevent the Bluebirds from completing a unique 'double' – i.e. the winning both the English and Welsh Cups in the same season. The goals in a 2-0 victory came from Len Davies and Sam Irving.

International honours were bestowed on five Cardiff City players during the 1926-27 season, viz. Fred Keenor, Willie Davies (before his illness) and Len Davies for Wales; Sam Irving and Tom Sloan played for Ireland.
In the final home programme of the season, it was announced that the Club had secured the unsold copies of the F.A. Cup Final programme. These were priced at 6d, but were on offer to supporters at 2d (1p)!

(Top) – Keenor with the lucky black kitten that was found by the players at Southport, and taken to Wembley.

(Middle) – George McLachlan being introduced to King George V by City skipper Fred Keenor.

(Right) – Arsenal captain Charles Buchan shakes hands with Keenor, before the start of the Cup Final.

THE 1927 F.A.

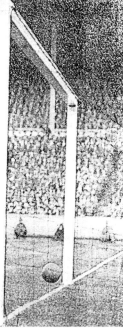

(Top) – Hughie Ferguson's shot, is fumbled by Lewis, the Arsenal Goalkeeper, and gently rolls over the line.
(Middle) – Billy Hardy takes his celebratory drink. Reserve Tom Pirie (right) looks on and Fred Stewart in the background smiles with satisfaction.
(Above) – The celebrations continue back in Cardiff, as entourage sets off through the crowded streets.
(Left) – Skipper Fred Keenor, with the Cup, leads the team down from the Royal Box.

CUP FINAL

1927-28 Season – Division 1:

During the Summer of 1927, Cardiff City appeared to be content to rest on their laurels, as far as the playing staff were concerned, preferring to invest much of the profits from their successful F.A. cup triumph into constructing a cover for 18,000 spectators at the Grangetown end of Ninian Park. Secretary-manager Fred Stewart's only pre-season signings were goalkeeper 'Joe' Hillier of Bridgend and John Ridgeway from local football in Sheffield.

As holders of the F.A. Cup Cardiff City were feted everywhere they went for they had not only won the trophy for the people of Cardiff but, so it seemed, the whole of the Principality. At Ninian Park, Mr. Watkin J. Williams was appointed Chairman, in place of Councillor Parker.

The crowds at Ninian Park improved for the opening games of the new season, (they had averaged only 14,000 the previous term), and the Bluebirds began their campaign with an unbeaten run of seven games, until coming down to earth with an almighty bump at Huddersfield on the 1st of October. The Yorkshiremen, League champions for three consecutive seasons and runners-up in the past season, showed merciless form as they smashed City by 8-2. But to their credit, the Bluebirds bounced back the following week when Ferguson and Len Davies scored in a 2-1 win over Tottenham Hotspur.

City were to remain in the top ten of the First Division for all of the campaign, mainly on the strength of their home form. When they played the return against Huddersfield on the 11th of February, the Bluebirds exacted full revenge for that 2-8 drubbing by winning handsomely - 4-0 - with goals from Thirlaway, Davies (2) and a Woodward own goal.

In a flurry of transfer activity defender, Bill Roberts was signed from Flint Town, as were Matthew Robinson, a forward from Pelaw in the North East, and Frank Harris (who cost £20) from Cradley Heath. Unfortunately, these players (good servants as they would turn out to be) hardly compensated for City selling quality players such as Sam Irving to Chelsea, Ernie Curtis to Birmingham City and Willie Davies - now recovered from his long illness - to Notts. County.

Just before the end of the season Mr Stewart signed Tom Helsby from Runcorn and local boy Walter Robbins on amateur forms. City's title challenge had evaporated by March and they suffered a shock 1-5 home defeat by West Ham on the 24th of that month. A week later they were sent crashing 1-7 at Derby, where the Rams who had drawn 4-4 at Ninian Park earlier in the season, displayed their best form of the term; Harry Bedford (4), George Stephenson (2) and Sammy Crooks beating Tom Farquharson.

In a topsy-turvy season, in which City had scored 70 goals but conceded 80, they still managed to finish sixth in the First Division. Only George McLachlan was ever present, Billy Hardy (now 36 years old), missed just one match, and there was consistency from Billy Thirlaway, Tom Farquharson and the redoubtable 33 year old Fred Keenor. Hughie Ferguson, with 18 goals from 32 matches, was top scorer, Len Davies notched 15 and there were 11 goals apiece for both wingers Billy Thirlaway and George McLachlan. The improvement in City's League form was mirrored by the average home attendances which rose to top 20,000.

F.A. Cup:

Cardiff City's defence of the trophy began on the 14th of January, with a home third round tie against Southampton. Regular scorers Hughie Ferguson and Len Davies netted for the Bluebirds and although Rawlings replied for the Saints, City ran out 2-1 winners. Two weeks later Liverpool visited Ninian Park in the fourth round. In the heaviest conditions imaginable, the City overcame the men from Anfield. Goals from George McLachlan and Jimmy Nelson (from a fiercely struck direct free kick), turned the match Cardiff's way, after Liverpool had taken the lead with a penalty from Dick Edmed.

It was on to Nottingham Forest for a fifth round tie on February the 18th. This was to be the day that the blue and white ribbons would be taken off the F.A.Cup, for City lost their grip on the trophy. Early signs had been promising as Cardiff, with Joe Jennings replacing the injured Tom Watson, appeared to be well in control, and their confidence was boosted further when Ferguson scored to give the Bluebirds an interval lead. The Forest team began to turn the tide, encouraged by 30,570 excited supporters, and spurred on by Welsh International Charlie Jones, who had played just one game for Cardiff City back in February 1921 before joining Oldham Athletic. They equalised via the penalty spot, when Jimmy Nelson was adjudged to have fouled Forest's Wadsworth. Thompson duly obliged from the spot, and with Troedyrhiw-born Jones in irresistible form, Forest finally forged ahead with a hotly disputed goal. The ball appeared to have gone for a City goal kick, when Gibson knocked it into the goalmouth and Stocks scored with the Cardiff players vainly appealing that the ball was 'out'.

Cardiff City had won the F.A. cup in controversial circumstances and now they had lost it in a dubious fashion. On the 5th of March, the trophy was returned to the F.A. Headquarters at Russell Square. In a simple ceremony, the case was unlocked, the Cup was inspected, and a receipt was issued to the Club.

Welsh Cup:

Cardiff City began the defence of the Welsh Cup with an emphatic 7-1 win at Oswestry with Len Davies (3), Fred Castle (2) and Thomas Potter-Smith (2) sharing the goals. On the 2nd of April, the City entertained Swansea Town in the next round, and in a tight encounter, eventually edged out their West Wales rivals, with Potter-Smith's lone goal.

The semi-final, on the 18th of April, saw City face Rhyl at Wrexham, and the non-League side almost caused an upset with a battling performance. City had cause to thank Ferguson, whose two goals earned a reply from a 2-2 draw. A week later, at Shrewsbury, City overcame their complacency to win by 2-0, with Len Davies and Harry Wake goals.

City met Bangor City in the Welsh Cup Final at the North Walians' own Farrar Road ground. The prolific goalscorer Ferguson was once again the matchwinner, netting both goals in the 2-0 victory that enabled the Bluebirds to retain the trophy.

1927 Charity Shield:

In 1927, The Charity Shield was not the showpiece that it has become in more recent times. The match was played in midweek at Stamford Bridge, where Cardiff City opposed the famous amateur side, Corinthians. The game proved to be a most difficult one for the Bluebirds as the Corinthians team was full of representative players, and just after the interval the amateurs took the lead through Ashton. City were tottering for a while but made their professional fitness tell by plugging away and wearing the amateurs down.

With twelve minutes left, Ferguson levelled the scores, and five minutes from time Len Davies scored the winning goal to delight the London Welshmen in the 15,000 crowd.

For a time at least, Cardiff City were the proud holders of the F.A. Cup, Welsh Cup and F.A. Charity Shield, a feat never achieved before – or since!

On the 3rd of October 1927, Cardiff City played Scottish Cup winners Glasgow Celtic in a special match at Hampden Park. A travel-weary City team, who had journeyed to Scotland following the 2-8 defeat at Huddersfield two days earlier, were beaten 1-4 by Celtic in front of a 6,000 crowd; Ernie Curtis netted the Bluebirds only consolation.

At long, long last, Englishman Billy Hardy received some recognition for his loyal service and unquestioned ability when, at the age of 36, he gained his only representative honour. Hardy was selected for the Football League to play the Irish League at Newcastle in September 1927. The joy at Cardiff City was such that his team-mates regarded Hardy's selection as the equivalent of winning a full international cap. Gaining International honours during the season were, Fred Keenor, Len Davies, Ernie Curtis and Willie Davies – all for Wales, with Sam Irving, Tom Sloan in Irish colours, and Jimmy Nelson who turned out for Scotland.

In 1928, Cardiff City undertook a successful tour of Denmark, where they defeated Aarhus 2-0, Aalborg 4-0 and Odense Combination 4-1. Agreement was made during the tour for substitutes to be used during matches – a previously unheard ofaction!

It was reported that Fred Stewart agreed terms with Jensen, who played centre-forward for Odense, but work permit problems curtailed transfer negotiations.

•••••••••••••••••••••••••••••••••••

1928-29 Season – Division 1:

Ninian Park was looking an absolute picture during the summer months as the construction of the covered end behind the Grangetown goal reached completion.

Fred Stewart made one significant signing when he bought Welsh international inside-forward Stan Davies from Birmingham City. Unfortunately for City, Davies had gone beyond his best having been an influential player with West Bromwich Albion, and his short stay at Ninian Park was not to be a happy one. Within months he was appointed player-manager of Rotherham United. Also arriving at Ninian Park was defender Emlyn John from Mid-Rhondda and inside-forward Leslie Jones, an amateur from Aberdare, who was destined to have a successful career in later years.

Cardiff City began the 1928-9 season with a 1-1 draw at Newcastle, Ferguson immediately getting off the mark, and a week later, on September the 1st, the Grangetown stand was officially opened at the home game against Burnley. The Lord Mayor, Alderman A.J. Howell, performed the opening ceremony. Then Hughie Ferguson took over the celebrations, with a sensational five goal salvo as City crushed Burnley 7-0, their highest-ever win in Division One. Who of the 25,000 spectators present would have predicted just how sour the season would turn on Cardiff City in the coming months?

Already without Tom Watson, plus an injury to Jimmy Nelson, the City were robbed of both International full-backs, and by November, Irishman Tom Sloan was also a long-term injury victim.

But probably worst of all, a series of niggling injuries meant that Hughie Ferguson played only 20 games throughout the season. It was becoming increasingly obvious that these players could not be replaced in terms of quality even though Frank Harris, Tom Helsey and Bill Roberts were all given their chance.

In a fourteen match sequence, from the 22nd of September – when they beat Bury 4-0 – to a Boxing Day 2-0 win over Leeds United, the City's only success was a 1-0 win at Portsmouth. The Fratton Park success was the last on foreign soil in Division One, a game in which Walter Robbins made his League debut. A week later Robbins scored on his home debut in a 1-1 draw with Bolton. The signing of former England international Frank Moss from Aston Villa did little to stem the flow, so Mr. Stewart invested in Scotland's leading scorer, Jim Munro of St. Johnstone, – but all to no avail. After a fine (and rare) 3-0 home win over Derby County on the 19th of January, when Hughie Ferguson (2) and George McLachlan were on target, City then went the rest of the season with only one win – 3-1 against Sheffield Wednesday – in their final sixteen games. To the chagrin of everyone concerned with the Club, Cardiff City annoyingly lost nine games by the odd goal, drew another 13 games and their defensive record of 59 goals against was the lowest in the First Division. The Bluebirds' undoing was their lack of scoring prowess for after that opening 7-0 win over Burnley they managed to total only 43 goals all season – and they failed to score at all in seventeen games! The loss of Hugh Ferguson at vital times obviously had had its effect.

Mr Stewart used 30 players with full-back Joe Jennings the only ever-present. Other good contributions came from Billy Thirlaway, Fred Keenor, Tom Farquharson and George McLachlan.

Hughie Ferguson was top scorer with 14 goals from only 20 games, followed by Len Davies who scored on 8 occasions. The 'golden era' was over for Cardiff City and, together with Bury, they were relegated to the Second Division. Not surprisingly the Ninian Park attendances had begun to drop towards the end of the season, but they still averaged 16,000 overall.

F.A.Cup:
Cardiff City suffered their heaviest defeat in the completion (only two years after winning the trophy), when they were humiliated 1-6 at Aston Villa. In this match veteran Billy Hardy scored his only F.A. Cup goal, whilst Villa's goals came from Tate, Durrell, Waring, Beresford (two) and York. By coincidence the referee, Mr W.F. Bunnell, who had taken charge of Cardiff City's finest hour at Wembley, was again the match official. City's sad fall from grace was witnessed by a crowd of 51,242.

Welsh Cup:
Cardiff City set out to retain the Welsh Cup for the third successive season with a home tie against Newport confectionery side, Lovell's Athletic. The Bluebirds managed to scrape through by 3-2 with Hughie Ferguson, Frank Harris and Len Davies scoring the goals. In the next round, on the 20th of March, City visited Somerton Park where Jim Munro's solitary goal was enough to beat Newport County. City's semi-final opponents were Rhyl and on the North Walians' home turf, they just managed to sneak into the final by virtue of goals from George Blackburn and Len Davies, in a narrow 2-1 victory.

The Welsh Cup Final, on 1st May, was played at Wrexham with City the clear favourites to beat Connah's Quay Nomads. In keeping with their sorry season the Bluebirds stumbled to a shock 0-3 defeat even though their team was packed with experienced campaigners! It was the first time in six Welsh Cup Final appearances, for City to lose, and seldom in the club's history can there have been a more humiliating defeat.

Five Cardiff City players were required for international duty:- Fred Keenor, Len Davies, Freddie Warren (a young winger in his first full season at Ninian Park) each played for Wales; Tom Sloan and Tom Farquharson turned our for Ireland.

1929-30 Season – Division 2:

Hughie Ferguson, so often a Cardiff City matchwinner and a huge favourite with South Walians, returned to his native Scotland when he joined Dundee during the Summer. Although not realised at the time, this transfer was to have a devastating effect on Ferguson's life. The popular Scot left behind fond memories of 76 First Division goals in 117 appearances (including his record setting 5 versus Burnley in September 1928), 10 F.A. Cup goals in 13 appearances (including the F.A. Cup Final winner versus Arsenal in 1927) and 5 Welsh Cup goals in 8 appearances. It was a phenomenal record and worthy of soccer immortality in the City 'Hall of Fame'. Faced with Second Division Football, Cardiff City secretary-manager Fred Stewart brought in Wilf Lievesley from Wigan Borough, Albert Valentine from Southport, William Bird (an amateur) from Llandrindod Wells and Paddy Moore of Mulingar (Ireland).

Moore, Lievesley and Valentine all played in the City opening 1-4 defeat at Charlton Athletic, but after a further two games none of these players appeared again during the season. The early months saw local boys Frank Matson (signed from Cardiff Corries in 1926), Walter Robbins and Freddie Warren all vying for regular places in the first team, as City still relied on veterans Tom Farquharson, Harry Wake, Fred Keenor and Len Davies.

On the 5th of October, the City and Swansea Town met for the first time in League Football, and attracted the seasons' biggest crowd, at Ninian Park, of 30,000. The game ended scoreless. The City's overall form was poor, until they won four successive home games during October and November, and during this period, the improvements included two outstanding personal performances. Billy Thirlaway hit a treble in a 5-2 win over Southampton on 16th November, and a fortnight later Treorchy-born reserve centre-forward Alf Miles helped himself to three goals against Oldham Athletic. Both these games drew crowds of around 12,000, and the drop in attendances started to have an inevitable effect on the Club's financial situation.

Just before Christmas, Cardiff accepted a substantial offer for George McLachlan, and the Scot, who had – at times – operated away from his customary left-wing berth, did not hesitate in making a return to the First Division when he joined Manchester United. Within a month the City were involved in an amazing bout of transfer action. They sold reserve goalkeeper 'Joe' Hillier, full-back Jack Jennings and emerging winger Freddie Warren to Middlesbrough in a triple deal worth £8,000. Mr Stewart immediately invested £800 to bring the goal scoring mercenary Ralph Williams from non-League Colwyn Bay.

It was during this mid-season burst of activity that the Bluebirds received a boost when Scottish international full-back Jimmy Nelson returned after a long injury lay-off. Aberdare-born Ralph Williams was quickly joined by Leslie Jones - another Cynon Valley discovery – in the first team, and City settled down to their best form of the season. Williams notched eight League goals in seven games, and schemer Jones weighed in with three, as the City won four home matches in a row:- Blackpool 4-2, Bradford (P.A.) 2-0, 'Spurs 1-0 and Millwall by 3-1.

By the end of the season the City were 8th in the Second Division, and in the final match Ralph Williams became the third City player to score a hat-trick during the term when he scored three times in a 5-1 home win against Bury. Williams finished as top scorer with 11 goals from 16 games and although Stewart had called upon no fewer than 29 players (a number of whom had departed Ninian Park during the season), Tom Farquharson, Bill Roberts, Harry Wake, Len Davies, Fred Keenor and George Blackburn all appeared regularly. Faced with Second Division football the public responded accordingly, and average home attendances were only 12,000.

F.A. Cup:

Cardiff City were drawn away to Liverpool in the third round before an Anfield crowd of 50,141. Despite having three reserve forwards, Jim Munro, Matthew Robinson and Jim McGrath in the team, the City shocked their First Division hosts by winning 2-1, with Len Davies scoring both goals. Archie McPherson had previously given Liverpool the lead in the 19th minute.

On the 25th of January, the Bluebirds travelled to Sunderland for their fourth round engagement, where Jack McJennett made his debut at full-back. Len Davies scored another F.A. Cup goal, but it was not enough as McLean and Gurney scored for Sunderland to put City out of the competition, before a crowd of 49,424.

Welsh Cup:

Cardiff City, for all their inadequacies, sailed through to reach their fourth successive Welsh Cup Final. On the 17th of March they travelled to Llanelly where goals from Len Davies (2), Alf Miles and Les Jones game them a 4-1 win. The City then met Swansea Town at Ninian Park, and hit another four goals through Billy Thirlaway, Les Jones, Len Davies and Jimmy Nelson without reply. Three weeks later City met Wrexham in the semi-final and goals from Miles and Les Jones, saw the Club into the final with a 2-0 win.

On the 3rd of May, City and Rhyl played out a 0-0 draw in the Welsh Cup Final at Wrexham, and the Football Association of Wales held over the replay until October 1930.

During the season, two Cardiff City players received international honours, with Fred Keenor and Len Davies playing for Wales.

Legendary manager Fred Stewart with the Bluebirds since pre-League days.

1930-31 Season - Division 2:

Fred Stewart shopped prudently during the summer months, making just one major signing, right wing George Emmerson from Middlesbrough replacing Billy Thirlaway, who departed for Tunbridge Wells Rovers. Bill Merry was signed from Fishguard Sports and Robert Weale from Troedyrhiw. Amateurs Len Evans from Lovell's Athletic, plus Eddie J. Jenkins and Tom Ware also joined the Ninian Park staff.

It was no great surprise that Cardiff City, with an ageing and weakened team, began the season with five successive defeats including a 3-6 reversal in their first home match, against West Bromwich Albion, for whom the prolific Jimmy Cookson scored four times.

Billy Hardy, in his 20th season at Ninian Park, was appointed player-coach and Jock Smith, a full-back, was bought from Middlesbrough for a small fee. City's next misery continued unabated and as they slipped down the table so their attendances suffered accordingly, by dropping below 10,000. The Bluebirds first victory came in their eighth match, when Walter Robbins (two), Ralph Williams and Len Davies scored in a 4-1 triumph over Plymouth Argyle.

By this time no fewer than eight players were on the injured list. Within a few weeks, Len Davies was also ruled out following an operation for appendicitis. City improved their position by winning 1-0 at Southampton through Fred Keenor's final goal for the Bluebirds, and a week later they beat Reading 5-0 with Robbins (2), Les Jones (2) and Valentine scoring. Robbins scored a hat-trick in a 4-4 draw with Millwall, but the City were leaking goals, and in three successive away games they lost 1-4 at Wolves, 0-7 at Preston and - on Boxing Day - 1-5 at Plymouth. New players were being tried at regular intervals and even the arrivals of former Irish international forward Jim McCambridge from Everton, inside-forward Albert Keating from Blackburn Rovers, and pivot John Galbraith from Clapton Orient did nothing to prevent the Bluebirds remaining entrenched at the foot of the Second Division. Galbraith, in fact, was seen as the ultimate successor for long-serving Fred Keenor.

In an amazing sequence of 17 games, from January the 17th - when they beat Port Vale 2-1 - City went all the way to the end of the season with only one more win. This solitary victory was against Stoke City, when Jim McCambridge scored all three goals in a 3-2 victory. City scored only eight goals in those seventeen matches, and they had already crashed out of the Second Division well before the end of the season. The support had ebbed away, and by the final game against Bury attendances had dropped to barely 5,000 - the lowest since 1910!

Mr Stewart had given League debuts to 15 players, and had used 32 in all, with only the ever loyal Tom Farquharson, George Emmerson and Jock Smith playing with consistency. Injuries, loss of form, and in the case of Billy Hardy and Fred Keenor - age - had all taken its toll, as the City dipped rather ignominiously into Division Three (South).

F.A.Cup:

Cardiff City were drawn to play at Brentford, of the Third Division (South), in the third round, on the 10th of January, and with twenty minutes remaining of the match, looked destined for victory as they led 2-0 with goals from Les Jones and Bert Valentine. The Bees staged a grandstand finish, and two goals in a three minute spell from Billy Berry and Jimmy Bain forced a replay. At Ninian Park, four days later, over 25,000 spectators (an amazingly high turnout), watched in disappointed silence as Brentford took a 2-0 lead in the opening 20 minutes through the two Lanes, Jack and Bill. A second-half reply from Walter Robbins was not enough to save the Bluebirds from defeat.

Welsh Cup:

On the 8th of October, Cardiff City and Rhyl met in the replay of the Welsh Cup Final, which had held been over from the 1929-30 season, and the Bluebirds made no mistake in recapturing the trophy that they had lost, so disappointingly, to Connah's Quay Nomads in 1929. Len Davies scored a hat-trick, and Les Jones the other, in a 4-2 victory.

The 1930-1 Welsh Cup campaign began for City with a runaway 7-3 win over Barry Town at Ninian Park, on the 4th of March. City's seven goals came from the three pairs of goals from Matthew Robinson, Len Davies, and Bill Merry, plus a single from George Emmerson. Three weeks later the Bluebirds travelled to Chester for the next round and emerged victorious, with Jim McCambridge on target in a 1-0 victory. City met with disappointment in the semi-final at Shrewsbury, then a non-League side, going down to a single goal defeat.

Two Cardiff City players received International honours, Fred Keenor and Walter Robbins, who each played for Wales.

On the 9th of January, Cardiff City and all their followers were stunned by the news from Scotland of Hughie Ferguson's suicide, who gassed himself after a training session at Dens Park, Dundee. Ferguson had struggled with injury and lack of goals since his return to Scotland. Unable to come to terms with his lack of success, and the barracking from the Dundee crowd, he had taken his own life in a fit of deep depression. Ferguson left a widow and two children.

Veteran Billy Hardy in training.
He was to play for Cardiff until 1932 - 21 years with the Club

CHAPTER 4

THE PRE-WAR SLUMP YEARS

1931-32 Division 3 (South):

In May 1931, Fred Keenor, Cardiff City's greatest player, severed his connections with Ninian Park when he joined Crewe Alexandra in the Division 3 (North). Keenor had joined Cardiff City as an amateur from Roath Wednesdays in 1911 and became a full-time professional a year later. He went on to play in 61 games for Cardiff in the Southern League (interrupted by the First World War, when he was twice wounded), and 369 Football League outings, plus 42 in the F.A. Cup and 32 Welsh Cup matches, to take his grand total to 504 appearances. Fred was the City's F.A. Cup winning captain in 1927, and a Welsh international on 31 occasions.

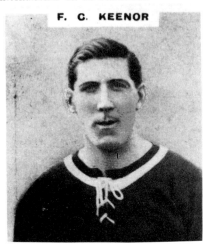

F. C. KEENOR

Another departure from the 'great' days was the popular Len Davies, one of Cardiff City's greatest ambassadors, and the holder of the record aggregate number of goals for the Club. The Welsh international forward surprisingly decided to join Thames Association, in their second (and final) season of League football. Len Davies scored 129 League goals in 304 games, plus 17 goals in his 33 F.A. Cup appearances and 32 goals from 32 Welsh Cup matches. His impressive final record for Cardiff read; 178 goals in 369 appearances (all competitions), and he was capped by Wales on 21 occasions.

Fred Stewart once again cast his net far and wide for players during the Summer, and succeeded in bringing Stan Holt of Macclesfield, Owen McNally of Bray Unknowns, Peter Ronan of Rosslyn Juniors and Harry O'Neill of Runcorn, to the Club. Unfortunately these players were not of the standard required to lift the ailing Bluebirds back to the Second Division.

The four new signings all made their debuts in Cardiff City's opening Third Division (South) match at Northampton on 29th August 1931, where the Bluebirds lost 0-1. Tom Farquharson was still going strong in goal and the City eventually managed to steady their downward trend, following a distressing spell between the 3rd of October and Boxing Day, when they won just once in ten games. The Bluebirds subsequently hit a rich seam of goals, particularly at home, with a 4-1 win over Luton, 5-0 against Northampton, 5-2 against both Torquay United and Exeter City and achieving their highest League victory of 9-2, against Thames Association. The goals were liberally spread between Walter Robbins, Jim McCambridge and Albert Keating, to the delight of the dwindling band of City supporters - now averaging less than 8,000.

Len Davies returned to Ninian Park on the 6th of February 1932, and ironically, in the light of his past goal-scoring exploits for the Bluebirds, found himself on the receiving end of Cardiff's record League win. The ill-fated Thames team wore ten of Davies' Welsh international jerseys at Ninian Park, in the hope that this would change their luck, but all to no avail! Walter Robins set a record of five goals from the left-wing, as City romped away to their impressive win, the other goals coming, as usual, from McCambridge, Keating, Jones, and a Burke own goal. As if fate had decreed it, Davies scored one of the Thames goals in this, his final appearance, at Ninian Park. City's record League victory came at just the right time, for the Bluebirds had dropped to 19th position in table, following three defeats. The 9-2 win over Thames was the first of five consecutive victories which pulled them to the security of 13th position.

Unable to make the first-team, Harry O'Neill joined Berne in Switzerland. On the 7th of April, the City, due to financial difficulties, were forced to accept a record offer of around £11,000 from West Bromwich Albion, for Welsh international winger Walter Robbins.

Towards the end of the season, McCambridge scored an amazing twelve goals in only seven League games, which included hat-tricks against Q.P.R. at the White City on Easter Saturday and Clapton Orient at Ninian Park on the 16th of April, as City finished the season on a high note. McCambridge led the City scorers with 26 League goals, a new club record. Walter Robbins hit 21 before his transfer to W.B.A., Albert Keating scored 19 and George Emmerson netted 10, in the Bluebirds' final tally of 87 goals. This was their highest number in their League history at that time.

The City ended the season in 9th position in Division 3 (South) as secretary-manager Stewart, had managed to find a more settled side in the second-half of the season. George Emmerson was ever-present and Bill Roberts missed just one game. Other notable contributions came from Galbraith, Farquharson, McCambridge and Harris.

A sporting carnival was arranged by other organisations in Cardiff during June 1932, when all proceeds went to aid the Cardiff City F.C. finances, which were at a low ebb. This reflected the sorry state of affairs that now existed at Ninian Park, following the club's rapid fall from grace and glory.

F.A. Cup:

Cardiff City's relegation in the 1930-31 season, meant that the Bluebirds were required to enter the competition in the first round. Seven thousand spectators were at Ninian Park to see City take on non-League Enfield on the 28th of November 1931, and they were rewarded by the Bluebirds, who ran up their record win in the F.A. Cup. Enfield were swept aside as City netted eight goals without reply, Albert Keating becoming the first Cardiff player to score a hat-trick in the competition. City's other goals came from O'Neill (two), Emmerson (two), and Harris. Amazingly, McCambridge and Robbins failed to find the net!

Clapton Orient were City's second round opponents at Ninian Park, on the 12th of December, where the Londoners met their match, as the Bluebirds, in fine form, galloped to a comfortable 4-0 win.

The goals were shared between McCambridge, Keating and Emmerson plus a Broadbent own goal. On the 9th of January, the City travelled to Bradford Park Avenue in the third round. The Yorkshiremen made their Second Division class tell as they beat the Bluebirds by 2-0, with goals from Irvine Harwood and Trevor Rhodes.

Welsh Cup:
Cardiff City played their first tie at Llanelly, and in a game of eight goals, won 5-3 with a hat-trick for Jim McCambridge plus a brace from Walter Robbins. In the next round City travelled to Chester, who were in their first season of League football in the Third Division (North). A goal from George Emmerson could not save the City from losing by 1-2 to the League newcomers.

Just one Cardiff City player received International recognition, with Walter Robbins representing Wales.

....

1932-33 Season - Division 3 (South):

There were two notable departures from Ninian Park in the early summer of 1932. Billy Hardy, who had been with Cardiff City since 1911 when he had been Mr Fred Stewart's first signing, left the club to take up a coaching position with Bradford Park Avenue. His bald pate and spring-heeled heading ability made Hardy one of the earliest recognised players in the Football League, and it was generally thought that it was only the fact that he was playing for a club outside the English Association, that had prevented him from becoming an English international. Hardy's amazing consistency for Cardiff City is best illustrated in his appearance record:- Southern League 143, Football League 353, F.A.Cup 49, Welsh Cup 37. A Total of 582 appearances.

If Billy Hardy was revered and loved by his adopted Cardiff public, then he had to share some of that affection with Captain George Latham M.C. Latham, an extraordinary character, had signed for Cardiff City from Stoke as player-coach on the 1st of March 1911. A Welsh international, Latham hailed from Newtown, Powys, where Cardiff City often played during the 1920's to raise funds for the local hospital, where George's mother was employed. Decorated for bravery in the First World War, Latham was awarded the Military Cross when serving with the 7th Royal Welsh Fusiliers and where he rose to the rank of Captain. Latham became one of football's best-known characters, as he trained the City players and made them one of the fittest teams in the Football League. He made his one and only League appearance for Cardiff City at the age of 42 in 1922, and was closely involved with everything at Ninian Park during all the great years. He left Cardiff City to take up a coaching appointment with Chester.

Cardiff City secretary-manager Fred Stewart signed two players from Q.P.R., full-back Robert Pollard plus outside-left Stanley Cribb, during the summer, and also invited Freddie Hill, a local amateur, to Ninian Park. All three new signings were in the Cardiff City team that lost 2-4 at Reading on the opening day of the season, where Stan Cribb scored a debut goal. Successive home wins, (3-0 against Bournemouth, 4-2 over Norwich City and 4-3 against Bristol Rovers), seemed to indicate a better season was in prospect for the Bluebirds. But their away form was disastrous and they failed to win a solitary match on foreign soil all season!

The defence was like a colander, particularly away from Ninian Park, and they suffered some heavy beatings, including; 1-8 at Luton, 2-6 at Swindon, 0-5 to Coventry, 1-5 against Q.P.R. and by 3-7 at Brentford. Even the return of former City favourite Jimmy Blair as coach in November 1932 did nothing to improve the City's away form, but it did coincide with a 2-1 home win over leaders Brentford, followed by a 1-1 draw with Bristol City and on the 17th of December, a 6-1 trouncing of Clapton.

Keating was transferred to Bristol City during November, and just before Christmas, a number of players arrived at Ninian Park. George Russell came from Bristol Rovers, plus amateurs Jack Collins and W.M. Burden appeared; trialists Jim Tennant and Roy Horton, made the move from Lovell's Athletic. Of these only Russell made any significant contribution.

Despite the many problems McCambridge scored well in the months before Christmas, and in order to help him in attack (when really it was the defence that needed strengthening), Stewart signed forwards Tom Maidment from Workington and Jim Henderson from St. Bernard's (Edinburgh). Both new players made an immediate impression, and Henderson had the rare distinction of scoring a hat-trick for the City at Brentford, on the 1st of April 1933, as the Bluebirds were stung 7-3 by the Bees.

On the 22nd of April, Jim Henderson wrote himself into Cardiff City's record books with his five goal haul in a 6-0 win over Northampton; Stan Cribb scored the other. Unfortunately only 7,000 saw Henderson's nap hand, which was just below City's average home attendance for the season.

Players had come and gone regularly throughout the season, and when amateur reserve goalkeeper Len Evans joined Birmingham Police, he was replaced by young Bristol Rovers' custodian Bob Adams. City ended the season in a disappointing 19th position, with McCambridge the leading scorer with 16 goals. Les Jones managed 13, the same as Jim Henderson whose strikes came in only 26 games, whilst Stan Cribb netted 11 times. Jim McCambridge missed just one match and other regulars were Tom Farquharson, George Emmerson, Leslie Jones, Frank Harris and Eddie Jenkins.

Cardiff City were sinking, with little signs of any improvement, and when secretary-manager Fred Stewart resigned in May 1933, it came as no surprise, for he had stated his intentions two months earlier. Mr Stewart had been secretary-manager of Cardiff City for 22 years, leading them into the Football League, to two F.A. Cup Finals and within a decimal point of the First Division championship. He was, and still remains, the most successful manager in Cardiff City's history. Over the years Mr Stewart had accumulated a number of business interests in the Roath district of Cardiff, including coal and corn merchant premises, and it was to these that he retired, until his death on the 1st of February 1954, aged eighty-one. Mr Stewart's resignation brought about Cardiff City's first managerial change since 1911. Club founder and assistant secretary Bartley Wilson took up the secretary-manager's post.

F.A.Cup:
Cardiff City were paired with Bristol Rovers in the first round on November the 26th, but failed to make home advantage count and had to be content with a 1-1 draw, right-half Frank Harris scoring City's goal. In the replay at Eastville four days later Cardiff City's woeful away form was again in evidence as they crashed out of the tournament, 1-4, McCambridge netting City's consolation goal.

Welsh Cup:
On the 22nd of February, Cardiff City had a rare meeting with Tranmere Rovers, in the Welsh Cup, and although the Merseysiders were a Third Division (North) team they came up against a City side having one of their rare good days. Two apiece from Leslie Jones and new signing Jim Henderson gave the Bluebirds a 4-2 home victory.

The next round, on March the 9th, saw City visiting Swansea Town, and they did well to earn a replay with a 1-1 draw, Tom Maidment scoring. In the replay a week later Maidment was again on target, together with Leslie Jones, as the City beat Swansea 2-1. City travelled to Chester, who were now coached by George Latham, in the next round, and the home side - who had dispatched City from the tournament during the previous season - did it again by defeating the Bluebirds 2-1, with Jim Henderson scoring City's single goal.

....

1933-34 Season - Division 3 (South):

New secretary-manager Bartley Wilson and his player-coach Jimmy Blair scoured the country for players during the Summer, but with little cash available they could not afford to bring any signings of note to Ninian Park. The popular George Emmerson was surprisingly exchanged for Ted Marcroft of Queen's Park Rangers, the latter having impressed the City officials with a hat-trick in Q.P.R.'s 5-2 win at Ninian Park the previous October. Other new arrivals included 'Eli' Postin of West Bromwich Albion, Robert Calder of Glasgow Rangers, Alex Hutchinson of Blackpool, Bill Marshalsey of St. Bernard's (Edinburgh), plus amateurs Harry Perks and Tommy Paget (who had played for Cardiff during the previous season), and John Duthie from Workington, the latter signing for the Club following a trial.

When Cardiff City won 2-1 at Watford on the opening day of the season, with left wing Alex Hutchinson having a two goal debut, nobody could have predicted that the Bluebirds were embarking on their worst-ever season in the Football League. Defender Calder, plus forwards Marcroft and Postin, were all debutants as City won four of their opening seven engagements.

Then, following a 4-0 home win against Crystal Palace on 7th October, the rot really set in, and City did not win again until the 30th of December, when they defeated Watford 4-1 at Ninian Park. As in previous seasons players came and went with unerring regularity, and of the 28 men to figure in Cardiff City's first team, no fewer than 18 were debutants. Of the men to join the Club, and there were quite a number during the season, the one big surprise was the signing of former City favourite Ernie Curtis from Birmingham City. Reg Reating (the brother of Albert) arrived from Bath City, Peter Molloy from Bristol Rovers and Enoch Mort from Gilfach Goch. These signings made absolutely no difference at all as City remained rooted to the foot of Division Three (South), and Bartley Wilson, after only ten months in the post, resigned in February 1934; he had found the job too demanding.

When City played at high-riding Coventry City, on Boxing Day, a record crowd of 27,589 enjoyed the Bantams' 4-1 win. Although the Bluebirds were rock bottom, Coventry Manager Harry Storer noted with interest the talents of both Leslie Jones and Ernie Curtis. Cardiff City had virtually nothing left, and sold their one prized asset, Leslie Jones, to Coventry City for £1,000 in January 1934.

The board of directors, realising that the nightmarish prospect of seeking re-election was looming ominously, invited Ben Watts-Jones, a former chairman of Swansea Town and a committee member of the Football Association of Wales, to take up the vacant secretary-manager's post, which he accepted on 7th March 1934. Known and respected throughout football Mr Watts-Jones' appointment did nothing immediately to improve the City's results. Indeed they won only once after he took office - a 3-2 victory at Aldershot where Reg Keating scored a hat-trick - and The Bluebirds finished the season rock--bottom of the Third Division (South) with attendances of only 2,000 for their final matches at Ninian Park. It was reported, when City lost 1-2 at home against Aldershot on 25th April, that there were no spectators on the 'Bob Bank'! It was inconceivable how this overall state of affairs had happened. Just seven years earlier, almost to the day, the Club had been F.A. Cup winners, respected in the First Division, and with a team full of international players. From the 1st of December 1933, the Bluebirds had been in the bottom two, and indeed they occupied bottom place from 3rd January until the end of this disastrous season. Yet they had been in the top 10 until October!

Cardiff City went cap in hand to the Football League A.G.M. and were immediately re-elected, and it was now up to the Club to recapture former glories. Eli Postin was the top marksman with 13 goals and Jim Henderson scored 12. Regular members of this poor team were the loyal Tom Farquharson in goal, full-back Bob Calder, centre-half John Galbraith, half-back Eddie Jenkins, centre-forward Eli Postin and defender George Russell.

F.A. Cup:
Cardiff City went no further than the first round. They drew 0-0 at home against Aldershot on 25th November, and four days later were beaten 1-3 in the replay, with Freddie Hill scoring City's consolation goal.

Welsh Cup:
The Club's interest in the competition was shortlived, for after drawing 2-2 against Bristol City at Ninian Park on 14th February (Jim Henderson and Ernie Curtis scoring), they bowed out 0-1 in the replay at Ashton Gate.

Division 3 (South) Cup:
On New Years' Day, Cardiff City entertained Aldershot in this new competition and their stay, as in the other Cup's, did not last until a second round, for they lost by 0-1!

....

1934-35 Season - Division 3 (South):

An old familiar face returned to Ninian Park in May 1934, when Captain George Latham M.C. came back from Chester to take over as club trainer from Jimmy Blair. Secretary-manager Watts-Jones cleared the decks for the new season - releasing all but five of his professional staff - and bringing in 17 new professionals plus two amateurs, during the Summer. Ernie Curtis had a dispute over wages and left, but the club kept his registration. The new arrivals consisted of, Stan Griffiths from Gillingham, Tommy Vaughan from Chester, Phil Griffiths from West Bromwich Albion, Jack Everest from Blackpool, former Welsh international Fred Whitlow from Exeter City, Arthur Granville of Porth, Walter Jennings from Bristol City, David 'Dai' Jones from Tottenham Hotspur, David Frater from Swindon, Billy Jackson from Bristol Rovers, Harold Riley from Notts. County, former Welsh international Wilf Lewis from Bath City, and amateurs Billy Moore, Syd Fursland and D.B. Lewis. It was the busiest close-season that Cardiff City had ever undertaken, and Mr Watts-Jones completely rebuilt the first team.

Cardiff City began their League season with no fewer that **eight** debutants in their line-up, only Reg Keating, John Gilbraith and the evergreen Tom Farquharson having previously played for the Club. To the delight of over 20,000 people, the Bluebirds won both their opening games at Ninian Park by 2-1 against Charlton Athletic and 1-0 versus Luton Town. But they quickly faced the stark reality of the situation, by losing away games at Crystal Palace 1-6 – where Palace's Albert Dawes scored five goals – and at Luton town with a 0-4 scoreline. With all the new faces, there were 15 newcomers in City's opening twelve games, one could never judge the mood of the team, brilliant one week, dismal the next.

When Jock Leckie replaced veteran goalkeeper Tom Farquharson on 29th September, it marked the beginning of the end for the legendary Irishman as a Cardiff City player. Although the City defence remained leaky, in spite of sterling work by left-back Jack Everest and pivot Bill Bassett, at least the forward line was not shy in front of goal.

On the 18th of October, Cardiff City unearthed a rare diamond when they signed 17 year old Reggie Pugh, an outside-right, from Aberaman. Two days later he made his League debut in a sparkling 3-1 win at Watford, which began a run of 97 consecutive appearances in City's first eleven.

By the season's end, Reg Keating led the scorers with 20 League goals, saving his best performance until City's final home game against Exeter City, on the 27th of April, when he netted four goals in a 5-0 win (Len Attley the other scorer). Jack Everest was ever-present and other regulars included Bill Bassett, Harold Riley and Reg Keating.

The 4th of May 1935, was one of the saddest days in Cardiff City's history, as goalkeeping legend Tom Farquharson played his final game for his beloved Bluebirds. Sadly, for the Irishman, it ended in a four goal win for Bristol City at Ashton Gate, but at least Tom's last appearance at Ninian Park the previous week had been in a 5-0 win over Exeter City. Farquharson had seen off allcomers since 1921, and had been a virtual ever-present in the intervening years. He stepped into retirement leaving behind a record of having made 445 League appearances, plus 34 in the, F.A.Cup, 39 games in the Welsh Cup, 1 showing in the Divisional Cup, which gave a grand total of 519.

The City ended the season in 19th position, with a lot of work still needed to improve their playing strength.

F.A.Cup:
Cardiff City's stay in the competition was very brief, for they lost the first round home match, against Reading, by 1-2 on the 24th of November. Wilf Lewis scored for the Bluebirds.

Welsh Cup:
Newport County were met at Ninian Park on the 13th of February, and in a five goal thriller against their fellow strugglers, the Bluebirds finally won by 3-2, with goals from Harold Riley (two) and Wilf Lewis. On the 27th of March, Cardiff City met Chester for the third successive season, and after a 2-2 draw at Ninian Park, City scoring through a Burke own goal and Jack Everest, they went to Chester on the 10th of April, and lost the replay 0-3.

Division 3 (South) Cup:
On the 17th of October, Cardiff slumped out of this competition by 1-3 at Crystal Palace, with Tommy Vaughan the solitary City scorer.

1935-36 Season – Division 3 (South):

Secretary-manager Ben Watts-Jones was not satisfied with the overall playing standards of his staff, and as a result he once again unloaded a large number of professionals during the close-season.

Arriving at Ninian Park in their place, were wing-halves Cliff Godfrey from Bradford Park Avenue and Harold Smith from Notts County, inside-forward Harry Roper from Leeds United, goalkeeper Jack Deighton from Everton, former Scottish international defender Hugh Hearty from Heart of Midlothian, and amateur goalkeeper George Poland from local football, plus centre-forward John Diamond from Barnsley and winger Fred Roberts from Luton Town.

An opening day hat-trick by Bob Bigg of Crystal Palace in a 2-3 defeat meant that the Bluebirds failed to get a good start, and six games had gone by before they recorded their first win, 4-1 at home against Clapton Orient. By this time Bill Bassett had switched temporarily to right-back and Enoch Mort had come in at pivot. Noted goalscorer Reg Keating was struggling with injury and loss of form, and it was just as well that John 'Legs' Diamond was finding the target fairly regularly, for it was the New Year before Keating opening his goal account for the season.

Young players George Poland, winger Doug Redwood and centre-forward Dai Williams were given opportunities in the first team. Williams, in particular, responded with some enthusiastic displays, netting five goals in four League matches, following his debut against Newport County at Ninian Park on the 18th of January. At least City seemed to be running into reasonably good form, despite the fact that Poland, Jock Leckie and Jack Deighton all had spells between the posts, and a number of players were used to full the outside-left position.

City's best League win of the season came on the 29th of February, when they beat Exeter City 5-2 at Ninian Park, and a four match unbeaten run during March kept the club out of the re-election waters. It was just as well, for the Bluebirds ended the season as they had begun it – with just one win in seven matches!

Reg Pugh had fulfilled his early promise and, although only 18 years old, was ever-present together with the experienced Cliff Godfrey. The City used 26 players during the season, with 14 of them making their League debuts, and it was little wonder that the club languished in 20th position in the table. Reg Keating was top scorer with 10 goals from 23 games, which included a hat-trick in a 4-2 win at Millwall on the 21st of March. There were identical goal returns from John Diamond and Dai Williams, who both scored nine in eighteen matches, and Reg Pugh notched up seven. The South Wales public had not entirely given up on the Bluebirds and had shown throughout the season that they were prepared to support the club, as the average home attendance of almost 11,000 demonstrated.

In May 1936 trainer Captain George Latham M.C. retired through ill-health. He had had an accident while riding to Ninian Park on his bicycle, and this left him severely shaken. He soon severed his Ninian Park connections and returned to his native Newtown in Powys.

F.A.Cup:
The 30th of November 1935, remains one of the darkest days in Cardiff City's history. Non-League Dartford came to Ninian Park in the first round and remarkably defeated the toothless Bluebirds by 0-3! The crowd of 9,000, still harbouring fond memories of the City's F.A.

Cup win only eight years previously scarcely believed it, and many saw the defeat as the lowest point in the club's existence.

Welsh Cup:
Cardiff were enjoying a good spell in the League when they faced Bristol City in the Welsh Cup at Ninian Park, and the run continued as they won 2-1 with goals from Reg Pugh and Reg Keating. The Bluebirds received a bye in the next round, and on the 12th of March, they lost 2-1 at Rhyl where Reg Pugh's goal was their only consolation.

Division 3 (South) Cup:
The City made yet another early exit from this competition, when John Diamond's goal was not enough to prevent them from losing 1-2 at Crystal Palace.

•••••••••••••••••••••••••••••••••

1936-37 Season – Division 3 (South):

The loss of the popular George Latham from Cardiff City's training staff was a major blow and created a gap which Mr Ben Watts-Jones quickly filled when he appointed Bill Jennings, the former Welsh international half-back. Jennings, a North Walian, had 19 years playing experience with Bolton Wanderers and had latterly been on the coaching staff at Notts County. His connections in football around Lancashire and the North did much to bring a number of new players to Ninian Park. Once again, Mr Watts-Jones, never one to let grass grow under his feet, turned over his playing staff – releasing all but a hard core of trusted professionals. Among the new faces for the season were:- Cecil Smith – a centre-forward from Burnley, David Ovenstone the Q.P.R. outside-left, winger John Prescott from Everton, full-back Bill Scott of Stockport County, goalkeeper Bill Fielding from Hurst (Lancs), Arthur Welsby – a forward from Sunderland and double signings Leslie Talbot plus Albert Pinxton, both from Blackburn Rovers.

There were **seven** debutants in Cardiff City's opening match at Walsall which, not surprisingly, was lost by 0-1. The Bluebirds then embarked on a sequence of five straight wins which put the club at the top of the table. New men Cecil Smith, Les Talbot and Albert Pinxton had all settled down and were scoring goals and playing well. The public response was excellent and almost 30,000 saw a 1-1 home draw with Southend on the 28th of September. The signing of experienced forward George Walton from Bolton Wanderers for a £1,550 fee in October demonstrated to the public that Cardiff City were well and truly back in business. With attendances often around the 25,000 mark at Ninian Park, it did look as if the Bluebirds were at last climbing out of the doldrums.

Then the bubble burst and City went down like a punctured tyre! On 21st November the Bluebirds crashed 1-5 at Bristol Rovers and it was not until 3rd March – when they beat Bournemouth 2-1 at Ninian Park – that they won again; a catastrophic run of 15 League games. Defeats included a 1-8 mauling at Luton (the eventual champions), and three successive away games which saw them slaughtered 0-6 at Q.P.R. on 13th February (where Fitzgerald and Charlton both scored hat-tricks), 1-8 at Southend – seven days later – plus 2-7 at Brighton, on the 6th of March.

The City rung the changes – perhaps too frantically – for in a six match period during December, no fewer than **nine** new players appeared in the first team.

Two new full-backs, John Mellor from Manchester United and former Scottish international Bob MacAulay from Chelsea, had the most daunting debuts in Cardiff City history when they faced that rampant eight-goal Luton attack on the 2nd of January. Other new players signed during this frenzied period were defender Jack Esler from Heart of Midlothian and centre-forward Eugene 'Ted' Melaniphy from Plymouth Argyle, plus a number of trialists. The full-back positions were proving a real headache as Arthur Granville, Louis Ford, Jack Esler, C. Turner, John Mellor and Bob MacAulay were all drafted in at one time or another. Bill Fielding and George Poland contested the goalkeeping position, and the only players to be unaffected by all the shuffling were wing-halves George Nicholson and Cliff Godfrey plus outside-right Reg Pugh – otherwise it was changes all the way!

A final surge of three wins in the last four League matches of the season dispelled any lingering fears of re-election, and the City ended the term in 18th position, an improvement of two places from a year earlier. But, after the encouraging start to their season, the Club must have been bitterly disappointed with the final outcome.

City's goal tally of 54 were evenly spread with George Walton leading the way with eight, and three players – Reg Pugh, Cecil Smith and Leslie Talbot – each scoring seven. Before the end of the season, Ben Watts-Jones resigned as secretary-manager after two hectic years in charge, and reverted to a place on the Board of Directors. Trainer Bill Jennings was appointed secretary-manager on the 1st of April 1937.

In the early hours of Monday the 18th of January 1937, the main centre stand at Ninian Park was completely destroyed by a fire. This was thought to have been caused by burglars who were after the takings of the F.A. Cup match against Grimsby Town that had been played the previous Saturday.

F.A. Cup:
The first round brought non-League Southall to Ninian Park on November the 28th, and, mindful of the Dartford fiasco twelve months earlier, Cardiff City made no mistake this time with a 3-1 win; George Walton, Leslie Talbot and Reg Pugh shared the goals. On the 12th of December, City entertained Swindon Town in the second round and emerged victorious following a close tussle. Goals from Arthur Granville and John Prescott, in only his second appearance for the club, took the Bluebirds to a 2-1 win.

The third round draw gave City another home tie and Grimsby Town visited Ninian Park on the 16th of January. By now Cardiff City were in that terrible mid-season slump, and in front of a marvellous crowd of 36,245, they put up a disappointing display. Grimsby won 3-1, with City's lone goal coming from Ted Melaniphy.

Welsh Cup:
Cardiff City did not last long in the competition, falling at the first hurdle to Barry Town at Jenner Park on March the 18th. The Linnets won 3-1 with George Walton scoring City's solitary goal.

Division 3 (South) Cup:
The City made what was their customary early exit, bowing out to Exeter City 0-1 at Ninian Park on the 28th of October!

•••••••••••••••••••••••••••••••••

Bill Bassett watches as Bill Fielding catches a high ball. The game, on the 10th of September 1936, was played at the Lea Bridge Road Ground of Clapton Orient.
City won the match (1-0) the third in a run of five successive victories - things then turned for the worst!

1937-38 Season - Division 3 (South):

Once again Cardiff City secretary-manager Mr Bill Jennings used his contacts in the game to strengthen the playing staff during the close season. He signed right-half Cecil McCoughey from Coventry City, outside-left Albert Turner from Doncaster Rovers, centre-forward Jimmy Collins from Liverpool, goalkeeper Bob Jones from Bolton Wanderers, Owen Evans from Aston Villa, Stanley Dibbert from Rhyl and Jimmy McMillan from Third Lanark.

The Club had a strong, experienced, and professional look about its team, and the Bluebirds made a blistering start to the new term. On the 28th of August, City had the honour of being the first League visitors to Brisbane Road, the new headquarters of Clapton Orient, and Jimmy Collins scored a debut goal in a 1-1 draw. In his home debut at Ninian Park two days later the chunkily-built Collins thrilled a 22,000 crowd with his hat-trick in a 5-2 win over Torquay United; George Walton and Bert Turner scoring the other goals. The following Saturday, the 4th of September, City went nap again with a 5-0 home win against Southend United, as Leslie Talbot (two), George Walton, Arthur Granville (penalty) and Bert Turner shared the goals.

The City duly won at Torquay, courtesy of Jimmy Collins, to complete a 'double' with the 1-0 win, before losing their first game, at Q.P.R. Then in successive home games, the City beat both Northampton and Brighton by 4-1, with Jimmy Collins continuing his spectacular start to his career at Ninian Park, when he scored a brace in each game. The South Wales public were thrilled by the team, and, despite the accommodation problems caused by the loss of the main stand through the fire of the previous January, 20,000 regularly attended the home games. This support was not surprising, for Cardiff were virtually impregnable at Ninian Park, and scored at a good rate on home soil. Jimmy Collins, Bert Turner and George Walton were a formidable trio of goalscorers. In November 1937, the one-time famous Sheffield Wednesday and ex-England international full-back, Ernie Blenkinsop, joined City as player-coach from Liverpool for a fee of £400. City were well placed in the Division until the turn of the year, but after February they lost momentum, the goals began to dry up and by the end of the season they had to settle for 10th position. On the 5th of March 1938, a record attendance for a Third Division (South) game of 38,066, saw City beat Bristol City at Ashton Gate through a Jimmy Collins goal.

The Club's overall performance over the campaign was a marked improvement on the previous four seasons, and City now had a base to work from. Custodian Bob Jones, although a veteran, had solved the goalkeeping problem, that was caused by Tom Farquharson's retirement, and was ever-present. In attack, Bert Turner, Reg Pugh, Leslie Talbot and Jimmy Collins missed very few games, and in defence the City were well served by Cecil McCaughey, Bill Bassett and Arthur Granville. Jimmy Collins led the scorers with 22 goals while Bert Turner secured 19 (oddly enough, all were netted at Ninian Park).

There was sadness at the club in October 1937, when 18 year old reserve half-back Trevor Williams, who had never made a first-team appearance, died at Cardiff Royal Infirmary following an operation.

F.A.Cup:
The first round draw had Cardiff City travelling to Northampton Town, and the mercurial Jimmy Collins rose to the occasion with both goals in a 2-1 win. City then met Bristol City at home in the second round on the 11th of December, and a hard-fought match ended 1-1 with Bert Turner scoring for the Bluebirds, before a crowd of 25,472.

The replay at Ashton Gate four days later produced a fine display by Cardiff City, and they ran out clear winners thanks to two goals from Jimmy Collins. On the 18th of January, the City faced Charlton Athletic at the Valley in the third round, but they were no match for the First Division side and crashed to one of their heaviest ever F.A. Cup defeats, for the Londoners triumphed by 5-0.

Welsh Cup:
On the 16th of February, Cardiff City slumped to a shock Welsh Cup defeat at Ninian Park, when non-League Cheltenham Town won the match by 1-0.

Division 3 (South) Cup:
After five years of trying to win a game in this competition, Cardiff City finally succeeded when a Bert Turner gave them a single goal victory at Northampton on the 27th of September 1937! In the next round, at Bristol City on November the 10th, the Bluebirds reverted to their usual form, and lost by 1-2; Jimmy Collins scoring City's goal.

Cardiff City played some interesting friendlies during the 1937-38 season. They journeyed to France and met Racing Club de Lens, on the 6th of October, winning 3-1, with George Walton, Jimmy Collins and Leslie Talbot sharing the goals. On the 4th of November, the Bluebirds recorded a fine victory when they were invited to meet Aston Villa in the Yeovil Challenge Cup, and beat the Midlanders conclusively 3-0 with Reg Pugh (two) and Jimmy Collins getting the goals. April the 27th, saw the visit of Hibernian to Ninian Park, and the Bluebirds beat the Scottish side 3-2 with goals from Jimmy Collins (two) and Leslie Talbot.

1938-39 Season – Division 3 (South):

Still trying to improve the overall quality of his playing staff the Cardiff City secretary-manager Bill Jennings signed wing-half Billy Corkhill and forward Ted 'Tex' Rickards from his former club Notts County. Mr Jennings solved the left-back problem by paying £1050 to Newport County for Jimmy Kelso, and when Gillingham failed to be re-elected to the Football League George Ballsom, their Welsh born right-back, came to Ninian Park. A £300 fee also brought Aberdeen's outside-left Ritchie Smith to Cardiff City.

Before the season started, the Football League's Fiftieth, City played Swansea Town at the Vetch Field in a Jubilee Benevolent Fund match. In a useful workout the teams shared six goals with Jimmy Collins (2) and a Simmons own goal claiming the City scores.

A marvellous crowd of around 30,000 were at Ninian Park for the Bluebird's opening League match against Exeter City, when Jimmy Kelso, Billy Corkhill and George Ballsom made their debuts. Despite a goal from Bert Turner, City got off to a disappointing start as the visitors scored twice to win 2-1. City's other two newcomers, wingers 'Tex' Rickards and Ritchie Smith, made their debuts in the Bluebirds' next match, at Mansfield, where two goals from Collins earned a point from a 2-2 draw.

Despite all the pre-season optimism at Ninian Park, the Bluebirds made a stuttering start to the new term, their best results being a 4-1 home win over Brighton on 1st October and 5-3 against Watford on 12th November, when Jimmy Collins netted a hat-trick.

After 56 consecutive appearances, Bob Jones lost his place in City's goal to Bill Fielding, and just before Christmas, popular hard-shooting winger Bert Turner – who had appeared only twice in the City's first team that season – was transferred to Bristol Rovers. Cardiff City paid Aldershot £1500 for their pugnacious forward Harry Egan, who had impressed City officials in a 1-1 draw at Aldershot on 3rd December. Egan made his City debut at Exeter on Christmas Eve and immediately began to repay his fee with a goal in a 1-1 draw.

City just could not string together a run good enough to make a promotion challenge, and following a 5-0 home win over Bournemouth on the 11th of February, a disappointing spell of only one win in nine games condemned them to the lower half of the table.

In March, Scotsman Ritchie Smith, who had been unable to settle and make an impact at Ninian Park, was transferred to Clyde. Billy Baker, a young outside-right or wing-half who hailed from Penrhiwceiber and had been signed from Troedyrhiw on amateur forms, came into the League team late in the season. He would go on to have an influential career at Ninian Park in later years.

Jimmy Kelso missed only one League match, and the mainstays of the City team were Bassett, Ballsom, Nicholson, Collins and Talbot. Collins was once again the leading scorer, with 18 goals, whilst both Harry Egan and Leslie Talbot each contributed 9. The season ended in dismal fashion – a 3-6 defeat at Walsall – and nobody could forsee that this fixture would be the last recognised League game for seven years!

In Europe war clouds were gathering which would soon erupt and plunge Great Britain into seven years of conflict.

F.A.Cup:
During the season, Cardiff City enjoyed their best run in the F.A. Cup competition for eleven years, which made up, in some way, for their inconsistency in the League.

On the 26th of November, the Bluebirds faced a tricky first round match at non-League Cheltenham Town, whose win at Ninian Park in the Welsh Cup the previous February was still fresh in everyone's minds. City didn't win, but they did manage to replay by drawing 1-1 through a goal from reserve winger Jack Prescott. It was Prescott who steered the Bluebirds through the replay four days later, as his lone goal was enough to win the tie.

The Bluebirds were drawn at home against Crewe Alexandra in the second round, and although the Northern team put up a stubborn performance, one flash of brilliance by Leslie Talbot earned City a 1-0 victory and a tilt at either First or Second opposition in the 3rd round.

To City's great delight the draw brought First Division Charlton Athletic to Ninian Park, and the Bluebirds were given a great chance of avenging the awful 0-5 beating they had suffered at The Valley the previous season. Much to the joy of the 22,000 crowd Cardiff City gave one of their best displays of the season, and they won far more handsomely than the narrow margin that was indicated by George Walton's single goal.

F.A. Cup fever gripped South Wales when it was learned that Cardiff City had been drawn at home to mighty Newcastle United in the fourth round on the 21st of January. In similar fashion to the Charlton Athletic match, the Bluebirds took the game to their more illustrious visitors, but try as they might they could not make a breakthrough. The magnificent turnout of 42,060 gave the City a marvellous ovation at the final whistle, but within their hearts they knew that any hopes of an upset had probably gone. And they were right, for the Bluebirds were no match for the rampaging Magpies in the replay at St. James' Park. United steamrollered City 4-1 with Reg Pugh scoring the consolation Cardiff goal.

F.A.Cup 4th round: Cardiff City 0 Newcastle United 0
Goalkeeper Bill Fielding looks up as Cardiff City centre-half Bill Bassett heads clear.
The attendance that day at Ninian Park was 42,060.

Welsh Cup:
Cardiff City had a busy season of Welsh Cup fixtures that begun with a home tie against Swansea Town on February the 8th. The game ended 2-2, with reserve Jimmy McKenzie and half-back Cec McCaughey scoring the City goals. The Bluebirds turned on the style in the replay at the Vetch Field a fortnight later, when two pairs of goals from Harry Egan and `Tex' Rickards gave them a runaway 4-1 victory. On the 8th of March, City met high-flying Newport County at Ninian Park, and they made ammends for the League `double' they had conceded to the promotion bound Monmouthshire side, with a crushing 5-1 win. Egan led the way with a hat-trick, and the other goals came from Rickards and McKenzie.

The City faced Oswestry in the semi-final, and it took three games before the tie was settled. Arthur Granville scored in a 1-1 draw on the 30th of March, and Leslie Talbot and Jimmy Collins both netted in the 2-2 drawn replay two weeks later. The deciding game on April the 26th, saw City edge out the gallant non-Leaguers 2-1, with Leslie Talbot and Jimmy Collins scoring the vital goals. All three semi-final games were played at Shrewsbury.

On the 4th of May, City faced South Liverpool in the Final, and although they fielded a strong line-up, the Bluebirds - who were strongly tipped to win the trophy - went down to a shock 1-2 defeat, Jimmy Collins being the lone City scorer.

Division 3 (South) Cup:
Cardiff City suffered their heaviest defeat in this competition when they selected an under strength team to play at Bristol City on 16th November, and were crushed 0-6.

On the 2nd of May, Cardiff City entertained Fulham in a benefit match for former 'warhorse' Billy Hardy. The Londoners won 3-2 with amateur Wilf Wooller and Freddie Hill scoring for the City.

There was a major development behind the scenes at Ninian Park in March, when Mr Herbert Merrett, a prominent Cardiff businessman, was elected to the Cardiff City board of directors. Within weeks Mr Merrett became Chairman, and his first action was to appoint Cyril Spiers of Wolverhampton Wanderers as secretary-manager, to replace Bill Jennings who had restored much of Cardiff City's lost credibility during his two years in office.

On the 9th of July 1939 all followers of Cardiff City's fortunes were dismayed to hear of the death of their legendary former trainer Captain George Latham M.C. at his home in Newtown, Powys. A former Welsh international, Latham had joined Cardiff City from Stoke on the 1st of March 1911 as player-coach. He trained the players hard, making all the team under his charge extremely fit for both Southern League and Football League matches.

Latham's bravery during the First World War, won him the Military Cross, and many of the tales surrounding him are now part of Cardiff City's folklore. The most repeated story, was when at the age of 42, he answered an emergency at Blackburn on the 2nd of January 1922. Following overnight illness which had incapacitated both Jimmy Gill and Jack Evans, Latham assisted the team to a 3-1 win, claiming afterwards that he had assisted in one of the goals by sitting on the Blackburn goalkeeper!

Latham trained both the 1925 and 1927 F.A. Cup Final teams, and he remained with the club until 1932, when he joined Chester - at that time a new club in the Football League. He returned to Ninian Park during Cardiff City's darkest days - in 1934 - but ill-health forced his retirement in May 1936. An example of George Latham's generosity and compassion was an episode in 1912, when he replaced centre-half Bob Lawrie, an injury victim, in the team for the Welsh Cup Final. Afterwards Latham gave Lawrie his winners' medal to make up for the pivot's disappointment at missing the game.

In George Latham's memory the ground of Newtown F.C. was named Latham Park.

1939-40 Season - Division 3 (South):

Despite the ever-threatening spectre of the War darkening the summer months of 1939, Cardiff City's new secretary-manager Cyril Spiers, a former goalkeeper with Aston Villa and Tottenham Hotspur, went about bringing in new players to Ninian Park.

Favourites such as centre-half Bill Bassett, wing-half George Nicholson and inside-forward Leslie Talbot - each of whom had made over 100 first team appearances for the Bluebirds - moved on. The new arrivals were left-half Jimmy Cringan from Wolves, teenage centre-half William `Sam' Booth from Port Vale, Tommy Anderson from Wolves, inside-forward Ernie Marshall from Sheffield United, inside-forward Trevor Morris from Ipswich Town (he would later become the secretary-manager at Cardiff City), winger George Sabin from West Bromwich Albion, left-back Ernie Sykes from Birmingham City, Cyril Reid from Newport County, amateur Wilf Wooler (later to become a famous Welsh rugby international plus a Glamorgan county cricketer and chairman), inside-left Laurie McPhillips from Albion Rovers and outside-left Jim Myers from Wolves.

Cardiff City played Swansea Town at Ninian Park in a Football League Jubilee Fund friendly on the 19th of August, and drew 1-1, thanks to Ernie Marshall's goal, before 9,000 spectators.

The ill-fated 1939-40 season began with the Country on the brink of war, and at Norwich on August the 26th, Cardiff City, with six debutants in their team (Ernie Sykes, Sam Booth, Jimmy Cringan, Ernie Marshall, Laurie McPhillips and Jim Myers), started with a 2-1 victory, obtained through goals from Jimmy Collins and Reg Pugh. The following Wednesday, the Bluebirds played at Swindon and earned their second away win in four days when Jimmy Collins' lone goal ensured the points.

There was increasing anxiety throughout the country as the British public awaited the outcome of the meeting between the Prime Minister Mr Neville Chamberlain and Adolf Hitler. But no mention was made of this in Cardiff City's match programme for the home game against Notts County on the 2nd of September.

A crowd of 20,000 watched a thrilling match of six goals, although the result - 4-2 - went against the City. Notts County, inspired by former Bluebird Jimmy McKenzie, made the most of their opportunities. Jimmy Collins scored both City goals.

On the following morning, at 11 a.m. (the 3rd of September 1939), came the fateful broadcast by the Prime Minister, and as the country went to War so the Football League was suspended. It would be seven years before football would return to normal and by then most of the players with clubs in 1939, would find their playing careers at an end.

On the 4th of September, former goalkeeper and assistant trainer Jack Kneeshaw, were made redundant. Cardiff City, like all their Football League counterparts, sought to arrange their affairs into some sort of order. Most of the contracted players left Ninian Park almost overnight, and the Government instructed that friendly matches and regional leagues only, would be set up in order to maintain the country's morale. Cyril Spiers introduced a number of young locals, plus a large number of `guest' players, to make up the bulk of Cardiff City's playing staff.

Welsh Cup:
The Football Association of Wales kept the competition open, and on the 16th of December, Cardiff City entertained and comfortably beat Ebbw Vale 4-0. Reg Pugh scored a hat-trick and Jack Court produced the other goal. By the time Cardiff City faced Newport County in the next round, the team had a very strange look about it, as players continued to come and go almost weekly. The game ended 1-1, with Bill Owen scoring for the Bluebirds. The replay on the 18th of March, was staged at Rodney Parade, the home of the Newport rugby union team, as Somerton Park had been taken over by H.M. Forces. City had no answer to County's forceful play, and they were well beaten by 0-5.

At the end of the season, Newport County who had been promoted to the Second Division at the end of the 1938-39 season, were forced to disband for the duration of the War. For the City, it was business as usual, so long as they could continue to field a full team.

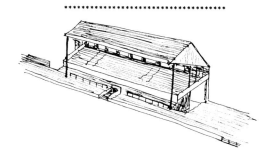

The centre-spread for the last peacetime programme (2nd September 1939) - Teams line-ups were as listed.

WARTIME FOOTBALL:

1939-40 Season:

Cardiff City kept together a hard core of professional staff in the early months of the War. After completing a number of friendlies, the City joined the newly-formed South-West League. This competition included Swansea Town, Plymouth Argyle, Swindon Town, Torquay United, Bristol City, Bristol Rovers and Newport County, the latter only competing during this first season.

Depending upon the availability of players, most clubs were pleased to be able to just field a full team, and this factor occasionally lead to scores of a freakish nature!

Secretary-manager Cyril Spiers called upon 55 players during this reduced 'season', of whom 21 were `guests'. Ernie Marshall, Sam Booth, Arthur Granville, Reg Pugh and George Ballsom made the most appearances, whilst teenage inside-forward Billy James appeared for the first time.

****

1940-41 Season:

The format of regional leagues and friendlies continued throughout the campaign. During this period, Cyril Spiers called upon forty-one players, including seven `guests'. It was around this time that Spiers' policy of introducing local teenage talent began to bear fruit. Springing to prominence were Billy Baker, Billy James (29 goals from 29 games), Beriah Moore (32 goals in 30 games) and Reg Parker. Others to make good contributions were goalkeeper Jackie Pritchard, centre-half John Pugh, inside-forward Bobby Tobin and half back Terry Wood.

The crowds, often pitifully thin on the terraces, saw plenty of goals, although sometimes the standard of football was indifferent; on the 2nd of November 1940, the City beat the Army XI 18-1 in a friendly encounter!

****

1941-42 Season:

Due to the call-up of a number of his young players, particularly for the Burma campaign, Cyril Spiers literally had to beg, borrow and steal players on occasions, to keep the Bluebirds in action. A grand total of 52 players represented the club and among a growing number of `guests' were some notable names including Johnny Carey, Raich Carter, Allenby Chilton, Benny Fenton and Ivor Lewis, some of whom made just a solitary appearance for the Bluebirds.

The City was best served by Beriah Moore (27 goals in 35 games), centre-half John Pugh, half-back Roy Phillips, centre-forward Reg Parker (27 goals from 25 games), and young wing-half Ken Hollyman. Making his first appearance during this season was a talented full-back, Alf Sherwood, a miner from Aberaman. Young Billy James played twice for Wales, versus England (scoring one goal), and this demonstrated his unquestioned ability. Within a few months, he became a Japanese P.O.W., and he never fully recovered from the results of this enforced captivity.

****

1942-43 Season:

Cardiff City were represented during this period, by an unprecedented 72 players, as the war effort saw ever increasing numbers of younger men joining the armed forces. Secretary-manager Cyril Spiers was helped by the appearances of 17 `guest' players, among them Sammy Chedgzoy, Jimmy Murphy and a certain Bill Shankly!

Many players made just a single appearance, and a substantial number played in only two or three games, as leave would allow. City were best served by winger Beriah Moore (13 goals in 32 games), full-back Alf Sherwood (who had been converted from wing-half), centre-forward Reg Parker, full-back A.H. Jones, defender J.A. Jones, goalkeeper Wyn Griffiths and a brilliant discovery on the left wing, Newport born Roy Clarke. Clarke was the top scorer with his 18 goals in 28 games. As usual there were plenty of goals, with City being involved in a number of these high-scoring matches, the most bizarre of which was a 4-8 defeat at Lovell's Athletic, who had a particularly strong team during the War years.

1943-44 Season:

Cyril Spiers at last began to recruit a regular band of professionals at Ninian Park - many of whom were in reserved occupations - and the basis of a solid team began to take shape.

Arriving at Ninian Park from local junior clubs were quality players such as centre-half Fred Stansfield, right back Arthur 'Buller' Lever, wing-half Danny Lester, goalkeeper Alan Smith and centre-forwards Bill Williams and Billy Rees. An Englishman (!), outside-right Colin Gibson, was spotted playing with Penarth Pontoons and was quickly snapped up by Mr Spiers. Gibson would prove to be a fine signing, before moving on and representing his country at full level.

Allied to regulars Alf Sherwood, Roy Clarke and Beriah Moore, the team did well in their regional league and cup completions. Beriah Moore was top scorer with 20 goals from 39 games, Billy Rees achieved 16 in 19, Bill Williams 14 from 31, and Roy Clarke notched 12 in 28 matches. Colin Gibson scored 7 goals from only 9 outings, and the City completed a satisfying season, as Spiers relied almost exclusively on home grown talent.

1944-45 Season:

The Cardiff City secretary-manager was once again grateful that he was able to rely on the blossoming talents of Alf Sherwood, Fred Stansfield, Terry Wood, Billy Rees, Alan Smith, Arthur Lever, Danny Lester, Colin Gibson and Roy Clarke.

Apart from defeats by the formidable Lovell's Athletic, in both the League Cup and League West Cup, the Bluebirds were impregnable at Ninian Park, and made a number of impressive displays. The star turn was centre-forward Billy Rees who returned 33 goals in 39 games, which earned him a War-time International cap against England at Ninian Park (but not officially recognised as a full international).

Towards the end of the season Cardiff City and Bristol City were involved in a two-legged League North 2nd round Cup tie which would go into the history books. The first leg at Ashton Gate on the 7th of April 1945, produced a good result for the Bluebirds, as Ernie Carless and Danny Lester scored in the 2-1 victory. The second leg turned out to be an epic struggle for after 90 minutes, Bristol City led 2-1 (Hollyman having scored for Cardiff), and so the aggregate score was even. Thirty minutes of extra-time were played - then another thirty - and, unbelievably, yet another thirty minutes. This meant that the game had progressed for three hours with the aggregate scores still level! Due to War-time restrictions the match had to be played to a finish, and with players of both sides down to walking pace - riddled with cramp and almost unable to kick the ball any distance - the tie was finally settled after a record 202 minutes, with a goal from City's Billy Rees, giving an eventual 4-3 aggregate score.

It was reported that a number of fans in the 25,000 crowd, who lived locally, went home for their teas and still had time to return to Ninian Park and see the end of the game! All the Bluebirds' efforts came to nothing however, as they lost in the next round to Wolves, 2-4 on aggregate.

The mainstays of the fine City team were:- Roy Clarke, Colin Gibson, Danny Lester, Arthur Lever, Beriah Moore, Billy Rees, Alf Sherwood, Alan Smith and Fred Stansfield - all of whom missed very few matches.

1945-46 Season:

The news that the whole of Great Britain and the allied countries wanted to hear so badly, finally arrived in the summer of 1945, when peace at last returned to Europe, after six strife-torn years of warfare.

The Football League decided to use the 1945-6 season as a watershed, by keeping the regional leagues that had been used during the War. This allowed the Football League clubs to reorganise their affairs, in order that they could make the transition to their various Divisions as smooth as possible, for League football to restart promptly in August 1946. Cardiff City were more fortunate than most, for having kept a full-time secretary-manager in Cyril Spiers, albeit on a reduced salary, they had managed to maintain a reasonably high standard, and a number of young players had become first-team regulars.

The war in the Pacific had taken its toll however, for reserve goalkeeper Jackie Pritchard did not return and the condition of Billy Baker, Bobby Tobin and Billy James - all of who had been prisoners of war with the Japanese - caused much concern.

Ken Hollyman joined regulars Fred Stansfield, Alf Sherwood, Arthur Lever, Roy Clarke and Colin Gibson in the first team. Billy Rees scored an impressive 25 goals in 25 games and Roy Clarke hit 24 in 36 matches.

Cyril Spiers made two significant signings towards the end of the season. Swansea Town inside-forward Bryn Allen and a 29 year old centre-forward from junior football - Stan Richards.

F.A.Cup:

The F.A.Cup competition resumed with a slightly different format, since from the third round - at which stage Cardiff City entered the competition - was a two-legged affair. The Bluebirds' opponents were West Bromwich Albion, and in a tingling first leg at Ninian Park on the 5th of January, the match ended 1-1 with Bryn Allen scoring the City goal, before 33,000 spectators. In the replay at the Hawthorns four days later, City were blown away 0-4, as Clarke and Newsome scored two goals apiece for an in-form Albion before 18,025 soccer-starved fans.

On the 17th of November 1945, Cardiff City were privileged to face the mighty Moscow Dynamo team, who were on a short tour of Great Britain. In an atmosphere of total disbelief the 31,000 at Ninian Park witnessed a display of awesome quality as the Dynamos ran City ragged, to inflict on the Bluebirds their worst ever home defeat, by 1-10! It was a makeshift City team, with reserve Kevin McLoughlin in goal, but even with regulars Alf Sherwood and Billy Rees also missing, it was a lesson in footballing skills that were not lost on secretary-manager Cyril Spiers. After the match a City player was asked why he thought the Bluebirds had not played well, to which he replied:
"To play well you have to have the ball - and I hardly had a kick throughout the match".

There may have been a certain amount of confusion for the players as the Dynamos turned out in all blue strip and City wore their customary blue shirts with white sleeves! Bobrov (three), Beskov (four) and Archangelski (three) were the visiting scorers, whilst Beriah Moore claimed the City's consolation goal.

In May 1945, the Club were honoured when Alf Sherwood and Roy Clarke were both selected to play for Wales for the first time. The match, versus Northern Ireland, was lost by 0-1.

Cardiff City Association Football Club, Limited.

PRESIDENT: THE RIGHT HON. THE EARL OF PLYMOUTH.

TELEPHONE: CARDIFF 3840
TELEGRAMS: "SOCCER, CARDIFF"

REGISTERED OFFICE & GROUND
NINIAN PARK,
CARDIFF.

C. H. SPIERS

16th May 1942

[handwritten letter signed Cyril Spiers]

S. WALES WAR CASUALTIES

Former City Goalie's Death

MRS. G. M. Pritchard, Greenhill-street, Splott, Cardiff, has been notified that her son, Gunr. Frederick John Pritchard, has lost his life at sea.

Aged 24, Gunr. Pritchard was goalkeeper for Cardiff City in the seasons 1939-40, 1940-41. He joined the Army in 1939 and was sent to Java, where he was taken prisoner at an early stage of the war. Before the war he was employed in the cold storage department of the Meat Supply Association.

GUNR. F. J. PRITCHARD

CITY PLAYER A PRISONER

Mr. and Mrs. James, of 183, Carlisle-street, Splott, Cardiff, have received news that their son, William John (Billy) James, the Cardiff City and Welsh international forward, is a prisoner of war in Japanese hands.

Nothing has been heard of James since November, 1941, but a month ago he was officially reported missing in Java. James was one of four Cardiff City players posted as missing in the same theatre of war. One of that number, Billy Baker (Penrhiwceiber) is also a prisoner of war.

Billy James.

Team line-ups changed dramatically during the War from match to match. Hence the use of many guest players. Above: An almost casual letter to Ken Hollyman from Cardiff manager Cyril Spiers.
It reads:
"*Dear Ken, You are selected to play for the Welsh X1 at Ninian Park on Saturday next. Kick-off 3-0 p.m. Letter enclosed from Mr. Rubbins F.A.W. and don't forget we play Swansea on Whit Monday at Cardiff, so try to arrange for that also.*" (!)

Some of the Bluebirds didn't return after the War, and some who did were unable to follow their football career:

Jackie Pritchard, a promising young goalkeeper, played just a handfull of games for the City in the early years of the War. Billy James was another exciting young prospect, and played for the Welsh team in the early War years. His experience in a Japanese P.O.W. camp badly effected his eyesight, and he played just six League matches for Cardiff before his premature retirement from the game.

CHAPTER 5

PEACETIME PROMOTIONS

1946-47 Season – Division Three South:

Cardiff City prepared for the resumption of League football by announcing the retained list, in May 1946:
B.Allen, W. Baker, D.Canning, R.Clarke, K.Devonshire, L.T.Evans, W.Foulkes, C.Gibson, C.Hill, K.Hollyman, W.James, N.Kinsey, D.Lester, A.Lever, E.Marshall, W.Mead, B.Moore, R.Phillips, G.Rayson, W.Rees, S.Richards, B.Ross, A.Sherwood, A.O.S.Smith, F.Stansfield, Tennant, R.Tobin, J.Williams, J.Skinner, T.Wood.

There was a huge shock for City followers on the 7th June 1946, when Secretary/manager Cyril Spiers resigned and joined Norwich City. It was believed that a disagreement over Mr. Spiers' contract pre-empted this decision, and Mr. Herbert Merrett, the Club Chairman, wasted no time in appointing William ('Billy') McCandless of Newport County – who had steered the Monmouthshire Club to the Second Division in the months before the War. McCandless had been a famous Irish International and had spent much of his playing career with Glasgow Rangers. The new Secretary/manager reinforced the playing staff before the season started, by signing Jim Pearce from Bristol City, wing-half Glyn Williams from Caerau, and re-engaging former City goalkeeper, George Poland.

The Football League fixtures for the 1946-47 were the same as those that had been intended for the disbanded 1939-40 season, and so Cardiff began the season at Norwich City (ironically against Cyril Spiers' new team), on the 31st of August. Of the Bluebirds team on duty, only goalkeeper George Poland had played League football before the War.

Spiers' knowledge of the Cardiff players was invaluable, and Norwich won this opening match, by 2-1, with Stan Richards finding the net for Cardiff. City also lost their next match, 2-3 at Swindon, before hitting the winning trail with 2-1 and 2-0 home wins over Notts. County and Bournemouth – Billy James scoring in both matches. However, the war had taken its toll on James, who had been a Japanese P.O.W., for he lacked stamina and his eyesight had deteriorated. Stan Richards took possession of the leaders' jersey, and from the 18th of September 1946 to March 1947, the Bluebirds had an incredible 21 match unbeaten run in the League, in which 19 victories were obtained.

The team virtually picked itself, and with ten Welshmen in the side (Colin Gibson from England being the odd man out), the soccer lovers of South Wales poured into Ninian on match-days. The defence, with captain Fred Stansfield, and full-backs Arthur Lever and Alf Sherwood outstanding, protected goalkeeper Dan Canning with great efficiency, and half-backs Ken Hollyman and Billy Baker (the latter happily recovered from his trials as a Japanese P.O.W.), prompted busily. Inside-forwards Bryn Allen and Billy Rees were inventive, and with Colin Gibson and Roy Clarke – a pair of fast, raiding, wingers – centre-forward Stan Richards benefitted greatly from such marvellous service, and responded with his prolific scoring rate.

(Above) Norwich goalkeeper Dukes punches clear as Cardiff number 9, Stan Richards challenges. The City won the Ninian Park contest by 6-1.
(Right) 'Pell' sums up the Walsall encounter in cartoon form.

(Left) Two of the City's key promotion players - Fred Stansfield (standing) and Billy Rees - in the Ninian Park boot room.
(Right) Cardiff City directors Dr. Alex Brownlea, Walter Riden, Herbert Merrett, Chris Page and Tudor Steer, pictured outside the Ninian Park Offices.

The sound of a large and happy crowd singing: " *Open the score Richards - and nod one in* ", became part and parcel of the Ninian Park scene, as Stan helped himself to a Club record haul of 30 League goals, from only 34 matches. Many teams came in trepidation of a visit to Ninian Park, where City remained unbeaten all season, as they recorded some outstanding victories: 5-0 versus Swindon, Exeter and Mansfield, 6-2 against Northampton, and 6-1 over Cyril Spiers' Norwich City team. The Bluebirds also established the record of eight successive away wins in the League. In League matches, they lost just six during the season, three of which were in the first half a dozen games! The statistics can continue, and when older supporters insist that the 1946/47 Bluebirds team was the best ever, it is very difficult to argue against the case, except to say that the team were, of course, only in the Third Division (South).

The harsh winter virtually wiped out all football throughout February 1947, but the enforced break had no effect on the team. The crowds flocked to Ninian Park, and peaked on Easter Monday, when a massive attendance of 51,626 were present for the derby match with Bristol City, which ended as a 1-1 draw. This ended the Club's poorest run of the season - four draws and one defeat in five games - for they then proceeded to return to their winning ways. These (generally) local born Bluebirds swept on to the Championship in no uncertain manner, and they finished the season nine points clear of second placed Queens Park Rangers.

Consistency was the key factor - Arthur 'Buller' Lever was an ever-present, both Billy Rees and Stan Richards missed just one match each, while Danny Canning appeared in all but two League matches. Bryn Allen and Roy Clarke were absent on three occasions, and Colin Gibson missed out on four games. Other reliable performers were Ken Hollyman and Stan Richards, as Billy McCandless enjoyed an almost trouble free season in charge. It was freely admitted that the team was the one which had been built by Cyril Spiers, but the honour of gaining promotion to the Second Division, went to McCandless.

Towards the end of the season, which had been extended into June due to the severe Winter, Cardiff bought winger George Wardle from Exeter City, and two days later they accepted an offer of £11,000 from Manchester City, for outside-left Roy Clarke. Capped by Wales, Clarke went on to a successful career at Maine Road.

F.A.Cup:
The City were drawn away to Brentford in the third round, but on the day the First Division Bees had too much sting for the Bluebirds, and won by 1-0, through Len Townsend's 25th minute goal, before a crowd of 32,894.

Welsh Cup:
Cardiff City stumbled at the first hurdle, when they went down by 2-4 at Merthyr Tydfil, a club that was emerging as a real force in the Southern League, after being relaunched following the dissolving of the pre-War Merthyr Town. Billy Rees and Billy James (in a rare appearance), scored City's goals.

At the end of the season, the enclosure in front of the Ninian Park Grandstand was extended and rebuilt in concrete terracing...... Alf Sherwood won his first full cap for Wales, in the match versus England, at Maine Road on the 13th of November (which Wales lost by 0-3)...... In a special match at Steboneath, Llanelly, on the 14th of June, a 'City Promotion XI', beat a strong William Hughes International team by 1-0, with a great goal from winger George Wardle; although only a 'Friendly', it nonetheless demonstrated the speed and quality of Cardiff City's Division Three (South) Championship side.

1947-48 – Division 2:

City Secretary/manager Billy McCandless was quite happy to stick with his successful 1946-47 team, on the Bluebirds' return to the Second Division – after an absence of sixteen years at this level. New arrivals at Ninian Park included amateurs Don Sheldon and David Leek, and joining the professional ranks were Harold Brain of Aberaman, Seamus McBennett from Belfast Celtic, Douglas Blair (the son of Jimmy Blair, the grand City full-back of the 1920's) from Blackpool, plus Beriah Moore who re-signed after spending a year at Bangor City.

The Bluebirds made a steady start to their Second Division return by drawing 0-0 with Chesterfield at Ninian Park on the 23rd of August. Two days later, when Doncaster Rovers were the visitors, the Ground was virtually full, with 47,000 spectators present to see the clash between the Champions of the Third Division Southern and Northern sections. Dougie Blair made his City debut at inside-left, replacing Bryn Allen, and his magical left foot inspired the Bluebirds to an emphatic 3-0 victory, with George Wardle (two) and Stan Richards being the marksmen. Before the game, much had been made of Clarrie Jordan, the Rovers' prolific centre-forward who had scored 44 goals in the 1946-47 season, but he was completely shut out by the City skipper, Fred Stansfield.

Beriah Moore, one of Cardiff City's mainstays during the War years, made his belated League debut in a 5-1 beating of Southampton, and scored twice. Two games later he was back in the Reserves - such was the competition for first-team places at Ninian Park. Seamus McBennett also scored twice in the return match, at Southampton, but like Moore, he failed to hold his place. Utility player Ron Stitfall, one of three Cardiff-born brothers on the playing staff, was released from H.M.Forces, and he made his debut at full-back on the the 18th of October. The match at Brentford ended as a 1-1 draw, and on the same day Alf Sherwood was called up as a reserve for the Wales team, for the International versus England at Ninian Park.

Two players, reserve Billy Lewis and Bryn Allen, were sold to Newport County for £4,500 and £5,000 respectively, within weeks of each other, as the City settled into their Second Division life.

There was a surprise in store when Secretary/manager Billy McCandless resigned on the 14th of November, and Club Chairman Herbert Merrett, immediately made overtures to Norwich City, for the Bluebirds former chief, Cyril Spiers. In the meantime McCandless had accepted a lucrative offer to take over at Swansea Town, and in 1949, he was to guide the Vetch Field team to the Second Division, thus completing a unique 'treble' of Third Division Championships - with Newport County (in 1939), Cardiff City in 1947 and then Swansea Town.

On the 3rd of December, Cyril Spiers was re-engaged as Secretary/manager, with a good contract, and his appointment coincided with City's best run of the season, during which time they knocked Millwall for six (without reply), on the 3rd of January, when Billy Rees and Stan Richards (two each) plus Doug Blair and Colin Gibson shared the goals. In early February, Cyril Spiers signed centre-forward Bill Hullett from Merthyr Tydfil, and (with Stan Richards suffering from knee injuries) he made an immediate impression by blasting seven goals in his first six League games which helped to take the City to the fringe of the promotion area. Cardiff then slumped badly, failing to win in eight matches, during which time they conceded the Easter 'double' to West Ham, and drew 1-1 with Newcastle United before a crowd of 50,000, with Derrick Sullivan making his debut in the latter game. In the final home match of the season, West Bromwich Albion cruised to a 5-0 victory at Ninian Park. Against the odds – and with nothing at stake – the City returned from Barnsley with a 2-1 victory, in the last game of the season, thanks to goals from Billy Rees and reserve Beriah Moore. In the final weeks of the campaign, reserve goalkeepers Wyn Griffiths and Roger Ashton both made their only first team appearances.

The Club ended their Second Division season in 5th place, a most creditable position. Arthur 'Buller' Lever was ever-present for the second successive time, and Danny Canning, Fred Stansfield, Alf Sherwood, Billy Rees, Dougie Blair, Billy Baker, George Wardle and Colin Gibson all appeared regularly. The top scorer was Billy Rees, with eleven goals, whilst George Wardle netted ten, and Stan Richards – in only 23 games – had nine successes. In common with most League Clubs in the immediate post-War era, Cardiff City attracted soaring attendances, with the average at Ninian Park of over 38,000.

F.A.Cup:
The City played a third round home tie against fellow Second Division opponents, Sheffield Wednesday, and in a quagmire which nullified all attempts to play constructive football, the Owls triumphed by 2-1, with Billy Rees scoring for the Bluebirds, in front of 48,000 spectators.

Welsh Cup:
Cardiff City were made to suffer for not taking the Welsh Cup competition too seriously, when they travelled to Lovell's Athletic, of the Southern League, on the 15th of January. With six reserves in their side, the City were turned over by the Newport confectionary factory team, who won 2-1. City's lone goal was scored by Beriah Moore.

At the end of the season Bernard Ross joined Sheffield United for £3,000...... Alf Sherwood and Billy Baker were both capped for Wales; it was to be the one and only occasion for Baker, and scant reward for such a fine player.

(Above left) Alf Sherwood challenges Fulham winger Thomas. The home match attracted a crowd of 35,000.
(Above) Canning punches clear during the Coventry City game.
(Below) A chatty and personal letter to Ken Hollyman!

Cardiff City Association Football Club, Limited

TELEPHONE CARDIFF 3840
TELEGRAMS
SOCCER CARDIFF

SECRETARY
TREVOR MORRIS

MANAGER
CYRIL H. SPIERS

REGISTERED OFFICE & GROUND

NINIAN PARK

CARDIFF

April 16th, 1948.

Dear Hollyman

    I have pleasure in informing you that your services have been retained for Season 1948-49.

                            Yours faithfully,

                                 Secretary.

1948-49 – Division 2:

One of Cardiff City's most popular post-War players, centre-forward Stan Richards and the holder of the greatest number of goals in a season (30), was now becoming quite injury prone; he travelled West, to link up again with Billy McCandless at Swansea Town. Richards had scored an incredible 40 goals in only 57 League matches for the Bluebirds.

Cyril Spiers needing an additional goalkeeper, signed Edwin 'Ted' Morris on amateur forms, and then bought Phil Joslin – Torquay United's vastly experienced custodian – to Ninian Park. This was the beginning of a seven year span, during which players of Cardiff City and Torquay United, were freely exchanged between the two Clubs. This situation was brought about by the friendship between the Cardiff Chairman, Herbert Merrett, and his counterpart in the Devon resort, at whose Hotel, Merrett spent his holidays.

Gordon Pembrey, a lively forward who had gone to Norwich City in 1946, was bought back to Cardiff, and in a shock move, Cyril Spiers exchanged City's reserve centre-forward, Reg Parker, for Bryn Allen, the latter having been with Newport County for only seven months. Alun Watkins, a prominent cricketer and a member of Glamorgan's Championship winning team of 1948, arrived from Plymouth Argyle. Willie McKay, Alex Gilchrist, John Barrie and Harry May were all recruited from junior football. It was to be a season during which Spiers would introduce no fewer than 14 new players to League football, in his efforts to improve the overall standard of the Cardiff City team.

In the opening match at Bradford (Park Avenue), where City lost 0-3, goalkeeper Joslin made his City debut, as did Gilchrist; for the latter this was to be his only League appearance. That first day of the season brought not the usual sub-tropical temperatures, but monsoon-like torrential rain which lashed the entire country. The deluge was so bad at Bargoed, in the Rhymney Valley, that Cardiff City's Welsh League game had to be abandoned after only 18 minutes!

Spiers juggled his forward line about in the early matches, and young reserves Ron Stitfall and Derrick Sullivan operated on the right and left wings respectively. Dougie Blair was switched to left-half, and Billy Baker to the right, as the City manager tried to strike the correct combination. On the 4th of September, the Bluebirds earned a remarkable point from a 1-1 draw at Barnsley, after injuries to George Wardle and Ron Stitfall had reduced the team to nine fit players in the second half.

Cecil Price, a local, stepped in at West Ham for his only first team appearance, and in a flurry of transfer activity, Spiers signed Tommy Best – Cardiff's first coloured player – from Chester, then paid a a new Club record fee of £10,000 to Wolves, for inside-forward Ernie Stevenson. Reserves, Seamus McBennett and John Barrie, moved on to Tranmere Rovers, and centre-forward Bill Hullett was sold to struggling Nottingham Forest. The left-wing was proving troublesome to Spiers, and Joe Nibloe, a reserve defender, made his only League appearance in that berth at Lincoln, on the 13th of November. The following week Albert Stitfall wore the number 11 shirt, with his brother Ron on the opposite wing, as City drew with Sheffield Wednesday at Ninian Park. It was the first time that a pair of brothers had appeared in a League match for Cardiff City.

Ted Gorin, a centre-forward from Grange Albion, was drafted into the first team, only weeks after joining the Club, as several players were laid low by injuries. Cyril Spiers made a night-time dash to sign George Edwards – Birmingham City's Welsh International outside-left – on Friday the 10th of December. The Football League were informed by telegraph, in order for Edwards to play at Leicester City the following day. The fee of £6,000, was to turn out to be one of Cardiff City's better investments. City drew 2-2 at Filbert Street, and a week later the hard shooting winger took only four minutes to celebrate his home debut with the first goal, as the Bluebirds hit Bradford (Park Avenue) for six. Ernie Stevenson, living up to his record fee, scored twice in this match, taking his tally to five in five League matches, as the Bluebirds started to march up the table.

Popular goalkeeper Danny Canning was sold to Swansea Town for £3,000 on the 6th of January. City received a set-back nine days later in the match at home to Barnsley – not only from the 0-3 defeat – but from the bad injury to Fred Stansfield which ruled him out for the rest of the season, and this resulted in his last appearance in a City jersey.

Spiers took immediate action and paid £6,000 to Southend United for tall centre-half Stan Montgomery, and he scored on his debut at Grimsby in a 2-2 draw. One week later and another centre-half was bought, Aldershot's much fancied pivot Alf Rowland, with the fee equalling the record £10,000 that had earlier been paid for Stevenson. Within a few days £5,000 was recouped when winger George Wardle was sold to Queens Park Rangers. Rowland and Montgomery played alongside each other on the former player's debut, but it was a chemistry that definitely did not mix, as Fulham – the eventual Second Division Champions – romped to a rousing 4-0 victory at Craven Cottage, with goals coming from Jezzard, Stevens and a Thomas brace. The following Wednesday (the 24th of February), Spiers fielded a strong Football Combination X1 for a cup match against the reserves of Bournemouth, selecting Montgomery at centre-half and Rowland at centre-forward. For the rest of the season, Montgomery became the first choice pivot, while Rowland – when he was not injured – languished in the second string.

After the heavy defeat at Craven Cottage, the Bluebirds won seven out of eight games, which put them fourth in the table, chasing Fulham, Southampton and West Bromwich Albion, but the task was too great, and by the end of the season they had to settle for this same final position; a slight improvement on the previous term. A number of amateur and junior players had been given trials, and Graham Hogg – a Welsh Amateur International – made his debut, as did utility forward Roley Williams from Milford United.

City's final game of the season was at home to Leicester City, a week after the the Midlanders had lost the F.A.Cup final to the Wolves. The Bluebirds had nothing to play for, but Leicester required one point at least to preserve their Second Division status. The match was a fiasco and was labelled as 'arranged', in order for Leicester to get their point. Certainly many end of season games are lack-lustre affairs, which end up as a draw, but the 35,000 crowd really gave vent to their feelings as neither side were prepared to win the match. Leicester continually pulled men back, and it was a great surprise when Billy Baker scored for Cardiff with a soft header after 65 minutes. The visitors were panic-stricken, but they secured an equaliser in the 78th minute, when a mistake by a City defender let in Leicester's Jack Lee to score. The match ended all square, but remains etched in the memories of those who saw it, as not being played in the spirit of the great game.

Alf Sherwood was an ever-present, and the Bluebirds were also well served by Phil Joslin, Ken Hollyman, Billy Baker and Doug Blair. Record signing Ernie Stevenson was top scorer with twelve, with the rest of the goals spread evenly among a number of players. Attendances at Ninian Park remained buoyant, averaging over 36,000, with the highest of 56,018 for the visit of Tottenham Hotspur on the 9th of October, followed by 50,000 for both the Christmas match with Brentford, and the visit of promotion bound West Bromwich Albion on the 26th of March.

F.A.Cup:

The City faced a tough third round tie when they travelled to Oldham Athletic, a doughty side then in the Third Division North. On a typically murky Northern afternoon at Boundary Park, the Bluebirds managed to withstand all that the Latics could throw at them, and it was a late goal from Ken Hollyman (his second of the match), plus one from Bryn Allen, that edged City to a narrow 3-2 victory.

By the time that the team travelled to Aston Villa, on the 29th of January, for the fourth round tie, they were without Sherwood, Stansfield and Blair. Ron Stitfall came in at left-back, Stan Montgomery was at centre-half, and Welsh Amateur International Graham Hogg played at left-half, in his only F.A.Cup appearance for the Club. Many thousands from South Wales helped swell the crowd to an astonishing 70,718, and they were delighted as City gave one of their best performances of the season to win by 2-1, with goals from Hollyman and Rees. A major factor of the victory was the manner in which new signing Montgomery exerted his mastery over Villa's fiery Welsh International, Trevor Ford.

The fifth round required the City to travel again, this time to Derby County, and with both Sherwood and Blair in the side, they were hopeful of a replay. The Rams, however, had other thoughts, and put out the Welsh fire by winning 2-1, City's goal coming from Ernie Stevenson.

Welsh Cup:

The City, with a mixture of first and second team players in the side, had a comfortable 3-1 home win over Welsh League, Troedyrhiw, Ted Gorin, George Wardle and Tommy Best scoring the goals. A strong team played at Milford United, but could only manage a 2-1 win, with Rowland - playing at left-back - and Edwards, on the goal sheet. City then faced Merthyr Tydfil at Swansea, in the semi-final on April the 7th, and met their match as the high powered Martyrs swept to a 3-1 win in 'gluepot' conditions, with Lowe, Powell and Jarman scoring, before Stevenson netted the Bluebirds consolation goal in the final minute. The Stitfall brothers, Ron and Albert, partnered each other in the full-back positions.

Alf Sherwood, Billy Rees, George Edwards and Fred Stansfield were all played for Wales during the season...... On Wales' tour of Portugal, Belgium and Switzerland, the first three players were each capped.

Ken Hollyman heads a sensational equaliser from George Edward's fierce cross. Cardiff stunned the mammoth 70,718 Aston Villa crowd when they went on to win the F.A.Cup 4th round tie on the 29th January 1949.

1949-50 Season – Division 2:

After all the movement of players during the previous season, the Cardiff manager was content to have a quiet summer. Only two players were signed, Caradoc 'Crad' Wilcox and, in May, Elfed Evans from Treharris Athletic of the Welsh League. A number of junior players were allowed to leave, as the Club cast its net for more local trialists. The most notable senior departures were Welsh Internationalist forward, Billy Rees – who was transferred to Tottenham Hotspur for £11,000 on his return from the Wales tour – and inside-forward Bryn Allen who left Ninian Park again, this time for Reading.

The City had no debutants in their line-up when they lost their opening fixture by 0-1 at Blackburn. The burden of goal scoring fell upon the shoulders of Tommy Best and Ernie Stevenson, neither of whom had the physique that was required for a centre-forward. Best, although he was built like a pocket battleship, lacked height when it came to aerial challenges. However, both players were soon on the goal scoring sheets, but the City's results were inconsistent, and Cyril Spiers was soon ringing the changes, particularly at centre-forward.

The visit of Swansea Town on the 27th of August, attracted a record crowd of 57,510 to Ninian Park. The Swans, under the guidance of Billy McCandless, had been promoted – as Champions of the Third Division (South) – and City won this clash of the South Wales 'giants', with a single goal from Tommy Best. After Best had scored five times in eight matches, Ron Stitfall was given the attack leader's berth, where he had a little success, and before the end of the season he was in his more accustomed full-back role, with Arthur 'Buller' Lever being tried at centre-forward. Elfed Evans, a smooth moving inside-forward, emerged as a player of quality, and when Tommy Best was transferred to Queens Park Rangers in December, Roley Williams took the opportunity to gain a first team place. Reserve players Bob Taggart, Bob Lamie – a Scot from Stonehouse Violets – Harold May, Gordon Pembrey and Bobby McLaren all made fleeting appearances, after Beriah Moore, Fred Stansfield and Graham Hogg each left the Club during the season.

On March the 9th, Cyril Spiers made his most significant deal of the season, when he traded record signing Ernie Stevenson – who was in a goal 'drought' – for Southampton winger Wilf Grant. Alf Steele, a goalkeeper from Walsall, was in the first team, as Cardiff City ended the season in a disappointing 10th position. The defence, well served as always by ever-present Alf Sherwood plus Stan Montgomery and Billy Baker, conceded only 44 goals, but the City attack had only scored 41, and that really was the story of the season. Elfed Evans was the top marksman with eight successes (the lowest top marksman in the City's history), whilst George Edwards managed seven and Ron Stitfall hit six.

Fred Stansfield, whose career at Ninian Park had come to a halt after his injury in January 1949, joined neighbours Newport County as player-manager, in September 1949, and he eventually became the manager at Somerton Park. Stansfield, one of Cardiff City's finest captains, played 106 League games after the second World War, and gained his only Welsh cap just before his tragic injury.

(Top) 10th of December, and Ron Stitfall (between the posts), slots the ball into the net, with the Preston defence bogged down in a sea of mud.
(Middle) Two weeks later and Phil Joslin punches clear (with the aid of Doug Blair) – but the match at Swansea ended in an embarrassing 5-1 defeat.
(Bottom) 5th of January 1950. The secretary – Trevor Morris – presents a gold pencil to Bartley Wilson, on the occasion of the Club's founder's 80th birthday. Looking on – Joslin, Stitfall, Lever, Baker, Sherwood and Hollyman.

F.A.Cup:

Cardiff City faced West Bromwich Albion in the third round, and looked to have missed their opportunity for victory when the game, before 38,000 at Ninian Park, ended at 2-2, with Elfed Evans and reliable half-back Glyn Williams scoring the goals. In the replay at The Hawthorns on January the 11th, the City stunned an Albion crowd of 37,400, by defending stubbornly, before winning the match with a goal from George Edwards.

On the 28th of January, the Bluebirds visited Charlton Athletic in the fourth round. Once again they played superbly against First Division opponents, drawing 1-1, with Elfed Evans scoring City's goal in front of a bumper 46,000 crowd at The Valley. Evans was in terrific form at this stage of the season, and his two goals settled the replay against Charlton, on the 1st of February. The City were full of optimism for their trip to Leeds United in the fifth round, but they finished well beaten with a 1-3 scoreline, the only consolation being Alf Sherwood's successful penalty; the crowd at Elland Road was a mighty 53,099.

Welsh Cup:

The third Stitfall brother on Cardiff's books, goalkeeper Bob, made his only appearance in the first team, when the Bluebirds defeated Ebbw Vale by 3-0 at Ninian Park in the sixth round. George Edwards scored twice, and Billy Baker netted the other. For the next round, the City travelled to Swansea, where they were well beaten by 0-3 before a crowd of 11,000.

Cyril Spiers obtained an important recruit on the 23rd of January 1950, when Albert Lindon - the former manager of Merthyr Tydfil - was appointed as chief scout...... During the season, Alf Sherwood and George Edwards were capped by Wales...... Sherwood was additionally awarded the 1949 Graydon Medal, in recognition of being voted the finest full-back in Europe.

● **DUGGIE BLAIR (left) shown here with George Edwards**

1950-51 - Division 2:

A number of reserve and junior players were released by Cyril Spiers during the close season, and the one major signing was the wing-half or inside-forward Bobby McLaughlin, from Wrexham at a fee of £5,000. Spiers also brought in Paddy McIlvenny from Merthyr Tydfil, whose father - of the same name - had been on the Cardiff City books during the 1924-25 season. Goalkeeper Ron Howells was signed from Barry Town, and others to arrive at Ninian Park were Colin Gale (a former amateur player), Gwyn George (who had experience as a part-timer with Swansea Town), Seward Smyth, John Comley, Fred Stevens and Alan Clissold.

There were two new faces in the Bluebirds' line-up which faced Grimsby Town at Blundell Park in the first game of the season - McLaughlin and centre-forward Ken Oakley, the latter having impressed in his performances with the reserves, and in the pre-season trials. The City still had a problem in the centre-forward position, and Spiers wanted to try out a few options, before having to enter the transfer market.

The team began the season in reasonable style, losing just twice in the opening ten matches - although five matches were drawn - as the manager began to ring the changes. Oakley scored on his home debut, which was won by 2-0 against Notts. County, but two games later inside-forward Elfed Evans took over the leader's role. Winger Bob Lamie came and went after several games, and, with a mounting injury list, half-back Glyn Williams filled in at centre-half for six games, until Stan Montgomery returned to the first team. On the 7th of September, the ever reliable Arthur 'Buller' Lever was sold to Leicester City for £10,000. He had been with Cardiff City since the War years, and had made 156 - near consecutive - League appearances. At the time of his transfer, Lever was unable to claim a first team place, and had appeared just once in the early games - at centre-half!

In the middle of November, Spiers brought Mike Tiddy from Torquay United, in the player exchange agreement that existed between the two clubs. The powerful right-winger was quickly accepted by the Ninian Park public at a time when City were finding it difficult to hit a winning run. Indeed, by that time the Bluebirds had played twenty games, of which half had been drawn. Easily identifiable by the grey streak in his dark hair, Tiddy's arrival allowed Spiers to switch the nippy ex-Southampton winger, Wilf Grant, into the problem centre-forward berth. It was a move that completely changed the City's fortunes, and in only his fourth game at number nine, Grant bagged a hat-trick in the 5-2 home win over Grimsby Town, on the 16th of December; inside-forward, Roley Williams scored twice. A week later, at Notts. County, the City gained their first away win of the season (by 2-1), with Grant scoring one of the goals.

The Bluebirds, and Grant, showed impressive form, and as the City climbed the Second Division table, it looked for a while as if promotion to Division One was a distinct possibility. Mr. Spiers tried to beef up his attack by introducing former Milford United forward Mars Marchant, and acquiring Don Mills, from Queens Park Rangers, in exchange for reserve Charlie 'Midge' Hill. Marchant scored on his debut, in the 3-0 victory at Chesterfield, where Wilf Grant netted the other two. On the 24th of February, there was a crowd of 38,000 at Ninian Park to see the defeat of second placed Blackburn Rovers. Grant scored his eleventh goal in twelve games, and the Bluebirds climbed to third in the table.

Elfed Evans, who had promised so much, went to Torquay on loan, and winger Bob Lamie was sold to Swansea for £1,000, as the season reached its peak. But the Bluebirds, who had drawn too many games, fell short of the promotion places and ended the season in third position. The defence, in which Ken Hollyman was an ever-present, conceded just 45 goals, and in attack, Wilf Grant emerged as the leading scorer with 14 goals, whilst George Edwards, the dependable winger, netted on nine occasions.

F.A.Cup:

Upton Park had never been a happy ground for Cardiff City, and the Bluebirds once again slumped to defeat, when they met West Ham United in the third round of the Cup on the 6th of January. City battled hard throughout the match, but Wilf Grant's goal was not enough, as the East-enders won by 2-1, with goals from Jim Barrett and Gerry Gazzard.

Welsh Cup:

On the 31st of January, Cardiff City entertained Barry Town, and gave the Southern League team an 8-0 walloping, with reserve inside-forward Leslie N.Evans scoring four times. Mars Marchant (two), Grant, and a Kelly 'own goal' completed the rout. The Bluebirds travelled to Bangor City in the next round, and they spoiled a big day for 12,000 North Walians, by cruising to a 7-1 win, with George Edwards (three), Mike Tiddy (two), Wilf Grant and Mars Marchant enjoying their day out.

City fielded their strongest team against Merthyr Tydfil, at Swansea, in the semi-final, where the match ended as a 1-1 draw. In the replay, which was also played at Swansea, Merthyr enjoyed one of their greatest days, as they won a titanic tussle by 3-2. Goals by George Edwards and Mike Tiddy were not enough, on a day that belonged to Bill Hullett's Martyrs, who scored through Jenkin Powell (penalty), Dai Lloyd and Harold Jarman.

The Festival of Britain was held in 1951, and most Football League clubs played matches against foreign touring sides to celebrate the event. On the 9th of May, Cardiff City entertained Eindhoven of Holland, where Mike Tiddy and Wilf Grant scored in the 2-2 draw...... Alf Sherwood was selected for all five Wales' International matches during the 1950-51 season...... On October the 20th, Coventry City's Bryn Allen was selected for the Wales versus Scotland match, this meant that all of Cardiff City's promotion forward line of the 1946-47 season, had been capped at full level; Roy Clarke, Billy Rees, Stan Richards and Bryn Allen for Wales, plus Colin Gibson for England.

(Left) Glyn Williams clears the ball from a Blackburn Rovers attack. The match at Ninian Park was won 1-0 by Cardiff City.

(Right) Swansea's Weston clears the ball from a muddy penalty area, as Ken Hollyman (left) and Wilf Grant (centre) close in. City won the match 1-0.

1951-52 Season – Division 2:

Cardiff City Chairman, Sir Herbert Merrett J.P., had gone on record as saying, after the club's promotion to the Second Division in 1947, that his ambition was to see the Bluebirds in the First Division within five years. This would be the season that the since knighted Merrett, and now President of the club that he had supported since boyhood, would realise his dream.

A quiet close season saw Elfed Evans return from Torquay United, and Cogan born Alan Harrington sign on junior forms. The public trial match, held a week before the start of the new season, was marred by a tragic incident, which saw goalkeeper Phil Joslin receive a badly broken leg in a goalmouth collision with Wilf Grant. This injury brought about an end to Joslin's career. Cyril Spiers acted swiftly, once the severity of Joslin's injury became apparent, for he agreed to pay a record fee of £15,000 for Iorwerth Hughes, Luton Town's Welsh International goalkeeper. The new custodian was the only new face in the first team, as City prepared for an historic season.

A cricketing injury meant that Stan Montgomery was unavailable for the opening week of the season. An old City favourite, Arthur 'Buller' Lever, returned to Ninian Park with Leicester City on the opening day, but his inclusion in the visiting side made little impact with a rampant Cardiff City team who won by 4-0 in splendid style, with George Edwards, Wilf Grant (two) and Roley Williams scoring the goals. The Bluebirds were well and truly 'grounded' two evenings later, when Rotherham United visited Cardiff, and won with the convincing scoreline of 4-2. Alf Sherwood received a rare roasting by Rotherham's Jack Grainger, who scored twice for the Millers. City's Welsh International full-back was later injured, and the Bluebirds ended the game with only ten men.

Five minutes into the first game of the season – and George Edwards rifles home the Bluebirds first goal in the match versus Leicester City.

Glyn Williams came in for Sherwood, and Stan Montgomery replaced young Derrick Sullivan for City's trip to Nottingham Forest, where the team bounced back with a brace of goals from George Edwards, and one from Roley Williams, in a stylish 3-2 victory. The return at Rotherham, on the 27th of August, provided another setback for the Bluebirds, as the Millers completed the double, with a 2-0 win, although it was an unusual incident that settled the match. With the score at 1-0, and City doing their best to draw level, Billy Baker unaccountably caught the ball inside his penalty area, convinced that he had heard the referee's whistle. It was in fact a whistle from the crowd, and Rotherham received a fortuitous penalty, after which the City never recovered.

The Bluebirds remained around mid-table, until two successive home wins against Sheffield Wednesday (2-1) and Coventry City (4-1), lifted them into the top five of the table. With twelve matches played, Wilf Grant had hit the target on thirteen occasions, and his quicksilver finishing ensured that the Bluebirds remained in contention. They received a jolt on the 27th of November, when they lost by 0-2 at Barnsley, where an injury to the dependable Glyn Williams reduced City to ten men for most of the game. Ironically it was at Barnsley during the previous season, that Ron Stitfall had received a severe knee ligament injury which continued to keep him out of the first team action.

The following week, Wilf Grant's single goal enabled the Bluebirds to pip Hull City at Ninian Park, but it was the run of former Welsh International winger George Edwards who provided the centre, for the goal, that thrilled the 23,500 crowd. Edwards hared down the 'Bob-bank' touchline, leaving a number of Hull players in his wake, and when he crossed from the byeline, Grant's header was purely academic. Seven days later, Edwards provided the match-winner at bottom placed Blackburn Rovers, when his goal, seven minutes from time, gave City only their second away win of the season. Oddly enough, the Bluebirds were subsequently unable to win on an opponents ground for the remainder of the campaign, but at Ninian Park, they were almost invincible.

Consecutive victories over Queens Park Rangers (3-1), Luton Town (3-0), Nottingham Forest (4-1) and on Boxing Day over Swansea Town by 3-0 – when Ron Howells took over in goal from Iowerth Hughes – kept City up with the leaders. Wilf Grant was still amongst the goals, and it was gratifying for manager Cyril Spiers to see inside-forward Dougie Blair, and outside-right Mike Tiddy, also hitting the target. On January the 5th, an excited crowd of 30,000 Ninian Parkites, in the match versus Doncaster Rovers, saw a 'Boy's Own' rescue act by skipper Alf Sherwood, who returned after dressing-room treatment to a badly gashed forehead, to play on the right wing. Wearing a heavy bandage around his head, like a badge of courage, Alf scored twice for City to ensure a vital 2-1 win which put the Bluebirds on top of the Second Division.

A poor performance at Everton, where the City crashed 0-3 before a crowd of 49.230, cost them the leadership, but they regained the top spot on the 26th of January, when Wilf Grant scored the only goal, against his former club - Southampton - at Ninian Park. It was the team's away form that caused concern. When the City played at Sheffield Wednesday on the 9th of February, both teams stood in silent tribute before the kick-off, to mark the passing away of King George VI. At the end of ninety minutes it was probably quieter in the City dressing-room, for after leading by 2-0 at half-time (through a brace of goals from Elfed Evans), the Bluebirds were swept aside in the second half. Jackie Sewell scored all four goals in Wednesday's remarkable 4-2 victory.

The Bluebirds crashed 1-2 at bottom placed Coventry City the following week, then drew at home 1-1 with West Ham. A return trip to Sheffield - this time to United - on March the 12th, appeared to shatter their promotion hopes. The first half at Bramall Lane was goalless, but in an amazing second period, the Blades cut the Bluebirds to pieces, and finished with a 6-1 victory! The reaction of Cyril Spiers was to sign Ken Chisholm, a strapping forward from Coventry City, and the big Scot repaid a large slice of his £12,000 transfer fee, with a two goal debut in City's 3-0 home win over Barnsley on the 15th of March; reserve Les Evans, scored the other goal.

The City drew 0-0 at Hull and 1-1 at Queens Park Rangers. In the Loftus Road match, both Ron Howells and Stan Montgomery were injured, and the Rangers equalised Wilf Grant's goal with a late penalty from Con Smith.

Wilf Grant's goal was equalised by the homesters in the this game with a late penalty that was converted by Con Smith. On Good Friday, sixth placed City played their third successive away game, at second placed Birmingham City, and, in a humdinger of a match, the Midlanders triumphed by 3-2. This left the Bluebirds with a mountain to climb!

Fortunately the City had games in hand over all the other promotion contenders, and of their last six League matches, five were at Ninian Park, where they had lost only once during the season. Ken Chisholm secured the points in a single goal victory over Notts. County on Easter Saturday, and in the home return match against Birmingham City, on the holiday Monday, the big forward provided two of the goals in a magnificent 3-1 win, with Wilf Grant scoring the other. A point from a 2-2 draw at Luton - Alf Sherwood's penalty and Roley Williams providing the goals - left the City with three home games to play. Victory in all three would place the Bluebirds above second placed Birmingham City, who had lost 0-5 at Notts. County.

There was to be no denying the flying Bluebirds, and in the re-arranged match with Blackburn Rovers, goals from Grant, Chisholm and Sherwood (penalty), gave them a 3-1 win. Over 40,000 were present at Ninian Park for Bury's visit, and the crowd went away in a buoyant mood after seeing a brace of goals from Blair and one from Grant provide the City with another win. Victory over Leeds United in the final match would return the Bluebirds to the First Division, after an absence of 23 years.

3rd May 1952, and the 52,000 crowd celebrate after the 3-1 win over Leeds United. A return to the First Division - after an absence of 23 years.

Chairman Sir Herbert Merritt (inset left) and Captain Alf Sherwood (inset right) address the massive crowd.

The third of May 1952 was Cup Final day, but at Ninian Park, over 52,000 rain soaked spectators were not interested in the events at Wembley, for this was to be one of the great days in the history of Cardiff City F.C. Conditions were heavy from the start, and after going close with long shots from Glyn Williams, Wilf Grant and Doug Blair, City had a narrow escape when Fidler clipped the crossbar with a header. The Bluebirds took the hint, and peppered the Leeds goal, but they still had to be careful, particularly when ex-City man Don Mills was in possession. In the 28th minute, City settled the nerves of the packed crowd, as Wilf Grant cleverly dribbled past McCabe and Hair, to place a left-footed shot into the corner of the net at the Canton end.

When Leeds tried to hit back, Ron Howells cleared his lines, and on the stroke of half-time, Wilf Grant got his second goal with another individual effort. The lightly built centre-forward jinked his way down the middle, feinted a pass to Chisholm, and went on to place his shot past Scott, and into the net, off the upright. City's pressure in the second half did not abate, and after 56 minutes, Roley Williams put over an inch perfect centre that Chisholm leapt upto, and headed past Scott's despairing fingertips. The promotion celebrations started, and the vast crowd did not seem to mind when Iggleden scored a consolation for Leeds, two minutes from time.

The scenes at the final whistle said it all, for nobody cared about the pouring rain as delirious supporters swept across the hallowed turf, and cheered wildly as Sir Herbert Merrett, Cyril Spiers, and City skipper Alf Sherwood addressed them from the Director's box.

Newcastle United defeated Arsenal by 1-0 in the F.A.Cup Final, but the massive Ninian Park crowd were oblivious to this Wembley scoreline!

Consistency had been the key factor for City's promotion, and no fewer than nine players had each appeared in at least thirty matches. Wilf Grant was the only ever-present and leading scorer, with 26 League goals. Both Doug Blair and Ken Chisholm contributed a further eight goals each, the latter from only eleven matches. City's home form was by far the best in the Second Division, where attendances averaged 30,000, but away from Ninian Park, they had one of the worst records! All this was incidental, as Cardiff City had come up on the rails to gain the runners-up spot, behind the Champions, Sheffield Wednesday.

F.A.Cup:
Cardiff City met Swindon Town at Ninian Park in the third round, and many West Countrymen travelled to South Wales to see the game which ended in a 1-1 draw, with Grant scoring for the Bluebirds. The replay on the 15th of January, was a close affair which necessitated extra time, before Maurice Owen won the match for the Third Division (South) team.

Welsh Cup:
A mixture of first and second team players visited Milford United on the 3rd of January where the City won by 3-1, with Crad Wilcox scoring two of the goals and Elfed Evans the other. On the 2nd of February, City faced a daunting task at Merthyr Tydfil, who were leading the Southern League by seven points. Although the Bluebirds fielded their first team, they were incapable of preventing a 1-3 defeat. George Edwards netted for the City, with Trevor Reynolds (two) and Jenkin Powell scoring for the Welsh Cup holders.

Alf Sherwood was selected for four Internationals...... Mike Tiddy was selected to play for the Football League...... Charlie Rutter and Wilf Grant were selected for the England 'B' team.

....

1952-53 – Division 1:

The Cardiff City manager, Cyril Spiers, did not make any major signings during the summer, but Keith Thomas (Sheffield Wednesday) Keith Norman (Aston Villa) and George Hazlett of Bury, were each invited to join the playing staff, after they had appeared in the public trial match.

Cardiff City's long awaited return to First Division action came at Wolverhampton Wanderers, on the 23rd of August 1952. Many thousands of Welshmen made the trip to Molineux in good heart, and swelled the attendance to around 50,000. But Jimmy Mullen's lone goal for the Wolves ensured that the travelling fans returned home unhappily. Four days later, City slumped to a 0-3 defeat at Middlesbrough, and therefore they required a big boost for their morale from their first home game, against Sheffield Wednesday, the following Saturday – and how they got it!

The Bluebirds never looked back after George Hazlett, making his home debut, scored from Alf Sherwoods's free kick. Further goals from Ken Chisholm (two) and Wilf Grant, wrapped up a fine 4-0 win over the Second Division Champions. The real hero of City's victory was centre-half Stan Montgomery who completely shut out Wednesday's ace marksman Derek Dooley. Later that season Dooley's career was tragically halted, when, following an injury at Preston, he had to have a leg amputated. The attendance for the opening match at Ninian Park was 43,478, and four days later there were 51,512 present for the 1-1 draw with Middlesbrough. On September the 6th, a mammoth 62,150 were at Tottenham to see City lose narrowly by the odd goal in three.

Young defender John Frowen came in at right-back for several games, and Keith Thomas made his debut, as the City experienced injury problems, and slumped to near the bottom of the table. But a fine 3-2 victory at Preston on the 20th of September, with Doug Blair in an unaccustomed centre-forward berth, restored some confidence to the team; the City goals were scored by Blair, Roley Williams and Ken Chisholm. A week later, two goals from Williams, earned a 2-0 home win over Stoke City, but only two points from the next three consecutive away matches ensured a lowly position in the table. Cyril Spiers exchanged reserve Griff Norman for Torquay's Tommy Northcott, and the stocky centre-forward celebrated his home debut with a goal in City's 2-2 draw, with Blackpool, on the 1st of November. In an amazing match at Chelsea, seven days later, the Bluebirds won by 2-0, despite having players at various stages of the match, needing to leave the field for treatment. One of the injured, George Edwards, scored while still feeling the effects of concussion. City's other goal came from an Alf Sherwood penalty. Twenty minutes from the end of this noteworthy match, misfortune struck the City utility defender Glyn Williams, when he broke his left leg, and this injury was to end his playing career.

Reserve defender Harry Parfitt took the well worn path to Torquay, and Spiers signed Jack Mansell, Brighton's experienced left-back, which was a surprise when one considers the wealth of defenders that were already at Ninian Park. Mansell made his debut in a fine two goal victory at Portsmouth (Northcott and Grant netting the goals), and then did not play again for the first team until four months later, apart from the ill-fated F.A. Cup-tie at Halifax.

After Sunderland had been comprehensively beaten by 4-1 – with goals from Grant (two), Edwards and Chisholm – the Bluebirds had the most barren spell in their history, for another goal was not scored until the 21st of February, a total of eight League matches. Five of the games in this sequence were goalless draws, but this lean spell did not affect the crowd numbers, and there were 51,592 at Ninian Park for the Christmas visit of Newcastle United. On the 21st of February, the goal drought was ended in no uncertain a manner when they hit Manchester City for six without reply. Roley Williams, Keith Thomas (two), Wilf Grant (two) and George Edwards had a field day against the First Division's tail-enders.

On the 7th of March, the Bluebirds visited Arsenal, who were destined to become the League Champions, and they stunned the Highbury crowd of 59,579, by winning with a headed goal from Blair, following Tiddy's corner in the eighth minute. City enjoyed a run of successes which lifted them to mid-table. The 4-1 victory at Manchester United on Easter Saturday spoiled the debut of the United's 15 year old, Duncan Edwards. A 4-0 thumping of Liverpool at Ninian Park two days later was City's last home win of the season, Grant and Chisholm scoring a brace apiece.

The visit of Arsenal on the 22nd of April attracted the highest Ninian Park attendance for a League match, when 57,893 witnessed an unfortunate dour and scoreless draw. Young goalkeeper Graham Vearncombe made his debut in the final game of the season, thus denying Ron Howells the distinction of being an ever-present.

Stan Montgomery and Alf Sherwood were regular choices, and Ken Chisholm led the goalscorers with thirteen, whilst Wilf Grant managed eleven.

The City finished their first season back in the First Division in a comfortable 12th position, after negotiating several traumatic experiences along the way. The South Wales' public responded to the return to the First Division with attendances which averaged over 38,000 at Ninian Park.

F.A.Cup:
Cardiff City were the unfortunate victims of a 'giant killing' in the third round, when they were well beaten by 1-3 at Third Division (North) Halifax Town. A reshuffled team, which included full-back Jack Mansell at inside-left, had no answer to the Halifax goals from Priestly, Murphy and Moncrieff. City's only consolation, on a bleak Northern afternoon, was a rare goal from the veteran Billy Baker.

Welsh Cup:
The Bluebirds at last managed to beat Merthyr Tydfil at Penydarren Park, when Tommy Northcott and Ken Chisholm netted two goals each – plus one from George Hazlett – in the 5-2 victory. At Barry, in the next round on the last day of January, Northcott managed another brace, plus one from Mike Tiddy, in a narrow 3-2 win. The semi-final at Rhyl caused embarrassment to a full strength City team, who were humbled by the non-Leaguers with their 1-0 win. An early injury to skipper Alf Sherwood, which required a hospital visit, upset the Bluebirds rhythm, but Rhyl were worthy winners.

Alf Sherwood, Ron Stitfall and Derrick Sullivan were all capped by Wales during the season

****

1953-54 Season – Division 1:

During the summer, Cyril Spiers re-signed the former City reserve centre-forward Ken Oakley from Ebbw Vale of the Welsh League, and brought in inside-forward Johnny Rainford, from Crystal Palace. A number of junior players were invited to Ninian Park, amongst them were Clive Burder, Graham Barnes and Mike McCarthy – all Welsh schoolboys – plus Ken Jones the former Wales schoolboy goalkeeper, Johnny Williams (ex-Wales Youth) and Bob Elston from Ely.

Before the start of the season, the Club received the sad news that Willie Davies, their former Welsh international of the 1920's, had died during a visit to his brother-in-law, in Llandeilo. Davies had been signed from Swansea Town in 1924 for a £2,500 fee, and he went on to make 87 appearances, score 17 goals, and appear in the 1925 F.A.Cup Final. A serious chest illness kept him out of the team for a year, which resulted in him missing the 1927 Cup triumph. In March 1928, he was transferred to Notts. County, and two years later he joined Tottenham Hotspur, where he was a great favourite for four seasons, before his return to Swansea Town in 1933, and where he ended his career; he won 17 Welsh caps during his football career.

Due to the proposed broadcasting and televising of the next F.A.Cup Final, all fixtures scheduled for the 1st of May 1954 were brought forward to the 19th of August, and so for the first time, the League season started on a Wednesday. Cardiff City, with new inside-forward Rainford making his debut, drew 0-0 at Middlesbrough, and three days later the Bluebirds opened their home programme with a 2-1 win over Aston Villa, when both right-winger Peter Thomas and Rainford scored in their home debuts, but before a somewhat disappointing attendance of 28,156. City made a stuttering start to the season, which was not helped by the absence of McLaughlin, Hollyman, Sullivan and Glyn Williams, who were all on the injured list. Skipper Sherwood was to join them when he contracted an infected leg following an insect bite!

Jack Mansell deputised for Sherwood at left-back, and the City enjoyed a run of ten matches with only one defeat - the reverse to the League Champions, Arsenal, who won 3-0 at Ninian Park on the 26th of September. By mid-October, the City rose to 7th in the First Division, and were going quite well following a 2-1 success at Preston, and a 1-0 home win over Tottenham Hotspur. Bobby McLaughlin, unable to win a regular first team place, was exchanged for the reliable goal-scoring Southampton inside-forward Frank Dudley. Only six months after joining Cardiff, Johnny Rainford returned to London, with Brentford, where he went on to have a long and successful career. Dudley scored on his home debut, against Charlton Athletic, when City won by 5-0 with the other goals coming from Tiddy and a Chisholm hat-trick. But Southampton made by far the better deal in the McLaughlin/Dudley exchange, for the former City player went on to make 169 appearances for the Saints, whereas Dudley was to make just four appearances for the Bluebirds, before he also moved on to Brentford, a week before Christmas. After the 5-0 victory over Charlton, City conceded an amazing 16 goals in just three games - 0-4 at Newcastle, 1-6 at home to Manchester United and 1-6 at West Bromwich. In the Albion game, Ronnie Allen scored four times, and Johnny Nicholls scored the other two. Cyril Spiers allowed Ken Hollyman, one of City's most popular players, to join Newport County, and accepted an offer of £12,000 from Portsmouth for Jack Mansell. Following a 3-1 home win over Liverpool, Cardiff City shook the football world when they swooped for the Wales' international centre-forward Trevor Ford, and paid a £30,000 transfer fee. The City had failed with their big offers for Barnsley's Tommy Taylor and John Charles of Leeds United, so the 30 year old Ford was hardly the first choice.

Sir Herbert Merrett later revealed that he did not sanction the purchase of the controversial Ford, and refused to endorse the cheque that brought him to Ninian Park.

Ford scores on his debut - versus Middlesbrough.

On his home debut, against Middlesbrough on the 12th of December, Ford scored the game's only goal. His charismatic presence added 10,000 more to the gate over the previous home attendance, so there was no doubting the public reaction to one of Wales' foremost personalities. Ken Chisholm lost his place almost immediately and was snapped up by Sunderland for a reasonable fee. The Roker Park Club saw Chisholm as a replacement for Ford, and the transfer fee that the City received went some way towards offsetting the outgoing money.

A mid-season slump, in which City scored just once in six League games, coincided with an injury crisis that saw eleven of the professional staff out of action. It was not surprising that the Bluebirds dropped into the lower half of the table, but they recovered in grand style following a 1-1 draw at Arsenal on the 13th of February, when Ford scored the City goal. City proceeded to win seven out of the next eight League games, which included a 3-2 victory at Manchester United (avenging the earlier 1-6 home defeat). The best performance was probably that which knocked West Bromwich Albion off the top of the First Division, when they won 2-0 at Ninian Park, on the 10th of April, before 45,000 delighted fans. On Easter Saturday, Cardiff visited the bottom club, Liverpool, and in a dramatic match they lost the services of goalkeeper Ron Howells through injury. Alf Sherwood took over in goal, and after Tommy Northcott had scored for the Bluebirds, Sherwood defied all that Liverpool could throw at him - including a penalty taken by the legendary Billy Liddell. The City won by 1-0, and the Anfield club were relegated!

City finished the season in 10th place, and manager Spiers was pleased that youngsters Graham Vearncombe, Colin Gale, Colin Baker, Cliff Nugent and Tommy Northcott had all tasted First Division action. Old hands, Billy Baker and Stan Montgomery, had been regulars in the City line-up, and the leading scorers were Wilf Grant and the departed Ken Chisholm, with 12 goals each. City had to pay £5,000 to bring defender Harry Parfitt back from Torquay, where he had gone, on loan (!), to answer the mid-season injury crisis. This unsatisfactory situation ended the transfer agreement that had existed between the clubs since the War. Despite City's erratic form, home attendances had still averaged over 33,000.

F.A.Cup

For the first time in sixteen years, the City met non-League opposition in the competition, when Peterborough United visited Ninian Park for a third round tie on the 9th of January. The attendance of 34,000 was one of the highest recorded for an F.A.Cup match involving a non-League club. The part-timers were a very good side, but against a City team with five Welsh International players in their line-up, it was no surprise when Trevor Ford - with two - and Tommy Northcott, provided the goals for the Bluebirds to win comfortably by 3-1, after Martin had given Peterborough a sixth minute lead.

The fourth round draw brought Third Division (North) Port Vale to Ninian Park, and in one of the major shocks of the day, the men from the Potteries took full advantage of the City's misfortune when goalkeeper Howells was knocked out on the bone hard pitch. Sherwood took over in goal, but was helpless as Port Vale won by 2-0, with goals from Bert Leake and Ken Griffiths, that were scored either side of half-time.

Ron Howells in action during the Cardiff City/Port Vale Cup match of 1954 challenged by Vale's Bert Leake.

Welsh Cup:

Cardiff City fielded a mainly reserve line-up for the tie at Barry, on the 20th of January, and were fortunate to escape with a 1-1 draw, after Clive Burden had scored for the City, and former Bluebird Bryn Allen, had replied for Barry. The Southern Leaguers had missed their chance of causing an upset, for a strengthened Cardiff team won the replay at Ninian Park by 4-2, with goals from Trevor Ford, Mike Tiddy and a pair from Cliff Nugent.

For the fourth consecutive season, City and Merthyr Tydfil met in the competition, and even with several reserves in the team, the Bluebirds were too strong for a Merthyr team that was now just past its peak. The City won by 5-2 at Penydarren Park, with a hat-trick from Wilf Grant, plus one from Tommy Northcott, and a Lowe own goal.

Cardiff City were now clear favourites to win the Welsh Cup, but in the semi-final at Wrexham, on the 24th of March, they crashed 1-2 to Flint Town, when Northcott's goal was not enough to save their blushes.

There was great sadness at Ninian Park on the 11th of February 1954, when it was learnt that former secretary/manager Fred Stewart had died at his home in Newport Road, aged 81 years. The greatest manager in the history of the Club had spent 22 years in charge at Ninian Park - from 1911 - during all of the Bluebirds greatest triumphs. He had brought many great players to South Wales, which led the Club to become a major force during the 1920's.

The dust had barely settled on the 1953-54 season when there was a great deal of activity behind the scenes at Ninian Park...... Former City favourite Walter Robbins, who had been the Club's trainer since 1947, resigned on the 26th of April, in order to concentrate on his business interests...... There was an even bigger shock when manager Cyril Spiers tendered his resignation. The reasons for this shock decision have never been made public...... Assistant secretary (and a founder member of the Club), Bartley Wilson, retired after a lifetime's service with the City, at the age of 85...... During the past season, Howells, Sherwood, Sullivan and Ford were capped by Wales.

****

1954-55 season - Division 1:

On the 30th of June, a number of administration and background changes were made:

New Director:	Ron Beecher
Secretary/manager:	Trevor Morris
Assistant/secretary:	Harold Grizelle
Head Trainer:	Eddie Nash (ex-Bristol City)
Chief Coach:	Bob John
Assistant Coaches:	Billy Jones and Glyn Williams
Physiotherapist:	John Evans
Chief scout/assist. manager:	Albert Lindon

Caerphilly-born Trevor Morris, who was once on the books of Ipswich Town, had his playing career ended due to a broken leg in a War-time match, whilst playing for Cardiff City. He had been assistant secretary, and then secretary, since the resumption of League football after the War, and was a surprise appointment to the vacant manager's chair. He had been awarded the D.F.M. during his War-time service with the R.A.F. Glyn Williams also had his playing career ended by a broken leg, at Chelsea in November 1952.

Albert Lindon introduced local youngsters, Don Clarke, Neil O'Halloran, John Davies plus Cecil Dixon from Trowbridge Town, to the Club, but there were no major signings for the new season.

City made the worst possible start to the campaign by losing at Burnley, where Les Shannon scored the winner, 90 seconds after the start of the game.

Shock waves ran through Ninian Park when the Bluebirds conceded 14 goals in the opening four games, the majority coming from Preston's astonishing League 'double', when they won by 5-2 in Cardiff, and 7-1 at Deepdale!

An unbeaten run of seven games, three wins and four draws, restored the City's confidence, as Trevor Ford got on the goal trail. Trevor Morris made his first major signing by paying £12,000 for Wolves' inside-forward Ron Stockin. Promising youngster Islwyn Jones was given his League baptism in the fine 3-1 victory at Sheffield United, and pacey blond-haired winger Cecil Dixon made his senior debut at Everton on the 25th of September, where City drew 1-1 before a crowd of 54,540, as Morris chopped and changed his players in order to find the best combination.

At Charlton, on the 23rd of October, Trevor Ford scored after only 15 seconds, but City crashed in the second half, with a final 1-4 scoreline. Never regarded as good travellers, the City achieved the rare feat of winning three successive away games, by 2-0 at Tottenham, 3-1 at Portsmouth and 2-0 at Aston Villa; in the latter match Ford scored twice against one of his former clubs. New boy, Ron Stockin, had responded to his change of environment, by netting seven goals in ten games besides having several efforts disallowed.

Trevor Morris signed Coventry winger Gordon Nutt for £12,000, and the new player made his debut in a bad 0-3 home defeat by Burnley, a week before Christmas. City were then relieved to beat West Bromwich Albion by 3-2 at Ninian Park, in what was to be the last League match to be played in the Welsh capital on a Christmas Day. The Bluebirds continued their annoying habit of dropping silly points and then putting together short unbeaten runs, until Charlton Athletic were beaten 4-3 in a thriller on the 12th of March. From then until the end of the season, City had a dismal run of results, which included four successive home defeats.

The goal that kept Cardiff City in the First Division, and effectively prevented Wolves from winning the Championship. Centre-forward Trevor Ford (hidden by Billy Wright) shoots past Wolves goalkeeper Bert Williams.

The Bluebirds tumbled into the relegation zone, and when they faced Wolverhampton Wanderers on the 30th of April, who were neck and neck with Chelsea in the race for the Championship, City were desperate for a victory, from this their final home game, in order to save themselves from relegation. Gerry Hitchens, a raw boned miner signed from Kidderminster Harriers for £1,500 four months earlier, made his League debut, and he rose to the occasion by scoring one of the goals in a thrilling 3-2 win. Trevor Ford netted the other two, to take his seasons' tally to 19, the top marksman for the Club, with Ron Stockin following with 12. City finished in 20th place, due mainly to the poor form late in the season. They were best served by Derrick Sullivan, Ron Howells, Trevor Ford, Alan Harrington and Alf Sherwood. Although they had lost eight League matches at Ninian Park, the home attendances still managed to average almost 27,000.

F.A.Cup:
Cardiff City faced a tough draw in the third round, with a trip to Arsenal. Despite battling in dogged fashion, the Bluebirds were finally beaten by a goal from Tommy Lawton, before a Highbury crowd that numbered 51,298.

Welsh Cup:
On the 12th of January, Cardiff enjoyed a trip to Pembroke Borough and won in a canter by 7-0, with Ford scoring four, and Nugent, Stockin and Tiddy netting the other three goals. City then made the trip to neighbours Cardiff City and, fielding a strong team, won by 3-1 before a crowd of 10,223. Ford, Stockin and Sullivan scored the goals. City's involvement in the competition came to an end in the semi-final which was played at Wrexham on the 13th of April, when Chester won 2-0.

At the end of the season, three of Cardiff City's finest post-war players - Billy Baker, Stan Montgomery and George Edwards - all left the Club. Baker had been a Cardiff City player since 1938, and had it not been for the intervention of the war, he would probably have nearly doubled his 293 League appearances for the Club. Baker moved on to Ipswich Town, where he stayed for two years before returning to South Wales, and non-League football. Montgomery had arrived at Ninian Park in December 1948, from Southend United, following a recommendation from his father-in-law, Jimmy Nelson - City's great full-back of the 1920's. Stan went on to make 231 League appearances, and was always a dominant figure in the City defence. He moved on to Worcester City, then Newport County, Llanelly and Ton Pentre. In 1962, he would return to Ninian Park as first team trainer. Ex-Welsh international winger George Edwards, who had been plagued by injury, decided to retire and concentrate on his business interests. He was to rejoin the Club as a director several years later. A popular hard-shooting winger, Edwards scored 34 goals in 194 League appearances, and won 12 Welsh caps.

During the season, Sherwood, Sullivan and Ford were capped by Wales.

1955-56 Season – Division 1:

The Cardiff City manager, Trevor Morris, reinforced his playing staff during the summer, by signing three men from Sunderland; inside-forwards Harry Kirtley and Howard Sheppeard, plus winger Johnny McSeveney, who together were involved in a triple deal that was worth £9,000. Controversy flared behind the scenes, when star centre-forward, Trevor Ford, refused to sign a new contract. The directors finally gave in to his demands, but Ford's career with Cardiff City became stormy after that period of dissatisfaction between Club and player.

New signings Kirtley and McSeveney made their debuts in the City's opening match of the season when, ironically, Sunderland were the visitors. McSeveney celebrated with two goals against his former club, and Trevor Ford - another former Sunderland player scored the other, in a 3-1 win. This was City's first success in a season opener since 1951. On the 3rd of September, the Bluebirds entertained Wolverhampton Wanderers, and before 45,000, they suffered their worst humiliation in League football at Ninian Park.

The Wolves won by 9-1, to equal the record away win in a First Division match, that was held by Sunderland who had beaten Newcastle with the same scoreline, in 1908. Four months earlier, City's 3-2 victory at Ninian Park over the Wolves not only saved the Bluebirds from relegation, but had gone a long way in preventing the Molineux men from winning the League Championship, which went to Chelsea.

The Wolves were thirsting for 'revenge', and within 15 *seconds,* diminutive winger Johnny Hancocks had fired the visitors ahead; by half-time they had cruised to a 5-0 lead. Hancocks, and centre-forward Roy Swinbourne, completed their hat-tricks; Peter Broadbent scored twice, and Alf Sherwood conceded an own goal, before Ron Stockin scored a late consolation goal for the City.

In their next home match, the Bluebirds hit back after Sheffield United had taken a 2-0 lead in the opening thirty minutes. Cecil Dixon laid on goals for Alan Harrington, Trevor Ford and Gerry Hitchens, to gain a final 3-2 victory for the homesters, for only their second win in nine matches. It was no surprise when the City sank to the depths of the First Division, and in late September, they accepted Arsenal's offer of the Gunners reserve outside-right Brian Walsh plus £20,000, for wingers Mike Tiddy and Gordon Nutt. Tiddy, a part-time lay preacher, had been a popular figure in his four years at Ninian Park, whereas Nutt had failed to come up to expectations following his arrival nine months earlier, from Coventry City. Walsh's debut on the 8th of October, coincided with the City's first away win of the season, when Ford and Stockin were on target in the 2-1 win at Preston. Home wins over Everton (3-1) and Birmingham City (2-1) kept the City just above the relegation zone - their plight not being helped by problems within the Club.

Ford was dropped for the home game against Birmingham City after refusing to play at inside-left. Amid much publicity he was suspended by the Club for two weeks, and placed on the transfer list. On the 8th of December, Morris finally signed a player that was needed so badly for the problem centre-half position, that had been caused by the summer departure of Stan Montgomery. Sullivan, Frowen and Gale had all been tried, but to no avail. Morris looked to Scotland, and signed Dundee's highly rated pivot, Danny Malloy, for £17,000. Malloy made his City debut in a sensational match, a 3-1 win over Charlton Athletic at Ninian Park on the 10th of December. Neil O'Halloran, a boiler-maker and part-time player also made his first appearance for the City, at inside-left, and stole Malloy's thunder when he became the only player in the Club's history to score a hat-trick, (all headers) in a League debut. Unfortunately the cumbersome O'Halloran had set too high a standard for himself, and after only four matches he returned to reserve team football. With Malloy as the king-pin in defence, and Ford recalled after a spell in the second team, City turned the corner and lost only once in fourteen games. During this period, Hitchens found his First Division feet by scoring ten goals. One of the Bluebirds finest performances came at Molineux on New Year's Eve, when they exacted revenge for that early season mauling, by beating Wolves 2-0, with goals from Hitchens and Ford, in front of a stunned 37,000 crowd. City had their best victory of the season - 4-1 over Manchester City on the 14th of January - and four consecutive wins during February saw the Bluebirds climb to the safety of mid-table.

Before the transfer deadline, inside forward Roley Williams, who had been with the City for six years (making 138 League appearances), and reserve defender Colin Gale, were exchanged for Bernard Jones, a Northampton Town inside-forward. After much early and mid-season strife, the Bluebirds finished the season in 17th place. McSeveney missed just one match, and Harrington, Kirtley, Hitchens and Stitfall all appeared regularly. Hitchens emerged as the leading scorer with 15 goals, and Ford (despite the controversies) managed 13. Average home attendances were maintained at over 28,000.

F.A.Cup:

Cardiff travelled to Second Division promotion chasers Leeds United for a third round tie. Despite fog warnings, the match was played at Elland Road in bright winter sunshine, before 40,000 spectators. It was twenty minutes from time when the City made the vital breakthrough with a drive from Hitchens. McSeveney made it 2-0 with just eight minutes remaining, and Leeds managed a late consolation goal from Brook in the dying moments. This strike was too late to prevent a City victory, and they inflicted on Leeds their first home defeat for 32 games! One of the main factors in City's victory had been the mastery of Danny Malloy over the mighty John Charles.

On the 28th of January, the Bluebirds faced Second Division West Ham United at Upton Park in the fourth round, and, in the worst 'glue-pot' conditions imaginable, they went down 1-2, with Ford scoring City's goal. Billy Dare and John Dick netted for the Hammers to delight a crowd numbering 35,500.

Welsh Cup:

Cardiff City began their Welsh Cup campaign at Pembroke Borough, where they had won 7-1 twelve months earlier. A full strength team almost went no further as, to their utter shame, the West Walian team forced a 2-2 draw, which must rank as one of Pembroke's finest hours; Ford and Hitchens spared the City's blushes. A week later, City, showing only two team changes - Vearncombe for the injured Howells and Sherwood replacing young Ron Davies - exacted full revenge with a runaway 9-0 win at Ninian Park. Ford scored four goals, Hitchens hit three, and Baker and McSeveney got one each.

The City were at home to Wrexham on the 29th of February, and in a game of eight goals, the Bluebirds overcame the gallant team from North Wales with a 5-3 scoreline, when Hitchens (three), Ford and McSeveney were on target. The semi-final was played at Wrexham on the 17th of March, with Oswestry facing City, and the League team roared to an easy 7-0 victory. Hitchens scored five goals and Ford managed two.

Cardiff City met Swansea Town in the final at Ninian Park, and the crowd of over 37,000 was the biggest in the history of the competition. Tragedy struck the City inside-forward Harry Kirtley, in the first half, when he was stretchered off with a broken leg. Ten man City put on a grand display, and two goals from Brian Walsh plus one from McSevenney put the Bluebirds 3-0 ahead. Swansea staged a grandstand finish, with Kiley and Palmer cutting the lead to 3-2, but City hung on to win the Welsh Cup, for the first time since 1930!

During the season, Alf Sherwood, Trevor Ford and Alan Harrington were all capped by Wales.

Trevor Ford about to shoulder-charge Swans keeper Johnny King

Rival captains Trevor Ford (left), and Swansea's Ivor Allchurch, with referee Mervyn Griffiths.

Scenes of celebration in the dressing-room. Standing at back: Harrington, Vearncombe and Hitchens. Front: Stitfall, Sullivan (drinking from Cup), Malloy, McSeveney, Baker, Walsh and Ford. Missing player, is Kirtley - with a broken leg - who had been taken to hospital.

30th of April: Cardiff City beat Swansea Town 3-2 in the Welsh Cup Final - before a record crowd of over 37,000.

1956-57 Season – Division 1:

During the close season veteran full-back Alf Sherwood moved on to Newport County. He had joined the City in 1941, and enjoyed fifteen years of almost total success as the Bluebirds went from Third Division (South) to the First Division. Sherwood was capped 39 times for Wales whilst with the City (he was selected twice more during his time at Newport), and made 353 League appearances for the Bluebirds. He remained one of Cardiff's best remembered players, particularly for his tussles in International and League encounters with Blackpool's immortal outside-right, Stanley Matthews. Brayley Reynolds, an inside-forward from Lovell's Athletic, who cost £2,500, was the only new player to arrive at Ninian Park in the summer.

Trevor Morris relied on the same squad to start the season, and following a scoreless draw at Arsenal on the opening day, City walloped Newcastle United 5-2 at Ninian Park in midweek. McSeveney (now operating at inside-right), Ford (with two) and a pair from utility forward Cliff Nugent scored the goals in an exhilarating performance. The following Saturday, City drew 3-3 at home to Burnley after leading 3-1, and suddenly all the old failings were back. On the 1st of September, the City crashed 0-6 at Preston, after conceding five first half goals. Ironically they had lost by 1-7 at Deepdale on the same date, two years previously.

Trevor Ford, who was the City captain following the departure of Sherwood, actually volunteered to play out of position, a complete turn about from the previous season when he refused to play anywhere but leader of the attack! Ford played on the right-wing at Birmingham City, where the Bluebirds lost 1-2, and was back in his more accustomed berth when Reynolds made his debut against Leeds United, at Ninian Park, on the 6th of October. City shook off their poor form and romped to a 4-1 win, with Hitchens (two), Ford and McSevenney finding the net. On the 3rd of November, Cardiff City fans saw the last of Trevor Ford in a Bluebirds jersey, when the home match against Manchester City marked his final appearance. A cloud of controversy quickly followed. Extracts from his, as then unpublished, autobiography entitled: *"I lead the attack"*, which dealt with illegal payments to players, were printed by a Sunday newspaper, and these soon led to him being banned by the Football League. In some quarters it was announced that Ford had retired, but he was in fact banned 'sine die', on the 30th of January 1957. He had the ban cut to three years, on his appeal on the 3rd of March 1958; three weeks later, he signed a three year contract with P.S.V. Eindhoven of Holland.

During this time, Cardiff City were left without one of their principal goal sources, and the mantle fell heavily on the broad shoulders of Gerry Hitchens. The youngster rose manfully to the challenge, but no matter how many goals City scored, the defence conceded more!

The team faced a daunting trip to Manchester United on Christmas Day, when they were forced to leave their snowbound coach outside Hereford. The players walked to the railway station, where they were reported to have indulged in Carol singing (!), while waiting for a train to take them to their overnight stop at Shrewsbury. They eventually reached the Hotel at 1.00 a.m. At Old Trafford the following day, Danny Malloy netted a second minute penalty, but the League Champions hit back to win by 3-1, with goals from Tommy Taylor, Denis Viollett and Billy Whelan.

Following a fine 2-1 win at West Bromwich Albion (goals by Hitchens and Baker), on the 9th of February, the City won only one more game during the remainder of the season – a disastrous run of 14 games. A 2-3 home defeat by already doomed Charlton Athletic on the 23rd of March, after Hitchens had fired City into a 2-0 lead, put the skids under the Bluebirds. But an Easter 'double' by Portsmouth, which saved the Fratton Park Club from the drop, condemned Cardiff City to the Second Division.

In their final home match on the 27th of April, City faced Manchester United a week before the 'Busby Babes' met Aston Villa in the F.A.Cup Final. Hitchens scored two fine goals to put City 2-1 ahead, but a much changed United side hit back to win 3-2. Scanlon's penalty winner from the game's last kick hit a post, and entered the net off goalkeeper Vearncombe! Perhaps the final act perfectly summed up City's traumatic season, which ended with them finishing 21st in the table, and relegation.

Danny Malloy was ever-present and Gerry Hitchens missed just one match, with Ron Stitfall and Graham Vearncombe appearing regularly. Hitchens was the top scorer with an impressive 21 League goals, and McSeveney, despite missing several vital penalties, scored on 12 occasions. Home support remained loyal, and averaged over 24,000 at Ninian Park.

F.A.Cup:
History repeated itself as Cardiff City returned to Elland Road for a third round tie on the 5th of January. Unbelievably the Bluebirds secured the same result as twelve months earlier, by winning 2-1, with goals from Stockin and McSeveney. City were drawn at home to Barnsley of the Second Division, in the fourth round. In a disappointing performance before a crowd of 32,000, they lost 0-1 to the unsung Yorkshiremen, whose goal from Frank Bartlett arrived just three minutes from time.

Welsh Cup:
Cardiff City took a full strength team to Haverfordwest, and, as at Pembroke twelve months earlier, found themselves facing a replay following an astonishing 3-3 draw. Hitchens (two) and Harry Kirtley – recovered from his broken leg – scored the City goals. A week later Cardiff swept Haverfordwest aside in a torrent of eight goals, from Hitchens (two), Walsh (two), Kirtley, Stockin, Sullivan and Williams' 'own goal'.

On the 27th of February, City met Chester at Ninian Park and suffered an embarrassing defeat at the hands of the Third Division (North) side, for whom Jepson and Davies scored in the visitors 2-0 victory.

During the season, Alan Harrington, Derek Sullivan, Trevor Ford and Ron Stitfall were capped by Wales.

A fateful penalty miss on the 20th of April. With the score at 0-0 McSeveney scuffs a spot-kick wide. The 0-3 final defeat helped City to relegation.

1957-58 season – Division 2:

George Edwards, the former Cardiff City and Wales outside-left, joined the board of Directors in May, and Bill Jones - ex-Worcester City and former Barry Town manager - was appointed to the Club's coaching staff three months later. Trevor Morris, realising the need to pep up the Bluebirds' attack, signed former England International Johnny Nicholls from West Bromwich Albion, where he had scored goals in abundance. Experienced Wrexham inside-forward Ron Hewitt was signed for £7,000 and Newport County's mercurial winger, Colin 'Rock' Hudson came to Ninian Park with Johnny McSeveny, Neil O'Halloran and Cecil Dixon moving to Somerton Park.

Former Wales goalkeeper Ron Howells dropped into non-League football at Worcester City, but in 1958 he returned to the Football League when he joined Chester. A number of reserve and junior players left Ninian Park during the Summer, as Cardiff City prepared for life in the Second Division.

The Bluebirds could not have faced a more daunting start to the season than a visit from Swansea Town, a side full of Welsh International players. Colin Hudson, Ron Hewitt and Johnny Nicholls all made their debuts in the City attack, and the 45,000 sun-soaked spectators must have been disappointed with the scoreless draw. City's early season form was poor, with a 1-0 home win over Huddersfield Town on the 11th of September being their only success in the first nine games. Full-back Ron Davies had been switched to the attack - he scored the goal against Huddersfield - and he was once again the only goalscorer in the victory at Doncaster on the 28th of September.

Alec Milne, a long-legged Scottish full-back, who had been signed from Arbroath the previous March, took over at left-back. City's results picked up during October - 2-2 at home to Rotherham and 3-2 versus Derby County, plus a 2-0 success at Bristol Rovers followed by another 3-2 home win (against Lincoln City). Morris confounded many observers when he signed Welsh International centre-half Ray Daniel from Sunderland for £7,500. City had a wealth of half-back talent on their books, and although Danny Malloy had struck a poor spell (during which he conceded several 'own goals'), it appeared to be only a matter of time before he would recapture his normal form.

To everyone's amazement, when the brawny Scot did return to the team – at home to Ipswich Town on the 9th of November – he appeared at centre-forward! Alongside Malloy, in the inside-left berth, was new signing Joe Bonson, a burly attack leader who had cost £7,000 from Wolverhampton Wanderers. He had been bought to replace Johnny Nicholls, who was transferred to Exeter City after failing to strike any form in his short stay at Ninian Park. Bonson had a goalscoring debut in the 1-1 draw with Ipswich, and suffice to say, Malloy did not play in the forward line again.

Following a 0-4 defeat at Blackburn Rovers, when all the goals came during a fifteen minute first half spell, young goalkeeper Ken Jones replaced Graham Vearncombe, and wing-half Bob Scott started to appear fleetingly. The much fancied Hitchens was missing on the 7th of December, when the Bluebirds achieved their highest post-War victory with a 7-0 win over Barnsley. On a bleak afternoon, and with a backdrop of construction cranes on the Ninian Park 'Bob bank', unsung utility forward Cliff Nugent grabbed the headlines with a hat-trick, the other scorers being Hewitt (two), Bonson and Hudson.

Two weeks later, Cardiff accepted an offer of £22,500 from Aston Villa for Hitchens, which brought cries of dismay from the disgruntled Bluebirds supporters. Hitchens was destined to become a leading goalscorer at Villa Park, and England international, followed by a lucrative career in Italian football. City secured their first ever League win at Swansea on the 21st of December, when Hudson scored the only goal in a largely undistinguished, yet historic game. The Bluebirds made it a very happy Christmas indeed for their followers, with the 5-2 Boxing Day victory over Stoke City, with Hudson, Bonson (two) Reynolds and Walsh sharing the goals.

The City followed that with an amazing 6-1 drubbing of League leaders Liverpool, at Ninian Park two days later. The Bluebirds led 5-0 at half-time with Colin Hudson (on his Wedding day), Reynolds (two), Hewitt and Joe Bonson (two) all getting on the scoresheet. The team had scored a Club record 18 goals in three successive home games.

The Bluebirds hovered in the lower half of the Second Division in the early months of 1958, and in that time reserve winger Ken Tucker moved on the Shrewsbury Town, full-back Ron Davies (who had been tried at centre-forward) was transferred to Southampton and former Welsh International Ray Daniel – who had done little during his short stay at Ninian Park – was sold to Swansea Town for £3,000. On the 26th of March, City nearly faced Bristol Rovers without goalkeeper Ken Jones, who was so engrossed in the televised F.A.Cup semi-final replay between Fulham and the post-Munich 'Busby Babes', that he managed to report to Ninian Park just before the teamsheets were presented to the referee!

Trevor Morris, suitably annoyed, watched the City lose by 0-2, their first home defeat for twelve games, and he relegated Jones to the Welsh League X1 for the match at Haverfordwest three days later. In this match he scored from the penalty spot in a 2-1 win, whilst at Ninian Park the Bluebirds were entertaining promotion bound Blackburn Rovers. The City beat the Rovers in a thrilling match by 4-3, with Hewitt striking a hat-trick, and Bonson scoring the other goal. Bristol City completed an Easter 'double' over the Bluebirds, and the eventual Second Division Champions, West Ham United, handed City a 3-0 thrashing at Ninian Park. Cardiff did end their home programme on a high note with a cracking 3-0 win over Fulham, on the 26th of April, with goals from wing-halves Baker and Sullivan (two), leaving Fulham's highly rated goalkeeper Tony Macedo clutching at thin air.

At Craven Cottage, centre-forward Gerry Hitchens challenges Fulham goalkeeper Tony Macedo. This was to be Hitchens last game for Cardiff, before his £22,000 transfer to Aston Villa.

City's final League game was at lowly Lincoln, a re-arranged match from the 8th of March which had been abandoned at half-time due to a blizzard, with the Bluebirds leading by 3-0! Two months later, Lincoln needed a victory to stay in the Second Division, and with a crowd of almost 20,000 urging them on, the Imps preserved their Second Division status with a 3-1 victory over a City team with nothing to play for; Cliff Nugent scored the consolation goal.

The Club finished the season in 15th place, but for long periods had looked like relegation material. Not surprisingly the home attendances were badly affected and the average was only a little over 16,000. The most consistent performers were Stitfall, Harrington and Malloy, and the leading scorer Hewitt with 14 goals, was followed by Bonson's 12 successes.

F.A.Cup:

A most amazing coincidence – unequalled in the F.A.Cup competition – resulted in Leeds United and Cardiff City being paired together at Elland Road, in the 3rd round, for the *third* consecutive season. Astonishingly the final score was once again 2-1 to the City, and the odds against such coincidences must surely have been millions to one! In order for the match to be played, the snowbound surface was rolled flat, and this proved to be a great leveller for the two teams. First Division Leeds were outfought by a Bluebirds team who did well on the day, with the goals coming from Harrington and Nugent.

The fourth round, on the 25th of January, brought Leyton Orient to Ninian Park, just a week after the teams had played out a 1-1 Second Division draw. The Londoners played in their old strip of white shirts with a broad red 'V' on the front, rather like a rugby jersey, but it did them no good as the City, in rampant mood, swept them aside with a 4-1 victory. The goals came from Walsh, two from Bonson, and a Bishop 'own goal', before a crowd of 35,849.

High flying Blackburn Rovers, who included fine players such as Billy Eckersley, Ronnie Clayton, Bryan Douglas, Peter Dobing, Roy Vernon and Ally McLeod in their ranks, were City's fifth round opponents at Ninian Park. A crowd of 45,580 were in full voice as Joe Bonson and Colin Hudson hit the woodwork in the opening minutes, and both players missed open goals a little later. Although the City pummelled the Blackburn goal, the match ended as a scoreless draw, and they had to replay the following Thursday, the 20th of February, at Ewood Park. Blackburn showed more of their true form in this second Cup encounter, and although the City scored through Hewitt, the Rovers won by 2-1.

Welsh Cup:

Cardiff City crashed at the first hurdle, and in embarrassing fashion, when Hereford United – then of the Southern League – won by 2-0 at Ninian Park, a performance which at that time was rated as one of the finest victories in Hereford's history. The goals were scored by prolific marksmen Roy Williams and Cyril Beech.

During the season, Harrington and Hewitt were capped, and later in the 1958 World Cup Finals that were held in Sweden, Baker, Sullivan and Hewitt all appeared for Wales.

....

1958-59 Season – Division 2:

When the Entertainment Tax on football was abolished in 1956, Sir Herbert Merrett (the Cardiff City President), promised to use the money to improve the facilities at Ninian Park, particularly for the 'Bob-bankers' for whom he had a special affection. During the 1957-58 season, construction work had been undertaken to put a full pitch length cover over the popular side, and this work was completed in time for the new season. It now meant that Ninian Park had covered accommodation on all four sides, and with a capacity for 62,000 spectators.

On the 20th of July, Secretary/manager Trevor Morris accepted an offer to join Swansea Town, and City coach Bill Jones was appointed to the vacant position. Stoke City's tall inside-forward George Kelly signed for the City before Morris' departure. After Bill Jones took over as acting manager, his first signing was goalkeeper Ron Nicholls of Bristol Rovers, who was also a County cricketer with Gloucestershire. Nicholls had been in dispute with Rovers over his cricketing commitments, and with Graham Vearncombe in the Merchant Navy, the City badly needed an experienced goalkeeper. Jones' offer of reserve defender John Frowen, and a small fee in exchange for Nicholls was accepted by the Rovers.

Just before the season began, full-back Charlie Rutter – who had been with the City since 1949 and whose long spells of injury had kept down his first team appearances to 118 – joined Exeter City on a free transfer; during his best spell he had been selected for the England 'B' team.

The season began disastrously, as City lost their opening three games without scoring a goal. Ken Jones was replaced in goal by new signing Nicholls, and the City recovered to win consecutive matches at Ninian Park, 3-2 against Huddersfield Town followed by 3-1 versus Sheffield United, with Kelly bagging two of the goals.

The new inside-right played only one more match before giving way to 18 year old Graham Moore, and the youngster marked his League baptism with a late equaliser in a 2-2 draw at Brighton on the 13th of September. Moore also scored on his home debut in a midweek disaster against Bristol Rovers, who won by 4-2. With the City staggering near the foot of the Second Division, Bill Jones made one of Cardiff's finest signings, on the 18th of September.

Derek Tapscott, Arsenal's Welsh international forward was languishing in the Gunners' reserves with injury problems, and Jones – who knew the player from their Southern League days together at Barry Town – gambled £10,000 to bring Tapscott to Ninian Park. For Tapscott's home debut against Grimsby Town, Jones recalled outside-right Brian Walsh, who had been at Arsenal with City's new signing, and introduced 17 year old wing-half Steve Gammon. City cruised to a 4-1 win, and although Tapscott did not score, his confidence flowed throughout the team. The goals came from Hewitt (two), Bonson, and flying left-winger Brian Jenkins, who was beginning to enjoy an extended run in the first team, after a couple of seasons as a high scoring reserve team player.

The following week, City overcame an early goal at Liverpool, and went on to win 2-1, with Bonson and Hewitt goals. Nicholls, with some fine goalkeeping displays, brought solidity to the defence, and when Steve Gammon was rested, Welsh international Derrick Sullivan demonstrated his great versitilty by switching from left-back to right-half.

The Cardiff City board of Directors had been sufficiently impressed by acting-manager Bill Jones, and on the 23rd of October offered him the permanent post, which he readily accepted. Jones made a popular appointment during November, when he brought Wilf Grant – City's former forward – from Llanelly (where he had been the manager), to become the City's new trainer-coach, where he worked with Bob John and Ernie Curtis. Two players with first team experience left Ninian Park for small fees – goalkeeper Ken Jones to Scunthorpe United, and utility forward Cliff Nugent with 117 City appearances in seven years, to Mansfield Town.

The Bluebirds home form was excellent, and with the forwards inspired by Tapscott's tenacity, the Club moved into the top ten places of the Second Division. Also, for the first time in several seasons, their away form showed signs of improvement, as demonstrated by the victories at Derby County (3-1), Sunderland (2-0) and the 3-2 win at Bristol City on Boxing Day. Bill Jones returned to his former Club, Worcester City, to buy the prolific scorer Harry Knowles for £2,500. In his Southern League career with Kidderminster and Worcester, Knowles had scored a multitude of goals, but he had a rude awakening in his first appearance on the 7th of February, when the Bluebirds were thumped 1-5 at Grimsby Town.

Following a 3-0 home win over Liverpool (Tapscott scoring twice and Reynolds netting the other goal), the season went rather flat for the City. They lost to Swansea for the first time in a League match at Ninian Park, on the 7th of March, when Mel Nurse's penalty settled the mud-bath of a game. Later in the season, on the 15th of April, the City exacted full revenge with a 3-1 win at the Vetch Field, when the recalled George Kelly scored twice and a Nurse 'own goal' dumped the Swans, on a morass of a pitch.

The season ended with Cardiff in 9th position in the League, Scotsmen Danny Malloy and Alec Milne both ever-present. Other regulars included Nicholls, Baker, Walsh and Sullivan. Hewitt led the goalscorers with thirteen, followed by Tapscott and Walsh who each netted ten. Attendances were a little higher than the previous season, with home gates averaging almost 18,000.

F.A.Cup:

Cardiff City travelled to Plymouth Argyle on the 10th of January for a third round tie, and they gave a great performance against the Third Division side, winning comfortably by 3-0, with goals from a Hewitt penalty, Reynolds and Bonson, in front of an impressive crowd of 36,247.

The fourth round took City to giant-killers Norwich City, who had beaten Manchester United in the third round. The Bluebirds were confident that they could topple the Canaries, but after leading by 1-0 at the interval (through a Hewitt goal), Cardiff were caught cold in the early part of the second-half, as Crossan and Bly put Norwich ahead, much to the delight of the partisan 38,000 crowd. When Bonson scored an equaliser, the game appeared to be destined for a replay, but three minutes from time the prolific Bly crashed home a shot from a narrow angle, to give Norwich the victory. The Canaries aroused national interest by reaching the semi-finals that season, when they lost to Luton Town in a replay.

Welsh Cup:

Cardiff travelled to Gloucester for a 5th round tie on the 5th of February, and even with a full strength side, apart from Kelly in place of Tapscott, could only manage a 1-1 draw, and that thanks to a Hewitt penalty. In the replay at Ninian Park a week later, City were more like their true selves, winning 3-0, with goals coming from Alec Milne, Joe Bonson and Colin Hudson. The Bluebirds faced Rhyl in the 6th round, and Tapscott, Reynolds and Knowles scored in the 3-1 victory. On the 19th of March, the City met Wrexham in the semi-final at Shrewsbury, and they completely overwhelmed the North Walians by winning 6-0, with Knowles (three), Tapscott (two) and Hewitt sharing the goals.

The Welsh Cup Final was played at Newport, with Cardiff City meeting Southern League Lovell's Athletic. In a typically hard fought match, the Newport confectionary factory side made City go all the way, before the Bluebirds won 2-0, with goals from Bonson and Hudson.

During the season, Derek Tapscott and Derrick Sullivan were capped by Wales.

••••••••••••••••••••••••••••••••••

1959-60 Season – Division 2:

In a relatively quiet season, two of Cardiff City's first team pool left the Club. Brayley Reynolds was transferred to Swansea Town (for a nominal fee), and Ron Hewitt, who had been the leading goalscorer in his two years at Ninian Park and had earned five Welsh caps, returned to Wrexham for £5,000. Bill Jones made only two signings of note. Steve Mokone, a black South African international inside-forward, was secured from the Dutch Club, Heracles, although he had been on Coventry City's books in 1956. The other newcomer was the experienced Bristol City outside-left Johnny Watkins, who had surprisingly been made available by his Club, and Bill Jones swooped quickly to complete the signing for a modest £2,500.

A week before the season began, young reserve player Graham Moore, scored four times in the public trial match, and he lined up alongside Mokone and Watkins in City's opening game of their Golden Jubilee season, at home against Liverpool. In a sensational match, Mokone made his mark only five minutes after the start, with a goal from close range, as City got off to a flying start. By half-time however, they had been overtaken, as Liverpool took the lead with two 'own goals' by City centre-half Danny Malloy! City's incessant pressure in the second half reaped dividends, after Graham Moore equalised in the 48th minute. In sweltering conditions, Liverpool melted away, and on the hour, Watkins celebrated his debut with the winning goal – a corking left-footed fifteen yard cross shot that swerved into the far post. It was to be the first of a number of such goals that Watkins would scored during the season. Moore and Watkins were the goalscorers when the City beat Middlesbrough in midweek, and although they lost 1-2 at Charlton, City were soon among the pace-setters, with a great run of results – both at Ninian Park and on their travels.

The Bluebirds bandwagon ground to a halt when Rotherham United visited Ninian Park on the 17th of September, and won 4-1, but the result could have been so different if Roy Ironside, in the Millers' goal, had not been in such inspired form. Ironside's display was to be remembered for many a long day by those who saw the match. This proved to be only a temporary hiccup, as City then went on to enjoy an eleven game unbeaten run.

Sadly, on October the 8th, the Club was informed of the death of its influential President, Sir Herbert Merrett, and when the City entertained Leyton Orient two days later, they produced a 5-1 victory that would surely have pleased their former Chairman, whose vision in the years each side of the War, saw the City team, and Ninian Park itself, rebuilt to such great effect.

At Huddersfield a week later, City were without Alan Harrington, Derrick Sullivan and Graham Moore, whose services were required by Wales, but they were still good enough to win by 1-0, thanks to a goal from Tapscott, although a teenage Denis Law missed a penalty for the Yorkshire side. Meanwhile, Graham Moore scored a last minute equaliser for Wales on his international debut against England, at Ninian Park. The Bluebirds' good run came to an end at Villa Park, on the 12th of December, when in a titanic top of the table encounter, before 54,000 spectators, Aston Villa won with two late goals, as fog engulfed the ground; one of Villa's goals was scored by Gerry Hitchens!

City's next game was at Liverpool, where the Club had just appointed Bill Shankly as manager, and the Bluebirds bounced back from their Villa defeat, with a resounding 4-0 victory. The City goals were scored by Tapscott (two), Watkins and Bonson, in a performance so stunning and full of power, that it had even the redoubtable Shankly purring in admiration.

City lost 1-2 at Sheffield United on the 28th of December, and then marched on with another ten match unbeaten run, that was full of goals and entertaining football. Bonson and Tapscott were an ideal pairing in attack, which was prompted by the young giant, Moore, and the skill and power of Walsh and Watkins on the wings provided an ideal balance. The usual half-back line of Baker, Malloy and Sullivan, reinforced on occasions by young Steve Gammon, was backed up by Milne, Stitfall and Harrington, who took it in turns to fill the full back berths, and Vearncombe in goal gave the City a defence full of International quality.

The Bluebirds appeared to be well in the running for the Second Division Championship when they went three points clear at the top following a spectacular 4-3 victory at Leyton Orient, on the 27th of February, and where teenager Barrie Hole made his League debut. Two goals behind in the first half (both scored by Tommy Johnston), City replied just before the interval when Tapscott converted a Watkins cross. In the 53rd minute City drew level when Bonson headed in from close range, following a Walsh centre. Both sides attacked in turn, but the power of the Bluebirds began to tell, and with twenty minutes left, they scored a goal that has become part of Cardiff City folk-lore! Tapscott chased Walsh's pass down the right and whipped over a chest high cross. Bonson pounding down the middle, launched himself at the ball, and horizontal to the ground, he met it in mid-air full on the forehead, to send the ball zooming into the Orient net from fully fifteen yards. It was a goal worthy of any match, and Derek Tapscott soon made it 4-2, before McDonald reduced the arrears for the stunned Londoners, near the end of a pulsating encounter.

The following week, over 40,000 saw City beat Huddersfield Town 2-1, after falling behind, and the winner from Watkins was acclaimed as one of the most fiercely struck goals ever seen at Ninian Park.

Promotion was all over, bar the shouting, for Aston Villa and Cardiff City opened up an eight point gap ahead of the chasing bunch. Maybe that was just as well, for the City unaccountably lost two home matches – by 1-4 in each, against Portsmouth and Brighton – and drew 3-3 at Swansea after at one time leading by 3-0!

On the 16th of April 1960, Cardiff City celebrated their 50th anniversary as a professional Club. By coincidence the visitors to Ninian Park were Championship contenders Aston Villa, who had been the first team to play at the ground in September 1910, when Ninian Park was officially opened. The Bluebirds made promotion a mathematical certainty, with a nail biting 1-0 win, in a dour contest before a 55,000 crowd.

The only goal, and one more in the keeping with *'Roy of the Rovers'* came after 12 minutes. Brian Walsh skipped a tackle near the touchline dug-outs and played the ball towards the corner flag for Colin 'Rock' Hudson (a late replacement for Joe Bonson), to chase. The Undy born forward slipped as he made his cross, but the ball fell right into the path of Graham Moore, and without checking his stride, the teenage Welsh international hammered a great shot high into the far corner of the Villa net!

There were ecstatic celebrations at the end of the game, and the team repeated the 1952 promotion heroes performance, when they addressed the crowd in turn as their names were chanted.

(Above) Inside-left Joe Bonson dives full length to score Cardiff's third goal in the 4-3 victory over Leyton Orient.
(Below) 16th April, and Graham Moore's 12th minute 'rocket' takes the Bluebirds back into the First Division, in the win over Aston Villa.

Three days later, City missed their chance of the Second Division Championship, when they lost 0-1 at home to Plymouth Argyle, and failing to score from two (Walsh and Malloy) penalties into the bargain. Ironically these were the first spot-kicks that City had been awarded all season!

The City were promoted, as runners-up to Aston Villa, and their 90 goals was one of their highest totals ever attained in a season. The team failed to score on only three occasions. Tapscott was the leading goalscorer with twenty, followed by Bonson's eighteen successes (in only 26 appearances), and ever-present Watkins cracked home fifteen; Moore notched thirteen, Walsh bagged ten, with wing-halves Sullivan and Baker scoring eight and six goals respectively. Ten players made over 30 appearances each, and the inclusion of teenagers Moore, Gammon, Hole and Durban, demonstrated Bill Jones' faith in youth. The promotion fever was reflected in the 25,000 average attendances for home games.

F.A.Cup:
In the third round, on the 9th of January, Cardiff entertained doughty Cup fighters Port Vale, when history repeated itself — as in 1954 — with the Potteries team pulling off a shock 2-0 victory.

Welsh Cup:
The City began on the Welsh Cup trail with a home tie against Lovell's Athletic, whom they had beaten in the previous season's final, and the Bluebirds had a comfortable 5-0 win, with goals from Moore, Bonson, Watkins plus a brace from Tapscott.

The sixth round, on Thursday the 25th of February, produced one of the most bitter and controversial ties in the history of the competition. City had been drawn to play at Swansea, and they tried to have the date changed, due to their important League fixture at Leyton Orient two days later. The Welsh F.A. refused to the request, and so Bill Jones fielded his Football Combination (reserve) team, which drew the wrath of the governing body. Bitterness showed itself on the field, as Swansea fielded their Second Division team. In very heavy conditions, the City reserve X1 took the lead when a shot from Steve Mokone was deflected past the massive figure of Johnny King in the Swansea goal. As tempers flared, so the tackles became more reckless, and there was more embarrassment for the Swans, when the Bluebirds doubled their lead, through Harry Knowles, with just a quarter of an hour left. The Swans put in a grandstand finish, and Ron Nicholls — who had been defiant in the Cardiff goal — was finally beaten, when former Bluebird, Brayley Reynolds, pulled a goal back. In the final ten minutes, Colin Hudson was sent off after committing a foul. Within minutes a bout of wrestling between Mokone and the late Harry Griffiths, of Swansea, ended with the two players flinging mud at each other. This incident resulted in the pair being dismissed as well.

The match ended in a 2-1 victory for the City, and following an inquiry by the F.A. of Wales, the Club were fined £350, and ordered to field their strongest available X1 in all future Welsh Cup games.

Cardiff City duly selected a strong team when they faced Bangor City in the semi-final at Wrexham on the 28th of March, and it took a Moore goal to earn the Bluebirds a 1-1 draw. The replay took place at Newport a month later, and although they included several reserves, the City were good enough to win 4-1, through two goals from Brian Jenkins (including one penalty), Graham Moore and Steve Mokone.

The Welsh Cup final took place at Ninian Park on the 2nd of May, and after a long season, City looked understandably jaded. The match ended 1-1 (Jenkins scoring the City goal), and three days later Wrexham completed the job when they beat the Bluebirds by 1-0, and so lifted the trophy.

Cardiff embarked on a tour of East Germany, but due to the U2 plane incident, the communists closed the border, and the tour had to be abandoned...... On the 11th of May, in Berne (Switzerland), a friendly match was played against Second Division Sunderland, who were also on tour. The game ended as a scoreless draw...... During the season, Sullivan, Baker and Moore were each capped by Wales.

****

1960-61 season – Division 1:

Floodlighting was installed at Ninian Park during the summer, Cardiff City being among the last clubs in the Football League to introduce this facility. But it was worth the wait for the system ranked with the best in the country.

Bill Jones set about reinforcing his first team pool when Joe Bonson was exchanged for Scunthorpe United's bustling forward, Peter Donnelly. A nominal fee bought Charlton Athletic's Welsh International full-back Trevor Edwards to Ninian Park. A fee of £5,000 was paid to Irish League Club Drumcondra for goalkeeper Maurice Swan, and £10,000 was spent on Brian Edgeley, the Shrewsbury Town inside-forward. Harry Knowles, who had scored goals by the bucketful for the reserves, but failed to hold down a first team place, returned to Worcester City, the Bluebirds receiving young winger Peter King in exchange.

The City travelled to Holland in early August, and lost by 0-3 to DWS Amsterdam, before moving on to Switzerland, where they lost 3-4 to Zurich Grasshoppers, despite a Johnny Watkins hat-trick.

The Club resumed their First Division career, after an absence of three years, at Fulham. They made an immediate impression, as they raced into a 2-0 lead through Walsh and Moore.

The Cottagers hit back in the second half, and Johnny Haynes made it 2-2 in the dying moments.

The new floodlights were seen to their best effect, when Sheffield Wednesday visited Ninian Park for a midweek fixture, but City disappointed the 35,000 crowd, when they lost 0-1. Tapscott gave the Bluebirds their first win of the season, when his two goals beat Preston North End at Ninian Park, and on the 3rd of September, City pulled off a dramatic win at League Champions Burnley, when a cannonball shot from Watkins - two minutes from time - secured a final 2-1 victory; Tapscott was the other Cardiff scorer.

City's results were not too encouraging, and they won only one of their next seven matches, and that victory came about in controversial circumstances. Derek Tapscott was alleged to have punched home the goal in the 1-0 victory over his former club Arsenal, at Ninian Park, on the 24th of September. City lost Graham Moore, who received a broken leg in a 0-5 defeat at Newcastle, and Trevor Edwards was switched from full-back to the forward line, in an experimental role.

Bill Jones looked to introduce some experience to the forward line and signed Derek Hogg from West Bromwich Albion, for £12,000. The frail looking winger put pen to paper before the television cameras, during a sports programme at the T.W.W. studios on the 26th of October. Hogg went on to make a stunning debut two nights later, for he scored the winning goal against Leicester City in a 2-1 win. The other goal came when Peter Donnelly barged Gordon Banks into the goal at the Canton end.

On the 2nd of November, the Bluebirds lost 2-3 at all-conquering Tottenham Hotspur, whose winner came near the end, via a dubious penalty decision. Following a 1-6 defeat at Blackpool three days later, Bill Jones decided to reinstate Ron Stitfall at left-back, switch Johnny Watkins to inside-left, and give Brian Edgeley the opportunity to fill in for the injured Graham Moore. The City drew 1-1 through Watkins' goal, against Everton at Ninian Park.

The City suddenly picked up, winning four home games on the trot, and these victories included a 3-0 triumph over Manchester United, who had ten men for much of the game, following an injury to Dennis Viollett. West Bromwich Albion were beaten 3-1 on Boxing Day, when Tapscott netted an impressive hat-trick. Goalkeeper Maurice Swan made his League debut in the return at The Hawthorns, which resulted in a 1-1 draw, and Graham Moore was back from injury when the City drew 1-1 again, this time at Preston.

The Bluebirds gave one of their finest performances when they completed the 'double' over Burnley, by winning 2-1 at Ninian Park on the 14th of January, after Ray Pointer had given the League Champions a first minute lead. Tapscott, in the middle of a purple patch, scored both the City goals, and in defence Malloy was proving to be one of the most accomplished centre-halves in the First Division; despite his ability, he did not figure in the plans of the Scottish team selectors.

The promising career of Steve Gammon, who was fast earning a reputation for shackling 'star' inside-forwards, ground to a virtual halt during City's home match with Manchester City, on the 4th of February. Gammon clashed with Denis Law, in front of the tunnel, and the particularly bad challenge left the Cardiff youngster with a compound fracture of the right leg. Unfortunately Gammon, who by then was close to full Wales honours, was never the same player again. He went on to break the same leg on another two occasions, in his attempted comebacks. In the February match, Cardiff were at one time 3-1 up, but Manchester City pulled back to gain a 3-3 draw, as the match ended as a bad tempered affair.

The hard shooting Johnny Watkins, and a balance payment of £11,000, were exchanged for the Bristol Rovers Welsh international forward Dai Ward. It was several weeks before Ward made his debut, and in the meantime the City had some fine results. The 'double' was completed over Arsenal when the Bluebirds won by 3-2 at Highbury, and they also gained 3-2 home victories over both Newcastle United and Wolves. In the Newcastle match, Irish goalkeeper Swan broke his collar bone, and Tapscott took over between the posts. For a while the City were down to only nine men, but fortunately Barrie Hole returned to the action, although still suffering from an earlier injury. Tapscott emerged as the hero of the hour, as Newcastle failed to find a way through for the equaliser.

On the 11th of March, City entertained the double-chasing Tottenham. In an electric atmosphere, which emphasised the spectacle of floodlit football, the Bluebirds triumphed 3-2 in one of Ninian Park's greatest nights. The 'Spurs made a great start when their tiny winger Dyson scored after only three minutes, but City replied in spectacular fashion through Derek Hogg in the 10th minute. The balding winger collected the ball in the centre circle, and in a fine dribble, took on and beat a number of Tottenham defenders before thrashing a superb shot into the top corner of the net. Les Allen restored the 'Spurs lead before the interval, but within ten minutes of the restart the Bluebirds had completely turned the match around. In the 48th minute Brian Walsh got the vital touch, in a packed goalmouth, to equalise, and with the aristocratic visitors visibly wilting, Derek Tapscott met a low cross at the near post to sweep home the winner. Danny Malloy plus his defence were superb, and goalkeeper Nicholls - in a rare first team appearance - overcame a buffeting from the over zealous Dave Mackay and Bobby Smith, to emerge as a real hero.

City's season just evaporated away after that historic night. They lost six of their remaining nine League matches, to finish in 15th place in Division 1. The Club were reasonably satisfied as they had been plagued by injuries for much of the term.

A memorable victory at Ninian Park. 'Spurs – on their way to a League and Cup 'double' – suffered only seven defeats in the 1960/61 season. The 11th of March match was watched by 45,938.

Malloy was ever present, and other regulars were Baker, Harrington, Tapscott and Walsh. Tapscott was way ahead the leading scorer with 21 League goals, and Peter Donnelly was next with 7. Despite a topsy-turvy season, Cardiff maintained an average attendance of over 23,000.

F.A.Cup:
Cardiff received a home tie with Manchester City in the third round, on January the 7th, and on a miserable afternoon they did everything but win! Tapscott put City ahead with a flying header from Johnny Watkins' driven corner, and the visitors equaliser was an unfortunate headed 'own goal' by Alan Harrington. Four days later, the replay at Maine Road (before 40,000), was the first played under floodlights at the ground, but it was a dour match with the defences well on top. Chances were few, and even extra time failed to bring a goal.

The second replay took place at Highbury on the 16th of January, with almost 25,000 present. Once again the defences dominated, and it was not until late in the game that Denis Law broke the deadlock. After another Manchester goal, from Hayes, the Bluebirds bowed owed of the competition.

(Manchester City played Luton Town in the fourth round, when Denis Law scored six goals before the match was abandoned. When the game was replayed, Law scored again, but Luton won by 3–1!)

Welsh Cup:
Cardiff City were involved in the most farcical Welsh Cup-tie ever played, when they fielded their First Division team against Knighton Town, of the Mid-Wales League, at Ninian Park, on the 28th of January. Under normal circumstances, City would have selected several reserve players , but due to the fine and severe censure imposed on the Club by the F.A. of Wales the previous season, the Bluebirds played their strongest team.

The final result of the match, 16–0, made a mockery of the situation, and sympathy went out to the poor Knighton team, who had become the unfortunate lambs to the slaughter. Derek Tapscott set up a new Club record, with six goals, and the other scorers were Moore (four), Donnelly (two), plus one each from Hogg and Malloy.

On the 16th of February, the City entertained Newport County in the 6th round, when the kick-off was delayed for 15 minutes, due to a power failure. There was no lack of power about the Bluebirds performance however, and they made light work of their neighbours, despite the narrowness of the final scoreline. A penalty by Hogg, and a goal from Moore, had the City well in control, and although Barrie Meyer (later to become a well known Test Match cricket umpire) replied for Newport, the result was never in doubt.

Cardiff City faced Swansea Town in the semi-final, at Newport, and in a disappointing match, the result finished 1–1, with Tapscott scoring for the Bluebirds. The replay took place at Steboneath, Llanelly, and before a 20,000 crowd of principally Swansea supporters, Cardiff lost by 0–1.

Football league Cup:
This was the inaugural season of the Football League Cup, and Cardiff City's first taste of the competition required a long trip to Middlesbrough, where, in a seven goal thriller before a crowd of 15,695, the Bluebirds overcame the Second Division side. The four Cardiff goalscorers, in the final 4–3 victory, were Walsh, Donnelly, Hudson and Edwards, with a penalty. Brian Clough bagged a brace, and Alan Peacock one, for the home side.

In the second round, City met Burnley at Ninian Park, and

they included several fringe players in their line-up, including Peter King, who made his first team debut, at inside-right. Torrential rain before the kick-off meant that it required a pitch inspection before the match could proceed, and Burnley showed their true League Championship form on a saturated surface. Several goalkeeping lapses by Ron Nicholls, and a series of defensive errors, resulted in Gordon Harris helping himself to a hat-trick, as Burnley won by 4-0.

Friendly matches:

Cardiff City officially opened their floodlighting system on the 5th of October 1960, with a visit from the Swiss Club, Zurich Grasshoppers, who the Bluebirds had played on their pre-season trip to Switzerland. The match, which attracted just under 15,000 to Ninian Park, was a breezy affair that ended in a 2-2 draw; the City goals coming from Trevor Edwards, and a solo effort by Danny Malloy, in the final minute.

Other foreign visitors to Ninian Park during the season were the French Club, Biel F.C.- who were beaten 3-0, with goals from Moore, Baker and Donnelly - and V.F.L. Osnabruck, who won 2-1, with Hogg scoring the Bluebirds' lone goal.

At the end of the season, Cardiff visited Eire, where they played two friendlies - a 2-2 draw with Shamrock Rovers and a 5-1 win over Waterford.

During the season, Vearncombe, Baker, Morre and Harrington were each selected to play for Wales.

1961-62 season - Division 1.

Cardiff City manager, Bill Jones, made only one major signing during the summer, that of Stoke City's centre, or inside-forward, Johnny King, who cost £11,500. Joining the Cardiff professional ranks were youngsters Alan McIntosh (a Welsh amateur winger), goalkeeper Dilwyn John, wing-half Gareth Williams and a winger released from Tottenham, Johnny Fleming. Departing from Ninian Park, were experienced goalkeeper Ron Nicholls, who moved to Bristol City, and inside-forward Brian Edgeley who joined Brentford.

Cardiff, along with the other League clubs, received a shock before the start of the new season, following the ban on maximum wages, which had been lifted, following the efforts of Fulham's Jimmy Hill and the Players Union. Bill Jones secured all his staff on the same pay scale, except the captain, Danny Malloy. The Club refused Malloy's request for extra money, and so the popular Scot, who had made 225 appearances for the City, left Ninian Park under a cloud. He accepted the player-coach position at unfashionable Doncaster Rovers, where he stayed for one year, before returning to Scotland. It was a sad loss to Cardiff of a player who had been one of the Club's best signings.

The City had a mixed start to the season, with uncompromising reserve centre-half Frank Rankmore, a local product, filling Malloy's shoes, and new signing King, leading the attack alongside Dai Ward. The Bluebirds had good home wins over Blackpool (by 3-1) and 5-2 over Chelsea, that were sandwiched between several defeats. Teenage goalkeeper Dilwyn John made his League debut as City completed the 'double' over Chelsea, by 3-2, at Stamford Bridge. This was the start of a good run, as the manager introduced Danny McCarthy, Peter King and Tony Pickrell to the first team, which by virtue of the already included Hole, Moore and Durban, had by now taken on a youthful look.

After fourteen years of excellent service, Welsh international Derrick Sullivan, who had played in **nine** different positions and made 276 League appearances for Cardiff City, moved on to Exeter City. Putting his faith in the young players, Bill Jones allowed Peter Donnelly to join Swansea Town for a small fee, and Brian Walsh - probably the most cultured outside-right to have represented the Club - was transferred to struggling Newport County for £2,500, following 206 League appearances for the Bluebirds.

When the City beat Sheffield Wednesday 2-1 on the 11th of November, with two goals from Derek Tapscott, the Club were seventh in the First Division, and surely nobody could have foreseen that the team would embark on a dreadful run of 21 games, during which time only one victory - 1-0 against Aston Villa on Boxing Day - would be obtained.

By this time the Cardiff public were already dismayed by the team's poor run, and were dealt a numbing blow when Graham Moore was transferred to relegation threatened Chelsea for £35,000, at that time a record transfer fee receipt. No amount of switching players around by Jones could stem the City's plunge into the relegation area, and one of the worst defeats was inflicted by fellow-strugglers Fulham, who won by 3-0 at Ninian Park, on the 23rd of March. By now, Cardiff had signed Mel Charles from Arsenal (for £28,000), but he failed to halt the Bluebirds slide. The City were thrown a thread of hope at Easter, when Tapscott's hat-trick beat Birmingham City 3-2 at Ninian Park, and two days later, on the holiday Monday, in what was to be the last First Division game to be played in the Welsh Capital, the Bluebirds beat West Ham United by 3-0 with goals from Ward (two) and Tapscott.

The following Saturday, the 28th of April, the Bluebirds' flight in the First Division ended in a crash landing at Everton, with an amazing 3-8 defeat, even though the City team included five Welsh iternationals in its ranks. Cardiff's final League game of the season was a re-arranged fixture at Aston Villa on the 1st of May. This match finished as a 2-2 draw, with Ward and Charles scoring the goals.

Full-back Alec Milne and half-back Colin Baker were ever present, and other regulars were Hole, Harrington and Rankmore, ironically all defenders. Dai Ward was the clear leading scorer, with 17 goals, and his impressive early season form had earned him a recall to the Wales team. Tapscott was the second leading goalscorer, with nine, in twenty-two games.

Early in the season, the Club had appealed for 'gates' to average 30,000, in order that the City could compete with the very best, but the dramatic slump towards relegation resulted in an average of less than 20,000.

F.A.Cup:

Inclement weather forced the postponement of the City's third round tie at Middlesbrough. When it was played, on the 10th of January, it came as no surprise when the out of form Cardiff lost 0-1, before an Ayresome Park crowd of 29,013, with Alan Peacock scoring the solitary goal.

Welsh Cup:

With Steve Gammon back in the team, and hoping to regain fitness from another broken leg, Cardiff beat a poor Newport side by 4-1 at Ninian Park on the 24th of January (goalscorers being Peter King, Durban, and two from Johnny King). Gammon later broke the same leg in a training accident and was again sidelined for a long period. On the 20th of February, the Bluebirds travelled to Bristol City for a sixth round tie. The lure of possible European competitive football had enticed several English cubs to be included in the Welsh Cup competition. The Bristol club's interest was ended by two goals from Dai Ward, in a 2-0 win, watched by an impressively large Ashton Gate crowd of just under 14,000.

The semi-final, against Bangor City, was played at Wrexham on the 20th of March, and the non-Leaguers capitalised on a shocking Cardiff performance, by defeating the team that included six Welsh internationals, with a 2-0 scoreline!

Football League Cup:

Cardiff City faced Wrexham in the first round, at Ninian Park, and with goals from Moore and Ward, they secured a 2-0 victory. The second round, at Mansfield Town on the 5th of October, coincided with the official opening of the Field Mill floodlights. Former Wolves and England captain Billy Wright performed the ceremony, and a hard fought match ended 1-1 with Johnny King scoring for the City. The replay was another close affair, the City winning 2-1 with goals from Johnny King again, plus Ward. On the 15th of November the Bluebirds travelled to Bournemouth for the third round tie, and they slumped to an embarrassing 0-3 defeat, much to the delight of the near 13,000 Dean Court crowd.

Friendlies:

Racing Club Lensois were played both at home and away, in what was termed the Anglo-French Friendship Cup. The City won both games, by 4-2 in France and 2-0 in Cardiff. The German Club, Offenbach Kickers, were also entertained at Ninian Park, with the City winning by 2-0 on the 27th of February.

Alan Harrington, Mel Charles and Dai Ward were each capped by Wales during the season...... Charles scored all four goals in Wales' 4-0 victory in Northern Ireland on the 11th of April.

(Above) Goalkeeper Dilwyn John played his first game for Cardiff at Stamford Bridge on the 20th of September.

(Left) Mel Charles made his City debut versus Manchester City at Ninian Park on the 24th of February.

CHAPTER 6

THE NOT SO SWINGING SIXTIES

1962-63 Season – Division 2:

During the close season two players left the Club. Welsh international forward, and leading scorer from the previous season, Dai Ward, was transferred to Watford for £8,000, and inside-forward Johnny King returned to Crewe Alexandra – his first club – for a fee of £7,000. Manager Bill Jones spent £7,000 on the Bristol Rovers hard shooting winger Peter Hooper, and the Welsh football public perked up when an £18,000 fee brought the 32 year-old – and much capped Welsh international inside-forward – Ivor Allchurch to Ninian Park, from Newcastle United.

With Hooper and Allchurch making their debuts against Newcastle (Ivor's former Club), the 'gate' at Ninian Park for City's first game of the season was an impressive 27,673. On a sweltering afternoon, the match was an exciting 4-4 draw, with Hooper, Charles and Barrie Hole (two) being the Bluebirds marksmen. A scoreless draw at Norwich and a 2-1 win at Derby – thanks to a Hooper penalty, and Ivor's first goal for the Club – signalled a good start to the season.

When Hooper blasted the City into a two goal lead against Norwich at Ninian Park, with two unforgettable shots, everything looked rosy, but the Canaries took full advantage of some dreadful defensive lapses, and in the final quarter went on to win the match 4-2. With further defeats – by 1-2 at home against Middlesbrough, 1-2 at Swansea and 0-1 at Huddersfield – it came as no real surprise when, on the 10th of September, Cardiff City dismissed both Bill Jones and Wilf Grant the trainer-coach. It was the first time in the Club's history that the Club manager had been relieved of his duties.

By one of those unanswerable quirks in football, the Bluebirds then embarked on an amazing run, with the 'double' over Grimsby Town (5-3 and 2-1 away), and a 5-2 home victory over Swansea Town. In the latter match, one of the finest solo goals ever seen at Ninian Park was achieved by Mel Charles. On the 29th of September, City won 6-2 at Preston – their highest ever away win (at that time) in the Football League. The previous best was 5-1 at Burnley in March 1922. At Preston, Tapscott, Hooper (two) Charles (two) and Durban were the record breaking goalscorers. The following week the City were routed by 0-6 at Chelsea!

Coach Ernie Curtis and veteran professional Ron Stitfall had control of the first team, but rumours were circulating about the appointment of a new manager.

The Bluebirds rolled along, beating Luton Town (with a goal scored from a 35 yard Hooper free-kick), defeating Scunthorpe United by 4-0 and winning 5-3 at Southampton; in the match at the Dell, the Saints forward George O'Brien bagged a hat-trick in vain.

On the 1st of November 1962, the three man board of Cardiff City directors, Messrs. Ron Beecher, Fred Dewey and George Edwards, met the Norwich City manager, George Swindin, at an hotel in Oxford. After negotiations, the salary terms were agreed – which was reported to be £5,000 per year – and Mr. Swindin accepted the Cardiff City managership, although he had been with Norwich for only five months.

Tapscott scored a hat-trick in a 4-2 victory at Charlton Athletic, and on the 24th of November, the immortal Stanley Matthews played in a rejuvenated Stoke City side that drew 1-1 at Ninian Park. The 50 year-old Matthews was believed to be the oldest player to play on the Cardiff ground, since the legendary Billy Meredith. Foggy conditions at Ninian Park are extremely rare, but on the 22nd of December the ground was blanketed, and many of the near 13,000 crowd did not see Hooper's late goal which was good enough to beat Derby County.

George Swindin appointed former Cardiff City centre-half Stan Montgomery as trainer-coach from his old club Norwich City, in December, a few weeks before the worst Winter since 1947 brought football to a halt. Following a 2-4 defeat at Plymouth on Boxing-Day, the City did not play for almost two months, and when they did return to action on the 23rd of February, they had a controversial 1-0 win over League leaders Chelsea, on a bone hard Ninian Park pitch, when Alan Harrington scored a rare goal.

For the rest of the season the City settled into a mid-table position, mainly due to their inconsistency, which upset Swindin greatly, particularly as he was selecting teams with as many as six Welsh international players in them. They did beat Sunderland by 5-2 at home, and Luton at Kenilworth Road with a 3-2 scoreline (Hooper scored a hat-trick), but overall the standard fell below expectations. Don Murray, a 17 year-old ground-staff boy, made his League debut at Middlesbrough, at the end of the season, and a week later, Swindin rocked the soccer world when he transfer-listed 13 players, six of whom had International experience. He explained that the Club had to sell in order to buy, and that a number of players had expressed their dissatisfaction at the terms offered in their new contracts. For some players it meant a drop in wages of around £10 per week, but as Mr. Swindin stated:

> " This Club cannot afford to pay First Division wages while in the Second ".

It all led to a summer of discontent which kept Cardiff City F.C. in the sporting headlines!

The Bluebirds had ended the 1962-63 season in 10th position, with Peter Hooper and Alan McIntosh missing one game apiece. Indeed, McIntosh would have been ever present had he not missed the team coach following a lunch stop at Shrewsbury on the way to the City's match at Stoke City; Mr. Swindin was not amused!

Other regulars in the first team included Harrington, Hole, Allchurch, Baker, Tapscott Charles and Rankmore, whilst Hooper was the top scorer with 22 goals.

F.A.Cup:

The harsh Winter meant that the City's third round tie at Charlton Athletic was postponed on no fewer than **fourteen** occasions. Originally scheduled for the 5th of January, the game was finally played on February the 18th! A series of missed chances cost City dearly when a Len Glover goal, five minutes from time, put Charlton through to the next round.

Welsh Cup:

Cardiff entertained leading Welsh League club, Abergavenny Thursdays, on March the 26th, and swept to an easy win with two pairs of goals from Allchurch and Durban, plus singles from Hole, Hooper and Tapscott, in their 7-1 victory.

On the 11th of April, City travelled to Swansea Town, and an early injury to Ivor Allchurch cramped the Bluebirds style. In a scrappy match, the Swans scored two second half goals. Barrie Jones dipped a far post cross inside the upright after 53 minutes, and twenty minutes later, a punch from goalkeeper Vearncombe went straight to Swansea's Eddie Thomas who headed the ball back into the City net to complete a 0-2 defeat for the Bluebirds.

Football League Cup:

Cardiff City were 'between' managers when they entertained Reading in the second round of the Cup on the 26th of September. A poor first half display by the Bluebirds was punished when Norton gave Reading a 27th minute lead. Whatever was said at half-time galvanised the City into urgent action, and within three minutes of the re-start Mel Charles equalised. Reading were made to pay for their poor finishing when Tapscott put City ahead, and in the final twenty minutes, two from Durban and a Hooper penalty, completed a 5-1 victory.

City visited Bristol Rovers in the third round and gave a most disappointing performance, even allowing for the fact that they had full-back Alec Milne a limping passenger, from the tenth minute onward. Rovers wrapped up the game in the first half, Williams heading home Jarman's corner after 30 minutes, and Jarman himself scoring a second, five minutes later. Sandwiched between the goals, Bobby Jones of the Rovers even missed a penalty. The City had no reply, and slumped to a 0-2 defeat.

During the season, Ivor Allchurch, Barrie Hole and Mel Charles were each capped by Wales.

....

1963-64 Season – Division 2:

Following the dramatic 'open to transfer' list issued by Cardiff City in April 1963, manager George Swindin had a busy summer!

Top scorer Hooper, who had asked for a transfer on three occasions during a year at Ninian Park – due to his dissatisfaction over wages – was sold to Bristol City for £11,000, thus earning the City a £3,000 profit. Promising inside-forward Alan Durban, who had progressed alongside Ivor Allchurch, was transferred to Derby County for £10,000, and City received £5,000 from Hull City for goalkeeper Maurice Swan.

There was a buzz of expectancy among the Bluebirds supporters, when the great John Charles arrived in Cardiff from his Italian club Roma, with views to talking over a proposed move to Ninian Park. Almost immediately centre-half Frank Rankmore was sold to Peterborough United for £10,000, and it became obvious that the 'Gentle Giant' would become a Cardiff player. The Bluebirds agreed to pay Roma a fee in the region of £25,000, and the player that they had tried to sign from Leeds United ten years earlier was finally theirs. A less spectacular signing was that of utility player Dick Scott from Norwich City for £4,000. Just before the new season began, Harrington and Mel Charles both came off the transfer list, and signed new contracts.

In a pre-season friendly match at Bath City, new boy Scott scored for City in a 1-1 draw, but the non-Leaguers goal was conceded by John Charles.

Scottish full-back Alec Milne, a long term absentee with cartilage trouble, broke a leg in training, but that was only the beginning of Swindin's pre-season problems. In the public trial match both Harrington and Trevor Peck received broken legs, with the unfortunate Jim Upton, a trialist from Glasgow, involved in each incident. Winger Tony Pickrell was still laid low with a chest illness, and the unlucky Steve Gammon who had earlier broken his leg for the **third** time, was not expected to be fit for some time.

The opening League match was versus Norwich City at Ninian Park, and there were six players with International experience for Wales in the line-up.

Peter King, now recovered from his chest illness, scored from close range in the 26th minute, but this opener was equalised 14 minutes later. The 22,078 crowd were drawn to the match by the appeal of John Charles, and the charismatic player conjured up a moment that they would remember forever. Charles took an indirect free-kick from all of 75 yards, and saw the ball sail deep into the Norwich penalty area, bounce wickedly, and finally go into the net via the shoulder of the debutant goalkeeper Kevin Keelan. Technically it was an 'own goal', but John Charles was given the credit, and nobody would ever forget that astonishing incident – least of all the mortified Keelan, for had he not touched the ball, the outcome would have been a goal-kick! In the second-half, Allchurch weaved through for City's third goal, to complete a final score of 3-1.

The Bluebirds maintained a good start to the season, drawing 2-2 at home to Manchester City, with the equaliser coming from the injured John Charles in the last minute, and obtaining a 2-1 victory at Scunthorpe. Mel Charles had also been hurt in the Manchester game, and both brothers were missing (youngsters Gareth Williams and Don Murray were the replacements) in the team that appeared at the Old Show Ground.

Injuries at the Club were rife, and Swindin could never field the same team two weeks running. Poor form resulted from these continual changes and, predictably, attendances dropped alarmingly. Fortunately the brilliant Allchurch maintained his customary flair, and Swindin was forced into giving debuts to full-backs Jim Upton and Peter Rodrigues – the latter player had been retained by the Club, in view of the broken legs sustained by others.

Allchurch scored a magnificent hat-trick at Sunderland on the 28th of September, all three goals coming in the first 22 minutes. After only six minutes the blond inside-left went from the halfway line, and beat two men before scoring with a low drive from 25 yards. Seven minutes later, Ivor received a pass from Alan McIntosh, made space, and then rocketed a great shot in off the upright from 20 yards. His hat-trick was completed when he dribbled in from the right-wing, completely wrong footed the Sunderland defence with his famous body swerve, and scored from the edge of the penalty area. Unfortunately, Sunderland also scored three goals and the game ended all square, before a crowd of 37,000.

The Bluebirds injury crisis deepened as Trevor Edwards and Derek Tapscott were both ruled out, and a trialist from Bermuda – Dick Mallory – came into City's beleaguered side, before Swindin signed forward Tommy Halliday from Dumbarton, for £5,000. By November, Cardiff were left with only twelve fit professionals on their staff, and those players did exceptionally well to win by 4-0 at Newcastle, and obtain home victories over Huddersfield Town (by 2-1) and Plymouth Argyle (3-1).

The bubble had to burst, and even as some of the injured players returned to fitness, the Bluebirds lost five League games in succession, including both the Christmas games, by 0-4, to Preston.

The depression surrounding Ninian Park deepened on Saturday the 4th of January, the day the City lost 0-1 at home to Leeds United in the third round of the F.A.Cup, when it was announced that Ron Beecher – the Cardiff City Chairman for the past seven years – had died at Llandough Hospital. Mr. Beecher had been ill for a long time, and at his death he was only 50 years-old.

Youngsters Phil Watkins and Graham Coldrick made their debuts in a dismal 0-5 defeat at Portsmouth on the 11th of January. Bernard Lewis, a winger and part-time player, had his League baptism when City beat Rotherham 2-1 at Ninian Park six days later, as Swindin continued to ring the changes. Before the transfer deadline, he signed winger Greg Farrell from Birmingham City for only £2,000, and the tall Scot helped the City achieve an Easter 'double' over Swindon Town, plus home wins versus Derby County and Scunthorpe United (when he scored twice), to allay any lingering doubts about relegation.

There was a major shock for supporters before the Bluebirds played their Welsh Cup Final replay, with the announcement that the Club had dispensed with the services of the manager, Mr. George Swindin. The decision was arrived at following a stormy Board meeting, when, it is understood, certain pertinent questions were asked by Swindin with regard to the future of both him and the Club! Fred Dewey (Chairman) and directors Vivian Dewey, Robert Williams and George Edwards, held an emergency meeting, and it was decided to ask the manager for his resignation. Swindin refused, whereupon the Board took the matter the next step further by terminating his contract. It was a totally unsatisfactory situation, and considering the limited cash resources at his disposal, plus the Club's injury plight during the season, George Swindin was understandably bitterly disappointed at the way he had been treated.

On the positive side, Swindin had given youngsters Gareth Williams, Don Murray, Peter Rodrigues and Bernard Lewis, their chances, and had restored Peter King to the first team after his long illness. He had been forced to 'blood' a number of newcomers, using 26 players in all during the season, but felt that he had been let down by some of the senior professionals. Swindin revealed that he had opposed the signing of John Charles, a Board decision and not his, as he believed that the player would only give a short term return on the money, and would considerably lift the average age of the side.

The Bluebirds ended a strife-torn season in 15th position, with Allchurch missing just one game, and also being the leading goalscorer with thirteen. Scott and King were other regulars when injuries had restricted the maximum number of possible appearances for some players.

F.A.Cup:

Old adversaries Leeds United were Cardiff City's third round opponents at Ninian Park on the 4th of January – a match best remembered for two players who each received a broken leg. After only eight minutes the City winger McIntosh suffered a double fracture of his left leg, through falling over the Leeds Welsh international goalkeeper Gary Sprake. Ten minutes later, the Leeds defender Freddie Goodwin also broke his leg when challenging John Charles. Both McIntosh and Goodwin ended up in adjacent beds at St. David's Hospital! Unfortunately for McIntosh, his injury brought an early end to a potentially brilliant career. With ten men a side, the match continued, and Leeds – emerging under the managership of Don Revie – scored the winning goal, when Billy Bemner fired in a speculative 30 yard shot which caught Dilwyn John off his line.

Welsh Cup:

Cardiff City played at Ebbw Vale on the 25th of January, and any hopes that the Welsh League team had of causing an upset were dashed in the opening six minutes, when Peter King scored twice. Bernard Lewis netted just before half-time, and in the second period, Mel Charles, with two, and Lewis, scored further goals. The loudest cheer of the afternoon at the Welfare Ground came when Ebbw Vale's Emrys Israel barged Graham Vearncombe into the net, for a consolation goal, in the 6-1 City victory.

On the 19th of February, City met Chester at Ninian Park, and the fans were shocked when Talbot gave the visitors a 10th minute lead. Barrie Hole equalised a minute later, and it was a 'cat and mouse' game' until the final 15 minutes, during which period Mel Charles and Tapscott scored to give the City a 3-1 victory.

Newport County were the Bluebirds opponents in the semi-final, and at the Vetch Field on the 11th of March, the teams fought out a 2-2 draw. Laurie Sheffield, plus ex-Bluebird Joe Bonson scored for the Gwent club, whilst Allchurch and Mel Charles got the City goals. The replay took place at Ninian Park two weeks later, and a game that could have gone either way was settled by a Mel Charles goal, after 57 minutes.

City faced Bangor City in the Welsh Cup Final, which was to be played over two legs. The North Walians had built up a reputation as 'giant-killers' and they lived up to this by upsetting the City with some forceful play. Bangor scored goals in the 6th minute through Robinson and a penalty from Edwards (after Trevor Peck had handled), in the 63rd. Just before the final whistle, Dick Scott and Kinsella were sent off, and the game ended 2-0 to Bangor. On the 29th of April, the Bluebirds won the second leg at Ninian Park, with a 3-1 scoreline (goals from Lewis, Allchurch and Mel Charles). But at this time the Final was decided on a points basis – rather than goal aggregate – over the two legs, and therefore a replay was necessary.

On the 4th of May, the City met Bangor, for the third time, at Shrewsbury. Two goals from Peter King won the Welsh Cup for the Bluebirds, and pointed the way towards European football, just one day after the Club had dispensed with the services of manager George Swindin.

Football League Cup:

Welsh rivals Wrexham were faced at Ninian Park in the second round. Tapscott scored in the first minute and headed a second after eighteen. But Wrexham hit back before half-time, through Myerscough, and with fourteen minutes remaining, young Arfon Griffiths scored to force a replay. At this time, the City were having their worst period for injuries, and they struggled in the replay, before King scored in the 70th minute. Just before the end, Dick Mallory was carried off with a leg injury, and Whitehouse equalised for Wrexham in stoppage time. The City battled gamely on, with ten men, in extra-time, but there were no further goals, and therefore another replay was necessary.

The third match was also played at the Racecourse, and within three minutes City went behind, as Barnes scored from the penalty spot. The Bluebirds, fielding an almost total reserve line-up, included teenagers Phil Watkins, Albert Burns and Alistair Brack, who were each making their first team debuts. When Metcalf scored another for Wrexham just before half-time, the tie was all but over. The North Walians wrapped it up, a few minutes into the second half, when Arfon Griffiths scored with a great shot, to give his side a final 3-0 victory.

Friendlies:

Cardiff City were invited to open Worcester City's new floodlights on the 4th of November, and they drew 2-2, with Tapscott scoring twice. The team played three matches in Italy during May, a short tour which was arranged as part of the John Charles transfer deal. The Bluebirds drew 3-3 with Juventus, before losing by 1-4 to Roma, and 3-4 at Latina.

Ivor Allchurch, John Charles and Barrie Hole were each capped by Wales during the season.

Pictured in the boardroom (from the left): Fred Dewey (Chairman), George Swindin (Manager), Graham Keenor (Secretary) and George Edwards (Director).

1964-65 Season - Division 2:

In June 1964, Cardiff City appointed former Portsmouth, Newcastle and Scotland wing-half Jimmy Scoular as the manager to succeed George Swindin. He had previously been the player/manager of Bradford (Park Avenue).

One of Cardiff City's finest goalkeepers, Graham Vearncombe, left Ninian Park during the Summer after 13 years service and 208 League appearances. He went on to concentrate on his Licensing business and to play as a part-time player with Merthyr Tydfil. Trevor Edwards, another former Welsh international emigrated to Sydney, Australia.

Aston Villa's reserve goalkeeper, Bob Wilson, was Scoular's first signing. He cost £2,000, and the tall custodian went straight into the Cardiff first team. Yorkshireman, Lew Clayton, was appointed trainer-coach. City's preparation for the new season consisted of two friendlies with Newport County, when they lost by 0-1 at Somerton Park, and won the return at Ninian Park by 3-1.

Scoular's beginning at the helm of the City could not have been more traumatic, as the team went **twelve** games before obtaining their first victory! By this time the manager had rung the changes, giving youngsters Gerald King and Clive Lloyd a fleeting run in the first team. Dick Scott was exchanged for Scunthorpe's burly forward Keith Ellis, while Alec Milne and Steve Gammon both failed to recapture their form after injury problems and were soon out of the first team picture.

The first win of the season arrived on the 10th of October, when the Bluebirds beat Derby County by 2-1 at Ninian Park, with goals from Peter King and Derek Tapscott. New signing Ellis made his presence felt with some important goals as City beat Charlton Athletic 2-1 at home, Leyton Orient (3-1 away) and Bury with a 4-0 scoreline at Ninian Park. Tapscott was also amongst the goals when City overcame Plymouth Argyle by 4-0, in December.

On the 15th of January, Cardiff City had one of their biggest ever victories, when they beat Middlesbrough 6-1, at Ninian Park. Peter King, now converted to an inside-forward role - to the exclusion of Ivor Allchurch - scored a hat-trick in this triumph, with Tapscott bagging two, and Gareth Williams scoring the other goal.

As the City remained in the bottom half of the table, Scoular reinstated Ivor Allchurch to the team. The maestro responded to his recall by scoring some vital goals. The young Scottish ground-staff boy, George Johnston, came into the team towards the end of the season, as did George Harris - a part-time full-back who had cost a fee of £2,000 from Forfar Athletic.

The Bluebirds surged up the Second Division with an end of season run of twelve games, in which they lost only three matches. A 5-0 home win over Swansea Town on the 6th of April, which helped to relegate the Vetch Field Club, was one of the City's better performances, with Allchurch netting a hat-trick, and John Charles scoring the other two goals. An Easter 'double' over Coventry City, and a 3-2 home win against Rotherham United - in which full-back Rodrigues was injured, was converted to a makeshift centre-forward, and scored a goal - were other highlights. The Bluebirds ended the season in far better form than they had started some eight months earlier.

They finished the campaign in 13th position, and Barrie Hole was ever present, with Rodrigues, Bob Wilson, Peter King and Gareth Williams forming the backbone of the team. Allchurch was the leading goalscorer, with 15 from the 27 games in which he played, short term signing Keith Ellis scored 10 goals in only 22 matches, and the 'veteran' Tapscott contributed 9 successes from 16 games.

● **IVOR ALLCHURCH (right)** heads the first goal of a hat-trick in Cardiff City's 5-0 Second Division win over Swansea at Ninian Park in April 1965. Swans 'keeper John Black and full-back Roy Evans (2) can only watch.

F.A. Cup:
Cardiff met Charlton in the third round at Ninian Park and although Tapscott scored for the Bluebirds, defensive lapses helped the visitors to a 2-1 victory, with goals from Frank Haydock and Mike Bailey.

Welsh Cup:
The City were the Cup-holders, and they visited Merthyr Tydfil for the first time in ten years, and made their experience tell in a 3-1 win. Peter King (two) and Tapscott scored the goals for the City, against their former team mate, Vearncombe, the Martyrs goalkeeper. On the 17th of February, another Southern League club - Hereford United - were entertained, and they were also beaten with a 3-1 scoreline; Allchurch, Ellis and Greg Farrell (a penalty) shared the goals.

The semi-final took place at Somerton Park on the 10th of March, and Farrell's penalty was enough to beat Swansea Town in a tense and scrappy encounter. City met Wrexham in the two-legged final, and in the home tie on the 12th of April, they swamped their opponents by 5-1, with teenager George Johnston scoring two goals, and Allchurch plus King (also a brace) completing a nap hand.

Normally that magnitude of victory would have been enough to ensure the winning of the Trophy, but the F.A. of Wales continued to work on the points system rather than that of goals aggregate. Therefore Wrexham's single goal victory at the Racecourse, on the 26th of April, was enough to ensure a replay! The third match was played at Shrewsbury on the 5th of May, and the City rid themselves of any lethargy they may have felt, winning the decider by 3-0. Allchurch, in his final appearance for the Bluebirds scored twice and King netted the third. The Bluebirds had retained the Trophy, and another entry into Europe beckoned.

Football League Cup:

The team fell at the first hurdle when they lost a second round match at Southampton by 2-3, with goals coming from Bernard Lewis and Peter King.

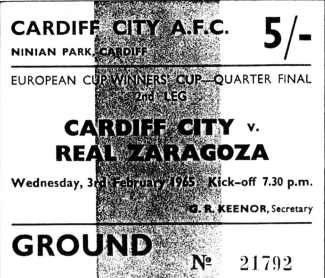

European Cup-Winners Cup:

The Welsh Cup holders had their first excursion into European competition with a rather tepid first round tie against Esjberg of Denmark. After a goal-less first leg, Peter King's goal at Ninian Park in the return match was enough to put the City through to the next round.

The Bluebirds drew a plum tie when they met the holders – Sporting Lisbon of Portugal. The Welshmen got a sensational result in the first leg in Lisbon on the 15th of December, when goals from Farrell and Tapscott – the latter a right-wing cross from 40 yards – gave them a marvellous 2-1 advantage to take back to Wales. Scoular's master plan had been to use John Charles as a 'sweeper', and rely on the big fellow's knowledge of Continental football to direct operations from the back.

The return leg in Cardiff, two days before Christmas, was anything but a classic, yet the 25,000 crowd enjoyed a full-blooded encounter, particularly as Tapscott threw himself wholeheartedly into the fray. The match ended as a scoreless draw, and Real Zaragoza from Spain were drawn in the next round, the quarter-finals.

The first leg on the 20th of January was played in Spain, and the City looked well and truly out of the competition when they trailed by 0-2, but in a terrific fightback, Gareth Williams and Peter King levelled the scores to set up the prospects of an epic battle at Ninian Park in the second leg, that was scheduled for the 3rd of February. A crowd of 38,458 saw City fight tooth and nail, knowing that a 0-0 scoreline would be enough to win the round. Unfortunately the Spaniards struck just once, and therefore they put the gallant Bluebirds out of the competition, by 2-3 on aggregate.

Barrie Hole, Ivor Allchurch, John Charles and Peter Rodrigues were the four Cardiff City players to win Welsh Caps during the season.

Peter King fires in the winning goal in our game against Esbjerg on October 13th

1965-66 season - Division 2:

Jimmy Scoular, the manager, had a mass 'clear out' during the Summer, which led to the departure of a number of senior professionals. Local born Ron Stitfall, now 39 years of age, retired after serving Cardiff City since the War years. He made 403 League appearances and had been one of the cornerstones of the Bluebirds defence during the 1950's. He took up a job on the coaching staff at Newport County, and in later years was employed by the Sports Council of Wales. Ivor Allchurch, after three years at Ninian Park, returned to his native Swansea Town, for a £6,000 fee. Ivor had given much pleasure to Club and supporters in his 103 League appearances and scored many great goals after 'wrong footing' defenders with his famous body swerves.

Alec Milne, still troubled by injury, emigrated to New Zealand, following 172 appearances in the League, and the unfortunate Steve Gammon - who had broken his leg on three occasions - was finally forced into quitting League football, and joined Kettering Town as their player-manager. Derek Tapscott, the goal hero of many City supporters, moved on to Newport County after seven years at Ninian Park, during which time he scored 79 goals in 194 League appearances. Mel Charles dropped into non-League football with Portmadoc, and Keith Ellis moved on to Lincoln City. Alan McIntosh retired from football - he broke a leg during the Leeds United match in January 1964 - and took up a teaching post in Gloucester, while Trevor Peck joined Southern League club Worcester City. Scoular was pinning his faith on young prospects and his only notable signing during the close season was that of Terry Harkin, the Crewe Alexandra prolific scorer, who cost £10,000. Harkin and John Charles were paired together in City's attack for the pre-season friendlies, which City won by 3-2 at Cheltenham, 4-2 at Hereford, and in a return match at Ninian Park, the Bluebirds swamped the latter team by 8-3.

The introduction of substitutes in English League football, initially to replace injured players only, commenced in the 1965-66 season. On the 21st of August, Cardiff City were at home to Bury, a match that was refereed by the future Minister of Sport, Denis Howell M.P., and a powerful header by John Charles secured the points in a single goal win. With just five minutes remaining, local youngster David Summerhayes became the first Cardiff City substitute in League football, when he replaced the injured veteran Colin Baker. There were goals a plenty in the City's opening matches, but not all were at the right end! Charles, Harkin and the teenage George Johnston were all prominent, as City were involved in this series of high-scoring matches.

Harkin scored on his debut, as the City beat Derby County by 2-1, and a week later the Bluebirds won the return at the Baseball Ground by 5-1. The defence, however, started to leak goals in frightening fashion and the City lost 1-4 at home to the Wolves, 4-6 at Rotherham, and 2-5 at Charlton, before the Bluebirds won a seven goal thriller (4-3) against Manchester City at Ninian Park, when Harkin scored the winner in the closing minutes.

The season gets off to a flying start, as John Charles scores after only 10 minutes, in the opening match, at Ninian Park, against Bury.

On the 6th of October, City met Coventry City at Ninian Park, in a match that was beamed back to Highfield Road, where an estimated 10,000 watched Coventry's 2-1 victory on two big screens. As City lurched into the relegation zone Scoular brought in two youngsters, the Davids' Summerhayes and Houston, besides introducing centre-forward George Andrews, who had been signed from the non-League club Lower Gornal. The sleek Andrews settled in quickly, scoring regularly as the City won three successive matches, the first of which was by 3-1 at home to Charlton, when Johnston scored two goals from penalties. On the 13th of November, the City beat Leyton Orient 3-1, the game being remembered for the appearance of the 16 year old apprentice, John Toshack, who came on as a substitute and scored the third goal. The following week, Toshack made his full debut, at Middlesbrough, where he and the 18 year-old Johnston, scored two goals apiece, in a great 4-3 victory.

The successes did not last, for Toshack was soon back in the reserves, and the 'gates' dropped. After a disastrous 3-5 home defeat to Southampton, on the 27th of December - when Chivers scored a hat-trick - the City accepted an offer of £40,000 from Leicester City, for their Welsh international full-back Rodrigues, on New Years Eve. Scoular immediately invested £5,000 on Derby County's experienced full-back Bobby Ferguson, who made his debut for the Bluebirds, along with teenage goalkeeper Lyn Davies, in a glorious 5-1 home win over Plymouth Argyle on New Year Day. Andrews and Harkin each scored two goals, with Hole scoring the other. One week later, at Leyton Orient, the City suffered another setback, when the classy, veteran, defender Alan Harrington broke his leg once again, after returning from a previous fracture and having made the right-back berth his own. Unfortunately for the Welsh international and one of City's finest servants (with 349 League appearances to his credit), this latest injury was to ultimately end his distinguished career.

Jimmy Scoular paid £11,000 for the Rotherham United full-back David Carver, and two weeks later he signed Ronnie Bird from Bury, for £5,000. Bird, a speedy left-winger, had been with the craggy Scoular, at Bradford. The City manager certainly knew his way around the transfer market, but he was still struggling to field a settled side, as his young players faded in the face of adverse results.

The Club were deep in trouble, right up until the 4th of May, when they met Middlesbrough at Ninian Park. It was the Boro's final match, and they had to win to have any chance of avoiding relegation. If Cardiff won, then they would be safe. The game became known as 'Farrell's Match', for the tall Scot gave a virtuoso right-wing performance that enthraled the Bluebirds' supporters, and which cut the Boro' to ribbons. In the 7th minute, Middlesbrough's strapping centre-half Dickie Rooks, stunned the City by heading home a corner. The Bluebirds roared back, with Farrell tormenting the Middlesbrough defence, and after 25 minutes Hole equalised, after being put clear by a slick move between King and Lewis.

Two minutes later, the City were again in arrears, when Rooks slammed home a penalty. Within five minutes the Bluebirds were awarded a penalty themselves, when Ian Gibson handled, and Farrell slotted home the spot kick. City took the lead for the first time, before the half-time whistle, with a brilliantly headed goal from Andrews, following a Lewis corner. The second half belonged to Cardiff, and particularly Farrell, as they took a total grip on the game. King finished off a combination between Williams and Hole to make it 4-2, and near the end of the game the effervescent Farrell laid on City's fifth goal for Andrews to score from close range. Rooks completed a remarkable hat-trick in the closing minutes, but Middlesbrough, despite a determined fight, were relegated, and Cardiff City were safe!

City finished the season in 20th position in the Second Division, with Hole, Farrell, Williams, King and Murray the mainstays of the team. George Johnston was leading scorer with eighteen, followed by George Andrews on fifteen, and Terry Harkin's ten. The following Saturday was one of the blackest in Cardiff City's history, as Preston North End whipped the Bluebirds by 9-0 at Deepdale. The Cardiff display was a shambles, and one that had Scoular growling afterwards:

" *If I were a Cardiff City player, I would be ashamed to walk down the street* ".

City finished the season in 20th position in the Second Division, with Hole, Farrell, Williams, King and Murray the mainstays of the team. George Johnston was leading scorer with eighteen, followed by George Andrews on fifteen, and Terry Harkin's ten.

F.A.Cup:
Inclement weather caused a postponement of Cardiff City's home third round tie with old adversaries Port Vale, who had beaten the Bluebirds in the F.A.Cup in 1954 and 1960. The game eventually went ahead, under floodlights and in pouring rain, on the 26th of January, and as the conditions got more heavy, so the match became a real slog in the mud. Port Vale took the lead, and Peter King tied the score at 1-1, before City's stylish wing-half Barrie Hole sent the soaked crowd of 18,898 into ecstasy with a last minute goal.

The fourth round draw sent the City to Fourth Division Southport, on the 12th of February, and for the third time in just ten days, the Bluebirds crashed out of a major competition (having already lost to West Ham in the League Cup and to Swansea Town in the Welsh Cup). This was a really low spot for the Club, as the Fourth Division side showed all the passion that the Bluebirds lacked, and won by 2-0. Mr. Scoular's after-match comments were unprintable!

Welsh Cup:
Cardiff City faced their greatest rivals - Swansea Town - in the fifth round at the Vetch Field, and in treacherous conditions - on a pitch that resembled a paddy field. The two teams finished level at 2-2 after an exciting and controversial match. City had led twice through goals by Andrews and King, only to be pulled back each time, firstly by a Don Murray 'own goal', and the second by former Bluebird Ivor Allchurch.

The replay at Ninian Park came just six days after the City had lost to West Ham in the League Cup. The Bluebirds sailed into a comfortable 3-0 lead through Gareth Williams and George Johnston's pair of goals, with only 53 minutes gone. The game then swung dramatically in the 64th minute, when referee Leo Callaghan sent off the City centre-half Don Murray for an alleged head-butt on Swansea's Jimmy McLaughlin. Within a minute, centre-forward Todd had scored for the Swans as City fell in disarray and lost their composure.

The diminutive Todd pulled back another goal, and six minutes from time the Swans Herbie Williams scored, sending the game into extra time. There was going to be only one winner now, and five minutes into the extended period, McLaughlin put the Swans in front. Within the next five minutes, winger Brian Evans netted Swansea's fifth, to complete one of the most sensational matches ever played between the two clubs.

Football League Cup:

Cardiff began on a long run in the competition with a nondescript second round match at Crewe Alexandra, where a goal from Bernard Lewis earned a 1-1 draw, after former Bluebird Johnny King had scored for the Railwaymen. The replay resulted in a comfortable 3-0 victory for the City, with a pair of goals from Peter King, and the other via former Crewe player, Harkin.

The third round brought Portsmouth to Ninian Park, and Scoular introduced new signing George Andrews into the team. City won 2-0 with King and Andrews scoring the goals. The fourth round draw favoured the City, for they entertained Reading. The Bluebirds romped to one of their best victories in the competition, as a hat-trick from teenage sensation Johnston, and two goals from Harkin, completed a 5-1 win.

The Bluebirds were favoured with home advantage yet again, when they played Ipswich Town in the fifth round. A youthful City team, with teenagers David Houston, George Johnston and John Toshack, brought a smile to Mr Scoular's face as they won by 2-1, with Andrews and Hole the marksmen.

The City faced West Ham United in the two-legged semi-final, and in all honesty they were no match, in either game, for the First Division aristocrats. The Hammers took full advantage of the first tie, at Upton Park, and won by 5-2, with Andrews scoring both the City goals. It came as no surprise that the second leg, at Ninian Park on the 2nd of February, was a purely academic exercise, and the Bluebirds received a thorough soccer lesson as West Ham cruised to a 5-1 victory – giving the aggregate score of 10-3. Bernard Lewis scored the City consolation goal.

European Cup-Winners Cup:

Cardiff faltered at the first hurdle when they went out in the first round to the Belgian Club, Standard Liege. A bad-tempered match at Ninian Park ended with the Belgians winning by 2-1 in unsatisfactory circumstances; Johnston scored the City goal. Liege completed the job on their home ground with a single goal victory, courtesy of a Harrington 'own goal', and hence went through 3-1 on aggregate.

During the season, Barrie Hole and Peter Rodrigues were capped by wales.

****

1966-67 Season – Division 2:

Cardiff City were involved in one major transfer during the Summer, when they accepted Blackburn Rovers' offer of £42,000 for Welsh international, wing-half, Barrie Hole. The player had been after a move for five years, and had been on and off the transfer list without attracting a realistic offer. Hole left Cardiff after making 211 League appearances, totally disillusioned at the Club's lack of progress since their relegation in 1962. Three former Welsh international players – John Charles, Alan Harrington and Colin Baker – all severed their connections with League football. The legendary Charles joined another former Bluebird, Ray Daniel, at Hereford United, where he was to become a great success. Harrington retired through injury, after making 349 appearances, and Baker ended his Cardiff career with 293 games in a City shirt. Both Harrington and Baker had been two of the City's greatest locally born products. Baker remained at Ninian Park, organising the Club Lottery, which also involved former Bluebird, Derek Tapscott. Two young Leeds United reserves, Derek Ryder and Jack Winspear, joined the Ninian Park staff, as manager Scoular resisted any excursion into the transfer market.

The opening League match against Ipswich Town, at Ninian Park, drew only 7,735 spectators, and they were in a disgruntled mood as City lost by 0-2. Although the Bluebirds won 2-1 at Bristol City, and beat Carlisle United 4-2 at Ninian Park in the following games, there was no denying that the team was in a bad shape overall. Soon the defeats, and goals-against, began to pile up, as Scoular gave League debuts to Derek Ryder and Gary Bell, who had been signed form Lower Gornal. Bell, in fact, had his baptism in an awful 1-7 mauling at Wolves, and Lyn Davies, who had replaced Dilwyn John in goal, had the mortification of conceding a total of 32 goals in just six games – twenty-four of these were in five Cardiff matches, and the other eight were conceded when he was the custodian for the Welsh Under-23 team that was thrashed by their England counterparts at Molineux! The shell-shocked youngster never appeared for the City again after Scoular had re-installed Bob Wilson, who had been out of favour.

During this awful spell, Scoular paid Northampton Town £15,000 for the former England Amateur international centre-forward Bobby Brown, and on Brown's home debut – against Hull City – Ken Wagstaff scored all four goals in the visitors 4-2 victory. Another £10,000 bought Everton's experienced half-back Brian Harris, who had played in the Toffees F.A.Cup winning team against Sheffield Wednesday just six months earlier.

The 32 year-old Harris must have doubted his wisdom in joining Cardiff City as he had the misfortune to make his debut at Plymouth on the day when the former milkman, Mike Bickle, scored four goals for Argyle, as they hammered the City 7-1!

It took time for the manager to get things sorted out, and, after selling Terry Harkin to Notts. County for a nominal fee, City beat Bury by 3-0 at Ninian Park on the 19th of November, with a brace of goals from John Toshack and one by Bobby Brown. This was only the third Bluebirds win in sixteen games. They began to turn the corner with a 2-0 home victory over Norwich City and a last minute 2-1 win at Birmingham City. In the St.Andrews match, for the first time in the Club's history, a full-back – Graham Coldrick – scored in successive games. A pulsating 4-2 win over fellow-strugglers Northampton Town, when both Williams and Brown scored twice each, finally lifted the Bluebirds off the foot of the Second Division table.

Crystal Palace completed a Christmas 'double' over Cardiff, and the City had Greg Farrell sent off, in the Boxing Day match at Ninian Park. But the Bluebirds ended the year in some style by beating Bristol City 5-1, with Brown and Bird scoring two apiece, and Bristol's Low, putting through his own net. It remained an uphill struggle, and as the transfer deadline approached Scoular had to 'wheel and deal' in the market, which he did to some effect. Young George Johnston was sold to Arsenal for £20,000, after impressing in a benefit match at Highbury which was played to aid the victims of the Aberfan Disaster. Greg Farrell joined Bury for £7,000, and Southport paid £6,000 for George Andrews. Jimmy Scoular used the money placed at his disposal to buy Welsh international winger Barrie Jones from Plymouth, for £25,000, and Southampton forward Norman Dean for £6,000.

The City manager's gamble paid off as the Bluebirds had a successful Easter, beating Plymouth 4-1, with goals from Toshack, Dean, Barrie Jones and Bobby Brown, before earning only their second away win of the season, 2-1 at Portsmouth; King and Williams scored the goals. A 4-0 home win over Preston North End, a 1-1 draw at Ninian Park with promoted Coventry City, and another home victory, by 3-0 versus Birmingham City, saved City from relegation. But for the second successive season, it had been a close thing.

The Bluebirds finished 20th in the table, with King, Williams, Murray, Ferguson and Coldrick as regulars, but nobody underestimated the influence that Brian Harris had exerted on the team. Brown was the top scorer with fifteen, and young John Toshack also made double figures with his ten goal contribution.

F.A.Cup:

Cardiff travelled to Barnsley in the Yorkshire coalfields for their third round tie on the 28th of January. On a typically dirty Northern afternoon the crowd of 21,464 at Oakwell were treated to a magnificent cup-tie. It looked as if Ronnie Bird had won the game for the City, but Barnsley battled back to earn a relay with a late goal from Johnny Evans.

The replay, at Ninian Park, was no less exciting, and an upset looked likely when Barrie Thomas headed the Fourth Division side into the lead after 49 minutes. City piled forward and were rewarded when a handling offence resulted in a penalty which George Thompson converted. In a tingling climax, Peter King raised the roof with a brilliant run and shot, which gave the Bluebirds a 2-1 victory.

The City had a home draw against First Division Manchester City in the fourth round, and 37,205 flocked to Ninian Park, on a dreadful day, to witness a titanic tussle in a sea of mud. An own goal by Coldrick put the visitors ahead, but the City stormed back to equalise through skipper Gareth Williams. A 'tank' of a wing-half, in the mould of manager Jimmy Scoular, the blond haired Williams ended a surging run with a blistering shot from a narrow angle. The match finished 1-1, with goalkeeper Bob Wilson a second-half hero. In the replay at Maine Road, City made a dream start when Johnston scored from a ninth minute penalty, and shortly afterwards Ronnie Bird was only inches away from making the score 2-0. But urged on by a crowd of 41,616, the Sky Blues' superior skill began to tell on the sticky surface. This class was to eventually tell, and goals from Neil Young, Johnny Crossan and Colin Bell, eventually put the Bluebirds out of the competition.

Johnston celebrates as Williams (between the posts) equalises.

F.A. Cup 4th round versus Manchester City

Welsh Cup:

Cardiff and Swansea met in the fifth round at the Vetch Field, and thankfully there was no repeat of the disgraceful tie of the previous season. The Bluebirds cast aside their indifferent League form and cooly swept to a 4-0 victory, with Bernard Lewis, Greg Farrell, and George Johnston (two) scoring the goals.

Big John Charles made an early return to Ninian Park with Hereford United in the sixth round. It was not to be a happy homecoming for the 'Gentle Giant' as the City won 6-3 – a score made much closer than it should have been as the visitors scored two late goals; King, Johnston (two), Coldrick, Ferguson and Brown were the five City goalscorers. The goals by Coldrick and Ferguson made history, for it was the first time that both full-backs had scored goals for Cardiff City in the same first team match.

The semi-final at Newport saw City lead with goals from Brown and King, and a penalty by County's Terry Melling came too late to prevent the Bluebirds from winning by 2-1.

The City met Wrexham in the two-legged Final, and the first match at The Racecourse on the 17th of April resulted in a 2-2 draw, courtesy of goals from Brown and King. The second leg at Ninian Park was a close encounter, but the City won the trophy with a 2-1 victory – 3-2 on aggregate – through Norman Dean and a Showell 'own goal'. This victory meant a return to Europe in the following season.

Football League Cup:

In the first round, Cardiff entertained Bristol Rovers, and a single goal by young Toshack was enough to win an uninspiring game. City were hosts to Exeter City in the next round and they gave an absolutely terrible performance. They were denied by former Bluebird Ken Jones between the Exeter posts, and a goal by defender Ray Harford put the Bluebirds out of the competition.

1967-68 – Division 2:

Manager Jimmy Scoular spent a quiet close season, and the only newcomer to Ninian Park was Malcolm Clarke, a reserve wing-half from Leicester City. Following a trial period, the Scot was offered a contract.

The opening game of the new season brought Plymouth Argyle to Ninian Park on the 19th of August, and a crowd of 17,343 – ten thousand more than the first League fixture of a year earlier – showed that they had faith in Scoular's policy at Cardiff City.

The team made a reasonable start, with Bobby Brown scoring five goals in six games, until four successive defeats sent them sliding downwards.

The heaviest defeat of these games was a 1-5 beating by Brian Clough's Derby County, at Ninian Park, when Kevin Hector got a hat-trick for the Rams. It was reported that Scoular and Clough had to be separated following an altercation in the tunnel at the end of the game. Apparently the controversial Derby manager had aired his views on the Bluebirds performance, within earshot of Scoular, which was indeed tempting fate!

To make matters worse, the Club accepted an offer of £45,000 (a new Club record) from Bolton Wanderers for the services of powerful wing-half Gareth Williams, who had made 161 League appearances for the Bluebirds. Free transfer signing Malcolm Clarke stepped into Williams' shoes (or boots) and did a good job as the City got back on song, with a 3-0 home win over Middlesbrough, a 2-1 success at Hull City, a 3-1 victory at Carlisle, and another home win – by 3-2 – against Blackburn; in the latter game Clarke netted a fortuitous deciding goal. Young John Toshack was beginning to establish a regular place in the first team, and the 18 year-old responded with seven goals in nine games. Another of Scoular's young prospects, defender Steve Derrett, came into the team during November, and in his search to improve the quality of his side, the City manager transferred Bernard Lewis to Watford for £7,000, and then paid £15,000 for Blackpool winger Leslie Lea, in early December.

An administrative error prevented Lea from making his debut at Plymouth on the 16th of December, and Scoular drafted in substitute Gary Bell. For the only time in the Club's history (since they were permissable), Cardiff City played a League match without a substitute on the bench, but they still managed to earn a scoreless draw.

On Boxing Day, City met Aston Villa at Ninian Park, and the match was both an extraordinary and tragic one. The Bluebirds were leading by 1-0 at half-time, thanks to new boy Leslie Lea, but full-back Graham Coldrick had to stay in the dressing rooms with an injury after the break. Gary Bell was substituted, and eleven minutes into the second half, Bobby Brown collided with Villa goalkeeper, Colin Withers. Even as Brown lay in agony in the penalty area, John Toshack jumped over his injured colleague, to head Don Murray's centre into the net. Brown was stretchered off with a severe knee injury that was to eventually end his playing career.

City carried on with ten men, until twenty minutes from the time, when an injury to David Carver reduced the Bluebirds to **nine** players. The crowd roared the depleted team on, and they incredibly increased the lead to 3-0, when Lea volleyed a cross from Toshack into the Villa net.

Hampered by the Club's excursions in Europe, their League form continued to suffer. Jimmy Scoular paid £10,000 for the Wolves goalkeeper Fred Davies, and within weeks he had spent a further £8,000 on the Huddersfield forward Brian Clark, by which time the full extent of Brown's earlier injury was confirmed.

Clark made a sensational debut for the City in a 4-3 win at Derby, on the 3rd of February, where the burly Bristol born striker scored twice, to add to Peter King's brace of goals. The big forward settled in quickly, with six goals in six games - although he was not eligible for European games - and the City maintained a mid-table position until the end of the season, with a run of just one defeat in the final seven games.

The Bluebirds finished the season in 13th place, with both Barrie Jones and Peter King ever present. Other regulars were Murray, Harris, Clarke and Toshack. King led the goalscorers with twelve, followed by Toshack's eleven, and the unfortunate Brown's contribution of nine goals before his injury. Scoular was beginning to get the Club into shape, and a combination of strict training and his change of tactics, by introducing a 4-3-3 formation, began to pay off.

F.A.Cup:

Drawn away to First Division Stoke City in the third round, Cardiff had no answer to the Potters razor-like finishing, and were well beaten with Barrie Jones scoring the Bluebirds consolation goal, as Stoke won 4-1.

Welsh Cup:

Cardiff City entertained Ebbw Vale from the Welsh League in the fifth round, and even at half pace, they mercilessly took apart the part-timers with their 8-0 win. Toshack and Bird both scored hat-tricks, with the City's other goals coming from King and Lea.

The City were again impressive in the next round, at Wrexham, where goals from Barrie Jones, Lea and Bird earned a comfortable 3-1 win, and the semi-final at Chester, proved to be no problem for a City team that were in good form. King, Toshack and Lea scored in the 3-0 victory.

The two-legged final saw Cardiff play Hereford, and the League team swept to victory in both games, with a 2-0 win at Edgar Street on the 6th of May (Jones and King were the scorers), and by 4-1 at Ninian Park, ten days later. In the second game, Norman Dean, Clarke, Lea and an own goal from Jones, the Hereford defender, all found the net. The Bluebirds therefore retained the Trophy, with an aggregate score of 6-1.

Football League Cup:

Cardiff travelled to Aldershot, for a first round tie, and in a see-saw match they emerged as 3-2 winners, with goals from Bobby Brown (two), and Peter King.

The Bluebirds visited Burnley in the second round and fought an uphill battle against the First Division side. Despite a goal from defender Graham Coldrick, they eventually lost the match with a 1-2 scoreline.

European Cup-Winners Cup:

The Bluebirds enjoyed a glorious run in Europe, which monopolised the campaign. It all began with a tie against Shamrock Rovers, and after Peter King's goal had earned a 1-1 draw in Dublin on the 20th of September, the City completed the job at Ninian Park a fortnight later, when Brown and Toshack scored the goals in the 2-0 win.

The next opponents were Dutch side, NAC Breda, and once again the City did well in the away leg, with a 1-1 draw, in which King scored. The Welshmen gave a superb display in the return, at Ninian Park, as Brown, Jones, Toshack and Clarke shared the goals in a 4-1 (5-1 aggregate) win.

The quarter-finals paired the Bluebirds with Moscow Torpedo, but none of Scoular's newest signings - Leslie Lea, Fred Davies and Brian Clark - were eligible, as all three had been signed after the third round deadline. There was no problem in the Ninian Park first leg on the 6th of March, as the City beat the defence-minded Russians 1-0, when Barrie Jones headed home the goal, two minutes before half-time.

The return in Russia, however, was fraught with all kinds of problems, with Torpedo having to switch their home leg match, to Tashkent - some 2,000 miles away - as Moscow was in the grip of its sub-zero temperature Winter. The venue was fairly close to the Chinese and Afghanistan borders, and with the indigenous population being in the majority, the packed 65,000 crowd were not Russians, but Asians.

It was now the City's turn to display a defensive strategy, until Torpedo scored, after 34 minutes, which levelled the aggregate score. The match was now up for grabs! Goalkeeper Bob Wilson, defied all that the Torpedo could throw at him, and at the final whistle, the large crowd applauded the City's defiant performance.

The play-off took place in Augsberg, West Germany, on the 3rd of April, and the match was a real 'do or die' cup-tie, with both teams missing chances, until Norman Dean scored the decisive goal. This dramatic win put the City into the semi-finals of the competition. It had been a fine performance, particularly as the team included reserve centre-half Richie Morgan - for his first team debut - in place of the injured Don Murray.

The famous West German team, S.V. Hamburg, with a host of International players - including Uwe Seeler - were waiting for the City in the semi-finals, with the first leg scheduled for Hamburg, on the 24th of April. City got away to a 'dream' start, when Dean fired them into a fourth minute lead. The Germans blazed away at the Bluebirds stubborn defence, which sometimes numbered nine men, and behind the front line, Bob Wilson was in inspirational form. The lanky 'keeper was finally beaten when the German full-back Sandemann, scored in the 69th minute. But the City managed to hold on for a final 1-1 draw.

Cardiff City versus S.V. Hamburg: Peter King just fails to score at Ninian Park in the European Cup Winners' Cup Semi-final.

The second leg, at Ninian Park, produced a match to live long in the memories of the 43,070 who watched it. Only ten minutes had elapsed, when Clarke's left-wing run set up a goal for Norman Dean. Just as the Bluebirds were dreaming of the Final, Hamburg brought them back to earth, with a short range equaliser, from Honig.

The cool night air of the May Day evening crackled with tension, as the nerves began to fray, and on the hour, Uwe Seeler – of whom little had been seen – whipped a bouncing ball over his shoulder, and to the crowds amazement the ball floated into the corner of the net. The City threw caution to the wind, and with twelve minutes left, Ninian Park exploded with noise, as Brian Harris scored his only goal in 88 appearances, to bring the teams level at 2-2.

But the game was still to have a sting in its tail, as, two minutes from time, Honig went forward from the halfway line without a challenge, and from about 30 yards, put in a hopeful shot. Wilson, so often the City hero, dived to save, but the ball squirmed from his grasp and rolled just inside the upright, and into the net.

Cardiff City were out, beaten at this hurdle by 3-4 on aggregate, and poor Bob Wilson - like Arsenal's Dan Lewis in the 1927 F.A.Cup Final - would be remembered for that one fatal error!

At the end of May, Cardiff embarked on a six week tour of New Zealand and Australia, and played 14 games. They lost just once, and scored many goals along the way.

****

1968-69 Season – Division 2:

After much of the close season that was actively spent on tour, Scoular appeared to be happy with his playing staff, and made no new signings.

The season started badly, as City, with young Leighton Phillips making his full League debut (he had been a scoring substitute in the match versus Rotherham on the 29th of January 1968), crashed 0-4 at Ninian Park to Crystal Palace. Mel Sutton, a former Aston Villa reserve, made his debut as City lost at home again four days later, this time to Charlton Athletic by the only goal of the game. The Bluebirds were defeated 1-3 at Norwich, and after these three reversals had dumped them at the foot of the table, they achieved their first point from a 3-3 draw at Bury; former Bluebird, Greg Farrell scored twice for the Shakers.

Unable to claim a regular place in the first team, European goal-hero Norman Dean was transferred to Barnsley for £7,000 during September. Suddenly the team burst into life, winning six of the next seven matches, with Brian Clark and John Toshack scoring regularly, but this run ended abruptly during October, with three successive defeats – at Millwall and Birmingham, and at home to Bolton Wanderers.

The manager's reaction was to switch the ball skills of Barrie Jones from the wing into midfield, where he joined Mel Sutton, Peter King and – another converted winger – Leslie Lea. The City boss implemented the 4-3-3 and 4-4-2 formations which were becoming more widely used in the Football League, in the wake of England's 1966 World Cup success.

With Don Carver and Gary Bell forming a new full-back combination, the City team began to take on a new shape. The impact was startling, as the Bluebirds leapt up the table, with some fine wins along the way.

A 4-1 beating of Sheffield United in the Ninian Park mud, and a 5-2 victory at Fulham, had the Cardiff public buzzing again, and almost 23,000 were at Ninian Park (with a frozen pitch), to see a great 2-0 victory over Millwall, who were the leaders of the Division. With a number of players wearing basketball shoes, City proved too nimble for the Londoners. Clark and Toshack demonstrated their blossoming partnership up front, with a heading duet that allowed Toshack to open the scoring. In the last minute, Clark scored one of the most unusual goals of his distinguished career, when he headed Brian King's weak goal-kick back over the mortified 'keeper, and into the net!

A 42,000 crowd were at snowbound Villa Park on Boxing Day, when the City slipped 0-2, with ex-Bluebird Barrie Hole scoring one of the Villa goals. But this was only a slight hiccup, as City kept up with the leaders by virtue of a string of home victories during the bad Winter. Unfortunately their away record prevented them from compounding their promotion potential, and by the end of their most successful League season for almost a decade, they had cause to rue their poor start, and the odd lapse afterwards. Frank Sharp's arrival from Carlisle, in late February, failed to add impetus to the team.

The Bluebirds had restored the public's interest, by finishing in 5th position, and Mr. Scoular had moulded together a hard-working team with a sound defence and reliable goalscorers. Indeed the City had rejected a bid of £70,000 from Bobby Robson at Fulham, for teenage sensation John Toshack.

Goalkeeper Fred Davies, plus Barrie Jones, and Don Murray were all ever-present, while Toshack missed just one match. Toshack was the leading goalscorer, with 22, followed by Brian Clark's contribution of 17.

Memories! Fred Keenor (Left), and Arsenal's goalkeeper Bob John, seated below the photo of the winning F.A.Cup final goal of 42 years earlier.

F.A.Cup:
The home third round tie with Arsenal revived memories of the 'good old days' of First Division soccer. The Bluebirds were having a great run in the Second Division, getting much media attention, and a mammoth crowd of 55,136 packed Ninian Park for this encounter.

The game failed dismally to live up to anticipation, and this can be gauged by the fact that neither City goalkeeper Fred Davies, or his Arsenal counterpart Bob Wilson, had a serious shot to save throughout the match. From very early on, it was apparent that the game would end in stalemate, and so it did with a 0-0 scoreline. It epitomised the way that the style of British football had changed, with more defensive tactics, cynical fouls and time wasting gamesmanship, all of which prevented the game to flow as it had done in previous years. The replay was a little better, and the Highbury crowd of 52,681 was relieved when two second-half goals for Arsenal put City out. Almost 108,000 people had seen the two ties, but sadly had had very little value for their money.

Welsh Cup:
Cardiff City, the holders, had little difficulty in sweeping through the competition. They accounted for Aberystwyth Town by 3-0 (goals by Lea, Toshack and Jones), and Bethesda Athletic, with a 6-0 scoreline, when the goals were scored by Clark (two), plus singles from Lea, Jones, Bell and Toshack. In the semi-final, two Toshack goals at Sealand Road, beat Chester.

The two-legged final paired the City with Swansea Town, and in the first game, on a rain-soaked Vetch Field, Toshack terrorised the Swans defence. The tall teenager scored twice, and forced Mel Nurse into conceding an own goal, as City won 3-1. The second leg, on the 29th of April, was a foregone conclusion, and the Bluebirds had little trouble in retaining the trophy. Lea and Toshack scored in the 2-0 victory to give an aggregate 5-1 win.

Football League Cup:
The team had to make a long midweek journey to Carlisle United, for a second round match, and their interest in the competition ended there, as the Cumbrians won by 2-0.

European Cup-Winners Cup:
The City faced a difficult task when they opposed F.C.Porto, the Portuguese Cup-winners. The writing was on the wall when the first leg at Ninian Park ended as a 2-2 draw. Toshack and Bird put the City ahead, but in a bruising, ill-tempered affair, the Porto substitute Pinto came off the bench and stunned the home team with two goals. The return in Oporto was no better, with the crowd throwing missiles at the visiting bench. On the pitch, the City – despite a goal from Toshack – lost by 1-2, and hence went out of the competition by 3-4 on aggregate.

The City undertook a six match – unbeaten – end of season tour of Mauritius and Zambia. Reserve forward, Sandy Allan, was in prolific goal-scoring form.

1969-70 season – Division 2:

The Cardiff City manager, Jimmy Scoular, kept a low profile on the transfer front during the close season, apart from the signing of Junior players Jim Eadie and Jimmy McInch (both Scots), and Freddie Pethard, who had been released by Glasgow Celtic.

The Club hit the national headlines on the 9th of August, when Toshack scored the fastest goal of the season – after only 28 seconds – in the opening fixture at Carlisle, and they went on to record a 3-2 victory. It was the Bluebirds first win on an opponents soil, on an opening day of the season, since the 26th of August 1933, when Watford were beaten 2-1! The City strike force of Toshack, Clark and King, were in impressive form as the Bluebirds began the season well, and the B.B.C. 'Match of the Day' cameras were at Ninian Park when the City drew 1-1 with Leicester City.

Toshack completes his first hat-trick (versus Q.P.R.)

John Toshack stunned Q.P.R. with a dashing hat-trick, in a 4-2 home win on the 27th of September, which was watched by the first League crowd of 30,000 plus, for eight years. Winger Frank Sharp dislocated his shoulder in the Rangers match, and a week later City were dealt a shattering blow, when not only did they lose by 2-3 at Blackpool (after leading 2-1), they also lost Barrie Jones. In the last minute, Jones paid for a moment of rashness when he made an awkward tackle on a Blackpool defender, and came off worse with a double fracture of his right leg. It was to be the 'twinkle-toed' ball artistes' last appearance in a City shirt, as he was ultimately forced to quit League football, two years later.

Scoular juggled his midfield players around, and although they beat Aston Villa by 4-0, and Hull City 6-0, they also slipped up with a single goal defeat at home to Norwich City, and a 0-3 defeat at Portsmouth. Realising that Jones' loss was to be a permanent one, the manager paid £25,000 to Crystal Palace for utility player Bobby Woodruff, the man with the longest throw in League football.

Woodruff made his debut on the 22nd of November, when City beat Preston North End by 2-1 at Ninian Park, and this was the first of seven successive victories – the best sequence by the Bluebirds since the 1946-47 season. After beating Sheffield United 3-0 in the Ninian Park mudbath on the 10th of January, they went to the top of the Division, and Clark completed a spell of seven goals in the same number of games.

The City were the Second Division leaders for only one week, for a disappointing run of ten games followed, which yielded just one victory, and dropped them outside of the promotion placings. They were to remain in this area for the remainder of the season. Amazingly, Scoular had introduced only two new faces into the team all season, viz. Woodruff and the big Scottish goalkeeper Jim Eadie, the latter having played just two games.

David Carver, Don Murray, and Brian Clark were all ever-present. Bell missed just one game, whilst Fred Davies and King were absent for two; Harris and Toshack appeared in all but three matches. It was the most consistent City team for a number of years, and the only disappointment for the 21,000 average crowd – the highest since the First Division days – was the Bluebirds finish of seventh in the League. Brian Clark topped the goalscoring list – with eighteen – Toshack scored seventeen, and King managed ten.

F.A.Cup:
The team were in terrific form in the League when they visited Fourth Division York City, in the third round on January the 3rd. An own goal by Swallow put the City into the driving seat, but Boyer equalised, as York fought back to earn a deserved draw.

The City could still not shake off the lower League battlers in the replay four days later. York equalised Toshack's first half goal, and after no further scoring in extra time, the tie went to a third meeting, at St. Andrews, Birmingham. Most of the neutrals' sympathy was directed to the York team, who again came from behind, after King had fired the City in front. In extra time, Swallow and Aimson scored for York, and City – who at this time were leading the Second Division – were beaten by 1-3.

Welsh Cup:
Relishing in their position as the Premier Club of Wales – in terms of League status – the City went straight through the competition to reach yet another Final. Clark enjoyed a five goal spree as the team beat Barmouth and Dyffryn by 6-1, and the big striker scored twice in City's 3-0 win over Wrexham.

Old rivals Swansea Town (but now renamed 'City'), visited Ninian Park, in the semi-final, and shook the Bluebirds by drawing 2-2. Toshack and Woodruff scored the City goals. The replay took place after the League season had ended, and in extra time, Bird and King scored the goals that earned the Bluebirds a place in the final, against Chester.

As Chester were an English Club, the Bluebirds were automatically guaranteed a place in Europe, but they made sure of their qualification credentials, by winning by 1-0 at Chester, through Ronnie Bird's strike, before strolling to a 4-0 second-leg win, with goals from Woodruff, Bird, Lea and Clark.

Football League Cup:
Cardiff City travelled to Crystal Palace for a second round tie, and on the night, were not quite good enough to prevent the recently promoted First Division team from winning 3-1, despite a Leslie Lea goal.

European Cup-Winners Cup:
The City enjoyed a comfortable first round tie versus the Norwegian team, Mjondalen, for after winning by 7-1 in Norway (a City record away score in the competition), the Bluebirds completed the job at Ninian Park, when reserve forward Sandy Allan headed a hat-trick in the 5-1 victory, giving Cardiff their record aggregate win of 12-2.

The second round proved too tough for the Bluebirds when they met the Turkish Cup holders, Goztepe Izmir, and a 0-3 defeat in Izmir in the first leg, effectively put the tie beyond the reach of the Welsh team. The City did not give up easily, and although they won the second leg at Ninian Park, Ronnie Bird's goal was insufficient to prevent the Turks from winning 3-1 on aggregate

John Toshack and Steve Derrett were capped by Wales during the season.

****

1970-71 Season – Division 2:

Toshack celebrates his third goal – versus Hull – his last game for Cardiff.

Mr. Scoular, realising that the City needed someone a little bit special to lift them into the First Division, spent a Club record sum of £35,000 for Coventry City's brilliant midfield player Ian Gibson. The chunky Scot, who had been with Scoular at Bradford Park Avenue in the early 1960's, had engineered Coventry's climb to the First Division in 1967, and was so confident that he could do the same for Cardiff City, that he place a sizeable bet on the Club getting promotion!

Barnsley paid £20,000 to take Leslie Lea and reserve player Frank Sharp to Oakwell, in a double deal. Goalkeeper Fred Davies was transferred to A.F.C. Bournemouth for a nominal fee, and reserve forward Sandy Allan, was sold to Bristol Rovers for £5,000. A week before the start of the season, Scoular paid Crystal Palace £15,000 for their reserve 'keeper Frank Parsons, and both new signings – Parsons and Gibson – were in the City starting line-up for the first match of the season.

The campaign began at Leicester City, who, along with the Bluebirds, were among the bookmakers' favourites for promotion. Cardiff lived up to their short odds with a fine victory, on a hot and sunny afternoon, before 27,578 spectators. Brian Clark, wearing an unfamiliar number '7' shirt, headed the game's only goal over a stranded Peter Shilton, and the Bluebirds were off to a great start.

The City let a two goal lead slip in a 2-2 home draw with Millwall, but at Sheffield Wednesday – four days later – they came back from a goal down, to beat the recently relegated Club. Prendergast had given the Wednesday a 10th minute lead, but straight from the restart, King passed back to Dave Carver, and the full-back's deep kick to the far post was headed back across goal by Toshack, for Clark – his co-striker – to head in. It was a tried and tested move by the City, direct from the kick-off, but the first time that it had produced a goal, after many attempts. Sutton scored the City's second goal after 23 minutes, and the Bluebirds had little difficulty in holding on for their first League win at Hillsborough.

A defensive error two minutes from time at Bristol City, let Jerry Sharpe in to score the only goal of the game. In the match one week later, a misjudgment by goalkeeper Frank Parsons, allowed Sheffield United to equalise through Alan Woodward, in the 1-1 home draw. Two Toshack goals defeated Birmingham City at Ninian Park, on the 5th of September, where the sixteen year-old Trevor Francis made his first League appearance for the visitors – as a second half substitute. At Bolton the following week, Gibson scored his first goal for the Club, and the Bluebirds went on to win the game by 2-0. One week later, another goalkeeping error by Parsons, resulted in Norwich City drawing 1-1 in a table-topping Ninian Park encounter, after Cardiff had led through Clark's first half goal.

On the 3rd of October, the home fans – and there were 21,072 of them – witnessed an amazing match when Middlesbrough were entertained.

The visitors took the lead with Hickton's diving header after 20 minutes, and ten minutes later, Peter King created a headed equaliser for Brian Clark. Twelve minutes into the second half, the City had seemingly broken the lowly Boro's resistance with two spectacular goals. The first, after 53 minutes, was a crashing 25 yard shot from midfielder Bobby Woodruff. But that effort was bettered four minutes later, when King scored one of Ninian Park's greatest ever goals. The midfielder was wide on the left as a clearance dropped to him, and he whacked an unbelievable bending volley into the far top corner of the Grangetown goal, from an almost impossible angle, to put Cardiff 3-1 ahead.

A few minutes later, there was further excitement, when Middlesbrough were awarded a penalty, and Frank Parsons kept out Hickton's shot, with a flying save. The cheers turned to groans five minutes later, as the goalkeeper fumbled Maddren's shot, and the ball rolled into the net. The sun-soaked crowd were shocked as the Boro' picked up the tempo, and when Parsons dived to save Downing's sharp angled drive, the ball ran free for Laidlaw to follow up and tap over the line, to bring the score level at 3-3.

The drama hadn't finished, for the City were to be hit by a sting in the tail, when Hughie McIlmoyle - who, over the years was a prolific goalscorer against the Bluebirds - headed the winning goal following a free-kick. The unfortunate Parsons had been slow in coming out to meet the ball, and McIlmoyle took full advantage to score his 12th goal against the City in eleven games!

Scoular's private reaction to this match was unprintable, but publicly the gruff Scot stated that:
" I brought Frank Parsons, and any fault is down to me. He will now go into the reserves to build up his game, and I will bring in Jim Eadie."

The giant Scottish goalkeeper came into a City team that won by the only goal at Watford, and the Bluebirds were featured on 'Match of the Day', when, for the second successive season, their home match against Leicester City was televised. It was a sweet game for David Carver who had conceded an own goal a year earlier, as on this occasion the brawny full-back grabbed a last minute equaliser in a 2-2 draw.

The manager made a tactical switch, by moving midfielder Woodruff into attack in place of Clark, who, in turn was demoted to substitute, and drafted Leighton Phillips into the midfield vacancy. Toshack responded with a flurry of goals, the highlight coming with a hat-trick in the 5-1 home win over Hull City, on the 31st of October. This game emphasised the growing maturity of the 21 year-old striker, and following the next League match at Q.P.R. - which City won 1-0 with a Phillips goal - Liverpool moved in with a £110,000 offer for Cardiff's current favourite son.

The offer was immediately accepted, and Toshack became a Liverpool player on the 8th of November. Bill Shankly, the Liverpool manager, told the Press:
" This must be one of my greatest signings. I think this boy has everything to become an idol on Merseyside. He'd be cheap at a million."

The public outcry in South Wales raged long and furious, some fans declaring that they would never put a foot inside Ninian Park again, and over the ensuing years, this particular transfer is the one that has left the Bluebirds fans with a feeling of bewilderment and anger!

Clark returned to the City team and scored twice against Blackburn Rovers, in a 4-1 home victory, that began with a goal from King after only 28 seconds! The City then stuttered and stumbled over the next six matches, losing to bottom placed Charlton Athletic, Oxford United and Millwall, until Scoular paid a new Club record fee of £42,000 - on Christmas Eve - for Sheffield Wednesday's abrasive striker, Alan Warboys. The new boy began to make things happen almost immediately with two goals against his former Club, in the 4-0 home win on the 9th of January, and another brace when City won by 3-1 at Portsmouth, a week later.

A pulled hamstring, against Brentford in an F.A. Cup-tie, restricted Warboys' appearances, and little John Parsons, the son of backroom employee Harry Parsons, came off the substitutes' bench to make several vital contributions. These included the only goal in the home win over Oxford United, a week before his full debut. Warboys returned, and scored a goal in the 1-1 draw at Hull, and on the 6th of March the six foot-two inch striker earned his legendary status when he scored all four goals, as the City beat Carlisle United in a top of the table clash at Ninian Park. The big man cracked home a hat-trick after just **ten** minutes, and each goal was brilliantly taken. After his third effort had thundered into the Carlisle net, Warboys raced to the dug-out - with hands held open - as a gesture demanding the extra payment that Scoular had said he would pay out of his own pocket to any player scoring a hat-trick! Warboys went on to smash home his fourth goal before half-time, and was substituted in the second period to protect his right thigh which was heavily strapped.

City's only defeat, in a run of 15 League games since Warboys debut (on Boxing Day), came in an epic match at St. Andrews, where Birmingham City won 2-0, before a crowd of 49,025. The Bluebirds, who had played at Real Madrid three days earlier, were caught cold by 16 year-old Trevor Francis' sixteenth goal in as many games, which was scored after only three minutes. A second-half header from Phil Summerhill completed the scoring.

The Bluebirds remained amongst the promotion places until the 17th of April, but on that day they crashed 0-1 at home to lowly Watford. The visitors had all the luck imaginable, as the City hit the woodwork on a number of occasions, and the Hornet's inspired Welsh 'keeper, Mike

Walker, kept everything else at bay, as they clung to the 60 minute lead given them by Woods. The City dropped to third place as Sheffield United beat Birmingham 3-0, and Leicester City stretched their lead at the top. The following week, City travelled to Norwich, and won by 2-1 with goals from Clark and Warboys. This victory put them just one point behind Sheffield United, and with a game in hand. It was to Bramall Lane that the City next travelled – on the 27th of April – needing to get at least one point to keep up their challenge; a defeat would almost certainly end their promotion hopes.

On a balmy evening, Bramall Lane was bursting at the seams, with 42,963 fans craning from every vantage point, including the old Yorkshire cricket pavilion on the open side of the – then – three sided stadium. The ninety minutes proved to be the most painful of the season for a shell-shocked City team, as Sheffield, urged on by the buzzing crowd, swept into an early lead when Dearden slotted home Hockey's cleverly lobbed pass. Cardiff fell further behind after 33 minutes, when Flynn headed in Badgers' flick-on, from Currie's free-kick. Derrett pulled back a goal for the City, just before the interval, with a deflected shot, but the second-half saw the Bluebirds cut to ribbons by the sharp-shooting Blades. Currie headed in Woodwards corner – for number three – then one-time City reject Gilbert Reece sped through a scattered defence to smash home the fourth. Nine minutes from time, Dearden scored his second, and so the United finished the match as 5-1 winners, and the Cardiff City promotion dreams were in tatters. Questions were asked about the validity of some of the Sheffield goals, but there was no doubting that the Blades overall performance was one that the City just could not cope with.

The Bluebirds beat Orient 1-0 in an anti-climatic atmosphere on the following Saturday, but Sheffield United overcame Watford in their final match to gain the runners-up spot, behind the Champions, Leicester City. Cardiff were left in third place.

The final game of the season, at Luton (re-arranged from January), saw Malcolm Macdonald scoring all three goals in Luton's 3-0 victory. Macdonald was then sold to Newcastle United for £180,000, making the fee that Cardiff had received for Toshack look like chicken-feed!

Full-backs David Carver and Gary Bell, plus Don Murray, were ever present. Mel Sutton and Peter King missed just one game each, and Ian Gibson was absent on two occasions. Brian Clark was the leading goalscorer with fifteen, and Alan Warboys had thirteen successes.

F.A. Cup:
The third round draw brought Brighton and Hove Albion to Ninian Park, and on a saturated pitch, the City had to thank the reliable Peter King for their narrow one goal win, which was scored after only three minutes. Fourth Division Brentford were the next visitors, in the fourth round, and the City – top of the Second Division – suffered one of the shocks of the day, as the Bees won by 2-0, on a mudbath of a pitch. The defeat was made all the more painful as City also lost Warboys with a hamstring injury.

Welsh Cup:
Cardiff travelled to the League's bottom Club, Newport County, in the fifth round, and nearly suffered total humiliation, but Clark's goal earned the Bluebirds a 1-1 draw. The replay was a much more formal affair, for City won by 4-0, with goals from Parsons, Gibson, Murray and King.

The City went one better in the sixth round, beating Bangor City 5-0 at Ninian Park – Gibson, Clark, Rees, Parsons and King sharing the goals between them. The semi-final brought Chester to Cardiff, and the visitors battled stubbornly, to earn a replay after a goalless draw. The Bluebirds had a hard fight in the replay at Sealand Road, but eventually they won the tie with a 2-1 scoreline, following goals from Clark and Derrett.

The two-legged final took place after the City had missed out on promotion, but they showed the right character, by beating Wrexham in both legs. Woodruff scored the only goal, before a crowd numbering 14,008 at the Racecourse, and Gibson's brace, plus one from Bird, were the marksmen in the 3-1 victory at Ninian Park.

Football League Cup:
After travelling to Q.P.R. for a second round tie, the City suffered one of their heaviest of defeats in the competition, as the Londoners – inspired by the brilliance of Rodney Marsh – won comfortably by 4-0.

European Cup-Winners Cup:
On the 16th of September, Cardiff City achieved their biggest (single leg) victory in a European Cup-tie, when they beat the Cypriots – P.O. Larnaca – 8-0 at Ninian Park. Sutton, Gibson, Woodruff, a pair from Clark, King, and another two scored by Toshack, shared the goal feast. The return match was played on a treacherous pitch in Cyprus, where the City were content to play out a scoreless draw, and so comfortably progressed to the next round.

The Club were then paired with F.C Nantes, from France, and over the two legs played some of their best football of the season. Toshack (two), Gibson, King and Phillips scored the goals in the 5-1 home leg victory. The job was completed in France, when Toshack's 100th first team goal, and Brian Clark's effort ensured a 2-1 win.

The quarter-final brought the plum draw that the City dearly wanted, matches against Real Madrid, with the first tie at home. Toshack had by now been transferred, and Warboys' arrival was too late for his eligibility, so Scoular had to revamp the forward line. 17 year-old outside-left Nigel Rees was brought in, although he had to beg his release from the Wales Youth squad, in order that he could play in one of Cardiff City's most important games.

In fairytail fashion, young Rees completed a clever dribble in the 32nd minute, and crossed perfectly for Clark to head in one of Ninian Park's best remembered goals, and enabled the City to win by 1-0. But this was Gibson's match, for the chunky Scottish midfield maestro was here, there, and everywhere. His performance had everything, as he teased and tormented the Real defence with his every touch. Years later, Gibson's contribution to a pulsating victory is as well remembered by the 47,500 crowd, as is Clark's winning goal.

The return match, in Madrid, was always going to be difficult, for the Bernabeu Stadium is a formidable fortress at the best of times. Although the Welsh team gave all they had, Real overcame the slender deficit, to win by 2-1 on aggregate.

Brian Clark's 31st minute winner versus Real Madrid

Both Leighton Phillips and Steve Derrett were capped by Wales during the season. The Cardiff City Youth side did the Club proud, by reaching the F.A.Youth Cup Final, only to lose to Arsenal in the two-legged final. Over 12,000 saw the home leg, and most of the boys were to be given an opportunity of first team football at a later date.

1971-72 Season - Division 2:

Two of Cardiff City's more popular players of the late 1960's left Ninian Park during the Summer. Brian Harris joined neighbours Newport County as player-manager, and Ronnie Bird moved to Crewe Alexandra. Manager Scoular paid Southampton £6,000 for full-back Ken Jones, who had once been at Bradford (Park Avenue) with the City boss. On the eve of the season's start, an on-off transfer saga involving the Newcastle winger Alan Foggon was finally completed when Scoular paid the fee of £20,000 to the United, one of his former clubs.

The League matches began badly as the City let a two goal lead slip in the opening game against Burnley, and the Lancashire team came back to force a 2-2 draw. Things went from bad to worse, as City plunged to heavy defeats at Blackpool and Orient. In the match in London, Roger Hoy made his City debut following his £20,000 transfer from Luton Town, and Ian Bowyer scored a hat-trick for the home side. It was not until the 11th of September, the seventh game of the season, that the first win was recorded, when the City came from 1-2 behind, to beat Sheffield Wednesday by 3-2. Alan Warboys scored twice against his old Club, for the second successive season.

Mr. Scoular busily rang the changes, particularly in midfield and attack, but it was usually a case of shuffling the same players around in differently numbered shirts! A £10,000 fee brought Irish amateur International goal keeper Bill Irwin from Bangor, Northern Ireland, to Ninian Park, and with Eadie out of form, and Parsons injured, the tall Irishman stepped straight into the Second Division, making his debut in a 1-2 home defeat by Millwall, on the 9th of October. A 6-1 home victory over Charlton Athletic came right out of the blue, and was the only victory in eight matches, during which time the youngsters Tony Villars and Alan Couch made their senior debuts.

As the City's form continued to deteriorate, so too did the state of the Ninian Park pitch, and by November, a large diamond shaped area was just a mudy morass. To make it playable a huge volume of sand was laid on the ground, but the surface was like a sponge, and Cardiff received complaints concerning the playing conditions, from every visiting club. Ian Gibson plugged away, often running himself to a standstill, and Brian Clark managed to keep scoring goals, as the City fought to stave off relegation. To make matters worse, the Bluebirds away record was abysmal. They could draw matches on their opponents grounds, but could not win, therefore a good home record was vital.

By the closing stages of the season Jimmy Scoular was selecting his more experienced players, apart from full-back Freddie Pethard, who had replaced Gary Bell in the team. The Club pulled itself out of the mire with a run of 12 games, of which only one was lost, but 7 were drawn.

A 5-2 home victory over Preston North End, in late March, began with Brian Clark heading a Woodruff throw-in directly into the net, after only 45 seconds. Warboys followed this with a hat-trick, and King also was on target, as the Bluebirds completed their only 'double' of the season.

On the 15th of April, the City beat Carlisle United 3-1 at Ninian Park, and this result virtually guaranteed safety from relegation. When this game was followed up with a 1-1 draw in the final home match, with Luton Town, any lingering worries were removed. In the last match of the season, at Q.P.R., the unlucky Frank Parsons was given an outing, but, as if fate had decreed it, the unfortunate 'keeper was stretchered off. Alan Warboys took over in goal, as the City were beaten by 3-0.

The Bluebirds finished in 19th position, and only Brian Clark was ever-present. Other regulars included Leighton Phillips, Ian Gibson, David Carver and Don Murray. Clark was the top marksman with 21 goals, followed by Warboys' 13 successes.

F.A.Cup:

Cardiff City returned to Bramall Lane on the 15th of January, the scene of their great disappointment in the promotion battle of a year earlier, to play Sheffield United in the third round. The Bluebirds gave a magnificent display, after taking the lead through Don Murray's header in the 20th minute. McKenzie equalised for the Blades fourteen minutes later, and after a 'ding-dong' battle, the City staged an amazing finish to the game. David Carver scored at his second attempt, and as the final whistle was about to be blown, Woodruff hit home the third City goal.

In the fourth round, Cardiff entertained Sunderland, and seemed set for victory when Peter King slammed home a great shot from 25 yards, in the 25th minute.

But midway through the second half, Chambers equalised for Sunderland from the penalty spot, after a trip on Malone. Although Clark hit a post near the end, the City had to travel to the North-east for the replay.

The Powerworkers dispute caused a ban on floodlighting, so the game at Roker Park, on St. Valentine's day, kicked off at 2 p.m., but with a staggering 39,348 in attendance. Youth player Brian Rees made his only first team appearance, when he replaced number '11', Alan Foggon. Once again the Bluebirds took a first half lead, when Clark netted after 26 minutes. The City withstood a real battering in the second period, and Bill Irwin gave an inspirational goalkeeping performance, until two minutes from time, when Bobby Kerr finally broke through for Sunderland. The extra-time period was both absorbing and exciting, but with the defences dominant, and the prospect of a home tie in the next round against the First Division leaders, Leeds United, no chances were taken, and the match went to a second replay.

Two days later, on February the 16th, Cardiff and Sunderland met at the neutral venue of Maine Road, and produced a pulsating match for the 8,868 crowd who managed to attend another midweek afternoon kick-off. For the third time, the City took the lead in the first half, when Clark once again tapped in a goal, after 25 minutes! But yet again the Roker Park Club came back, and McGiven equalised barely four minutes later. The match seesawed up and down, and with time running out, it looked as if extra-time, or even another game, would be required. Scoular sent on substitute Alan Warboys, and his bustling set up a goal for Bobby Woodruff, with just two minutes left.

In injury time, young Billy Kellock, in only his third first team match, sent a 20 yard shot through a packed goalmouth, to make the final score 3-1.

Woodruff scores Cardiff's second goal.
16th February 1972

Clarke acknowledges Kellock's last minute winner
F.A.Cup 4th round second replay.

The visit of the all conquering Leeds United on the 26th of February, in the fifth round, certainly caught the imagination of the South Wales public, and over 50,000 packed into Ninian Park. The City gave all they had, but it was never going to be enough, against a Leeds team that boasted many international players. Little Ian Gibson took them on, but was continually fouled whenever he threatened danger, and Bill Irwin performed heroically in goal. One of his saves, from Allan Clarke, earned him the 'Save of the Season' award from T.V. pundit Bob Wilson. But all of the City fire was extinguished as Johnny Giles scored a goal in each half, and so Leeds won by 2-0.

Welsh Cup:

Cardiff played at Swansea in the fifth round, and gave a hard working performance in heavy conditions, to win by 2-0. Warboys, after only two minutes, and Clark - seven minutes from time - were the scorers. Welsh League club Llanelli welcomed the City in the sixth round, and gave a good account of themselves, as they held the Bluebirds to a single goal victory (scored by Alan Foggon after 25 minutes).

The City played at Rhyl in the semi-final, and both Clark and Warboys were on the mark, in a narrow 2-1 victory, which assured Cardiff of another Welsh Cup final appearance. The Bluebirds met Wrexham in the two-legged final, and at The Racecourse, the City were not too downhearted after losing 2-1, with Woodruff scoring from a last minute penalty. The second leg at Ninian Park was a tale of continual misfortune for the Bluebirds, as chance after chance went begging, with Warboys as the main culprit. Foggon scored after 51 minutes, only for Kinsey to equalise 2 minutes later, and with the game ending as a 1-1 draw, City's hold on the Welsh Cup was relinquished (a 2-3 defeat on aggregate) after six years in the Ninian Park Boardroom.

Football League Cup:

The City faced a tough second round tie when they visited First Division West Ham United. Despite their poor League form, the Bluebirds showed what they were capable of and equalised after 63 minutes, to earn a deserved replay. At Ninian Park, on the 22nd of September, the teams served up another fine match to delight a crowd of over 30,000. Brian Clark fired the City into a first-half lead, but the Bluebirds eventually succumbed to two late goals, from moves that bore the West Ham trademark. In the 82nd minute, England captain Bobby Moore swung a 50 yard crossfield pass to Redknapp, and his near post cross was converted by Hurst. The crowd could well have been experiencing 'deja-vu' two minutes later, when an identical move resulted in Hurst scoring the winning goal.

European Cup-Winners Cup:

A long and expensive journey was necessary for the first round tie, to East Berlin, for the away leg at Dynamo Berlin. Only 12,000 saw the City play well in difficult circumstances, and the Bluebirds seemed to have gained control when Ian Gibson put them ahead twelve minutes from time. The East Germans made a late rally, and with just seconds remaining, centre-forward Schutze equalised.

The attendance of only 12,676 for the second leg at Ninian Park was disappointing, considering that over 30,000 had watched a League Cup match only seven days earlier. Clark put the Bluebirds into a 58th minute lead, only for Labes to bring the aggregate level, four minutes later. The game went into extra time, and with no further scoring, the City faced their first penalty shoot-out experience. The visitors started, and the shots by both teams were successful, until the scoring read 5-4. Don Murray blazed his kick high into the Grangetown stand, and so the City bowed out, after leading in both of the ties.

••••••••••••••••••••••••••••••••••••

1972-73 Season - Division 2:

Several players left Ninian Park during the close season, the most notable being hard running midfielder Mel Sutton, who joined Wrexham for a bargain fee of £15,000. Scoular paid out money for just one player, Irishman Albert Larmour of Linfield, a defender who cost £10,000.

A start was made on the Grandstand extensions, with the construction of the foundations, and a new pitch was laid after the under-soil drainage system had been installed.

The opening match of the season - at home to Luton Town -saw Larmour make his debut in a game best remembered for the way in which the City tried to play Continental-style possession football, which had the sun-soaked 16,364 Ninian Park crowd slow handclapping and hooting in derision. During the first half the City seldom crossed the halfway line. Luton went ahead with a 39th minute penalty, and Gary Bell equalised, also from the spot, a minute before half-time. Warboys headed a 60th minute winner, after the City had changed their tactics to more orthodox methods, but the crowd went away somewhat bemused!

City led in their next two games, against Portsmouth and Blackpool, and lost them both. But a Clark goal gave the Bluebirds a 1-0 victory over Millwall on the 30th of August. Larmour had lost his place by now, and goalkeeper Frank Parsons was given another chance, but a 0-2 home defeat to Aston Villa (during the game Parsons saved a Willie Anderson penalty) and a 0-4 thrashing at Carlisle, saw the 'keeper omitted once again, as the manager began to take drastic action.

In a surprise exchange deal with Sheffield United, the City boss swapped Warboys for Welsh internationals David Powell and Gil Reece. The move completed a full circle for the locally born Reece, who had been on the Ninian Park staff in the early 1960's, but never made the first team, and had left on a free transfer. Both players made their debuts in a shocking 1-3 home defeat by Bristol City, on the 23rd of September, and within days

Scoular accepted a £100,000 offer from Bournemouth for Clark and Gibson. It was good business for the City, as both had lost form, and the Club stood to make a profit of £60,000 on the pair. They had been two of the City's most popular players, but the money was needed for Scoular to finance further incoming transfers. Youth product Phil Dwyer replaced long-serving right back David Carver, and the latter eventually went to Swansea on loan, before joining Hereford United. Dwyer made his debut in a nondescript goalless draw at Orient. Nobody was likely to have guessed that Dwyer would be embarking on a career which would result in him eventually holding the record for the most appearances for Cardiff City. The Orient match saw the dismissal of Alan Foggon, and this was to be his last Cardiff game, for he moved on to Middlesbrough for a £10,000 fee.

On the 12th of October, Jimmy Scoular paid £35,000 for Middlesbrough's stylish midfield player Johnny Vincent, who made his City debut against his former team-mates, only two days after joining the Bluebirds. He thrilled the 10,430 crowd with a superb display, capped with the first goal, as City defeated Boro' by 2-0.

Shortly afterwards, Scoular, needing striking power to fill the gaps left by the departure of Clark and Warboys, paid a new Club record fee of £45,000 for Andy McCulloch from Queens Park Rangers. The new boy received an ankle injury, but still scored on his debut, as Preston were beaten 3-0 on the 28th of October. Bobby Woodruff substituted for the injured McCulloch, and netted twice in the second half.

Around this time there was a flurry of activity and movement at the Boardroom level, as Chairman Fred Dewey was incapacitated following a road accident. The Chairman's son, Vivian, invited David Goldstone - who had been in the Chair at Swansea City- to become a director at Cardiff, and this suggestion was accepted by the London businessman.

Reserve player Peter Morgan came into the City defence, lining up alongside his brother Richie for several games. The City did show some slight improvement, although their away form continued to be poor, and with McCulloch scoring consistently, they picked up some points at Ninian Park. The main problem revolved around McCulloch (or 'Super Mac' as some fans dubbed him), for when he was not on target, the Bluebirds invariably struggled.

David Goldstone took over as Chairman, from Fred Dewey, after only a short spell at the Club, and he sanctioned a move on the 23rd of February, for the Aston Villa winger Willie Anderson. A new Club record fee of £60,000 was agreed, for the player that Scoular had tried to sign a year earlier. Unfortunately Anderson's debut was made in a bad 0-3 defeat at Swindon, one of City's 'bogey' grounds. In a sixteen match spell, the City failed to score in ten of the games. Ironically, on the 31st of March at Fulham, McCulloch netted after only 18 seconds, one of the fastest of goals in the Club's history; he was later sent off in the final 1-1 draw.

The visit of Huddersfield Town, on the 21st of April, produced a relegation dogfight, in which the Bluebirds gave one of their best performances of the season. After persistent injury problems, Roger Hoy - a forgotten man at Ninian Park - took over from the indisposed Johnny Vincent, and battled gamely in midfield. Willie Anderson terrorised a poor Huddersfield defence, whilst both McCulloch and Reece profited up front. They scored two goals apiece in a sparkling 4-1 victory, and Andy's second goal, scored after a long surging run had taken him past a number of tackles, was one of the finest seen at Ninian Park for a long time.

McCulloch's late equaliser in the 1-1 draw at Millwall, resulted in the City requiring at least one point from their home match against Sunderland, to avoid relegation. This game was played only two days after the Rokerites had beaten Leeds United by 1-0 in an emotional F.A.Cup Final. The pace of the game was never greater than 'friendly' proportions, as the Sunderland men – who had been applauded onto the pitch by the City players and the 22,005 crowd – played with the celebration champagne still coursing through their veins! Woodruff put the Bluebirds ahead, Vic Halom equalised, and a rare meeting of the F.A.Cup and Welsh Cup holders ended 1-1, and the City staved off relegation by finishing 20th in the Second Division.

Leighton Phillips was ever present, and Gary Bell missed just one match. Other regulars included Bill Irwin, Don Murray and Bobby Woodruff, of the 30 players that Scoular had used during the season. Andy McCulloch scored fourteen goals in twenty-six games, and Woodruff netted on eight occasions, but the total of only 43 was the lowest in the League for the City since 1929.

F.A.Cup:

The third round draw produced a tricky tie at Fourth Division Scunthorpe United. In an atmosphere that was bristling with Cup fever, Billy Kellock shot the City into a 13th minute lead, which they held until half-time. Scunthorpe came roaring back after the interval, and Duncan Welbourne equalised on the hour, only for McCulloch to restore the City's lead five minutes later. With fifteen minutes remaining, Scunthorpe left-winger Harry Kirk had the 6,379 crowd at the Old Showground shrieking with delight, as a net busting drive left Bill Irwin helpless. It looked like a Ninian Park replay, until Phillips smote a dramatic winner, with a fierce drive, just 90 seconds from the end.

The fourth round sent the Bluebirds to Bolton, where they had not lost in four visits since 1967. In front of 25,000, the home team certainly had the City tottering for long periods, and finally four minutes before half-time, Gary Jones put the Third Division side ahead. The match continued in pulsating fashion, and with ten minutes remaining Kellock blasted home the equaliser. The contest reached boiling point just five minutes from time, when Reece and Bolton's Warwick Rimmer were dismissed for fighting. Within seconds John Ritson put the Wanderers back in front, but with the excited crowd urging the referee to blow the final whistle, Phillips silenced Burnden Park with an unstoppable shot, deep in injury time, to force a replay.

The replay, four days later, was another fine match. McCulloch gave the City a 28th minute lead, and Bolton struck back in the second half, to equalise through Gary Jones. Extra time was goalless, so the team met at The Hawthorns on the 12th of February, for another match.

This game was played in a snowstorm, and braved by only 6,609 fans, many of whom had come from Bolton.

It was the Lancastrians who went home with smiling faces, for Stuart Lee scored the winner for the Wanderers in the 37th minute.

Welsh Cup:

Cardiff City travelled to Aberystwyth in the fifth round and won comfortably 7-1, before a 3,500 crowd at Park Avenue. The Bluebirds faced a vastly improved Newport County (since Brian Harris had joined them as player-manager) in the sixth round, at Somerton Park. The City cast aside their poor League form, by racing into a 3-0 interval lead, with goals from Vincent, Phillips and Showers. Wynne Hooper replied for the County in the second half, but the City held on to their 3-1 lead, before a crowd of 11,350.

The semi-final was at Sealand Road, where the City managed to overcome Chester with a solitary McCulloch goal, and so reached the two-legged Final that was to be played against Bangor City.

The City gave a shambolic display in the Farrar Road first leg match, and a 70th minute Marsden goal gave Bangor a 1-0 advantage to take to Ninian Park. With the competition ruling that goal aggregate – instead of points – for overall victory now in force, City had to score twice to win the tie. In the event they netted five without reply, to regain the Welsh Cup on a 5-1 aggregate score. Reece notched a hat-trick, with Phillips and Bell completing the scoring.

Football League Cup:

Cardiff City met Bristol Rovers at Ninian Park in the first round. This produced a match that was full of excitement and drama, and was thoroughly enjoyed by a 14,450 crowd. Wayne Jones put Rovers ahead before half-time, and City struck back with two goals in ten minutes, from Showers and a Bell penalty. The Rovers finished strongly, and with three minutes remaining, Welshman Brian Godfrey equalised with a dramatic long range shot.

The replay at Eastville was a stormy affair. Brian Clark gave the Bluebirds an early lead, which Godfrey cancelled out in the 18th minute. The match turned sour on the City in the second half, as Murray was sent off, followed by Bannister and Jones goals for the Rovers in the final 13 minutes. Much to the delight of the 14,559 crowd the Rovers had won by 3-1.

Gil Reece was the only player to be capped by Wales during the 1972-73 season.

1973-74 Season - Division 2:

The new Grandstand was completed during the Summer, and it was unveiled to the public at a pre-season friendly match against Birmingham City. A magnificent structure costing £225,000, it contained 3,300 seats, and stretched the whole length of the ground, thereby cover was provided on all four sides of Ninian Park.

Reserve players Nigel Rees, Ken Jones, Jim Hobby and Alan Couch moved on to non-League clubs. Billy Kellock was sold to Norwich City for £20,000, and long-serving David Carver made his loan move to Hereford United a permanent one. Carver, well liked by the City fans and respected by his fellow professionals, had made over 250 appearances for the Bluebirds. George Smith, a powerful wing-half in the Scoular mould - who had seen service with Barrow, Portsmouth and Middlesbrough - was signed from Birmingham City for £45,000, and local boys Peter Sayer and Brian Attley were given full professional contracts.

Cardiff began the season in fine fettle, with three consecutive 1-1 draws, before a McCulloch hat-trick on the 12th of September demolished Oxford United in a 5-0 win at Ninian Park. The Bluebirds featured in a pulsating 3-3 draw at Selhurst Park a week later against a much publicised Crystal Palace team. Recovering from a 0-2 deficit (conceded after only 11 minutes), the City were level by half-time, through a Mel Blythe 'own goal', and Woodruff's 45th minute equaliser. Don Rogers put the Palace back in front after 72 minutes, but Vincent equalised within a minute, and earned the City a point.

Suddenly, from fifth place in the League, the City's form deserted them, and they plunged down the table. In an extraordinary match against Hull City, at Ninian Park, Ken Wagstaff - so often a scourge of the Bluebirds - put the Tigers into a sixth minute lead. Both teams were reduced to ten men, after Jim McGill of Hull and City skipper Murray were sent off. To complete an unbelievable first-half, the City were awarded a penalty, and Gary Bell's shot was initially saved by Jeff Wealands. The ball looped back off the 'keeper, and Bell - following up his spot-kick - headed the rebound into the net, and thereby became only the sixth player in League history to be credited with a headed penalty! Cardiff were stunned in the second-half, as Malcolm Lord scored twice, to give Hull a 3-1 win.

The next week at Villa Park, Woodruff gave the home side a great start with a sixth minute headed 'own goal', from all of 40 yards! Villa romped on to a 5-0 victory. Reece's goal gave the City a single goal victory over Blackpool on the 13th of October, but the Bluebirds were floundering as Scoular rang the changes in an attempt to restore the confidence of the team. A last minute goal scored by Ken Knighton gave Sheffield Wednesday a 1-0 win at Ninian Park, and a fortnight later, with on-loan Peter Grotier in goal, the City crashed 0-1 to West Bromwich Albion, after a Tony Brown late winning goal.

That weekend saw the end of Jimmy Scoular's nine years tenancy of the manager's chair at Cardiff City. He was dismissed by chairman David Goldstone on the 9th of November. Trainer Lew Clayton took over in a caretaker capacity for just one match, a 0-2 defeat at Millwall. Watching that game from the anonymity of the crowd, was the former Leicester City and Manchester United manager, Frank O'Farrell. Four days after Scoular's sacking, the Irishman was appointed as the new manager of Cardiff City F.C., and he immediately brought in Jimmy Andrews as the first team coach. Andrews had been a playing colleague of O'Farrell at West Ham in the late 1950's, and in the London area had built up a good reputation as a coach, following his appointments with Q.P.R. and 'Spurs.

O'Farrell watched a makeshift team lose by 0-3 at Middlesbrough and acted swiftly by engaging Willie Carlin, a vastly experienced midfield player, on loan from Notts County. He then paid a new Club record fee of £62,000, for Leicester City's highly rated winger John Farrington. Both newcomers featured in a 1-0 home win over Bolton Wanderers, and the following week - on the 1st of December - City at long last won on their travels, with a 2-1 victory at Orient. Woodruff and McCulloch were the scorers in the Bluebirds first League win on 'foreign' soil since a 2-1 success at Preston on the 2nd of October 1971; a lapse of over two years! That same week manager Frank O'Farrell negotiated Willie Carlin's loan spell to run to the end of the season, by which time the diminutive midfield man was intending to retire.

The Bluebirds had a good Christmas, drawing 1-1 at Hull, and beating both Swindon Town (2-1) and Sunderland (4-1) at Ninian Park. The Sunderland match was a classic, as the City recovered from Halom's third minute goal, to thrash the F.A. Cup holders. A flashing hat-trick from John Farrington - making it 5 goals in 3 games for the City's record signing - and a 30 yard 'wonder' goal from Willie Anderson, ensured the comfortable victory.

Powell, McCulloch and Dwyer show their delight. Out-of-picture Farrington scores the first goal in the Sunderland victory.

Former chairman Fred Dewey, and his son Vivian, resigned from the Board of Directors at the end of the year, and Lewis Walters – the Club solicitor – was elected to serve on a reconstructed Board, which had David Goldsmith as Chairman, and George Edwards as a director. At the annual general meeting, Mr. Goldstone aired his fears for the Club, in the light of the lack of success, and falling attendances.

On the field, the City were pulling themselves into a mid-table position, with McCulloch's goal earning them a 1-0 win at Fulham, followed by a 2-2 home draw with Carlisle, and a single goal victory against Notts County. The latter win was achieved in monsoon conditions, with a last gasp goal from Leighton Phillips, who celebrated by flashing two-fingered salutes at the crowd who had been barracking him!

The Bluebirds lapsed back into their bad old ways when they lost to a 66th second goal at Ninian Park, scored by Ray Graydon of Aston Villa. Although they beat Preston 2-0, with Phil Dwyer scoring his first goal for the Club in 81 consecutive matches, the City received a 0-5 drubbing at Sheffield Wednesday, and an alarming 1-3 home defeat to Millwall.

O'Farrell decided urgent action was needed, and before the transfer deadline, he brought in goalkeeper Ron Healey of Manchester City, and West Ham defender Clive Charles – both players on loan, but with a view to a permanent move. The new boys had a torrid debut at West Bromwich, as the Albion – through a Don Murray 'own goal' and David Shaw – raced into a 2-0 lead after only seven minutes. The City staged a tremendous second-half recovery, and on the hour, Johnny Vincent reduced the arrears. With five minutes remaining Cardiff were awarded a penalty, but Reece's shot was saved. However, the referee had spotted an infringement. Vincent stepped forward and rifled home the retaken spot-kick, and earned the visitors a point.

The Bluebirds kept themselves 'alive', with a fine 1-1 draw at Bolton, and a magnificent 3-2 home win over runaway League leaders Middlesbrough. The goals in the home game came from Reece, Carlin (a brave diving header amongst flying boots), plus a thrilling solo run and exquisite finish from a rejuvenated Vincent.

In a shock statement from the Club, it was revealed that Frank O'Farrell was leaving Cardiff City after only 158 days in office, in order to take up an appointment in the Middle East! Jimmy Andrews took over as acting-manager, as the Bluebirds tottered on the brink of relegation.

City drew 1-1 at Notts County, but lost by 1-2 at Nottingham Forest four days later, when – in the latter game – they had no answer to an absolutely superb virtuoso performance by Forest's brilliant forward Duncan McKenzie. The Bluebirds ended the season with two home games, drawing the first with promotion-hunting Orient by 1-1 (this result made it virtually impossible for the Londoners to be promoted to the First Division). This left the City needing at least a point from their final match on the 30th of April, against fellow-strugglers Crystal Palace. The Palace had to win in order to avoid their own relegation!

In an electric atmosphere at Ninian Park, the crowd of 26,781 were treated to a nerve jangling ninety minutes. Stewart Jump put Palace ahead in a goalmouth scramble after 28 minutes, and as the City stood with one foot in the Third Division, the enigmatic Tony Villars linked superbly with Gil Reece, to score with a superb low drive ten minutes later. There was no further scoring, and amid great scenes of joy, the City had hung on to their Second Division status by a whisker.

The Bluebirds final League placing was 17th, but relegation had been only a point away. In an unsettled season which had seen the City playing under four managers, only Phil Dwyer was ever-present. Other regulars were Leighton Phillips and Don Murray. Andy McCulloch – dropped before the end of the season – was the top scorer with ten goals, whilst Gil Reece collected seven. Willie Carlin, as promised, retired, and entered a supermarket business near Derby.

On the 1st of May 1974, Jimmy Andrews, who had been temporarily in charge, was appointed the new manager of Cardiff City F.C.

F.A.Cup:
Cardiff City crashed out at the first hurdle, when they ran into the potent scoring power of First Division Birmingham City at St. Andrews.

Trevor Francis fired the Blues into a third minute lead, and before half-time Bob Latchford had made it 2-0. Two goals in a minute from Impey and McCulloch on the hour, dragged the City back to 2-2, but Latchford restored Birmingham's lead. Two late goals from Bob Hatton produced a final scoreline of 2-5. It had been a game of many chances, in which Cardiff had played their full part, and they were unlucky that the margin of defeat was so wide.

Welsh Cup:
The visit of Welsh League side Ton Pentre to Ninian Park for a 5th round tie produced the lowest recorded attendance – 856 – for a competitive first team match. The midweek afternoon kick-off did not help, which had been brought about by the Power workers dispute and a ban on floodlit games. The City struggled for victory, and at the end only John Impey's 26th minute goal separated the sides. The City travelled to Oswestry for the sixth round tie, and had little difficulty in running up a 3-0 lead, through Reece and Farrington's brace of goals. In the last minute Oswestry were awarded a penalty that drew such protestations from goalkeeper Irwin, that the normally placid Irishman was sent off.

This dismissal gave Irwin the dubious distinction of becoming the first City custodian to be given his marching orders. Oswestry scored, and the City won by 3-1.

The semi-final was at Shrewsbury, with another afternoon kick-off. After an interesting match, the City once again reached the Welsh Cup Final - with goals from Showers and Murray - before ex-City man Alan Durban replied for the Town.

The two-legged Final saw Cardiff as the clear favourites for the matches against Southern League side Stourbridge. But the Bluebirds had to battle all the way to win by 1-0 at The Memorial Ground, with the goal scored by Showers. They fared no better in the second leg at Ninian Park, as Reece scored the only goal in an unsatisfactory game, and so Cardiff City retained the trophy with a 2-0 aggregate score.

Football League Cup:

Cardiff City entertained Hereford United in the 1st round, and they were in good form as McCulloch scored both goals in a 2-0 win. First Division Burnley were the attractive visitors in the next round, and the game turned out to be an excellent encounter. Welshman Leighton James fired Burnley into a first-half lead, but City surged back, and McCulloch headed in a 57th minute equaliser. Eight minutes later James raced through to net Burnley's second goal, but the Bluebirds refused to capitulate. In the last minute, Vincent levelled the scores with a rocket-like drive from 25 yards, which flew into the top corner of the net.

The replay at Turf Moor was equally exciting, and after a goalless first-half, Ray Hankin put Burnley in front in the 69th minute, only for Woodruff to equalise five minutes later. With substitute Dave Powell replacing the injured Johnny Vincent, the match went into extra-time. In the 94th minute, James fired Burnley ahead, from the penalty spot, but three minutes later Cardiff were also awarded a 'spot-kick'. Gary Bell converted, to make the scoreline 2-2. In a ding-dong finish, James settled it Burnley's way with nine minutes left to play, when his intended cross drifted into the City net.

European Cup-Winners Cup:

Portuguese Cup-holders Sporting Lisbon were entertained in the first round, a team that Cardiff had beaten back in 1964. In a spoiling first leg match at Ninian Park, the City were thwarted time and time again by Sporting's giant goalkeeper Damas, and had to eventually settle for a scoreless draw. The second leg, in Lisbon, was always going to be difficult, and after only 14 minutes Yazalde put the home side into the lead. Five minutes before half-time, Villars equalised, but the Bluebirds were finally knocked out, when Fraguito scored Lisbon's winner five minutes after the interval.

Don Murray (right) and Vitor Damas shake hands at the beginning of the European Cup-winners Cup match versus Sporting Club of Portugal.

1974-75 Season - Division 2:

Even before a ball was kicked many Cardiff City supporters feared the worst for the Club. For it was revealed that the Chairman, David Goldstone, had refused to release any money for new manager (Jimmy Andrews) to strengthen the team.

Major departures from Ninian Park, were leading goalscorer Andy McCulloch who joined Oxford United for £73,000, a record fee for the Headington Club, and thus realising a profit for the City of £28,000. Veteran Bobby Woodruff made the short trip to Newport County on a free transfer, after being virtually a Bluebirds regular over five years, during which time he had made almost 200 Cardiff appearances.

Another free transfer departure was the reliable full-back Gary Bell, who also joined Newport County, after spending the closing weeks of the previous season on loan to Hereford United. In eight years at Ninian Park, Bell had amassed over 250 appearances for the Club.

On the 31st of July, City played Arsenal at Ninian Park in a pre-season friendly match, for the 'Fred Keenor' Cup. The game attracted over 10,000 fans, and the result went Arsenal's way with a 2-1 scoreline. Jack Whitham scored the lone Cardiff goal.

The season commenced with a home game against Oxford United, therefore providing a quick return for 'old boy' McCulloch. Clive Charles became the first black player to captain Cardiff City, and he scored the equaliser in a

1-1 draw. A shocking run of results, in which the team gained only three points from ten games (including four consecutive defeats at home), dumped the team down at the bottom of the table.

At York City, where the Bluebirds lost by 0-1, the Club physiotherapist – Ron Durham – was apprehended by the Law, for throwing a bucket of water into the crowd, after the Cardiff bench had received prolonged vocal abuse! He was subsequently fined by the York magistrates, and the normally mild-mannered Mr. Durham later left football, to concentrate on his profession in his own Practise.

Leighton Phillips who had continually expressed his desire for a transfer over a period of several seasons, finally got his wish, when the City accepted Aston Villa's offer of £80,000 for the talented utility player. Phillips had been a product of City's youth team, and had scored with his first kick when, on his initial first team appearance in 1966, he came on as a substitute. He played for a number of years in a midfield position, before settling into a defensive role, and received Under-21, Under-23 and full International Caps for Wales. During his Cardiff playing career, he made over 200 appearances for the City.

Manager Jimmy Andrews was not allowed any of the money received from the McCulloch or Phillips fees to invest in new players, and in order to bring in necessary new faces, he exchanged the City record signing John Farrington, for Northampton's midfielder John Buchanan. In addition he obtained the Chelsea reserve striker, Steve Finnieston, on loan. Departing Ninian Park at this time was long serving centre-half Don Murray, who joined Swansea City for a month's loan. It was a quiet and permanent exit for a great clubman, who had given his all in the Cardiff City cause.

Both Buchanan and Finnieston made their Cardiff debuts in an amazing midweek match at Ninian Park against York City. Early in the game, Dave Powell had to retire with a leg injury, and Johnny Vincent – who had been guilty of an outrageous miss in front of an open goal in the previous match against West Bromwich Albion – came on as substitute. Within minutes of his entry onto the field, Vincent received a short pass from a Buchanan free kick, and blasted a low left-footed shot into the far corner of the net.

York had a 'goal' disallowed and also hit a post, before Ian Holmes scored the equaliser from the penalty spot. A second penalty was awarded to York before half-time, and the man on target was Holmes once again, this time after having to retake the spot kick. The unhappy home crowd reacted in an unfortunate manner, when they abused the referee as he left the pitch at half-time, and threw tea over him! The City restarted the match at full throttle, and after going close with a number of good efforts, they equalised on the hour, when Crawford could only parry Finnieston's shot, and Reece made no mistake with the chance. The game see-sawed each way until the City received a penalty 15 minutes from time, following a foul on Reece. Although the kick had to be taken twice, Vincent remained cool, and shot home the winner.

The City form showed much improvement, and after losing 1-2 at Bolton on the 19th of October, they had a run of twelve games in which they suffered just one defeat. During this period they had notable home victories over Oldham (when Vincent, after scoring an early goal, suffered a broken leg), Sunderland, Aston Villa and Norwich City. The bubble finally burst following Finnieston's return to Chelsea, and in their 1,000th League match, on the 25th of January, the City crashed 1-5 at Millwall. From then, until the end of the season, it was one disappointment after another. In seventeen matches they won only twice (2-0 at Notts County and 1-0 at home to Portsmouth), on their route down to the Third Division.

In a scoreless draw against fellow relegation strugglers Sheffield Wednesday, Johnny Vincent missed a penalty, and when George Smith was substituted he angrily hurled his shirt at the City bench, thereby emphasising the unrest and frustration that was felt by the players, as relegation loomed. The exciting prospect, Peter Sayer, received a broken leg at Southampton, and young Irishman John McClelland made a fleeting goalscoring appearance in a 2-2 home draw with Bristol Rovers. McClelland would emerge, years later, as a World Cup centre-half for Northern Ireland!

Andrews had faced the impossible task of trying to win games with little, or no, striking power, and had been forced to give a number of reserve and young players a 'blooding'. Such measures did nothing to stem the flow of defeats.

Scottish full-back Freddie Pethard missed just one game, and Phil Dwyer, Willie Anderson, Bill Irwin plus Derek Showers all appeared regularly. Richie Morgan replaced Don Murray, after the latter had gone on loan to Swansea City during the season before returning to his native Scotland and joining the Heart of Midlothian Club. Murray had been a magnificent clubman, and one of the greatest defenders in the City's history. Including all cup matches he made 529 appearances for the Bluebirds, including 406 League games.

Cardiff scored only 36 League goals during the season, their worst ever tally. Reece scored nine and Showers five, as the Club's returned to the Third, a Division in which they last appeared in 1947.

F.A. Cup:

A trip to Elland road for an F.A.Cup-tie was no new experience for Cardiff City, the fifth such game since the War! On this occasion they had little to offer against the might of the First Division giants, who swept smoothly to an unassailable 4-0 half-time lead, with goals from Eddie Gray, Allan Clarke (two) and Duncan McKenzie. The City plugged away in the second-half, and in the last minute Showers grabbed a consolation goal.

Welsh Cup:
The City began their defence of the trophy, at Ninian Park, against Hereford United. The Bluebirds won with second half goals from Reece and Showers. In the 6th round they were drawn at home to Oswestry, and young David Giles celebrated his first call-up to the senior team, with a goal after 39 minutes. Second-half goals from Buchanan (two) and Showers saw the Bluebirds comfortably through the tie, with a final 4-0 score.

In the semi-final, the City visited Newport County, and had a torrid match with their Fourth Division neighbours. Dwyer, playing as an emergency centre-forward, headed the only goal of the game, from Vincent's 53rd minute free kick, after former Bluebird Gary Bell had tripped Willie Anderson.

Cardiff met Wrexham in the two-legged Final, and in the first game, at The Racecourse, Buchanan fired City into a 4th minute lead. John Lyons equalised 14 minutes later, and after a further 9 minutes Brian Tinnion scored for Wrexham, to give the North Walians a 2-1 lead, which they held until the end of the match. At Ninian Park a week later, the City received a dreadful shock, when, after 10 minutes, a catalogue of mishaps presented Wrexham with a vital goal. Villars lost the ball to ex-City man Mel Sutton, who proceeded to set up an attack that ended with Ashcroft shooting against the post. The ball rebounded, and City goalkeeper Bill Irwin - in a terrible tangle - somehow contrived to put it over his own goal line!

Cardiff's performance was no better than mediocre, and only improved a little when Reece replaced the raw novice, John McClelland. Fifteen minutes before the final whistle, the City produced a surprise equaliser, when Albert Larmour emerged from a goalmouth melee, to shoot into the net. Wrexham recovered their poise, and with Mel Sutton in determined mood, they scored twice in the final three minutes to win 3-1, and 5-2 on aggregate. It was Cardiff's first Welsh Cup home defeat, for nine years.

Football League Cup:
The City made an early exit when they lost by 1-2 at Ashton Gate, to Bristol City. Jimmy McInch scored his only first team goal for the Bluebirds, 12 minutes from time.

European Cup-Winners Cup:
Cardiff City faced formidable first round opponents - the crack Hungarian team Ferencvaros. In the first leg, in Budapest, they went down to a goal in each half, scored by Nyilasi and Szabo. The second leg, at Ninian Park, was simply academic, and the brilliant Hungarians gave the Cardiff team a footballing lesson with a scintillating display of one-touch football. The first half was goalless, but when Ferencvaros stepped up a gear in the second period, Takecs, Szabo and Pusztai scored three goals in a ten minute spell. Dwyer managed a consolation goal, but in the final minute, Mate scored the Hungarians' fourth, to complete a 4-1 victory (6-1 on aggregate). This was the worst European competition defeat that had been inflicted on Cardiff.

During the 1974-75 season, Gil Reece and Derek Showers were capped by Wales.

••••••••••••••••••••••••••••••••••

1975-76 Season – Division 3

During the summer, Cardiff City chairman David Goldstone sold his holdings in the club to a consortium of businessmen moulded together by local man Clive Griffiths. Local politician and hotelier Stefan Terleski was elected Club Chairman, and the directorate consisted of Tony Clemo, Eddie Jones, Hyman `Tiny' Latner, North-eastern businessman Bob Grogan, and Jack Leonard of the Kenton Utilities Group. Also involved was entertainer Stan Stennett, a lifelong City supporter and friend of former Bluebird Trevor Ford.

Manager Jimmy Andrews and his assistant Ken Whitfield cleared the decks at Ninian Park in the close season. Of the relegated playing staff George Smith joined Swansea City, John Impey moved to AFC Bournemouth, Johnny Vincent, Jimmy McInch and Jack Whitham all joined non-League clubs, and Dave Powell enlisted in the Police Force at Bridgend. Andrews re-engaged former City favourite Brian Clark on a free transfer from Millwall, and little known Blackpool forward Tony Evans was obtained on a free transfer, following a recommendation by City`s Northern scout Fred Whittle. Goalkeeper Len Bond and winger Joe Durrell, both of Bristol City, joined the club on loan agreements. In an effort to introduce some `Star' quality to the side the City manager persuaded former Welsh international and Tottenham Hotspur centre-half Mike England to join the Bluebirds, after the London club had granted the big pivot a free transfer in recognition of his past services.

England missed the City's opening League game at Grimsby, where the home side wasted little time in demonstrating what Cardiff could expect in the Third Division! The Bluebirds played pretty football, but Grimsby were always the more direct, and consigned City to a 2-0 defeat. In midweek Mike England played his first game in the League Cup tie, and Andrews, realising that City's midfield needed a solid anchor man, was allowed to purchase Doug Livermore from Norwich City for £18,000. Both England and Livermore made their home League debuts for the City against Bury, before a 6,664 crowd, on a dim and drizzly afternoon. Tony Villars illuminated the gloom with a magnificent solo goal, but the Bury hit back to draw 1-1.

Villars was again on the mark in City's 1-0 win at Brighton a week later, where summer signing Tony Evans made his full debut.

The Bluebirds had no luck in their home match against Crystal Palace, as Mike England hobbled off after 25 minutes and both goalkeeper Ron Healey and Tony Villars struggled after collecting injuries. The final blow came in the last minute when Palace pinched the points with a goal from David Kemp. A reshuffled side had a great win at Mansfield, where David Giles, Phil Dwyer and Gil Reece (two) - all Cardiff born - shared the goals. But the following week, the team stuttered at home against Halifax and it took a penalty save by Ron Healey from Ray McHale to ensure a 0-0 draw.

Defeats at Port Vale and Preston deflated the Bluebirds, but the return of Willie Anderson, after a brief dispute with the club following his summer in America, and the switching of Tony Evans to centre-forward (shades of Wilf Grant in the early 1950's), inspired City to a 3-0 home win in their first League meeting with Wrexham, on the 4th of October. Phil Dwyer, in great form, scored twice but missed a last minute penalty which would have given him the only hat-trick of his career.

For all their constructive and enjoyable football, the City were still lacking a cutting edge as the reliable Brian Clark had lost his old - goal - touch. Eventually, in late October, Mr Andrews was allowed to sign former Australian World Cup striker, Adrian Alston, from Luton Town for £20,000. He made a sensational start to his City career in his home debut against Chesterfield, scoring two brilliant goals in the opening 23 minutes, and laid on City's third for Tony Evans on the half hour. Chesterfield hit back with two goals, before Willie Anderson netted City's fourth with a blistering shot following a sweeping move. Although Chesterfield scored near the end, the City triumphed 4-3, and Alston's arrival had the fans buzzing.

Physiotherapist Ron Durham made the headlines at Gillingham where his prompt intervention prevented Phil Dwyer from choking, after swallowing his tongue, following a collision during City's 2-2 draw. True to form the abrasive Dwyer was back in action the following week. Four consecutive wins elevated the Bluebirds to a top six placing, as Tony Evans and Adrian Alston began to build up to a remarkable partnership. It all turned sour on Boxing Day, when City crashed 0-4 at Swindon, but the following day the Bluebirds - watched by a 16,094 crowd - overcame an early conceded goal, to swamp Peterborough United 5-2, in one of the finest displays of all round attacking football seen at Ninian Park for a very long time.

Almost 18,000 were at Ninian Park when City played promotion hopefuls Brighton, and Adrian Alston gave the `Match of the Day' cameras a marvellous moment, when directly from the kick-off, he spotted `keeper Grummitt out of position and put in a shot from the centre-circle that drifted just wide, which had the crowd gasping. City's big day - Jimmy Andrews received the Divisional `Manager of the month' award - was spoiled when Ian Mellor's 76th minute goal won the match for Brighton. The City had two patchy home wins before coming a real cropper on February the 4th, at runaway leaders Hereford. In freezing conditions, at a packed Edgar Street, the United swamped the Bluebirds by 4-1, with all their goals coming from set pieces.

Andrews dropped Irwin and England for the trip to Walsall three days after the Hereford debacle, and at half-time at Fellows Park, City found themselves 0-2 down and facing another hiding. But, in a thrilling second-half recovery, Alston scored twice and Dwyer headed in a John Buchanan corner, to complete an unexpected victory. A 4-1 home romp against Gillingham, watched approvingly by former favourite John Toshack, kept City on the promotion trail, but the Bluebirds then began to drop points both at home and away. It seemed as if the promotion dream was fading, but in their final nine games the City, boosted by the £20,000 arrival of Birmingham City midfielder Alan Campbell, returned to their best form and conceded just one goal in some remarkable performances. A magnificent win at Crystal Palace, was described in a Croydon newspaper as " A 1-0 massacre", and four days later City fans enjoyed one of the great nights at Ninian Park with the visit of leaders Hereford United, the champions elect.

The Crystal Palace manager, Malcolm Allison, had been quoted as saying that Cardiff were incapable of attracting over 20,000 fans, but in the event a mammoth crowd of 35,549 packed Ninian Park for the titanic struggle. It was obvious that it would take something special to break the deadlock and so it proved, after 54 minutes. Ron Healey threw the ball out to Freddie Pethard, and the full-back played the ball down the left touchline for Tony Evans to clear. The centre-forward put over a chest high cross, and Doug Livermore, who had run 50 yards through the middle, dived full length to send a stunning header past the rooted Kevin Charlton. The City never allowed Hereford any latitude and two minutes from time the influential Livermore declined a shooting chance, to slip a neat pass for Alan Campbell to sidestep Charlton and score from only two yards.

A great night ended with City virtually assured of promotion and, following scoreless draws with Swindon and Peterborough, they made absolutely sure with a 1-0 win at Bury. Immediately after this match, centre-half Mike England departed for America, stating that Cardiff City had not kept their promise regarding a proposed coaching post - which the Club later refuted.

In a fine season Dwyer and Livermore missed just one match; other regulars included Evans, England, Larmour and Charles. Evans led the scorers with 21 goals, Adrian Alston got 14, and Phil Dwyer, who had played in a variety of roles, netted 8 times.

F.A. Cup:

Cardiff City's first appearance in the first round of the F.A. Cup for 29 years saw them entertain Fourth Division Exeter City. The visitors began well and took an 8th minute lead through Alan Beer, which Gil Reece equalised eight minutes later. By half-time the City had shown their superiority and two headers from Adrian Alston put them 3-1 up. Robertson pulled one back in the 62nd minute, but a minute later Alston completed a headed hat-trick, and within two minutes Tony Evans raced clear to make it 5-2. Gil Reece scored the City's sixth in the 88th minute, and this 6-2 victory was their highest in the competition since the Bluebirds had their record 8-0 win over Enfield in 1931. Alston's hat-trick was the first by a City player in an F.A. Cup tie since Reg Keating's treble in that Enfield match.

The second round brought non-League Wycombe Wanderers to Ninian Park and the Bluebirds had an almighty job in beating them. The vital breakthrough came just before half-time when the livewire Tony Evans had a header blocked, which he followed up to net from close range. It was the game's only goal and Cardiff were mightily relieved to see the backs of the gallant amateurs.

The Bluebirds travelled to Orient on the 3rd of January to meet the Second Division outfit in the third round, with Richie Morgan and Tony Villars deputising for the injured Mike England and John Buchanan. The City played neat inventive football, and it came as no surprise when they took a 35th minute lead, after Alston and Reece had combined sweetly for the former to net with a crisp half volley. The second-half was mainly a rearguard action with goalkeeper Bill Irwin inspiring confidence, and the Londoners could find no way through, as the visitors held on to win by the only goal.

Disappointingly, the fourth round draw sent the Bluebirds to Southend, on January the 24th, but the match turned out to be a thriller with a nasty sting in its tail. City were well on top when Tony Evans put them ahead after 43 minutes, but on the stroke of half-time, Southend replied through Stuart Parker.

The second period was a real battle and looked destined for a replay, until Parker popped up in injury time to score a controversial goal which had the City players questioning the referee as to its legality. The official stood firm and City lost 1-2.

Welsh Cup:

Cardiff City cantered through the fifth round with a 5-0 home win over Welsh League Sully, managed by former Bluebird Alan Harrington.

City met struggling Swansea City in the sixth round and looked on course when Dave Bruton put through his own goal. The Swans, rebuilding in the Fourth Division, hit back and Bruton made amends for his earlier lapse to score a 57th minute equaliser, and hence force a replay, at the Vetch Field on the 2nd of March.

The second match found the City in a determined mood and they swept aside Swansea's challenge with a sound performance, before a crowd of 10,056.

A journey to Chester for the semi-final was made, where a dull and uninspiring match ended 0-0. The replay on the 1st of April was little better, and it took a fortuitous own goal from Chester defender Chris Dunleavy to give City a 1-0 win.

The Bluebirds faced Hereford United in the two-legged Final, and on the 29th of April the teams played out a 2-2 draw at Ninian Park. But the match was declared void when it was learned that Peter Spiring - who scored both the Hereford goals - was ineligible. On May the 18th, the teams met at Edgar Street and played out a thrilling 3-3 draw. Tony Evans put the City ahead in the first-half, and in a rip-roaring second-half, Dwyer scored another goal for the Bluebirds. Hereford struck back with three goals in an eight minute spell to go 3-2 ahead, only for Dwyer to level matters three minutes from the end.

The following day the teams replayed the void match at Ninian Park where only 2,648 were in attendance, in stark contrast to the 35,000 who witnessed the League match only a month earlier. Those present were treated to an exciting match which was played in appalling conditions. Freddie Pethard, with his first senior goal, gave the City a 12th minute lead, which Clark doubled with a fine goal - in his final appearance for the club - after 33 minutes. Lindsay pulled a goal back for the visitors in the second-half, Tony Evans then made it 3-1, and Byrne scored a late consolation. The 3-2 victory, 6-5 on aggregate, meant that City had regained the Welsh Cup and would again play in European competition.

Football League Cup:

Cardiff City met Bristol Rovers in the two-legged first round, and in the initial tie at Ninian Park, Mike England appeared for the first time in the City's colours. With ex-Bluebirds Jim Eadie and Alan Warboys in their ranks, the Rovers were too strong for the home team, and Warboys put them ahead in the 40th minute.
Gil Reece equalised from the penalty spot just before half-time, but three minutes into the second-half Bannister gave the visitors a 2-1 victory.

The second leg at Eastville was a close affair and Brian Clark levelled the aggregate score in the 31st minute. But the Rovers recovered and eleven minutes later Stephens scored to put Cardiff out on a 2-3 aggregate.

Herefordshire Senior Cup:

Cardiff City accepted Hereford United's invitation to play in this long established event but the match turned out to be a rather tepid affair with Hereford winning 2-0.

****

1976-7 Season – Division 2:

Following Mike England's surprise departure to America, Jimmy Andrews announced that there would be little change to his playing staff during the summer. Two former Welsh internationals, Gil Reece and Tony Villars, departed Ninian Park. Reece joined Swansea City on a part-time basis and Newport County paid a small fee for Villars. One arrival at Ninian Park was Leicester's reserve forward Peter Jackson on a free transfer. It was felt that the club had wasted a great opportunity to strengthen a few positions in the City team which would have made them a force to be reckoned with. Former West Ham winger Alan Sealey, who had scouted for City near the end of the previous term, was appointed a full-time member of the coaching staff.

City opened their League programme on a bright sunny afternoon at Charlton, where young centre-half Keith Pontin made his League debut. They gave an impressive display in winning 2-0 with two goals from Showers, whose goal ratio unfortunately never matched his prodigious work rate. The Bluebirds slumped to a 1-2 home defeat by Bristol Rovers on the 25th of August, and it took the introduction of substitute Adrian Alston for City to overcome Blackburn Rovers 2-1 at Ninian Park three days later.

The centre-half position was giving rise for concern and Morgan replaced the inexperienced Pontin, but the City's results remained poor, and it was soon apparent that Andrews would have to take drastic action. At this time Portsmouth were in dire straits financially and were forced to accept Cardiff's offer of £30,000 for their highly-rated pivot Paul Went. The big centre-half had a torrid baptism in City's colours, as he conceded a third minute penalty in the home match with Bolton Wanderers on the 9th of October, which was the first sponsored game at Ninian Park, thanks to Barr Soft Drinks Ltd. Went had an uncomfortable afternoon but his blushes were spared. From 1-2 down the City carried on to win 3-2, with two goals in the final twelve minutes.

Poor Went conceded another penalty at Plymouth the following week, but City recovered twice to draw 2-2. City's form remained inconsistent and Andrews paid Norwich City £7,000 for winger Steve Grapes, while at the same time Adrian Alston, whose form had been disappointing, joined the exodus of British footballers to America by signing for Tampa Bay Rowdies for £20,000.

City were struggling in the lower half of the table, and in an amazing pre-Christmas match at Carlisle they were coasting at 3-1, when home striker Billy Rafferty scored a dramatic hat-trick in the final seven minutes of the game and condemned City to a 3-4 defeat! The Bluebirds beat Hereford 3-1 on Boxing Day in a strange match that could have ended 6-6, such was the wasteful finishing – particularly by the visitors.

Andrews used the money received from Alston's transfer when he purchased Reading's colourful striker Robin Friday for £20,000, and at the other end of the scale, obtained Hengoed born Ray Bishop from Cheltenham Town for £1,000. The shaggy haired Friday immediately captured the hearts of the Cardiff public with a two goal home debut in a 3-0 victory over Fulham. Over 20,000 were at Ninian Park, and their only disappointment could have been the non-appearance of George Best.

Willie Anderson, out of favour with Jimmy Andrews, returned permanently to America with a £20,000 move to Portland Timbers, and before the end of the season, full-back Clive Charles would also go Stateside. Friday, who had a shocking disciplinary record in his days with Reading, did not take long to tot up a series of bookings as City's League form went from good to bad, whereas they enjoyed success and publicity in the F.A. Cup. In the League, after beating Oldham Athletic 3-1, the City won only once – 2-0 at Millwall – in the next seven matches and they slumped into relegation trouble. For defensive stability, Andrews signed Crewe defender Phil Nicholls for £10,000 just before the transfer deadline.

Cardiff beat Hereford United 3-1 on the 27th of December. Tony Evans (who scored twice) is watched by Hereford's John Galley.

Within hours however, the transfer was cancelled when Nicholls' wife categorically refused to move house!

At fellow strugglers Hereford, the City were 0-2 down and had Robin Friday sent off when they staged an unlikely comeback, when Peter Sayer scored twice to finally draw 2-2. Three days later the City were outclassed at Ninian Park by Wolves, and were losing 0-2, when Friday came off the substitutes' bench. He helped the Bluebirds steal a point, with goals from Sayer and Went that were both scored in the closing three minutes. Friday enjoyed a good day when City beat Luton Town 4-2 at home, and in a game reminiscent of 'Rorke's Drift', the Bluebirds pulled off a fantastic 1-0 win at First Division bound Nottingham Forest, with a goal from in-form Peter Sayer. Healey and his defenders repelled all that Forest could throw at them, and it was be the last time for Brian Clough's team to lose at home for almost two years, during which time they would win the League Championship and the European Cup.

A 1-4 defeat at Wolves and a 0-1 home reversal against Burnley put Cardiff back in trouble, eased only by a vital 2-1 win at Hull City. After losing at Bolton, City's final League match was against Carlisle United at Ninian Park, which was of great importance to both clubs, for the Bluebirds needed one point to be safe and condemn the Cumbrians to relegation.

Buchanon beats Wrexham's Lloyd to score the injury time F.A.Cup winner.

It was almost a carbon copy of the situation in 1974 between the City and Crystal Palace. In a tension charged atmosphere, Alan Campbell - after 19 minutes - scored his first League goal for a year, but just sixty seconds later, Les O'Neill equalised for Carlisle with a stunning long shot. That ended the scoring but City were at times hanging on for grim death, and were mightily relieved to hear the final whistle, and hence their safety.

City regulars that season included Livermore, Evans, Dwyer and Larmour. Top scorer was Evans with 14, and both John Buchanan and Peter Sayer getting 9 each.

F.A. Cup:

Cardiff City faced First Division Tottenham Hotspur at Ninian Park in the third round on the 8th of January, and this was the match that shot Peter Sayer to national stardom. 'Match of the Day' cameras perfectly captured Sayer's seventh minute winner, which he blasted past Pat Jennings to give City a famous victory, before 27,868 delirious fans.

Three weeks later City were drawn at home against Wrexham in the fourth round, and this game has gone down as one of the most exciting ever staged at Ninian Park.

Almost 29,000, and millions more on television, saw young David Giles score after 20 minutes. When Sayer put the Bluebirds 2-0 ahead in the 56th minute, many must have thought that the tie was over, but a fine hooked shot from Whittle four minutes later kept the Wrexham hopes alive. City attacked furiously but Lloyd made some outstanding saves, and nobody left the ground early, which was just as well as the game was to have a real sting in the tail. In the last minute Wrexham received a controversial corner and fuzzy haired striker Billy Ashcroft headed home at the near post, which provoked great scenes of celebration among the Wrexham players and their fans.

The North Walians were still congratulating themselves when the City restarted, and Grapes jinked his way to the bye-line, before pulling back a neat pass which John Buchanan calmly sidefooted past Lloyd's despairing dive, for the most dramatic injury-time winner! The scenes as the final whistle sounded almost immediately after this goal were remarkable by any standards, to climax a match that was a credit to Welsh football.

The City were rewarded with a plum fifth round tie when they entertained Everton, which attracted a crowd of 35,582 and was featured on national television.

The Bluebirds made a great start, Tony Evans heading a superb goal following a flowing move after only ten minutes, and City controlled much of the first-half. Everton hit back after the interval, and in the 52nd minute, Latchford headed an equaliser from close range. Midway through the half Everton scored the winning goal when Albert Larmour made a mess of passing back (on a sticky surface) to Ron Healey, and McKenzie took full advantage by nicking the ball and skipping past the City 'keeper to score easily. City were out, but their emerging young players - Sayer, Giles, Attley and Evans - had enjoyed coming under the national microscope.

Welsh Cup

Cardiff City skated through to yet another Welsh Cup Final appearance. Late goals ended Stourbridge's resistance at Ninian Park in the fifth round. And it was second-half goals by Giles and Grapes that saw the Bluebirds win at Bangor in the sixth round. City had a tough fight at Welsh League Bridgend in the semi-final. After the part-timers had equalised Sayer's early goal, the Bluebirds were thankful for Evans' 65th minute winner which took them into the final.

The City were guaranteed a place in Europe, as they faced (England based) Shrewsbury Town in the final. It took a late flourish for the Bluebirds to win the home leg, after Hornsby had given Shrewsbury an eighth minute lead. Four minutes from time the City full-back Freddie Pethard equalised with his second goal in successive finals. In the last minute Robin Friday popped up with the winning goal to give City a 2-1 advantage. The second leg, played just two days later was an absolute nightmare for the Bluebirds. Griffin brought the aggregate scores level within two minutes, and in the second-half the City caved in as a Pontin own goal and a Roberts goal gave Shrewsbury a 3-0 victory – 4-2 on aggregate. This meant that Cardiff City qualified for Europe as losing finalists!

• Ron Healey

• Bill Irwin

Cardiff had two goalkeepers of International quality.
Healey played for Eire, and Irwin had been considered for Northern Ireland.

Football League Cup

The Bluebirds faced old adversaries Bristol Rovers once again in the first round. At Ninian Park, Rovers went ahead with a 10th minute penalty, which was equalised by Evans, on the hour. In the 87th minute Alston confidently struck the winning goal from the penalty spot. In the second leg three days later, Evans made history by becoming the first City player to score four goals in the competition. David Williams put Rovers ahead after 5 minutes, and Evans replied by scoring in the 23rd and 30th minutes, only for Bannister to hit back within two minutes, from the penalty spot. Rovers surged forward after the break, and further goals from Prince and Bannister made it 4-2 (5-4 on aggregate); the City appeared dead and buried. But then Evans took over, completing his hat-trick in the 68th minute, and then going one better with his historic fourth goal nine minutes from time.

The City were rewarded with a home tie against Queen's Park Rangers in the second round, but met their match as the Londoners, inspired by Stan Bowles and Dave Thomas, romped to a 3-1 win, with Tony Evans scoring City's late consolation.

European Cup Winners' Cup

Cardiff City met the Swiss cup holders Servette Geneva in the preliminary round.

The Bluebirds showed signs of distinct rustiness in the first leg at Ninian Park, which they won with an 88th minute goal from Tony Evans. In Geneva, the Welsh team looked to be in control, when Showers increased the aggregate score to 2-0. The Swiss side hit back and second-half goals from Bizzini and Pfister won the match by 2-1, but the City went through on the away goal ruling, as the aggregate stood at 2-2.

Cardiff faced Russian side Dynamo Tbilisi in the first round, and in the first leg at Ninian Park, the Russians displayed much quality but were caught by a late sucker punch, when substitute Alston volleyed a spectacular winner, 15 minutes from time. A reported 100,000 watched the second leg in Tbilisi, and Dynamo took only 22 minutes to draw level on aggregate, through Gutsaev. The Russians superiority came through late in the match when Kipiani and Kanteladze (penalty) made it 3-0, 3-1 on aggregate.

The controversial Robin Friday.

1977-8 Season - Division 2

Jimmy Andrews did little on the transfer front during the close season, recruiting only Manchester City reserve forward Graham O'Shea, on a free transfer. Striker Derek Showers, who had been at Ninian Park for almost ten years, was transferred to A.F.C. Bournemouth for a small fee.

The Safety of Sports Grounds Act came into being and Cardiff City were refused a safety certificate by the local council, until the club had taken relevant action to make the stadium safe for spectators. This meant that Ninian Park's capacity was drastically reduced and the Club could not stage any floodlit matches.

Tony Evans scored all four goals in a 4-1 pre-season home friendly with Swindon, but three days later the Bluebirds had a worrying 1-4 defeat at Reading. Even more worrying for manager Jimmy Andrews was the absence of striker Robin Friday, who was reported to be suffering from a serious illness, which caused him to miss the start of the new season.

Following a lack of striking power in the opening day 1-1 draw with Bristol Rovers at Ninian Park, Andrews paid £25,000 for West Ham's abrasive forward Keith Robson. The new boy lined up alongside another debutant, Ray Bishop, when the City slumped 0-3 at Blackburn. A week later reserve defender Gerry Byrne made his debut in a scoreless home draw with relegated Tottenham Hotspur. The Club's start was disappointing, with only one win in the opening ten League matches, and the much publicised Peter Sayer was sent off at Blackpool, where Bob Hatton scored a hat-trick in a 3-0 win for the Seasiders.

The City defeated Oldham 1-0 at home, and the following week they welcomed back Robin Friday, for the match at Brighton. The wayward striker lasted only an hour before being sent off for kicking Mark Lawrenson, and when the City team reached the dressing rooms – after a 0-4 mauling – Friday had disappeared. This prompted an angry outburst from manager Andrews.

Safety work was still being carried out at Ninian Park, and the crowd capacity was cut further, to only 10,000! The club, on and off the pitch, was in turmoil. In the boardroom, Stefan Terleski was relieved of the chairmanship after some heated exchanges between the directors, and Bob Grogan, whose Kenton Utilities Company was undertaking much of the ground safety work, was elected into the chair.

An injury crisis, which saw the loss of Tony Evans with a leg injury, had Jimmy Andrews switching players about almost weekly, and the squad was weakened further after Chester had signed Doug Livermore for £12,000. In an effort to stabilise his defence, the City manager paid Derby County £10,000 for veteran Welsh international full-back Rod Thomas, and the much-capped defender made his debut in a 2-0 home win over Stoke City, on the 5th of November. A week later the City crashed 1-4 at Hull City, and although they managed to pip Burnley by 2-1 at Ninian Park, they remained firmly entrenched in the relegation dogfight. A humiliating 1-6 defeat by Sheffield United (the worst at home since 1955), was followed by a 3-6 beating at Bolton a week later. In the latter match Robin Friday made his last Cardiff appearance, and was substituted by Ray Bishop. These results had the club lurching from one crisis to another.

Following a poor 0-0 home draw with Hull City, Bluebirds' coach Alan Sealey and striker Keith Robson were involved in a publicised scuffle in the staff car park, which again reflected the poor state of affairs that existed within the Club, although the two men were pictured making up their grievances a few days later.

At the end of the year the City managed to win consecutive home games against Millwall and Charlton – when Talgarth born Chris Williams made his debut. The youngster failed to make his mark and, with Friday now stating his intention of retiriring (!), it was a surprise when Keith Robson was sold to Norwich for £18,000, after only four months at Ninian Park. Andrews had to turn to centre-half Paul Went, and occasionally Phil Dwyer, to bolster an attack that was still missing Evans. Went's switch did the trick for a while, and Cardiff thrashed Sunderland 5-2 at Ninian Park, drew at snowbound Mansfield, and beat Blackpool with a (rare) late goal from Steve Grapes.

In an amazing statement to the Press in February, Jimmy Andrews announced that his entire playing staff was up for sale, but the only one to leave Ninian Park was Welsh international Sayer, who joined Brighton for £100,000. Some time later, goalkeeper Bill Irwin left the club for Vancouver Whitecaps.

Matters began to improve when Buchanan's penalty beat Brighton, and striker Ray Bishop scored the goals that earned a point at Millwall and beat Southampton at Ninian Park. Tony Evans, although still not fully fit, returned for the vital run-in, and after Bishop had produced the 85th minute goal to beat Bolton, Evans popped up with a last minute winner at Sheffield United.

On the 3rd of May, Cardiff came from behind to overcome Notts County, with goals from Buchanan and Went, to ensure Second Division safety. The Bluebirds still had a say in the relegation stakes, however, when they entertained Orient in the last game of the season, the Londoners having to win to stay up and thus condemn Blackpool to relegation instead. The 90 minutes on that sunny May evening turned out to be a mockery of professional football. Cardiff took it so easy that they were soon being heckled by their own supporters in the 8,270 crowd. The match defied description, and Peter Kitchen scored a scrambled 34th minute winner that saved Orient in most unsavoury circumstances.

Dwyer, Went and Campbell were regulars in that strife-torn season. Buchanan was leading scorer with 10 goals, whilst both Robson and Went scored eight.

F.A. Cup

Cardiff City entertained Ipswich Town in the third round, and two goals from England international Paul Mariner knocked the Bluebirds out of the competition.

Welsh Cup

A trip was made to Worcester City in the fifth round, and Cardiff nearly came to grief against the non-Leaguers. Shaw twice put the home side into the lead, and it took a Went penalty, plus a late strike by Ray Bishop, to earn the Bluebirds a replay.

A crowd of only 963 at Ninian Park watched the afternoon replay. The Bluebirds made no mistake as Bishop, Robson and a Barton own goal gave them a 3-0 victory.

The City faced Kidderminster Harriers at Ninian Park in the sixth round and the non-Leaguers earned a replay with a great show, and a 1-1 scoreline. A fortnight later, City cast aside all their problems to win the replay. Giles gave the Bluebirds a 29th minute lead, which looked to have settled the tie, until Griffiths forced extra time with an equaliser in the 86th minute. Cardiff took charge, and in the fifth minute of the extended period, Buchanan netted with a penalty, and Giles' goal gave a final 3-1 score with almost the last kick of the match.

Wrexham visited Ninian Park in the semi-final and soon put the skids under the Bluebirds when Les Cartwright scored direct from a corner, after only two minutes. The City never recovered, and near the end Alan Dwyer scored Wrexham's second, thus relieving the Bluebirds of the Trophy.

Football League Cup

The City met Torquay in the 1st round, and gave a very shoddy performance in the first leg at Plainmoor, where an own goal by Doug Livermore gave victory to the Fourth Division side. The second leg was played four days later, and in slippery conditions, Torquay doubled their aggregate lead through Lee, Phil Dwyer bundling a goal for the City ten minutes later. David Giles then scored from close range to put City 2-1 up, and 2-2 on aggregate, before Brown replied to restore Torquay's advantage. The Bluebirds play was rewarded in the second half, when Peter Sayer scored to bring the aggregate scores level once again, and force a replay, which took place at Ninian Park.

Just 1,711 – City's lowest attendance in the competition at that time – saw another ding-dong affair. Lawrence put Torquay into a 36th minute lead, and it took a second-half penalty from Sayer to bring the home team level. In the 73rd minute John Buchanan scored a remarkable winning goal, when his direct free-kick from all of 40 yards sailed over a packed penalty area and straight into the Torquay net, to make the result 2-1 to the City.

The Bluebirds travelled to Swindon in the second round and were defending stubbornly until Guthrie scored on the half hour. The floodgates opened in the second-half as Anderson scored two quick goals. Buchanan pulled one back but Moss and McHale, with a spectacular effort, scored in the final three minutes, and the City crashed out 1-5.

European Cup Winners' Cup

F.K. Austria Memphis were faced in the first round, and the first leg at Ninian Park attracted just 3,631, Cardiff's lowest attendance for a European cup tie up to that time. The City were already having injury troubles and never caused any problems for the Austrians, who were delighted with the 0-0 scoreline. A makeshift City team played in Austria and, despite a gallant defensive performance, they bowed out to a single goal.

(Above) George Best, playing his first game at Ninian Park, is beaten by Buchanan, in the Bluebirds 3-1 victory over Fulham. (Right) Paul Went scores the 4th minute match-winner versus Oldham.

1978-9 Season – Division 2:

Throughout the summer months work continued at Ninian Park in order to bring the stadium up to the required standards laid down by the Safety of Sports' Grounds Act. The demolition of the Grangetown Stand, which had been constructed following Cardiff City's F.A. Cup win in 1927, was completed, and a new standing enclosure with concrete terracing took its place. This meant that, with the loss of their beloved covered end, the main body of City supporters transferred their vantage point to the 'Bob Bank', leaving the new open area for visiting fans.

Bob Grogan continued with the chairmanship, despite protests being lodged in some quarters about him living in the North East of England. Cardiff City manager Jimmy Andrews, was allowed to spend more money than any previous manager when he set a new club record of £75,000, for Newcastle's Micky Burns, a player of the highest pedigree. Burns, it was revealed would become player-coach to the first team. Andrews then reinforced the Bluebirds' defence by paying Hull City £70,000 for Welsh international Dave Roberts. Before the season began Cardiff City played in the Anglo-Scottish Cup! Their section contained Fulham and both Bristol clubs. Although the Bluebirds defeated Fulham 1-0 they lost at Eastville and Ashton Gate in games that were little more than pre-season friendlies.

Right from the start of the new season City were struggling, particularly as injury ruled out Tony Evans, and Paul Went was sold to Orient for £20,000. Goalkeeper Ron Healey also picked up an injury, and with Bill Irwin having joined Vancouver Whitecaps, Andrews blooded young John Davies, and Keith Barber who had been borrowed from Swansea City. Barber, a former Luton goalkeeper, returned to Kenilworth Road with the City on the 16th of September, and was helpless as the Bluebirds were crushed 1-7, one of the clubs' worst post-war defeats. Making his debut on that forgettable sunny afternoon was lanky striker Gary Stevens, a £3,000 signing from Evesham, and the following week, Mr. Andrews dropped both expensive summer signings Burns and Roberts.

In a reshuffle the manager gave a baptism to Tredegar-born John Lewis, a part-timer, who had been progressing in the reserves after being spotted at Pontllanfraith in the Welsh League. Both players contributed in a 2-0 win over Blackburn Rovers, with Stevens scoring on his home debut, and the following Saturday, the Bluebirds beat Wrexham, with Buchanan scoring both goals.

In a shock move, City regained the £75,000 spent on Micky Burns, when Middlesbrough who had wanted him badly during the summer, took the unhappy player to Ayresome Park. It had been a disastrous, but short stay, at Ninian Park for Burns, who unfortunately did not have the coaching qualities that Andrews had expected.

Evans returned, and Stevens settled down quickly with some vital goals, but generally the overall quality was poor and with gates running at a low level, Jimmy Andrews was dismissed on the 6th of November, two days after a shocking 1-4 home defeat by Charlton Athletic.

The manager still had two and a half years left on his five year contract, and the club was committed to making a cash settlement, as they has done with Jimmy Scoular. Much to the surprise of many observers the board of directors appointed long-serving clubman Richie Morgan as caretaker/manager, whose playing career was virtually over, and who had been employed at Ninian Park in a commercial capacity. Morgan brought in Middlesbrough's Irish international goalkeeper Jim Platt on a months' loan, and although City's results hardly improved, the board were so impressed by Richie Morgan's enthusiasm that on the 9th of December they appointed him team manager. Aged 34, he became the youngest man at the helm in the club's history.

It was not until the 23rd of December that the Bluebirds won again, when they beat Fulham 2-0 at Ninian Park. City them played three away games, first losing badly 0-5 at Brighton - where Teddy Maybank scored a hat-trick - then drawing at Burnley, and finally a catastrophic 0-5 defeat at Cambridge, for whom Alan Biley scored a hat-trick. In the latter match the loyal band of City fans did a conga on the terraces, and chanted, 'what a load of rubbish'! It was the clubs' lowest point for some time, and as the freezing winter took a grip, the team did not play a League match for six weeks.

During this period Morgan made great strides towards turning the club around. He surrounded himself with experience, appointing former Ninian Park favourites Doug Livermore and Brian Harris, along with former Newport manager Dave Elliott, as his assistants. Morgan strengthened his playing staff by paying £70,000 to Norwich for left-back Colin Sullivan, a former England under 23 international. The City manager then broke the club record fee by signing the prolific Tranmere centre-forward Ronnie Moore for £100,000, before recouping some of the outlay by selling David Giles to Wrexham for £30,000, and Brian Attley to Swansea for £20,000.

When the City restarted in League action on the 24th of February, both Sullivan and Moore made their home debuts, alongside the youth team full-back Linden Jones, in a 1-0 win over Orient. In the next match, at Blackburn, Jones had the unfortunate distinction of being sent off, together with Rovers' John Bailey, as the Bluebirds romped to a magnificent 4-1 at snowy Ewood Park. The tide was turning and the team began to climb out of the relegation zone, attaining an unbeaten run in their final eleven League games, eight of which were at Ninian Park. There was a fine 4-0 home win over Sheffield United, when top scorer Buchanan bagged a hat-trick, and a superb 2-1 win at Sunderland, the victory denying the Roker men a place in the First Division.

Home and away draws with West Ham also helped keep the Londoners in the Second Division. It had been a complete turn around for the Bluebirds who, before the Winter freeze, had looked destined for relegation – yet at the end of the season had recovered so well that they finished in 9th place – the highest position since 1971!

Richie Morgan, who had performed a minor miracle, was rewarded with a deserved 'Manager of the Month' for April 1979.

Campbell, Dwyer and Buchanan appeared regularly, and the latter was the top marksman with 16 goals, followed by Stevens who scored 13 times.

F.A. Cup

The Bluebirds were at their lowest ebb when they lost 0-3 at Swindon in the third round.

Welsh Cup

Despite the inclement January weather, Cardiff City managed to fit in their 5th round Welsh Cup tie against Merthyr Tydfil at Ninian Park. With an afternoon kick-off and treacherous driving conditions, only 694 attended. The City overcame Pratt's goal, for Stevens and Evans (with a penalty) to ensure a 2-1 win.

With Britain in the grip of its worst weather since 1963, the City were surprised to learn that their sixth round match at Worcester would go ahead. In poor conditions, they soon found themselves 0-3 behind, and a late rally which saw Buchanan and Dwyer scoring, failed to prevent an embarrassing defeat at the hands of the non-Leaguers.

Football League Cup

Cardiff City crashed out of the competition by losing both legs of the first round tie with Oxford United, to go out 2-4 on aggregate.

Tony Evans ends a lean scoring spell, as he heads this goal in the home match versus Brighton.

A painful debut for £100,000 striker Ronnie Moore. Orient's former City player Paul Went, was booked for this foul.

1979-80 Season - Division 2:

After the encouragement of Cardiff City's improved form at the end of the previous season, Richie Morgan created a new Club record transfer fee when he signed Blackpool's midfield dynamo, Billy Ronson, for £130,000. In order to pay that sum, Cardiff received £120,000 from Birmingham City for popular striker Tony Evans, which beat the previous record (received) fee of £110,000 for John Toshack, set in 1970. Evans, much loved by Cardiff fans had scored 47 goals in 120 League matches, since his arrival from Blackpool on a free transfer in 1975.

The City had a good pre-season tour of Denmark, winning three and drawing one of their four matches, before drawing 2-2 with First Division Wolves at Ninian Park.

For the first time in League history three Welsh clubs, Swansea, Wrexham and City, were in the 2nd Division.

For the Bluebirds the new season began at Notts County, where three goals in the final ten minutes condemned City to a 1-4 defeat. Gary Stevens then scored in five consecutive League games; Tony Evans returned to Ninian Park in one of these, and scored twice in the opening ten minutes, enabling Birmingham City to win 2-1. Stevens' first minute goal won the points at Wrexham on the 1st of September, and his strike in the last minute earned a point at Watford, as City lost only three of their first eleven games.

Bishop emerged as a striking partner for Stevens, scoring some vital goals, but poor Ronnie Moore had little success, netting just once in the opening twelve games, despite being a regular in the number nine shirt. Morgan surprisingly paid American club Tulsa Roughnecks £70,000 for utility player Wayne Hughes, a Welshman, who had previously been with West Bromwich Albion.

It was a strange buy, for City needed strengthening in attack, as they were barely averaging one goal per game, thus ensuring that the Club remained around mid-table. With Ron Healey experiencing further injury problems, Morgan signed goalkeeper Peter Grotier from Lincoln City, initially on loan, and later making the transfer permanent by paying £25,000. Grotier had previously played two games on loan for Cardiff in October 1973. The Bluebirds suffered a mid-season slump, that was lifted by Ronnie Moore scoring the only goal against Wrexham on the 12th of January, thus giving them the 'double' over the Robins. It was the much-maligned Moore's second goal in 25 League games, and prompted the City fans to wear button badges proclaiming - 'I saw Ronnie Moore score!' The hard-working striker took this good naturedly, and was reported to be carrying his house number as a talisman on match days. A week later Moore scored a late winning goal at Shrewsbury, giving him two in two games, but he never scored another League goal in the City's colours!

On the 2nd of February, almost 8,000 Ninian Parkites stood in silent tribute before the game against Watford, in memory of former chairman Mr. Fred Dewey, and ex-goalkeeper Phil Joslin, both of whom had died during the previous week. A last minute goal from John Lewis beat Watford, which gave the City their third consecutive win. The Bluebirds maintained a mid-table position, and they had great satisfaction in beating Swansea on Easter Monday, with a rare goal from the busy Billy Ronson, for they had lost in controversial circumstances to David Giles' injury time goal at the Vetch Field, on New Years' Day.

Sunderland visited Ninian Park in the final game of the season and, with one foot in the First Division, they brought massive support with them, swelling the crowd to 19,340 - City's biggest of the term. The kick-off was delayed to accommodate the visiting fans who saw 'Pop' Robson secure the required point in a 1-1 draw, after Ray Bishop had put the City ahead.

Cardiff ended the season in 15th position, which represented a pretty mediocre term. Campbell was ever-present, Ronson missed one game through suspension; Pontin and Moore made regular appearances. The team could only manage a meagre 41 goals, but conceded just 48, with Bishop and Stevens sharing the leading scorers position with 11 goals each.

F.A. Cup

Cardiff City drew a real plum in the third round, with a home tie against Arsenal, the F.A. Cup holders. Memories of the 1927 F.A. Cup Final came flooding back when City produced a facsimile of the famous Wembley programme as a collectors item, to go with their normal matchday issue. The match was almost a non-event, defensive tactics ruling the day, and the 21,972 crowd were left disappointed with a boring scoreless draw.

Ronnie Moore heads towards goal in the F.A.Cup match versus Arsenal.

The replay at Highbury was a better game for the crowd of 36,582, if only on account of the three goals. It was little consolation to the Bluebirds that Buchanan scored the best goal of the game, as Alan Sunderland scored twice to win the tie for Arsenal.

Welsh Cup

The team crashed out in the fifth round to a buoyant Newport County, on their way to a promotion, and a Welsh Cup 'double'. Without the suspended Billy Ronson, the City lost the midfield tussle, and eventually Newport made the breakthrough when John Aldridge completed a flowing move, to score in the 65th minute. County wasted a number of chances, until the final minute, when substitute Tommy Tynan headed a spectacular goal to make it 2-0, which had Somerton Park in rapture.

Football League Cup

Cardiff City entered the competition in the second round, now two-legged, and faced Everton. In the first leg at Goodison Park, City had no answer to the finishing power of former England international Brian Kidd, who scored a goal in each half, to give Everton a 2-0 advantage.

The second leg at Ninian Park saw the Bluebirds thwarted by a fine goalkeeping display from Everton's Scottish international George Wood. He saved a penalty from Ronson in the first-half, and made a number of timely interceptions, until being finally beaten by a low drive from the City substitute, Buchanan, three minutes from time. It was too late and City bowed out 1-2.

During the season, Keith Pontin was capped by Wales.

CHAPTER 7

NOT MUCH RESPITE IN THE EIGHTIES

1980-81 Season - Division 2:

At the end of the 1979-80 season, Cardiff City appointed Ron Jones, a former Olympic athlete, in the new role of General Manager. It was a similar position to that which he had held at Queen's Park Rangers during the previous four years. The Club chairman Bob Grogan, under criticism due to his base being in Newcastle, felt that Jones could run the club on a day to day basis, with all the monetary business coming under the newcomer's control. It was believed that Jones was in charge of all the Clubs' commercial activities, but did not wish to be called the 'Commercial Manager'. Due to a shortage of cash flow, team manager Richie Morgan was told that in order to buy new players, some of the existing staff would have to be sold. Craig Richards of Wimbledon and Miah Dennehy of Bristol Rovers were taken on trial, but later released.

City made a three match tour of Scotland, winning all three games - at Hamilton, Cowdenbeath and Montrose - by 1-0. The Bluebirds also beat First Division Stoke City at Ninian Park, in another pre-season friendly.

A week before the new season began, the City accepted an offer of £100,000 from Rotherham United for Ronnie Moore. The big striker had had a traumatic spell at Ninian Park, and ironically became well-known and popular with the fans for his lack of goals! At Rotherham, Moore later became a feared scorer as he spearheaded the Millers to the Third Division Championship! Colin Sullivan, Dave Roberts, Ron Healey and Linden Jones remained long-standing injury victims, and the team began the season with a disjointed look, having midfield players Steve Grapes and John Lewis in the full-back berths. It was no real surprise when the Bluebirds lost their opening match 1-2 at home to Blackburn, although it was Rovers' first win at Ninian Park since the 18th of December 1926! Ray Bishop's goal secured the now customary City win at Wrexham.

With the money received from the sale of Ronnie Moore, Richie Morgan completed the purchase of Fulham's unsettled striker Peter Kitchen for £100,000, who had a proven scoring record with his previous clubs - Doncaster Rovers and Orient. Kitchen slotted in quickly, helping the Bluebirds to home wins over Orient, Bristol Rovers, and Watford. With the emergence of starlet Paul Maddy, City allowed veteran Alan Campbell to join Carlisle United for a small fee. The Scottish midfield player had been a model of consistency for four years, and had made over 200 first team appearances for the Bluebirds. With the City still striving to make economies, Coaches Brian Harris and Doug Livermore were relieved of their duties, Harris entering the licensing trade, and Livermore joining Norwich City's coaching staff.

The Bluebirds' away form was appalling until the 15th of November, when they won 3-2 at Blackburn with goals from Kitchen (two) and Buchanan; young winger Paul Giles, the brother of David, made an impressive debut. City now had their best run of results, winning three games, before **six** consecutive draws in a nine-match unbeaten spell.

The best remembered of these games was a 3-3 home draw with First Division bound Swansea City who were managed by former Bluebird John Toshack. The Swans were well in control, and with five minutes remaining, were leading 3-1, when Peter Kitchen cut the deficit. Injury time brought one of Ninian Park's greatest moments, as Buchanan blasted a tapped free-kick from all of 40 yards into the top corner of the Swansea net, and so earn the City an unlikely draw. Toshack was reported as saying he was hoping Buchanan would shoot - 'as he could never score from such a distance'!

The City then slumped to four successive defeats, and Morgan signed left-back Tim Gilbert from Sunderland for a small fee, which was payable after twenty Cardiff appearances. The Bluebirds hovered above the relegation zone, and they were thankful for winning goals from Stevens at Chelsea and Grimsby, and a late equaliser at Swansea.

Before the transfer deadline, Ray Bishop - who earlier in the season had been involved in a serious nightclub incident with team-mate John Lewis which almost cost Lewis the sight of one eye - moved on to Newport County for £5,000.

Goalless draws in the final home matches with Derby and West Ham were sufficient for a 19th final placing, but on goal difference only, above Preston - who were relegated. The public showed their apathy by average gates of only 6,700 for home matches.

Ronson and Pontin were ever-present and other regulars included Kitchen, Stevens, Buchanan, Dwyer (who passed the 300 League appearances point) and Lewis. Kitchen was top scorer with 13 goals, Stevens scored 7 and Buchanan 6.

F.A. Cup
Cardiff City made no progress in the competition, for in the third round they were well beaten by Jock Wallace's highly fit Leicester City, by 0-3 at Filbert Street.

Welsh Cup
Cardiff City entertained their amateur neighbours, Cardiff Corinthians, in the fifth round, and had a comfortable passage with a 6-0 victory. Kitchen emulated Brian Clark's feat of five goals in a match - set ten years previously - and Wayne Hughes also scored.

The City came a cropper at the Racecourse in the 6th round, as Wrexham rattled in three goals without reply.

Football League Cup

Torquay United were met in the first round, and the first leg ended 0-0 at Plainmoor. The Bluebirds struggled in the return until Ray Bishop gave them a 55th minute lead. Torquay replied through Fell, and ten minutes from time Stevens scored City's winner.

The Bluebirds met Chelsea in the next round, and Ray Bishop's goal in the 42nd minute won the first leg for the home team at Ninian Park. The return at Stamford Bridge did not reach any great heights until Droy scored for Chelsea. Kitchen nicked a goal and City went through 2-1 on aggregate.

The third round produced a highly controversial and bad-tempered match at Barnsley. There were a spate of bookings, and with Barnsley leading 2-1, John Lewis equalised for City in injury time. Amazingly, referee Mr. McNally allowed the game to continue, and in the **seventh** minute of stoppage time, Ian Banks scored a spectacular winner for the Yorkshiremen, which provoked much comment and argument afterwards!

································

1981-82 Season – Division 2:

The supporters of the Football Club were dismayed that all the publicity during the summer centred around the formation and launch of the Cardiff City Blue Dragons Rugby League Club, who were to play at Ninian Park. Former Rugby Union and League star, David Watkins, was appointed manager of the Rugby League outfit. The estimated cost of forming the Rugby League team was believed to be in the region of £100,000, which meant that there were no funds available for Richie Morgan to strengthen the City team.

Cardiff City were not re-elected to the Football Combination, and they also withdrew from the Welsh League, which resulted in a lack of competition for the reserve and young players. Richie Morgan appointed Colin Prophett and former City players Bobby Woodruff and Fred Davies to his coaching staff, and signed Paul Sugrue from Manchester City on a free transfer. For all their backroom problems the City had a good pre-season run of results.

Cardiff began the season at Oldham, where they found themselves 0-2 down in only six minutes, but the Bluebirds pulled a point out of the bag with goals from Stevens and Dwyer. Three successive defeats followed, including a 0-1 reverse at Rotherham - where Ronnie Moore scored against his old club. This prompted Morgan to sign defender Gary Bennett of Manchester City on trial, former Bluebird Peter Sayer from Preston - on a months' loan - and Norwich goalkeeper Roger Hansbury also on trial. Sayer scored one of the goals when the City dramatically won by 3-2 at Luton, and Morgan rapidly completed the signing of Manchester City winger Dave Bennett, the brother of Gary, for £120,000. Together with Sugrue, the new boy made his debut as Cardiff completed the rare distinction of two away wins in four days, when a Gary Stevens goal gave them victory at Barnsley on the 26th of September.

A week later City were crushed 0-4 at home by Newcastle United, for whom Inre Varadi completed a hat-trick, in the Magpies first-ever win at Ninian Park!

This was to be the last match that Billy Ronson was to play for the Bluebirds as the unsettled midfield dynamo - who had missed just one match in two years at Ninian Park - moved on to Wrexham for £90,000. After speculating on Dave Bennett, the Club were only too happy to recoup most of that fee by selling the unsettled Ronson, as Ninian Park attendances were now dropping to crisis point. At the same time John Buchanan, who had dropped out of first-team contention, rejoined Northampton for £12,000, following a distinguished career at Ninian Park where he scored many a spectacular goal in over 250 first-team appearances.

When City beat Bolton Wanderers at Ninian Park on the 17th of October, it was their first home win since the 25th of February, and only 3,879 were present. Sayer returned to Preston after four games on loan, and with injuries ruling out Sugrue and Sullivan, Wayne Hughes plus Tim Gilbert came into the line-up. Peter Kitchen, who wanted a move, was not considered. Ron Jones made football history in October, by becoming the first paid director of a Football League club, and his title was changed from general manager/secretary to Managing Director, at a salary reputed to be £25,000 per annum. Unfortunately for Mr. Jones, the gamble of having a Rugby League side in the Welsh capital was not paying off, and with gates of barely 1,000, the public expressed more concern with regard to the soccer club.

It came as a shock to many followers, when after winning home matches against Wrexham and Norwich City, Richie Morgan was relieved of the team managers' post and moved into an administrative position - for the team had just entered the top section of the Second Division.

On the 9th of November, the former West Bromwich Albion and Wales defender Graham Williams, was surprisingly appointed first team coach, although he was effectively regarded as the manager. Williams had been out of football, after working extensively abroad, and at the time of his appointment was running a health club in Weymouth. His first game in charge was a 'Match of the Day' scoreless draw at Watford. One week later, the City beat Leicester City 3-1, all the goals coming in the final 15 minutes, after Leicester centre-half Scott had been sent off. On the 4th of December, the Bluebirds defeated a poor Derby team with a Tarki Micallef goal, but that was to be their last win until the 20th of March - a total of eleven League matches of which nine were lost. On the 3rd of March both Morgan and Williams were dismissed.

Not unnaturally Mr. Morgan - locally-born and a Cardiff City clubman since 1966 - took the decision badly. He felt aggrieved, quite rightly, for while he was in charge of the first-team affairs they had attained their highest position for several seasons. Cardiff had also managed to avoid relegation the previous season, despite a crippling injury list, and at the time of Mr. Williams' appointment the team were once again 9th in the Second Division. It had been a sad interlude in the club's history, and many supporters had a lot of sympathy for the way in which Richie Morgan had been treated.

Cardiff City's board looked to Newport County's recently deposed Manager Len Ashurst as the man to pull them out of trouble. He had all the right credentials, being a thorough professional, and who, after a long playing career with Sunderland, had gained managerial experience at Hartlepool, Gillingham, and Sheffield Wednesday.

His exploits in four years with Newport County were well known to City followers. The new Manager's first game at Ninian Park turned out to be a sensational one, as City beat Cambridge 5-4. Stevens completed a headed hat-trick, and Peter Kitchen scored twice, but sadly the match was watched by only 3,243, Ninian Park's lowest League crowd since the War!

Coach Colin Prophett resigned for domestic reasons on the 11th of April, as the City enjoyed three successive home wins over Grimsby, Watford and Orient. Ashurst had raided the transfer market, bringing in the experienced Jimmy Mullen of Rotherham (on loan), Mick Henderson of Watford (a free transfer), and Andy Polycarpou – the latter an ex-Cambridge player (on trial). At the same time goalkeeper Peter Grotier departed for Grimsby Town and Paul Giles went to Exeter City on loan. All this activity, on and off the field, gave the City supporters some hope that relegation could be averted. It was only a pipe dream however, as the Bluebirds slumped back into the bottom three.

Young goalkeeper Andy Dibble made his debut as City lost 0-1 at home against Crystal Palace, and relegation appeared odds-on. A week later however, City pulled off a win at Grimsby, and once again had to win their last match in order to save themselves from the drop.

The Bluebirds had long built up a reputation for brinkmanship, and the biggest home crowd of the season – 10,277 – turned up to see if City could perform another of their famed 'Houdini' acts. The visitors, Luton Town, were the clearcut Second Division champions, and they gave a display of lovely simplistic football, that saw them take a 3-0 lead, besides missing a number of clear chances. The Bluebirds showed a little spirit with late goals from Kitchen and Micallef but by then it was all over, and Cardiff City were back in the Third Division.

Pontin, Stevens and Dave Bennett made the most regular appearances, and Stevens was top scorer with 13 goals; both Kitchen and Micallef netted 8 each. In a traumatic season, Cardiff had used 28 players.

F.A. Cup
A journey was made to Manchester City for the third round, and it was a quick return to Maine Road for the Bennett brothers and substitute Paul Sugrue. There were no happy home comings as the Bluebirds lost by 1-3.

Welsh Cup
The third round tie was played at Bridgend, and a comfortable 4-1 win was attained; it was the City's first Sunday match. The next round brought Newport County – who at this time were still managed by Len Ashurst – to Ninian Park in the fourth round. On a frozen pitch, the Bluebirds skated to a surprisingly easy victory with goals from Dwyer, Dave Bennett and Stevens.

The fifth round saw Billy Ronson return to Ninian Park with Wrexham, and the crowd would not let him forget that his move to North Wales had not furthered his ambitions, for Wrexham, like City, were struggling at the foot of the Second Division. Gary Stevens answered his personal 'Bob Bank' hecklers with the first goal, which he accompanied with a two fingered salute, before Peter Kitchen took over with a neat hat-trick. Ronson had the last word, with a late consolation, and the City won 4-1.

The Bluebirds met Hereford United in the two-legged semi-finals. The game at Edgar Street was marred by mindless crowd trouble, totally divorced from the match on view, which ended in a tame 0-0 draw. The second leg was a little better, and goals from Micallef and Stevens enabled a City win by 2-1 and hence they reached their first Welsh Cup final for five years.

Len Ashurst took the unprecedented step of signing the former Norwich forward Phil Lythgoe from Witney Town and Stan McEwan – on trial at Birmingham – just to play in the two-legged Welsh Cup Final against First Division Swansea City. The first leg at Ninian Park saw the Bluebirds go perilously close to toppling their deadliest rivals, in a match that saw both goalkeepers – City's young Andy Dibble and Swansea's Welsh international Dai Davies – distinguish themselves.

The City had a great start in the second leg when Gary Bennett scored an early goal. Swansea's superior class eventually showed through, even though they had skipper Ante Rajkovic sent off for a bad foul on Phil Lythgoe, and two goals from Bob Latchford put the Welsh Cup on the Vetch Field sideboard. There was an unusual sight at the end of the game when Rajkovic, who had been dismissed, came forward to accept the trophy!

Football League Cup
Cardiff City met Exeter City in the first round, and in the first leg at Ninian Park, two goals from Stevens gave them a 2-1 advantage. In the second leg the City took the lead through Paul Sugrue, but Exeter hit back twice to take the game into extra time, where they scored again to win 3-1, and 4-3 on aggregate.

••••••••••••••••••••••••••••••••••••

1982-3 Season – Division 3:

During the close season Len Ashurst appointed Jimmy Goodfellow, his former assistant at Newport County, as trainer-coach, and proceeded to turn over the playing staff in a no uncertain manner. To make room for new recruits, the City manager released Steve Grapes, who went to Torquay after making over 150 first-team appearances, expensive signing Peter Kitchen (who joined the exodus to Hong Kong), Wayne Hughes to Bath City, Tim Gilbert to Darlington, Mick Henderson to Sheffield United and Andy Polycarpou, who was not offered terms. Regular scorer Gary Stevens, who had suffered unnecessary barracking by some so-called City supporters, was signed by Shrewsbury for a tribunal set fee of £20,000. Stevens had cost just £3,000 from Evesham, and in four years had scored 44 goals in 150 League games, plus a number of Cup goals.

Long serving clubman, Phil Dwyer, who had been experiencing a niggling leg injury, was made available on a free-transfer, whilst on a monthly contract, as was Paul Sugrue. A number of other players were retained on reduced terms – in respect of appearance money – as Managing Director Ron Jones looked at all avenues to reduce expenditure. With little, or no money available, Mr. Ashurst raided the free-transfer market like no other City manager before him.

Arriving at Ninian Park were forward Jeff Hemmerman from Portsmouth, midfielder David Tong from Shrewsbury, utility player Roger Gibbins from Cambridge

United, full-back Paul Bodin from Newport County and goalkeeper Martin Thomas from Bristol Rovers – on a six month loan. Another goalkeeper, Steve Humphries of Doncaster, was given a trial period, as was Swindon midfielder Kenny Stroud, who joined Newport County, after appearing in several pre-season games.

In the boardroom, Cardiff City chairman Bob Grogan invited former player and director, George Edwards, to rejoin the directorate. Richie Morgan and Graham Williams were paid compensation in lieu of the contracts at the time of their dismissals. It was reported that Morgan received £8,000, and Williams £3,000. Seldom had Ninian Park experienced such a hectic summer.

With Andy Dibble and Martin Thomas sidelined with hand injuries, trialist goalkeeper Steve Humphries was one of five debutants in City's opening League match against Wrexham at Ninian Park, which the Bluebirds lost by 1-2. Thomas took over in goal, Humphries being released, and the City went to Millwall on the 5th of September, where they won spectacularly by 4-0, with goals from John Lewis, Dave Bennett (two) and Roger Gibbins. Three days later City were brought back to earth when they lost 0-4 at Orient!

The Bluebirds then put together four League wins in a row, beginning with an exciting 3-2 home victory over Wigan Athletic, which saw the winning goal coming via the head of triallist Billy Woof, just two minutes from full time. Three days later Woof, the former Middlesbrough striker, walked out on Cardiff City following words with Mr. Ashurst!

Jeff Hemmerman scored his first League goal for Cardiff City at Walsall the following week, where veteran Dwyer – on his return to first-team duty – was the hero with the winning goal. Home victories over Sheffield United and Exeter City elevated the Bluebirds to the top three, and sitting on the Cardiff substitutes' bench was Godfrey Ingram, who reputedly had cost £200,000 from San Jose Earthquakes, yet could not get into the team! The so-called record buy was City's matchwinner in a 1-0 home win against Gillingham.

Three days later, Gary Bennetts' lone goal took the Bluebirds to the top of the Third Division, as City beat Bradford City at Ninian Park. The thrill of leading a section of the Football League after a number of years lasted just four days, as City crashed 0-4 at Huddersfield, where Mark Lillis scored all four goals for the Yorkshiremen. Jeff Hemmerman was the happiest man at Ninian Park on the 30th of October, after heading the winner against his former club, Portsmouth. It was on the recommendation of former Pompey boss, Frank Burrows, that Ashurst had signed Hemmerman, and the nimble striker was fast becoming a favourite with the 'Bob-Bankers'. The Bluebirds won at Reading, and then defeated Preston North End 3-1 at Ninian Park, when Godfrey Ingram scored the third City goal, in what transpired to be his last appearance for the club.

The reputed record signing returned to San Jose Earthquakes for the £200,000 that the City supposedly had paid for him nine weeks earlier – and in subsequent years – few, if any, Bluebirds' supporters have accepted that Ingram had been the Club's record transfer fee (incoming and outgoing) player – although some prestigious football records books have recorded this as fact!

The City lost 1-2 at Lincoln in a tempestuous match that saw Dave Bennett being dismissed, after he had opened the scoring. It was to be Martin Thomas' final appearance for the Club, as he was recalled by Bristol Rovers, after enquiries from other clubs. Cardiff were not prepared to meet Rovers asking price, and following spells at 'Spurs, Southend and Newcastle, Thomas eventually joined the Magpies. Mr. Ashurst therefore pinned his hopes on 18 year old Andy Dibble, who had now recovered from injury.

The City manager reinforced his attacking options by obtaining the veteran and much-travelled goalscorer Bob Hatton, on a free transfer from Sheffield United. The 36 year old had been a regular scorer against Cardiff for a variety of clubs down the years. Hatton made his City debut on the 4th of December, in a 2-2 draw at Doncaster, and three days later, he marked his home debut with the City goal in a 1-1 draw versus Chesterfield. Hatton's influence brought about a marked improvement in the team's strike power, and he scored regularly as the Bluebirds enjoyed a good Christmas/New Year period.

After winning at Southend, the City entertained neighbours Newport County on the 27th of December, and produced a thriller for a crowd of 15,972. Hatton's close range lob gave City an interval lead, and with ten minutes left, Hemmerman's looped header gave the Bluebirds what appeared to be an unassailable 2-0 margin. But within six minutes Bailey and Vaughan had struck back for County. Cardiff were stunned, but Hatton headed on Dibble's deep kick, for Hemmerman to lob the ball over the outrushing Kendall and score a magnificent winner, which silenced the thousands of County fans at the Grangetown end.

The following day the Bluebirds let a 2-1 half-time lead slip at Home Park, as Plymouth Argyle roared back to win 3-2. But on New Years' Day, the Bluebirds returned to winning ways, beating Bristol Rovers 3-1 at Ninian Park, with Gary Bennett and Hemmerman (two) on the mark; one of Hemmerman's goals coming from the penalty spot. It was a sad match for Rovers' left back Brian Williams, who missed a penalty, and was sent off following a foul on Dave Bennett.

City's promotion bandwagon kept on rolling as the Bluebirds won at Brentford, drew at Wrexham, beat Walsall 3-1 at Ninian Park, won 2-0 at Exeter – where Gary Bennett and Exeter's Ray Pratt were sent off – and defeated Millwall at Ninian Park. Much to the dismay of the City boardroom the crowds were not returning in great numbers to Ninian Park as they had hoped, and less than 7,000 turned up to see City beat another promotion hopeful, Oxford United by, 3-0.

The Club's small squad was now beginning to be tested, as various players were ruled out through injury and suspension. The situation was aggravated further when young Dibble received a bad injury in collision with Bradford City's Bobby Campbell, at Valley Parade. Dwyer and Linden Jones took turns in goal, to no avail, and the City crashed 2-4.

Ashurst quickly brought in former Scottish international goalkeeper Jim Brown, on loan from Chesterfield, but he hardly inspired confidence in his three games as City drew at home with both Reading and A.F.C. Bournemouth which sandwiched a nail-biting 3-2 win at Gillingham.

Newport's Nigel Vaighan challenges City's David Tong, in the one goal defeat on the 4th of April 1983. An enormous crowd totalling 16,052 was at Somerton Park.

The manager released Brown and secured the experienced Eric Steele on loan from Watford, and City's fifth 'keeper of the season produced a magnificent display in his debut at Fratton Park, where 24,354 watched a table-topping scoreless draw.

The momentum was beginning to wane, and they won only twice in ten games, the last of which was a mammoth encounter at Somerton Park that Newport County won with a lone goal from John Aldridge, before 16,052 people. The Gwent club went to the top of the table and City dropped to fourth, but they were unlucky to lose this match, which had a number of controversial decisions, not least of which surrounded Aldridge's goal.

It was to be the last time that City would taste defeat that season and they powered back towards the Second Division in the final seven matches. David Tong scored twice as they beat Doncaster Rovers 3-0, and with Eric Steele returning to Watford, fit again Dibble was restored for a 0-0 draw at Wigan, where Gary Bennett was sent off for the second time that season.

The Bluebirds surged into the top three following an emphatic 4-1 home win over Southend, and a week later a reshuffled team – with Phil Dwyer, Gary Bennett and Linden Jones all suspended – still managed to win at bottom placed Chesterfield. Now the public became aware of the City's serious promotion intentions, and on May day, almost 10,000 saw them overcome a resilient Brentford 3-1 at Ninian Park, where man-of-the-match Bob Hatton scored a magnificent goal and laid on another for Dave Bennett, which helped propel City into second place.

Victory over Orient at Ninian Park on the 7th of May would ensure promotion, and 11,480 were there to see the Bluebirds do the job in style.

Orient made life difficult, even after defender David Peach had been sent off, and the City were relieved on the stroke of half-time, when John Lewis completed a length of the pitch breakaway and scored from Dave Bennett's low pass. Fifteen minutes from time the crowd broke into song when Bennett took Hemmerman's pass to shoot City's second goal, and ensure the Bluebirds' return to the Second Division. The pouring rain did nothing to hamper the enthusiasm of those supporters who clamoured before the Grandstand, demanding to see their favourites, who all appeared to a hero's reception in the directors' box.

Their final League match of the season was played at Bristol Rovers, on the 14th of May, and the many Welshmen in the 10,731 crowd were pleased to see Roger Gibbins score in the first-half. Platnauer equalised for Rovers midway through the latter period, but tragedy struck Jeff Hemmerman in the 70th minute when he was stretchered off following a collision with Kite, Bristol's 'keeper. The City top scorer had severely damaged knee ligaments, and it was a sad ending to the season for the popular striker and his many fans.

The Bluebirds finished as runners up to Portsmouth. Gibbins was the only ever-present, but appearing regularly were Hemmerman, Tong, Dwyer, Dave Bennett, Linden Jones, John Lewis and Jimmy Mullen. This was the third time that Mullen had captained a team promoted to the Second Division – a unique achievement. Hemmerman was top scorer with 22 goals, Dave Bennett notched up 12, with both Roger Gibbins and the evergreen Bob Hatton netting 9 each.

Sadly, however, the public did not respond, even though the City lost just one League match – the first – at home. The average attendance was 7,681, demonstrating that the Welsh capital would not support Third Division football.

F.A.Cup

Cardiff City were drawn away at little Wokingham Town in the first round and the tie was marred by mindless crowd trouble, caused by so-called Cardiff supporters, which spoiled the Surrey club's big day. The non-Leaguers were close to causing an upset until a rare goal from David Tong made it 1-1, and a replay which the Bluebirds had little trouble in winning at a rain-sodden Ninian Park.

City faced non-League opposition again in the second round, when Weymouth visited Ninian Park. The match turned out to be the major Cup shock of the day, and the 11th of December 1982 was to be remembered, for the City suffered their most humiliating post-war home defeat. There seem little likelihood of this happening as the home team raced into a 2-0 interval lead. Weymouth adopted a 'death or glory' attitude after the interval, and it certainly paid off, as they knocked a complacent City right out of their stride. Nine minutes into the second-half Iannone headed a fine goal and the non-Leaguers poured forward in pursuit of an equaliser. With twelve minutes remaining Iannone cashed in on an error by Dwyer, and from his pass Finnegan brought Weymouth level. As time ran out, and a replay looking likely, Baker collected a weak kick from Dibble and his deep cross from the left was met perfectly by Pearson, who volleyed Weymouth to an historic 3-2 win.

Welsh Cup

Cardiff City faced a tough hurdle in their fifth round tie at Newport County. Dave Bennett was suspended, and the Bluebirds wasted several opportunities, eventually paying the price, by losing to a Nigel Vaughan goal.

Milk Cup (Formerly Football League Cup)

Cardiff City's first round opponents in the newly named Cup, were Hereford United. In the first leg at Ninian Park, the Bluebirds gained a 2-1 advantage, which they improved in the second leg at Edgar Street, where goals from Gibbins and Hemmerman gave City another 2-1 win. The seeding system meant that City were guaranteed a good draw in the two-legged second round, and they were paired with old rivals, Arsenal. The Bluebirds put up a spirited display at Highbury, and although they lost 1-2, Gibbins' goal gave them encouragement for the second leg at Ninian Park. In the event however, Arsenal's poise and class proved too much for City's team of free-transfer signings. The Bluebirds did enjoy one brief spell when Hemmerman scored and George Wood, the Arsenal 'keeper, pulled off several fine saves, but the Gunners strode to a 3-1 win on the night, and 5-2 on aggregate.

****

1983-4 Season – Division 2

The Cardiff City Blue Dragons Rugby League side had completed two seasons at Ninian Park and had not achieved the level of success expected of them, with attendances now averaging around 600. A lot of money had been spent on the Rugby League project to the detriment of the soccer side of the club, for although Ashurst had brought the Bluebirds back to the Second Division on meagre resources, he still had no money available for strengthening his squad.

In fact, the team was severely weakened when Bot Hatton decided to retire, Jeff Hemmerman's injury put his future in grave doubt and the club accepted an offer from Coventry City for Dave Bennett, which took him back to the First Division. A tribunal set the fee at £120,000 – the figure the City had paid Manchester City for him. Also leaving the club was Paul Maddy, a frustratingly inconsistent player who had spent loan spells at Stoke and Hereford in the previous season. He joined Swansea City, who had just been relegated from the First Division, for a modest fee.

Ashurst had to raid the free-transfer market. He signed winger Gordon Owen from Sheffield Wednesday – who had loan spells previously with Rotherham, Doncaster and Chesterfield – and goalkeeper Gary Plumley from Newport County. Andy Crawford, a forward with A.F.C. Bournemouth, was taken on a three months' trial, and striker Chris Rodon of Brighton, was obtained on loan. Len Ashurst supplemented his weak looking squad with a number of Y.T.S. signings.

As the new term dawned there was a surprise announcement from the boardroom, when, due to a serious illness, Bob Grogan stepped down from the Chair; it was Mr. Grogan's act of attaching the football club to his Kenton Utilities Group in 1982 which had kept Cardiff City from being declared bankrupt. Jack Leomard took over the chair with Kenton directors, Arthur Conway and Ray Cobb, being drafted on to the board.

The Bluebirds began the new campaign at Charlton, where Owen, Crawford and Rodon all made their debuts, but the City slumped 0-2. Then the Bluebirds produced two fine home wins in defeating Manchester City and Grimsby Town, but this proved to be false dawn as they paid for their lack of goal power in the next couple of games.

Events on the field were overshadowed in early September, when it was learned that former chairman Bob Grogan had died from cancer. The man who, it transpired, had effectively been the saviour of the Club, had been the butt of some supporters and had, on at least one occasion, a nasty confrontation in the Grandstand after a poor showing by the team, which necessitated a police presence near the director's box for future games. Grogan, who had no particular affiliation with South Wales, had been with Cardiff City since the take-over of 1975, and proved that he wanted success for his adopted club. This became apparent to supporters, but only shortly after his untimely death.

On the 29th September, Len Ashurst and Colin Addison – the manager of Newport County – constructed an highly unusual transfer 'swap', which involved five players! County's highly-rated midfielder Nigel Vaughan, and utility player Karl Elsey, arrived at Ninian Park, with the experienced Linden Jones and John Lewis, along with Tarki Micallef, joining the Gwent club. Jones, a committed full-back, had made almost 200 appearances, as had the versatile Lewis, both of whom hailed from Tredegar, Gwent. Micallef, a frustrating player who never quite fulfilled his potential, had made over 100 appearances, many as substitute. Ashurst paraded Vaughan and Elsey, along with Phil Walker, a striker on loan from Rotherham, in the City home game against Barnsley on the 1st of October. But the Bluebirds gave a terrible performance, before a jeering crowd of 6,433, and were well beaten by three clear goals.

Two thousand fewer fans were at Ninian Park a week later, when the manager brought in former Nottingham Forest defender Colin Smith – who had been playing in Hong Kong. City got their first win and goals in five games, by beating Carlisle United 2-0, with Owen and Vaughan the scorers.

City were struggling, and won only once in the next five games, four of which were goalless, a victory at Fulham being the only shaft of daylight. The Bluebirds threw off their worries with a thumping 5-0 win over Cambridge United, when young winger Wayne Matthews made his home League debut. Len Ashurst then secured 19 year old striker Ian Baird on loan from Southampton, and although they defeated Huddersfield 3-1 at Ninian Park, three consecutive defeats before Christmas kept the Bluebirds near the relegation zone. City beat struggling Swansea 3-2 at Ninian Park on Boxing Day, with Trevor Lee, signed from A.F.C Bournemouth, scoring the deciding goal on his debut. This match marked the return of former idol John Toshack, and true to legend, he scored an outstanding goal, for his ailing Swans. A day later the City secured a rare win at lowly Derby County.

They looked to be turning the corner, until successive home defeats in February, to Leeds United, when Jeff Hemmerman re-appeared after his long injury lay-off, and 0-4 against Fulham, (the first League match to be played on a Sunday at Ninian Park), pitched them head-long into the relegation mire once more. Ex-Cambridge striker Martin Goldsmith was given a one-month trial, and former Sheffield Wednesday left-back David Grant was signed on a free transfer from Oxford United. Goldsmith came off the substitutes's bench to score the winner in a scrappy 2-1 home win over Middlesbrough, which put City back on the winning trail.

The next day, the 4th of March, Cardiff City manager Len Ashurst resigned his post to take the managers' position at Sunderland, where he had been a player between 1957-71. He had been offered the post at Roker Park during his time with Newport County, but turned it down for domestic reasons. The Cardiff City board, under the advice of managing director Ron Jones, appointed Jimmy Goodfellow and Jimmy Mullen to take temporary charge of team affairs, a situation which was to be reviewed at the end of the season.

On the last day of March, the City featured in an extraordinary match against high-flying Chelsea, at Ninian Park. A huge following from London in the crowd of 11,060 watched in amazement as the Bluebirds took the favourites apart, to such an extent, that with only nine minutes left, City held a comfortable 3-0 lead through goals from Gibbins, Owen and Vaughan. Dixon scored what appeared to be a consolation for the visitors, but it spurred Chelsea into belated action, and with the excitement of their supporters increasing, they pulled another goal back through Lee in the 87th minute. In injury time, David Tong was deemed guilty of an handling offence in the City penalty-area, and although the penalty awarded appeared highly dubious – in increasing intimidatory circumstances – Chelsea scored, and so drew drew 3-3, which probably avoided a crowd disturbance.

Gordon Owen was enjoying a run of six goals in eight games, and, although the City surrendered a 2-0 lead before losing 2-3 to a doomed Swansea, the Bluebirds reached their safety target on Easter Monday, when a single goal by Owen helped push Derby County into the Third Division.

On the 4th of May, Jimmy Goodfellow was appointed team-manager, and Jimmy Mullen was made his player-coach, a decision which had much support among the players. The end of season was spoiled by visiting Sheffield Wednesday who won by 2-0. This clinched the Second Division championship for them, and a carnival atmosphere was generated by their many supporters in the crowd of 14,171, which had realised record gate receipts.

Cardiff ended a disjointed season in 15th place, with more headlines being made about the club's financial situation than team affairs. The balance sheet showed that although the club made a working profit of £248,000, gained from transfers and stringent cuts on the wage bill, the overall debt was £1.4 million, of which over £1m. was owed to the parent company, Kenton Utilities. This meant that promising young players would have to be sold, and Mr. Goodfellow would not be allowed to buy players during the summer.

Three players, Dwyer, Gibbins and Tong were ever-present, and Dwyer became the new record holder of most Cardiff City appearances in all competitions, passing Don Murray and Tom Farquharson's totals. Goalkeeper Andy Dibble missed just one match. Gordon Owen was top scorer with fifteen League goals and Nigel Vaughan scored eight.

At the end of the season Jeff Hemmerman took a specialist's advice and decided to retire from League football, for his attempted comeback proved that he no longer had his former sharpness. He decided to continue his physiotherapy training and assist Cardiff City in the medical department.

F.A. Cup
Cardiff City faced First Division Ipswich Town in the third round, and were sent tumbling to a 0-3 home defeat, with Eric Gates completing a marvellous hat-trick for the visitors.

Welsh Cup
The City entertained Taff's Well of the Welsh League in the fifth round, and won by five clear goals. The next round brought another Welsh League club, Maesteg Park – managed by former Bluebird Brian Clark – to Ninian Park, and the City sailed through with a 4-0 score.

At home to Hereford United in the quarter-final, Cardiff suffered an embarrassing defeat as the Fourth Division side won 3-1.

Milk Cup
Exeter City were met in the first round, and the City won the first leg 3-2 at St. James Park. They then completed the job, by 2-1 at Ninian Park, thanks to Crawford and Gary Bennett. In the second round, the City faced First Division Norwich City, and in the first leg at Ninian Park, a youthful team which included Chris Townsend, Wayne Matthews and Russell Heycock as sub., did well to draw 0-0. Sadly the game was watched by less than 5,000 spectators. The Bluebirds were outclassed in the second leg at Carrow Road as Norwich won 3-0, with a hat-trick from former England player Mick Channon.

Generally considered the 'Goal of the 1983/84 season'. Roger Gibbins' brilliant volley, in the Chelsea match.

1984-5 Season - Division 2:

Cardiff City were seldom off the back pages of the local press during the close season, due to the hive of activity going on behind the scenes at Ninian Park.

The Blue Dragon Rugby League club, after three years without ever attaining the level of success that had been hoped for, departed Ninian Park to set up home at Bridgend. This brought relief among Cardiff City supporters, who held the belief that not only had the funding on the project been to the detriment of the soccer team, but the Ninian Park surface had suffered by having two different codes played on it, often on consecutive days.

Transfer speculation ran high and, with City deep in debt, they were in no position to turn down offers for goalkeeper Andy Dibble, defender Gary Bennett, and leading scorer Gordon Owen.

Dibble was signed by First Division Luton Town for £125,000, a new record incoming fee for City. Independent tribunals set fees of £75,000 for Bennett, who joined Len Ashurst at Sunderland, (City had wanted in excess of £100,000) and £27,000 for Owen to join Barnsley, his home-town club. City had valued Owen at £100,000, Barnsley offered just £10,000, and not for the first time the tribunal favoured the buying club. Jimmy Goodfellow retained most of his playing staff, releasing forwards Martin Goldsmith and Trevor Lee, so the decision of Jeff Hemmerman to accept his insurance settlement resulted in a desperate shortage of strikers. Goodfellow had no money to spend - the incoming fees for Dibble, Bennett and Owen going to appease the bank manager - and the manager scoured the lists of released players for new recruits. He did quite well, reinforcing City's depleted squad with utility defender Vaughan Jones from Newport County. Also signed were forwards Kevin Summerfield from Walsall and John Seasman from Rotherham, plus goalkeeper Lee Smelt from Halifax Town, who had been at City in 1979, when he was released by Richie Morgan after the pre-season tour of Denmark. Other players such as Russell Irving, Nyrere Kelly and Birmingham's Mark Kendall were released by Mr. Goodfellow following trial periods.

City had a mixed bag of pre-season games but did well in the final one at Ninian Park when they beat Stoke City 3-0. Just over 5,000 spectators were at City's opening League match against Charlton Athletic, when Smelt, Vaughan Jones, Seasman and Summerfield all made their debuts. The air was full of relegation talk as Derek Hales, with a hat-trick, swept the Londoners to a 3-0 victory. The Bluebirds slumped to the foot of the table as Goodfellow introduced Y.T.S. goalkeeper Mel Rees, loan signing Paul Bannon of Bristol Rovers and former England captain Gerry Francis - now a free agent - in a 2-4 home defeat by Brighton. But against the odds they then beat table-topping Leeds United in an exciting clash, and a well merited victory, at Ninian Park.

Five consecutive defeats kept the Bluebirds rooted to the bottom of the table, and the only pleasurable moment came at Blackburn on the 18th of September 1984, when Phil Dwyer passed the Club's League appearance record of 445 set by Tom Farquharson. Typically, Dwyer's historic match was spoiled when Blackburn scored a winning goal, with only ten seconds left to play.

The Bluebirds equalled their worst-ever start to a season, six defeats in seven games in 1921-2, when they crashed to three second-half goals at home against Manchester City after which Mr. Goodfellow made this ill-timed quote:-

> 'You can blame me for this is my team. The board said money would be made available for the right players. I recommended certain players but all were rejected for one reason or another'.

Former Cardiff City manager Jimmy Scoular, attending the Manchester City match, following a severe stroke which restricted his speech, was asked how many new players he thought City needed, and in typically wicked fashion, the craggy Scot held up all ten fingers and smiled wistfully! Five days later, on the 27th of September, 1984, Jimmy Goodfellow was dismissed at Cardiff City manager.

Alan Durban, the ex-Shrewsbury, Stoke City and Sunderland manager – who began his football career with Cardiff City and became a Welsh international whilst starring with Derby County – was appointed the new manager within hours of Goodfellow's departure. Local newspapers had linked Durban with the post during the previous April; Jimmy Mullen was retained as player-coach. Managing director Ron Jones, with regard to Goodfellow, said:-

'Kenton Utilities were never happy about Jimmy's appointment as he had little experience. The chairman, Jack Leonard, did not have confidence in Jimmy's judgement to buy players. Jimmy Goodfellow was given a chance. It did not work out, and we are very sorry about that. I suspect that Alan Durban will be more dynamic and determined as a manager and hopefully will push the club up the table'.

Jimmy Goodfellow later joined his former colleague Len Ashurst at Sunderland.

Durban's first match in charge was a relegation dog-fight at Middlesbrough, which City lost 2-3, and indeed the Bluebirds showed no improvement in their results, for in six games there was only a 2-0 win at Notts. County to lift the gloom. Former City player Tarki Micallef, a free agent, was re-signed after a trial. Durban's first purchase was for much-capped Welsh international midfielder, Brian Flynn, who he signed for £15,000 from Burnley.

City collected only their seventh point in 14 games when they came back, in sensational fashion, after being 0-2 down at home against Oldham Athletic, with Nigel Vaughan scoring twice in the last three minutes. Alan Durban brought in on trial the former Irish international Mick Martin, who had been with Vancouver Whitecaps. With barely 3,000 at Ninian Park, The City secured only their third win in 15 games when Tong scored an injury time winner in the 2-1 victory over Carlisle.

Welsh international goalkeeper David Felgate – on loan from Lincoln City, full-back King (ex-Shrewsbury and Wrexham), plus non-League players Kevin Meacock, Mike Ford and Paul McLoughlin all came into the team and Durban paid £20,000 for Coventry striker Graham Withey, after a loan spell. Despite these changes, The Bluebirds did not win again until the 2nd of February, when Meacock scored twice in a 2-1 home win over Middlesbrough – before City's lowest post-war League crowd of only 2,564. The Bluebirds recovered from a 3-6 beating at Grimsby on the 2nd of March, to record an unlikely 4-1 triumph at Charlton three days later. It was to be the last time that the reliable Dwyer would score for his beloved City, for following successive home defeats by Fulham and Notts. County, Durban released him, plus Lee Smelt, Vaughan Jones, and David Grant.

Thirteen years a first-team player it was sad to see Dwyer leave Ninian Park under a cloud. Capped ten times by Wales the locally-born Dwyer had set a new appearance record for the Bluebirds with 471 Football League appearances, plus 23 in the F.A. Cup, 43 in the Welsh Cup, 28 Football League Cup games, and 5 European Cup-winners Cup appearances; a total of 570. He also played three games in the Anglo-Scottish Cup which are not always recorded. Dwyer joined Fourth Division Rochdale, third from bottom of the League, where he played out the season, before enlisting in the South Wales constabulary.

The Bluebirds drew 0-0 at promotion chasing Portsmouth, and hit back from 0-2 down at leaders Manchester City, to earn a surprise point. Just on the transfer deadline Durban brought loan signings Dean Saunders from Swansea and David Hamilton from Blackburn, both of whom made their debuts at Maine Road. City however, remained rooted to the foot of the Division until three successive wins, at Carlisle and at home against Barnsley plus Huddersfield – during which time Nigel Vaughan scored five goals – offered a fleeting lifeline to safety. But it was not to be, as the Bluebirds lost their final three games of the season. So it was a black day in Cardiff on the 11th of May 1985, when City dropped back into the Third Division. To add to the gloom, the popular *'Football Echo'* after its birth in 1919, was published for the last time.

In-an instantly forgettable season which saw the City use 30 players, Gibbins, Vaughan, Tong and Dwyer made the most regular appearances. Vaughan was top scorer with sixteen goals and Withey netted six.

F.A. Cup

Cardiff were drawn to play at Gillingham in the third round, who were near the top of the Third Division, and it was no real surprise when the Bluebirds were knocked out at the rain-sodden Priestfield Stadium. Eight minutes from time Leslie rewarded the volunteers – who had helped clear the pitch of eight inches of snow – with Gillingham's winner.

Welsh Cup

Cardiff City were drawn at home against Merthyr Tydfil in the fifth round. Although the part-timers had seven players with Football League experience they were no match for the Bluebirds, after David Tong had scored a fluke goal. Further strikes saw City romp to a 5-0 win.

Hereford United visited Ninian Park in the sixth round and the Fourth Division side repeated their feat of the previous season by dumping City out of the competition, with a 0-4 scoreline. Two goals in each half inflicted upon City their worst Welsh Cup defeat since they had lost at Swansea in 1925 by the same margin. Embarrassment was the word banded freely around Ninian Park on one of the saddest nights in Cardiff City's history.

Milk Cup

For the third time in four seasons, the Bluebirds met Exeter City in the first round. City lost to a Viney penalty in the first leg at St. James' Park, but went through 2-1 on aggregate, when Roger Gibbins scored twice at Ninian Park.

The second round paired the City with First Division Watford, and the first leg at Vicarage Road was quite a torrid affair. Three minutes after Gibbins had headed the Bluebirds in front, John Seasman had a weak penalty kick saved by Sherwood. The City then had defender Colin Smith sent off. A minute before half-time, John Barnes equalised and went on to complete a hat-trick in the second half, and City were faced with a 1-3 deficit.

The second leg saw the City produce a battling display, even though Watford missed a number of chances with Blissett twice hitting the woodwork – one a penalty kick which struck the bar. Just after half-time Grant moved up to head in Bodin's free-kick, and although the home team won, they bowed out 1-3 on aggregate.

Phil Dwyer bids farewell to Ninian Park with a looping header from Mullen's free-kick, and gets the equaliser against Wimbledon.

1985–86 Season – Division 3

Cardiff City found themselves plunging even deeper into debt following their relegation to Division Three, and attendances were running at the lowest ebb since the dark days of the 1930's, with 4,395 as the average over the previous season. With precious few assets, Durban released goalkeeper Gary Plumley, full-back Paul Bodin and utility player Karl Elsey. Both Nigel Vaughan and Roger Gibbins were unsettled and had not signed renewed contracts. Lee Smelt, who had previously been made available, re-signed for the club with a special role in charge of the youth team. Alan Durban, upset by City's lack of reserve competition, organised the Club's election to the newly-founded Macbar League. He also brought former Bluebird Stan Montgomery – a player in the late 40's and 1950's and trainer in the early 1960's – back to Ninian Park to 'spot' and coach local youngsters. It was a role 'Monty' had done to great effect for Bristol Rovers over a number of years. Durban signed Norwich reserve forward Mark Farrington on a free transfer, and gave successful trials to full-back John Carver of Newcastle United, forward Rob Turner of Huddersfield Town, defender Carleton Leonard of Hereford United and goalkeeper Chris Sander of Swansea City. Goalkeeper Ray Cashley – ex-Bristol City – and Hamilton Academicals' midfielder Brian Wright, played in several pre-season games, but were then released.

Some of Cardiff City's pre-season matches were labelled the *Welsh Friendly Cup*, which meant nothing, as there was no trophy to play for! The Club began the season without any shirt sponsorship, and seldom can the Bluebirds have prepared for a new term at such a low ebb. It therefore came as an almighty shock when the Bluebirds walloped Notts County 4-1 at Meadow Lane on the 17th of August, to record their best opening day victory since their first League match in 1920 (when they won 5-2 at Stockport). Sander, Carver, Farrington and Turner made their debuts, and although City then lost 0-2 at home to Chesterfield, they secured another away win on August Bank Holiday, when Nigel Vaughan's late goal pipped Newport County at Somerton Park.

From a comfortable 8th position in the Third Division, the Bluebirds then embarked on a dreadful run that yielded just one win in seventeen matches, results which anchored them firmly to the foot of the table, and sent the attendances tumbling to around the 2,000 mark. When Reading beat the City 3-1 at Ninian Park on August the 31st, Durban refused to give the match ball to Trevor Senior – who had scored a hat-trick – but a Reading supporter later purchased the ball for the player!

Players came and went at an alarming rate. Ex-City player David Giles rejoined the Club, youngsters Jason Gummer, Paul Wheeler, Wayne Curtis, Allen Price and Tim O'Connor were given debuts. Loan signings David Corner from Sunderland and Andy Spring from Bristol Rovers made brief appearances, John Carver was released and Roger Gibbins (after good service for Cardiff over three seasons and in a number of positions), was exchanged for Swansea's Welsh international midfielder Chris Marusti. Also leaving the Club was David Tong for Cambridge United (who had made over 100 appearances), and Graham Withey – who had cost £20,000 – joined Bath City. In November, Brian Flynn, a major disappointment, was transferred to Doncaster Rovers, whilst Welsh international defender Nigel Stevenson, from Swansea City, and winger Derrick Christie of Reading, both arrived for loan spells.

It was during Stevenson's stay at Ninian Park that the Bluebirds enjoyed their best form of the season, which began with a 4-0 win at Lincoln on the 14th of December. A week later, the City won 4-3 at Chesterfield, at the same time as neighbours Swansea City were being wound up in the High Court. The Swans frantically launched a lifeline appeal in the city and the public response was such that they had a stay of execution – which was granted on Christmas Eve. It was in this atmosphere that the City and the Swans met on Boxing Day at Ninian Park, and the Bluebirds notched their third successive League win when Nigel Vaughan's goal two minutes from time settled a passionate match before a crowd of 9,373.

The Bluebirds then drew 1-1 at home with Newport County, before featuring in a breath-taking match in monsoon conditions at Plymouth, on New Year's Day, which ended with a 4-4 scoreline. The Bluebirds astonishingly moved up and out of the relegation places in which they had been entrenched, when Nigel Vaughan's goal beat Brentford. A week later they earned a 1-1 draw at all-conquering Reading, after leading through Mike Ford's goal.

Nigel Stevenson then returned to Swansea, the clubs failing to agree a deal; in fact, the centre-half wanted to remain at the Vetch Field as it was his testimonial year. Almost without warning the Bluebirds dipped back into their previously hopeless form - with only two wins in sixteen games! Centre-half Phil Brignull came from AFC Bournemouth on loan, and was eventually signed for £9,000 - with half the fee subscribed by supporters - and it was reported that Alan Durban also contributed to the sum.

It was becoming obvious that Cardiff were on the slide to the Fourth Division, and as the crowds dipped, Kenton Utilities put the club up for sale. Amid much speculation, vice chairman Tony Clemo and managing director Ron Jones were reported as putting together a package deal to take over the club. Following a reported incident involving Club supporters, Mark Farrington had his contract terminated, which further depleted City's squad. Durban, who was now facing the wrath of City supporters on a daily basis, brought in forwards Will Foley and Gerry Nardiello in a last ditch attempt to stave off the inevitable.

But nothing could arrest the City slide. On the 5th of April, the lowest League crowd (to that date), 1,777, watched City's home match with Walsall, during which Chris Sander became the first City goalkeeper to save two penalties in a game, which ended with a 1-1 scoreline. Not for the first time the City teased their diehard supporters that they may earn a last gasp reprieve, when they won 2-0 at Doncaster, and beat Bristol Rovers 2-0 at home. But on the 26th of April, a 1-3 defeat at Wolves (who were themselves relegated), saw the Bluebirds reach their nadir as they dropped into the basement of the Football League.

On May the 1st, Alan Durban was sacked after reaching a settlement on the remaining seventeen months of his contract, and news of the Tony Clemo ownership of the club, that was to take effect on the 2nd of June 1986, became public. It had been a traumatic two years for Alan Durban, who had seen the club sink like a stone from the Second to the Fourth Division. Player-coach Jimmy Mullen took charge for the City's final home game of the season, against Lincoln City (who were also relegated), which they won 2-1, with two goals from Rob Turner. The crowd was a meagre 1,904, and the average attendance during this awful season was only 3,061!

An astonishing thirty two players had represented Cardiff City during the season, of which Jimmy Mullen, Mike Ford and Nigel Vaughan appeared most often. Vaughan was top scorer with twelve goals and Mullen netted eight times (all penalties). On May the 21st, the new Club chairman Tony Clemo approached Sunderland with regard to the availability of their coach, Frank Burrows. The Roker Park club had no objections to City's enquiry, and Frank Burrows agreed to become the new manager of Cardiff City.

F.A. Cup

Cardiff City visited Exeter City, in the first round, and came away empty handed after former Swansea striker Darren Gale scored twice for the Fourth Division side. On loan Nigel Stevenson got a late consolation, and at the final whistle, hundreds of disenchanted City fans vented their feelings by calling for the resignation of Mr Durban.

Welsh Cup

Cardiff City played at Caerleon in the fourth round, and the Welsh Leaguers made the Bluebirds work hard for a hollow victory. Vaughan scored twice, and with the score at 2-2, Marustik capped a wriggling run to score the winning goal from the narrowest of angles, five minutes from time. This effort silenced a group of spectators, who had chanted for Durban's resignation throughout the second-half.

There was a pleasant surprise for the crowd of 604, the lowest in the City's history for a recognised first-team game, when Jeff Hemmerman was included in the team to face Mold Alexandra at Ninian Park in the fifth round. Hemmerman, now working in physiotherapy, was registered for cup games, and both he and Rob Turner scored in the first-half. Mold replied, but two goals from Vaughan in the final seven minutes gave Cardiff a flattering 4-1 win.

Welsh League champions Barry Town, managed by former Bluebird Richie Morgan, visited Ninian Park in the quarter final, and they came close with a gritty performance which earned a replay from a goalless draw. Two days later the teams met again, at Jenner Park, and the City had to thank Hemmerman for their interval lead, following a near post diving header. Midway through the second-half, David Giles operating at left-back scored for City to win by 2-0.

The Bluebirds faced Wrexham in the two-legged semi--final and they were humiliated at the Racecourse, as Wrexham romped to an emphatic 4-1 win. This result virtually put City out of the competition. A week later Wrexham completed the job when they comfortably beat a woeful City 2-1!

Milk Cup

Cardiff and Swansea met in the first round, and at Ninian Park, two poor sides produced an exciting match which the Bluebirds won by 2-1. Cardiff appeared to be in control of the second leg at the Vetch Field, when Mark Farrington headed them into a 40th minute lead. The Swans scored a disputed goal on the stroke of half-time through Randell, and the same player scored again just after the break. In the 55th minute, Swansea completed a great rescue act when Pascoe put them 3-1 ahead. That was the end for the Bluebirds.

Freight Rover Trophy

Cardiff City's first excursion in the competition created for Third and Fourth Division clubs, with a Wembley Final on offer, saw them in a three club group, along with Newport County and Swansea City. The Bluebirds made no impression at all, losing 0-1 at Newport, and 0-2 at home against Swansea, the latter watched by a crowd of only 1,006.

1986-7 Season – Division 4:

The summer of 1986 was a very hectic one as far as Cardiff City were concerned. The agreed take-over of the club was completed on the 2nd of June, when Kenton Utilities released control of the club ownership to Tony Clemo, a Cardiff City director since 1975. At the same time directors Dewi Evans and George Edwards, resigned from the board. On the following day, the former Newport County manager Bobby Smith was appointed as Youth and Reserve team coach.

Frank Burrows, the new manager of Cardiff City, was well known in football circles, and he began to recruit busily for the coming season. Jimmy Mullen accepted the post of player-manager at Newport County, after giving the City four years excellent service, during which which he made well over 150 appearances and captained the Bluebirds to promotion in 1982-3. Keen to bolster his first team squad with seasoned professionals, Burrows signed experienced left back Steve Sherlock from Stockport County, Welsh international Alan Curtis from Southampton, winger Alan Rogers (Southend United) and Graham Moseley, a former Cup Final goalkeeper with Brighton. These players were obtained on free transfers, but Cardiff had to pay neighbours Newport County £22,000 for former Welsh international defender Terry Boyle, the fee being fixed by a tribunal.

Burrows also drafted in Andy Kerr of Shrewsbury, and Paul Wimbleton of Portsmouth – on trial – and both players were later signed permanently. Another major appointment was made when former City manager Jimmy Goodfellow returned to the Club as physiotherapist and assistant to Mr. Burrows.

So in a very short space of time the new manager had overhauled his first team pool and created what was probably the most experienced back room staff in the Fourth Division.

The City played a mixed bag of pre-season friendlies, in which Paul Wheeler scored freely, but Alan Curtis suffered a broken cheekbone, which caused him to miss the Bluebirds' first game in the Fourth Division. This match was at Hartlepool, and ended 1-1, with Rob Turner scoring the Clubs' first goal in the Football League's basement. Unfortunately disturbances by some City 'supporters' attracted unwanted publicity for the Club.

Less than two hours after the Hartlepool game had ended, Middlesbrough, bankrupt and locked out of Ayresome Park, played their home Third Division fixture with Port Vale at the Victoria Ground – a gesture from Hartlepool which went a long way towards keeping their neighbours in business.

The Bluebirds lost just once in their opening nine games of Fourth Division football, a 0-2 home defeat by Tranmere, but with five draws City hardly surfaced above mid-table. Just as it seemed that they had come to terms with life at the bottom, bad defeats at Wrexham (1-5), and by 1-3 at Colchester, rocked the Bluebirds, and the attendance for a 1-1 draw with Scunthorpe at Ninian Park barely reached 2,000. Triallist Nicky Platnauer came into the team after a run of substitute appearances, scoring on his full debut in a 1-1 draw at Halifax, and young Mel Rees emerged as a serious contender for Graham Moseley's position in goal.

Fortunately for the Club, their exploits in the Littlewoods Cup, diverted attention away from their less than mediocre League form, as the team cried out for a proven goalscorer.

Kevin Bartlett, once at Portsmouth under Mr. Burrows, was signed from non-League Fareham Town. After scoring twice in a Welsh Cup tie, the quicksilver black forward made a sensational two goal League debut four days later, as the City beat Cambridge United 3-0. Burrows borrowed Fulham's Cardiff-born striker Chris Pike, who had escaped City's notice when he played locally, and the burly six footer scored several vital goals during his two month loan. The Bluebirds were unable to make Fulham an offer for the player and he returned to Craven Cottage.

On the 28th of December Graham Moseley became the second goalkeeper to be sent off in the City's history, when the Bluebirds crashed 1-4 at runaway leaders Northampton Town. The club received £1,000 from Bristol Rovers for Rob Turner, who would later be involved in several substantial transfer moves, and Steve Sherlock had a loan spell at Newport County.

Cardiff were proving to be a real 'Jekyll and Hyde' outfit, with good performances in the F.A. Cup and Littlewoods Cup competitions. But in League matches they seemed incapable of making home advantage tell, whereas their away record was almost on a par with promotion form. The Bluebirds failed to win a League match at Ninian Park for over four months, for after beating Aldershot 2-0 on the 13th of December, their dwindling band of hardcore supporters had to wait until the 18th of April before witnessing another home victory. During this same period however, the Bluebirds won five away games.

It really was a ludicrous state of affairs that not even the arrival (on loan) of Reading's Dean Horrix and Rotherham's Tony Simmons, could alter – although both players did, in fact, get on the score-sheet. A proposed exchange deal involving Horrix and Cardiff's unsettled Nigel Vaughan failed to materialise, and after 16 year old Jason Perry made a brief appearance as one of the City's youngest debutants, at right-back against Exeter City on the 31st of March, Vaughan ended the season in that position. This was an amazing selection by Burrows, for an attacking left-sided midfielder! Before the transfer deadline, Steve Sherlock joined Newport County on a permanent basis, and forward Steve Mardenborough arrived from the Gwent club.

Public apathy showed in the final game of a mediocre season, when only 1,510 – the lowest ever home League attendance – watched a 4-0 win over Hartlepool! The average for home games dipped below 3,000 for the first time, as the City finished in 13th position. The lowest point since the dark days of the 1930's. had been reached!

Midfielder Paul Wimbleton, an ever present, was the top scorer with only eight goals – four of them penalties. Vaughan scored six goals, despite his eight appearances at right back at the end of the season.

F.A. Cup

The first round provided a unique occasion, for the City travelled to Welsh League club Ton Pentre – in the heart of the Rhondda Valleys – and a traditional stronghold of the Bluebird's support.

The City overcame the non-Leaguers by 4-1, although they had the occasional scare along the way. Brentford came to Ninian Park in the second round, and the visitors never recovered from Wimbleton's first minute goal. The speedy Kevin Bartlett later added a second, as the City - in heavy ground conditions - triumphed 2-0.

The Bluebirds faced a tough hurdle in the third round, when they travelled to the Den, the intimidating home of Millwall. Cardiff gave a gritty defensive display to earn a replay from a 0-0 draw, and at Ninian Park ten days later, the teams played out a ding-dong F.A. Cup tie in the traditional mould, which also ended all square, at 2-2. The Bluebirds won the toss for choice of venue for the second replay and, on the 26th of January, they made home advantage tell by winning 1-0, from Chris Pike's rapier-like header.

Five days later a large number of City supporters were in the 20,423 crowd at First Division Stoke City, for the fourth round tie. Despite taking the lead with a Paul Wimbleton goal, the Welshmen finally cracked, as Stoke came back to win 2-1.

Welsh Cup

Cardiff City met Taff's Well at Ninian Park in the third round, and the crowd of only 581, became the lowest recorded for a home match, in any competition. Kevin Bartlett marked his first appearance in the City's colours, with two goals, as the Bluebirds beat the Welsh League team 4-0. The City bowed out of the competition in the fourth round tie at Wrexham, on the 3rd of February, when the Robins won by a solitary goal.

Littlewoods Cup (Formerly Milk Cup)

Cardiff City's first game (on the 26th of August), in the newly titled competition was a first round first leg match, against recently promoted Second Division Club Plymouth Argyle. The match proved to be one of the most remarkable games ever seen at Ninian Park.

Burrows' reshaped City team, which included six summer signings, made a disastrous start when Matthews fired Argyle into an early lead, with a fierce 30 yard free-kick. In the 22nd minute Coughlin doubled the Plymouth lead, but seven minutes later Nigel Vaughan reduced the deficit with a well constructed goal.

A memorable night for Nicky Platnauer. After scoring the equaliser in the Littlewoods Cup match versus Chelsea, he (behind the post) nets the winner from close range.

The visitors scored a third when Coughlin hammered a stunning shot past Graham Moseley from all of 35 yards, and just before half-time, former City player Kevin Summerfield nipped in to give Argyle an apparently unassailable 4-1 lead!

The Bluebirds powered back after the break, and two goals in three minutes from Rob Turner and Nigel Vaughan, brought City back to 3-4. The small crowd was now behind the Bluebirds, and there was delight on the terraces when new skipper Terry Boyle forced home the equaliser from Alan Rogers' free-kick. With the match wide open, both sides continued to create chances. Cardiff completed possibly the greatest fight back in their history, when Paul Wheeler made it 5-4 with a close range shot seven minutes from time.

The second leg saw Argyle in rousing form, but the City defence stood firm in the face of hectic pressure. They made sure of winning the tie when David Giles sent a long centre into the Plymouth net to score a freak goal.

The Bluebirds were drawn against Luton Town in the two-legged second round, and in an unprecedented situation in football history, they were awarded the tie after Luton had refused to issue a ticket allocation for Cardiff City supporters. Luton took the severe and drastic action of banning all away supporters from Kenilworth Road for League matches, following incidents two years earlier. But this action could not be implemented for Cup matches. Cardiff asked for their rightful ticket allocation - Luton refused - and the League Management Committee had no option other than to award Cardiff a bye.

The decision became a major talking point at a time when the Government wanted action to be taken by the clubs against the hooligan element, which was not helped by Cardiff City - *'supporters'* - causing problems in the early weeks of the season at both Hartlepool and Exeter!

The Bluebirds entertained Chelsea in the third round, and with the threat of hooligan problems the policing was stringent. Ninian Park resembled a fortress as all supporters underwent a search on entry to all parts of the ground, and thousands of genuine supporters suffered this inconvenience and embarrassment. Fortunately for the 8,018 at Ninian Park, the game turned into an emotional occasion, as the City hit back after the struggling First Division side had taken the lead through Jones' penalty. Nick Platnauer, making his first full appearance, headed home a classic equaliser, and later bundled home a close-range winner.

All roads lead to Shrewsbury on the 18th of November, for the fourth round tie, and in monsoon conditions the Bluebirds had by far the better of the game. They paid for their lack of finishing power however, when McNally scored for Shrewsbury with just three minutes remaining - to net the game's only goal.

Freight Rover Trophy

In their group matches they lost 0-1 at home to Wolves, and by the same score at A.F.C.Bournemouth, and so slipped quietly out of the competition.

During the 1986-7 season, Alan Curtis was recalled to the Wales' squad, and played in the match versus Russia, at the Vetch Field.

1987-88 Season – Division 4:

Cardiff City manager Frank Burrows scoured the transfer marker during the summer, following his teams' poor position in the Fourth Division. It was imperative that the Bluebirds showed a lot of improvement as attendances had reached crisis level, and promotion from the Fourth Division had to take precedence over all else. Among the departures from Ninian Park were Andy Kerr, Chris Marustik, Alan Rogers and Phil Brignull. The cash flow was eased by a £100,000 package deal from Watford for teenager goalkeeper Mel Rees, whose performances at the end of the past season had alerted the First Division club. It was believed that the deal consisted of a £60,000 down payment, with the balance payable after a specified number of first team appearances.

Burrows signed rookie midfielder Mark Kelly from Shrewsbury, where he had made just two Welsh Cup appearances, and then brought in former Welsh international defender Nigel Stevenson from Swansea City, who had played 14 League games on loan for the Bluebirds, during the 1985-66 season. Other free transfer recruits were Oxford winger Brian McDermott, once a First Division player with Arsenal, and Cardiff born defender Phil Bater from Brentford – who had played over 400 games in a career spanning spells with Bristol Rovers and Wrexham. Halifax forward Paul Sanderson was given a three month trial. Finally the manager spent £17,000 on the much travelled 24 year old striker Jimmy Gilligan, who found himself out of the Football League, after finishing bottom of the table with Lincoln City; the first club to suffer automatic relegation to the G.M. Vauxhall Conference. The squad looked useful, laced with experience and no little quality, and they had a good pre-season tour of East Anglia.

Nigel Vaughan was still in dispute over the terms of his contract, and Burrows stated that he did not intend to select the former Welsh international midfielder until the problems were resolved. The City opened the season at home to Leyton Orient, on the 15th of August, with five debutants – Stevenson, Sanderson, Gilligan, McDermott and Kelly – in the line-up. Jimmy Gilligan headed the equaliser in a 1-1 draw, on a sweltering afternoon. That same evening saw the return, by public demand, of the popular pink *'Football Echo'*, after an absence of two years.

After slumping to defeat at Bolton, the City roared into winning ways in the 'derby' match with Swansea at Ninian Park, on the 29th of August. Jimmy Gilligan smote a fierce winner but a keen encounter was marred by the sending off of Swansea's Joe Allen for striking Terry Boyle. Mindless hooliganism on the 'Bob Bank' made the television news and forced the new Membership scheme to be rigorously enforced.

The Bluebirds earned their first away point in a dour 0-0 draw at Cambridge, before returning to Ninian Park to win a thrilling match with Wolves by the odd goal in five. One of the visitors' goals was scored by substitute Nigel Vaughan, who had joined the Midlanders two days earlier for a bargain £12,000 fee. Only 2,258 saw the game, due to a ban on Wolves' supporters after incidents at Scarborough on the opening day of the season.

On the 12th of September, Phil Bater and Youth Team captain Gareth Abraham, made their debuts in an unhappy 0-3 defeat at Wrexham. Bater had the unwanted statistic of becoming the first Cardiff City player to be sent off on a debut appearance!

Abraham scored on his home debut as the City beat Darlington, and four days later they overcame Carlisle. A 1-0 success at Tranmere elevated the bobbling Bluebirds into second place, and almost 4,500 were at the home game with Hereford on the 10th of October. But it was a poor match and the visitors took the points through Spooner's penalty, after the normally mild mannered Alan Curtis had been sent off.

A week later City lost a remarkable match at Peterborough 3-4, despite taking the lead three times! After the match, hospital X-rays revealed that goalkeeper Graham Moseley had sustained a broken arm, and Burrows moved quickly to borrow Oxford's Alan Judge in time for him to play against Torquay three days later. The on-loan 'keeper, in borrowed kit after his car had been burgled overnight, made a winning start as City came from behind to beat Torquay 2-1.

Jimmy Gilligan, whose popularity among the Bluebirds fans was increasing, headed a last minute winner against Rochdale at Ninian Park. The City kept up their good work, by drawing 1-1 at Scarborough, and Gilligan was again the hero as the Bluebirds came from behind to beat Exeter City 3-2 at Ninian Park. The strikers' first goal followed some instinctive ball juggling and shot from 20 yards, and he netted the winner just seven minutes from time.

Young John Roberts stepped between the posts for his League debut when City won 2-1 at troubled Newport County, and a week later Brian McDermott's late equaliser spared the Bluebirds' blushes in a 1-1 home draw with Hartlepool United. As Christmas approached, the City – in fourth place – were well placed. Successive home wins over Burnley and Tranmere kept up the momentum. Following Alan Judge's recall to Oxford, Burrows borrowed York goalkeeper Scott Endersby, and also recruited former Welsh international forward Ian Walsh (from Grimsby), where he had suffered long spells with injury.

Cardiff lost at the leaders, Colchester United, by 1-2 on the 28th of December, but on New Years' Day they drew 2-2 at Swansea. Amidst torrential rain and gale force winds, all the goals came in the final half-hour, with Gilligan's equaliser arriving deep into injury time.

A car accident, and the consequential injuries received, ultimately put goalkeeper Graham Moseley out for the season (he retired six months later), and Burrow signed the experienced George Wood, a former Scottish international from Crystal Palace, until the end of the season.

City swept Cambridge aside at Ninian Park, scoring four goals without reply, on the 30th of January. After drawing 0-0 at Darlington, the Bluebirds had a magnificent 4-1 victory at Molineux against League leaders Wolves, where Gilligan and Paul Wimbleton scored two apiece, which put the City at second place in the table.

A solo goal from utility player Mike Ford was enough to beat Colchester, at a rain-swept Ninian Park, but seven days later they crashed 1-4 at Leyton Orient, a bitter disappointment for the club's followers, for if the Bluebirds had avoided defeat, they would have competed at

Wembley at the end of the season, as one of the two Fourth Division representatives at the Football League centenary celebration tournament. This overshadowed the fact that the City's defeat at Brisbane Road was only their second League loss in sixteen games.

Kevin Bartlett hit a rich seam of goals, with six in five away games, that helped the team to win at Halifax, Hereford and Exeter, and draw at Rochdale. But the Bluebirds struggled at Ninian Park, until Easter Monday when they demolished a beleaguered Newport 4-0. After a 0-2 defeat at Torquay, Cardiff ended the season in great style with five straight wins, and this put the club back into the Third Division, as the runner-up behind Wolves. There was delight at Ninian Park when Frank Burrows was nominated as Bell's *'Manager of the Month'*, for April 1988 - a worthy award and a popular one.

Over 10,000 expectant supporters were at the City's final home game, with Crewe Alexandra on the 2nd of May, and they saw Kevin Bartlett, and Brian McDermott (direct from a corner kick), score the goals that brought rejoicing on the terraces as promotion was secured.

Jimmy Gilligan and Terry Boyle were ever-present and both Brian McDermott and Mike Ford missed just one match. There were good contributions from Phil Bater, Alan Curtis, Paul Wimbleton, Nicky Platnauer and Nigel Stevenson - who all appeared regularly. Gilligan was leading scorer with 20 League goals, followed by Kevin Bartlett with 12.

It had been a good season with the manager skilfully utilising his small squad to the best of their abilities, although he had had to use no fewer that five goalkeepers. Although the financial situation had apparently stabilised, the Club still needed improved attendances and major sponsorship in order to be a viable concern.

F.A. Cup
Cardiff City bowed out at the first hurdle, when they lost 1-2 at Peterborough, for whom midfielder Mick Gooding scored a goal in each half.

Welsh Cup
The Bluebirds were drawn at Welsh League champions Ebbw Vale in the third round, but the local police, unhappy with crowd segregation arrangements, would not allow the game to be played at the 25,000 capacity Eugene Cross Park.

Manager Burrows and Chairman Clemo proudly hold the Welsh Cup.

The dressing-room scene after the promotion victory over Crewe.

The match was switched to Ninian Park and Ebbw Vale took the honours with a gutsy display in a 0-0 draw. The replay, also at Ninian Park, was settled by an early goal from Kevin Bartlett, as the City struggled to overcome the worthy Welsh League champions. Steve Morris, an impressive goalkeeper for Vale in both games, was later offered an extended trial period by Burrows.

City met non-League opposition again in the fourth round, when Port Talbot Athletic visited Ninian Park. Heavy rain and a saturated pitch, which was covered in small puddles, made conditions difficult, but two opportunist first half goals from Mike Ford put Cardiff on the road to victory. In the second-half Gilligan classically headed City's third, before the gallant Welsh Leaguers scored a late consolation, for a final 3-1 scoreline. Welsh Cup fever gripped the Glamorgan valleys when Cardiff and the holders, Merthyr Tydfil, met at Ninian Park in the fifth round. Over 7,000 saw the Bluebirds romp to a 3-1 win in a match that was more one sided than most people had expected. In the closing stages Webley scored a consolation for the disappointing Martyrs, whose rough house tactics were not appreciated by the crowd!

Caernarfon Town were met in the two-legged semi-final, and Cardiff were made to struggle in the first leg at Ninian Park. A Paul Wimbleton penalty put the City ahead, but Caernarfon soon equalised through Looker. Just before half-time Mark Kelly powered in what was to be the deciding goal, to give the City a 2-1 advantage. The second-leg at Caernarfon eight days later, saw the Bluebirds doing a thoroughly professional job to win 1-0, and the 3-1 aggregate score put Cardiff into their first Welsh Cup Final for six years.

Wrexham were their opponents in the Final at the Vetch Field on the 17th of May, and the Bluebirds, on a balmy evening, were determined to complete a promotion and Welsh Cup 'double'. They achieved their objective with ease after Alan Curtis put his side ahead in the 13th minute, with one of the finest of individual goals to be scored in the competition. The winger made a fine run from the half-way line to the right touchline, before he suddenly veered infield, beat two men, and fired a stunning left footed shot into the top corner of the net. Twenty minutes later Gilligan converted McDermott's corner kick, and the Welsh Cup was on it's way to Ninian Park. The second-half was an anti-climax but nobody cared as the City completed the 'double' with a 2-0 scoreline.

Littlewoods Cup

Cardiff City met troubled neighbours Newport County in the two-legged first round, but with Somerton Park not complying with safety regulations, both games had to be played at Ninian Park. County overcame this disadvantage, winning the first game 2-1, with two goals from former City reserve player Paul Evans, and Alan Curtis replying for the Bluebirds. City had only to win the second leg 1-0 to go through and Gilligan gave them a sixth minute lead.

Five minutes later the County levelled with a great goal from Taylor, but Cardiff regained the lead before half-time, through triallist Paul Sanderson.

Much to the home team's disappointment, Tupling made it 2-2 three minutes into the second-half, and with no further goals, the Bluebirds tumbled out of the competition.

Freight Rover Trophy

Cardiff City were drawn with Wrexham and Walsall in the preliminary group, and they scored their first goals in the competition through Wheeler, McDermott and Gilligan, when they beat Wrexham 3-2 on a wet and windy night at Ninian Park. Although they lost 1-3 at Walsall, the City went through to the first round on goal difference. They met Notts County at Meadow Lane on the 20th of January, and lost 0-2.

1988-9 Season - Division 3:

There was an air of optimism among Cardiff City supporters that the Bluebirds could challenge for a return to the Second Division, if the squad that had won promotion and the Welsh Cup 'double' the previous season, could be strengthened in one or two areas. With summer wages and bonuses to be found, it still came as something of a surprise when Oxford United made a staggering offer of £150,000 for utility player, Mike Ford. The money was just too good to turn down, and the player who was getting married readily agreed to the move. The transfer became a new record fee received by Cardiff City. Although only 22, Ford was the Club's longest-serving player, having been at Ninian Park for four years, during which he had made over 180 appearances. It was a good return for someone who had cost the club nothing.

Unfortunately for Frank Burrows, little of the Ford money came his way for new players. But he did sign veteran goalkeeper George Wood on a permanent basis, and also recruited the experienced Steve Lynex - a forward who had played at the highest level - from West Bromwich Albion on a free transfer. Burrows paid ailing Newport County - who had lost their League status and now found themselves in the G.M. Vauxhall Conference - £7,000 for midfielder Steve Tupling. The Club's major deal involved Hereford United's Ian Rodgerson, who could operate at full-back or midfield, and he came to Ninian Park for a tribunal set fee of £35,000. Going in the opposite direction was Steve Mardenborough, who joined Hereford United on a free transfer.

Another major departure from Ninian Park that summer was Managing director/secretary Ron Jones, who had been with Cardiff City for eight years. Jones accepted an offer from Jim Gregory, the Chairman of Portsmouth, to take up an executive position at Fratton Park; the two had previously been at Q.P.R. The supporters of Cardiff City were not too dismayed at Jones' departure, for the relationship between them had never been a popular one. In fact, many had often queried how a club - continually pleading poverty - could afford to pay a large salary to an administrator, while at the same time employing a number of cost-cutting exercises!

Eddie Harrison, an experienced administrator with the F.A. of Wales, accepted the post of secretary. Harrison's administrative skills were quickly put to the test, as Cardiff City were back in European football for the first time in eleven years. They were drawn to play Derry City, but due to the delicate nature of the Northern Ireland situation - particularly in Londonderry - Cardiff City refused to take their permitted allocation of tickets and implored their supporters to stay at home.

With English clubs banned, much media attention was being focused on Cardiff and the Scottish representatives, in the three European competitions.

The Bluebirds' return to the Third Division was disappointing, as they began with a 1-2 home defeat against Fulham - after taking an early lead - before a crowd of over 6,000. A week later midfielder Mark Kelly was sent off as the City were hammered 0-4 at Bolton, but things looked up when Huddersfield visited Ninian Park on the 10th of September, and inspired by two opportunist strikes from Ian Walsh, the Bluebirds won by three first-half goals.

Jimmy Gilligan scored his first League of the season at Port Vale seven days later, but it made little difference as the team crashed 1-6 to a Potteries' side who demonstrated the art of spot-on finishing.

Steve Tupling, yet to make the starting line-up, joined Torquay on loan, and young Jon Morgan made his League debut on the 8th of October, as the City slumped to a 1-2 home defeat by Reading. Burrows drafted in Leyton Orient's Steve Ketteridge on loan, and the midfielder scored at Mansfield, where Cardiff let a 2-0 lead slip, and the game ended at 2-2.

The Bluebirds did themselves a power of good during November when they played four League and two Cup games at Ninian Park, and scored twelve unanswered goals.

The twelve points gained, catapulted the team out of the bottom four to 17th position in the table, and the cause was helped with a 3-3 draw on Preston's plastic surface in a rip-roaring match, on the 3rd of December. In this match, goalkeeper George Wood made his 500th League appearance. It was not until the 2nd of January that the City gained their first away win in the Third Division, with an Alan Curtis goal securing all three points at Aldershot. The striking form of both Jimmy Gilligan and Kevin Bartlett gained more notice and publicity, and after Cardiff had rejected a £100,000 pre-Christmas bid from Scarborough for Gilligan, improved offers were reported to have been made for the player from Bristol City and Queen's Park Rangers among others.

It was something of a surprise therefore, when it was Kevin Bartlett who left the club, as Cardiff accepted an offer of £125,000 from West Bromwich Albion for the speedy forward. Two weeks before his transfer Bartlett had scored an exquisite goal, as the City romped to their best home win of the season – 3-0 over promotion-seeking Port Vale – on the 28th of January. Within days of Bartlett's sale, Cardiff City chairman Tony Clemo, under fire from supporters for allowing another quality player to be sold, announced that the club itself was up for sale, and that he would listen sympathetically to any realistic offers. At that time City's boardroom housed only Mr. Clemo himself, and his wife, Lynda, following the resignation of businessman, Gerald McCarthy.

Although Cardiff remained rooted in the lower half of the table, the Bluebirds were still in sight of the play-off positions, and following a 2-1 win at Gillingham on the 11th of March, there was even some optimistic comment to that effect. The reality was much different however, for that success over Gillingham represented the team's only win in seven League matches.

There was an announcement that among the first parties reputedly interested in formulating a take-over package to buy Mr. Clemo's controlling share holding in the club, were former directors, Gerald McCarthy and Craig Burgin. With as much activity off the field as on it, Cardiff City were seldom out of the local news, and in the midst of all this turmoil, their Third Division standing became threatened further by a 0-4 thrashing at lowly Chesterfield, for whom giant striker Andy Morris bagged a hat-trick.

Burrows managed to keep Jimmy Gilligan at Ninian Park, despite continued overtures from Terry Yorath at Bradford City, with bids that reached £330,000! Gilligan, it was reported, did meet and agree terms with the Bradford manager, but mindful of the Club's position and the possible repercussions amongst the City supporters so soon after Kevin Bartlett's transfer, Clemo and Burrows decided to keep their leading scorer to the terms of his contract, which still had several months to run. Before the transfer deadline the manager engaged former Blue-bird Roger Gibbins, now a free agent following Newport County's demise, and young Matthew Holmes of A.F.C. Bournemouth on loan.

On the 25th of March, the team won their first home League match in two months, beating Aldershot. A 1-1 draw at Swansea on Easter Monday, with only ten men after Terry Boyle's dismissal, was followed by two successive 1-1 home draws. After a surprise 1-0 win at promotion bound Sheffield United, through a Garath Abraham goal on the 11th of April, the City looked at the prospect of six home games in their remaining nine fixtures to get them out of trouble.

Four days later, Cardiff slumped by 0-1 at Bury, but events at Hillsborough that afternoon overshadowed all other football events. The City supporters rallied to the Hillsborough Disaster Fund, and in seven days collected £3,455.98p. There was a one minute silence before Notts County's visit on the 18th of April. Four days later, Cardiff City and Southend United lined up at six minutes past three, to observe a further – and moving – one minute silent tribute to the ninety five Liverpool supporters who perished so tragically at Hillsborough.

Cardiff beat Southend 2-0, and they finally clambered out of the relegation mire on the 9th of May. Terry Boyle and Jimmy Gilligan (his 14th League goal of the season) earned the Bluebirds a 2-0 home win over Chester City, before a disillusioned crowd of only 3,002!

It had been a frantic season, when the City's lack of consistency and goals away from home almost cost them dearly. Only 14 goals on their travels in a poor total of 44, told its own story.

The hoped for improvement in gate receipts, had not materialised and before the end of the season, Mr. Clemo revealed that the Club was losing £2,000 a week, and that the only way to placate the bank was to sell players such as Kevin Bartlett. Jimmy Gilligan was ever present and the top scorer.

F.A. Cup
Cardiff City were enjoying their best form when they entertained Hereford in the first round and they duly cantered to a comfortable 3-0 win,

On Sunday the 11th of December, City played at non-League Enfield, in the second round. Reports of City supporters' misbehaviour at motorway services, and in Enfield, distracted from a thoroughly professional job, which saw Wimbleton (penalty), Lynex and Gilligan (two) score the goals in a 4-1 win over the G.M. Vauxhall Conference side.

The City were well on their way to beating second Division Hull City in the next round, when Gilligan headed a superb early goal, but Hull hit back to level through full-back Brown. In the second-half, veteran Keith Edwards put the Bluebirds out by scoring an opportunist goal.

Welsh Cup
Non-League Bath City were no match for a rampant Cardiff City in the third round at Ninian Park, on the 15th of November. Kevin Bartlett was a constant thorn in the side of the Beezer Homes outfit, scoring twice in a 3-0 win, with Paul Wimbleton getting the other. City faced a sterner test against Worcester City in the fourth round, and despite home advantage, only a Mark Kelly shot separated the sides.

The Bluebirds made an ignominious exit at Kidderminster Harriers on the 8th of February, crashing 1-3 to the G.M. Vauxhall Conference team, who were in charge throughout. Kevin Bartlett, who was watched by a representative from West Bromwich Albion, scored his final goal for the City, before joining the Midlands club.

Littlewoods Cup
Cardiff City slumped to rivals Swansea City in the first leg of the first round at Ninian Park on the 30th of August, when Steve Thornber scored the only goal. But much to everyone's surprise, City overtook the Swans in the second leg, on a 2-1 aggregate.

The Bluebirds met Q.P.R. in the second round and suffered a 0-3 reversal in the first leg at Loftus Road, which all but put them out of the competition. Rangers completed the job at Ninian Park on the 11th of October, beating a youthful City team 4-1 to complete a 7-1 aggregate rout, although veteran Alan Curtis did score a marvellous consolation, with a free-kick from 22 yards. The crowd was a lowly 2,629, which reflected City's poor home form and the hopelessness of overcoming the Rangers' first leg advantage.

European Cup Winners' Cup
Despite advice against it, a small number made the trip, to see Cardiff's first game in Europe for eleven years. Despite the emotion generated by Derry City's 10,500 crowd, the game seldom reached any heights, and the Bluebirds were happy to play out a 0-0 draw.

The second leg was a one-sided affair once Brian McDermott had headed City in front after 20 minutes. Gilligan then proceeded to make a little bit of club history by becoming only the second City player to score a hat-trick in European competition, (Sandy Allan was the first in October 1969), as the Bluebirds cruised to a 4-0 win. Indeed Frank Burrows was less than complimentary about Gilligan's treble, stating:-

"He (Gilligan) is too easily satisfied, that is why he is here and not in the 1st Division. I could have scored them".

The City manager refused to sign the match ball, and although Gilligan was clearly upset by the remarks, it was seen as Burrows' way of 'geeing-up' the star striker. The second round brought the visit of the Danish club I.K. Aarhus, who provided some stylish football. Gilligan scored first, for the City, the visitors then stepped up a gear and proceeded to score twice with scintillating one-touch soccer to win 2-1, before a crowd of 6,156. As expected, the City were seldom a threat in the second leg, as Aarhus strolled to a 4-0 win.

Sherpa Van (formerly Freight Rover) Trophy
In a three club preliminary group, Cardiff defeated Swansea City at Ninian Park 2-0, and lost 1-3 at Torquay. The format of the competition allowed two clubs to progress, and Cardiff went on to face Bristol Rovers at Twerton Park in the first round, where they lost 1-2.

22nd April 1989. Before the Southend match, the City team pay silent tribute to the victims of the Hillsborough Disaster.

1989-90 Season – Division 3:

Once again it was a summer of discontent and transfer activity at Ninian Park, as Cardiff City manager Frank Burrows – whose own contract was due for renewal in June but remained unsigned – had to sell several players in order to balance the books, as the Club reported increased debts. Club captain Terry Boyle did agree a new contract, but the City's popular skipper moved to Swansea for about £12,000. Nick Platnauer, exercised his right under freedom of contract to negotiate a move, and he joined Notts County – for he considered that they had more ambition than Cardiff City – for a tribunal set fee of £50,000. Cardiff had rescued Platnauer from the scrap heap in 1986, and his successful conversion into an attacking left-back had resurrected his ailing career. Earlier in the summer City had accepted Bristol City's offer of £60,000 for midfielder Paul Wimbleton. Also leaving Ninian Park were Nigel Stevenson (to Merthyr), Phil Bater and Ian Walsh. Cardiff born striker Chris Pike – who had been at Ninian Park on loan during the 1986-7 season – joined the City from Fulham on a free transfer, and Hull City's left-back Ray Daniel was obtained for a tribunal set fee of £40,000.

Former Bluebird Paul Maddy, and Robbie Taylor (ex-Newport County), played several pre-season games on a trial basis, but were not offered terms. Leading goalscorer Jimmy Gilligan was still at the club, but like his manager he had not signed a new contract. Overall the squad looked weak, and one which appeared to be likely relegation candidates.

It came as no surprise to followers of the club's fortunes when the Bluebirds began the season in horrendous fashion. By the time that they had chalked up their first League victory, on the 7th of October (which constituted City's worst-ever start to a campaign), a further six players had arrived at Ninian Park, seven had departed, there had been a change of manager and a new record incoming transfer fee had been set!

Cardiff had lost the opening game 0-2 against Bolton at Ninian Park on the 19th of August, and following a 0-3 pasting at Tranmere seven days later, Frank Burrows accepted an offer to become an assistant manager to John Gregory at Portsmouth.

Almost immediately Cardiff City chairman Tony Clemo appointed Len Ashurst for his second spell as manager at Ninian Park. Ashurst, who proclaimed that he had the 'Midas touch', quickly brought in Ian Love on non-contract forms and two players on loan – Richard Sendall of Carlisle, and David Kevan of Notts County.

Even so, the City's form was abysmal, and when Frank Burrows instigated a Portsmouth bid of £215,000 for the unsettled Jimmy Gilligan – which was much too good an offer to turn down – the popular striker (who had never missed a game in any competition during this career with Cardiff City), moved to Fratton Park. Ashurst immediately invested £60,000 in Kettering striker Cohen Griffith, paid £25,000 for Swindon midfielder Leigh Barnard, and gave a trial period to former West Bromwich Albion goalkeeper Gavin Ward, since George Wood had picked up a wrist injury. On the 3rd of October, former Welsh international Alan Curtis joined Swansea City for £5,000 – his third spell at the Vetch Field.

Cohen Griffith took only 19 minutes to mark his League debut, with a spectacular goal, as City gained a splendid first victory of the season, 3-2 at Huddersfield. The Bluebirds, however, remained rooted to the foot of the table with four draws in five matches, before they won again. By this time, goalkeeper Roger Hansbury, who had been on loan from Birmingham City, was signed for £25,000, and Ashurst also paid £15,000 for Bolton winger Jeff Chandler, an ex-Eire international, who made his debut in the spanking 3-1 win over Bury.

A week later, aided by a little good fortune, the City pulled off a remarkable 5-2 win at Fulham, where Pike and Griffith both scored twice in the Bluebirds' highest away win since the 7th of December 1968 ...... at Fulham! It could have been even better, but Chandler missed a late penalty. On the 25th of November, Cardiff won their third successive League victory, with goals from Rodgerson, and one apiece for Pike and Griffith who were beginning to forge a deadly partnership.

Successive away wins were gained at Swansea, where Leigh Barnard's goal after only 45 seconds gave City their first League win at the Vetch since 1959, and at Walsall four days later. Suddenly the bubble burst, Griffith's goals dried up, and the City's only win in the next nine games was a surprise 1-0 victory at Brentford, where young giant defender Gareth Abraham was the scorer. A 2-0 home win over Rotherham on the 6th of March, offered some respite, but eleven days later they suffered an embarrassing 1-5 home defeat at the hands of Huddersfield Town, and relegation looked to be odds-on. There was still time for Cardiff to make a belated late salvage effort to stave off the inevitable, but a 0-2 home defeat by Swansea on Easter Monday made the situation almost impossible. However, a 3-1 home win over Walsall which virtually booked relegation for the Midlanders, was followed by an amazing 3-3 home draw with Fulham, and their point saved the Londoners. The City's third home game in seven days saw them defeat Reading 3-2 on May Day, which gave the Bluebirds a mathematical life-line of reaching safety.

But a limp 0-2 defeat at Bury four days later, where an impressive number of City supporters had travelled, condemned the Bluebirds to their second spell in the Fourth Division, after only two seasons in the Third. The Club's eight home defeats had cost them dearly.

F.A. Cup
Cardiff City struggled to overcome non-League Halesowen Town in the first round at Ninian Park, and it took a controversial first-half penalty (scored by Chris Pike), following a dubious trip on Jeff Chandler, to put the Bluebirds through. The City were only minutes from elimination against Gloucester City at Ninian Park, when young reserve striker Morrys Scott scored twice, to force a replay from a 2-2 draw. Three days later Scott again emerged as City's hero by heading the only goal of the game, on a night marred by shocking crowd scenes which involved Cardiff 'supporters'.

The Bluebirds drew a plum 3rd round tie with the visit of First Division Queen's Park Rangers. In the light of their poor season, an excellent crowd of 13,834 turned out to see what became a dour 0-0 draw.

There were more headlines concerning the weekend robbery of the Ninian Park offices, and the theft of the £50,000 gate receipts. Questions were asked regarding the existence of an alarm system, and an insurance against such loss, which caused the club considerable embarrassment. The money was eventually found on an hillside near Pontypridd, and the thief revealed to be Anthony Clement, a club employee, whose similarity of names, caused embarrassment to chairman Tony Clemo! The City, urged on by good support, fought hard in the replay at Loftus Road, but missed several chances, and were eliminated when Wegerle and then Wilkins scored for the Rangers.

Welsh Cup
The third round brought a visit to Ninian Park from the newly formed Newport A.F.C. and the part-timers played exceptionally well, only to go down narrowly to a goal from City centre-half Gareth Abraham.

Welsh League Port Talbot visited Ninian Park in the fourth round, and the City swept to a 4-1 victory. On the 6th of February, Cardiff faced Aberyswyth Town in the fifth round. The visitors almost took a first minute lead when player-manager Tommy Morgan's shot struck a post, but the home team eventually won 2-0. The Bluebirds met Hereford United in the semi-final, and at Ninian Park, they were swept away as Hereford won 3-0. Two nights later, at Edgar Street, Cardiff put up a more resilient performance and came close to turning the tables, but their 3-1 win was not enough.

Littlewoods Cup
Cardiff City met Plymouth Argyle in the first round and were well beaten 3-0 in the first leg at Ninian Park. They then dumbfounded their critics by winning the return at Home Park 2-0, with goals from Pike and Steve Lynex, but a victory that was insufficient to allow further progress.

Leyland Daf Cup
City were in a preliminary group with Walsall and Shrewsbury, and lost an extraordinary game to Walsall by 3-5 at Ninian Park, and then crashed 0-4 at Shrewsbury. In the latter match, Ashurst selected a side made up of Reserve players, including a West German triallist Merio Miethig.

The advent of Fanzines mushrooming all over the country saw no fewer than four such publications covering Cardiff City, and they had a field day in their criticism of chairman Tony Clemo, who had kept the club up for sale all season, but had not received any offers to interest him.

CHAPTER 8

BOTTOM BASEMENT... BUT READY FOR A RISE AGAIN!

1990-91 Season – Division 4:

The 1990-91 season turned out to be one of the most traumatic in Cardiff City's history. Throughout the Summer, a number of proposed consortiums interested in buying out Tony Clemo's holdings in the Club received much publicity, but none of them got past the planning stage. Amid all this unrest, there appeared dissention among certain City players, who began to wonder in which direction the Club was going, and quotes to this effect were made public.

Len Ashurst scoured the free transfer market, and managed to bring Pat Heard from Rotherham and Mark Jones from Swindon. Heard had played at the top level with Aston Villa, Everton, and Newcastle among others; Jones had experienced injury problems in the past. Neil Matthews, a utility player at Blackpool, came to Ninian Park, but his signing was delayed until a tribunal decision was made.

The City dumped Merthyr Tydfil 2-3 in a pre-season friendly, and then beat Portsmouth 1-0, through a Heard goal. But any optimism among the City faithful, and there were 3,819 of them at the season's opening game – a tepid scoreless draw with Scarborough – quickly evaporated, with some cynics remarking that it was just as well that automatic relegation to the G.M. Vauxhall Conference would not occur for two seasons!

Therefore, it was quite a surprise as the Bluebirds embarked on an eleven match (League and Cup) unbeaten run, which ended unceremoniously when Rochdale won at Ninian Park by 1-0 on the 2nd of October. The stark reality of that run revealed that the City had still to win a home League game, having had two remarkable 3-3 draws with Torquay and Stockport (despite being three goals up after 12 minutes in the latter match).

Following Bobby Smith's departure to Hereford, Ashurst eventually filled the vacancy, on the 7th of October, to his coaching staff, by appointing the much-travelled Eddie May.

The City were hovering in mid-table when they embarked on what has become known as *Black November*, with only a 2-1 home win over Chesterfield illuminating the gloom in the month which saw shock Cup defeats at the hands of Merthyr Tydfil (Welsh Cup), Hayes (F.A.Cup), Exeter City, (Leyland Daf) and heavy League defeats at Maidstone and Gillingham. Ashurst rang the changes giving opportunities to youngsters Damon Searle, Lee Badderley, Lee Stevens and, fleetingly, to Chris Summers.

Ray Daniel, heavily criticised for his dressing-room attitude, joined Portsmouth for £80,000, while Ian Rodgerson – still hankering for a move – joined Swindon and Birmingham for loan spells, after bearing brunt of heavy barracking from the terraces. He was eventually to sign permanently for Birmingham for a £40,000 tribunal fee.

The City's financial plight was worsening weekly, and following revelations that some players signing-on fees had still not been settled, the Football League put an embargo on any further deals.

Once this unsatisfactory state of affairs was resolved Ashurst moved quickly to bring in, on loan, Ken DeMange (Hull City) and Mark Taylor (Blackpool). The City manager had the later embarrassment of being 'sent off' at Northampton just before Christmas! Successive home wins over Carlisle and Halifax lifted supporters hopes of a revival, but once DeLange and Taylor had rejoined their clubs, the City slumped once again.

On the 1st of February, the Club hit their lowest ebb. They were by then being sued by the local council for unpaid interest bills on a previous loan, and a winding-up order meant a visit to the High Court. Against this background, and on a pitch cleared of snow, the Bluebirds crashed to an all-time low by losing at home to struggling Aldershot. Many observers believed that the 1,692 crowd was the lowest for a League match in the Club's history, but that unwanted statistic was still held by the 1,510 fans present for the match with Hartlepool in May 1987.

Kevin Russell, on loan from Leicester City, must have wondered what was going on, for following the Aldershot defeat, it was revealed that the players pay cheques had bounced. It was reported that demands for unpaid bills from the likes of printers, bus companies, etc., were being made, and emergency matchday programmes were issued for a number of home games. It looked as if the Club had literally very little time left. Once again, consortium and takeover rumours were rife, but with the Club's affairs in such turmoil, and Chairman Tony Clemo under increasing pressure to let the Club go, the football team were almost overlooked. It was therefore a pleasant surprise when the team picked itself up, following the Aldershot debacle, and went on an unbeaten run of nine games, to the fringe of the play-off places.

The young players in the squad – Jason Perry, Natham Blake, Damon Searle and Nick Matthews – were seen as major assets, despite their immaturity, and gave the City supporters optimism for a promotion push. Cameron Toshack, the son of former idol John, made his full debut (following a few substitute appearances) when the City played at rock-bottom Wrexham on March the 22nd. The Bluebirds fell to Chris Armstrong's early header. Needing to reinforce his team, Ashurst was allowed to bring Oxford's Phil Heath, Coventry's Kevin McDonald and re-engage Ken DeMange, all three on loan.

It was revealed that Rick Wright, the millionaire owner of Barry Island's Majestic Holiday Camp complex, had emerged as a financial benefactor, having wiped out the Club's immediate debts, and was prepared to pay the wages of the new recruits.

The Club and local media were optimistic that the promotion play-offs, held at Wembley, could be reached, which at least would promise a lucrative pay-day for the Bluebirds. The reality was far different, for after successive wins – at home against Northampton, and away at Halifax – the City failed to taste victory in the last eight games of the season. It was all a big let down, for in the matches that mattered – at Torquay and Blackpool, and at home to Champions Darlington – the Bluebirds proved to be not good enough. The season ended on a farcical note when Len Ashurst selected reserve goalkeeper Gavin Ward as substitute for the final two games!

In the away match at promoted Peterborough, the City *followers* were in the process of a pitch invasion when Paul Culpin broke away, and with twenty to thirty people in his wake, he cracked home Posh's third goal. It was an unsavoury incident which thankfully had no repercussions.

Against Maidstone, at home, Ward replaced Hansbury in the first half, and during the latter period, the visitors 'keeper Nicky Johns, was sent off for a 'professional' foul, with defender Mark Golley taking over in goal. The match had four goalkeepers – but no goals – and for the City supporters, it was a case of 'this is where we came in', as the season ended as it began, with a goalless stalemate.

Roger Hansbury was ever-present with regular contributions from Roger Gibbins, Pat Heard, Cohen Griffith, Jason Perry and Chris Pike; the latter was the leading scorer with 14 goals. The one redeeming feature of arguably the Club's worst season, was the potential revealed in its young talent. Nathan Blake had drawn much interest and Damon Searle's emergence totally overcame the loss of Ray Daniel.

It came as no surprise to the Club's followers, when Len Ashurst left, for he had lost his way, and quite understandably had grown disillusioned with his position.

His extreme frustration had shown on several occasions, for he had been sent from the touchline twice during the season, and his selection of a reserve goalkeeper as a substitute certainly raised a few eyebrows!

F.A. Cup:
The City failed to make home advantage pay in the first round when non-League Hayes earned a replay from a 0-0 draw. The attendance of 1,844 was the lowest for an F.A. Cup tie at Ninian Park.

In the replay at Griffin Park, Brentford, the City lacked urgency, and paid for their slackness, when Paul Clarke dumped them out of the competition, with a goal five minutes from time.

Welsh Cup:
Cardiff were humbled by Merthyr Tydfil at Ninian Park in the third round. Prolific marksman David Webley poached a hat-trick, and Russell Lewis also netted, as the Martyrs completed a rout. The City's only reply was a Pike penalty. The defeat was one of the worst in most supporters living memories.

Rumbelows Cup:
Mansfield Town were overcome in the first round, with a 1-1 draw at Field Mill, followed by a 3-0 win at Ninian Park in the second leg.

Second Division Portsmouth, then managed by Frank Burrows, were City's second round opponents. A hard fought home leg ended 1-1, and the City were unlucky to be pipped at Fratton Park, when late goals helped Pompey to a 3-1 victory, 4-1 on aggregate.

Leyland Daf Cup:
The City were in a group with Exeter City and Hereford United, but a 0-1 home defeat by the former team effectively ended their interest. A 1-1 draw at Hereford was not enough, and the City were eliminated.

1991-92 Season – and beyond......

> *Rick Wright took over as financial controller, but did not have ownership of the Club in total. He promised that Ninian Park would become all-seater, and also introduced a revolutionary sliding scale admission fee, this being dependant upon the team's standing in the Fourth Division.*
>
> *A number of managerial candidates were considered, but just before the start of the 1991-92 season, the Club appointed from within, by naming Eddie May as Club coach. It was the first time that Cardiff had no manager in name, but May's position gave him full control of first team affairs.*
>
> *Within weeks Rick Wright demonstrated his willingness to back the Club by allowing Eddie May to buy Port Vale's Paul Miller (for £60,000), Carl Dale from Chester at £90,000 and Paul Ramsey from Leicester for £40,000.*
>
> *In a matter of months the gloom had been lifted, and with Ninian Park undergoing a facelift, the future could now be faced with optimism........*

CHAPTER 9

GROUND - WORKS

The Club's original ground was little more than an open area within Sophia Gardens – currently the Glamorgan County Cricket Ground – and the facilities consisted of nothing more than a shed which served as dressing-rooms. Other temporary venues were used for prestigious friendly games at Cardiff Arms Park and the Harlequins Ground in Newport Road.

By 1910 the Club had been accepted into the Southern League, and a 5 acre area of waste ground lying between Sloper Road and railway sidings – which was being used for refuse – was acquired from the Corporation, initially on a seven year lease. With the aid of voluntary and Corporation workers, the ground was levelled. The pitch was enclosed with a white picket fence and shallow ash banking was raised on all four sides. A small wooden grandstand – with a canvass roof and an initial capacity for around 200 – was built on the Sloper Road side, with changing rooms and offices adjacent. The intended name of the Ground was 'Sloper Park' but was eventually titled 'Ninian Park', after Lord Ninian Crichton-Stuart – who was a benefactor to the Club.

The first match was played at Ninian Park on the 1st of September 1910, when Aston Villa were entertained, before a crowd of 7,000, in a prestigious Friendly game.

One year later the facilities were improved slightly, and these included the installation of gas and water to the manager's office and the dressing-rooms.

1910 – The first season at Ninian Park, and the ground development and facilities were sparse.

Little more in the way of improvements were made to the ground until after the First World War, despite the ground accommodating crowds of over 20,000, and also being used to stage International matches – the first in 1911.

During the summer of 1920, the Canton Stand was built behind the North goal. As well as being covered, it also had bench seating for several thousand spectators (an advanced facility for its time).

(Training for the 1925 Cup Final) By now the Canton Road covered and seated stand had been built. The 'Bob Bank' was still an open, ash bank.

It was a further eight years before any further substantial improvements were made to the ground, although access from the City and other districts was made easier, in 1925, when the Corporation tramlines were extended to the area.

In 1928, work at the Grangetown end was completed, and a simple flat cover was initially provided; this was officially opened on the 1st of September. Although still somewhat basic, the ground was able to accommodate large numbers (of upto 50,000), and continued to be the first choice for staging Welsh International matches.

On Monday the 18th of January 1937, the grandstand was burnt down (the fire was thought to have been started by burglars), and the wooden structure was rebuilt in brick and steel, and extended approximately one third pitch length.

1931: By now the Grangetown end had a conventional pitched roof. Three days after this photograph was taken (3rd of February) the Bluebirds had their biggest League victory – 9-2 versus Thames Association.

There were no further alterations or improvements of note until after the Second World War, the pre-War days being a period of 'ups and downs' for the Club.

The 1947 view at ground level shows the Sloper Road side prior to the paddock extension........

.........but this is apparent in the 1948 aerial view; the 'Bob Bank', was still a basic raised embankment and uncovered.

At the end of the 1946/47 season, the paddock in front of the grandstand was extended, and concrete was used to provide a raised terrace. This in effect moved the touchline nearer the railway, and hence the Canton stand was no longer symmetrical with respect to the pitch!

On the 22nd of April 1953, the record (Club) attendance of 57,893 was reached with the visit of Arsenal.

In 1958, the popular ('Bob Bank') side was extended in depth, raised in height, and a new roof was added. By now the ground could boast of having cover on all four sides.

Surprisingly, in view of the Club's League status, they were one of the last clubs in the Football League to introduce floodlights, in 1961. The first match under the modern lights – which ranked with the best in the League at that time – were used for the friendly match with Zurich Grasshoppers on the 5th of October. Nine days later, the record ground attendance was attained when a crowd of 61,566 was present for the Wales versus England match.

During the summer of 1972, improved under-soil drainage was installed, a new pitch was laid, and substantial alterations were started on the Grandstand. These extensions provided seated cover along the complete Sloper Road side of the ground, and this work was finally completed during the summer of 1973. The work had cost £225,000 and provided seating for 3,300.

With the Safety of Sports Grounds act being instigated in 1977, the Club suffered tremendously. An over-zealous local Authority ensured that the Act was complied with in every detail, without any leeway or commonsense being applied. Although very large Ninian Park was still somewhat basic, and the capacity was drastically cut to 10,000 – until substantial and expensive modifications were undertaken – and the staging of floodlit matches was temporarily banned. The most drastic visual alteration was the removal of the cover over the Grangetown end, and this concrete terrace was subsequently given over to visiting supporters. A total of £600,000 was spent on the modifications, with only one third of the costs being met by the Grounds Improvement Trust, plus a £27,000 grant from the Welsh F.A.

There has been little money available for ongoing modifications, to what is an essentially outdated stadium, and the introduction of Rugby League football to Ninian Park in 1981 did not improve the situation, for it ensured that the pitch was over used, and consequently suffered!

With the 1980's being generally years of austerity and boardroom changes, what little money that has been available has been used more to improve the team rather than the ground. Although still theoretically able to accommodate very large crowds it has been difficult to ensure that improvements keep pace with the ever demanding safety requirements. Probably the greatest snub to the Club was the decision of the Welsh F.A. to take away from Ninian Park its unwritten right to stage the majority of International Matches, at the 'home' of Welsh football.

1990 and the ground is now covered on only three sides.

(Photo: Chris Ambler)

CHAPTER 10

THE MEN WHO KICKED THE BALL

Every player who appeared in the Football League for Cardiff City has been given. More detailed information (upto 1987) can be found in the earlier book:

The Bluebirds. A Who's Who of Cardiff City Football League Players (by John Crooks).
These earlier details have been updated, to include players to the end of the 1990/91 season.

The first column gives – in alphabetical order – the surname, followed by Christian name, and (shown in brackets where applicable), the player's more popular nickname. The second column provides the place or area of birth (where known), or Country of birth (in brackets). The third column gives the date or year of birth (where known), and finally the fourth column, the period spent as a Cardiff player; additional years (in brackets) refer to a player's second spell with Cardiff City. Brief details of the more prominent players (generally those who have made in excess of 100 Football League appearances for Cardiff City) have been added. Players have been included who were with the Club in the 1990/91 season and continued into the next.

Although not given here, the number of appearances for Cardiff City – in various competitions, plus goals scored – can be obtained from the Statistical Section.

ABRAHAM, Gareth	Aberfan	Feb 69.	1986–
ABRAMS, Laurence	Southport	c.1895	1920–21
ADAMS, Robert	Coleford	28/2/17	1932–34
ADLAM, Leslie	Guildford	c.1906	1933–34
AITKEN, Fergus	Glasgow	4/6/1896	1922–23
ALLAN, A. (Sandy)	Forfar	29/10/47	1967–70
ALLCHURCH, Ivor M.B.E.	Swansea	16/10/29	1962–65

Welsh international – Known throughout British Football only by his christian name. There can be no higher accolade. A player who would have been great in any era.

IVOR ALLCHURCH

ALLEN, Bryn	Gilfach Goch	28/3/21	1946–47
			(1948–49)
ALSTON, Adrian	Preston	6/2/49	1975–76
ANDERSON, J.E. (Ernie)	Scotland	c.1896	1920–22
ANDERSON, R.S.	London	1914	1938–39
ANDERSON, Willie	Liverpool	24/1/47	1972–77

A winger who was capable of creating havoc on either flank. Beame a popular figure with the 'Bob Bankers'. In 1977 signed for Portland Timbers in the U.S.A.

ANDREWS, George	Dudley	23/4/42	1965–67
ASHTON, Roger	Llanidloes	16/8/21	1948–49
ATTLEY, Brian	Cardiff	27/8/55	1973–79
ATTLEY, Leonard	Cardiff	1910	1934–36

BADDELEY, Lee	Cardiff	12/7/74	1990–
BAILLIE, Jim	Hamilton	1902	1926–28
BAIRD, Jim	Southampton	1/4/64	1983–84
BAKER, Colin	Cardiff	18/12/34	1953–65

Welsh international – One of the finest wing–halves in the Club's history. A strong, relentless player – typical of the classic wing-half. Had the virtue of a good shot, with either foot.

COLIN BAKER

BAKER, William, G. (Billy)	Penrhiwceiber	3/10/20	1938-55

Welsh international – A constructive player, keen in the tackle and a clever tactician.
He deserved more than his one Welsh Cap. Joined Ipswich for two seasons from 1955.

BALLSOM, William, George	Trealaw		1938-40
BANNON, Paul	Dublin	18/11/56	1984-85
BARBER, Keith	Luton	21/9/47	1978-79
BARNARD, Leigh	Worsley	29/10/58	1989-91
BARNETT, Albert	Co.Durham		1914-22
BARTLETT, J.W.	S. Wales		1933-34
BARTLETT, Kevin	Portsmouth	12/10/62	1986-89
BASSETT, W.E.G. (Bill)	Brithdir	8/6/12	1934-39

A tough as teak pre-War pivot, who was loved by supporters, and feared by opponents.
In 1939, after 150 League games for Cardiff, he moved on to a former club – Crystal Palace.

BATER, Phil	Cardiff	24/19/53	1987-89
BEADLES, Harold	Newtown	28/9/1898	1924-26
BEARE, George	Southampton	2/10/1888	1914-21
BELL, Gary	Stourbridge	4/4/47	1966-74

Converted from a winger in to a full-back. Noted for his accurate passing and crossing
from the left. An ability that was near international quality.

BENNETT, David	Manchester	11/7/59	1981-83
BENNETT, Gary	Manchester	4/12/61	1981-84
BEST, Tommy	Milford Haven	23/10/20	1948-49
BIRD, Donald W.	Llandrindod Wells		1930-31
BIRD, Ronnie	Erdington	27/12/41	1966-71
BISHOP, Ray	Hengoed	24/11/55	1977-81
BLACKBURN, George	London		1926-31
BLAIR, Doug	Sheffield	26/6/21	1947-54

A fine football artist with an educated left foot, deceptive body swerve, superlative ball control,
and an astute football brain. In 1954 moved to Hereford but continued work as a Quantity Surveyor.

BLAIR, Jimmy	Glenboig, Lanarks.	11/5/1888	1920-26

Scottish international – Returned to Cardiff as a Coach (1932-34). A stylish full-back,
calm and composed in all situations. His son – Doug – became a top Cardiff player.

BLAKE, Nathan	Cardiff	27/1/72	1989-91
BLAKEMORE, R.	(England)		1930-31
BYLAND, W.H.	Leeds	1904	1934-35
BLENKINSOP, Ernie	Cudworth, Yorks.	20/4/02	1937-39
BODIN, Paul	Cardiff	24/3/56	1982-84
BONSON, Joe	Barnsley	19/6/36	1957-60
BOOTH, W.S. (Sam)	Hove	7/7/20	1939-46
BOYLE, Terry	Ammanford	29/10/58	1986-89

Welsh International – A commanding defender, strong in the air, who was a natural leader.
A player who was capable of spending more of his career in the higher divisions.

BRACK, Alistair	Aberdeen	27/1/40	1961-64
BRIGNULL, Phil	London	2/10/60	1986-87
BRITTAN, R.C. (Charlie)	Porstmouth		1913-23

A major signing during the Southern League days. He was instrumental in City's
rise to the Football League.

BROWN, Alec	St.Monance, Fife		1936-38
BROWN, Jim	Coatbridge	11/5/52	1982-83
BROWN, L. (Tom)	(England)		1921-22
BROWN, R. (Bobby)	Streatham	2/5/40	1966-68
BUCHANAN, John	Dingwall	19/9/51	1974-78

It defied logic how one so slight could posess such a canonball shot.
He put it down to his timing – an explanantion which is difficult to disagree with!

BURKE, Marshall	Glasgow	26/3/59	1983-84
BURNS, Micky	Blackpool	21/12/46	1978-79
BYRNE, Gerry	Glasgow	10/4/57	1975-78

CALDER, Robert	(Scotland)		1933-34
CALLAN, Dennis	Merthyr	27/7/32	1952-55
CAMPBELL, Alan	Arbroath	21/1/48	1976-80

Made the game look easy, particularly when short passing was required. Became a popular
player with supporters for almost five years. Moved on to Carlisle in 1980.

CAMPBELL, Hugh	(Ireland)		1936-37

CANNING, Danny	Pontypridd	21/2/26	1946-48
CARLESS, Ernie	Barry	9/9/12	1932-46
CARLIN, Willie	Liverpool	6/10/40	1973-74
CARVER, David	Rotherham	16/4/44	1966-72

A strong and well balanced player with two good feet. He was the complete full-back and well respected in the 2nd Division. Came to Cardiff in 1966 - became a regular first-teamer for 6 years.

CARVER, John	Newcastle		1985-86
CASHMORE, Arthur	Birmingham	30/10/1893	1919-21
CASSIDY, Joe	Calder, Lanarks.	10/8/1896	1925-26
CASTLE, Fred	Pontypridd		1926-28
CHANDLER, Jeff	Hammersmith	19/6/59	1989-91
CHARLES, Clive	Bow	3/10/51	1974-77
CHARLES, John	Swansea	27/12/31	1963-65

Welsh international - The greatest Welsh footballer of his generation. A Giant in stature but his approach to football was that of a ballet dancer. Moved from Juventus to Cardiff for £25,000 in 1963.

CHARLES, Mel	Swansea	14/5/35	1961-64

Welsh international - Younger brother of John. Made his name with Swansea and Arsenal - a much better player than given credit for. A centre half or forward, and scored regularly as an attacker.

CHISHOLM, Ken	Glasgow	12/4/25	1952-54
CHRISTIE, Derrick	Bletchley	15/3/57	1985-86
CLARK, Brian	Bristol	13/1/43	1968-72
			(1975-76)

A model professional, whose effort and goals made him one of the most popular of all Cardiff City players. Returned in 1975, before later moving on to Newport County.

CLARKE, Joe	Durham		1912-22
CLARKE, Malcolm	Clydebank	29/6/44	1967-69
CLARKE, Roy	Newport	1/6/25	1946-47
CLENNELL, Joe	New Silksworth, Co.Durham		1921-25

A silky inside-forward, with the ability to glide past opponents. Often described as 'the little demon and a terror for his size'! For four years he scored regularly for the City in the First Division.

COLDRICK, Graham	Newport	6/11/45	1962-70
COLLINS, Chas. Elvet	Rhymney	16/10/02	1924-28
COLLINS, James	(England)		1932-33
COLLINS, J.H. (Jimmy)	London		1937-40
CORKHILL, William Grant	Belfast	23/4/10	1938-40
CORNER, David	Sunderland	15/5/66	1985-86
COUCH, Alan	Neath	15/3/53	1970-73
COURT, Harold John	Tirphill	13/6/19	1938-39
CRAWFORD, Andy	Filey	30/1/59	1983-84
CRIBB, S.R. (Stan)	Gosport		1932-33
CRINGAN, Jimmy	Douglaswater	Dec 1918	1939-40
CURTIS, Alan	Rhondda	16/4/54	1986-89

Welsh International - His skill and ability won over the bigots who resented his long association with Swansea City. An oasis in the desert of the Fourth Division!

CURTIS, Ernie	Cardiff	Jun 1907	1925-28
			(1933-34)
CURTIS, Wayne	Port Talbot	22/2/69	1985-87

DALE, Ceri			
DANIEL, Ray	Swansea	2/11/28	1957-58
DANIEL, Ray	Luton	10/12/64	1989-91
DAVIES, Albert Bryn	Cardiff		1935-38
DAVIES, Ben	Middlesbrough		1920-23
DAVIES, Fred	Liverpool	22/8/39	1968-70
DAVIES, Gary	Cardiff	6/10/59	1986-87
DAVIES, John	Llandyssul	18/11/59	1978-80
DAVIES, Len	Splott, Cardiff	1900	1919-31

Welsh International - One of Cardiff's greatest sons and ambassadors. The Club's all time leading goalscorer with 129 in the League.

DAVIES, Lyn	Neath	29/9/47	1965-67
DAVIES, Paul	Kidderminster	9/10/60	1979-81
DAVIES, Ron	Merthyr	21/9/32	1952-58
DAVIES, Stan	Chirk		1928-29
DAVIES, Willie	Troedyrhiwfuch	16/2/1900	1924-28
DAVIES, W.J. (Jim)	S. Wales		1938-39
DEAN, Norman	Corby	13/9/44	1967-68
DEIGHTON, Jack	(England)		1935-36

DEMANGE, Ken	Dublin	3/9/64	1990-91
DERRETT, Steve	Cardiff	16/10/47	1965/72
DIAMOND, John. J.	Middlesbrough	30/10/10	1935-36
DIBBLE, Andrew	Cwmbran	8/5/65	1981-84
DIXON, Cecil	Trowbridge	28/3/35	1954-57
DONNELLY, Peter	Hull	22/9/36	1960-61
DUDLEY, Frank	Southend	9/5/25	1953-54
DURBAN, Alan	Port Talbot	7/7/41	1958-63
DURKAN, Jack	Bannockburn	1915	1933-35
DURRELL, Joe	London	15/3/53	1975-76
DUTHIE, John Flott	Fraserburgh	7/1/03	1933-34
DWYER, Phil	Cardiff	28/10/53	1971-85

Welsh International – One of Cardiff's greatest players who made the current record number of League appearances for the City (471). An opponent to be feared!

EADIE, Jim	Kirkintilloch	4/2/47	1966-72
EDGLEY, Brian	Shrewsbury	26/8/37	1960-61
EDWARDS, George	Treharris	2/12/20	1948-55

Welsh International – Played some of the best football of his career at Cardiff. A great left foot and his direct style made him a crowd pleaser. Retired in 1955 but returned as a Director.

EGAN, Harry	Tibshelf, Derbys.		1938-40
ELLIOT, Mark	Rhondda	20/3/59	1979-80
ELLIS, Keith	Sheffield	6/11/35	1964-65
ELSEY, Karl	Swansea	20/11/58	1983-85
EMMERSON, George	Bishop Auckland	15/5/06	1930-33
ENGLAND, Mike	Prestatyn	2/12/41	1975-76
ESLOR, Jack	(Scotland)		1936-37
EVANS, A. (Tony)	Liverpool	11/1/54	1975-79

His pace and instinct made up for his lack of physique. One of the Club's fastest forwards. Scored four goals in a League Cup match – a Club record in the competition.

EVANS, A.H.	S. Wales		1931-33
EVANS, Chas John	Cardiff	1897	1922-24
EVANS, Elfed	Rhondda	28/8/26	1949-51
EVANS, Herbie	Llandaff, Cardiff	1901	1921-26
EVANS Jack	Bala		1910-26

Welsh International – Became a legend in his time with his level of consistency. Superb left foot shot and capable of pinpoint centres. Became a popular and frequent visitor to the Club, as a reporter.

EVANS, T.J. (Trevor)	S. Wales		1938-39
EVEREST, Jack	The Curragh, Eire		1934-36
FARQUHARSON, Tom	Dublin		1922-35

Irish International – Considered to be the greatest of all the many Cardiff goalkeepers. Capped by both Northern Ireland and Eire. Played in both F.A.Cup finals, holder of the 2nd most appearances.

FARRELL, Greg	Motherwell	19/3/44	1964-67
FARRINGTON, John	Lynemouth	19/6/47	1973-74
FARRINGTON, Mark	Liverpool	15/6/65	1985-86
FELGATE, David	Blaenau Ffestiniog	4/3/60	1984-85
FERGUSON, Hughie	Motherwell	1898	1925-29

His £5,000 transfer fee from Motherwell was a staggering sum in 1925. A prolific goalscorer; scored the 1927 F.A.Cup Final winner. Moved to Dundee, but depression led him to take his own life in 1930.

FERGUSON, R. (Bobby)	Dudley	8/1/38	1965-68
FIELDING, William (Bill)	Braodbottom	17/6/15	1936-40
FINLAY, Jim	(Scotland)		1937-38
FINNIESTON, Steve	Edinburgh	30/11/54	1974-75
FLYNN, Brian	Port Talbot	12/10/55	1984-85
FOGGON, Alan	Chester-le-Street	23/2/50	1971-72
FOLEY, Will	(Scotland)		1985-86
FORD, Francis	Bridgend	3/2/67	1984-85
FORD, Louis	Cardiff	18/5/14	1936-39
FORD, Mike	Bristol	9/2/66	1984-88

A utility player who was plucked from obscurity, and later sold for an incredible £150,000! Played the game with boundless enthusiasm.

FORD, Trevor	Swansea	1/10/23	1953-56

Welsh International – One of Welsh football's greatest characters. A record fee of £30,000 was paid for one of the game's most feared centre-forwards. Later, his football revelations led to a 3 year ban.

FRANCIS, Gerry	Chiswick	6/12/51	1984-85
FRANCOMBE, Peter	Cardiff	4/8/63	1981-82

FRASER, Gordon	Elgin	27/11/43	1961-63	
FRIDAY, Robin	London	27/7/52	1976-78	

Made more headlines off the field than on it! His unsavoury lifestyle ultimately cost him his life.

FRIEND, Harold	Cardiff		1933-34	
FROWEN, John	Trelewis	11/10/31	1951-58	
FRY, Chris	Cardiff	23/10/69	1986-91	
FURSLAND, Syd	Llwynypia		1934-35	

GALBRAITH, John	Renton		1931-35

Came to Cardiff at the early 'veteran' stage as a replacement for the great Fred Keenor. Although past his best, he tried to shore up a leaky defence. Missed few matches during his four year stay.

JOHN GALBRAITH

GALE, Colin	Pontypridd	31/8/32	1950-56
GAMMON, Steve	Swansea	24/9/39	1958-65
GAULT, William	Wallsend		1920-21
GIBBINS, Roger	Enfield	6/9/55	1982-85 (1988-)

Came to Cardiff on a free transfer from Cambridge United. A model of consistency, dependable in any position – a good all-rounder. Returned in 1989 to carry on where he had left off.

GIBSON, Colin	Normanby	16/9/23	1946-48
GIBSON, Ian	Newton Stewart	30/3/43	1970-72
GILBERT, Tim	South Shields	28/8/58	1981-82
GILCHRIST, Alex	Hollytown	28/9/23	1948-49
GILES, David	Cardiff	21/9/56	1974-78 (1985-87)

Welsh International – Moved to Wrexham for £20,000 in 1978, and after other moves returned to Cardiff in 1985. Had many highs and lows in his career.

GILES, Paul	Cardiff	21/9/56	1979-83
GILL, Jimmy	Sheffield	9/11/1894	1920-25

First player to be signed after the City's Football League entry. A prolific goalscoring inside-right of exceptional ability – a Cardiff City 'great'. Played in the 1925 F.A.Cup Final.

JAMES GILL

GILLIGAN, Jimmy	Hammersmith	24/1/64	1987-89

Signed for only £17,500 – having formerly moved from Watford to Grimsby for £100,000 – Jimmy rebuilt his goal-scoring career at Ninian Park, and was later sold for a record fee of £215,000.

GODFREY, Clifford	Baildon, Yorks.	17/2/09	1935-38
GODWIN, Don	Bargoed	5/7/32	1953-57
GOLDSMITH, Martin	Carmarthen	25/5/62	1983-84
GORIN, Ted	Cardiff	2/6/24	1948-50
GRANT, David	Sheffield	2/6/60	1984-86
GRANT, Wilf	Ashington	3/8/20	1950-54

A winger converted to successful centre-forward. Appeared for England 'B' once, and regarded as one of Cardiff City's finest forwards. Later reverted to the wing, and moved to Ipswich in 1954.

GRANVILLE, Arthur	Llwynypia	1911	1934-46
GRAPES, Steve	Norwich	25/2/53	1976-82

£7,000 was paid to bring him from Bournemouth. Changed from a winger to a midfielder. A Stocky player with excellent distribution. Was released in 1982, and joined Torquay.

JIMMY GILLIGAN

GRAY, Alex	Arbroath	7/11/36	1957-60
GRIFFITHS, Cohen	Georgetown	26.12.62	1989-
GRIFFITHS, Philip A.	Tylorstown	25/10/08	1934-35
GRIFFITHS, Stanley	Pentre	1911	1934-35
GRIFFITHS, Wyn	Blaengwynfi	17/10/19	1947-50
GRIMSHAW, Billy	Burnley		1919-24

A pacey player whose combination with Jimmy Gill was a joy to watch. Joined Cardiff in 1919, and went on to earn Football League representative honours.

GROTIER, Peter	London	18/10/50	1973-74 (1979-82)
GUMMER, Jason	Tredegar	27/10/67	1985-87

HAGAN, Alfred	Washington, Co.Durham	10/11/1895	1923-26
HAIG, Richard	Pontypridd	29/12/70	1988-90
HALLIDAY, Tommy	Ayr	28/4/40	1963-64
HAMILTON, David	South Shields	7/11/60	1984-85
HAMPSON, Tom	Bury	1900	1926-29
HANSBURY, Roger	Barnsley	26.1.55	1989-
HARDY, Billy	Bedlington	1891	1911-32

Virtually an ever-present during the Club's early days, and his name will always be remembered when the great days are recalled. A superb competitor and keen defender.

HARKIN, Terry	Londonderry	14/9/41	1965-66	
HARRINGTON, Alan	Cardiff	17/11/33	1951-66	

Welsh International - One of the Cardiff all-time greats. Became a permanent fixture in the team for a decade, latterly playing at full-back. A stylish player blessed with speed of recovery.

HARRIS, Brian	Bebbington	16/5/35	1966-71

A master signing when transferred from Everton for £10,000 in 1966. Returned to Ninian Park for two years as Assistant Manager in 1978. His cool authority instilled confidence.

HARRIS, Frank	Birmingham	1908	1928-33

Started as an inside-forward, but later converted to wing-half. An ill-judged transfer when he moved on to Charlton Athletic in 1933, where he shone in the Londoners rise to the 1st Division.

HARRIS, Gordon	Perth	19/2/43	1964-65
HARRINGTON, J.	Bolton		1937-38]
HAZLETT, George	Glasgow	10/3/23	1952-53
HEALEY, Ron	Manchester	30/8/52	1974-82

Eire International - After two seasons competition with Irwin as the first choice goalkeeper, enjoyed five years as the number one. Made up for the odd lapse with many acrobatic performances.

HEARD, Pat	Hull	17/3/60	1990-
HEARTY, Hugh	(Scotland)	1912	1935-36
HEATH, Phil	Stoke	24/11/64	1990-91
HELSBY, Tom	Runcorn	1904	1928-31
HEMMERMAN, Jeff	Hull	25/2/55	1982-85
HENDERSON, Mick	Gosforth	31/3/56	1981-82
HENDERSON, W.J.	Kilbirnie		1932-34
HEWITT, Ron	Flint	21/6/28	1957-59
HILL, Charlie (Midge)	Cardiff	6/9/18	1938-47
HILL, Fred	Cardiff	1914	1932-36
HILLS, Joseph John	London	14/10/1897	1924-26
HITCHENS, Gerry	Rawnsley	8/10/34	1955-57

English International - Soon after his transfer for a modest fee of £1,500, he became a regular in the first team, and formed a successful goal-scoring partnership with Trevor Ford.

HOGG, Derek	Stockton	4/11/30	1960-62
HOGG, Graham	Neath	15/1/22	1948-49
HOLE, Barrie	Swansea	16/9/42	1959-66

Welsh International - A stylish player whose career was hampered by poor moves after he left Cardiff. A frail looking player who was a superbly confident artiste on the ball.

HOLLYMAN, Ken	Cardiff	18/11/22	1946-53

One of City's most popular post-war players, with his buzzing, high energy displays. Made up for his lack of size by his shear ability and reading of the game.

HOLT, Stan	(England)		1931-32
HOLMES, Matthew			1988-89
HOOPER, Peter	Teignmouth	2/2/33	1962-63
HORRIX, Dean	Taplow	21/11/61	1986-87
HORTON, Roy	S. Wales		1932-33
HOUSTON, David	Glasgow	7/7/48	1965-67
HOWELLS, Ron	Port Henry	12/1/27	1950-57

Welsh International - a tall reliable goalkeeper, with a safe pair of hands. A regular custodian for six years, during which period he won 2 'Caps'.

HOY, Roger	London	6/12/46	1971-73
HUDSON, Colin	Undy	5/10/35	1957-61
HUGHES, Iorwerth	Llanddulas	26/5/25	1951-53
HUGHES, Mike	Llanidloes	3/9/40	1958-61
HULLETT, Bill	Liverpool	19/11/15	1947-48
HUMPHRIES, Steve	Hull	29/5/61	1982-83
HUTCHINSON, Alex	(Scotland)	1908	1933-34

IMPEY, John	Exeter	11/8/54	1971-75
INGRAM, Godfrey	Luton	26/10/59	1982-83
IRVING, Sam	Belfast	1894	1926-28
IRWIN, Bill	Newtonards	23/7/51	1971-77

This tall and agile Irish goalkeeper was signed for a modest fee - the City had good value for money. He was an Irish Amateur International.

JACKSON, William	Farnsworth		1934-35
JAMES, Billy	Cardiff	18/10/21	1941-47
JENKINS, Brian	Treherbert	1/8/35	1956-61

JENKINS, Eddie	Cardiff	1900	1921–24
JENKINS, E.J.J. (Eddie)	Cardiff	1911	1930–34
JENKINS, John (Jack)	Platt Bridge, Wigan	27/8/05	1925–30
JENNINGS, Walter	Bristol	1911	1934–36
JOHN, Dilwyn	Cardiff	3/6/44	1960–67
JOHN, Emlyn	Rhondda Valley		1928–32
JOHNSTON, George	Glasgow	21/3/47	1964–67
JONES, Barrie	Swansea	10/10/41	1967–70

Welsh International – A winger when bought from Plymouth for £25,000. His switch to midfield was a master stroke. One of the classiest of close dribblers to have represented the Club.

JONES, Bernard	Coventry	10/4/34	1956–57
JONES, Bryn	Llandrindod	8/2/48	1966–69
JONES, Charles	Troedyrhiw		1911–21
JONES, D.G. (Dai)	Cardiff	1913	1934–35
JONES, Islwyn	Merthyr	8/4/35	1952–56
JONES, Jimmy	Ton Pentre		1922–24
JONES, John	Wrexham	12/9/39	1957–59
JONES, Ken	Aberdare	2/1/36	1953–58
JONES, Ken	Havercroft	26/6/44	1971–72
JONES, Leslie	Aberdare	1913	1930–34

Welsh International – A stocky, clever and constructive player. In his football career he scored over 100 League goals. As manager of Scunthorpe, he led them into the Football League.

JONES, Linden	Tredegar	5/3/61	1978–83

Product of the youth team, who at 18, and in his second League match, became the youngest Cardiff player to be sent off! A regular for five years, until part of the multi-exchange deal with Newport.

JONES, Mark	Berinsfield	26/9/61	1990–
JONES, Robert	Liverpool	9/1/02	1937–39
JONES, Vaughan	Tonyrefail	2/9/59	1984–85
JONES, V.		1900	1922–23
JOSLIN, Phil	Kingsteignton	1/9/16	1948–51

After gaining a big reputation at Torquay, came to Ninian Park in 1948 and became the first choice goalkeeper. His career was ended in a tragic accident during a pre-season public trial in 1951.

JUDGE, Allan	Kingsbury	15/5/60	1987–

KEATING, Albert	Swillington, Leeds	28/6/02	1931–33
KEATING, Reg	Swillington, Leeds		1934–36
KEENOR, Fred	Cardiff	31/7/94	1913–31

Welsh International – quite simply the greatest Bluebird of them all! He led the Club to two F.A.Cup Finals and the runners-up spot in the Football League. He signed as an amateur in 1911, turned professional two years later, and after the great War returned to Cardiff until 1931.

KELLOCK, Billy	Glasgow	7/2/54	1971–73
KELLY, Mark	Blackpool	7/10/66	1987–
KELSO, Jimmy	Inchinnan	8/12/12	1938–40
KERR, Andy	West Bromwich	7/4/66	1986–87
KETTERIDGE, Steve	Stevenage	7/11/59	1988–91
KEVAN, David	Wigtown	31/8/68	1989–91
KING, Gerald	Cardiff	9/4/47	1963–65
KING, Jake	Wrenbury	9/8/32	1961–62
KING, Peter	Worcester	3/4/43	1960–73

Without doubt Cardiff's most loyal Clubman. In an era when wingers went out of fashion and were converted to midfielders, he successfuly made the change. A consistant and adaptable player.

KIRTLEY, Harry	Washington, Co.Durham	23/5/30	1955–57
KITCHEN, Peter	Mexborough	16/2/52	1980–82
KNEESHAW, Justin (Jack)	Beckhill, Bradford	1883	1912–35
KNOWLES, Harry	Hednesford	6/9/32	1959–61

LAMIE, Bob	Newarthill	28/12/28	1949–51
LANE, E.		1908	1934–35
LARMOUR, Albert	Belfast	27/5/51	1972–79

Signed from Irish club Linfield. After two seasons he became a first team regular, for four seasons. Although not the fastest of players he was a dependable sweeper.

LATHAM, M.C. Capt. George	Newtown	1880	1911–36

Cardiff's legendary trainer, who made his one appearance for the first team – his debut – aged 42!

LAWSON, Dennis	Lennoxtown	11/12/1897	1923–26
LAYTON, A.E.	Durham		1914–21

LEA, Leslie	Manchester	5/10/42	1967-70
LECKIE, J.T. (Jock)	Alva, Eire		1934-36
LEE, Trevor	London	3/7/54	1983-84
LEONARD, Carleton	Oswestry	3/2/58	1985-86
LEVER, Arthur (Buller)	Cardiff	25/3/20	1946-50

Welsh International – In the first two post-war seasons he was an ever present, and only missed a handful of games until his transfer to Leicester. An outstanding full-back.

Arthur Lever

LEWIS, Allan	Pontypridd	31/5/71	1989-
LEWIS, Bernard	Aberfan	12/3/45	1963-67
LEWIS, D.B.	S.Wales		1934-35
LEWIS, E.G.	S.Wales		1933-34
LEWIS, John (Jack)	Newport	1902	1924-26
LEWIS, John	Tredegar	15/10/55	1978-83

Transferred from Welsh League side Pontllanfraith, almost immediately became a first team regular. He was one of those involved in the 1983 five man player exchange with Newport County.

LEWIS, Terry	Newport	22/10/50	1967-70
LEWIS, Wilfred	Swansea	1905	1934-36
LEWIS, William	Cardiff	4/7/23	1946-47
LIEVESLEY, Wilfred		6/10/02	1929-30
LIVERMORE, Doug	Liverpool	27/12/47	1975-77
LLOYD, Clive	Merthyr	4/9/45	1964-65
LLOYD, Kevin	Wolverhampton	12/6/58	1979-80
LOVE, Ian	Cardiff	1/3/58	1989-90
LYNEX, Steve	West Bromwich	23/1/58	1988-90

MacBENNETT, Seamus	Newcastle	16/11/25	1947-48
McCAMBRIDGE, Jim	Larne	1905	1931-33
McCARTHY, Danny	Abergavenny	26/9/42	1960-62
McCAUGHEY, Cecil	Bootle		1937-39
MACAULAY, Robert	Wishaw	28/8/04	1936-37
McCLELLAND, John	Belfast	7/12/55	1974-75
McCULLOCH, Andy	Northampton	3/1/50	1972-74
McDERMOTT, Brian	Slough	8/4/61	1987-
McDONAGH, C.	(England)		1935-36
McDONALD, Ken	Llanwrst	24/4/1898	1922-23
McDONALD, Kevin	Inverness	22/12/60	1990-91
McGRATH, James	Washington, Co.Durham	4/3/07	1929-32
McGUCKIN, George	Dundee	11/8/38	1955-58
McILVENNY, Paddy	(Eire)	1900	1924-25
McINCH, Jimmy	Glasgow	27/6/53	1970-74
McINTOSH, Alan	Llandudno	29/7/39	1961-64
McJENNETT, G.J. (Jack)	Cardiff	1906	1929-32
MacKENZIE, Jimmy	Sudbrook		1935-39
McLACHLAN, George Herbert	Glasgow	21/9/02	1925-29

He was the replacement for the legendary Jack Evans. A winger who combined speed with superb ball control. Recovered from a broken leg and played in the 1927 F.A.Cup Final.

GEORGE McLACHLAN

McLAREN, Bobby	Chryston	5/8/29	1949-51
McLAUGHLIN, Bobby	Belfast	6/12/25	1950-53
McLOUGHLIN, Paul	Bristol	23/12/63	1985-86
McMILLAN, John	Dumbarton	14/4/37	1958-61
McNALLY, Owen	Eire		1931-32
McPHILLIPS, Laurence	Bathgate, Scotland		1939-40
McSEVENEY, Johnny	Shotts	8/2/31	1955-57
MADDY, Paul	Cwmcarn	17/8/62	1980-83
MAIDMENT, Tom	Sunderland		1933-34
MAIN, Walter (Bill)	St. Monance, Fife		1936-39
MALLORY, Richard	Bermuda	10/8/42	1963-64
MALLOY, Danny	Dennyloan	6/11/30	1955-61

£17,500 brought him to Cardiff from Dundee, and he became one of the City's finest pivots. Was ever present for three seasons. Was surprisingly overlooked by the Scottish selectors.

DANNY MALLOY

MANSELL, Jack	Manchester	22/8/27	1952-53
MARCHANT, Marwood	Milford	19/6/22	1950-51
MARCROFT, E.H. (Ted)	Rochdale		1933-34
MARDENBOROUGH, Steve	Birmingham	11/9/64	1987-88
MARSHALL, Ernest	Dinnington		1939-47
MARSHALSEY, W.H.G. (Bill)	(Scotland)		1933-34
MARTIN, Mick	Dublin	9/7/51	1984-85
MARUSTIK, Chris	Swansea	10/8/61	1985-87
MASON, F.O. (Frank)	(England)		1921-24

MATSON, Frank	Cardiff	21/11/05	1926-30
MATTHEWS, Neil	Manchester	3/12/67	1990-
MATTHEWS, Wayne	Cardiff	11/9/64	1982-84
MAY, Harry	Glasgow	15/10/28	1948-50
MAYO, A.			1930-31
MEACOCK, Kevin	Bristol	15/9/63	1984-85
MIETHIG, Mario	(West Germany)		
MELANIPHY, Eugene (Ted)	Westport, Ireland		1936-39
MELLOR, John	Oldham		1936-38
MELVILLE, A.	(Scotland)		1921-22
MENZIES, Ross	Glasgow	31/10/34	1957-59
MERRY, W.	Fishguard		1930-31
MICALLEF, C. (Tarki)	Cardiff	24/1/61	1977-83 (1984-86)
MIETHIC, Mario	W.Germany		1989-90
MILES, Alfred	Treorchy		1927-30
MILES, Idris	Cardiff		1930-31
MILLAR, Paul			
MILLS, Don	Rotherham	17/8/26	1950-51
MILNE, Alec	Dundee	4/6/37	1957-64

A tall lanky Scot, who was keen in the tackle and sure in the air. He was signed from Arbroath and was an ever present for two seasons. Ankle injuries curtailed his playing career.

MITCHELL, J.W. (Jimmy)	Barry		1937-47
MOKONE, Steve	South Africa	23/3/32	1959-60
MOLLOY, Peter (Paddy)	Rossendale	1911	1933-35
MONTGOMERY, Stan	London	7/7/20	1948-55

Signed from Southend United as a replacement for fred Stansfield – also an accomplished cricketer, playing for Glamorgan. Missed few first team matches during his stay at Ninian Park.

MOORE, F.B. (Beriah)	Cardiff	25/12/19	1947-48
MOORE, Graham	Hengoed	7/3/41	1957-61
MOORE, P. Paddy	Dublin		1929-30
MOORE, Ronnie	Liverpool	29/1/53	1979-80
MOORE, William	S. Wales		1934-35
MORGAN, Jon	Cardiff	10/7/70	1988-91
MORGAN, Peter	Cardiff	28/10 51	1969-74
MORGAN, Richie	Cardiff	3/10/46	1966-76
MORRIS, Edwin	Pontypool	6/5/21	1948-50
MORRIS, E.L. (Eric)	S. Wales		1931-33
MORT, Enoch	Ogmore Vale	1912	1933-38
MOSELEY, Graham	Manchester	16/11/53	1986-
MOSS, Frank	Aston, Birmingham		1928-29
MULLEN, Jimmy	Jarrow	8/11/52	1982-86

Had played over 200 games for Sheffield Wednesday, before his move to Rotherham and then Cardiff. Was hampered by injury for two seasons, and by 1985 had become a player/assistant manager.

MUNRO, James	Glasgow	20/5/05	1929/30
MURRAY, Don	Duffus	18/1/46	1962-74

Made his debut for the City aged 17, and within two years became the regular first choice centre-half. Gave his all for Cardiff for over a decade.

MURPHY, Jerry	Rhymney		1927-28
MURPHY, Pat	Merthyr	19/12/47	1927-28
MYERS, James H.	Barnsley		1939-40

NARDIELLO, Gerry	Oldbury	5/5/66	1985-86
NASH, Harry E.	Troedyrhiw		1921-24
NELSON, Jimmy	Greenock	7/1/01	1922-30

Scottish International – One of the greatest of all Cardiff's full-backs. Played in both of City's F.A.Cup Finals, and also in the team which beat England by 5-1 at Wembley in 1928.

NEWTON, William	Cramlington	14/5/1893	1921-22
NIBLOE, Joe	Glasgow	10/12/26	1948-49
NICHOLLS, Jack	Cardiff	14/12/1898	1924-25
NICHOLLS, Johnny	Wolverhampton	3/4/31	1957-58
NICHOLLS, Ron	Sharpness	4/12/33	1958-61
NICHOLSON, George	Pelaw, Co. Durham		1936-39
NICHOLSON, J.R. (Joe)	(England)		1924-26
NOCK, A. (Jack)	Birmingham	1900	1921-24
NORMAN, Griff	Cardiff	20/2/26	1950-52
NORTHCOTT, Tommy	Torquay	5/12/31	1952-55

NUGENT, Cliff	London	3/3/29	1951-58

For several seasons he was unable to command a regular first team place, and although finally making well over 100 League appearances, is probably one of the least remembered of players.

NUTT, Gordon	Birmingham	8/11/32	1954-55
OAKLEY, Ken	Rhymney	9/5/29	1950-53
O'CONNOR, Tim	Port Talbot	1967	1985-86
O'HALLORAN, Neil	Cardiff	21/6/33	1954-57
O'NEILL, Harry	(England)		1931-32
OVENSTONE, David Guthrie	St. Monance, Fife	17/6/13	1936-37
OWEN, Gordon	Barnsley	14/6/59	1983-84

FREDDIE PETHARD

PAGE, Jack	Liverpool		1920-26
PAGET, W.S.T. (Tom)	Cardiff	1909	1932-34
PAGNAM, Fred	(England)		1921-22
PARFITT, Harry	Cardiff	26/9/29	1949-54
PARKER, Reg.	Pontyclun	10/6/21	1941-48
PARSONS, Frank	Amersham	29/10/47	1970-72
PARSONS, John	Cardiff	10/12/50	1968-73
PECK, Trevor	Llanelli	25/5/38	1958-65
PEMBREY, Gordon	Cardiff	10/10/26	1948-50
PERKS, Harry	Cardiff		1933-34
PERRY, Jason	Newport	2/4/70	1986-
PETHARD, Freddie	Glasgow	7/10/50	1969-79

After a spell in the reserves - and cover for the full-back positions - he settled at left-back. A defender who loved to go forward.

PHILLIPS, Joe R.W.	Cardiff	8/7/23	1946-47
PHILLIPS, Leighton	Briton Ferry	26/9/49	1967-74

Welsh International - Signed as an apprentice and scored on his first team debut. Was a midfield player until settling into a defensive sweeper role. Later starred with Aston Villa and Swansea City.

LEIGHTON PHILLIPS

PICKRELL, Tony	Neath	3/11/42	1960-62
PIKE, Chris	Cardiff	19/10/61	1986-87
			(1989-)
PINXTON, Albert	(England)		1936-37
PIRIE, Tom	(Scotland)		1926-27
PLATNAEUR, Nicky	Leicester	10/6/61	1986-89
PLATT, Jim	Ballymoney	26/1/52	1978-79
PLUMLEY, Gary	Birmingham	24/3/56	1983-85
POLAND, George	Penarth		1935-37
			(1946-47)
POLLARD, Robert	Exeter	25/7/01	1932-33
POLYCARPOU, Andy	Islington	15/8/58	1981-82
PONTIN, Keith	Pontyclun	14/6/56	1974-83

Welsh International - Had a two year wait for his first team debut, and a two more before becoming a regular choice. A disagreement with manager Ashurst led to a premature drop into non-League football.

KEITH PONTIN

POSTIN, Eli	Birmingham	1911	1933-34
POWELL, Cliff	Watford	21/2/68	1989-90
POWELL, Dave	Dolgarrog	15/10/44	1972-74
PRESCOTT, Jack	Waterloo, Lancs.		1936-39
PRICE, Allen	S. Wales		1985-86
PRICE, Cecil	Cardiff	2/12/19	1948-49
PUGH, Reg.	Aberaman	July 1917	1934-40

One of Cardiff's most loyal of players in the 1930's. Made his first team debut aged 17 and soon became the regular right-winger. The War effectively curtailed his football career.

REG PUGH

RAINFORD, Johnny	London	11/12/30	1953-54
RAMSEY, Paul			
RANKMORE, Frank	Cardiff	2/7/42	1957-63
REDWOOD, Douglas	Ebbw Vale	1918	1935-37
REECE, Gilbert	Cardiff	2/7/42	1972-76
REED, Ebor	Spennymoor	30/11/1899	1925-26
REES, Mel.	Cardiff	25/1/67	1984-87
REES, Nigel	Bridgend	11/7/53	1970-72
REES, W. (Billy)	Blaengarw	10/3/24	1943-49

Welsh International - Joined the Club during the War as a centre-forward but soon switched inside. Always capable of snatching vital goals - which he did in the 1945 'marathon' Bristol City match!

REID, George	Belfast		1922-23

Billy Rees

146

REYNOLDS, Brayley	Newport	30/5/35	1956-59
RHODES, Albert	Devon	1920	1938-39
RICHARDS, Len	Cardiff		1932-33
RICHARDS, Percy	Merthyr	1908	1926-27
RICHARDS, Stan	Cardiff	21/1/17	1946-48
RICKARDS, C.T. (Tom)	Giltbrook, Notts.		1938-39
RILEY, Harold	Oldham	22/11/09	1934-36
ROBBINS, Walter	Cardiff	24/11/10	1928-32

Welsh International – Holds the record for scoring five goals in a match – from the left wing. A superb player who became the Club trainer in the decade following the War.

ROBERTS, Dave	Southampton	26/1/49	1978-80
ROBERTS, Jason	Ferndale	1971	1987-89
ROBERTS, John	Ferndale	1969	1987-
ROBERTS, Joseph	Birkenhead		1935-36
ROBERTS, William (Bill)	Birmingham		1928-32

Made his Cardiff debut a year after signing – the last match (for some years) in the First Division! Formed a solid, though somewhat ponderous, full-back partnership with John Smith.

Bill Roberts

ROBINSON, Matthew	Felling, Co.Durham		1928-32
ROBSON, Keith	Hetton	15/11/53	1977-78
RODGERSON, Ian	Hereford	9/4/66	1988-90
RODON, Chris	Swansea	9/6/63	1983-84
RODRIGUES, Peter	Cardiff	21/1/44	1961-66
ROGERS, Alan	Plymouth	6/7/54	1986-87
ROGERS, T.W.	S. Wales		1933-34
RONAN, Peter	Dysart, Scotland		1931-33
RONSON, Billy	Fleetwood	22/1/57	1979-81
ROPER, Harry	Romiley, Cheshire		1935-37
ROWLAND, Alf	Stokesley	2/9/20	1949-50
RUSSELL, George	Altherstone		1932-34
RUSSELL, Kevin	Portsmouth	6/12/66	1990-91
RUTTER, Charlie	London	22/12/27	1949-58

A full-back who made his debut a year after signing, and within two years was the regular choice (during which time he gained an England 'B' Cap). Later became a tropical bird dealer.

RYDER, Derek	Leeds	18/2/47	1966-68

SANDER, Chris	Swansea	11/11/62	1985-86
SANDERS, Alan	Newport	29/10/63	1981-82
SANDERSON, Paul	Blackpool	16/12/66	1987-
SAUNDERS, Dean	Swansea	21/6/64	1984-85
SAYER, Peter	Cardiff	2/5/55	1973-78
			(1981-82)
SCOTT, Morry	Swansea	1971	1989-90
SCOTT, R. (Dick)	Thetford	26/10/41	1963-64
SCOTT, R. (Bob)	Dundee	16/3/37	1957-61
SCOTT, W.J.(Bill)	(Ireland)		1936-37
SEARLE, Damon	Cardiff	26/10/71	1990-
SEASMAN, John	Liverpool	21/2/55	1984-85
SEMARK, Robin			
SENDALL, Richard	Stamford	10/7/67	1989-90
SHARP, Frank	Edinburgh	28/5/47	1969-70
SHAW, W.	Kilnhurst	3/10/1898	1928-29
SHERLOCK, Steve	Birmingham	10/5/59	1986-87
SHERWOOD, Alf	Aberaman	13/11/23	1941-56

Welsh International – Arguably the greatest Cardiff full-back. After his War-time selection, became the City's most capped player. Moved on to Newport County, for 5 years, after 353 Cardiff games!

ALF SHERWOOD

SHOWERS, Derek	Merthyr	28/1/53	
SIMMONS, Tony	Sheffield	9/2/65	1986-87
SLOAN, Tom	Portadown	11/9/1900	1924-29
SMELT, Lee	Edmonton	13/3/58	1984-86
SMITH, Cecil F.	Marchwiel	30/10/04	1936-37
SMITH, Colin	Ruddington	3/11/58	1983-84
SMITH, E.E. (Bert)	Donegal		1919-24

Irish International – One of Cardiff's greatest centre-halves. For the first 3 seasons of League football was the first choice. Of two League goals scored, one was the first in the 1st Division.

SMITH, George	Newcastle	7/10/45	1973-75
SMITH, Harold R.	Wealdstone		1936-37
SMITH, James	Worcester		1936-38
SMITH, John	Beith, Ayrshire		1930-32
SMITH, Ritchie	Aberdeen		1938-39

Bert Smith

SMITH, Samuel J.W.	Stafford	7/9/04	1925–27
SMITH, Thomas, Potter	Newcastle-upon-Tyne	July 1901	1925–29
SPRING, Andy	Gateshead	17/11/65	1985–86
STANSFIELD, Fred	Cardiff	12/12/27	1943–49

Welsh International – Settled down at centre-half. Tenacious and keen in the tackle, a tower of strength in the air, he was one of the finest pivots to have played for the Club.

STEEL, Alf	Glasgow	15/8/25	1950–51
STEELE, Eric	Newcastle	14/5/54	1982–83
STEPHENS, Lee	Cardiff	30/4/71	1990–91
STEVENS, Gary	Birmingham	30/8/54	1978–82

A long striding, splindly player, who was strong in the air. Entered League football at the age of 24, and for four years was the City's regular choice centre-forward.

STEVENSON, Ernie	Rotherham	28/12/23	1948–50
STEVENSON, Nigel	Swansea	2/11/58	1985–86
STITFALL, Albert	Cardiff	7/7/24	1948–52
STITFALL, Ron	Cardiff	14/12/25	1942–64

Welsh International – Cardiff born and bred and joined the City during the War finally settling in at full-back. In the late 1940's was one of 3 brothers on the books. A loyal Club man and unsung hero.

STOCKIN, Ron	Birmingham	27/6/31	1954–56
SUGRUE, Paul	Coventry	6/11/60	1981–82
SULLIVAN, Colin	Saltash	24/6/51	1979–81
SULLIVAN, Derek	Newport	10/8/30	1947–61

Welsh International – Made his League debut at 17 years, as at outside-left, and although regarded as a half-back was one of the most versatile of Cardiff's players. A post-war 'great'.

SUMMERHAYES, David	Cardiff	21/3/47	1965–67
SUMMERFIELD, Kevin	Walsall	7/1/59	1984–85
SUMMERS, Chris	Cardiff	6/1/72	1990–91
SUTTON, Mel.	Birmingham	13/2/46	1967–72

Came into the first team during the 1968/69 season, and became a a near ever present for four years. A round shouldered and hunched appearance belied his abilities. Was often in trouble with referees!

SWAN, Maurice	Dublin	25/2/32	1960–63
SYKES, E.A. (Ernie)	Chesterfield		1939–40

TAGGART, Bobby	Torbush	10/3/27	1949–50
TALBOT, F.L. (Les)	Hednesford	3/8/10	1936–39

A big, strong, and constructive inside-forward who had a tremendous shot. The War effectively ended his career with Cardiff City, and he moved on to Walsall in 1945, before retiring at 37.

TAPSCOTT, Derek	Barry	30/6/32	1958–65

Welsh International – having missed an earlier chance of signing 'Tappy', he eventually came to Ninian Park, from Arsenal, in 1958, to become one of the best Cardiff players. A brave opportunist.

TAYLOR, Mark	Hartlepool	20/11/64	1990–91
TAYLOR, S.G.	(England)		1934–35
TENNANT, Jim	(Canada)		1932–33
THIRLAWAY, William J. (Billy)	Durham	10/10/1896	1927–30
THOMAS, Keith	Oswestry	28/7/29	1952–53
THOMAS, Martin	Senghenydd	28/11/59	1982–83
THOMAS, Peter	Treforest	18/10/32	1953–54
THOMAS, Rod	Glyncorrwg	11/1/47	1977–81
THOMPSON, Chris	Walsall	24/1/60	1989–90
TIDDY, Mike	Helston	4/4/29	1950–55

A winger who combined power with pace, yet was a lay preacher in his spare time! Came straight into the first team after his transfer from Torquay, and became the regular right-winger for 5 years.

TOBIN, Bobby	Cardiff	29/3/21	1941–48
TONG, David	Blackpool	21-9/55	1982–85

A consistant, if unspectacular, midfielder, who gave good service afer joining the Club on a free transfer. Notable for his careful passing and deadball accuracy.

TOSHACK, Cameron	Cardiff	7/3/70	1990–
TOSHACK, John M.B.E.	Cardiff	22/3/49	1964–70

Probably the most charismatic player ever produced by the Club. At 16, he scored on his (substitute) debut. His transfer to Liverpool stunned the City fans. Later, at Swansea, was awarded the M.B.E.

TOWNSEND, Chris	Caerleon	30/3/66	1983–84
TUCKER, Ken	Merthyr	15/7/35	1955–58
TUPLING, Steve	Wensleydale	11/7/64	1988–89
TURNBULL, William (Billy)	Blyth	1900	1922–23
TURNER, Albert	Sheffield	3/9/07	1937–38
TURNER, C.	(England)		1936–37
TURNER, Rob	Durham	18/9/66	1985–87
TYSOE, G.F.	Northampton		1926–28

UNSWORTH, Jamie	Bury	1/5/73	1990-
UPTON, Jim	Coabridge	3/6/40	1963-64
VALENTINE, Albert, Finch	Higher Ince	3/6/07	1929-31
VAUGHAN, Nigel	Caerleon	20/5/59	1983-87

Welsh International – A waif-like midfield player, he joined Cardiff as the 'lynch-pin' in the multi-player Newport deal in 1983. Was top-scorer for two seasons, and later joined Wolves.

VAUGHAN, Thomas	Cardiff		1934-35
VEARNCOMBE, Graham	Cardiff	28/3/34	1952-64

Welsh International – Debut made in the final match of the 1952/53 season, eventually becoming first choice goalkeeper three years later, although only capped on five occasions.

VILLARS, Tony	Cwmbran	24/1/52	1971-76
VINCENT, Johnny	West Bromwich	8/2/47	1972-75
WAKE, Harry	Seaton Delavel	21/1/01	1923-31

The regular choice right-half from 1924. Was at fault with the 1925 F.A.Cup Final goal, but 2 years later scored one of the semi-final goals; a serious injury however kept him out of the Wembley team.

WALKER, Phil	Kirkby	27/1/57	1983-84
WALSH, Brian	Aldershot	26/3/32	1955-61

A brilliant right-winger, who on his day was of International standard; a maker rather than taker of chances. Qualified as a Chartered Accountant, which he practised on his retirement in 1962.

WALSH, Ian	St. Davids	4/9/58	1987-89
WALTON, George	Burnley		1936-40
WARBOYS, Alan	Goldthorpe	18/4/49	1970-72
WARD, Dai	Barry	16/7/34	1961-62
WARD, Gavin	Sutton Coldfield	30/6/70	1989-
WARDLE, George	Durham	24/9/19	1947-49
WARE, Thomas	Cardiff		1930-31
WARREN, Freddie	Cardiff		1927-30
WATKINS, Johnny	Bristol	9/4/33	1959-61
WATKINS, Phil	Caerphilly	2/1/45	1962-64
WATKINS, Tom	Belfast	4/10/02	1925-29
WATSON, Bill	Swansea	11/6/18	1947-48
WEALE, Robert H.	Troedyrhiw		1930-31
WELSBY, Arthur	Ashton in Makerfield	17/11/02	1936-37
WENT, Paul	Bromley-by-Bow	12/10/49	1976-78
WEST, George	Wardley		1913-22
WEST, Joseph	Walker on Tyne	1910	1933-34
WHEELER, Paul	Caerphilly	3/1/65	1985-89
WHITHAM, Jack	Burnley	8/12/46	1974-75
WHITLOW, Fred	Barry		1934-35
WILLIAMS, Chris	Brecon	25/12/55	1977-78
WILLIAMS, D.R. (Dai)	Cardiff		1935-37
WILLIAMS, Gareth	London	30/10/41	1961-67

A tank of a player, who was renowned for his thrustful drives and crossfield passes. Soon became a first choice half-back, alongside Allchurch, and made team captain by 1964.

WILLIAMS, Glyn	Caerau	3/11/18	1946-52

Welsh International – A quick tackling, hard working defender. Became a regular first-teamer at either full or half-back. Won only one Cap, and following a badly broken leg, became a coach.

WILLIAMS, Ralph Shipley	Aberdare	2/10/05	1929-31
WILLIAMS, Rowland	Swansea	10/7/27	1949-56

A forward, whose skills and intelligent play were a pleasure to watch. Hampered by niggling injuries and a protracted illness, but was a regular first team member during the early 50's.

WILLIAMS, Thomas D.	Cardiff		1937-46
WILSON, Bob	Birmingham	23/5/43	1964-69

A lanky and extremely agile 'keeper, whose many fine games will always be clouded by his late mistake in the Cup winners Cup match v. Hamburg. Moved to Exeter where he made 200+ appearances.

WILSON, Thomas H.	London	1905	1930-31
WIMBLETON, Paul	Havant	13/11/64	1986-89
WINSPEAR, Jack	Leeds	24/12/46	1966-67
WITHEY, Graham	Bristol	11/6/60	1984-86
WOOD, George	Douglas	26/9/52	1987-89
WOOD, Terry	Newport	3/9/20	1946-47
WOODRUFF, Bobby	Highworth	9/11/40	1969-74

A talented midfielder who for many years was considered to have the longest throw in football. After 180 appearances for Swindon he was bought by Cardiff, and added 141 League games to his total.

WOODS, Jonathon	Gwent	5/10/66	1983-85
WOOF, Billy	Gateshead	16/8/56	1982-83
YOUDS, Eddie	Liverpool	3/5/70	1989-90

CHAPTER 11
THROUGH THE PLAYERS EYES

FRED STEWART (Cardiff City Manager 1911–33)
(Extracts from an interview published in the Athletic News – Monday, the 14th of January, 1924.)

I am a proud man to have seen my club, Cardiff City, at the top of the First Division. Many have asked the secret behind the success we have enjoyed in our short history. Let me say, here and now, there is no secret beyond this – we get players of decent ability, and each man does his best, with unity of feeling and purpose. The big point is that we are all such good friends – not only the players but the directors also. We take each other's opinion. We never make a change in the team without consulting with the players. Their opinion is worth having.

When I came to Ninian Park in 1911 we only had eleven competition matches on our ground as the main source of support. The area was a Rugby stronghold and our years' income was less than £1,000. Compare that to our situation today at the top of the First Division, where over the recent Christmas-New Year period our games with Sheffield United, Aston Villa and Middlesbrough were watched by almost 150,000 people. In those early pre-war days at Cardiff the game in the Southern League was much like that played in the Scottish League, very pretty to watch. Prior to the war the Southern League was stronger than the Second Division, in my opinion.

We were fortunate that the War did not take a great toll on us, we lost just one player, reserve Tom Witts, and everyone at Cardiff City were united on achieving Football League status.

In George Latham, we have, as you know, a wonderful trainer--coach who is held in the utmost respect of all the players. He is Cardiff City through and through, he even stepped in at Blackburn and helped us to avert a crisis a couple of years ago. He would play today if I asked him to! Our players never give us any trouble. There are old heads among them; wise old owls, if you like that phrase better. James Blair, for instance, is a thoughtful and an earnest man, who knows football from top to bottom.

He is one of the easiest men in the world to get on with, and James Nelson – from Belfast Crusaders – is another. Jimmy Gill was a marvellous capture and Clennell, I believe, has been the making of our team, combining as he does with that marvellous servant, Jack Evans. Len Davies has been a great find and there are others to look out for. I have been asked many times *'who is the best footballer you have had through your hands'.* I have had, and still have, so many – but Billy Hardy I suppose is a bit special. Let me tell you how he came to us, for it is a queer story. I transferred Abrams and reserve half-back Burden to Hearts when I was at Stockport. This left Stockport without a full complement of players, and Hearts agreed that I could take two of their reserves. I could not believe my luck for I was able to sign Hardy and an inside-left, Brown. Hearts did not want me to take Hardy for he was not a regular reserve, but I held them to our agreement. There was a fee of £200 involved should Stockport take up Hardy's registration the following year, but they could not pay the £200 and the player went home to Bedlington, with Hearts holding his registration. I moved to Cardiff City that year, and I desired to get Hardy, and Hearts let me have him for £25. Hardy has never failed. He has never played a bad game in his life. Therefore it is not surprising that he has never been left out of the team as a matter of form. Cardiff City would rejoice if he were to be honoured by the English Association for he is a wonderful half-back.

Fred Keenor sums up the attitude of our team. I honestly do not believe the word 'beaten' is in his vocabulary. We shall be there, or thereabouts, at the end of the season. Our players are determined to succeed on behalf of the wonderful support they receive in South Wales.

In conclusion may I quote from Shakespeare:-
'I profess not talking, only this – Let each man do his best'.

FRED KEENOR (Player: 1913–33)
(Extracts from a feature interview in the Sports Budget, on the 27th of August, 1927.)

Let me show you around Ninian Park where we are preparing for the new season. After winning the F.A. Cup in April we have had a hectic summer I can tell you. As captain, I have eaten more free suppers than I ever imagined possible but I am ready for Bolton Wanderers at Ninian Park this Saturday.

Doesn't the ground look a picture. It hardly seems possible that it was a rubbish tip in 1910 – but it was! Today Ninian Park holds 60,000, the concrete stand cost £8,000 and we are having another built in the near future. The pitch is looked after by old David Gouldstone, an excellent groundsman. He has to suffer a lot of leg-pulling, but he's an old soldier and takes it well. Dave likes a bet but none of the lads have made a fortune from his tips.

The chap with that big cheery grin is George Latham. Everyone knows George and the dog with him is Bonzo, his pet bull-terrier who doubles-up as night watchman. Wait until you see our dressing room. George keeps it full of flowers and his eight canaries are always in good voice.

The players will be coming in for a massage soon. We call Jim Nelson and Tom Watson the Siamese Twins. Always together and always up to no good! One of their favourite tricks is to wait until we are all in the showers and then turn on the cold water. And when we stay away they regularly manage to sew up one of the lad's pyjamas! Quite a few of the lads like a game of snooker or billiards and you'll often find Len Davies, Ernie Curtis, Billy Hardy and myself on the table in the recreation room. But our billiards prize must go to Sam Irving, who also enjoys a game of golf. We've got several musicians at the club. Jack Jennings, Ernie Curtis and Harry Wake can all tinkle the ivories a bit, while Tommy Sloan thinks he is the best singer in all of Cardiff. Tommy Farquharson is a keen dancer, always up to the latest fads, and he claims to be able to pick up any music station in the world on that wireless of his. Hughie Ferguson and George McLachlan also have musical tastes but of the gramophone variety. Both claim to be keen collectors and George, like myself, is a motorist. Harry Wake is a good friend of mine and he acts as secretary of the Cardiff City Benevolent Fund, a scheme originated by the directors, by which the players subscribe now and again for the poor and needy of the Cardiff district.

I don't know whether any other clubs practise the same sort of idea: I havn't heard of any who do.

Winning the F.A. Cup was a great ambition of mine. I pledged our return after losing to Sheffield United in 1925. My sympathies then went out to dear old Harry Wake who was unfairly blamed for our defeat. Then fate capped it all when Harry was injured and had to miss the Final success over Arsenal. I think it helped spur the boys on to victory. As a Cardiff boy, I was overwhelmed with our home-coming, and Len Davies, Ernie Curtis and myself felt ever so proud to be natives of this great City. The scenes outside City Hall will remain with us long after our playing days are over.

ERNIE CURTIS (Player: 1925-28 & 1933-34)

Fred Stewart signed me for Cardiff City, he was a coal merchant and a very nice man. He did not have anything to do with training – that was left to George Latham and some of the senior players. What a character that George was! Always ready with a joke, and it was he that kept things going, no doubt about that. The directors were a boozy lot and weren't wealthy men, and not many people know that George put money in the club from time to time. He liked a drink mind, in fact he was drunk for a week following our F.A. Cup win, but he was always at the ground. Sometimes he would stay there all night preparing our equipment for important matches. George was so dedicated and we all liked him immensely.

The Club was full of great players in the 1920's, and we all got on well together. Bert Smith, an Irish centre-half, was quite mad. He used to mesmerise centre-forwards – or so he said. One night some of us convinced Bert that he must have hypnotic powers, and we persuaded him to stand in the middle of Canton High Street and see if he could stop the traffic. Oh, he stopped the traffic all right – I don't know what today's newspapers would have made of that little caper! Bert was a well built chap, and an excellent centre-half, but as I say, quite mad.

Tom Farquharson used to change next to me. He was such a pleasant type but secretive about his past back in Ireland. One day Tom began telling me about being on the move from house to house, and that he always carried a gun. He opened up his kit bag and there it was! I often wonder if he still had it when he had his tobacconist kiosk near the Capitol Cinema in Queen Street years later.

Although my natural position was inside-forward I played at outside-right in the Cup Final, due to Willie Davies' illness and an injury to Harry Wake. Both these players were short and slight, Harry was a good passer but a little slow, and I remember we all visited Willie at the Chest Hospital in Talgarth. He was such a nice chap and ever so glad to see us. Of course he recovered his fitness and moved on to Tottenham.

People often ask me about Fred Keenor. Well, he was one of the hardest tacklers in the game, some said he was dirty but he was just hard. Nobody took liberties with old Fred. I would have liked to have seen him against today's fancy dans with their elbowing, shirt-pulling and poking out tongues. Fred would have tackled them once – they wouldn't come back for more. And he was fit considering he was virtually a chain smoker.

He would lap Ninian Park in a pair of old heavy army boots while we were doing ball practise. Fred could run all right, he couldn't run with the ball mind you, but he could run all day. And talk, Fred would mouth and curse at us, urging us on, a great leader. He had this big car and some of the other lads would block his way out with their vehicles just to get him going. The air would be blue!

You could not wish to meet a nicer man than poor old Hughie Ferguson. I felt so sorry when I heard of his suicide. The Dundee crowd drove him to it so I was told, but they loved him here in Cardiff. Some said he wasn't a brilliant player but look at his goals – all in the First Division – he would have earned a fortune today. That's what I will remember about Hughie, his goals and his shooting power.

George McLachlan could shoot too, a marvellous left foot but Jack Evans was the more accurate crosser of the ball. He was great, but so thin you would have thought a gust of wind would blow him over. When Fred swore at Jack, he would swear back in Welsh, and Fred would just wave and nod. He didn't have a clue what Jack was saying. Billy Hardy had a reputation in the game for his heading power – and it was all true. He was only about five feet six inches and he would outjump six footers. It was incredible really. Billy was a quiet type. He never bothered that much, just played his football and went home. Len Davies was a bit like that as well. He came from Canton, liked a drink, and had his own mates. Funnily enough, I didn't have much to do with Len, although we were both local lads. He was a bit older than me though. Herbie Evans was another local and a good friend. He was so unlucky with injury, and eventually joined Tranmere. I became friendly with reserve full-back Jack McJennett, and eventually married his sister.

I remember my transfer to Birmingham. Fred Stewart came up to me during training and asked me to call in at the office later. He told me that the Club were up against it and that Birmingham had made an offer which had been accepted. He advised me to go as City were in financial trouble – and this wasn't that long after we had won the F.A. Cup mind. Mr. Stewart told me that other players would probably have to be sold – so I went. It was the beginning of the break up of a good team. We all played for each other and got on well. Travel was always by rail and we favoured certain hotels. No late nights and no monkey business in those days. If you were caught straying, you were immediately fined a fortnight's wages, and no appeal. We had a couple of drinkers in the team but everything was done in moderation.

I suppose winning the F.A. Cup was the biggest thrill. I was on £8 a week, £6 in the summer, but there was no bonus for beating Arsenal, just our winners' medals. When we came back from London, every station on route was packed, and we stopped at the back of Somerton Park, where Newport County were playing, to show them the Cup. There must have been 300,000 waiting for us in Cardiff and we had a great reception. I know Fred and Len were quite overcome, but as a 19 year old, I thoroughly enjoyed it all.

How it had all changed when I rejoined the City in 1933. Ben Watts-Jones brought me back, but it was a shambles and the team were in a poor state. He took me out on the pitch and told me that he intended to have advertising here and there, and things like that. I said to him: *'don't you want to talk to me about football and what we can do on the pitch to get out of trouble'*. I didn't have much time for him. I got on well with Les Jones though. He was a talented player, a small, tricky inside-forward, who could score goals. He was sold to keep the Club in business. I didn't hang about and quickly moved, and it was twenty years before I came back to help out training the reserves. Say what you like about Cyril Spiers, and he wasn't everybody's cup of tea, but he was a professional, and whereas it had been so happy-go-lucky in my playing days, he had the club organised. And of course Mr. Spiers had recruited many of the great players during the War who went on to take City back to the First Division. Bill Jones and Wilf Grant were good men but they were treated shabbily at Swansea, in September 1962, when they were told in the dressing rooms that they were being sacked.

Ron Stitfall and myself took charge and we won eighteen points from twenty four, with plenty of goals along the way. We decided that we couldn't tell the team how to play and they got on with it. Ivor Allchurch, what a great player, and that Peter Hooper. He was a smashing bloke with a great left foot. His two goals when we won 6-2 at Preston were two of the hardest shots I've ever seen. The directors brought in George Swindin and I continued on the coaching staff until Jimmy Scoular came to the club. I didn't agree with his methods. Some of his coaching antics were crazy and over-robust, and, after one particular incident regarding a young player, I told him so. We ended up having an almighty row and I was finished at the club. I didn't want it to end that way. Of course I still go down there with my friend Ted Gorin, and I'm treated well, but the style of football isn't what I like to see. I preferred it along the ground where players could show their ability. Alex James of the Arsenal was the best I ever saw. I can remember seeing him beating eight men on a mud-heap, he was brilliant. Now it's all changed and it's all in the air - and not for the better.

Just before I finished at City, John Toshack came on the ground staff. I didn't think he had the pace to make it, there were times when he looked rubbish. But Jimmy Scoular started the high ball game and young John fitted the bill. He certainly made the most of his opportunities and has become a great success, but like a lot of the players since my era, was sold for a quick profit.

No matter what everyone says City have had great players and I've been honoured to have known most of them.

BERIAH MOORE (Player 1940-49)

I didn't see Cardiff City much in the days before the War as I was usually playing myself. But I got to know a number of the players, if only briefly, when I signed as an amateur from Cardiff Corries. By then, of course, only the likes of Arthur Granville and Jimmy Collins were still there and the City manager, Cyril Spiers, was already looking to local talent for his team. Jimmy Collins was a smashing centre-forward, at his peak he would have been brilliant, but his career was ended by the War.

I came to Ninian Park with Billy James, Bobby Tobin and Len Parker (not to be confused with Reg Parker). Billy was a 'boy wonder' - what a player at such a young age, and in my opinion Bobby Tobin was the best player, not to play for Wales. He had such skill and close ball control. Of course Billy, Bobby, Billy Baker and Jackie Pritchard ended up as prisoners of war with the Japs. When they returned I played with both Bobby Tobin and Billy James in the reserves, and it was sad to see them trying to recover their lost careers.

I played my first game for City up in the valleys and scored three or four goals. Mr. Spiers selected me for the first-team the following Saturday and we were playing a War-time regional match at Torquay. We had a special compartment on the train and were due to pick up a couple of lads from Everton at Newport station. Well, they didn't turn up - it was like that in the early days of the War. We had to play the match with ten players and our trainer, who was a chap called Smith and who had played for Bolton in the 1923 F.A.Cup Final. Torquay were a good team, with quite a few 'guest' players, but that day, it was in May 1940, we beat them 4-2. I got one goal on my full debut and Billy James, Ernie Marshall and Len Parker also scored.

As an amateur I was allowed 7/6d.(37p) tea money for away games and 5/- (25p) at home, but when Mr.Spiers signed me on professional forms - in August 1940 - I was on 30/- (£1-50p) a match, which was pretty good in those days.

City did not rely on 'guest' players but for a while we had a lot of lads - who were stationed at St.Athan - turning up and playing the odd game. I can remember the likes of Bill Shankly, Raich Carter, Johnny Carey, Allenby Chilton, Roy Paul, Benny Fenton and Charlie Mitten playing just once or twice. We were a bit cut off in Wales, and the West, and non-League clubs such as Bath City, Aberaman and Lovell's Athletic were allowed to play in our section. Some of these, Bath City in particular, would pay good appearance money, and as a result they often had several top international players in their team; people like Stan Mortenson played regularly for them. And Bristol City believed in using 'guest' players - I played for them four times!

By 1943 Cardiff City had the likes of 'Buller' Lever, Alf Sherwood, Fred Stansfield, Billy Rees, myself and Ken Hollyman (when he was home from the Navy), and Mr.Spiers had us playing the way he wanted. He liked to play four forwards with one support player. In the early days it was Bobby Tobin who filled that role and later on he signed Bryn Allen for that purpose. Some times the standard of football was poor but that was because clubs were relying on 'guest' players, who seldom fitted in to a game plan. We attracted quite good crowds and there was some keen rivalry in our region. In the 1944-5 season, when we won the Western Regional Championship, the supporters got right behind us and we played some good stuff.

I played in the long Cup-tie against Bristol City and we were told that they announced over the radio that the game was continuing, just in case people at home were worried about their husbands or sons!

Then, of course, there was the match against the Moscow Dynamos. They were good, not 10-1 better than us, but they were also crafty and clever off the ball. Gamesmanship, I suppose you would call it today. After the War the Club had a terrific playing staff and I found myself unable to get into the Third Division (South) championship team. Roy Clarke was the regular outside-left, and then George Wardle and Derrick Sullivan came in. I did play in the Second Division, and scored twice on my League debut against Southampton when we won 5-1.

Eventually, in 1949, I moved to Bangor City and then a year later joined Newport County where I linked up again with some old pals from Cardiff. I felt Newport were a better club than Cardiff in their treatment of players. Cardiff was professionally run and you only got what you were due, but County would give bonuses and arrange functions for the players and their families. I really enjoyed my time there.

I don't think my career was harmed by the War. In fact, if anything, I was a player who benefitted during those six years. I was a first team player – and the club leading scorer – and played with some unusual characters. It all helped me have a long career in the professional game and I'm grateful for that.

RON STITFALL (Player: 1942–64)

I enjoyed watching Cardiff City in the late 1930's when they had some good players such as goal-keeper Bob Jones, centre-half Bill Bassett – what a hard man he was – outside-right Reggie Pugh and inside-forward Leslie Talbot. Jimmy Collins was a good, old fashioned centre-forward who could shoot with either foot, and one of the most popular players was winger 'Pluto' Prescott, who was deaf.

I played for the Welsh schoolboys in 1939-40 but due to the outbreak of war we never received our caps. I understand that someone quite recently has tried to put that right, but I do not know how many of that team are still around. I went straight to Ninian Park as an amateur outside-right, and was only 15 years old when I made my first appearance for Cardiff City. I got 5/- (25p) tea money for home games and 7/6d. (37p) when we played away, and I trained on Tuesday and Thursday evenings with whoever turned up. In those days City were relying heavily on servicemen and guest players, you hardly saw the same men two weeks running.

I spent four years in the Army, based mainly overseas when I played intermittently. As I grew bigger so I moved backwards, centre-half, and then full-back. When I rejoined City in 1947, I played in those positions for the reserves and made my debut at Brentford, when Alf (Sherwood) was called up by Wales, and I took his place at left-back. It was a hard game, we got a draw, and a little later I came into the side again at West Bromwich. That day I saw an unbelievable performance by Dougie Blair, who I hardly knew at the time. What a player and character Dougie was, but the players who impressed me most were the half-back line of Ken Hollyman, Fred Stansfield and Billy Baker.

'Holly' was a real livewire, absolutely non-stop, Fred was strong and solid, while Baker could put the ball through the eye of the needle with the accuracy of his passes – and what a runner with the ball. The funny thing was, I never felt Baker was fully fit as the War had taken its toll on him, he had been a P.O.W. with the Japs. I came in for Alf when we played that F.A. Cup tie at Villa Park. I wasn't worried about the big crowd but Dougie couldn't play, and Graham Hogg, an amateur, came in at left-half and I had to cover him. The first 20 minutes was like El Alamein but Phil Joslin was inspired and made some great saves that probably broke the Villa's hearts. We had a great spirit which saw us through and that goal of 'Holly's' was a beauty.

There was great competition for places in those days and the reserve players were always out to catch Cyril Spiers' eye in practice matches. I've seen really heated arguments, even the odd fight, between some players – that's how competitive it was.

For a while I played all over the place but I never minded as long as I was in the team. I was on less money than some of the lads and the club had to ask permission from the Football League to raise my wages during the season. They agreed to let me be paid £10 per week in the winter and £9 in the summer, still £2 a week behind the others!

Our coaching staff were great characters. Walter Robbins, a marvellous player, Bob John, one of the greatest Welsh players, Bob Allison, who never kicked a ball in his life, and Jim Merrett, who did much valuable work, particularly with the youngsters.

Bob John and Derrick Sullivan were great characters together. They used to be at loggerheads all the time, each trying to put one over on the other, and even when Bob was mad, 'Sully' would make him laugh. I remember when Bob put 'Sully' in a sweat suit as he was overweight, and after training in it, 'Sully' telling Bob where to stick it and that he would soon put back what he had sweated off! Bob Allison was one of those larger than life blokes. I think he was heart-broken when he finished at the City. He lived on his own in Broad Street, near the ground, and was a keen gardener. He was found dead in his garden and all of us who knew him were devastated.

I picked up a cartilage injury at Barnsley which caused me to miss almost the entire 1951-2 promotion season. I had it wrongly diagnosed and, as a result, was out of action for 15 months. I watched that team a lot. What a revelation Wilf Grant turned out to be, a really clinical finisher. Big Ken Chisholm was a real darling with a wicked streak in him. 'Chis' always ran out second behind Alf Sherwood, and at the dressing room door he would call over his shoulder:- 'Good luck boys, see you at the far post!' He loved terrorising goalkeepers and his pet rabbit was Charlton's Sam Bartram. I remember 'Chis' telling us before we played Charlton at home in 1953: *'I'll murder Bartram tomorrow'* and he was as good as his word, for after putting Bartram, ball and all, into the net for a disallowed goal in the first minute, 'Chis' headed a first-half hat-trick as we won 5-0.

I didn't expect to play in that 9-1 defeat by Wolves but Charlie Rutter was late and I stepped in. They were brilliant, no doubt about that, in fact they could have scored 12! We had nothing to lose when we played at Molineux, but we rolled our sleeves up and really upset them by winning 2-0 – and it was no fluke either.

As a full-back I faced some great wingers and the one who gave me the biggest run around was Vic Metcalfe of Huddersfield. I remember him getting me fit in one early season game as I chased him all afternoon and I never fouled him once – I never got near enough to him for that! I'm proud to say that I was never 'booked' during my career, and Stanley Matthews once thanked me for playing him so cleanly

In 1959 Bill Jones told me that he wanted me to help the reserve side, but a few weeks later, Bill called me in to play at inside-right at Middlesbrough, as the team needed an anchor in midfield. We drew 1-1, and the following Saturday, the same team went 4-0 up in only 20 minutes against Bristol City, at Ninian Park. In the second half I was on the point of collapse but Bill urged me to carry on, and I missed the next two games with calf strain. I then came back and played at full-back for the rest of the season, as we went up into the First Division. That was a good team. Alec Milne, with his sliding tackles, seemed to spend most of his time on his backside. Colin Baker was vastly under-rated, I loved playing behind him. 'Daisy' Walsh could be brilliant and ruin a full-back.

I remember him crucifying poor Ronnie Moran when we won 4-0 at Anfield. Graham Moore was such a strong player and should have gone on to greater things. John Watkins gave us power on the left and both 'Tappy' and Joe Bonson could score great goals. I remember Joe arriving from Wolves and thinking he should be the fittest player in the Club. He would make himself ill trying to win races in training. Danny Malloy was a good centre-half but he would kick his own Granny. I often wonder if Brian Clough thinks of his duels with Danny when he was with Middlesbrough. I can remember one game when Danny was marking Alan Peacock, and Derrick Sullivan was taking Cloughie. Peacock scored with a header and Danny went mad. Cloughie started mickey-taking, telling Peacock he would get a hatfull, and riling Danny even more. He wouldn't keep quiet, and all of a sudden I heard a whack behind me.

When I turned around there was Cloughie face down on the penalty spot and Danny swaggered past me saying, *'I chinned him, I chinned him!'* The funny thing was, that nobody in the ground saw it!

Just as my career was winding down Bill Jones and Wilf Grant were sacked, and for a while, Ernie Curtis and myself took charge and we had a good run, but I had no managerial ambitions. I had rejected offers to be player-manager at Wrexham, Chester and Yeovil. The club appointed George Swindin and he and I never really hit it off. He once told me at half-time that I was playing 'higgledy-piggledy', I didn't have a clue what he meant, and no-one else did either. George was like that, he would use these expressions that had no meaning! By now Don Murray was coming in and I rated him better than Malloy. He was so brave, hard, and determined. Peter King was showing a lot of promise but the daddy of them all was Ivor Allchurch. I could enjoy watching Ivor have any off day, which wasn't often. Ivor was like a gazelle, a great dribbler and could shoot with both feet, and to a man, I never heard anyone have a bad word to say against him. The arrival of Jimmy Scoular saw a lot of changes begin to take place. He didn't rate Ivor, and a lot of us senior players didn't see eye to eye with him. It was win at all costs with Jimmy Scoular and he used to frighten some of the youngsters to death. I suppose that was what I resented most, for I was running the Youth side at the time – lads like George Johnston and John Toshack – and there were times when would lay into them instead of using words of encouragement. He finished me at the Club, although it was secretary Graham Keener who broke the news to me. I was part-time, and I left with obvious regrets.

After twenty-five years I had had three benefits as a loyal clubman, and I later had some enjoyable seasons at Newport County. Even now I am involved in the game, assisting Terry Yorath and the Wales' set-up. And I love telling Ian Rush of the days when Cardiff City beat Liverpool 6-1 at Ninian Park, and when we won 4-0 at Anfield!

KEN HOLLYMAN (Player: 1946–53)

I was soccer-mad as a boy and loved the thrill of watching Cardiff City and being at Ninian Park. As a schoolboy I was allowed in on a complimentary ticket. Although they were in the Third Division, this was about 1937, the atmosphere was terrific and City had players like Arthur Granville, Bill Bassett, Reggie Pugh, Fred Talbot and 'Pluto' Prescott – I loved watching them.

Just as the War began I joined Cardiff Corries and I I must emphasise what an important role the Corries played towards making Cardiff City a great team. Mr.Pritchard, the father of Jack who perished at Java, was running the Corries and he was responsible for recruiting some really fine players. I was playing for Corries under 17's, against their 19 year olds, when Albert Lindon, the Arsenal scout, approached me about going to Highbury. I was all set to go, when Mr.Cyril Spiers arrived at our home and persuaded me to join Cardiff City, as an amateur. I had left the family bakery business by then, and was working at Preston's, so that I could have Saturdays off for football, and with 5/- (25p) 'tea money' at Cardiff City, I was doing well. I made my City debut at Coventry in 1940 against a team full of big experienced men. Afterwards Cyril Spiers told me to go back to the Corries and build myself up, and you can imagine my surprise a week later, when a taxi with a City official came to Llandaff Fields, where I was warming up for a Corries match, to take me to Ninian Park, and play in the return match with Coventry. That was the start of it really and I can remember Jock Weir from Hibs., Allenby Chilton of Manchester United and Bill Shankly (then of Preston) all turning out for City. Bill only played one match, and I remember him having a row with Mr.Spiers about his appearance money. Apparently City gave him thirty shillings, and Shankly argued that he could get £5 playing for Lovell's Athletic, so he left. One of our turning points came when Mr. Spiers agreed to take a team to the Army barracks on Rumney Hill and play a special match. Afterwards, Mr.Spiers made an agreement with the C.O., that if any City players enlisted they would be stationed in Cardiff for the duration! It all backfired five weeks later when the battalion was shipped out, and players like Billy James, Billy Baker, Bobby Tobin, Roy Phillips and Jackie Pritchard were captured by the Japanese. Goalkeeper Jackie Pritchard unfortunately lost his life, and all these were ex-Corries' players.

I enlisted in the Navy, and while waiting for my demob. in Oxford, in November 1945, Mr.Spiers contacted me by telephone to get back to Cardiff where City were due to play the Moscow Dynamos. I hitch-hiked to Cardiff in my demob. suit and trilby hat, and played the following day. But we were no match for the Russians whose technique and support play had us chasing-shadows.

I think that we learned from that lesson though, and much of the Dynamos style came out in our 1946-7 team that won the Third Division championship. When I returned from the Navy, Mr.Spiers had brought in Arthur 'Buller' Lever, Fred Stansfield, Colin Gibson, Bryn Allen, Billy Rees, Roy Clarke, etc. All were great players including the marvellous Stan Richards. What a character Stan was, he always played in these taped up boots that kept falling apart, but he would not go on the pitch without them! Our trainer was Jim Merrett, who became my father-in-law, and when Mr. Spiers went to Norwich he took Jim with him.

Billy McCandless was the secretary-manager for our championship season, and what a marvellous chap he was. He didn't do anything like training with the players – absolutely nothing – but he knew how to handle us, and he was able to manage an extra win bonus for us. It wasn't 'under-the-counter', or anything like that, but Mr.McCandless managed it. Once we got going we were unstoppable. Our only thought was to win and score goals, which we did. We wouldn't have lost our long unbeaten record at Bristol Rovers if it hadn't been for the snow and mud. The match only went ahead because there were over 30,000 there, and it was a benefit for their trainer. We were persuaded to go out, and once they scored there was no way they would call it off.

Stan Richards loved scoring, he would guide the ball home with his feet and head – a great leader. Billy Rees was like a tank, all power and strength, but for me Bryn Allen was exceptional, he was our Ivor Allchurch if you like, a marvellous goalscoring inside-forward. Billy Baker did not look like a footballer but could he play. He was like Bobby Tobin since you could not get close enough to him to make a tackle. Bobby, another ex-Corrie, would have been great had it not been for the War – the same as Billy James, who suffered badly from malnutrition. Cyril Spiers came back from Norwich and continued with his youth policy, and in the late 1940's we had a big staff, and it didn't matter where you played, the competition for places was terrific.

I suppose scoring for City in that F.A.Cup-tie at Aston Villa in 1949, before over 70,000, was one of my finest moments. I started the move in the centre-circle, and George Edwards went clear on the left wing. All I could think of was to get to the far post as I ran through the middle. I don't know whether George tried a shot or not, but the ball came over like a bullet, and I thought 'Bloody Hell lookout', as I jumped up and it went like a rocket from my head into the net. What a feeling, what a noise, I went crazy. Billy Rees got another and we won 2-1. I was never nervous about those big crowds, all you did was concentrate on the opposition and get on with it. It was at the start of that season that Mr.Spiers and H.H.Merrett, the chairman, came to see me during training. I had to be introduced to 'H.H.' as I had never met him, and he told me that I was going to Blackpool to be coached by Stanley Matthews, as they thought I would make an outside-right. Stanley had an open cheque, but how can you be taught anything by a genius. Still he did give me a few tips, including one for his horse, which came nowhere!

Bob Allison was the trainer who gave us manipulation and rub downs. A friend of 'H.H.', Bob was a former professional boxer and borstal boy, and had really rough hands. He once gave Dougie Blair a rub-down which left Dougie looking like he'd had a cat of nine tails, and when I once complained of stomach pains, Bob's remedy was to punch me in the midriff! Whatever it was it seemed to work and I was O.K., but it moved Dougie to call Bob a 'thug'. He wasn't really – but Dougie Blair came from a far different background. Now Dougie Blair was unique. When my late brother-in-law came back from being a P.O.W., he badly wanted to see us play, so he went to West Bromwich Albion when we won 3-2, and Doug. scored two phenomenal goals. Doug. was like that, he could be quiet for long periods, but when he got in the mood, look out. Quite simply one of Cardiff City's 'greats' and with his father and brother both Scottish internationals, Doug. had the pedigree.

Our training was mainly running, running, and more running. Road runs to Barry and back, and Doug. would simply refuse to do them. He was employed by John Morgan (Builders), and trained in the evenings, and when we stayed overnight somewhere, Doug. would simply say: *'I don't fancy that, I'll travel up by car in the morning';* and he would.

They were great years at Cardiff City and, after I had torn ligaments, I was approached by my old mate Fred Stansfield to join Newport County. I hesitated over the move as I was due another benefit at City and did not know if I would last any time through the injury. My benefit was sorted out and I went on, incredibly, to have eight marvellous seasons with the County, and three years as player-coach with Ton Pentre. The atmosphere was more relaxed at Somerton Park, but we had no success, whereas at Ninian Park you showed respect and discipline to the seniors and management, but we had a winning team which was a pleasure to be part of.

My wife has often criticised me for always wanting to win whether it be at soccer, baseball, bowls, golf or even cards. But winning brings enjoyment; if you lose, so what, there's always another game, another day. That was our rallying cry at Cardiff City, as any of the 30,000 plus who watched regularly would tell you. Quite often little things happen in football that prove to be turning points. One such incident occurred at Ninian Park on the 11th of November 1950, when we were playing Hull City.
I was centre-forward, and Bobby McLaughlin was injured before half-time. In the dressing room it was decided that I would switch to my regular right-half position and Bobby Mac to outside-right. Someone said: *'What will we do with that bugger-?',* pointing at Wilf Grant. I spoke up: *'He can have a go at centre-forward'.* At this time, mind you, anyone coming in for Wilf could have had him for £2,000. Well, it is history what happened after that. We won the match 2-1, Wilf became one of the coolest and deadliest leaders in the game, and a year later, he scored the goals to take us to the First Division. I can proudly say that my chance remark went some way in changing the course of history.

ARTHUR 'BULLER' LEVER (Player: 1946-50)

I watched the City in the late 1930's when they had some good players but were not a successful team. I remember big Bill Bassett, the centre-half – who would have kicked his Granny if she'd been on the pitch – little Reggie Pugh with his darting in and out running, and left-wing 'Pluto Prescott, who was deaf. Many was the time that 'Pluto' did not know the whistle had been blown and would carry on playing. I suppose his deafness had its advantages though, as he never knew what the crowd were calling him! I was signed by Cardiff City in 1943 from local team Machine Products, and more or less, went straight into the team that Cyril Spiers was building from scratch. Teams like Lovell's Athletic and Bath had international 'guests' and it was a great experience playing against them. That war-time Cup-tie against Bristol City which went on and on, as we had to get a result, was something you do not forget. Three hours forty minutes I think it was – it's true that people who lived near Ninian Park were popping home for their tea! And it was a great relief when Billy Rees literally fell into the net with the ball, for us to win.

The Moscow Dynamo game taught us a great lesson. It's a funny thing but I swear we had as much of the ball as them, but they had the techniques. That Dynamo side was probably one of the greatest ever put together, but remember, we were still rebuilding after the War, and lads like McLoughlin, Raybould, Danny Lester and Ernie Carless were not in our 1946-7 championship team. Now that **was** a team which I was proud to be a part of. Great players and great characters too. Billy McCandless had taken over from Cyril Spiers, and he got us going and kept us happy. A great chap, Billy Mac, and my abiding memory of him is seeing him sat in his office, glass of whisky in one hand, and this black cat on his knee. If ever you went in to see him, that's how he would be. Bob Allison, the trainer, was a real one-off. A former prize fighter he kept us in shape, literally. Ask any of the lads who had one of his massages, he wasn't too subtle and had hands like pancakes.

Walter Robbins, a great player in his own right, was in charge of training, although much of it was based on running and sprinting. Walter believed in ball work, and we used to have head tennis games the length of the pitch – and this with the old leather ball, mind. In those days you would know a lot about your opponents, and if they were a bit on the light side a few balls would be kept in a bucket of water, and thrown on from time to time – it was all part of the 'kidology'. I got on well with the chairman, H.H.Merrett, and when I was first married we lived in a cottage on his estate, Alf Sherwood and his wife lived there too. It was a crescent of six, named after his son who had died during the War. When my son was seriously ill, old 'H.H.' would call in every evening for a report on his condition – he was a nice chap – although players and directors did not mix much, and some of our boys never really got to know him. 'H.H.' had a soft spot for Stan Richards who would often turn up looking like a tramp. Stan was a real rough diamond and 'H.H.' would give him the odd dinner jacket and suit, so that he would be turned out properly. They were second-hand mind, and Stan often looked like old 'H.H.' himself. It's amazing to think of the crowds we had. Over 51,000 when we played Bristol City in the Third Division, that was the day that a chap fell through the stand roof and survived, and over 70,000 for that F.A.Cup-tie at Villa in 1949. All my nerves would disappear once I was running out, and you did not really notice the crowd, except for a sort of humming noise in the background.

Hillsborough, and St.James's Park, Newcastle, were my favourite grounds. I remember Billy Baker being given a runaround by Len Shackleton up there. No disgrace in that, 'Shack' was a great player, but he kept bouncing the ball up on his knee in front of 'Puffer', and there was nothing that he could do. For a month afterwards the rest of us would taunt 'Puffer' – 'look out, Shack's about'!

We played a Cup tie at Derby in 1949 and stayed overnight at Matlock or Buxton. Anyway, we removed this small statue and placed it in Cyril Spiers bed, who saw the joke. That match with Derby at their closed-in ground was a real epic. We thought that we had got a replay, until Jackie Stamps dumped Phil Joslin into the net to score a late winner, which put us out. He was a rough handful, Stamps, and all teams had centre-forwards who thought nothing of going in on the goalkeeper. It all added to the goalmouth excitement and the crowds loved it – I'm not so sure that the goalkeepers did though.

I didn't like playing on small tight grounds, and I hated it at Barnsley who had this bandy-legged Scotsman, Johnny Kelly, on their left wing. You could drive a pig up the passage between his legs, but what a player, certainly one who I feared yet respected. Talking of characters, I'm almost sure that Tommy Best was the first coloured player in League football, who in the right mood was a hell of a player. We played at Tottenham and he was up against Bill Nicholson, *'Don't worry about me'*, he told us with a smile on his black face, *'I'll give him the soft shoe shuffle!'* Bestie was as good as his word and we had an extremely rare win over the 'Spurs. The name of Dougie Blair will always be linked with Cardiff City. He was brilliant when switched on, with one of the best left feet I've ever seen. Everybody talks about the game at West Brom, when Dougie scored two phenomenal goals, well I don't think I've ever seen better. Anyone who was at that game was privileged to see Doug at his peak. He had his own way, which was tolerated by Mr.Spiers. Mr.Spiers knew how to handle us. He thought of all the players as 'his boys', and I swear that on the morning of my transfer to Leicester in 1950, he had a tear in his eye. Whenever I played against the City after that, Mr. Spiers would be the first to welcome me with open arms. I played twice against the 1951-2 promotion team, they beat us 4-0 in the opening game, and we won 3-0 at Leicester. I was not sure that they were promotion material, they seemed to blow hot and cold, but Wilf Grant kept scoring, and the signing of big 'Chis' (Ken Chisholm) – and that late run – settled it. I had three good years at Leicester – playing with Arthur Rowley, Derek Hines and Johnny Morris – but I picked up an ankle tendon injury, and eventually ended my career at Newport County, with old friends like Alf Sherwood and Ken Hollyman. It was a happy go lucky club with some fine players, particularly Ray Wilcox and centre-forward Tommy Johnston. Although I played mainly at right back in my days at Cardiff, Leicester and Newport, when I was with the City I had a run at centre-forward at the end of the 1948-9 season, and managed a few goals. One that I'll never forget came at West Ham, which won us the game. Their goalkeeper, Ernie Gregory, wasn't a great kicker of the ball off the deck, and he scuffed a goal-kick which tamped towards me. Dick Walker, the centre-half, was already looking upfield for the ball, and when he turned around, my shot was rebounding back off the stanchion which held the net up. There was a deathly silence in the ground: *'What the bloody hell's going on'*, Bull, Walker said to me, *'You didn't score did you?'* I nodded, and Dick went on: *'Well you'll never get another one like that!'* He was right, I didn't!

STAN MONTGOMERY (Player: 1948-55)

I came to Cardiff City in 1949, after poor old Fred Stansfield had broken his leg, and made my debut at Grimsby where I scored following a corner-kick, in a 2-2 draw. There were many fine players at Ninian Park in those days and most of our opponents also had good players. I remember just after joining City we played at Aston Villa in an F.A. Cup tie. I was marking Trevor Ford, and we won the game in front of over 70,000 people. We used to play before some tremendous crowds and I was lucky in that I did not suffer from nerves. I suppose I got used to it and in my time as a Cardiff City player we had some very good teams.

Alf Sherwood was quite simply the best full-back I ever played with or against. He was absolutely terrific, a marvellous bloke and not even great players such as Stanley Matthews could better him. Alf Rowland joined the City after me, and he was a good centre-half but I kept him out of the side. He didn't move into the area, and it seemed a strange signing at the time but these things happen.

Dougie Blair was fantastic. I wouldn't have liked to choose between him and Ivor Allchurch. But Doug had such a cultured left foot and when he had the ball he was like poetry in motion. In those days we used to have full scale practice matches on Tuesday mornings and they were taken seriously, I can tell you. Well Dougie would take control, and if he was really buzzing he would run those games as only he could – he was some player and he could talk his way through ninety minutes. The best all-rounder would have to be Derrick Sullivan. He started as an outside-left and eventually played in about nine positions for the City. In those days, if you were chosen to play at right-back or centre-half or whatever, that's where you played. Not like today where players go anywhere. Derrick was popular and played excellently in every position. I think he was playing left-back for us one week, and then played at centre-half for Wales the next, he was that good.

We had a fantastic team spirit at Ninian Park in my playing days, and trainers Bob John and Walter Robbins were really nice men. Bob, in particular, was well respected and a joy to work with. Cyril Spiers was a real gent. We didn't see that much of him and when we did he wouldn't tolerate bad language or players stepping out of line. He had been a goalkeeper with Aston Villa and he was aware of what players got up to. Not that anything did, Cyril was too cute for that. He used to believe in giving young players their chance.

I remember Alan Harrington, Colin Baker, Islwyn Jones, and others, coming into the side at an early age. I think he picked Charlie Rutter after only two trial games. If you were good enough, Cyril Spiers would give you a chance. He used to come out near the end of training and take four of five players, in what we called the shooting box, for special work, otherwise it was all down to Bob John and Walter Robbins. Ernie Stevenson was a good inside-forward. He could beat a man and pass the ball, and players like Tommy Best and Tommy Northcott were not only good players, but they were great characters. We used to call Tommy Northcott, 'Sammy the Seal', because of his shape. He used to go into that rubber suit to sweat it off, but he could play.

I remember us playing Wolves and Billy Wright was marking 'Sammy', who kept flicking the ball past him and leaving him standing. Poor old Billy just did not know what to do to stop him.

Tommy Lawton was the best player I ever had to mark. He had everything and would have been worth a fortune today. We used to get to know our opponents during matches – quite often we would be chatting away as it really was man to man marking in those days. Stan Mortensen liked a chat, and then – whoosh, he would be gone. One of the quickest off the mark was 'Morty'.

I had the greatest admiration for Brian Walsh. Not only was he a brilliant outside-right but all the time that he was with us Brian was studying for his accountancy exams. On away trips he would be deep into his books and his dedication paid off for he qualified as a chartered accountant. Not many professionals I know ever did that sort of thing. When I was with Ton Pentre I almost took a job as a rep., but chose to take a coaching course at Lilleshall instead. I've never regretted it, as it changed my life and kept me in the game – I only wish more players from my era had done the same, but very few did. For example, we had about 45 professionals at Cardiff City and I was the only one to take up full time coaching.

As I say they were great times but we did have a few black days. In our promotion year, in 1952, we were 2-0 up at half-time at Sheffield Wednesday, and Jackie Sewell scored four in the second-half. I'll never forget the look on poor Billy McLaughlin's face, he was supposed to be marking Jackie. And that F.A. Cup defeat at Halifax the following year! We had a disjointed team out, with Jack Marshall – a full-back – at inside-left. They poured all over us and we were never in it.

Games up North were hard, you never got much from the likes of Grimsby and Rotherham for example, where it always seemed to be raining and very cold. Barnsley had this left-winger, Johnny Kelly; he was a fabulous dribbler, and a great left foot. Poor 'Buller' Lever used to have nightmares about him. Most teams had ball artists though, and there were not many easy matches.

I came back to Ninian Park in 1962, as a trainer under George Swindin, who I thought was a good manager. These weren't easy days at Cardiff City, they had just been relegated from the First Division, and the previous manager and coach – Bill Jones and Willy Grant – had been popular with the players. There was not a lot of money available, but George was astute in the transfer market, and carried on giving young players such as Don Murray, Peter Rodrigues and George Johnston their chance. We weren't helped by injury either. We had six players in plaster at the start of the 1963-4 season, and at one time had only about 14 fit players to pick from; and we were trying to run three teams!

Alan Durban was manager on my return. He was concerned that young players were not coming through at that time. We managed to re-introduce a youth policy which has since borne fruit, but when Len Ashurst was appointed I was informed that the club could no longer afford me! It was a sad way for me to sever my connections with the club, but I'll remember always the great players and many friends that I made by being with Cardiff City.

ALAN HARRINGTON (Player: 1951-66)

I had two soccer-mad uncles who took me to Ninian Park just after the War, when Cardiff City won the Third Division championship. They were a great team and I knew Colin Gibson, who had played local football for Penarth Pontoons. After two years as captain of Cardiff schoolboys, I joined Cardiff Nomads - a nursery side for the City. The Nomads were run by two smashing blokes, Harry Goulding and Jack Nicholson, who worked hard with the youngsters. Eventually I joined Cardiff City and was part-time for a while, and I used to train with Dougie Blair on Tuesday and Thursday evenings. He was such a laid back character and if he had had to really play for a living - he was a part-timer - he would have played for England, I'm sure of that. I made my first appearance in the first team in a Welsh Cup tie at Merthyr, on a Thursday afternoon in January 1953. We won 5-2, big Ken Chisholm scored twice, and I must have done well as I was picked to play against Spurs at Ninian Park, in the First Division, two days later. I was given a specific job to follow Eddie Bailey, and the crowd gave me great encouragement. The game ended 0-0, and to his credit, Bailey complimented me as we shook hands. That was more than Joe Mercer, Alex Forbes and other Arsenal players did when we beat them 1-0 at Highbury! They were the League leaders and did not like us beating them. Doug Blair scored our goal and Tommy Northcott was outstanding that afternoon. He ran their defence ragged.

There were some great characters and players about then. I grew up quickly playing against the likes of Jimmy Hagan, Wilf Mannion and Raich Carter. I remember a match at Sunderland when Len Shackleton sat on the ball in the centre-circle to take the mickey out of us. Dougie Blair was our nearest player to 'Shack', and he went up behind him, and proceeded to practise imaginary golf swings. It was Doug's way of taking the mick out of 'Shack'. Alf Sherwood had been an early idol of mine, and as a youngster, I walked to Alf's house on a Sunday afternoon just to get his autograph. It was a great thrill to be in the same team as the great man, to whom I always showed the utmost respect, and I became great friends with Alf and his wife Joan later on. Ron Stitfall was a marvellous full-back to have behind you, a vastly underrated player who should have played for Wales many times, but just couldn't break through. I became friendly with goalkeeper Ronnie Howells, we were both single, and when Colin Baker arrived in the first team we began a friendship that has lasted to this day. A smashing bloke and a good player.

I was very fortunate during my National Service in the R.A.F., for I was originally posted to the Isle of Man, but a phone call to Trevor Morris worked wonders, and I was at St.Athan forty eight hours later. Time off was no problem and I could train regularly. I was refused leave only once, and that was to play in an Inter Service semi-final at Gloucester. Unfortunately we lost 2-1.

Wolves were the outstanding team of the mid-50's and I remember Gerry Hitchens making his debut against them in the final home game of the 1954-5 season, when we had to win to stay up. Gerry was really fired up and raced around like a stag. He scored, and Trevor Ford got two, as we won 3-2, and Wolves missed the Championship, which I think went to Chelsea. The next time we played Wolves was the record 9-1 defeat just a few months later. They steam-rollered us and I remember when they were 8-0 up, Billy Wright urging them on for more. I've always maintained that Wolves scored all the goals that day because our scorer - Ron Stockin - had just been signed from them.

I went to the New Theatre that evening, and Stan Stennett appeared in a hat with an arrow through it, and told the audience that he had just come back from Ninian Park! When we played the return at Molineux, the media turned out in force; T.V. Cameras everything, anticipating another 9-1, but by then Danny Malloy had joined us and we were playing quite well. Trevor Morris was ill so Albert Lindon and Walter Robbins were in charge. That afternoon Fordie and Gerry Hitchens really rattled them, and we pulled off a 2-0 win. Stan Montgomery had been a good centre-half, and following his retirement City needed someone, and in Danny Malloy they had a marvellous buy. He was powerful, took no prisoners, and slotted in straight away. Danny made his debut against Charlton when Neil O'Halloran had three touches - three goals - on his first appearance, quite remarkable. I don't think the loss of Trevor Ford cost us relegation in the 1956-7 season. We had too much inexperience, and down we went.

The Club brought in Ronnie Hewitt, Colin Hudson, and later, Joe Bonson. I was best man at 'Rocky's' wedding on the day that we beat Liverpool 6-1. 'Rocky' scored the first goal with a hell of a shot, and everything went for us that day. Derrick Sullivan was a great reader and anticipator of the game, but never got fit until October, and for a while, he and Joe Bonson lived together, quite a mix that was.

I received a dislocated shoulder in 1958, and instead of having it pinned as was normal, I had an operation which shortened a muscle but restricted my arm movement. When I came back there was an injury to someone and I slotted in at right-back, where I stayed - more or less - for the remainder of my career, and I was capped for Wales in that position. An injury before the game at Aston Villa - Gerald King caught my ankle in a practice match - caused me to miss half of the 1959-60 promotion season. That was a good team, full of experience and power. Graham Moore played a deep-lying role, much like Don Revie at Man. City. He could pass and come off his man well, and could be found easily. Brian Walsh and Johnny Watkins were a good pair of wingers. John, in particular, was a nice lad and he gave us width, could cross a great ball with that marvellous left foot, and of course, just about everything he hit that season went in.

When I was out of the first team I played in that Welsh Cup tie at Swansea, where City decided that it was worth the fine to play the reserves rather than risk some of the senior players. Trevor Morris had joined Swansea by then and, for some reason or another, relationships between the Clubs were strained. It was a dreadful afternoon, we were ankle deep in mud, and I suppose the conditions gave us a 50-50 chance, as Swansea were a bit lightweight. On a dry day they would have beaten us. All the trouble started after an injury to Trevor Peck. We were hanging on to our lead, they were getting ratty, and the atmosphere was not good.

We all remember our win over 'Spurs' in 1961, a great night. I always enjoyed playing them as they would allow you to play. When we beat Knighton 16-0, I ended up with two cracked ribs, this young lad had caught me near the end - can you imagine getting injured in a match like that?

We were relegated in 1962, and we had a vital match against Fulham on a Friday night. Bill (Jones) and Wilf (Grant) took us to the Water's Edge, Barry, for the afternoon to 'psych' us up. We had nothing to do except get tense and nervous.

Fulham arrived in Cardiff after tea-time, laughing and joking, and they ended up beating us 3-0. If we had won, I'm sure that we would have stayed up.

Bill and Wilf were a decent management team with Wilf the driving force. Bill's sacking came after Ron Beecher and Fred Dewey had come into the dressing room, at Swansea, during half-time. Wilf was giving us a rollicking, they felt that was Bill's job, and words were said. The following Monday, I heard of Bill's dismissal, and secretary Graham Keenor rang me to ask if Wilf could contact the club. Wilf had just moved in near me and was not on the telephone. He thought the Club were going to make him manager, but when he came back he told me that he was also sacked! We had a great run then, Ronnie Stitfall and Ernie Curtis were picking the team, but the club appointed George Swindin. I didn't think he did much for Cardiff, he couldn't forget the Arsenal, and it showed. He did bring Donald Murray to the Club, as a 15 year old full-back, and Don's conversion to centre-half was a shrewd move for he did not have the pace for a full-back.

The 1963-4 season was a non-event for me as I received a broken leg in the public trial, and as I lay in the hospital bed, they brought in Trevor Peck, and then Alec Milne, all of us having been put there by Jim Upton, a triallist full-back! Jimmy Scoular had become manager by the time I had recovered, and although I was picked for the first team – and played in Europe against Sporting Lisbon, Real Zarragossa and Standard Liege – the following year I knew my life at the Club as running out. For some reason or other Jimmy Scoular and I did not get on that well, in fact all the senior pro's had difficulties with him, and Ivor Allchurch probably suffered the most. They had been at Newcastle together and just did not get on. Ivor was a marvellous chap and became a great friend. All that year I was out he would pop around in the afternoons for a chat, and when he played a charity match at Aston Villa one evening he packed me, plaster cast and all, into his car and took me along. As a player he was a one-off, brilliant to play with and great to play against. I remember our duels when he was at Swansea, you just had to be on top form, otherwise he would murder you.

I will always be sorry that Cardiff City have never bothered with me since my playing days. I am sure that any number of former players still living in the area would have helped out scouting, or coaching schoolboys, but we have never been asked. I spent sixteen years with Cardiff City, and am proud to have been part of some of the greatest times in the club's history.

COLIN BAKER (Player: 1953-65)

Like many other young players of the late 1940's and early 1950's I graduated through Cardiff Nomads, a nursery team set up by secretary-manager Cyril Spiers, before arriving at Ninian Park.

Everywhere I looked there were fine players and the drop-out rate was very high as hundreds of young players filtered through the junior sides. In those days you began in the 'A' team, then the Welsh League, Football Combination and, if you were lucky enough, the League side. Each team was a separate entity, reports would be forwarded on your form and gradually you would move upwards. I was in the Welsh League side before I was 16, and what a League that was. Every team wanted to beat Cardiff City and most clubs had ex-pro's, seasoned veterans and lads who might not have made it with City, Swansea or Newport County, and had a point to prove. It was hard but you quickly learned it was a man's game, and of course we had the honour of Cardiff City to uphold.

Mr. Spiers had a reputation of giving young players their opportunity, and I made my League debut against Sheffield Wednesday at Ninian Park, in the last game of the 1953-4 season. The half-back line consisted of Alan Harrington, Colin Gale and myself; Alan was 20, Colin 21 and I was 19. We had Ron Stitfall and Alf Sherwood behind us, two of the best full-backs in the game and I remember it being a 2-2 draw. A number of us were doing National Service, we did not have problems having time off to play for our clubs, but you did miss the training, practice matches and day-to-day involvement.

In my time at Cardiff City there was a wealth of half-back talent. Alan Harrington, Billy Baker, Ken Hollyman, Islwyn Jones, John Frowen, Stan Montgomery, Colin Gale - and Dougie Blair could play left-half as well. I worked with Doug when I was a 16 year old at John Morgan (Builders), he was in the surveying department. But the best of all was probably Derek Sullivan, who could play anywhere. We all knew Duncan Edwards of Manchester United was a 'great' in the making, but 'Sully' – in many ways - was the equal of Duncan.

After Stan Montgomery had left the club, Trevor Morris bought Danny Malloy from Dundee and what a player he was. The wing-halves may have switched around but Danny seemed to be always there at centre-half, hard as nails but he could also play. Although we were relegated in 1957, Danny played in every game, I think, and Gerry Hitchens had come through and scored over 20 goals. Some people say Gerry was a bit raw, but he was a good bustling centre-forward who got goals. He didn't become an England international and have a career in Italy without being something special. Ronnie Hewitt was a good goalscorer as well. He was also a fitness fanatic and always doing extra training. I remember a game against Notts County at Ninian Park, when one of their guys threw a lump of mud at the ball just as Ronnie was taking a penalty, from which he scored. The referee saw what happened and ordered the kick to be retaken, and this time the shot was saved - Ronnie was livid. It didn't matter though, we still won 2-0.

Our promotion side of 1960 was a good team to play in, very strong and a nice blend. Graham Moore and outside-left Johnny Watkins had a great season. Watkins and Brian Walsh developed this wing to wing passing which no other team were doing. That 4-0 win at Liverpool was an outstanding performance. I think that was Bill Shankly's first game as Liverpool manager and he wasn't too happy as I recall. The 1-0 home win over Aston Villa before 54,000 was a great occasion, how can you forget moments like that? And the 3-2 win over 'Spurs in the First Division was another lasting memory. It was played under lights on a Saturday night following a Rugby International. Derek Hogg scored a marvellous goal and then Brian Walsh and 'Tappy' won it for us in the second-half. I was ever-present when we were relegated in 1962, and our world just caved in. Once the rot set in there seemed nothing would go right. I do remember us being beaten 8-3 at Everton at the end of the season but I think we had gone by then.

That story about our trip to Manchester on Christmas Day 1956 is completely true. The bus got stuck in deep snow near Hereford and we walked to the station singing carols. We ended up staying the night at Hereford, and caught an early train on Boxing Day for Manchester. United were League champions and beat us 3-1, although Danny (Malloy) gave us the lead with an early penalty. We had a lot of travelling in those days. We would go overnight to most games, even London. If it was Newcastle or Sunderland, we wouldn't get back until Sunday lunchtime, otherwise it would be midnight or the early hours of Sunday morning. Almost everywhere we played there seemed to be a train leaving half an hour after the final whistle, and with big crowds, you can imagine the rush to get to the station. Quite often they would hold the train for us.

We used to stay at the Queen's Hotel in Manchester for most of our Northern games and I've known six or seven teams to be staying there.

You got to know one another, not closely but well enough to have a brief chat. No telly in those days, or at least not much, and Friday night would be a night at the pictures. We would ring up to find what was showing and order our tickets – not a really glamorous life. We all became film buffs though! Just before my career finished I was involved in one little bit of Cardiff City history. I was the injured player to come off for David Summerhayes to become the first ever substitute. Of course in those days you **had** to be injured.

In one of my last appearances John Toshack made his full League debut at Middlesbrough, where we won 4-3, with 'Tosh' and Georgie Johnston scoring two goals each. By then Jimmy Scoular was manager and was getting his team together, but I had a good run and loved every minute of my time with Cardiff City – even the travelling.

ALEC MILNE (Player: 1957-65)

I came to Ninian Park, together with another full-back – Alex Gray – in March 1957. City's Scottish scouts had watched us play for Arbroath and I believe our joint fee was about £3,000. The City were in the First Division at the time and I remember Portsmouth beating us twice over Easter to push us into the Second Division. I made my first-team debut against Middlesbrough at Ninian Park the following September, not a happy day as we lost 2-0 with Brian Clough scoring both goals. I was lucky enough to have several good runs in the first-team, and that season we reached the fifth round of the F.A.Cup, only to go out at Blackburn in a replay. Over 50,000 had been at Ninian Park for the first game – but I was not too bothered about playing in front of so many – once you are out there you have got to get on with it. We beat Liverpool 6-1 that season, in fact they were not a particularly good team at the time, and we always seemed to have their measure. Alan Harrington was not too happy against Alan A'Court and I would be switched to right back to mark him. I'm pleased to say A'Court never caused me too many problems.

I always seemed to play well against the likes of Cliff Jones and Bryan Douglas, but even now I shudder at the thought of the roasting that a lesser known player, such as Grimsby's Jimmy Fell, who also played for Newcastle, gave me. He was a natural left footer, who wanted to take you on, and was very difficult to mark. I was ever-present in the 1958-9 season, and remember our F.A. Cup tie at Norwich when they knocked us out with a late goal from Terry Bly. Their winger Bobby Brennon was a real handful and I should have heeded some advice to knock him into the crowd, for he laid on one of the Norwich goals. If we could have brought them back to Ninian Park I am sure that we would have won.

Managers such as Trevor Morris and Bill Jones left the training to blokes like Wilf Grant, Bob John, Ernie Curtis and Jim Merrett, and Wilf was really the brains behind our promotion winning side of 1959-60. He encouraged us to play 4-2-4, although we had some stick in the local press at the time. I don't think they understood what was going on! That promotion team were a really good bunch of lads, we got on really well and set out to win every match. When we lost successive games, 1-4 at home against Brighton and Portsmouth, people said we did not want promotion. That was utter rubbish and we answered them with that 1-0 win over Aston Villa. It was not a classic match, more like a Cup-tie really, but what an occasion and what a crowd. They could not have got any more into Ninian Park if they had tried.

I don't think I have ever seen a goal as brilliant as the diving header Joe Bonson scored at Leyton Orient. He was feet off the ground when he met John Watkin's cross and the ball simply flew in. Joe was a good centre-forward, and Derek Sullivan the best all-round player at the Club. He should have been a true 'great' but he enjoyed a drink or two which led to weight problems and eventually caught up with him. They had a special rubber suit at the club for Derek, and it was incredible the amount that he sweated off in training.

It certainly was a different game then. As a full-back I always had a winger to mark, and when the ball was on the opposite flank I would act as cover for the centre-half. It was as physical, if not more so, as today's game but with far less bookings for fouls, because players just did not roll over faking injuries when tackled. It was a man's game with few cheats and sendings off were extremely rare.

There were characters in the game, Colin 'Rocky' Hudson and Harry Knowles were two who were lively chaps, even if they weren't exactly brilliant players. In fact Bill Jones had a great deal when he exchanged Harry for Peter King of Worcester, as Peter could play in a variety of positions, and went on to do really well for Cardiff City. He was a quiet type and kept to himself but became a good team player.

Even after the lifting of the maximum wage Cardiff City were not amongst the highest payers in the First Division. We were on £30 a week, and the Club did not pay us a bonus for promotion in 1960 – that wouldn't happen today. I remember receiving one rise, and that was when Mel Charles came from Arsenal. He obviously wanted more than we were being paid so the club gave us all a rise.

That was the season, 1961-2, when we were relegated. I was ever-present and even today cannot understand how we fell so dramatically after being seventh in the First Division. We should never have gone down for we were playing well, but a lot of youngsters had come in and as we kept losing, so a certain amount of panic crept in. Then Bill Jones and Wilf Grant brought back the veteran players, but it was too late. I still cannot believe it all.

The club cut our money following relegation and in some cases it was by quite a bit. I remember strike action being called for. Most of the first-team did not sign contracts until the start of the season.

My career at Cardiff City began to wane when I had cartilage trouble which kept me out for some time, and then two broken legs, and an ankle injury, knocked my confidence. In 1963 I can remember five of us in plaster and we had a terrible run of injuries. George Swindin was manager then but he had little rapport with most of the players.

He was a bit aloof, and probably after being with a club like Arsenal, must have felt that Cardiff City was a little beneath him. I may be wrong but that was the way that he came across to us. Injuries finally finished me a Cardiff, but I enjoyed my time there, particularly winning promotion and playing in the First Division before large crowds.

I remember playing at Rotherham in 1958, when a blizzard forced the game to be abandoned at half-time. It was so cold I can remember the snow actually freezing on my arms, and when we came off the hot showers were not working and we had to wash in cold water. Oh, they were happy days!

DON MURRAY (Player: 1962–74)

It was Cardiff City's Scottish scout Jimmy Shanks who spotted me and sent me to Ninian Park for a trial. Before then I knew very little about Cardiff City, or South Wales in fact, as I had grown up near Elgin and supported Aberdeen as a boy. I was signed by Bill Jones, but it was George Swindin who gave me my first-team debut at Middlesbrough, in April 1963. I marked Alan Peacock, an England centre-forward, and he scored twice before I knew what was going on, and we lost 3–2.

The arrival of big John Charles had a big influence on me, for the 'Gentle Giant' took me under his wing and helped me greatly. He also gave me an introduction to hard liquor on an end of season trip to Italy where, at his villa, I was ill on Benedictine! Besides 'Charlo' there were a number of household names at Cardiff City in those days, John's brother Mel, Ron Stitfall, Derek Tapscott, Alan Harrington, Colin Baker, Graham Vearncombe – all Welsh internationals – and of course, the great Ivor Allchurch.

I got on well with George Swindin and coach Stan Montgomery – who was one of the most comical characters I've ever met. George rarely swore, and instead of giving someone a real effing and blinding his stock phrase was – 'Christopher Columbus, what are you playing at?' There couldn't have been a more different character than Jimmy Scoular who I maintain was a man's man and ruled with a rod of iron. Although our basic wage was average, Jimmy looked after his players by negotiating our bonus system, and very few were dissatisfied during my time at Cardiff City.

If John Charles was an early influence, then Jimmy Scoular and Brian Harris went a long way in helping me have such a long career at Ninian Park. John played sweeper in our first European run in 1964–5 and proved what a great player he was. For some reason known only to himself Jimmy left Ivor Allchurch out, preferring Peter King, who was a non-stop runner. We had great respect for Ivor and there was a saying among the players – 'if you are in trouble, give it to Ivor'.

I had some of my worst moments as a Cardiff City player in the 1965–66 season. I was sent off in a Welsh Cup match against Swansea at Ninian Park. Jimmy McLaughlin and myself had been at it during the game, and when he finally invited me to hit him I went up close and made as if to butt him. Unfortunately for me Jimmy cheated and went down pole-axed, although I swear to this day that no contact was made. I was sent off by Leo Callaghan, and as if that wasn't bad enough, we lost 5–3 in extra-time after leading 3–0 at the time of my dismissal. Club chairman Fred Dewey told Jimmy Scoular and myself afterwards that any recurrence of that type of incident, then I would never play for Cardiff City again! It was a hard lesson but one which I learned from.

Later that season we were hammered 9–0 at Preston, a match which I think was my first as captain. It was a day when some of our lads did not give of their best and Preston seemed to score almost at will. It would be easy to say that our 5–3 win over Middlesbrough three days earlier, which saved us from relegation, had caused complacency but I can make no excuses for that 9–0 defeat. In that victory over Middlesbrough, Greg Farrell gave the best display by any winger I've ever seen, he was brilliant. It was such a pity that Greg could never maintain a level of consistency just below that performance, which was a one-off, because then money could not have bought him.

Youngsters like John Toshack and George Johnston began to emerge. 'Tosh' was full of goalscoring potential and certainly made the most of his abilities, but George had the skill to have been a great player and wasted it after his transfer to Arsenal. Looking back, he should have stayed with us, for the bright lights dazzled him and his career suffered.

Although good players like Peter Rodrigues, Barrie Hole and Gareth Williams were sold, Jimmy Scoular began to build a solid team with players like Bobby Brown, Brian Harris, Barrie Jones, Norman Dean, Fred Davies, Brian Clark and others coming into the club. Brian Harris was by far the greatest playing influence on my career. We built up a good understanding, and he gave me such a lot of belief and confidence in my ability. Brian was one of the great characters at Ninian Park, there was seldom a dull moment with him about.

Down the years I've kept in touch with Bob Wilson, who was crucified for that fatal mistake in the European Cup Winners' Cup semi-final with Hamburg. If it hadn't been for Bob's brilliance against Moscow Torpedo, and in the first leg in Hamburg, we would never have gone so far, and I felt really sorry that Bob ended his City career so tragically. We got used to travelling around Europe. This was a great period for Cardiff City and Jimmy Scoular only wanted players who were proud to represent the club.

The loss of a quality player such as Barrie Jones was a huge blow, and it took the arrival of Ian Gibson to fill the enormous gap left by Barrie's tragic injury. 'Gibby' was an exceptional player and for a small player certainly knew how to handle himself. He liked his horses and a gamble, but he was a great team man and another lively character, like Brian Harris and Jim Eadie.

Big Jim (Eadie) got his chance following a series of errors by Frank Parsons, who, unknown to City supporters at the time, was experiencing problems within his marriage. Anyway Jim came in and one of Jimmy Scoular's biggest problems with Jim was to get him in goal during training, because Jim thought he was the best centre-forward in the club!

Our victory over Real Madrid remains a great memory, to beat a club with all those European Cup triumphs was marvellous for Cardiff City. On the other side of the coin was our 5-1 defeat at Sheffield United in the promotion run-in. We lost Brian Harris with injury, a big blow, and they ran all over us. No excuses, the best team won and possibly, in hindsight, we weren't quite good enough. I know people point to the transfer of John Toshack, but Alan Warboys was a good replacement. There had been speculation about 'Tosh' for some time which caused some unrest, and it wasn't a matter of if he would go, but when. Years later Jimmy Scoular told me that he wanted to bring in two or three players to guarantee promotion but the directors stood firm. If we had reached the First Division they would have had to buy new players — but that is all speculation now. There were offers for me, some big ones I understand, but Jimmy Scoular wanted me to form a cornerstone of his team in the First Division. Perhaps I should have insisted on going to another club, but we all thought that promotion would eventually come, but as everyone now knows City never came as close again.

The following year the Ninian Park pitch became a quagmire and it was heartbreaking to see little 'Gibby', Peter King and Mel Sutton trying to play on it. That season we lost to Dynamo Berlin on penalties and I've never forgotten my crucial miss in that game. Some of the other players 'bottled' out, and as captain, I felt the responsibility was mine. I had never taken a penalty in my life and look what happened. I was reconciled when I heard Alan Ball say: *'only great players miss penalties because only great players take them!'* Jimmy Scoular had to change personnel and although good players like Willie Anderson, Johnny Vincent, Andy McCulloch and George Smith arrived, things did not improve.

A major influence on the Club came when David Goldstone bought out the Deweys, for the Club had never had such caring people in the boardroom since then. David Goldstone certainly had no feeling for the City and it hurt terribly when he sacked Jimmy Scoular. Frank O'Farrell simply used the club as a resting place, and although Jimmy Andrews was a good coach, I sometimes doubted his appointment as manager, although he did bring the Club up from the Third Division after I had left.

I knew my days were numbered when Jimmy Andrews allowed me to join Swansea City on loan. I was stunned when the club refused me a free transfer, and Hearts had to pay a fee after all my years of loyalty, and around 500 appearances. I had two enjoyable years with Hearts, we had an unbeaten run of 22 games after I joined them, but I developed a calf injury in my second season and they did not stand in my way when Jimmy Scoular wanted me to join Newport County. Times were bad at Somerton Park, I once got paid in small change(!) When Colin Addison took over he used to continually remind us ex-Cardiff players of Sheffield United's win in 1971! After a spell with Barry Town, Richie Morgan asked me to help out City's youngsters in the Welsh League, something I found hard but very enjoyable. I couldn't believe it when I took my sons to a match at Ninian Park — and was refused a couple of complimentary tickets — I have never felt so humiliated. The Club resigned from the Welsh League and I then concentrated on a full-time job away from football.

Like a number of former players living in the area, I still retain an affection for Cardiff City which I doubt will ever die. I had some great times, travelled the world and met some great people. One of the funniest characters was Bill Donovan, who must have been one of our most devout supporters. He came with us to Moscow and some of us went to the State Circus, the rest to the Bolshoi Ballet. Bill went to the Ballet resplendent in blue and white bobble hat and scarf. When we met up back at the hotel I asked Bill what he thought of the ballet: *'Oh it was O.K. Don',* he said: *'But there was a bit too much dancing!'*

RICHIE MORGAN (Player: 1966-76. Manager: 1978-81)

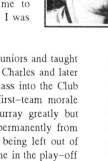

It must have been around the mid 1950's when I first went to Ninian Park, in the First Division days of 'Daisy' Walsh, Danny Malloy and all those other fine players of that time. I spent seven months at Leeds United in 1965, but like so many Welsh teenagers suffered homesickness and came back. That lovely man, the legendary Harry Parsons, who has been with Cardiff City longer than Methuselah, took me to Ninian Park and, after a series of trial games, I was signed by Jimmy Scoular.

Another unsung hero, Jim Merrett, trained the juniors and taught me a lot, and we looked up to the likes of John Charles and later on Brian Harris, who brought First Division class into the Club on his arrival from Everton, at a time when first-team morale was rock-bottom. I also admired Donald Murray greatly but knew deep down that I would never oust him permanently from the first-team. Despite my disappointment at being left out of the trip to Tashkent in 1968, my big chance came in the play-off match against Moscow Torpedo in Augsburg. Donald failed a late fitness test and I was in for my first appearance with the seniors in such a vital game. I did not have time to be nervous, anyway Jimmy Scoular's words to me were: *'Freeze on the night and we've lost!'* I'm pleased to say that I didn't — we won with a goal from Norman Dean — and I did well against their international centre-forward who had been in prison for rape, G.B.H., and much more. The only thing he didn't try on with me that night was .... rape!

Jimmy then picked the same team to play Blackpool at home three days later, which meant ineligible European players like Fred Davies and Brian Clark were not included, and my home League debut ended in a 3-1 defeat, although I had a good match against Tom White, Blackpool's centre-forward. I know that down the years criticism had been levelled against me concerning a lack of ambition, and to a certain degree it is true. But honestly, it was as much a club decision as mine. They were content, in my ability to step in for Donald and do a job, and by offering me a few quid more each season, I was more than happy to stay. After all we had developed into a useful Second Division side with European football virtually every year. How many other clubs could offer that? I appreciate and indeed sympathise with the supporters' claims concerning John Toshack's move to Liverpool. But from a playing point of view Alan Warboys could not have done more — he played like 'superman' for a spell.

The problems were at boardroom level where the Dewey family ran the club. Jimmy (Scoular) needed two players and it was apparent they would not go out on a limb for the club.

Fred Dewey, the chairman, was not well following a broken hip and his son Vivien wanted out. It was the way things were but supporters never really know the full story and some of us players are also in the dark.

Really since then the club has been in a downward spiral and the sacking of Jimmy Scoular was the end of an era. He wasn't everybody's favourite, some players couldn't stand him, but he looked after his men even if you had to suffer a real mouthful at times. I know that I was really sorry to see Jimmy go, and his replacement, Frank O'Farrell, simply used the club to get back into football. David Goldstone had bought out the Deweys, had no feeling for the club, and soon began to look for a buyer himself, while all the time we were struggling in the Second Division. Jimmy Andrews, a marvellous coach and a smashing bloke, was more or less pressed into the manager's chair, and although he did his best for the club, in some ways Jimmy was not a strong enough personality to stick in the job. I always remember him saying to me when we were in the West Country in pre-season: *'This is the time I love the most, being with all the players and not having to pick sides!'* I believe that statement described Jimmy fully.

We were relegated, and immediately bounced back, but the team that gained promotion in 1976 just weren't good enough for the Second Division. We were always a couple of players short and it was a great disappointment that someone like Adrian Alston could not play at that level, and Jimmy's signing of Robin Friday was a disaster. The Club knew his background and reputation in the game, and if a giant like Reading's manager Charlie Hurley couldn't handle him, then what chance Jimmy.

I appreciate that my appointment as manager came as a shock to the City Supporters, but rumours concerning Jimmy Andrew's future were circulating around the club when I was called to the boardroom and asked to take over in a caretaker capacity. When the board told me that Jimmy was leaving the club I accepted, but felt that I was keeping the chair warm for someone else. We were terrible and getting worse, and my appointment wasn't taken well by all the first team pool who saw me as just a reserve team player with little or no experience, which was basically true. I brought Brian Harris, Doug Livermore and Dave Elliot to the club, and Graham Reynolds did our scouting, and gradually we turned the thing around after signing Ronnie Moore and Colin Sullivan. The team finished in 9th position, and I was voted 'Manager of the Month' for April. I knew several players – may be three or four – would have to be replaced, but I let my heart rule my head because some of the lads had played out of their skins to get us out of trouble, and probably – on hindsight – I should have been more ruthless.

Although we had to sell Tony Evans, I was allowed to buy Billy Ronson who, unfortunately, did not do all I expected of him. Billy's wife just would not live in Cardiff, despite consistent overtures, and as a result his performances fell short of what we wanted. His mind was always on getting back to Blackpool, and although he hardly missed a game in two years, he did not develop into the great player I believed he would become. Another major disappointment was Wayne Hughes, a player who was full of potential in his early days with West Bromwich Albion. I went to Holland to watch him and he was the only one that night who was trying, and we gambled that he would give us some good seasons. We needed competition for places, and with a niggling injury list, required more depth in the squad, but Wayne's signing was unsuccessful and I received a lot of stick over it. But these things happen in football.

The team held its own despite a lack of goals, Ronnie Moore's contribution is well documented, and we finished 15th, which should have been about 12th really. I was told to sell in order to buy and we got a good deal for Ronnie Moore, which enabled us to buy Peter Kitchen who I had wanted two years earlier when he scored four goals against us in a reserve match. This was a season of change behind the scenes as both Doug Livermore and Brian Harris left the club. I brought in Tony Book, who had just been dismissed by Manchester City, and Ron Jones had been appointed to oversee the commercial activities under the title of general manager. Injuries and a team that quite frankly were not too good saw us end in 19th position. Then the Club decided to bring Rugby League to Ninian Park, which alienated a lot of our supporters. Not only that but we lost our long established place in the Football Combination and withdrew from the Welsh League, decisions which had a detrimental overall effect on the standard of play within the club.

Despite all that we found ourselves in 9th position after thirteen games, and it was then that the chairman Bob Grogan suggested that I became football administrator, and that someone else would run the team as coach. I was not too happy – but Mr. Grogan implied that my position was secure – and after talking to Frank Burrows, Len Ashurst and Barry Lloyd, Graham Williams was appointed. I was dubious because Graham had been out of British football for some time and it wasn't long before I realised what a mistake had been made. Our results went from bad to worse, confidence was drained, the supporters were disenchanted and I pleaded with Mr. Grogan to have the team back – all to no avail.

When Graham and I were sacked I admit that I did not handle it too well. A one-club man, Cardiff born and bred, I was being dismissed for something I had no control over. The City had been 9th in the Second Division when I handed the team over, and the Club has not been as high since then. I look back and wonder if I could have done things differently, but deep down there were certain factors conspiring against me. Some people believed that I was still naive – but I **had** been manager for three years. I remember Tony Book recommending Gary Bennett to me, which I admit I disregarded since with so many clubs around Manchester, I thought that if he was any good one of them would snap him up. Tony persisted and eventually he sent Gary down on the train, and as we were on a pre-season tour, Colin Prophett met him, and he went on to become a great capture. Just to emphasise the fine line that exists in footballing fortunes, I remember a pre- Christmas game at Leicester in 1979, and Ian MacFarlane telling Brian Harris that Leicester manager Jock Wallace had two reserve players he was not keen on, and they could be obtained cheaply. One was Steve Lynex and the other, yes you've guessed, was Gary Lineker, but Mr. Grogan would not allow me any money – I think it would have required about £20,000. That was the same price I could have paid for Alan Smith, then in non-League, but once again I could not buy him – although I wanted him badly. Our former full-back Bobby Ferguson, then at Ipswich, rang me to say that they had a forward who Bobby Robson did not know what to do with, and for £60,000, he would be a steal. Mr. Grogan told me to offer £15,000 and more after a certain number of games. I did not even make the offer. The player? oh yes, it was Alan Brazil!

These are just a few of the examples of missing out, but as I say every manager can quote similar stories. Time goes on and wounds heal, and I had five successful years with Barry Town before leaving football for a stress-free lifestyle. But I have some great memories of Cardiff City and the marvellous players who were there in my time.

GIL REECE (Player: 1972–76)

I was a schoolboy with Cardiff City, and in a three year spell – from 1958 – I graduated through the ranks to play in the Football Combination. I was part-time while I did an apprenticeship in plumbing and went on loan to Ton Pentre. Ken Hollyman was there then, and we had a good season. There was a change of manager at the City, George Swindin came in, and before he had a good look at me, I was released on the recommendation of Ernie Curtis, who was on the coaching staff. I don't suppose I've ever really forgiven Ernie for that!

Newport County picked me up from Pembroke Borough – and in no time at all, that wily old fox Billy Lucas accepted an offer from Sheffield United after I had been spotted in the County team. It was incredible really, on the scrapheap, and then into the First Division in such a short time, and a year later, I won my first Welsh Cap. They were great days at Sheffield United. It is a real football city, especially with the rivalry with the Wednesday, and even shopping trips were difficult. I enjoyed my games against Cardiff, and in 1968 scored the only goal against them at the Lane which many claimed was yards offside, but I still say I was onside when the ball was played. Matches at Ninian Park were wet affairs as I recall, and we had a couple of hidings. But of course, the one that mattered was at the Lane in 1971, when we won 5-1 and went up to the First Division. That was a great night for me as I scored our fourth goal. The City lads did not know what has hit them after Billy Dearden had scored twice in the opening ten minutes, but we always started our home matches like that. We were notorious for going at our visitors like a red and white tide, it was great to play like that, for most managers were developing defensive tactics at that time. Alan Woodward, Geoff Salmons, Tony Currie and Billy Dearden were such positive players. We were backed up by Len Badger and Trevor Hockey – the latter player was a character, long hair, beard and headband, he was like a pirate to look at. But do you know, that for all his aggression he couldn't tackle!

Quite recently I was shown the 'Echo' newspaper after that 5-1 game, and typically, there was Scoular raving and ranting about offside goals and fouls on his goalkeeper, and so on. It was the usual nonsense, most managers do it. I mean, would anybody run into a big guy like Jim Eadie on purpose? That defeat was probably a blessing in disguise for that City team, as it was not quite good enough for the First Division, whereas we went straight to the top of the League the following season.

My move to Cardiff came at just the right time for I had been at Sheffield for eight years, and had begun to consider some business propositions in Yorkshire. Dave Powell and myself came in an exchange deal for Alan Warboys – which in itself was unusual for 'Warby' was an ex-Wednesdayite – and I wasn't surprised that he didn't last long at Bramall Lane, such is the rivalry between the Sheffield clubs. He lives near Doncaster now, and the last I saw him, he was looking in great shape.

It was quite a difference at Cardiff compared to Sheffield. The players did not socialise much, there were hardly any supporters' functions, and the whole atmosphere around the city was low key. In Sheffield we would always be out on Monday nights for darts, dominoes etc., at a supporters' branch, and the Wednesday lads did the same. Quite often we would have functions together. Sadly, there was nothing like that in Cardiff.

The City team were undergoing a lot of changes as Jimmy Scoular tried to rebuild, but all the chopping and changing was unsettling, and it was a struggle. Some nice lads came into the Club – Andy McCulloch, Johnny Vincent, Willie Anderson besides youngsters like Phil Dwyer. I enjoyed playing up front with Andy. I don't think I've ever seen anyone quite like him. There were times when you would be thinking, 'what's he doing in the first team', and he'd turn round and score the most unorthodox goal. He was incredible, but a great fellow and you just could not dislike him. Johnny Vincent could play. His trouble was that he had been around a bit and become known as a good time Charlie. On his day though he was terrific.

The club seemed to have a number of ball-players whose level of consistency let them down. Look at Tony Villers. What a player he could have been, if only his attitude had been right. I remember that night when we drew with Crystal Palace in a relegation match and Tony's goal kept us up. I can see it now, for he played it into me, and I gave him the return and he hit a beauty on the run into the bottom corner.

Ron Heeley and Clive Charles came in and they were good mates, and good company too. Frank O'Farrell had replaced Jimmy Scoular as manager and I think I saw him once. Jimmy Andrews did all the coaching and I got on well with him. I'm sure that if I had met Jimmy earlier in my career he would have made me a better player. He respected me as a senior player and knew that even if I had been injured, my level of fitness would be maintained without bullying me. He trusted me and I respected him for that. Unfortunately for Jimmy, David Goldstone – who was chairman – didn't allow him to strengthen the side, and it was obvious that without new players we would be relegated in 1975. It was a dire season all round and the highlight for me was scoring two goals when we beat Norwich, who were promoted.

Down in the Third Division, Jimmy had more leeway after the 'Mafia' had taken control of the club from Goldstone. That bunch of directors were a mixed lot and some of the players did not know what to make of them. Players of stature like Mike England, Doug Livermore, Brian Clark, Alan Campbell, and later on, Adrian Alston, came into the club. Jimmy got us playing, and although I wasn't a regular, I did enjoy some of the games that season. I was sub. for the great game with Hereford, and it made us realise what great support there could be for Cardiff City.

This was the time when I began having trouble with my breathing. I thought it was asthma related, and after a lot of tests, I was diagnosed as having an over-active thyroid. I went part-time with Swansea for a while, as I concentrated on my business. Had I known about the thyroid sooner, I would most probably have played on for another three or four years at some level. As it is, I am still fit enough to play charity matches in Sheffield with the old United and Wednesday boys and it is quite hard to get selected!

I have often said to people like Harry Parsons, that it seems a shame that no-one in this area has organised teams of former Cardiff, Swansea and Newport players to play Sunday matches. There are more than enough of us around and I'm sure we would be well supported.

Unfortunately I don't have much time to visit Ninian Park these days, but I do follow what is going on. I'm sure that I speak for all the ex-players when I say that we all want to see the City back in the higher divisions, where they belong.

PHIL DWYER (Player 1971-85)

I joined Cardiff City on schoolboy forms in 1968, and never thought that I would one day go on to become the club's record appearance holder. Harry Parsons was there then and did a lot with the youngsters. He's still there, of course, and tells me that he is indispensable!

The professionals were great, there was no 'them and us' and we all took part in the five aside matches. Jimmy Scoular was the boss and he knew everybody, and kept his eye on everything. He was hard, but fair, and I will always be grateful to him for giving me my chance. He still lives just down the road from me, and obviously we keep in touch.

Our youth team of 1971, which lost to Arsenal in the F.A. Youth Cup Final, was a good side and it was a surprise that very few of them really made it. Nigel Rees, Alan Couch, Jimmy McInch didn't quite make it, while John Impey and 'Danny' Showers did reasonably well.

The first team were having a bad run when I made my League debut. In fact, I had been the junior player in the squad a week earlier, when we lost 3-0 at Q.P.R., and the following Friday Jimmy told me that I would play at Orient. The game ended 0-0, and we had Alan Foggon sent off. That was the start of my League career, but in all my years the Club never had too much League success. The atmosphere in the Club was generally good, although it suffered when we were relegated a few times.

In my early days the signings of Andy McCulloch, Johnny Vincent and Willie Anderson gave the place a lift, they were good players and fun to be with.

Jimmy Scoular's sacking was not a real surprise to most of us. David Goldstone wanted a new big name manager, and we hadn't been playing well. It's usually the players who get managers the sack, and we had let Jimmy down. I admit that I had a tear in my eye when I went in to thank him for all he had done for me.

Frank O'Farrell was the complete opposite to Jimmy. We hardly saw him, in fact we reckoned he wore his tracksuit over his suit. He wasn't there long, but had brought in John Farringdon and Willie Carlin. 'Farro' was a pigeon-fancier and a quiet chap. Willie was a tremendous influence and not afraid of anyone. He upset a few people at the Club, for he had been used to winning things at places like Derby. In my time I played with a lot of goalkeepers, and oddly enough, two of the best were at the club at the same time. Ron Healey was a good talker and we used to call Bill Irwin, a 'big dopey Irishman', which he was not I can tell you. It's amazing the number of people that I saw come and go, and that includes managers, but there were some great characters.

I can remember John McClelland at the Club. What was he, 6'2" or 6'3", yet he couldn't head a ball. He went on to become a centre-half for Rangers and Ireland, and now he's at Leeds United. Ian Baird came on loan and later had several half million pound transfers. And Paul Bodin, what a rags to riches story. Mind, what happened to him at Crystal Palace after they had paid all that money for him, was disgraceful. Dean Saunders came to City just as I was leaving, but we trained together a few times. He told me that the City wanted to offer him a years' contract at £90 a week! Deano went to Brighton, and the rest is history, as they say. The two promotion years from the Third Division were my main highlights I suppose. In 1975-76, Mike England was a great influence.

We all looked up to him, for he had achieved everything at Tottenham. That was a good team, we played football and in Willie Anderson, big Adrian Alston, Tony Evans and John Buchanan we could attack. I remember scoring twice against Wrexham, and taking a last minute penalty for my hat-trick. Big Lloydy saved it and I had a right rollicking from Jimmy Andrews. He said that if we missed promotion by a goal he'd hang, draw and quarter me. I didn't play in the 4-1 defeat at Hereford, as I was with the Wales' under 23 team at Wrexham, and I thought it was a wind-up when they told me the score! I think the Walsall match was the turning point of the season. We ran all over them, big Ade scored two, and I headed the winner from a corner - and all this after being 2-0 down at half-time! One of my best moments.

By a strange coincidence I also scored the winner at Walsall in the 1982-83 season. That was my first game back after nearly being off-loaded to Plymouth, where I had played some trial matches. Len Ashurst was the City manager then, and he sent someone to watch me, to see if I had recovered from my knee injury. I came back and stayed a regular in the side until I finished at the Club. The turning point in that promotion season had to be the Weymouth defeat at home in the F.A. Cup. Nowadays no end of League clubs lose to part-timer,s but that defeat made the national headlines on T.V. We had no excuses, 2-0 up at half-time, they came right back and steamrollered us. I gave them one of the goals. We watched the video over and over, and on the following Thursday, Len had us all in his little office and told us we could either fight back or go down. The next night we won 2-1 at Southend and I don't think any one of us even considered being beaten there. That was another good team with Jeff Hemmerman, Roger Gibbins, David Tong, the Bennett brothers - Dave so flash, Gary so quiet - and later on, Bob Hatton.

Things had been going wrong at the club for a long time. The appointment of Ron Jones was not popular, nor was the decision of having Rugby League at Ninian Park. Looking back, the moving of Richie (Morgan) and the inclusion of Graham Williams only helped to lower morale.

Len (Ashurst) did the best that he could but we were going nowhere, and he got out when Sunderland came for him. I had always got on well with Alan Durban, who took over from Len, and I was ever-present until we lost 4-1 at home to Notts County. I wasn't prepared to sit there and mope about it. I knew that I had a bad game but Alan decided to release David Grant, Colin Smith, myself and one or two others. I felt rotten but immediately took up an offer to help Vic Halom at Rochdale, who were fighting re-election. David Grant and I went to Spotland and signed within hours. It was only going to be a temporary thing so far as I was concerned, although by then a number of clubs, including Swansea and Newport expressed an interest. At one time at the City, I had been asked about helping out with the youngsters, which would have been great, but Alan Durban changed all that.

My record appearance game came at Blackburn, and although the Club didn't officially recognise it, I did receive a presentation from the supporters' clubs for which I'll always be grateful. Although I left City on a sour note I'll always remember our Welsh Cup victories in the 1970's which gave us European football. I played in front of 100,000 at Tbilisi.

What a journey that was, particularly the plane ride from Moscow on a real boneshaker, where they gave you boiled sweets for the air sickness. Georgian people were some of the nicest I ever met. Playing at Old Trafford and Elland Road (the Leeds United team were my boyhood idols) were great thrills, but my favourite ground was Sunderland. When I played at right-back, Luton's John Aston gave me the most trouble. Later on, at centre-half, Peter Withe and Malcolm MacDonald were difficult opponents but I wouldn't say there were too many easy games.

City were reasonable payers during my time, people like Jimmy Scoular and Richie Morgan did their best for you and when Billy Ronson came to us, he was the first player at Cardiff to have an agent. There was a time when I would have moved on but the club refused. I even had an enquiry from Panathinaikos, which came to nothing, but generally I was happy to stay. My main injury problem concerned my knee which had a piece of bone floating around in it. It nearly finished me, but once I had it removed, I went on for several more seasons. I suppose my career could have ended at Gillingham in 1975 when I swallowed my tongue, but prompt action from dear Ron Durham saved my life. I can only remember trying to head on Bill Irwin's kick and taking a knock in the back. The next thing I knew, I was waking up at the side of the pitch where, somehow, they had managed to bring an ambulance.

Back home, my wife was not too happy when the accident was reported on 'Grandstand', as she thought I could have died!

Ron Durham, who had heart trouble, was one of the nicest people in football, and I remember him getting into trouble at York, when he threw a bucket of water over some hecklers. It was so out of character and, for weeks afterwards, we kept winding him up about going to jail! Fortunately all charges were dropped.

A lot of City supporters have mentioned that final game of the season in 1977-78, when we lost 1-0 at home to Orient. Many have wondered if the game was bent. Well I was having a go, but we were so bad it was embarrassing, and if there were any brown envelopes or cheques going around, I didn't get one!

Due to my commitments with the South Wales Police I've seen only two matches at Ninian Park since I finished. But I still drop in for a cup of tea and a chat with Harry Parsons, Jimmy Goodfellow and Eddie May.

I am proud of the fact that I hold the appearance record, especially when one considers what great players have been with Cardiff City. I expect my record will be beaten one day, but at the moment, it does look a long way off.

JOHN LEWIS (Player: 1978-83)

It was Jimmy Andrews' assistant, Ken Whitfield, who spotted me in Welsh League football, and I initially joined Cardiff City on a part-time basis. I'll never forget my first experience of being with the first team, for although I would not be playing, I travelled to Luton with them to taste the atmosphere. We stayed overnight at Heathrow, and I roomed with Gary Stevens who was making his debut. I remember chairman Bob Grogan coming to wish us all the best and then telling us, just like a schoolteacher, to: 'Go on to bed like good boys!'

I sat with Ken (Whitfield) in the stand, and at half-time the lads were 0-3 down. The dressing-room atmosphere was awful, Jimmy Andrews was not there, he had gone to watch Derby's Colin Chesters, but Ken told me that it would be better in the second-half. We went 0-4 down, 0-5, 0-6 when we got one back and the final score was 7-1 to Luton. Now Ken was a great chap but when he was annoyed he could fly into a rage. Micky Burns, who was coach, asked him to cool down but Ken was too worked up, and everyone had a rollicking. He had told me during the second-half that I would be in the team the following week, and honestly, I didn't know whether to laugh or cry! Anyway, I made my debut at home against Blackburn, we won 2-0, I played the entire match and the rest of the lads were brilliant towards me. Blokes like Ron Healey, Rod Thomas, Phil Dwyer and John Buchanan could be so funny, and they made me feel right at home.

I signed a full-time contract about a month later. It wasn't an easy decision for I had a secure job, but the opportunity was there, and at 23 years of age I had to take it. Before I really got to know Jimmy Andrews he was gone, sacked, following a terrible 4-1 home defeat by Charlton. He was a quiet man and an excellent coach.

Just before Jimmy's dismissal, Richie Morgan, who was the senior professional and union rep. had walked me around Ninian Park saying that if I had any grievances to see him.

A few weeks later, he was manager! Richie's appointment wasn't taken too seriously at first for everyone, including Richie himself I think, believed it would be only a temporary one. He brought in Brian Harris, Doug Livermore and Dave Elliott, and I was one of the players to be dropped as they changed the team. Brian didn't fancy me at first and it was Doug Livermore who restored my confidence when I had a spell in the reserves. Things went better the following season, even though Richie signed Wayne Hughes to replace me. Wayne was a disappointment, and when Colin Sullivan was injured, Brian Harris persuaded me to give it a go at left-back where I enjoyed a good run. It was probably at this point that I became one of the Club's established players.

For me, Alan Campbell was the best player in my time at Cardiff City, you could almost see his brain ticking, he was so confident and a great professional. Amongst others who I was proud to be friendly with, were Keith Pontin and 'Joe' Dwyer, yet the club, to my way of thinking, let them down badly later on - but in football you live with other people's opinions and influences. 'Pont' had a heart like a lion, he was Cardiff City through and through, and what more can be said about 'Joe'? He was a battler and the one person you could depend upon in a scrap. I remember a game at Crystal Palace when 'Pont' was elbowed in the face after fouling Dave Swindlehurst. Suddenly 'Joe' burst on the scene, laid Swindlehurst out, and we had a situation where all three players were sent off.

John Buchanan, who had been watching from the stand, raced to the touchline, got involved with someone, and was arrested! Richie had to go to the police station on our way home to bail 'Buchie' out! 'Buchie' was a great lad and the best kicker of a ball I've ever seen. His goal against the Swans is legendary but I saw him hit an absolute beauty at Luton. And at Highbury in an F.A. Cup-tie he beat Pat Jennings all ends up with a terrific bending shot into the top corner. The trouble with 'Buchie' was that he couldn't pass to you, he would **shoot** the ball in your direction!

We came back from Newcastle via London one day and 'Buchie' organised a case of lager as we switched trains. He and Colin Sullivan were together and began to have a row when 'Sully' refused to have a drink. Just as it was getting heated, Richie walked in and 'Buchie' gave him a mouthful, and ended up being fined two weeks' wages. They were an expensive couple of lagers for 'Buchie'.

Tony Evans was a fine striker but after recovering from a serious injury, 'Evo' was a re-christened 'Zebedee', as he kept hopping out of tackles. Believe it or not, in training 'Joe' Dwyer was the best finisher in the club, and Ronnie Moore could also rattle them in. The only trouble with 'Mooro' was that he couldn't score in the League. He took some stick off the lads, if you couldn't take the banter you were dead, and he often gave as good as he got.

The atmosphere around the club changed dramatically when, in a short space of time, we lost the Football Combination and Welsh League sides, and gained a Rugby League team and a general manager in Ron Jones. We had no animosity towards the rugby boys, in fact a lot of our lads watched them for a while, but Ron Jones was not popular, and in fact I don't think he got on with anyone very well. He was on a large contract and could only justify his salary with a number of cost cutting exercises.

The appointment of Graham Williams was a disaster. His training methods tended to be bizarre, some of the lads called him 'Mr. Punch' as his stock phrase was: *'That's the way to do it'*. He did for me though, as I went over on my ankle carrying Gary Stevens up the Bob Bank! I was out for about eight months. In that time Richie and Graham were sacked, and Len Ashurst came in. I thought Len was a good manager, particularly during our promotion year in 1982-3, when he was either shrewd or extremely fortunate to bring in some experienced lads like David Tong, Roger Gibbins and Jeff Hemmerman. Due to us being relegated, players like Linden Jones and myself lost our appearance money, and we were on very low wages. Len did his best for us and finally got it back, but we knew then that the football club was in financial trouble.

That promotion season was full of good memories, apart from the Weymouth nightmare, but at least we were then able to concentrate on the League. The Bennetts – Dave and Gary – were brilliant and when Godfrey Ingram was there we called them the Three Degrees. Godfrey's record fee was a joke, we all knew that, but it was set up between Ron Jones and Gordon Jago apparently. Bob Hatton made a big difference to us. He took the knocks for Jeff Hemmerman and did well himself. Bob had this trick of coming off his man, then turning him, the lads in training never really fathomed it.

Not that we saw a lot of Bob, he always seemed to be either coming or going. He was a great pro. though. We had some smashing games against Newport County. To be truthful I thought they were a better side than us, but we had the edge in experience. I was fortunate enough to score the first goal in the promotion clincher against Orient, and after the game, Dave Bennett – who laid on my goal and scored our second – and myself were interviewed on television. When asked to describe my goal, I praised Dave for doing the 'spadework', I'm still not sure whether he gave me a black look or not! In the dressing room we had just four bottles of celebration champagne between all of us – hardly a mouthful!

I am of the opinion that the promotion season was probably part of the Club's downfall. For one reason or another, Len lost his strike force and had no money to rebuild, and when Linden Jones and myself did not receive an acceptable pay rise for achieving promotion, Len told us that the club just did not have any money. We were offered the chance of joining Newport County, with Nigel Vaughan and Karl Elsey going to City. County's offer was just too good to turn down, it meant that I was on a higher basic wage and was better off in the summer.

Things had altered so much at Ninian Park in five years, the professional staff had been slashed from over 40 to about 18, and there was nobody at the club, apart from 'Joe' Dwyer, who had been there when I signed. Of course the indestructible Harry Parsons was still around the place. It's hard to imagine Ninian Park without Harry and everybody who has had contact with the big fellow have their own stories. I think the only time that I saw him speechless was when the lads had a whip round to pay the insurance on that big Rover he had. He knew nothing about it and when we gave him the cash it almost moved him to tears – but not for long – as he was soon having a go at us again. I'll always be grateful for having the opportunity of playing at stadiums like Highbury and Maine Road, and against some great players.

But my favourite venue was St. James's Park Newcastle, where there was a great atmosphere and an appreciative crowd. I can't say the same for Barnsley though. I remember a League Cup-tie there, when some of their crowd were having a bit of a go at me. We had this free-kick near the touchline and someone called out: *'Get on with it gummy'*, referring to the fact that I played without a couple of false teeth. *'Watch this one go in'* I said, and as my free-kick curled in, Ronnie Moore ran across it, and with the goalkeeper unsighted, the ball went in at the far post. You can imagine my delight as I turned to the crowd with arms aloft and gave them a very special toothy grin.

HARRY PARSONS ('H')

I can remember Cardiff City winning the F.A. Cup in 1927 and the great homecoming the team had on their return. Although I saw all those great players, unfortunately I cannot remember in detail what they were like – it's a long time ago. I watched the team in the 1930's and they had good men like Jimmy Collins – a fine centre-forward – and Les Talbot, plus strong men in Arthur Granville and Bill Bassett. I became involved with Cardiff City when a kids' team I was running beat their youth side 4-0, and when Jimmy Scoular came to the club he asked if I would look after his youngsters. He said that I would be paid more than I was getting in the fruit market where I was working, and from that day on I've never looked back.

I have been asked many times who is the best manager in my time. I can honestly say that I got on with all of them, except Graham Williams, in his short spell at the club. I didn't know him before his appointment and for some reason he just didn't seem to require my services, and was the only person to stop me travelling with the first-team. From Jimmy Scoular to Eddie May, they were all good men, although Frank O'Farrell wasn't around long enough to get to know anyone. Jimmy Scoular was a gem and was the biggest character, at a time when the Club was full of characters. I remember when the ground was frozen solid and he was desperate to get a match played as the team were going well. He called me in and said:

'Can you drive a five ton truck, Harry? I want you to go to Cowbridge and pick up a flame-thrower that I can have a loan of, and then we can melt the ice.

Well, we go to Cowbridge, the Bell pub it was, and asked the lady there for the flame-thrower. She pointed to the corner and there was a bit of pipe with these nozzles on – that was it! And I'd driven a bloody five ton truck for it, when a car would have done! Back at the ground we fitted it up and Jimmy took over. The ice was inches thick at the Grangetown end and I kept telling him it was useless, but he wouldn't give up. Suddenly someone called him from the tunnel and as he swung around the nets caught fire, and that was the end of it – the match had to be called off then!

Jimmy was the sort of boss who wanted to run the club from top to bottom and Heaven help anyone who kept anything from him, or did things behind his back, which of course happened from time to time. We were preparing to play a European match in Lisbon when the kit came back from the laundry and I found the jock straps were damp. In order to have them ready I left them overnight on a steam boiler. I asked Lew Clayton to make sure they were collected the following morning and thought that was that. Well the next day we loaded up and set off, and it wasn't until the coach met us at Lisbon airport to take us to the hotel that I remembered the jockstraps. I managed to attract Lew's attention without Jimmy seeing me, but he shook his head when I asked him if they had been packed. We were staying at Fulham chairman Ernie Clay's hotel in the hills outside Lisbon, and I couldn't wait to get off the coach to find him and see if he could help us out.

Ernie, a millionaire, was a smashing bloke, and he whipped me to the town in his Jag. Jock-straps were out of the question so I bought 18 pairs of women's briefs at a department store and charged it to the hotel. I handed them to the players an hour before the kick-off, and told them to get them on before Jimmy noticed, and to take them home for their wives and girlfriends afterwards. Anyway the lads played in them, we didn't lose, and I thought no more about it until, months later, Jimmy suddenly said: *'Oh Harry, I know something you think I don't know, regarding women's knickers'* – and I had to come clean. He probably knew all along!

The best player in my time has to be Brian Harris who was absolutely outstanding, great on the pitch and a hell of a character off it. He was class through and through, he'd won everything at Everton, and it rubbed off on our lads, particularly Don Murray. I was caddying for Brian at St. Mellon one day when he popped the ball over the green and into a bunker. He had played the course many times and told me to get the ball as it was out of bounds. I jumped into the bunker and sunk all the way up to my chest – it was only a bloody bog, wasn't it, and there was Harris almost wetting himself at my attempts to get out! The more I tried – the deeper I got.

Brian Clark was the best professional, a model through and through. His father had been a star with Bristol City after the war, and Brian had picked up all the right habits. The same couldn't be said about Ian Gibson, who was a fabulous player, but who would bet on anything. We used to leave a gate open on the far side of the ground so that 'Gibby' could dodge the bookies, and if Jimmy (Scoular) had known half of what he was up to, there would have been murder.

If 'Gibby' was a lovable rogue then I'm afraid Robin Friday was just a rogue. He was bad through and through and definitely the worst character I've ever encountered in football. Robin already had a bad reputation in the game before he joined us, and I can remember the first time he stripped in the dressing rooms, he had 'mild' and 'bitter' tattooed under his nipples. I thought to myself: 'what the Hell have we got here!' He was already well into drugs, of which we had little knowledge – not like today, – and Jimmy Andrews, who was manager then, asked me to keep an eye out for him. It was a nightmare and the Press would have had a field day if they had known all that was going on concerning Robin at that time. I put him to bed after he had wrecked a snooker room in an hotel where we were staying. When I took him to view a bungalow the Club wanted him to have at St. Athan, he only nicked some of the family silverware! I blew my top but made a joke of it when I returned the stuff to the owners – otherwise Cardiff City Football Club would have been crucified in Court. It may seem like a bit of a lark to younger supporters, but Robin was to be pitied for he could have been a world beater, and where did his lifestyle get him? Dead at 38, that's the tragedy, and nothing we could do about it!

Down the years most of our players have relied upon me to supply them with their boots, as I could get them at cost. I would keep a book on who had the boots and, even though he may be a millionaire today, John Toshack still owes me for a pair – and I've got the proof!

I'm pleased to say that successful lads like 'Tosh' have always remained friends and it was gratifying that so many old pals turned up at my Testimonial dinner in 1991.

Certain people, like Frank Burrows, will always be special to me. Frank was totally unpredictable, and the Press boys never knew what mood he would be in. I think he used to have them on, but he would always give them an angle. When he comes back to Ninian Park, he always looks me up, and on one visit he gave me a parcel. *'That's for you to wear'* he said. When I opened it up I found an XL tee-shirt with the words, 'You fat t..t' written on it. That was Frank all over, he knew that I couldn't take it home and wear it in the garden.

I'll keep working at Ninian Park as long as the Club need me, and one day, maybe, I'll be able to do my memoirs, although a lot of it will be unprintable!

STATISTICAL SECTION:

The statistics pages have been designed for easy reference and are generally self-explanatory. The full details can be easily extracted, however the following notes explain the various specific details.

The first page for each season includes a summary of the League matches played, and lists the full details of the Football League (or Southern League and Glamorgan League where applicable) games, complete with match numbers in the left hand column. The figure in the top box of this column, refers to the accumulative number of Football League matches played (including the matches for that season); these figures ignore the three games played in the aborted 1939/40 season. The second page refers to all first team cup matches and known 'friendly' games. Since many 'friendly' matches consisted of mixed first team, reserve and other players, then the team members have not been included, however other details (where known) have been added.

The fixture dates, results ('Res'), attendances ('Attend.') and Cardiff City goalscorers for each match are self explanatory ('o.g.' refers to an own goal, and the scorer's name generally follows). 'pen' or 'p', refers to a goal scored from a penalty. Attendances are official numbers where known, 'rounded up' numbers (usually to the nearest one thousand) are generally based on newspaper estimates for those seasons before precise figures were available.

The opposition shown in upper case (capital letters) refers to a Cardiff City 'home' match, lower case opposition to an 'away' match.

All players that appeared in any League or Cup match (including substitutes for later seasons), are listed in the right hand table for each season. Players who made Football League appearances are listed in alphabetical order, with players that appeared in Cup, or made substitute appearances only, following. Each player is given a letter reference for each season, and this letter is substituted in the columns showing the team line-ups (columns headed 1 to 11, or 1 to 14 for later seasons), therefore each player's position (or shirt number) is readily identified. Ditto marks indicate that the same position (or number) was held by that same player, and therefore a change in letter in any column refers to a different player taking over the position for that match, and any subsequent ones (where dittos are shown below). A player's League debut performance (for Cardiff City) is shown by an asterisk (*), and an asterisk used in the substitute columns (under numbers 12 and 12+14) indicate that although only a substitute, he played for at least part of the match, and that this game has been considered as his debut performance. The numbers alongside each player (in the 'Players' table) refers to the number of Football League appearances/ Cup appearances/ and total number of goals scored in League and Cup matches – for that season. Hence 12/4/6 would signify 12 League appearances, 4 cup appearances and 6 goals scored in that season. (a '0' for League or Cup appearances, in later seasons, refers to a player that was only listed as a substitute in League or Cup matches and did not appear in any starting line-up).

The first column in the 'Cup' tables gives the round number for that competition, e.g. 3rd = 3rd round. Typical abbreviations include '1st/2 Leg', i.e. 1st round, 2nd leg and 'Prelim.' refers to a preliminary round.

1910-11

Player/Manager: Davy McDougall

Southern League Division 2 (Plus: Glamorgan League – 'GL') Withdrew From Glamorgan League at end of season.
(Southern Lge.) P:22 W:12 D:4 L:6 48-29 Pts:28 Pos:4th

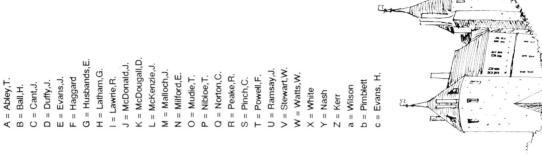

Players:
A = Abley,T.
B = Ball,H.
C = Cant,J.
D = Duffy,J.
E = Evans,J.
F = Haggard
G = Husbands,E.
H = Latham,G.
I = Lawrie,R.
J = McDonald,J.
K = McDougall,D.
L = McKenzie,J.
M = Malloch,J.
N = Milford,E.
O = Mudie,T.
P = Nibloe,T.
Q = Norton,C.
R = Peake,R.
S = Pinch,C.
T = Powell,F.
U = Ramsay,J.
V = Stewart,W.
W = Watts,W.
X = White
Y = Nash
Z = Kerr
a = Wilson
b = Pimblett
c = Evans, H.

	Date	Opposition	Res	Attend.	Goalscorers	1	2	3	4	5	6	7	8	9	10	11
GL	5 Sep	Ton Pentre	3-2	4800	Peake 3	G	L	D	I	U	K	J	A	R	W	E
GL	10	MARDY	1-1	4000	Ramsay	"	"	"	"	"	"	"	"	"	"	"
GL	12	Aberdare Athletic	2-2	3000	Peake 2	"	"	"	"	"	"	"	"	"	M	"
1	24	TON PENTRE	4-1	8000	Peake 2 Watts J.Evans	*"	*"	*"	*"	*	*"	*"	*W	*"	*"	*"
GL	26	Cwm Albion	0-1	1200		"	Y	N	a	V	"	c	"	"	"	"
2	8 Oct	Treharris Athletic	0-0	4000		"	L	D	*T	I	"	J	O	"	"	"
GL	10	Merthyr Town	0-1	6000		"	"	"	"	"	"	"	"	"	"	"
GL	17	Cwmparc	2-2	1000	Peake 2	X	"	"	a	"	U	"	A	"	"	"
3	5 Nov	Aberdare Athletic	1-1	4600	McDonald	*"	"	"	I	"	K	"	*W	Y	"	"
4	12	TREHARRIS ATHLETIC	2-1	6000	J.Evans 2	"	"	"	"	U	"	"	*S	*P	A	"
GL	19	Barry & District	2-1	4000	Nibloe J.Evans (pen)	G	Y	"	"	"	"	R	C	"	"	"
GL	26	CWM ALBION	5-0	6000	Nibloe 3 Cant 2	"	L	"	"	"	"	"	"	"	"	"
5	3 Dec	Salisbury City	4-1	4000	J.Evans 2 Pinch Cant	"	"	"	"	"	"	J	S	"	*C	"
6	7	ABERDARE ATHLETIC	1-2	6000	Pinch	"	"	"	"	"	V	R	"	"	"	"
7	17	CWMPARC	3-0	2500	Peake Lawrie Pinch	"	"	"	b	I	K	"	"	"	V	"
7	24	Kettering Town	7-4	5000	Pinch 2 J.Evans Peake 3 McDonald	"	"	"	I	U	"	J	"	R	W	"
8	26	Reading	0-0	8000		"	"	"	"	"	"	"	"	"	C	"
9	27	Stoke	0-5	9000		"	"	"	"	"	"	"	"	M	W	"
GL	31	TREDEGAR	2-1	3000	Ramsay Stewart	"	"	"	"	"	"	"	V	"	"	"
GL	2 Jan	BARRY & DISTRICT	5-1	4000	Pinch Ball 2 Lawrie Peake	"	Q	"	"	"	"	"	S	R	B	K
10	7	KETTERING TOWN	2-0	5000	Peake Lawrie	"	L	"	"	"	K	"	"	"	*"	E
11	14	Chesham	7-1	2500	Peake 4 J.Evans 3	"	"	"	"	"	"	"	"	"	"	"
12	21	SALISBURY CITY	3-1	4000	Peake 2 Ball	"	"	"	"	"	"	"	S	"	B	"
13	28	CROYDON COMMON	1-0	8000	Pinch	"	"	"	"	"	"	"	"	"	"	"
14	4 Feb	Croydon Common	3-1	6000	Abley 2 Peake	"	"	"	"	"	"	"	A	"	A	"
GL	8	ABERDARE ATHLETIC	1-1	5000	J.Evans	"	"	"	"	"	"	"	Y	"	"	"
15	11	Walsall	1-1	4000	Pinch	"	*Q	"	"	"	"	"	S	"	"	"
GL	25	Treharris Athletic	0-2	2500		"	L	"	"	"	"	"	"	"	"	"
16	1 Mar	MERTHYR TOWN	1-1	5500	J.Evans	"	N	"	"	"	"	"	"	"	"	"
GL	4	WALSALL	2-1	6000	Abley Peake	"	*"	L	"	"	"	"	M	"	"	E
17	11	Ton Pentre	2-4	14000	Peake Abley	"	L	*H	"	"	"	"	S	"	"	"
18	18	MERTHYR TOWN	1-0	6000	Peake	"	"	D	"	H	"	"	A	"	B	"
19	25	Merthyr Town	0-1	8000		"	"	"	"	"	"	"	"	"	"	"
20	1 Apr	CHESHAM	6-0	4000	Evans 2 Pinch 2 Latham Peake Peake	"	"	"	"	"	"	"	S	"	A	"
GL	6	Mardy	1-1	2000	Peake	"	Z	"	F	"	"	C	"	*F	"	"
GL	15	Tredegar	2-0	1000	Watts Cant	X	N	"	I	"	"	"	"	"	"	"
21	17	READING	0-2	10000		G	L	"	"	"	"	K	"	S	A	"
22	18	STOKE	1-2	6000	Ramsay	"	"	"	"	"	"	W	"	"	"	"
GL	19	TREHARRIS ATHLETIC	2-1	3000	Cant Abley	"	"	"	"	U	"	"	C	R	"	"
GL	28	TON PENTRE	0-0	4000		"	"	"	"	"	"	"	S	"	"	"

Other Matches

F.A.Cup

	Date	Opposition	Res	Attend.	1	2	3	4	5	6	7	8	9	10	11
4th	17 Sep	BATH CITY	3-1	5000	G	L	D	I	U	K	J	W	R	M	E
3rd Pre	1 Oct	MERTHYR TOWN	0-1	12000	"	"	"	"	"	"	"	A	"	"	"

Peake 2 Watts

Welsh Cup

	Date	Opposition	Res	Attend.	1	2	3	4	5	6	7	8	9	10	11
1st	13 Oct	Mardy	1-0	3000	"	"	"	"	"	"	V	A	R	"	"
2nd	29	TREDEGAR	4-1	4000	"	"	"	"	"	"	J	W	V	"	"
3rd	10 Dec	TON PENTRE	2-2	5000	"	"	"	"	T	"	"	"	P	A	"
3/R	15	Ton Pentre	0-1	8000	"	"	"	"	"	"	"	"	"	S	"

Abley
Watts Evans,J.Stewart Malloch
Powell Abley

Friendlies

	Date	Opposition	Res		
	1 Sep	ASTON VILLA	1-2		Evans.J
	3	BRISTOL LEAGUE X1	6-0		Peake 4 Watts O.G.
	21 Oct	POST OFFICE X1	2-1		Evans.H. Bainton
	15	READING	0-1		
	19	SWINDON TOWN	1-4		Malloch
	22	NEWPORT LEAGUE X1	6-1		Evans.J. McDougall Malloch Stewart 2 Ramsay
	10 Nov	TREDEGAR	3-0		Evans.J.2 Pinch
	24 Feb	Rhymney	3-2		Cant Ramsay Watts
	8 Apr	Merthyr Town	0-0		
	14	EXETER CITY	1-0		Evans.J.
	27	Swansea league X1	1-0		Abley
	29	NORTHAMPTON TOWN	3-0		Abley 3

The Earliest known Cardiff City Team Group – Pre-1910.

(Back) H. Rawlinson (Referee), Bartley Wilson (Hon.Sec.), C.Kyd (Chairman) E. Pocock, W. Oldfield, C. Hockey.
(Middle) F. Burfitt (Vice-Chair), S. Sheppard, L. Nash, H. Evans, V. Jones, W. Boon, W. Johnson, D. Jenkins (Trainer)
(Front) A. Fogg, F. Good, N. Wilson (Captain), R. Thomas.

1911-12

Southern League – Division 2

Player/Manager: Fred Stewart.

P:26 W:15 D:4 L:7 55-26 Pts:34 Pos:3rd

#	Date	Opposition	Res	Attend.	Goalscorers	1	2	3	4	5	6	7	8	9	10	11
1.	2 Sep	KETTERING TOWN	3-1	6000	Burton,J. Abley Tracey	M	*U	*P	Q	*S	*K	*T	*D	*H	A	G
2.	23	Pontypridd	2-3	4000	Burton,J. Hiffle	"	F	"	"	"	"	*L	"	"	*B	"
3.	7 Oct	CWM ALBION	5-1	4200	Featherstone 4 Burton,J.	"	"	"	"	"	"	T	"	"	A	"
4.	21	PORTSMOUTH	0-0	6000		"	"	"	"	N	"	"	"	"	"	"
5.	28	Cwm Albion	4-2	2000	Burton,J. Burton,G. Evans 2	"	"	"	A	O	"	"	*C	"	D	"
6.	11 Nov	Ton Pentre	4-3	2000	Featherstone 2 Evans Burton,G.	"	"	"	"	"	"	"	"	"	"	"
7.	18	TREHARRIS ATHLETIC	0-0	4000		"	"	"	"	"	"	"	"	"	"	"
8.	16	Chesham Town	4-0	3000	Burton,G. Evans 2	*J	"	"	"	"	"	"	"	"	"	"
9.	23 Dec	Kettering Town	2-0	5000	Featherstone Evans	"	"	"	"	"	"	"	"	"	"	"
10.	25	CROYDON COMMON	4-0	8000	Featherstone Abley Burton,G. & J.	"	"	"	"	"	"	"	"	"	"	"
11.	26	Croydon Common	0-2	2500		"	"	"	"	"	"	"	"	"	"	"
12.	13 Jan	ABERDARE ATHLETIC	3-1	5000	Thompson Featherstone Burton,G.	"	"	U	"	"	S	"	"	"	"	"
13.	20	MARDY	1-1	6000	Featherstone	"	"	"	"	"	K	"	"	"	"	"
14.	27	Aberdare Athletic	2-0	4000	Evans,J. 2	"	"	"	"	"	"	"	"	"	"	"
15.	10 Feb	TON PENTRE	3-0	7000	Tracey 2 Lawrie	"	"	"	"	"	"	"	"	"	"	"
16.	17	Portsmouth	2-3	11000	Evans,J. Tracey	"	"	"	"	"	"	"	"	"	"	"
17.	24	MERTHYR TOWN	1-2	15000	Evans	"	"	"	"	"	"	"	"	"	"	"
18.	29	Mardy	1-0	2000	Douglas	M	"	"	"	*Q	"	"	"	*E	"	"
19.	9 Mar	CHESHAM TOWN	5-0	2000	Abley Tracey Douglas 3	"	H	"	"	O	"	"	H	"	"	"
20.	16	PONTYPRIDD	0-0	4000		"	F	"	"	Q	"	"	"	"	"	"
21.	18	Walsall	3-0	4000	Burton,J. Burton,G. Duffy	"	"	"	"	"	"	"	R	C	"	*I
22.	5 Apr	SOUTHEND UNITED	0-2	10000		"	E	"	O	"	S	"	A	"	"	G
23.	6	Merthyr Town	0-2	9000		"	"	"	A	S	K	"	R	"	"	I
24.	10	WALSALL	5-1	5000	Burton G.& J. Latham	"	"	I	"	O	N	A	"	"	"	"
25.	24	Southend United	1-0	2000	Featherstone	"	E	"	A	S	K	"	C	H	"	"
26.	27	Treharris Athletic	0-2	2000		J	"	"	"	"	"	"	"	"	"	"

Players:

A = Abley,T.
B = Bates,J.
C = Burton,G.
D = Burton,J.
E = Douglas,W.
F = Duffy,J.
G = Evans,J.
H = Featherstone,H.
I = Gaughan,W.
J = Germaine
K = Hardy,W.
L = Hiffle,J.
M = Husbands,E.
N = Latham,G.
O = Lawrie,R.
P = Leah,R.
Q = Newton,L.
R = Pinch,C.
S = Thompson,E.
T = Tracey,H.
U = Waters,A.

Other Matches

F.A.Cup

	Date	Opposition	Res	Attend.	Goalscorers	1	2	3	4	5	6	7	8	9	10	11
1 Qual.	16 Sep	CARDIFF CORINTHIANS	3-0	3000	Featherstone Latham Abley	J	U	P	O	N	K	T	A	H	D	G
2 Qual.	30	MARDY	2-0	3000	Featherstone Abley	M	F	"	"	S	"	"	"	"	"	"
3 Qual.	14 Oct	Merthyr Town	1-1	8000	Evans	"	"	"	"	"	"	"	"	"	"	"
4 Qual.	18	MERTHYR TOWN	1-2	5200	Evans	"	"	"	"	N	"	"	"	"	"	"

Welsh Cup

	Date	Opposition	Res	Attend.	Goalscorers	1	2	3	4	5	6	7	8	9	10	11
3rd	10 Jan	TREHARRIS ATHLETIC	1-0	3000	Featherstone	J	"	U	A	O	"	"	C	"	"	"
4th	3 Feb	Wrexham	2-1	3500	Featherstone Burton,J.	"	"	"	"	"	"	"	"	"	"	"
Semi/Fin	23 Mar	CHESTER	1-1	3000	Burton,J.	M	K	"	"	"	S	"	"	R	"	"
S/F Rep.	27	Chester	2-1	3500	Tracey Burton,G.	"	"	"	"	"	"	"	"	E	"	"
Final	8 Apr	PONTYPRIDD	0-0	18000		"	E	K	"	"	"	"	"	R	"	"
F/Replay	18	Pontypridd	3-0	6648	Featherstone Tracey 2	"	N	U	"	S	K	"	"	H	"	"

Friendlies

	4 Sep	Treharris Athletic	2-2	Thompson Featherstone
	9	Pontypridd	1-1	Waters
	20	PLYMOUTH ARGYLE	3-1	Burton,J. Bates Featherstone
	3 Oct	Exeter City	1-0	Abley
	11	Plymouth Argyle	0-6	
	25	EXETER CITY	1-1	Evans
	4 Nov	WEDNESBURY	4-0	Bates 2 Evans Featherstone
	25	CHESTERFIELD	4-1	Featherstone 3 Pinch
	9 Dec	CHELSEA	5-1	Burton, G. Evans 2 (1 pen) Featherstone 2
	1 Jan	BRISTOL CITY	2-0	Featherstone Tracey
	30 Mar	Treharris Athletic	3-2	Pinch Gaughan Burton, J.
	20 Apr	CARDIFF & DIS. LGE.	2-1	Tracey Burton, G.
	29	Barry & District	4-0	Thompson 3 Burton, G.
	30	Llanelly	3-0	Bates Evans Burton, J.

1912-13

Southern League – Division 2. Secretary/Manager: Fred Stewart

P:24 W:18 D:5 L:1 54-15 Pts:41 Pos:1st.

	Date	Opposition	Res	Attend.	Goalscorers	1	2	3	4	5	6	7	8	9	10	11
1.	7 Sep	Swansea Town	1-1	8000	Burton, J.	*R	*G	T	*O	*E	N	W	D	L	*Q	K
2.	12	Mid-Rhondda	1-0	4000	Keggans	"	*I	"	"	"	"	"	"	"	"	"
3.	14	NEWPORT COUNTY	2-0	8000	Tracey Featherstone	"	"	"	"	"	"	"	"	"	"	"
4.	21	Ton Pentre	1-0	6000	Burton, J.	"	"	"	"	"	"	"	"	J	"	"
5.	28	CROYDON COMMON	3-1	7000	Burton, J. 2 Keggans	"	"	"	"	"	"	"	"	*H	"	"
6.	5 Oct	Treharris Athletic	2-0	2000	Devlin Keggans	"	"	"	A	"	O	"	C	"	"	"
7.	19	MARDY	5-2	6500	Burtons G.& J. Cassidy, Devlin	"	"	"	"	"	"	"	"	"	D	"
8.	9 Nov	Croydon Common	2-1	3000	Evans Burton, G.	"	"	"	Q	"	N	"	"	L	"	"
9.	7 Dec	TREHARRIS ATHLETIC	2-1	7000	Cassidy Tracey (pen)	"	"	"	"	"	"	"	"	H	"	"
10.	21	SOUTHEND UNITED	1-0	8000	Evans	"	"	"	"	"	"	"	"	"	"	"
11.	25	PONTYPRIDD	1-1	10000	Featherstone	"	"	"	"	"	"	"	"	L	"	"
12.	26	Luton Town	0-2	6000		"	"	"	"	"	"	"	"	"	"	"
13.	1 Jan	LLANELLY	5-0	8000	Devlin Featherstone 2	"	"	"	"	"	"	"	H	"	"	"
14.	15	TON PENTRE	9-0	7000	Devlin3 Tracey2(1o) Cassidy2 Evans Burton,J	"	"	"	"	"	"	"	"	"	"	"
15.	8 Feb	Newport County	3-1	8000	Cassidy Tracey Burton, G.	"	"	"	"	"	"	"	"	"	C	"
16.	12	ABERDARE ATHLETIC	3-0	4000	Harvey Devlin Burton, J.	"	"	"	"	"	"	"	"	"	D	"
17.	22	Southend United	1-1	7000	Burton, G.	"	"	"	"	"	"	"	C	*F	"	*B
18.	1 Mar	MID RHONDDA	1-0	6000	Burton, G.	"	"	"	*U	"	"	M	"	"	"	K
19.	8	Mardy	2-1	3000	Burton, G. Clarke	"	"	S	"	"	"	*P	"	"	"	"
20.	15	SWANSEA TOWN	0-0	10000		"	"	G	"	V	A	"	"	"	J	"
21.	21	LUTON TOWN	3-0	21000	Burton, J. 2 Burton, G.	"	"	T	O	E	N	W	"	H	D	"
22.	24	Pontypridd	1-1	7500	Hardy	"	"	"	"	"	"	B	"	"	"	"
23.	29	Llanelly	2-0	1500	Devlin Burton, J.	"	S	"	"	"	"	W	"	"	"	"
24.	5 Apr	Aberdare Athletic	3-2	2000	Evans Burton, G. Devlin	"	L	"	"	"	"	"	"	"	"	"

Players:

A = Abley,T.
B = Bennett,K.
C = Burton, G.
D = Burton, J.
E = Cassidy,P.
F = Clarke,J.
G = Croft,R.
H = Devlin,W.
I = Doncaster,T.
J = Douglas,W.
K = Evans,J.
L = Featherstone,H.
M = Gaughan,W.
N = Hardy,W.
O = Harvey,H.
P = Holt,A.
Q = Keggans,H.
R = Kneeshaw,J.
S = Latham,G.
T = Leah,R.
U = McKechnie
V = Newton,L.
W = Tracey,H.

Other Matches

F.A.Cup

	Date	Opposition	Res	Attend.	Goalscorers	1	2	3	4	5	6	7	8	9	10	11
1st Qual.	12 Oct	Merthyr Town	5-1	10000	Devlin 3 Harvey Burton, J.	R	I	T	O	E	N	W	Q	H	D	K
2nd	2 Nov	PONTYPRIDD	2-1	12000	Burton, J. Burton, G.	"	"	"	"	"	"	"	C	L	"	"
3rd	16	Llanelly	4-1	3000	Burton, G. Evans Tracey O.G.(Gough)	"	"	"	"	"	"	"	"	"	"	"
4th	30	EXETER CITY	5-1	14000	Devlin 2 Burton, J. Burton, G. Harvey	"	"	"	"	"	"	"	"	H	"	"
5th	14 Dec	SOUTHEND UNITED	0-3	8000		"	"	"	"	"	"	"	"	"	"	"

Welsh Cup

	Date	Opposition	Res	Attend.	Goalscorers	1	2	3	4	5	6	7	8	9	10	11
3rd	4 Jan	TON PENTRE	4-2	2000	Douglas 2 Burton, G. Featherstone	"	"	"	"	S	"	B	"	L	J	M
4th	25	Bangor City	4-0	3000	Devlin Featherstone Burton,J. Cassidy	"	"	"	"	"	"	W	H	"	D	K
Sem/Fin.	15 Feb	SWANSEA TOWN	2-4	12000	Cassidy Burton, J.	"	"	"	"	"	"	"	"	"	"	"

Friendlies

4 Sep	TREHARRIS ATHLETIC	5-0		Douglas 2 Keggans 3
11 Nov	Cwm Albion	1-2		Gorman
25 Mar	Newport County	1-1		J.Evans
2 Apr	Bridgend X1	9-0		Douglas3 D.Evans2 J.Evans Newton Bennett Keenor
28	Pontypridd	1-1		Douglas
30	Mid-Rhondda	1-1		Burton, G.

(Back) W. Douglas, T. Doncaster, K. Bennett, J. Duffy, J. Kneeshaw, J. Evans, R. Croft, P. Cassidy (Middle) T. Abley, G. Burton, H. Featherstone, S. Nicholls (Chairman), J. Burton, A. Hall (Director), W. Hardy, H. Tracey, R. Leah. (Front) H. Keggans, H. Harvey.

1913-14

Southern League – Division 1. Secretary/Manager: Fred Stewart
P:38 W:13 D:12 L:13 46-42 Pts:38 Pos:10th

#	Date	Opposition	Res	Attend.	Goalscorers	1	2	3	4	5	6	7	8	9	10	11
1.	1 Sep	Bristol Rovers	0-1	7000		S	I	T	M	E	L	O	C	H	D	J
2.	6	Plymouth Argyle	0-1	8000		"	"	"	"	"	"	"	R	"	"	"
3.	13	SOUTHAMPTON	1-2	10000	Devlin	"	"	"	"	"	"	"	"	"	"	"
4.	20	Reading	0-1	4000		"	"	K	"	"	"	Y	C	"	"	"
5.	27	CRYSTAL PALACE	1-2	8000	Devlin	"	"	T	"	"	"	"	"	"	"	"
6.	4 Oct	Coventry City	2-2	7000	Robertson 2	"	"	"	"	"	"	A	*N	*Y	H	"
7.	11	WATFORD	2-0	7000	Robertson Henderson	"	"	"	"	"	"	"	"	"	"	F
8.	18	Norwich City	2-2	7000	Robertson 2	"	"	"	"	"	"	"	"	"	D	J
9.	25	GILLINGHAM	2-0	11000	Evans Henderson	"	"	"	"	"	"	"	"	"	"	"
10.	1 Nov	Northampton Town	1-2	6000	Burton,J.	"	"	"	"	"	"	"	"	"	"	"
11.	8	SOUTHEND UNITED	3-0	8000	Hopkins 2 Harvey	"	"	"	"	U	"	"	"	*P	"	"
12.	15	Brighton	1-2	6000	Hopkins	"	"	"	"	"	"	"	"	"	"	"
13.	22	PORTSMOUTH	1-3	15000	Devlin	"	"	*b	"	"	"	"	"	H	"	"
14.	6 Dec	EXETER CITY	1-1	8000	Hopkins	*X	"	T	"	E	*Q	H	V	P	*Z	F
15.	13	Q. P. RANGERS	3-0	12000	West,G. 3	"	"	"	"	"	L	Y	H	"	"	"
16.	20	Swindon Town	2-1	10000	Devlin 2	"	*B	"	*G	"	"	"	"	"	"	J
17.	25	MERTHYR TOWN	1-1	20000	Evans,J.	"	"	"	"	"	"	"	"	"	"	"
18.	26	Merthyr Town	2-2	12000	Hopkins Burton,G.	"	"	"	"	"	"	C	"	"	"	"
19.	27	PLYMOUTH ARGYLE	2-1	20000	West,G. Tracey	"	"	"	"	Q	"	Y	"	"	"	"
20.	1 Jan	BRISTOL ROVERS	2-0	16000	West,G. Burton, J.	"	I	B	"	E	"	"	D	"	"	"
21.	3	Southampton	0-2	8000		"	"	"	"	"	"	"	"	"	"	"
22.	17	READING	1-0	13000	West,G.	"	"	"	"	"	"	"	"	"	"	"
23.	24	Crystal Palace	0-4	11000		"	"	"	M	"	"	H	N	"	"	"
24.	7 Feb	COVENTRY CITY	2-1	8000	Harvey West,G.	"	"	"	"	"	"	*W	"	"	"	"
25.	14	Watford	2-3	4000	Cassidy Hopkins	"	B	T	"	"	"	"	"	"	"	"
26.	21	NORWICH CITY	3-0	14000	Burton,G. West,G. Robertson	"	"	"	"	"	"	"	C	V	"	"
27.	28	Gillingham	0-0	8000		"	"	"	G	"	"	"	D	"	"	"
28.	7 Mar	NORTHAMPTON TOWN	0-0	12000		"	"	"	M	"	"	"	"	"	"	"
29.	14	Southend United	1-2	12000	West,G.	"	"	"	"	"	"	"	"	"	"	"
30.	21	BRIGHTON	0-0	12000		"	"	I	"	"	"	"	"	"	"	"
31.	28	PORTSMOUTH	1-1	14000	Evans	"	"	"	"	"	"	"	"	H	"	F
32.	4 Apr	Millwall	0-3	9000		"	"	"	"	"	"	"	"	V	"	J
33.	10	WEST HAM UNITED	2-0	13000	Devlin 2	S	"	"	"	"	"	"	*a	H	"	"
34.	11	Exeter City	1-0	5000	Devlin	"	"	"	"	"	"	"	"	"	"	"
35.	13	West Ham United	1-1	15000	Doncaster (pen)	"	"	"	"	"	"	"	H	"	"	"
36.	18	Queens Park Rangers	2-0	9000	Evans West,J.	"	"	"	"	"	"	"	"	V	"	"
37.	25	SWINDON TOWN	0-0	11000		X	"	"	"	"	"	"	"	H	"	"
38.	29	MILLWALL	0-0	6000		"	"	"	"	Q	"	"	"	"	"	"

Players:

A = Bennett,K.
B = Brittan,R.
C = Burton,G.
D = Burton,J.
E = Cassidy,P.
F = Clarke,J.
G = Davidson,W.
H = Devlin,W.
I = Doncaster,T.
J = Evans,J.
K = Featherstone,H.
L = Hardy,W.
M = Harvey,H.
N = Henderson,J.
O = Holt,A.
P = Hopkins,L.
Q = Keenor,F.
R = Keggans,H.
S = Kneeshaw,J.
T = Leah,R.
U = McKenzie,K.
V = Roberston,T.
W = Seymour,E.
X = Stephenson,J.
Y = Tracey,H.
Z = West,G.
a = West,J.
b = Witts,T.
c = Dr.McBean

Other Matches

F.A.Cup

	Date	Opposition	Res	Attend.	Goalscorers	1	2	3	4	5	6	7	8	9	10	11
4th qual	29 Nov	Swansea Town	0-2	12000		S	I	c	M	E	L	A	N	V	D	J

Welsh Cup

3rd	3 Jan	Oswestry Town *	1-2		Gaughan											

* City fielded Reserve team.

Friendlies

†	17 Nov	BLACKBURN ROVERS	1-2	15000	Evans
	31 Jan	OLDHAM ATHLETIC	1-1	10000	West.G

† Senghenydd Disaster Fund.

(Top) K. McKenzie, G. West, J. Evans, J. Kneeshaw, P. Cassidy, J. Stephenson, E. Milford, W. Davidson, T. Witts, T. Robertson.
(Middle) T. Doncaster, J. Bennett, A. Holt, H. Featherstone, J. Burton, H. Harvey, W. Hardy, H. Ward, R. Leah, J. Clarke.
(Bottom) G. Burton, H. Tracey, W. Devlin, H. Keggans, W. Gaughan, J. Henderson, F. Keenor.

1914-15

Secretary/Manager: Fred Stewart.

Southern League - Division 1.

P:38 W:22 D:4 L:12 72-38 Pts:48 Pos:3rd

Players:
- A = Barnett,A.
- B = Beare,G.
- C = Brittan,R.
- D = Burton, G.
- E = Burton, J.
- F = Cassidy,P.
- G = Davidson,W.
- H = Devlin,W.
- I = Doncaster,T.
- J = Evans,J.
- K = Goddard,A.
- L = Hardy,W.
- M = Harvey,H.
- N = Henderson,J.
- O = Hopkins,L.
- P = Keenor,F.
- Q = Kneeshaw,J.
- R = Layton,A.
- S = Stephenson,J.
- T = West,G.
- U = West,J.

#	Date	Opposition	Res	Attend.	Goalscorers	1	2	3	4	5	6	7	8	9	10	11
1.	2 Sep	Watford	1-2	8000	Cassidy	Q	C	*R	M	F	L	*B	U	Q	T	J
2.	5	NORWICH CITY	1-0	8000	Evans	"	"	"	"	"	"	"	P	"	U	"
3.	12	Gillingham	1-1	6000	Burton,J.	"	"	"	"	"	"	"	N	E	"	"
4.	19	BRIGHTON	0-1	10000		"	"	"	"	P	"	"	"	"	"	"
5.	26	Crystal Palace	2-0	9000	Hopkins Evans	"	"	"	P	F	"	"	*K	O	"	"
6.	3 Oct	Exeter City	0-2	7000		"	"	"	"	"	"	"	"	"	"	"
7.	10	LUTON TOWN	3-0	8000	Hopkins West,G. Cassidy	"	"	"	"	"	"	"	"	"	T	"
8.	17	Portsmouth	1-0	14000	West,G.	"	"	"	M	"	"	"	"	"	"	"
9.	24	SWINDON TOWN	3-0	16000	Cassidy Evans(p) West,G.	"	"	"	"	"	"	"	"	"	"	"
10.	31	Southend United	1-2	7000	Beare	"	1	"	"	"	"	"	"	H	"	"
11.	7 Nov	Q.P.RANGERS	2-0	9000	Beare Evans	"	C	"	"	"	"	"	"	O	"	"
12.	14	Millwall	1-2	6000	Beare	"	"	"	"	"	"	"	"	H	"	"
13.	21	BRISTOL ROVERS	7-0	10000	Devlin 3 West,G. Goddard Beare Evans	"	"	"	"	"	"	"	"	"	"	"
14.	28	Croydon Common	1-0	2000	Cassidy	"	"	"	"	"	"	"	"	"	"	"
15.	5 Dec	READING	3-2	12000	Devlin 2 O.G.(Crawford)	"	"	"	"	"	"	"	"	"	"	"
16.	12	Southampton	1-1	8000	West,G.	"	"	"	"	"	"	"	"	"	"	"
17.	19	NORTHAMPTON TOWN	5-0	12000	Beare Devlin 2 Goddard 2	"	"	1	"	"	"	"	"	"	"	"
18.	25	Plymouth Argyle	0-2	8000		"	"	"	"	"	"	"	"	"	"	"
19.	27	PLYMOUTH ARGYLE	2-0	9000	Goddard Beare	"	"	R	"	"	"	"	"	"	"	"
20.	1 Jan	WATFORD	2-3	4000	Beare Evans	"	"	"	"	"	"	"	"	"	"	"
21.	2	Norwich City	1-2	4000	Beare	"	"	"	"	P	"	"	N	"	"	"
22.	16	GILLINGHAM	3-1	8000	West,G. Devlin	"	"	1	"	F	"	"	K	"	"	"
23.	23	Brighton	1	3000	Evans	"	"	R	"	P	"	"	"	T	*A	"
24.	30	CRYSTAL PALACE	5-0	10000	Barnett West G. Evans Beare	"	"	"	"	"	"	"	"	"	"	"
25.	6 Feb	EXETER CITY	1-0	5000	Barnett	"	1	"	"	"	"	"	"	"	"	"
26.	13	Luton Town	1-2	9000	West,G.	S	"	"	P	F	"	"	H	"	"	"
27.	20	PORTSMOUTH	3-2	6000	Evans Keenor Barnett	Q	"	"	"	"	"	"	K	"	"	"
28.	27	Swindon Town	0-0	5000		"	C	"	M	"	"	"	"	P	"	"
29.	6 Mar	SOUTHEND UNITED	3-0	10000	Keenor Evans Goddard	"	"	"	"	G	"	"	"	"	"	"
30.	13	Q.P. Rangers	0-3	7000		"	"	"	"	"	"	"	"	"	"	"
31.	20	MILLWALL	4-1	9000	Hopkins 3 Goddard	"	L	"	"	F	P	D	"	O	"	"
32.	27	Bristol Rovers	1-0	11000	Beare	"	C	"	"	P	L	B	"	"	"	"
33.	2 Apr	West Ham United	1-0	10000	Goddard	"	"	"	"	"	"	"	"	"	"	"
34.	3	CROYDON COMMON	1-0	9000	West,G.	"	L	"	"	F	P	"	H	"	"	"
35.	5	WEST HAM UNITED	2-1	13000	Goddard Barnett	"	C	"	M	"	"	D	K	"	"	B
36.	10	Reading	2-1	6000	West,G. Evans	S	"	"	"	P	L	B	T	T	"	"
37.	17	SOUTHAMPTON	1-1	12000	Barnett	Q	"	"	"	"	"	"	"	"	"	J
38.	24	Northampton Town	5-2	5000	Evans West,G. Barnett Beare Cassidy	"	"	"	"	F	"	"	"	"	"	"

Other Matches

F.A.Cup

	Date	Opposition	Res	Attend.	Goalscorers	1	2	3	4	5	6	7	8	9	10	11
1.	9 Jan	Bristol City	0-2	15000		Q	C	R	M	F	L	B	K	H	T	J

Welsh Cup

3rd		Pontypridd †														

† Cardiff City withdrew from the Competition (believed to 3rd round, no date agreed before withdrawal)

(Back Row) T. Witts, J. Stephenson, F. Keenor. (Middle) W. Davidson, A. Fish, R. Leah.
(Front) E. Seymour, G. Burton, W. Devlin, W. Henderson, J. Clarke, W. Canter (Asst. Trainer)

1915-16

Friendlies

	Date	Opposition	Res	Attend.	Goalscorers	1	2	3	4	5	6	7	8	9	10	11
1.	4 Sep	BRISTOL ROVERS	4-1		Seymour Beare 2 Stone	R	E	N	P	Z	M	B	c	H	f	U
2.	11	BRISTOL CITY	1-0		Seymour	"	"	"	"	"	"	"	"	"	—	"
3.	18	Bristol City	1-1		Beare	"	"	"	S	"	"	"	"	"	f	"
4.	25	PORTSMOUTH	2-0		Seymour Stone	"	"	"	P	"	"	"	"	"	"	"
5.	2 Oct	FOOTBALL BATTALION X1	0-1			"	"	"	"	b	"	"	"	"	"	"
6.	9	Bristol Rovers	2-3		Millard Beare	"	N	h	A	Z	"	"	"	W	"	"
7.	16	BRISTOL LEAGUE X1	2-0		Davies Seymour	"	B	"	"	N	"	"	"	"	H	"
8.	23	Portsmouth	2-3		Beare Millard	e	L	"	J	I	O	"	H	"	f	"
9.	6 Nov	BARRY & DISTRICT	1-1		Evans (pen)	R	?	?	?	?	M	"	"	?	?	"
10.	13	Southampton	2-2		Collier Stone	"	N	d	K	Z	"	c	f	a	X	"
11.†	20	WELSH FIELD AMBULANCE X1	6-1		Davies 4 Stone Hardy	"	V	h	N	"	"	"	"	H	M	"
12.	27	Mid-Rhondda	2-3		Hardy Davies	"	c	"	"	"	Y	B	"	"	"	"
13.	11 Dec	WELSH REGIMENT X1	6-3		Hardy 2 Stone 2 Hewitt Davies	"	?	"	"	"	?	?	"	"	"	"
14.	18	Barry & District	0-1			"	G	"	"	Z	M	B	Q	"	f	"
15.	25	Merthyr Town	2-1		Stone Beare	d	"	"	Y	"	"	"	"	"	"	"
16.	27	BARNSLEY	0-0			R	E	"	"	"	"	"	"	"	q	"
17.	1 Jan	SOUTHAMPTON	1-0		Evans (pen)	"	T	N	"	"	D	"	"	M	f	"
18.	5 Feb	Barry & District	0-3			"	G	h	"	M	N	"	"	F	"	"
19.	19	BARRY & DISTRICT	0-1			"	"	"	N	Z	M	"	"	"	"	"
20.	22 Apr	NOTTINGHAM FOREST	2-1		Coates 2	"	"	"	"	"	Y	"	"	"	P	i
21.	24	SWINDON TOWN	3-2		Coates 2 Jones	"	"	"	Z	"	P	"	"	"	C	"

† Due to play Southampton but missed connection at Bristol.

South-West Combination

	Date	Opposition	Res	Attend.	Goalscorers	1	2	3	4	5	6	7	8	9	10	11
1.	8 Jan	Swindon Town	2-0		Beare Coates	R	G	h	N	Z	Y	B	Q	F	f	U
2.	15	SWINDON TOWN	1-0		Coates	"	"	"	"	M	"	"	"	"	"	"
3.	22	BRISTOL CITY	1-0		Jones	"	"	"	"	Z	M	"	"	"	"	"
4.	29	BRISTOL ROVERS	1-2		Evans (pen)	"	"	"	"	"	"	"	"	"	"	"
5.	12 Feb	Southampton	3-6		Coates Jones Stone	k	N	G	Z	Y	n	"	"	"	"	"
6.	4 Mar	SOUTHAMPTON	2-0		Beare Jones	R	G	h	N	Z	"	"	"	"	"	"
7.	11	Newport County	5-1		Jenkins 4 Jones	"	"	"	"	"	"	"	"	"	"	"
8.	18	NEWPORT COUNTY	3-1		Jones 2 Coates	"	"	G	"	"	M	"	"	"	P	"
9.	25	Portsmouth	0-4			i	"	"	"	m	o	"	p	q	"	M
10.	1 Apr	Bristol Rovers	2-0		Pinch Stone	R	G	h	"	Z	M	"	Q	F	F	P
11.	8	Bristol City	0-2			"	"	"	"	"	Y	"	"	"	f	"
12.	15	PORTSMOUTH	1-2		Coates	"	"	"	"	"	"	"	"	"	"	"

Players:

A = Allden
B = Beare
C = Bennet
D = Bratley
E = Brittan
F = Coates
G = Dalton
H = Davies
I = Doran
J = Fenwick
K = Fish
L = Ford
M = Hardy
N = Hewitt
O = Hunter
P = Jenkins
Q = Jones
R = Kneeshaw
S = Lt.G. Latham
T = Layton
U = Evans
V = L/Cpl. Smart
W = Millard
X = Mitchell
Y = Mortimer
Z = Pinch
a = Pte. Collier
b = Pte. Keenor
c = Seymour
d = Sgt. Tinsley
e = Somers
f = Stone
g = Vizard
h = Walton
i = L/Cpl. Evans

Players (Additional)

j = Gibbons
k = Holly
l = Ordell
m = Lee
n = Jones, C.
o = Emerson
p = Quinn
q = Hood

War-Time Friendlies

1916-17

	Date	Opponent	Score	Scorers
	11 Nov	INTERNATIONAL ARMY X1	4-0	Beare 3 Henderson
	23 Dec	SWINDON TOWN	3-1	
	26	Barry & District	0-1	
	3 Feb	VICTORIAS (Cardiff)	4-1	
	7 Apr	Barry District	1-2	
	9	BARRY DISTRICT	0-1	
	28	SWANSEA TOWN	4-1	

1917-18

	Date	Opponent	Score	Scorers
	25 Dec	Barry District	4-6	
	4 May	BARRY DISTRICT	1-1	
	11	Barry Town	2-2	

1918-19

	Date	Opponent	Score	Scorers
	25 Dec	Newport County	1-2	
	26	NEWPORT COUNTY	3-0	Philpott Pinch Beare
	11 Jan	Barry District	1-2	
	1 Mar	GLAMORGAN X1	1-2	
	8	Pontypridd	0-3	
	15	PONTYPRIDD	1-1	
	22	BARRY DISTRICT	1-3	
	29	Bristol Rovers	0-3	
	5 Apr	Newport County	4-1	
	12	MAERDY	1-0	
	18	COVENTRY CITY	2-0	Rutherford 2
	19	NEWPORT COUNTY	7-1	Grimshaw 3 Beare 2 Clarke West, G.
	21	SWANSEA TOWN	3-0	Rutherford West, G. Harvey
	26	BRISTOL ROVERS	1-0	Beare
	28	BRENTFORD	3-0	Beare Beaumont Jones, E.
	30	Aberdare Athletic	0-0	

1919-20

Secretary/Manager: Fred Stewart

Southern League – Division 1.   P:42   W:18   D:17   L:7   70-43   Pts:53   Pos:4th

Players:
A = Barnett,A.
B = Beare,G.
C = Brittan,R.
D = Cashmore,A.
E = Cassidy,P.
F = Clarke,J.
G = Cox,W.
H = Davies,L.
I = Devlin,W.
J = Evans,J.
K = Grimshaw,W.
L = Hardy,W.
M = Harvey,H.
N = Hewitt,W.
O = Hopkins,L.
P = Jenkins,E.
Q = Johnstone,
R = Jones,C.
S = Keenor,F.
T = Kneeshaw,J.
U = Layton,A.
V = Smith,E.
W = Stewart,A.
X = West,G.

	Date	Opposition	Res	Attend.	Goalscorers	1	2	3	4	5	6	7	8	9	10	11
1.	30 Aug	Reading	0-2	6000		T	C	U	M	E	S	B	*K	X	*R	J
2.	1 Sep	Bristol Rovers	4-4	6000	Evans(p) Grimshaw2 Jones	"	"	"	"	"	"	"	"	O	"	"
3.	6	SOUTHAMPTON	3-0	11000	West Evans Keenor	"	"	"	"	"	L	"	"	S	"	"
4.	9	BRISTOL ROVERS	0-0	7500		"	"	"	"	"	"	"	"	"	I	"
5.	13	Luton Town	2-2	10000	Grimshaw 2	"	"	"	"	"	S	*H	"	T	A	"
6.	20	GILLINGHAM	5-0	8500	Grimshaw2 Evans2 Devlin	"	"	"	"	"	"	B	"	"	"	"
7.	27	Swansea Town	1-2	15000	Evans	"	E	"	"	"	"	"	"	"	"	"
8.	4 Oct	EXETER CITY	1-0	12500	Cox	"	C	"	"	"	"	"	"	G	"	X
9.	11	Watford	0-0	8000		"	"	"	"	"	L	"	"	"	"	J
10.	18	Q.P.Rangers	0-0	10000		"	"	"	"	"	E	"	"	"	"	"
11.	25	SWINDON TOWN	3-3	15000	Cox 2 Grimshaw	"	"	E	"	"	S	"	"	"	X	F
12.	1 Nov	Millwall	2-1	12000	Grimshaw 2	"	"	A	"	"	"	"	"	"	"	J
13.	8	BRIGHTON	2-0	14000	Harvey Grimshaw	"	"	"	"	"	"	"	"	"	"	"
14.	15	Newport County	3-1	10000	Hopkins West Smith	"	"	"	"	"	"	"	"	O	"	F
15.	22	PORTSMOUTH	0-1	16000		"	"	U	"	"	"	"	"	"	"	"
16.	29	Northampton Town	2-2	7000	West Grimshaw	"	"	"	"	"	"	"	"	G	"	J
17.	6 Dec	CRYSTAL PALACE	2-1	13000	Cashmore Evans	"	A	"	"	"	"	"	"	*D	"	"
18.	13	Southend United	1-1	9000	Cashmore	"	"	"	"	"	"	"	"	"	G	"
19.	25	Merthyr Town	1-1	10000	Cashmore	"	"	"	L	"	"	K	G	"	R	"
20.	26	MERTHYR TOWN	3-2	18000	Beare Evans O.G.(Chamberlain)	"	"	"	"	"	"	B	"	"	X	"
21.	27	Brentford	2-1	10000	Evans Cashmore	"	"	"	*P	"	"	"	"	"	"	"
22.	1 Jan	NORWICH CITY	1-0	12000	Hardy	"	C	A	L	"	L	"	"	"	S	"
23.	3	READING	4-0	15000	Clarke 2 Cox 2	"	"	"	"	"	S	"	"	"	R	F
24.	17	Southampton	2-2	10000	Cashmore Beare	"	"	"	"	"	"	"	"	"	F	"
25.	24	LUTON TOWN	2-1	15000	Cashmore West	"	"	"	M	"	"	K	"	"	X	"
26.	7 Feb	SWANSEA TOWN	1-0	23500	Beare	"	"	"	L	"	L	"	G	"	"	"
27.	14	Exeter City	1-1	8000	Clarke	"	"	*W	M	"	L	"	"	"	"	F
28.	28	Q.P.RANGERS	4-0	17000	Beare 2 West Cashmore	"	U	A	L	"	S	K	"	"	R	J
29.	6 Mar	Swindon Town	2-2	9000	Cashmore 2	"	"	"	"	"	"	"	"	"	F	"
30.	13	MILLWALL	4-2	12000	Grimshaw 2 Clarke West	"	"	"	M	"	L	"	"	G	"	F
31.	16	Gillingham	0-3	5000		"	C	U	S	"	"	"	"	D	F	J
32.	20	Brighton	1-1	13000	Cashmore	U	"	A	"	"	"	"	"	"	"	"
33.	27	NEWPORT COUNTY	0-0	18000		*N	U	"	"	"	"	"	G	"	"	"
34.	2 Apr	Plymouth Argyle	0-1	16000		T	C	U	"	"	"	"	K	"	X	"
35.	3	Portsmouth	0-0	24600		"	"	A	"	"	"	"	G	"	"	"
36.	5	PLYMOUTH ARGYLE	0-2	25000		"	"	"	"	"	"	"	"	"	"	F
37.	10	NORTHAMPTON TOWN	6-1	12000	Hopks2 West Evans Grim,w Keenor	N	"	W	M	S	"	K	G	O	"	J
38.	14	WATFORD	0-1	11000		"	"	"	L	V	S	B	"	"	"	"
39.	17	Crystal Palace	1-1	16000	Cashmore	T	"	U	K	"	L	"	K	G	"	F
40.	24	SOUTHEND UNITED	1-0	16000	West	"	"	"	S	"	"	B	G	D	"	J
41.	29	Norwich City	1-1	10000	West	N	"	"	"	"	"	K	Q	"	"	"
42.	1 May	BRENTFORD	2-0	12000	Evans(pen) Cashmore	T	A	"	"	"	"	B	"	"	"	"

Other Matches

F.A.Cup

	Date	Opposition	Res	Attend.	Goalscorers	1	2	3	4	5	6	7	8	9	10	11
1st	10 Jan	OLDHAM ATHLETIC	2-0	20000	West Evans	T	C	A	L	Y	S	B	K	G	X	J
2nd	31	Wolverhampton W.	2-1	37000	Smith Beare	"	U	"	"	"	"	"	"	"	"	"
3rd	21 Feb	Bristol City	1-2	32432	Beare	"	"	"	"	"	"	"	"	"	"	"

Welsh Cup

	Date	Opposition	Res	Attend.	Goalscorers	1	2	3	4	5	6	7	8	9	10	11
3rd	14 Jan	MERTHYR TOWN	5-0		Clarke 3 Harvey Cox	T	C	W	M	E	S	B	G	Q	F	J
4th	11 Feb	CHESTER	5-0		Cashmore 2 Evans Smith Keenor	N	L	"	Y	V	"	"	"	D	X	"
S/Final	24 Mar	SWANSEA	2-1		Evans(pen) West	U	C	A	S	"	L	"	"	"	"	"
Final	21 Apr	Wrexham	2-1		West 2	T	"	U	"	"	K	"	"	"	"	"

Friendlies

	Date	Opposition	Res	Attend.	Goalscorers
†	6 Oct	SWANSEA TOWN	1-1		Devlin
	20 Dec	PLYMOUTH ARGYLE	5-1		Cashmore 2 Jones Keenor Evans
	3 May	BRISTOL CITY	2-0		Beare Hopkins

† Geo. Latham Benefit Match

(Identified players) Back Row: Fred Keenor – in suit.
Front Row: W. Davidson, C. Hewitt (with ball), J. Kneeshaw, J. Clarke.

1920-21

Football League – Division 2

Secretary/Manager: Fred Stewart

P:42 W:24 D:10 L:8 59-32 Pts:58 Pos:2nd (Prom'd.)

42	Date	Opposition	Res	Attend.	Goalscorers	1	2	3	4	5	6	7	8	9	10	11
1.	28 Aug	Stockport County	5-2	10000	Gill 2 Grimshaw Keenor Evans	*R	*E	*S	*O	*X	*Q	*N	*M	*F	*Y	*K
2.	30	CLAPTON ORIENT	0-0	25000		"	"	*B	"	"	*A	"	"	"	L	"
3.	4 Sep	STOCKPORT COUNTY	3-0	22000	Cashmore 2 Grimshaw	"	"	"	Q	"	O	"	"	"	Y	"
4.	6	Clapton Orient	0-2	12000		"	"	"	"	"	"	"	"	"	"	"
5.	11	BIRMINGHAM CITY	2-1	30000	Gill Cashmore	"	"	S	"	"	"	"	"	"	"	"
6.	18	Birmingham City	1-1	45000	Gill	"	"	B	"	"	"	"	"	"	"	"
7.	25	WEST HAM UNITED	0-0	30000		"	"	"	"	"	"	"	"	"	"	"
8.	2 Oct	West Ham United	1-1	26000	Gill	"	"	"	"	"	"	*C	"	"	L	"
9.	9	Fulham	3-0	30000	Beare Gill West	"	"	"	"	"	"	"	"	"	Y	"
10.	16	FULHAM	3-0	20000	Cashmore 2 Keenor	"	"	"	"	"	"	"	"	"	"	"
11.	23	Notts County	2-1	22000	Cashmore Gill	"	"	"	"	"	"	"	"	"	"	"
12.	30	NOTTS COUNTY	1-1	30000	Gill	"	"	"	"	"	"	"	"	"	"	"
13.	6 Nov	Leicester City	0-2	25000		"	"	"	"	"	"	"	"	"	"	"
14.	13	LEICESTER CITY	2-0	20000	Cashmore Gill	"	"	"	"	"	"	"	"	"	"	"
15.	20	Blackpool	4-2	23000	West Cashmore Gill O.G.(Baker)	"	"	*D	"	"	"	"	"	"	"	"
16.	27	BLACKPOOL	0-0	24000		"	"	"	"	"	"	"	"	"	"	"
17.	4 Dec	The Wednesday	1-0	18000	West	"	"	"	"	"	"	"	"	"	"	"
18.	11	THE WEDNESDAY	1-0	28500	West	"	"	"	"	"	"	"	"	"	"	"
19.	18	BURY	2-1	27500	Gill Cashmore	"	"	"	"	"	"	"	"	"	"	"
20.	25	Coventry City	4-2	22000	Gill 2 Cashmore Beare	"	"	"	"	"	"	"	"	"	"	"
21.	27	COVENTRY CITY	0-1	42000		"	"	"	"	"	"	"	"	"	"	"
22.	1 Jan	Bury	1-3	14000	Cashmore	"	"	"	"	"	"	"	"	"	"	"
23.	15	Bristol City	0-0	33672		"	"	"	"	"	"	"	"	"	B	"
24.	22	BRISTOL CITY	1-0	43000	Barnett	*H	"	"	"	"	"	*Z	*J	"	"	"
25.	5 Feb	STOKE CITY	0-1	27000		"	"	"	*U	"	"	C	"	"	*P	"
26.	12	Barnsley	2-0	16000	Gill Nash	"	"	"	Q	"	"	Z	"	*I	*T	*G
27.	14	Stoke City	0-0	12000		"	"	"	Q	Q	"	"	M	"	G	K
28.	26	Nottm. Forest	2-1	16000	Gill Keenor	"	"	"	U	"	"	C	"	*W	T	G
29.	9 Mar	BARNSLEY	3-2	20000	Gill Beare Pagnam	"	"	B	Q	X	"	C	"	"	"	K
30.	12	Rotherham County	0-2	20000		"	"	D	U	Q	"	N	F	"	"	"
31.	26	PORT VALE	1-2	30000	Grimshaw	"	*Y	"	Q	X	"	*Z	*J	"	"	G
32.	28	LEEDS UNITED	1-0	25000	Pagnam	"	"	"	Q	"	"	C	"	"	B	"
33.	29	Leeds United	2-1	20000	Pagnam Keenor	"	"	"	"	"	"	"	"	"	"	"
34.	2 Apr	Port Vale	0-0	17000		"	"	"	"	"	"	"	"	"	"	"
35.	4	NOTTM. FOREST	3-0	27000	Pagnam Evans,S. Clarke	"	E	"	*U	"	"	Z	"	*I	*T	*G
36.	9	SOUTH SHIELDS	1-0	30000	Gill	"	"	V	Q	"	"	"	M	"	G	K
37.	11	ROTHERHAM COUNTY	1-0	30000	Evans,H.	"	V	D	Q	"	"	"	"	"	T	G
38.	16	South Shields	1-0	17000	Hardy	"	E	"	"	"	"	C	"	*W	"	"
39.	23	HULL CITY	0-0	30000		"	V	"	U	"	"	"	"	"	T	"
40.	30	Hull City	0-2	10000		"	E	"	Q	"	"	N	"	"	Y	K
41.	2 May	WOLVERHAMPTON W.	2-0	40000	Gill Pagnam	"	Y	"	"	"	"	"	"	"	T	G
42.	7	Wolverhampton W.	3-1	20000	Pagnam Nash Gill	"	E	V	Q	"	"	"	"	"	"	G

Players:

- A = Abrams,L.   1/1/0
- B = Barnett,A.   17/4/1
- C = Beare,G.   23/7/4
- D = Blair,J.   24/7/0
- E = Brittan,R.C.   36/7/0
- F = Cashmore,A.   26/7/13
- G = Clarke,J.   13/2/1
- H = Davies,B.   19/7/0
- I = Davies,L.   3/1/1
- J = Evans,H.P.   5/0/1
- K = Evans,J.   30/6/1
- L = Gault,W.   2/0/0
- M = Gill,,J.   37/6/20
- N = Grimshaw,W.   15/2/3
- O = Hardy,W.   42/7/1
- P = Jones,C.   1/1/0
- Q = Keenor,F.   38/7/5
- R = Kneeshaw,J.   23/1/0
- S = Layton,A.   2/0/0
- T = Nash,H.   13/2/2
- U = Newton,W.   5/1/0
- V = Page,J.   8/1/0
- W = Pagnam,F.   14/0/6
- X = Smith,E.E.   40/7/0
- Y = West,W.   21/0/4
- Z = Evans,S.   4/1/1
- a = Sayles,T.   0/1/0
- b = Wilmott,T.   0/1/0
- c = Hopkins,L.   0/1/0

City open League career with 5-2 win at Stockport -- Fred Stewart's former Club !...... Jimmy Blair signed for £3,500, record fee for a full - back.... Fred Pagnam's signing boosts City into 1st Division -- at first attempt......

Other Matches

F.A.Cup

	Date	Opposition	Res	Attend.	Goalscorers	1	2	3	4	5	6	7	8	9	10	11
1st	8 Jan	Sunderland	1-0	35000	Beare	R	E	D	Q	X	O	C	M	F	B	K
2nd	29	Brighton & H.A.	0-0	20260		H	"	"	"	"	"	"	"	"	"	"
2nd Rep.	2 Feb	BRIGHTON & H.A.	1-0	31000	Cashmore	"	"	"	"	"	"	"	"	"	"	"
3rd	19	Southampton	1-0	21360	Gill	"	"	"	"	"	"	N	"	"	C	G
4th	5 Mar	CHELSEA	1-0	45000	Cashmore	"	"	"	"	"	"	C	"	"	B	K
S/Final †	19	Wolverhampton W.	0-0	42000		"	"	"	"	"	"	"	"	"	T	"
S/Final ††	23	Wolverhampton W.	1-3	45000	Keenor (pen)	"	"	"	"	"	"	"	N	"	"	"

Welsh Cup

						1	2	3	4	5	6	7	8	9	10	11
1. †	15 Jan	Pontypridd	1-3	2000	Davies,L	"	Y	a	U	b	A	Z	c	I	P	G

† City fielded Reserve X1 due to fixtures clash.

Friendlies

	Date	Opposition	Res													
††	22 Sep	Bristol City	0-0													

†† J. Nicholson Benefit.

● This Cardiff City team, shown at Birmingham in September 1920, had played against Stockport County at Ninian Park a few weeks earlier shortly after their debut in League football.... BACK (from left): Billy Hardy, Dr. Alex Brownlee (Chairman), Jack Page (reserve), Sid Nicholls (Director), Bert Smith, Fred Stewart (Secretary/Manager), Jack Kneeshaw, Lewis Williams (Director), Charlie Brittan (Captain), Walter Parker (Director), Fred Keenor. FRONT (from left): Billy Grimshaw, Jimmy Gill, Arthur Cashmore, George West, Jack Evans, Albert Barnett.

1921-22

Football League – Division 1.   P:42   W:19   D:10   L:13   61-53   Pts:48   Pos: 4th   Secretary/Manager: Fred Stewart

84	Date	Opposition	Res	Attend.	Goalscorers	1	2	3	4	5	6	7	8	9	10	11
1.	27 Aug	TOTTENHAM HOTSPUR	0-1	50000		T	D	b	S	d	Q	P	O	c	e	L
2.	29	Aston Villa	1-2	30000	Smith	"	"	B	"	"	"	"	G	"	"	"
3.	3 Sep	Tottenham Hotspur	1-4	31771	West	"	"	*W	"	"	"	"	"	"	"	"
4.	5	ASTON VILLA	0-4	40000		I	"	"	"	"	"	"	M	"	G	*E
5.	10	OLDHAM ATHLETIC	0-1	25000		"	"	b	"	"	*A	M	K	J	X	"
6.	17	Oldham Athletic	1-2	17276	Grimshaw	"	"	C	"	"	X	P	"	c	G	L
7.	24	MIDDLESBROUGH	3-1	40000	Gill 2 Nash	"	"	"	K	S	*R	"	O	"	X	"
8.	1 Oct	Middlesbrough	0-0	33000		"	"	"	"	"	Q	"	"	"	e	"
9.	8	BOLTON WANDERERS	1-2	40000	Gill	"	"	"	"	"	"	"	"	"	X	"
10.	15	Bolton Wanderers	2-1	35000	Gill 2	"	"	"	"	"	R	"	"	"	"	"
11.	22	West Bromwich Alb.	2-2	20969	Gill Keenor	"	"	"	"	"	"	"	"	"	*H	"
12.	29	WEST BROMWICH ALB	2-0	35000	Gill 2	*Y	"	"	"	"	"	"	"	"	"	"
13.	5 Nov	MANCHESTER CITY	0-2	38000		"	"	"	"	"	"	"	"	"	"	"
14.	12	Manchester City	1-1	25000	Gill	"	D	"	"	"	"	"	"	"	"	"
15.	19	EVERTON	2-1	35000	Davies,L 2	"	"	"	"	"	"	"	"	J	"	"
16.	26	Everton	1-1	50000	Davies,L	"	"	"	"	d	Q	"	"	"	"	"
17.	3 Dec	SUNDERLAND	2-0	33000	Davies,L Gill	"	"	b	"	"	"	"	"	"	"	"
18.	10	Sunderland	1-4	24000	Gill	"	"	"	"	"	"	"	"	"	"	"
19.	17	HUDDERSFIELD TOWN	0-0	25000		"	"	C	"	"	"	M	"	"	"	"
20.	24	Huddersfield Town	1-0	15000	Grimshaw	"	b	"	"	"	"	P	"	"	"	"
21.	26	Arsenal	0-0	40000		"	"	"	"	"	"	"	"	"	"	"
22.	27	ARSENAL	4-3	41000	Davies,L 2 Gill Grimshaw	"	"	"	"	"	"	"	"	"	"	"
23.	31	Birmingham City	1-0	30000	Davies,L	"	"	"	"	"	"	"	"	"	"	"
24.	2 Jan	Blackburn Rovers	3-1	30000	Davies,L Grimshaw 2	"	"	"	"	"	"	*U	P	Y	X	"
25.	14	BIRMINGHAM CITY	3-1	35000	Clennell 2 Grimshaw	T	"	"	"	"	"	P	S	"	"	L
26.	21	BRADFORD CITY	6-2	20000	Davies,L,3 Gill2 Clennell	"	"	"	Z	"	"	"	O	"	"	"
27.	4 Feb	PRESTON NORTH END	3-0	27000	Gill 2 McDonald	"	D	"	S	"	"	"	"	*V	"	"
28.	8	CHELSEA	2-0	25000	Clennell Gill	"	"	"	"	"	"	"	"	J	"	"
29.	11	Preston North End	1-1	21000	Davies,L	"	"	b	"	"	"	"	"	"	"	"
30.	25	Chelsea	0-1	65000		"	"	"	K	"	"	"	"	"	"	"
31.	11 Mar	Sheffield United	2-0	33000	McDonald Clennell	"	"	C	"	S	"	"	H	Y	X	"
32.	15	Bradford City	0-1	12000		"	"	"	S	d	"	"	"	"	"	"
33.	18	Burnley	1-1	25000	Hardy	"	"	"	K	S	"	M	Q	J	"	F
34.	25	BURNLEY	4-2	35000	Davies,L 2 Evans,J Gill	"	b	"	"	"	d	"	"	"	"	L
35.	1 Apr	Newcastle United	0-0	25000		"	D	b	R	d	Q	P	"	V	"	"
36.	8	NEWCASTLE UNITED	1-0	25000	Davies,L	"	b	C	S	"	"	"	"	J	"	"
37.	15	Liverpool	1-5	50000	Clennell	"	"	b	"	"	"	"	O	"	"	"
38.	17	BLACKBURN ROVERS	1-3	30000	Clennell	"	D	C	K	"	"	"	"	"	"	"
39.	22	LIVERPOOL	2-0	37000	Davies,L Gill	"	b	"	S	d	"	"	"	"	"	"
40.	26	SHEFFIELD UNITED	1-1	15000	Clennell	T	"	"	K	"	"	"	"	"	"	*a
41.	29	Manchester United	1-1	18000	Davies,L	"	"	"	S	"	"	"	"	"	"	"
42.	6 May	MANCHESTER UNITED	3-1	16000	Gill Clennell 2	*N	"	"	K	"	"	"	"	"	"	X

Players:

A = Anderson,J.   1/0/0
B = Barnett,A.   1/0/0
C = Blair,J.   31/9/0
D = Brittan,R.C.   27/4/0
E = Brown,T.   2/0/0
F = Clarke,J.   1/1/0
G = Cashmore,A.   4/0/0
H = Clennell,J.   32/8/13
I = Davies,B   33/9/0
J = Davies,L.   25/10/30
K = Evans,H.   29/6/0
L = Evans,J.   36/8/2
M = Evans,S.   4/1/0
N = Farquharson,T.   1/0/0
O = Gill,J.   34/8/26
P = Grimshaw,W.   38/9/8
Q = Hardy,W.   32/7/1
R = Jenkins,E.   8/0/0
S = Keenor,F.   27/5/3
T = Kneeshaw,J.   8/0/0
U = Latham,G.   1/0/0
V = McDonald,K.   4/0/2
W = Melville,H.   1/0/0
X = Nash,H.   8/4/3
Y = Nelson,J.   2/0/0
Z = Newton,W.   1/0/0
a = Nock,J.   1/0/0
b = Page,J.   22/7/0
c = Pagnam,F.   13/0/0
d = Smith,E.E.   30/9/1
e = West,G.   4/0/1

City fail to win any of first six matches in 1st Division . . . . . Len Davies bursts into scoring action - - nets first Bluebirds hat-trick in League football . . . . Tom Farquharson appears for first time - - in final match of season.

Other Matches

F.A. Cup

	Date	Opposition	Res	Attend.	Goalscorers	1	2	3	4	5	6	7	8	9	10	11
1st	7 Jan	Manchester United	4-2	25000	Davies,L. 2 Nash Clennell	I	b	C	K	d	Q	P	H	J	X	F
2nd	28	Southampton	1-1	19291	Gill	"	"	"	"	"	"	"	O	"	H	L
2nd Rep.	1 Feb	SOUTHAMPTON	2-0	40000	Gill Clennell	"	"	"	"	"	"	"	O	"	"	X
3rd	18	NOTTM. FOREST	4-1	50470	Davies,L. 2 Gill Clennell	"	"	"	"	"	"	"	"	"	"	L
4th	4 Mar	TOTTENHAM HOTSPUR	1-1	51000	Davies,L.	"	"	"	"	"	"	"	"	"	"	"
4th Rep.	9	Tottenham Hotspur	1-2	53626	Gill	"	"	"	"	S	"	"	"	"	"	"

Welsh Cup

						1	2	3	4	5	6	7	8	9	10	11
3rd	10 Jan	NEWPORT COUNTY	7-1	5500	Davies,L. 4 Grimshaw 2 Keenor	T	D	b	"	"	"	"	"	"	X	"
4th	22 Feb	MERTHYR TOWN	5-0	3500	Davies,L. 3 Nash O.G.(Jackson)	J	"	C	"	"	"	M	S	"	"	"
S/Final	10 Apr	Pontypridd	3-0	2000	Keenor Evans,J. Gill	"	"	"	"	"	S	M	O	"	"	"
Final	4 May	Ton Pentre	2-0	2000	Davies,L. Gill	"	"	"	"	"	"	P	"	H	"	"

Friendlies

		Ton Pentre	1-2		Meston
	7 Sep				
	26	Merthyr Town	1-1		Gill
†	31 Oct	Bristol City	2-2		Hardy Davies,L.
‡	30 Nov	Brighton	3-0		Brown Nash Evans,J.
	3 Apr	Heart of Midlothian	0-1		
	1 May	Plymouth Argyle	2-4		Evans, S. Latham

† Keenor Benefit

‡ Ballingham Benefit

CARDIFF CITY 1922 – ENGLISH CUP TEAM.

Top Row, left to right :— H. P. EVANS, SMITH, BEN DAVIES, PAGE, LEN DAVIES, CLARKE. Bottom Row, left to right :— GRIMSHAW, GILL, BLAIR, HARDY, CLENNELL. Insets :— EVANS (J.) (left), BRITTAN (Capt.) (centre), KEENOR (right). [Evening Express Photo.

1922-23

Secretary/Manager: Fred Stewart

Football League – Division 1. P:42 W:18 D:7 L:17 73-59 Pts:43 Pos:9th

126	Date	Opposition	Res	Attend.	Goalscorers	1	2	3	4	5	6	7	8	9	10	11
1.	26 Aug	Tottenham Hotspur	1-1	43168	Gill	E	C	B	P	Y	M	L	K	F	D	H
2.	28	ASTON VILLA	3-0	45000	Clennell 2 O.G.(Smart)	"	W	"	"	"	"	"	"	"	"	"
3.	2 Sep	TOTTENHAM HOTSPUR	2-3	50000	Davies,L 2	"	"	"	"	"	"	"	"	"	T	"
4.	4	Aston Villa	3-1	25000	Nash Grimshaw 2	"	"	"	G	"	Q	"	"	"	T	"
5.	9	ARSENAL	4-1	30000	Davies,L 2 Grimshaw Nash	"	"	"	"	"	"	"	"	"	"	"
6.	16	Arsenal	1-2	40000	Davies,L	"	C	W	P	"	M	"	"	"	D	"
7.	23	EVERTON	0-2	30000		"	W	B	"	"	"	"	"	"	"	"
8.	30	Everton	1-3	50000	Smith	"	"	"	"	"	"	"	"	"	"	"
9.	7 Oct	SUNDERLAND	2-4	31000	Clennell 2	"	"	"	G	"	"	"	P	"	"	"
10.	14	Sunderland	1-2	35000	McDonald	J	C	W	"	P	"	"	D	S	T	"
11.	21	Liverpool	1-3	39000	Clennell (pen)	"	"	"	"	"	"	"	"	F	"	"
12.	28	LIVERPOOL	3-0	32000	Grimshaw McDonald Clennell	"	"	B	"	"	"	"	K	S	D	"
13.	4 Nov	Birmingham City	0-0	26000		"	"	"	"	"	"	"	"	"	"	"
14.	11	BIRMINGHAM CITY	1-1	30000	Gill	"	W	"	"	"	"	"	"	F	"	"
15.	18	Huddersfield	0-1	16500		E	"	"	"	"	"	"	D	"	Y	"
16.	25	HUDDERSFEILD	0-1	27000		"	"	C	"	Y	"	"	G	"	D	"
17.	2 Dec	STOKE CITY	2-1	29000	Gill Clennell	"	"	"	P	P	"	"	K	S	"	"
18.	9	Stoke City	1-3	20000	McDonald	J	"	W	G	"	"	"	"	"	"	"
19.	16	MANCHESTER CITY	3-1	15000	Gill McDonald 2	"	"	"	P	Y	"	*A	"	"	T	"
20.	23	Manchester City	1-5	18000	Reid	"	"	B	"	"	"	"	"	"	*X	"
21.	26	WEST BROMWICH ALB.	3-0	44000	Gill 2 Reid	"	W	"	"	"	"	L	"	X	D	"
22.	27	West Bromwich Albion	0-3	14898		"	"	"	"	"	"	"	"	"	T	"
23.	30	Bolton Wanderers	0-0	32000		"	U	"	"	"	"	"	P	"	D	"
24.	6 Jan	BOLTON WANDERERS	1-0	25000	Reid	"	"	"	"	"	"	"	"	"	"	"
25.	20	Blackburn Rovers	1-3	28000	Nash	E	C	W	"	"	P	"	"	F	T	"
26.	27	BLACKBURN ROVERS	5-0	22000	Davies,L 2 Gill 3	"	U	B	G	"	"	"	"	"	D	"
27.	10 Feb	NEWCASTLE UNITED	5-0	27000	Davies,L 2 Gill 2 Grimshaw	"	"	"	"	"	"	"	"	"	T	"
28.	17	Nottm. Forest	2-3	12000	Davies,L Gill	"	"	"	"	"	M	"	P	"	D	"
29.	28	Newcastle United	1-3	10000	Davies,L	"	"	"	"	P	N	"	"	W	"	"
30.	3 Mar	Chelsea	1-1	35000	Gill	"	"	W	"	Y	P	"	"	F	"	"
31.	10	CHELSEA	6-1	25000	Davies,L 3 Gill 2 Evans,J	J	"	B	"	"	M	"	"	"	T	"
32.	17	MIDDLESBROUGH	2-0	22000	Gill Reid	"	"	W	"	"	"	"	"	X	"	"
33.	24	Middlesbrough	1-0	20000	Gill	"	"	B	P	"	"	"	"	F	"	"
34.	30	Burnley	5-1	20000	Clennell3 Davies,L Keenor	"	"	"	G	"	"	"	P	"	"	"
35.	31	PRESTON NORTH END	1-0	20000	Davies,L	"	"	"	"	"	"	"	"	W	"	"
36.	2 Apr	BURNLEY	2-2	34000	Keenor 2	"	"	"	"	"	"	"	"	F	"	"
37.	7	Preston North End	0-3	15000		"	"	W	"	"	"	"	L	*O	"	*Z
38.	14	SHEFFIELD UNITED	1-0	17000	Clennell	Q	"	*R	"	W	"	"	"	F	"	"
39.	21	Sheffield United	0-0	27000		E	"	P	P	Y	M	"	L	K	F	H
40.	25	NOTTM. FOREST	3-1	16000	Davies,L 2 Clennell	"	W	"	G	"	"	"	K	"	"	"
41.	28	OLDHAM ATHLETIC	2-0	13000	Clennell 2 (1 pen)	J	U	"	P	"	"	"	*a	"	"	"
42.	5 May	Oldham Ahletic	1-3	4051	Davies,L	"	C	"	G	"	"	"	K	"	"	"

Players:

A = Aitken,F. 2/0/0
B = Blair,J. 33/8/0
C = Brittan,R.C. 14/1/0
D = Clennell,J. 35/7/17
E = Davies,B. 20/6/0
F = Davies,L. 27/8/28
G = Evans, H.P. 27/8/1
H = Evans,J. 41/9/3
I = Evans,S. 1/2/1
J = Farquharson,T. 21/3/0
K = Gill,J. 31/8/25
L = Grimshaw,W. 40/7/7
M = Hardy,W. 35/3/0
N = Jenkins,E. 1/1/0
O = Jones,V. 1/0/0
P = Keenor,F. 37/8/5
Q = Kneeshaw,J. 1/0/0
R = Mason,F. 1/0/0
S = McDonald,K. 7/1/5
T = Nash,H. 8/0/3
U = Nelson,J. 17/7/0
V = Nock,J. 1/1/1
W = Page,J. 22/2/0
X = Reid,E. 7/1/7
Y = Smith,E.E. 32/8/1
Z = Taylor,W. 1/0/0
a = Turnbull,W. 1/0/0

City score consistantly all season - - Davies, Gill and Clennell net regularly . . . . 6-1 home win over Chelsea - - record victory for Bluebirds . . . . 6 reserves due to International call-up in 1st Division match v. Sheffield Utd. - - City win 1-0 !

Other Matches

F.A. Cup

	Date	Opposition	Res	Attend.	Goalscorers	1	2	3	4	5	6	7	8	9	10	11
1st	13 Jan	WATFORD	1-1	34000	Evans,J. (pen)	J	W	B	P	Y	M	L	K	S	D	H
1st Rep.	17	Watford	2-2	12727	Davies,L. Clennell	E	C	"	G	"	"	"	"	F	"	"
1st Rep. †	22	Watford	2-1	15000	Davies,L. Evans,H.	"	U	"	"	"	P	"	"	"	"	"
2nd	3 Feb	Leicester City	1-0	35690	Davies,L.	"	"	"	"	"	"	"	"	"	"	"
3rd	24	Tottenham Hotspur	2-3	54000	Evans,J. (pen) Gill	"	"	"	"	N	"	"	"	"	"	"

† Played at Villa Park

Welsh Cup

	Date	Opposition	Res	Attend.	Goalscorers	1	2	3	4	5	6	7	8	9	10	11
4th	7 Feb	RHYMNEY	7-0	3000	Gill 3 Davies,L. Nock Keenor Evans,S.	"	"	"	"	"	"	"	"	"	"	"
5th	14 Mar	OSWESTRY	10-0	3000	Davies,L.3 Gill 3 Reid 3 Keenor	"	"	W	"	Y	"	I	"	X	V	"
S/final	11 Apr	Swansea Town	3-2	12000	Clennell 2 Davies,L.	J	"	"	"	"	M	L	P	"	F	"
Final	3 May	Aberdare Athletic	3-2	8000	Grimshaw Gill Davies,L.	"	"	"	"	"	P	"	K	"	D	"

Friendlies

	Date	Opposition	Res	Goalscorers
††	2 Oct	Newcastle United	4-0	McDonald 2 Keenor Grimshaw
‡‡	9	Rest of South Wales	1-1	Turnbull
	16	Chesterfield	3-3	McDonald 2 Brittan
‡	1 May	CITY Internationals v. THE REST	2-1	
	10	Montgomery X1	6-2	Davies,L.2 Jones,J.3 Gill

†† Wigan Disaster Fund   ‡ Barnett Benefit Match   ‡‡ Played at Swansea

● This was Cardiff city's Line-up at Aston Villa on September 4th, 1922 in a season which saw six of the Club's players in action for three Home Counties on the same day ..... BACK (from left): Jack Nock (reserve), Jack Page, Ben Davies, Bert Smith, Fred Stewart (Secretary/Manager), Billy Turnbull (reserve), Joe Clennell (reserve). SEATED (from left): Billy Grimshaw, Jimmy Gill, Len Davies, Jimmy Blair (Captain), Harry Nash, Jack Evans. ON GROUND (from left): Fred Keenor, Herbie Evans.

1923-24

Secretary/Manager: Fred Stewart

Football League – Division 1.   P:42   W:22   D:13   L:7   61-34   Pts:57   Pos:2nd

168	Date	Opposition	Res	Attend.	Goalscorers	1	2	3	4	5	6	7	8	9	10	11
1	25 Aug	BOLTON WANDERERS	3-2	30000	Gill 2 Clennell	I	T	B	P	V	M	K	J	E	C	H
2	27	SUNDERLAND	2-1	26000	Gill Evans,J.(pen)	"	"	"	G	P	"	"	"	"	"	"
3	1 Sep	Bolton Wanderers	2-2	31000	Davies Hardy	"	"	"	"	"	"	"	"	"	"	"
4	5	Sunderland	3-0	24000	Gill Davies Clennell	"	"	"	"	"	"	"	"	"	"	"
5	8	West Ham United	0-0	20000		"	"	"	"	"	"	"	"	"	"	"
6	15	WEST HAM UNITED	1-0	35000	Davies	"	"	"	"	"	"	"	"	"	"	"
7	22	Newcastle United	1-1	37000	Davies	"	"	"	"	"	"	"	"	"	"	"
8	29	NEWCASTLE UNITED	1-0	45000	Davies	"	"	"	"	"	"	"	"	"	"	"
9	6 Oct	Chelsea	2-1	40000	Gill Clennell	"	"	"	"	"	"	"	"	"	"	"
10	13	CHELSEA	1-1	42000	Davies	"	"	"	"	"	"	"	"	"	"	"
11	20	PRESTON NORTH END	1-1	37000	Davies	Q	"	"	"	"	"	"	"	"	"	"
12	27	Preston North End	1-3	23000	Davies	I	"	"	"	"	"	"	"	"	"	"
13	3 Nov	WEST BROM. ALBION	3-0	20601	Gill 2 Evans.H.	"	"	"	"	"	"	"	"	"	"	"
14	10	West Brom. Albion	4-2	15143	Davies 4	"	"	"	"	"	"	"	"	"	"	"
15	17	Manchester City	1-1	25000	Grimshaw	"	"	"	"	V	P	"	"	"	"	"
16	24	MANCHESTER CITY	1-1	22000	Davies	"	"	"	"	"	"	*R	"	"	"	"
17	1 Dec	Nottm. Forest	1-0	15000	Evans,J.	"	"	"	"	P	M	"	"	"	"	"
18	8	NOTTM. FOREST	4-1	29000	Gill 2 Clennell Davies	"	"	"	"	"	"	"	"	"	"	W
19	15	Liverpool	2-0	32000	Clennell Gill	"	"	"	"	"	"	"	"	"	"	H
20	22	LIVERPOOL	2-0	25000	Davies 2	"	"	"	"	"	"	"	"	"	"	"
21	25	Sheffield United	1-1	45000	Hardy	"	"	U	*X	N	"	"	L	O	"	"
22	26	SHEFFIELD UNITED	3-1	50000	Davies 2 Keenor	Q	"	B	G	P	"	"	J	E	"	W
23	29	Aston Villa	1-2	54775	Davies	"	"	"	X	"	Y	*D	"	L	"	"
24	1 Jan	Middlesbrough	1-0	35000	Clennell	"	"	"	"	"	M	"	*Q	"	C	"
25	5	ASTON VILLA	0-2	40000		"	"	"	"	"	"	"	J	"	"	"
26	19	Arsenal	2-1	35000	Davies Clennell	"	"	U	"	"	"	"	"	"	"	H
27	26	ARSENAL	4-0	20000	Gill 3 Davies	"	"	"	"	"	"	"	"	"	"	"
28	9 Feb	BLACKBURN ROVERS	2-0	21000	Gill Hardy	"	"	B	"	"	"	R	"	O	"	"
29	16	Tottenham Hotspur	1-1	32478	Hagan	"	"	U	"	N	"	"	J	E	"	"
30	1 Mar	Huddersfield Town	0-2	21000		Q	"	B	G	P	"	"	J	"	"	"
31	15	NOTTS. COUNTY	0-2	24000		"	"	"	X	N	"	"	L	O	"	"
32	20	Blackburn Rovers	1-2	10000	Clennell	I	"	"	G	P	"	"	J	"	"	"
33	22	Notts. County	0-1	20000		"	"	"	X	"	"	"	"	"	"	"
34	29	EVERTON	0-0	21000		"	"	"	"	"	"	R	L	E	L	"
35	5 Apr	Everton	0-0	40000		"	"	"	"	"	"	"	"	"	C	"
36	7	TOTTENHAM HOTSPUR	2-1	25000	Jones Clennell	"	"	U	"	"	"	J	O	"	"	"
37	12	BURNLEY	2-0	10000	Evans, J. Davies	"	"	"	"	"	"	"	"	"	"	"
38	14	HUDDERSFIELD TOWN	0-0	30000		"	"	"	"	"	"	"	"	"	"	"
39	19	Burnley	2-1	15000	Gill Davies	"	"	B	"	"	"	E	J	E	"	"
40	21	MIDDLESBROUGH	1-0	30000	Clennell	"	"	"	"	"	"	"	"	"	"	"
41	26	BIRMINGHAM CITY	2-0	18000	Jones Clennell	"	"	"	"	"	"	"	J	O	"	"
42	3 May	Birmingham City	0-0	49000		"	"	"	"	"	"	"	"	"	"	"

Players:

- A = Barnett,A.   0/1/0
- B = Blair,J.   36/9/0
- C = Clennell,J.   40/9/14
- D = Collins,E.   2/3/0
- E = Davies,L.   38/9/24
- G = Evans H.P.   29/8/1
- H = Evans,J.   38/10/3
- I = Farquharson,T.   39/12/0
- J = Gill,J.   39/8/19
- K = Grimshaw,W.   15/0/1
- L = Hagan,A.   5/5/1
- M = Hardy,W.   39/11/4
- N = Jenkins,E.   3/2/0
- O = Jones,J.   12/3/3
- P = Keenor,F.   39/10/1
- Q = Kneeshaw,J.   3/0/0
- R = Lawson,D   18/8/0
- S = Lewis,E.   0/1/0
- T = Nelson,J.   42/11/0
- U = Page,J.   6/4/0
- V = Smith,E.E.   4/0/0
- W = Taylor,W.   4/2/0
- X = Wake,H.   12/1/0
- Y = Nock,J.   0/1/0

City miss Championship by narrowest margin - - Davies misses late penalty in last match, at Birmingham . . . . Davies first City player to score four goals in League match. . . One point from 5 matches in March proves costly !

Other Matches

F.A.Cup

	Date	Opposition	Res	Attend	Goalscorers	1	2	3	4	5	6	7	8	9	10	11
1st	12 Jan	GILLINGHAM	0-0	20000		I	T	B	G	O	M	R	J	E	C	H
1st Rep	16	Gillingham	2-0	17000	Gill Davies	"	"	"	"	"	"	"	"	"	"	"
2	2 Feb	ARSENAL	1-0	35000	Gill	"	"	U	"	"	"	"	"	"	"	"
3rd	23	BRISTOL CITY	3-0	50000	Gill 2 Clennell	"	"	B	"	"	"	"	"	"	"	"
4th	8 Mar	Manchester City	0-0	76166		"	"	"	"	"	"	"	"	"	"	"
4th Rep *	12	MANCHESTER CITY	0-1	50000		"	"	"	"	"	"	"	"	"	"	"

Welsh Cup

	Date	Opposition	Res	Attend	Goalscorers	1	2	3	4	5	6	7	8	9	10	11
4th	14 Feb	Shrewsbury Town	0-0	4000		"	"	"	"	"	"	"	"	"	"	"
4th Rep	27	SHREWSBURY TOWN	3-0	3500	Clennell 2 Hardy	"	"	"	"	"	"	"	L	"	"	"
5th	17 Mar	Newport County	1-1	5500	Jones	"	U	A	X	N	S	D	"	O	Y	"
5th Rep	24	NEWPORT COUNTY	0-0	5000		"	"	B	S	P	M	"	T	"	L	"
5th 2/Rep	31	Newport County	0-0	4000		"	T	"	"	"	"	"	Q	E	"	W
5th 3/Rep	10 Apr	Newport County	0-3	2000		"	"	"	N	"	"	J	L	O	C	"

Friendlies

	Date	Opposition	Res	Goalscorers
	2 Oct	Pontypridd	1-2	Davies
	29	Newport County	1-3	Nock
	21 Nov	Llandudno	7-0	Davies 3 Gill 2 Clennell Hardy(pen)
Tour	7 May	Sparta Prague	2-3	Jones Davies
"	8	Sparta Prague	3-2	Davies 2 Beadles
"	11	First Vienna	2-0	Nock Evans,J.
"	14	Borussia	2-0	Nock Nicholls
"	18	S.V. Hamburg	2-2	Nock Jones

(Standing) Page, Evans, Jones, Farquharson, Hardy, Blair, Davies, Wake.
(Front) Beadles, Nelson, Keenor, Nichols.

1924-25

Football League – Division 1. Secretary/Manager: Fred Stewart

P:42 W:16 D:11 L:15 56-51 Pts:43 Pos:11th

#	Date	Opposition	Res	Attend.	Goalscorers	1	2	3	4	5	6	7	8	9	10	11
1.	30 Aug	Burnley	0-0	20000		H	Q	B	W	M	K	N	I	E	C	G
2.	1 Sep	SHEFFIELD	1-1	25000	Davies,L	"	"	"	"	"	"	"	"	"	"	"
3.	6	LEDDS UNITED	3-0	30000	Davies,L 2 Lawson	"	"	"	*S	"	"	"	"	"	"	"
4.	8	Sheffield United	0-1	35000		"	"	"	"	"	"	"	"	"	"	"
5.	13	Birmingham City	1-2	28000	Gill	"	"	"	"	"	"	"	"	"	"	*F
6.	15	Preston North End	3-1	15000	Davies,L Gill Clennell	"	T	"	"	"	"	"	"	*P	"	"
7.	20	WEST BROM. ALBION	0-1	20000		"	"	"	"	"	"	F	"	"	*A	G
8.	27	Tottenham Hotspur	1-1	38324	McIlvenny	"	Q	"	"	"	"	"	"	"	C	"
9.	4 Oct	BOLTON WANDERERS	1-2	30000	Davies,W	"	"	"	W	S	"	"	"	"	"	"
10.	11	Notts. County	0-3	15000		"	"	"	S	M	"	"	"	"	"	"
11.	18	EVERTON	2-1	20000	Davies,L 2	"	"	"	"	"	"	"	A	E	"	"
12.	25	Newcastle United	2-1	28000	Davies,L 2	"	"	T	"	"	"	"	*R	"	A	"
13.	8 Nov	Nottingham Forest	1-2	10000	Beadles	"	"	"	"	"	"	"	"	"	"	"
14.	15	BURY	4-1	18000	Davies,L 3 Beadles	"	"	B	W	"	S	N	"	"	"	"
15.	22	Manchester City	2-2	33000	Davies,L Beadles	"	"	"	"	"	"	"	F	"	"	"
16.	29	ARSENAL	1-1	22000	Beadles	"	"	"	"	"	K	"	"	"	"	"
17.	6 Dec	Aston Villa	2-1	40000	Davies,L 2	"	"	"	"	"	"	"	"	"	"	"
18.	13	HUDDERSFIELD TOWN	2-2	25000	Davies,L Beadles	"	"	"	"	"	S	"	"	"	"	"
19.	15	LIVERPOOL	1-3	17000	Gill	"	"	"	"	"	"	"	I	"	"	V
20.	20	Blackburn Rovers	1-3	25000	Beadles	"	"	K	"	"	"	"	F	"	"	G
21.	25	West Ham United	2-3	20000	Davies,L Gill	"	"	B	"	"	"	F	I	"	"	"
22.	26	WEST HAM UNITED	2-1	30000	Davies,L Beadles	"	"	"	"	"	"	F	"	"	"	"
23.	1 Jan	Sunderland	0-1	18000		*L	"	"	"	"	"	N	"	"	"	"
24.	3	Leeds United	0-0	19000		"	"	K	"	"	"	F	"	"	"	"
25.	17	BIRMINGHAM CITY	1-0	16000	Davies,L	H	"	B	"	*U	"	N	F	S	"	"
26.	24	West Brom. Albion	0-1	22508		"	Q	"	"	M	K	"	I	"	A	F
27.	7 Feb	Bolton Wanderers	0-3	20000		"	T	"	"	U	"	F	"	"	P	G
28.	11	BURNLEY	4-0	7000	Davies,L 2 Gill Nelson	L	Q	"	"	M	"	"	"	"	A	F
29.	14	NOTTS. COUNTY	1-1	21000	Nicholson	"	"	"	"	"	"	N	"	E	F	G
30.	25	Everton	2-1	13000	Beadles Davies,W	"	"	"	*O	"	"	F	"	S	A	"
31.	28	NEWCASTLE UNITED	3-0	25000	Nicholson 2 McIlvenny	"	T	W	"	"	"	"	I	"	"	"
32.	14 Mar	NOTTINGHAM FOREST	2-0	25000	Nelson (pen) Gill	"	"	B	"	"	"	F	"	S	"	"
33.	18	TOTTENHAM HOTSPUR	0-2	31126		"	"	"	"	"	"	"	"	"	"	"
34.	21	Bury	1-4	22000	Nicholson	"	"	"	"	"	"	E	F	"	J	F
35.	1 Apr	MANCHESTER CITY	0-2	25000		L	"	"	"	U	"	N	I	S	A	"
36.	4	Arsenal	1-1	20000	Beadles	"	"	"	"	"	"	F	"	"	"	"
37.	11	ASTON VILLA	2-1	18000	Nicholson Gill	H	"	"	"	"	"	F	I	S	"	N
38.	13	SUNDERLAND	2-0	25000	Hagan Davies,W	"	"	"	"	"	"	E	"	"	"	"
39.	15	BLACKBURN ROVERS	3-0	12000	Gill Davies,W Nicholson	"	"	"	"	U	"	N	I	"	J	F
40.	18	Huddlefield Town	0-0	15500		"	"	"	"	"	"	D	"	"	"	N
41.	29	Liverpool	2-1	20000	Beadles Gill	"	"	"	"	S	"	N	"	E	A	G
42.	2 May	PRESTON NORTH END	0-0	17000		"	"	"	M	"	"	"	"	"	"	"

Players:

- A = Beadles,H.   26/9/12
- B = Blair,J.   37/7/0
- C = Clennell,J.   12/0/1
- D = Collins,E.   1/0/0
- E = Davies,L.   30/5/22
- F = Davies,W.   31/7/6
- G = Evans,J.   33/7/0
- H = Farquharson,T.   37/9/0
- I = Gill,J.   32/6/11
- J = Hagan,A.   3/0/1
- K = Hardy,W.   35/8/0
- L = Hills,J.   5/0/0
- M = Keenor,F.   37/8/0
- N = Lawson,D.   26/6/1
- O = Lewis,J.   1/0/0
- P = McIlvenny,P.   5/0/2
- Q = Nelson,J.   37/9/2
- R = Nicholls,J.   2/0/0
- S = Nicholson,J.   28/6/8
- T = Page,J.   9/1/0
- U = Sloan,T.   4/1/0
- V = Taylor,W.   1/0/0
- W = Wake,H.   31/9/0
- X = Whitcombe,E.   0/1/0

Although only a mid-table team, City appear in F.A.Cup Final - - beaten by Sheffield Utd. when Fred Tunstall punishes Harry Wake for moment of fatal hesitancy!

Other Matches

F.A. Cup

	Date	Opposition	Res	Attend.	Goalscorers	1	2	3	4	5	6	7	8	9	10	11
1st	10 Jan	DARLINGTON	0-0	21150		H	Q	K	W	M	S	N	I	E	A	G
1st Rep	14	Darlington	0-0*	18808		"	"	"	"	"	"	"	"	"	"	"
1st 2/Rep†		Darlington	2-0	22465	Davies,L. Davies,W.	"	"	B	"	"	K	"	F	"	"	"
2nd	31	FULHAM	1-0	20000	Davies,L.	"	"	"	"	"	"	"	I	"	"	"
3rd	21 Feb	Notts. County	2-0	39000	Nicholson Gill	"	"	"	"	"	"	F	"	"	"	"
4th	7 Mar	LEICESTER CITY	2-1	50272	Beadles Davies,W.	"	"	"	"	"	"	N	"	S	"	F
S/Final ††	28	Blackburn Rovers	3-1	20000	Nicholson Gill Beadles	"	"	"	"	"	"	F	"	"	"	G
Final ‡	25 Apr	Sheffield United	0-1	91763		"	"	"	"	"	"	"	"	"	"	"

† At Anfield †† At Meadow Lane ‡ At Wembley Stadium

Welsh Cup

	Date	Opposition	Res	Attend.	Goalscorers	1	2	3	4	5	6	7	8	9	10	11
5th	2 Mar	Swansea Town	0-4	15000		"	"	T	"	"	X	"	U	N	"	"

Friendlies

	Date	Opposition	Res	Goalscorers
(Tour)	6 May	Distillery	3-0	Davies,L. 2 Gill
(Tour)	7	Portadown	2-2	Beadles McIlvenny
(Tour)	9	Dublin City		
(Tour)	11	Newtown	2-2	Keenor Beadles

25th April 1925. F.A. Cup Final versus Sheffield United. The Duke of York (later King George VI) accompanied by Sir Charles Clegg shakes hands with J.Evans before kick-off.

(Standing) G. Latham (Trainer), F. Keenor, J.Nelson, J. Hills, J. Nicholson, J. Evans, H. Wake. (Seated) W. Davies, J. Gill, J. Blair, H. Beadles, W. Hardy.

1925-26

Football League – Division 1. Secretary/Manager: Fred Stewart

P:42 W:16 D:7 L:19 61-76 Pts:39 Pos:16th

#	Date	Opposition	Res	Attend.	Goalscorers	1	2	3	4	5	6	7	8	9	10	11
1.	29 Aug	Manchester City	2-3	42000	Beadles, Gill	I	S	B	Z	P	M	Q	K	E	A	F
2.	31	West Ham United	1-3	20000	Nicholson	"	"	"	"	"	"	"	"	"	T	"
3.	5 Sep	EVERTON	2-1	13914	Gill, Beadles	"	"	"	"	"	"	"	"	"	A	"
4.	7	WEST HAM UNITED	0-1	20000		"	"	*a	"	"	"	"	"	"	A	"
5.	12	Huddersfield Town	1-1	19033	Davies,W.	"	"	B	"	"	"	"	"	"	F	H
6.	14	Tottenham Hotspur	2-1	26716	Lawson, Davies,W.	N	"	"	"	"	"	"	"	"	"	"
7.	21	TOTTENHAM HOTSPUR	0-1	20698		"	U	"	"	"	"	"	"	"	"	"
8.	23	SUNDERLAND	0-1	27000		"	"	"	"	"	"	"	"	T	"	"
9.	26	Blackburn Rovers	3-6	18042	Nicholson 2, Beadles	I	"	"	"	"	W	"	"	"	A	F
10.	3 Oct	BURY	3-2	25000	Nicholson, Davies,L. Beadles	"	M	"	*O	*V	"	"	"	"	"	"
11.	10	Birmingham City	2-3	30000	Davies,W. Keenor	"	"	"	Z	P	"	F	E	P	K	"
12.	17	Arsenal	0-5	40000		"	U	a	N	"	M	Q	K	T	A	E
13.	24	MANCHESTER UNITED	0-2	15846		"	S	"	T	"	V	"	L	E	*C	H
14.	31	Aston Villa	2-0	36000	Nicholson, Smith,S.	"	"	"	M	W	"	"	*Y	T	"	E
15.	7 Nov	LEICESTER CITY	5-2	30000	Cassidy 3, Davies,W. Ferguson	"	"	"	"	"	"	F	E	*J	"	*R
16.	14	Leeds United	0-1	19360		"	"	"	T	"	"	"	"	"	"	"
17.	21	NEWCASTLE UNITED	0-0	35000		N	"	"	"	"	"	"	"	"	"	"
18.	28	Bolton Wanderers	1-0	20000	Ferguson	I	"	"	"	"	M	"	"	"	"	"
19.	5 Dec	NOTTS. COUNTY	2-1	22000	Ferguson 2	"	"	"	"	"	"	"	"	"	"	"
20.	12	Liverpool	2-0	30000	Davies,L. Ferguson	"	"	"	"	P	"	D	Y	"	"	"
21.	19	BURNLEY	2-3	17678	Ferguson, Davies,L.	"	"	"	"	"	W	F	E	"	"	"
22.	25	WEST BROM. ALBION	3-2	15225	Ferguson 2, Davies,W.	"	"	"	"	"	T	"	"	"	"	"
23.	26	West Brom. Albion	0-3	31554		"	"	B	O	W	M	"	"	"	"	"
24.	1 Jan	Sheffield United	2-11	30000	Davies,L. Davies,W.	"	"	a	P	"	"	"	"	"	*X	"
25.	2	MANCHESTER CITY	2-2	12000	Cassidy 2	"	"	"	"	"	"	Q	"	"	C	F
26.	16	Everton	1-1	26553	Nicholson	N	a	B	"	"	V	"	F	"	X	"
27.	23	HUDDERSFIELD TOWN	1-2	13049	Ferguson	"	"	"	"	"	M	"	"	"	"	"
28.	6 Feb	BLACKBURN ROVERS	4-1	16484	McLachlan 2, Davies,L. Cassidy	"	"	"	G	"	"	"	"	"	"	"
29.	13	Bury	1-4	20000	Ferguson	"	S	a	"	"	"	"	E	"	"	"
30.	20	BIRMINGHAM CITY	2-0	18000	Davies,L. Ferguson	I	"	"	"	P	"	"	Y	"	"	"
31.	27	ARSENAL	0-0	21000		"	"	B	O	"	W	"	E	"	"	"
32.	13 Mar	ASTON VILLA	2-0	25000	Ferguson 2	"	"	a	P	W	M	"	"	"	"	"
33.	20	Leicester City	2-1	23000	Davies,W. 2	"	"	"	"	"	"	"	"	"	"	"
34.	27	LEEDS UNITED	0-0	18300		"	"	"	"	"	Q	"	"	C	"
35.	31	Sunderland	3-1	5000	Davies,W. Davies,L. Ferguson	"	"	"	"	"	"	"	"	X	"
36.	3 Apr	Newcastle United	1-0	18000	Ferguson	"	"	"	Z	"	"	"	"	"	"	"
37.	5	SHEFFIELD UNITED	0-1	30000		N	a	B	"	"	"	"	"	"	C	H
38.	10	BOLTON WANDERERS	0-1	20000		I	"	"	P	W	"	"	"	"	"	"
39.	17	Notts. County	4-2	12000	Ferguson 3, Keenor	"	S	a	Z	P	"	D	S	T	X	F
40.	24	LIVERPOOL	2-2	18000	Ferguson, Hardy	"	"	"	P	W	"	"	E	J	"	"
41.	28	Manchester United	0-1	9116		"	"	"	C	"	"	"	"	"	"	"
42.	1 May	Burnley	1-4	16381	Davies,L.	"	"	"	Z	"	"	"	C	E	"	"

Players:

A = Beadles,H. 6/0/4
B = Blair,J. 16/2/0
C = Cassidy,J. 24/4/7
D = Collins,E. 6/0/0
E = Davies,L. 37/1/0
F = Davies,W. 36/3/9
G = Evans,H. 3/10/0
H = Evans,J. 7/0/0
I = Farquharson,T. 33/1/0
J = Ferguson,H. 26/3/21
K = Gill,J. 11/0/2
L = Hagan,A. 1/0/0
M = Hardy,W. 37/2/1
N = Hills,J. 9/3/0
O = Jennings,J. 2/0/0
P = Keenor,F. 25/0/2
Q = Lawson,D. 20/3/1
R = McLachlan,G. 19/4/2
S = Nelson,J. 34/4/0
T = Nicholson,J. 18/4/6
U = Page,J. 3/0/0
V = Reed,E. 6/1/0
W = Sloan,T. 28/3/0
X = Potter–Smith,T. 8/0/1
Y = Smith,S. 2/1/0
Z = Wake,H. 15/1/0
a = Watson,T. 30/3/0
b = McCracken,W. 0/1/0

Nelson becomes first City player to be sent off in League match – – on first day of season … Over £7,000 paid for Ferguson from Motherwell, and McLachlan from Clyde…. Depression affects attendances … City crushed 2-11 (record defeat) at Sheffield Utd. on New Year's Day… Jack Evans plays last game for City.

Other Matches

F.A.Cup

	Date	Opposition	Res	Attend.	Goalscorers	1	2	3	4	5	6	7	8	9	10	11
3rd	9 Jan	BURNLEY	2-2	30000	Cassidy Davies,L	N	S	a	T	W	M	F	E	J	C	R
3rd Rep	13	Burnley	2-0	26811	Ferguson 2	"	"	"	"	"	B	Q	F	"	"	"
4th	30	NEWCASTLE UNITED	0-2	42000		"	"	"	"	"	M	"	Y	"	"	"

Welsh Cup

						1	2	3	4	5	6	7	8	9	10	11
5th	3 Mar	Merthyr Town	1-2	4000	o.g. (Ferrans)	"	"	B	Z	Y	T	"	F	b	C	R

Friendlies

	30 Sep	Bristol City	1-2	3328	Nicholson
	28 Dec	CRUSADERS	2-2		McCracken Evans
	26 Apr	Abercynon United			
		Kenfig Hill	4-1		

All the players who appeared in the 1925 Cup Final team appeared frequently for the City during the 1925/26 season.

1926-27

Football League – Division 1.

Secretary/Manager: Fred Stewart

P:42 W:16 D:9 L:17 55-65 Pts:41 Pos:14th

294	Date	Opposition	Res	Attend.	Goalscorers	1	2	3	4	5	6	7	8	9	10	11
1.	28 Aug	Burnley	3-4	20000	Ferguson 2 Davies,L	H	K	Z	Y	N	*B	G	F	L	V	P
2.	30	Leeds United	0-0	14242		"	"	"	*L	"	"	"	"	"	"	"
3.	4 Sep	WEST BROM. ALBION	1-1	18000	Davies,L	"	"	"	"	"	"	"	"	"	"	"
4.	6	LEEDS UNITED	3-1	13653	Ferguson2 Smith,P Davies,W	"	"	"	"	"	"	"	"	"	"	"
5.	11	ASTON VILLA	2-3	8000	Ferguson 2 (1 pen)	"	Q	K	"	"	"	"	"	"	"	"
6.	18	Bolton Wanderers	0-2	20000		"	"	"	"	"	"	"	"	"	"	"
7.	20	NEWCASTLE UNITED	1-1	15000	Smith,P.	"	"	"	"	"	"	"	"	"	"	"
8.	25	MANCHESTER UNITED	0-2	17267		"	"	"	*A	T	"	"	*R	"	*E	F
9.	2 Oct	Derby County	3-6	21508	Ferguson Davies,L Curtis	"	"	Z	L	N	K	"	F	"	"	P
10.	9	SHEFFIELD UNITED	3-0	13000	Ferguson Irving Davies,W.	"	"	"	"	"	"	"	"	"	"	"
11.	16	Huddersfield Town	0-0	17000		"	"	"	"	"	"	"	"	"	"	"
12.	23	SUNDERLAND	3-0	12000	Ferguson 2 Curtis	"	"	"	"	"	"	"	A	"	"	"
13.	30	Bury	3-2	180005	Ferguson McLachlan 2	"	"	"	K	T	B	D	F	"	"	"
14.	6 Nov	BIRMINGHAM CITY	1-0	15000	McLachlan	"	"	"	"	N	"	G	"	"	"	"
15.	13	Tottenham Hotspur	1-4	15350	Curtis	"	"	"	"	"	"	"	"	"	"	"
16.	20	WEST HAM UNITED	1-2	8000	Davies,W.	"	"	"	Y	"	K	"	"	"	"	"
17.	29	Sheffield Wednesday	0-3	16986		"	"	"	B	"	"	A	"	"	"	"
18.	4 Dec	LEICESTER CITY	0-1	15000		"	"	"	A	"	B	D	"	"	"	"
19.	11	Everton	1-0	27181	Ferguson	"	"	"	N	T	K	"	U	"	F	"
20.	18	BLACKBURN ROVERS	0-1	12254		"	"	"	L	N	"	*O	"	"	"	"
21.	25	Newcastle United	0-5	40000		"	"	"	N	T	"	"	*C	"	"	"
22.	27	ARSENAL	2-0	25000	Ferguson Curtis	"	"	"	L	"	"	I	Y	F	E	*S
23.	1 Jan	Arsenal	2-3	40000	Curtis Davies,L	*J	"	"	"	"	"	"	"	"	"	"
24.	15	BURNLEY	0-0	14647		H	"	"	N	"	"	"	"	"	"	"
25.	31	Aston Villa	0-0	10000		"	"	"	L	"	"	"	Y	"	"	P
26.	5 Feb	BOLTON WANDERERS	1-0	10000	Davies,L	"	"	"	N	"	"	"	L	"	"	"
27.	12	Manchester United	1-1	26213	Ferguson	"	"	"	Y	"	"	*X	"	I	"	"
28.	21	West Brom. Albion	2-0	10068	Davies,L. McLachlan	"	"	"	N	"	B	I	"	F	"	"
29.	26	Sheffield United	1-3	28000	Davies,L	"	"	"	Y	"	"	X	F	I	"	"
30.	12 Mar	Sunderland	2-2	15000	Irving 2	"	"	"	N	T	"	*W	"	"	F	"
31.	16	DERBY COUNTY	2-0	8000	Ferguson 2	"	"	M	"	"	"	"	"	"	"	"
32.	19	BURY	2-1	13000	Ferguson McLachlan	"	"	"	"	"	"	"	"	"	"	"
33.	21	HUDDERSFIELD TOWN	2-0	15000	Ferguson 2	"	"	Z	"	"	"	"	"	F	"	"
34.	2 Apr	TOTTENHAM HOTSPUR	1-2	13384	o.g. (Skitt)	"	"	"	"	"	"	"	"	"	"	"
35.	7	Leicester City	1-3	12000	Ferguson	"	"	"	Y	"	"	"	Y	I	"	"
36.	9	West Ham United	2-2	18000	Ferguson Wake	"	"	M	B	R	"	"	F	"	E	"
37.	15	Liverpool	0-5	35037		J	"	Z	N	T	"	"	L	C	"	"
38.	16	SHEFFIELD	3-2	13426	Ferguson 2 Wake	H	"	"	B	"	B	"	Y	I	"	"
39.	18	LIVERPOOL	2-0	15000	Ferguson Irving	"	"	"	R	R	K	E	L	"	F	"
40.	27	Birmingham City	2-1	35000	Ferguson 2	"	"	"	N	"	"	W	"	"	"	"
41.	30	EVERTON	1-0	18341	Keenor	"	"	"	B	T	"	"	Q	N	E	"
42.	7 May	Blackburn Rovers	0-1	11000		"	"	"	N	R	"	"	L	O	"	"

Players:

A = Baillie,J.   4/0/0
B = Blackburn,G   18/3/0
C = Castle,F.   2/1/2
D = Collins,E.   4/0/0
E = Curtis,E.   26/10/7
F = Davies,L.   34/12/17
G = Davies,W.   15/0/3
H = Farquharson,T.   40/11/0
I = Ferguson,H.   39/8/31
J = Hampson,T.   2/1/0
K = Hardy,W.   40/10/0
L = Irving,S.   26/12/5
M = Jennings,J.   5/0/0
N = Keenor,F.   33/9/1
O = Matson,F.   3/0/0
P = McLachlan,G.   38/11/7
Q = Nelson,J.   38/12/0
R = Pirie,T.   5/2/0
S = Richards,P.   3/1/0
T = Sloan,T.   20/11/0
U = Smith,S.   2/0/0
V = Potter–Smith,T.   8/0/2
W = Thirlaway,W.   12/0/0
X = Tysoe,F.   2/0/0
Y = Wake,H.   10/4/3
Z = Watson,T.   33/12/0

City's greatest triumph - - Arsenal beaten 1-0 in F.A.Cup Final . . . . Miner's strike drastically reduces home gates - - some fans walk from Valleys to Ninian Park ! . . . . . . Ferguson credited with winning goal in Cup Final sets new goalscoring record . . . . City complete unique 'double' - - also win Welsh Cup.

Other Matches

F.A.Cup

	Date	Opposition	Res	Attend.	Goalscorers	1	2	3	4	5	6	7	8	9	10	11
3rd	8 Jan	ASTON VILLA	2-1	30000	Davies,L. Curtis	H	Q	N	L	T	K	I	Y	F	E	S
4th	29	Darlington	2-0	12986	McLachlan Ferguson	"	"	"	"	"	"	"	"	"	"	P
5th	19 Feb	Bolton Wanderers	2-0	49463	Ferguson (pen) Davies,L.	"	"	"	N	"	"	"	L	"	"	"
6th	5 Mar	Chelsea	0-0	70184		"	"	"	"	"	"	"	"	"	"	"
6th Rep	9	CHELSEA	3-2	47853	Irving Davies,L. Ferguson (pen)	"	"	"	"	"	"	"	"	"	"	"
Semi–Fin.†	26	Reading	3-0	39476	Ferguson 2 Wake	"	"	"	"	"	"	Y	"	I	F	"
Final ††	23 Apr	Arsenal	1-0	91206	Ferguson	"	"	"	"	"	"	E	"	"	"	"

† At Molineux   †† At Wembley Stadium

Welsh Cup

	Date	Opposition	Res	Attend.	Goalscorers	1	2	3	4	5	6	7	8	9	10	11
5th ‡	29 Mar	Ebbw Vale	0-0	10000		"	"	"	"	"	"	Y	"	"	"	"
5th Rep	4 Apr	Ebbw Vale	6-1	8000	Davies,L. 2 Castle 2 McLachlan Curtis	J	"	"	B	R	"	E	"	C	"	"
6th	28	BARRY TOWN	2-0	5000	McLachlan Davies,L.	H	"	"	K	"	T	N	"	F	E	"
Semi-Final	2 May	Wrexham	2-1	14600	Davies,L. 2	"	"	"	B	T	K	"	"	"	"	"
Final	5	Rhyl	2-0	9600	Davies,L. Irving	"	"	"	"	"	"	"	"	"	"	"

‡ Venue switched, gate receipts to Marine Colliery Fund.

Friendlies

	Date	Opposition	Res		Goalscorers
Benefit	14 Apr	Northampton Town	1-4		McLachlan
	29	Merthyr Town	0-1		
	14 May	Montgomery X1	6-2		Davies,W. 2 Hardy Pirie Curtis Smith

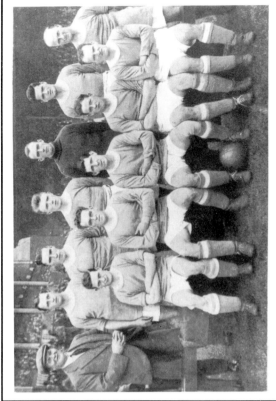

(Back) G. Latham(Trainer), L.Davies, J.Nelson, T.Potter-Smith, T. Farquharson, G.McLachlan, W.Hardy. (Front) W. Davies, S. Irving, F. Keenor, G. Blackburn, H. Ferguson.

1927-28

Football League – Division Secretary/Manager: Fred Stewart P:42 W:17 D:10 L:15 70-80 Pts:44 Pos:6th

336	Date	Opposition	Res	Attend.	Goalscorers	1	2	3	4	5	6	7	8	9	10	11
1.	27 Aug	BOLTON WANDERERS	2-1	25000	Davies,L. McLachlan	G	R	X	K	M	I	U	E	H	D	N
2.	3 Sep	Sheffield Wed.	3-3	17944	Ferguson Curtis Thirlaway	"	"	"	"	"	"	"	"	"	"	"
3.	5	Blackburn Rovers	0-0	14343		"	"	"	"	"	"	"	"	"	"	"
4.	10	MIDDLESBROUGH	1-1	23033	McLachlan	"	"	"	"	"	"	"	"	"	"	"
5.	12	BLACKBURN ROVERS	1-1	16000	Davies,L	"	"	"	"	"	"	"	"	"	"	"
6.	17	Birmingham City	3-1	32000	Ferguson 2 Thirlaway	"	"	"	"	"	"	"	"	"	"	"
7.	24	NECASTLE UNITED	3-1	35000	Ferguson Davies,L Curtis	"	"	"	"	"	"	"	"	"	"	"
8.	1 Oct	Huddersfield Town	2-8	12975	Ferguson Davies,L	"	"	"	"	"	"	"	"	"	"	"
9.	8	TOTTENHAM HOTSPUR	2-1	21811	Ferguson Davies,L	"	"	"	"	"	B	"	"	"	"	"
10.	15	Manchester United	2-2	31094	Thirlaway Curtis	"	"	I	"	"	"	"	"	"	"	"
11.	22	PORTSMOUTH	3-1	1000	Ferguson(p) Thirlaway McLachlan	"	"	"	V	"	"	"	"	"	"	"
12.	29	Leicester City	1-4	26000	Smith	"	"	X	K	S	I	"	O	"	T	"
13.	5 Nov	LIVERPOOL	1-1	10000	Smith	"	"	"	"	M	"	"	E	"	"	"
14.	12	West Ham United	0-2	25000		"	"	"	"	"	"	"	"	"	D	"
15.	19	DERBY COUNTY	4-4	10000	Davies,L,2 Matson Davies,W.	"	"	"	"	"	"	F	O	"	E	"
16.	26	Sheffield United	4-3	30000	Ferguson McLachlan 2 Davies,L	"	"	"	"	"	"	U	F	"	"	"
17.	3 Dec	ASTON VILLA	2-1	16000	Ferguson 2	"	"	"	B	"	"	"	"	"	"	"
18.	10	Sunderland	2-0	12000	Davies,L Thirlaway	"	"	"	K	"	"	"	"	"	"	"
19.	17	BURY	0-1	15000		"	"	"	"	S	"	"	D	"	"	"
20.	24	Burnley	1-2	14000	Ferguson	"	"	"	"	M	"	"	"	"	"	"
21.	26	Everton	1-2	56305	Wake	"	"	"	V	"	B	"	"	"	"	"
22.	27	EVERTON	2-0	25387	Davies,L Wake	*J	"	L	B	S	I	"	Y	*P	"	"
23.	31	Bolton Wanderers	1-2	28000	Miles	"	"	"	"	"	S	"	"	"	"	"
24.	7 Jan	SHEFFIELD	1-1	9208	Ferguson	G	"	I	"	M	"	"	K	H	"	"
25.	21	Middlesbrough	2-1	21728	Ferguson Thirlaway	"	"	X	V	"	"	"	D	"	T	"
26.	4 Feb	Newcastle United	0-2	26000		"	"	L	"	I	B	"	K	E	D	"
27.	11	HUDDERSFIELD TOWN	4-0	25000	Thirlaway Davies,L2 o.g.(Woodward)	"	"	"	"	M	I	"	D	H	E	"
28.	22	BIRMINGHAM CITY	2-1	22000	Ferguson McLachlan	"	"	"	B	"	"	"	"	"	"	"
29.	25	MANCHESTER UNITED	2-0	260001	Ferguson Davies,L	"	"	"	Y	"	"	"	"	"	"	"
30.	3 Mar	Portsmouth	0-3	26000		"	"	"	"	"	"	"	"	"	"	"
31.	5	Tottenham Hotspur	0-1	15559		"	"	"	"	"	"	"	"	"	"	"
32.	10	LEICESTER CITY	3-0	15000	Ferguson 2 McLachlan	"	"	"	"	"	"	"	Q	E	D	"
33.	17	Liverpool	2-1	35000	Davies,L Thirlaway	"	"	"	"	"	"	"	E	H	T	"
34.	24	WEST HAM UNITED	1-5	18000	Ferguson	"	"	A	"	"	"	"	"	C	"	"
35.	31	Derby County	1-7	15810	Thirlaway	"	"	B	"	"	"	"	"	H	"	"
36.	6 Apr	Arsenal	0-3	27000		J	"	L	"	S	"	"	T	P	*Q	"
37.	7	SHEFFIELD UNITED	2-1	18000	McLachlan 2	"	R	"	M	"	"	"	V	H	T	"
38.	9	ARSENAL	2-2	25000	Smith Wake	"	"	"	"	"	"	"	"	"	"	"
39.	14	Aston Villa	1-3	16140	McLachlan	G	"	"	"	"	"	"	E	N	E	*W
40.	21	SUNDERLAND	3-1	20000	Davies,L Warren McLachlan	"	"	"	"	"	"	U	"	"	T	"
41.	28	Bury	0-3	10000		"	"	"	"	"	"	"	"	"	"	"
42.	5 May	BURNLEY	3-2	8663	Davies,L 2 Warren	"	"	"	"	"	"	"	"	"	"	"

Players:

A = Bailie,J. 1/0/0
B = Blackburn,G. 11/3/0
C = Castle,F. 1.1.2
D = Curtis,E. 20/2/3
E = Davies,L. 37/9/21
F = Davies,W. 5/1/1
G = Farquharson,T. 37/9/0
H = Ferguson,H. 32/8/25
I = Hardy,W. 41/8/0
J = Hillier,E. 5/0/0
K = Irving,S. 21/3/0
L = Jennings,J. 18/6/0
M = Keenor,F. 36/9/0
N = McLachlan,G. 42/8/12
O = Matson,F. 4/0/1
P = Miles.A. 3/0/1
Q = Murphy,J. 1/0/0
R = Nelson,J. 41/8/1
S = Sloan,T. 12/3/0
T = Potter-Smith,T. 13/4/6
U = Thirlaway,W. 40/9/11
V = Wake,H. 16/5/4
W = Warren,F. 4/0/2
X = Watson,T. 22/2/0

City win Charity Shield and Welsh Cup . . . . Crash 2-8 to Champions Huddersfield - - win return 4-01 . . . . record home defeat suffered - - 1-5, to West Ham United.

Other Matches

F.A.Cup

	Date	Opposition	Res	Attend.	Goalscorers	1	2	3	4	5	6	7	8	9	10	11
3rd	14 Jan	SOUTHAMPTON	2-1	23000	Ferguson Davies,L	G	R	I	K	M	B	U	D	H	E	N
4th	28	LIVERPOOL	2-1	20000	McLachlan Nelson	"	"	X	V	"	"	"	K	"	"	"
5th	18 Feb	Nottm. Forest	1-2	30500	Ferguson	"	"	L	"	"	"	"	"	"	"	"

Welsh Cup

	Date	Opposition	Res	Attend.	Goalscorers	1	2	3	4	5	6	7	8	9	10	11
5th	15 Mar	Oswestry	7-1	4000	Davies,L,3 Castle 2 Smith 2	"	L	X	"	"	"	"	T	C	"	F
6th	2 Apr	SWANSEA TOWN	1-0	10000	Smith	"	R	L	M	"	S	"	"	H	"	N
Semi-final	8	Rhyl	2-2	3000	Ferguson 2	"	"	"	"	"	B	"	K	"	"	"
Semi	25	Rhyl	2-0	5000	Wake Davies,L	"	"	"	"	V	"	"	"	"	"	"
Final	2 May	Bangor City	2-0	11000	Ferguson 2	"	"	"	"	S	"	"	V	"	"	"

F.A. Charity Shield

	Date	Opposition	Res	Attend.	Goalscorers	1	2	3	4	5	6	7	8	9	10	11
At Chelsea	12 Oct	Corinthians	2-1	15000	Ferguson Davies,L	"	"	"	I	K	M	B	E	"	D	"

Friendlies

	Date	Opposition	Res	Goalscorers
	19 Sep	Wigan Borough	6-2	Ferguson 2 Davies,L 2 Curtis Thirlaway
	3 Oct	Glasgow Celtic	1-4	Curtis
(Tour)	13 May	Aarhus	2-0	Smith Ferguson
(Tour)	16	Aalberg	4-0	McLachan Ferguson 2 Smith
(Tour)	19	Odense Combination	4-1	
(Tour)	24	Montgomery X1	5-1	McLachan Ferguson 3 Smith

The match versus Exeter, on the 5th of November.

1928-29

Football League – Division 1. Secretary/Manager: Fred Stewart

P:42 **W:**8 **D:**13 **L:**21 **43-59** **Pts:**29 **Pos:**22nd (rel.)

378	Date	Opposition	Res	Attend.	Goalscorers	1	2	3	4	5	6	7	8	9	10	11
1.	25 Aug	Newcastle United	1-1	46000	Ferguson	D	T	K	M	Y	G	a	b	E	*C	P
2.	1 Sep	BURNLEY	7-0	20174	Ferguson 5 Davies,L 2	"	"	"	"	"	"	"	"	"	B	"
3.	8	Derby County	0-2	20577		"	"	"	"	"	"	"	C	"	"	"
4.	10	WEST HAM UNITED	3-2	22000	Ferguson 2 Thirlaway	"	"	"	"	"	"	"	"	"	"	"
5.	15	Sheffield United	1-3	30000	Davies,S.	"	"	"	"	"	"	"	"	"	"	"
6.	17	West Ham United	1-1	18000	Ferguson	"	"	"	"	"	"	"	"	"	"	"
7.	22	BURY	4-0	20000	Ferguson Davies,L2 Davies,S.	"	"	"	"	"	"	"	"	"	"	"
8.	29	Aston Villa	0-1	30000		"	"	"	"	"	"	"	*H	"	"	"
9.	6 Oct	LEICESTER CITY	1-2	15000	Harris	"	"	"	"	"	"	"	"	*X	"	"
10.	13	Manchester United	1-1	26010	McLachlan	F	K	G	"	"	A	"	C	"	"	"
11.	20	SUNDERLAND	0-1	20000		"	"	"	"	"	"	"	"	H	"	"
12.	27	Sheffield Wed.	0-1	20116		D	"	"	*I	"	"	"	"	"	"	"
13.	3 Nov	ARSENAL	1-1	25000	Sloan	"	"	"	M	"	"	"	H	P	Z	c
14.	10	Everton	0-1	25994		"	"	"	I	M	"	"	"	E	B	P
15.	17	HUDDERSFIELD TOWN	0-0	13845		"	"	*V	"	G	"	"	N	"	"	c
16.	24	Manchester City	1-1	15000	Smith,P.	"	T	K	"	M	G	"	B	P	Z	"
17.	1 Dec	BIRMINGHAM CITY	1-4	15000	Thirlaway	"	"	V	A	"	"	"	C	B	"	P
18.	8	Portsmouth	1-0	15000	Miles	"	"	G	I	"	A	"	Z	Q	*U	c
19.	15	BOLTON WANDERERS	1-1	14000	Robbins	"	"	"	"	"	"	"	"	B	"	"
20.	22	Blackburn Rovers	0-2	12000		"	"	"	"	M	"	"	H	"	"	"
21.	25	Leeds United	0-3	28188		"	"	"	"	"	"	"	"	B	"	"
22.	26	LEEDS UNITED	2-1	20409	Wake Thirlaway	F	"	V	"	"	"	"	b	E	P	"
23.	29	NEWCASTLE UNITED	2-0	18000	Thirlaway Wake	"	T	K	"	P	"	"	"	"	Z	"
24.	1 Jan	Bolton Wanderers	0-1	34000		"	"	V	"	M	"	"	"	"	"	"
25.	5	Burnley	0-3	20000		"	"	"	"	"	P	"	"	"	"	"
26.	19	DERBY COUNTY	3-0	15000	Ferguson 2 McLachlan	D	"	"	b	"	*R	"	C	"	"	P
27.	26	SHEFFIELD UNITED	0-0	16600		"	"	"	"	"	"	"	"	B	"	"
28.	2 Feb	Bury	1-4	13000	Ferguson	"	"	"	b	*O	"	"	"	"	"	"
29.	9	ASTON VILLA	0-2	15000		"	"	"	R	"	"	"	B	E	U	"
30.	21	Leicester City	0-2	21000		"	"	"	"	Y	"	"	"	*S	Z	"
31.	23	MANCHESTER UNITED	2-2	13070	Ferguson Davies,L.	"	"	"	R	M	A	"	S	E	B	c
32.	2 Mar	Sunderland	0-1	21500		"	"	"	"	"	G	"	H	S	"	"
33.	9	SHEFFIELD WED.	3-1	18636	Davies,L. Thirlaway Warren	"	"	"	b	"	A	"	"	"	"	"
34.	16	Arsenal	1-2	42000	Davies,L.	"	"	"	R	"	"	N	"	"	"	"
35.	23	EVERTON	0-2	14681		"	"	"	b	"	"	"	b	"	"	"
36.	29	Liverpool	0-2	30000		"	"	"	R	"	"	"	"	B	P	"
37.	30	Huddersfield Town	1-1	13332	Davies,L.	"	"	"	"	Y	"	"	"	"	"	"
38.	1 Apr	LIVERPOOL	1-2	12000	Wake	"	"	d	I	"	"	a	"	"	"	"
39.	6	MANCHESTER CITY	1-3	10000	Munro	"	"	R	"	M	"	"	H	S	U	"
40.	13	Birmingham City	0-0	18000		"	"	V	"	"	"	N	B	"	P	"
41.	20	PORTSMOUTH	1-1	10000	Munro	J	T	K	M	*L	G	a	H	"	"	*W
42.	4 May	BLACKBURN ROVERS	1-1	5738	Harris	D	"	"	"	"	"	"	"	"	U	c

Players:

A = Blackburn,G. 22/3/1
B = Davies,L. 28/4/10
C = Davies,S. 13/1/2
D = Farquharson,T. 35/5/0
E = Ferguson,H. 20/3/15
F = HampsonT. 6/0/0
G = Hardy,W. 24/2/1
H = Harris,F. 13/2/3
I = Helsby,T. 13/2/0
J = Hillier,E. 1/0/0
K = Jennings,J. 42/5/0
L = John,E. 2/0/0
M = Keenor,F. 36/5/0
N = Matson,F. 7/0/0
O = McGrath,J. 1/0/0
P = McLachlan,G. 31/4/2
Q = Miles,A. 2/1/1
R = Moss,F. 12/0/0
S = Munro,J. 11.1.3
T = Nelson,J. 11/0/0
U = Robbins,W. 6/1/1
V = Roberts,W. 21/4/0
W = Robinson,M. 1/0/0
X = Shaw,W. 2/0/0
Y = Sloan,T. 15/0/1
Z = Smith,T.P. 14/0/1
a = Thirlaway,W. 36/5/5
b = Wake,H. 18/4/3
c = Warren,F. 22/2/1
d = Watson,T. 1/0/0

Relegation - despite conceding fewest goals in First Division ! .. Injury prevents Ferguson from scoring more goals (record five in 7-0 win over Burnley)... Grangetown stand opened.... 6-1 defeat to Villa - worst defeat in F.A.Cup ... Lose to Connah's Quay in Welsh Cup !

Other Matches

F.A.Cup

	Date	Opposition	Res	Attend.	Goalscorers	1	2	3	4	5	6	7	8	9	10	11
3rd	12 Jan	ASTON VILLA	1-6	51242	Hardy	D	K	G	I	M	P	a	b	Q	U	c

Welsh Cup

	Date	Opposition	Res	Attend.	Goalscorers	1	2	3	4	5	6	7	8	9	10	11
5th	27 Feb	LOVELL'S ATHLETIC	3-1	5000	Ferguson Harris Davies,L	"	"	V	"	"	G	"	H	E	B	"
6th	25 Mar	Newport County	1-0	4000	Munro	"	"	"	b	"	"	"	C	S	"	"
Semi/fin	25 Apr	Rhyl	2-1	7000	Blackburn Davies,L	"	"	"	"	"	A	"	N	"	"	"
Final	1 May	Connah's Quay Nomads	0-3	10000		"	"	"	"	"	"	"	"	"	"	"

Friendlies

	Date	Opposition	Res	Attend.	Goalscorers
	10 Apr	Bristol City	1-1	3,000	Ferguson
Benefit	16 May	Mongomery X1	9-3		Matson 3 Smith,P. 3 Warren Davies,L

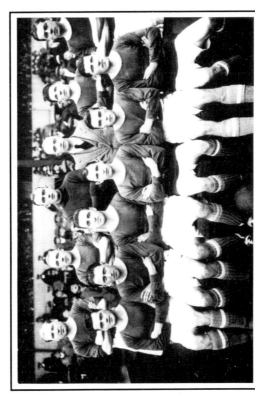

(Back) F. Moss, J. Jennings, T. Farquharson, H. Wake, W. Roberts, G. Blackburn.
(Front) G. McLachlan, F. Matson, J. Munro, L. Davies, F. Warren, F. Keenor.

1929-30

Football League – Division 2. Secretary/Manager: Fred Stewart

P:42 W:18 D:8 L:16 61-59 Pts:44 Pos:8th

420	Date	Opposition	Res	Attend.	Goalscorers	1	2	3	4	5	6	7	8	9	10	11
1.	31 Aug	Charlton Athletic	1-4	25000	Robbins	D	U	I	L	*R	E	T	*M	*Z	W	b
2.	2 Sep	PRESTON NORTH END	2-0	18000	Robbins 2	"	I	V	a	L	B	"	"	"	"	"
3.	7	HULL CITY	0-1	12664		"	"	"	"	"	"	"	"	"	"	"
4.	9	Preston North End	3-2	17000	Matson Warren Harris	"	"	"	"	"	E	"	F	C	"	"
5.	14	Stoke City	1-1	14000	Davies	"	"	"	"	"	"	"	"	"	"	"
6.	16	NOTTS. COUNTY	3-1	15000	Matson Warren Harris	"	"	"	"	"	"	"	"	"	X	"
7.	21	WOLVERHAMPTON W.	0-0	17000		"	"	"	"	"	B	"	"	"	"	"
8.	25	Notts. County	1-2	16000	Warren	"	"	"	"	"	E	"	"	"	"	"
9.	28	Bradford City	1-0	10000	Blackburn	"	"	"	"	"	B	"	"	"	"	"
10.	5 Oct	SWANSEA TOWN	0-3	30000		"	"	"	"	"	"	"	"	"	W	"
11.	12	Blackpool	1-0	15000		"	"	"	"	"	"	"	"	"	"	"
12.	19	BARNSLEY	1-0	12000	Harris	"	"	"	"	"	E	"	"	"	"	"
13.	26	Bradford (P.A.)	0-2	18743		"	"	"	"	J	B	"	"	Q	"	"
14.	2 Nov	WEST BROM. ALBION	3-2	15027	Miles Davies Thirlaway	"	"	"	"	L	"	Y	"	"	C	P
15.	9	Tottenham Hotspur	2-1	23071	Robinson Miles	"	"	"	"	"	"	"	C	"	X	"
16.	16	SOUTHAMPTON	5-2	12000	Thirlaway 3 Davies Roberts	"	"	"	"	"	"	"	"	"	"	"
17.	23	Millwall	0-2	15000		H	"	"	"	"	"	"	F	"	"	"
18.	30	OLDHAM ATHLETIC	5-0	12112	Miles 3 Thirlaway McLachlan	"	"	"	"	"	"	"	C	"	"	"
19.	7 Dec	Nottingham Forest	1-3	4385	McLachlan	"	"	"	"	"	"	"	"	"	"	"
20.	14	CHELSEA	1-0	14000	Davies	D	"	"	"	"	"	"	"	"	"	"
21.	21	Bury	2-4	8000	Warren Thirlaway	"	"	"	"	"	"	"	"	S	"	"
22.	25	Bristol City	0-2	16350		"	"	"	"	"	"	"	"	"	X	"
23.	26	BRISTOL CITY	1-1	27000	Wake	"	U	I	"	"	E	"	"	Q	W	B
24.	4 Jan	CHARLTON ATHLETIC	1-0	10000	Miles	"	I	V	"	"	B	"	"	"	V	N
25.	4 Jan	Hull City	2-2	11695	Davies Munro	"	"	"	"	"	"	"	"	S	X	"
26.	18	STOKE CITY	1-2	11000	Robinson	"	U	"	"	"	"	"	"	"	"	"
27.	1 Feb	BRADFORD CITY	0-1	9000		"	*O	V	"	"	"	"	*c	W	C	"
28.	8	Swansea Town	0-1	20000		"	U	"	"	L	"	"	C	c	*K	X
29.	15	BLACKPOOL	4-2	10000	Davies Blackburn Williams Harris	"	"	"	"	"	"	C	F	"	"	"
30.	22	Barnsley	2-2	9000	Williams 2	"	"	"	"	"	"	"	"	"	"	"
31.	1 Mar	BRADFORD (P.A.)	2-0	11442	Jones Williams	"	"	"	"	"	G	"	"	"	"	W
32.	8	West Brom. Albion	2-0	5889	Williams Robbins	"	"	"	"	"	"	"	"	"	"	"
33.	15	TOTTENHAM HOTSPUR	1-0	15404	Jones	"	"	"	"	"	B	"	"	"	"	"
34.	22	Southampton	1-1	14000	Williams	"	"	"	"	"	"	"	"	"	"	"
35.	29	MILLWALL	3-1	12000	Williams 2 Jones	"	"	"	"	"	"	Y	C	"	"	"
36.	5 Apr	Oldham Athletic	1-4	18596	Robbins	"	"	"	G	"	"	"	"	W	C	"
37.	12	NOTTINGHAM FOREST	1-1	10000	Davies	"	"	"	"	"	"	"	"	c	*K	X
38.	14	Wolverhampton W.	0-4	7000		"	"	"	a	"	"	C	F	"	"	"
39.	18	READING	2-1	8000	Davies Williams	"	"	"	"	J	"	"	"	"	"	"
40.	19	Chelsea	0-1	30000		"	"	"	"	"	"	"	"	"	"	Y
41.	21	Reading	0-2	17000		"	"	"	G	"	"	"	"	"	*	*A
42.	26	BURY	5-1	8000	Williams 3 Bird Davies	"	"	"	"	"	"	"	"	"	"	"

Players:

A = Bird,W. 2/0/1
B = Blackburn,G. 35/6/1
C = Davies,L. 37/6/15
D = Farquharson,T. 39/6/0
E = Hardy,W. 6/0/0
F = Harris,F. 24/2/5
G = Helsby,T. 4/2/0
H = Hillier,E. 3/0/0
I = Jennings,J. 26/1/0
J = John,E. 6/2/0
K = Jones,L. 15/4/6
L = Keenor,F. 36/5/0
M = Lievesley,W. 3/0/0
N = McGrath,J. 4/3/0
O = McJennett,J. 1/1/0
P = McLachlan,G. 9/0/2
Q = Miles,A. 10/4/8
R = Moore,P. 1/0/0
S = Munro,J. 4/2/1
T = Matson,F. 13/0/2
U = Nelson,J. 18/4/1
V = Roberts,W. 40/6/1
W = Robbins,W. 21/2/5
X = Robinson,M. 16/2/2
Y = Thirlaway,W. 18/3/7
Z = Valentine,A. 3/0/0
a = Wake,H. 39/5/1
b = Warren,F. 13/0/5
c = Williams,R.S. 16/0/11

Scoring legend Hughie Ferguson makes ill-fated transfer to Dundee during the close season . . . . George McLachlan sold to Manchester Utd. . . . Ralph Williams and Les Jones make their mark in the second half of a mediocre season.

Other Matches

F.A.Cup

	Date	Opposition	Res	Attend.	Goalscorers	1	2	3	4	5	6	7	8	9	10	11
3rd	11 Jan	Liverpool	2-1	50141	Davies 2	D	U	V	a	L	B	Y	C	S	X	N
4th	25	Sunderland	1-2	49424	Davies	"	O	"	"	"	"	"	"	"	"	"

Welsh Cup

	Date	Opposition	Res	Attend.	Goalscorers	1	2	3	4	5	6	7	8	9	10	11
5th	17 Mar	Llanelly	4-1	5000	Davies 2 Miles Jones	"	U	"	"	"	"	C	F	Q	K	W
6th	2 Apr	SWANSEA TOWN	4-0	8000	Thirlaway Jones Davies Nelson	"	"	"	"	"	"	Y	C	"	"	"
Semi-final	23	Wrexham	2-0	4000	Miles Jones	"	"	"	G	J	"	"	"	"	"	N
Final †	3 May	Rhyl	0-0	5000		"	"	"	"	"	"	L	a	"	"	C

† Replay held over until 1930/31 season.

Friendlies

	Date	Opposition	Res	Goalscorers
	12 Mar	Colwyn Bay	3-1	Jones Williams 2
	28 Apr	Swansea Town	2-6	Jones 2

(Back) W. Robbins, W. Thirlaway, F. Keenor, T. Farquharson, W. Roberts, F. Stewart (Manager) T. Helsby, G. Latham (Trainer).
(Front) L. Davies, F. Harris, R. Williams, J. Nelson, L. Jones, H. Wake.

1930-31

Football League – Division 2.
Secretary/Manager: Fred Stewart

P:42　W:8　D:9　L:25　47–87　Pts:25　Pos:22nd (Rel)

462	Date	Opposition	Res	Attend.	Goalscorers	1	2	3	4	5	6	7	8	9	10	11
1.	30 Aug	Swansea Town	2-3	20000	Williams 2	G	S	X	c	P	B	*E	J	f	N	W
2.	3 Sep	Bury	0-3	8000		"	"	"	K	"	"	"	"	"	"	"
3.	6	WEST BROM. ALBION	3-6	12088	Jones Bird Helsby	"	I	"	"	"	"	"	"	"	"	A
4.	8	EVERTON	1-2	11463	Bird	"	X	M	"	"	"	"	N	"	W	"
5.	13	Port Vale	0-2	10000		"	*a	X	"	"	"	D	J	"	"	"
6.	17	Everton	1-1	17564	Williams	"	"	"	c	M	"	E	"	"	"	"
7.	20	BRADFORD CITY	1-1	8000	Bird	"	"	B	"	"	P	"	K	"	"	"
8.	22	PLYMOUTH ARGYLE	4-1	6615	Robbins2 Williams Davies	"	"	"	K	"	"	"	D	"	"	"
9.	27	Charlton Athletic	1-4	12000	Williams	"	"	M	"	"	"	"	"	"	"	"
10.	4 Oct	BARNSLEY	2-0	8000	Helsby Jones	"	"	"	"	"	B	"	N	"	D	W
11.	11	Bristol City	0-1	18720		"	"	X	"	"	"	"	"	"	W	A
12.	18	Oldham Athletic	2-4	8911	Harris Emmerson	"	"	"	"	*g	"	"	K	J	N	W
13.	25	NOTTINGHAM FOREST	1-1	8000	Jones	"	"	"	c	K	"	"	*V	b	"	A
14.	1 Nov	Southampton	1-0	12202	Keenor	"	"	"	"	P	"	"	K	"	"	W
15.	8	READING	5-0	9000	Robbins 2 Jones 2 Valentine	"	"	"	"	"	"	"	"	"	"	"
16.	15	Stoke City	0-1	9000		"	"	"	"	"	"	"	"	"	"	"
17.	22	BRADFORD (P.A.)	0-3	5475		"	"	"	"	K	"	"	J	"	"	A
18.	29	Wolverhampton W.	1-4	7000	Valentine	"	"	I	"	P	"	"	K	"	"	W
19.	6 Dec	MILLWALL	4-4	8000	Robbins 3 Emmerson	"	"	"	K	"	"	"	c	"	"	"
20.	13	Preston North End	0-7	14000		"	"	*d	"	"	"	"	V	"	*Y	"
21.	20	BURNLEY	4-0	7485	Robbins 2 Jones Emmerson	"	"	"	"	"	"	"	*V	f	N	"
22.	26	Plymouth Argyle	1-5	31106	Williams	"	"	"	"	"	"	"	b	"	"	"
23.	27	SWANSEA TOWN	1-0	31000	Jones	"	"	"	"	"	"	"	"	"	"	"
24.	3 Jan	West Brom. Albion	2-3	24028	McCambridge 2	"	"	"	"	"	R	"	"	*Q	"	A
25.	17	PORT VALE	2-1	8000	Robbins 2	S	"	"	"	"	"	"	"	"	W	*e
26.	31	CHARLTON ATHLETIC	0-2	3500		a	"	"	J	"	B	"	N	"	"	"
27.	4 Feb	Bradford City	1-2	14000	McCambridge	"	"	"	K	*L	R	"	b	"	N	W
28.	7	Barnsley	0-4	7000		"	"	"	B	"	"	"	*O	"	"	"
29.	14	BRISTOL CITY	0-1	16000		"	"	"	K	*H	B	"	"	"	D	"
30.	21	OLDHAM ATHLETIC	0-0	11663		"	"	"	J	"	"	"	"	"	"	e
31.	28	Nottingham Forest	1-3	3565	Davies	F	"	"	"	"	"	"	"	"	"	"
32.	7 Mar	SOUTHAMPTON	0-1	7000		"	"	"	"	"	I	"	*U	"	"	"
33.	14	Reading	0-3	6000		"	"	"	"	P	B	"	D	"	Z	N
34.	21	STOKE CITY	3-2	8000	McCambridge 3	"	"	X	"	H	R	"	U	"	N	A
35.	28	Bradford (P.A.)	0-3	6503		"	I	"	"	"	B	"	"	"	"	R
36.	3 Apr	Tottenham Hotspur	2-2	41547	McCambridge 2	"	"	"	"	"	L	"	"	"	"	e
37.	4	WOLVERHAMPTON W.	0-3	8000		a	"	"	"	"	"	"	b	"	N	W
38.	6	TOTTENHAM HOTSPUR	0-0	6666		"	"	"	K	P	B	"	D	"	D	R
39.	11	Millwall	0-c	15000		"	"	I	B	H	L	"	*O	"	"	"
40.	18	PRESTON NORTH END	0-0	5000		"	"	"	"	H	"	"	"	"	D	"
41.	25	Burnley	0-1	4108		"	"	"	"	"	"	"	O	"	"	e
42.	2 May	BURY	1-3	5000	Jones	"	*C	"	"	"	"	V	"	*T	"	"

Players:

A = Bird,W. 11/0/3
B = Blackburn,G. 28/3/0
C = Blakemore,R. 1/0/0
D = Davies,L. 10/2/7
E = Emmerson,G. 39/6/5
F = Evans,L. 3/0/0
G = Farquharson,T. 39/6/0
H = Galbraith,J. 11/3/0
I = Hardy,W. 12/4/0
J = Harris,F. 19/3/1
K = Helsby,T. 27/3/2
L = Jenkins,E. 10/1/0
M = John,E. 6/0/0
N = Jones,L. 32/5/9
O = Keating,A. 6/0/0
P = Keenor,F. 25/3/1
Q = McCambridge,J. 18/2/9
R = McGrath,J. 13/4/0
S = McJennett,G. 3/1/0
T = Mays,A. 1/0/0
U = Merry,W. 6/3/2
V = Miles,A. 3/0/0
W = Robbins,W. 26/3/12
X = Roberts,W. 17/1/0
Y = Robertson,J. 1/0/0
Z = Robinson,M 1/1/2
a = Smith,J. 35/4/0
b = Valentine,A. 13/2/3
c = Wake,H. 10/1/0
d = Ware,T. 12/2/0
e = Weale,R. 6/1/0
f = Williams,R.S. 14/2/6

City begin miserable season with five straight defeats.... Lack of goals in latter stages condemn City to relegation.... Welsh Cup won in October -- held over from past season -- fail to keep trophy 6 months later.... Fred Keenor makes final appearance in 0-0 draw.

Other Matches

F.A.Cup

	Date	Opposition	Res	Attend.	Goalscorers	1	2	3	4	5	6	7	8	9	10	11
3rd	10 Jan	Brentford	2-2	16500	Jones Valentine	G	a	d	K	P	R	E	b	P	N	W
3rd Rep.	14	BRENTFORD	1-2	25000	Robbins	"	S	"	"	"	"	"	"	"	"	"

Welsh Cup Final (Held over from 1929/30 season)

	Date	Opposition	Res	Attend.	Goalscorers	1	2	3	4	5	6	7	8	9	10	11
Final	8 Oct	Rhyl	4-2	7000	Davies 3 Jones	"	a	I	"	B	E	E	e	D	"	"

Welsh Cup (1930/31 season)

	Date	Opposition	Res	Attend.	Goalscorers	1	2	3	4	5	6	7	8	9	10	11
5th	4 Mar	BARRY TOWN	7-3	3000	Robinson 2 Davies 2 Merry 2 Emmerson	"	"	"	J	H	"	"	U	"	Z	e
6th	25	Chester	1-0	12000	Mc Cambridge	"	I	X	"	"	"	"	"	Q	"	R
Semi-fin.	13 Apr	Shrewsbury Town	0-1	4000		"	a	I	"	"	L	"	"	"	"	"

Friendlies

	Date	Opposition	Res	Attend.	Goalscorers
	20 Apr	Llanelly	1-2		Keating

(Back) H. wake, J. Smith, T. Farquharson, W. Hardy, G. Helsby.
(Front) G. Emmerson, A. Valentine, W. Robbins, F. Keenor, L. Jones, G. Blackburn.

1931-32

Football League – Division 3 South. Secretary/Manager: Fred Stewart

P:42 W:19 D:8 L:15 87-73 Pts:46 Pos:9th

504	Date	Opposition	Res	Attend.	Goalscorers	1	2	3	4	5	6	7	8	9	10	11
1.	29 Aug	Northampton Town	0-1	8000		D	V	T	G	*H	*U	C	*P	*Q	M	S
2.	31	BRIGHTON & HOVE A.	1-1	10435	O'Neil	"	"	"	"	E	"	"	"	"	"	"
3.	5 Sep	READING	5-1	12000	Jones Robbins3 McCambridge	"	"	"	"	"	F	"	"	M	K	"
4.	7	Coventry City	1-2	8000	McCambridge	B	"	"	"	"	"	"	"	Q	M	"
5.	12	Southend United	1-1	6000	o.g.	D	"	"	"	"	"	"	"	"	M	"
6.	14	COVENTRY CITY	6-1	7000	Keating2 Robbins2 Jones McCamb:	"	"	"	"	"	"	"	L	M	K	N
7.	19	FULHAM	0-3	6000		"	"	"	"	"	"	"	"	"	"	S
8.	26	Thames Assoc.	2-1	4000	Keating McCambridge	"	"	"	"	"	N	"	"	"	P	"
9.	3 Oct	BRENTFORD	3-2	15000	Emmerson Keating Robbins	"	"	"	"	"	"	"	"	"	K	"
10.	10	Exeter City	1-3	5000	Emmerson	B	"	"	A	"	"	"	"	"	"	"
11.	17	MANSFIELD TOWN	2-0	6000	Emmerson Robbins	"	"	"	G	"	"	"	G	"	"	"
12.	24	Watford	0-3	7000		"	"	"	"	"	"	"	L	"	"	"
13.	31	CRYSTAL PALACE	1-3	6757	Emmerson	D	F	"	"	"	J	"	"	M	"	N
14.	7 Nov	Bournemouth	0-3	8000		"	V	"	"	"	F	"	"	"	"	S
15.	14	Q. P. RANGERS	0-4	2000		"	O	"	"	H	U	"	A	Q	M	"
16.	21	Bristol Rovers	2-2	9000	O'Neil Ronan(pen)	"	V	"	"	E	"	"	"	"	"	"
17.	5 Dec	Clapton Orient	1-1	6524	Keating	"	"	"	"	"	"	"	"	"	L	K
18.	19	Norwich City	0-2	7690		"	"	"	"	"	"	"	"	"	M	S
19.	25	Luton Town	1-2	8000	Keating	"	"	"	"	"	"	"	L	"	K	"
20.	26	LUTON TOWN	4-1	16000	Robbins 2 Keating McCambridge	"	"	"	"	"	"	"	"	M	"	"
21.	2 Jan	NORTHAMPTON TOWN	5-0	5000	McCamb2 Harris Robbins Emmer'n	"	*R	"	"	"	"	"	"	"	"	"
22.	13	TORQUAY UNITED	5-2	3000	Emmer'n2 McCamb.Keating Robbins	"	V	"	"	"	"	"	"	"	"	"
23.	16	Reading	1-5	5000	McCambridge	"	R	"	I	"	"	"	"	"	"	"
24.	23	SOUTHEND UNITED	2-3	8000	Robbins o.g.(French)	"	V	"	G	"	"	"	"	"	"	"
25.	30	Fulham	0-4	10000		"	"	"	"	E	"	"	A	"	"	"
26.	6 Feb	THAMES ASSOC.	9-2	6000	Robbins5 McCamb.Jones Keel.	"	R	"	"	"	"	"	L	M	"	K
27.	13	Brentford	3-2	18000	McCamb. Keating Robbins	"	"	"	"	"	"	"	L	"	"	S
28.	20	EXETER CITY	5-2	9000	Robbins2 Emmer'n McCamb. Jones	"	"	F	"	"	"	"	"	M	K	"
29.	27	Mansfield Town	2-1	7500	McCambridge 2	"	"	"	G	"	"	"	"	"	"	"
30.	5 Mar	WATFORD	2-1	8000	Robbins Jones	"	"	"	"	"	N	"	"	"	"	"
31.	12	Crystal Palace	0-5	13206		"	"	"	"	"	I	"	"	"	"	"
32.	19	BOURNEMOUTH	0-0	6000		"	"	"	"	"	"	"	"	"	"	"
33.	25	Gillingham	1-1	6000	Emmerson	"	V	"	"	"	"	"	"	"	"	"
34.	26	Q.P. Rangers	3-2	8279	McCambridge 3	"	"	"	"	"	"	"	"	L	"	"
35.	28	GILLINGHAM	1-0	11000	McCambridge	"	"	"	"	"	"	"	"	M	"	"
36.	2 Apr	BRISTOL ROVERS	3-1	8000	McCambridge Keating 2	"	R	"	F	"	"	"	"	"	"	"
37.	9	Torquay United	2-2	5000	McCambridge 2	"	"	"	G	"	"	"	"	"	"	"
38.	13	SWINDON TOWN	3-1	5000	Keating Emmerson	"	V	"	"	"	"	"	"	"	U	N
39.	16	CLAPTON ORIENT	5-0	5290	McCambridge 3 Keating	"	"	"	"	"	"	"	"	"	K	"
40.	23	Swindon Town	4-1	4000	McCambridge 2 Keating	"	"	"	"	"	U	"	"	"	"	"
41.	30	NORWICH CITY	0-2	5000		"	"	"	"	"	"	"	"	"	"	"
42.	7 May	Brighton & Hove A.	0-0	5447		"	"	"	"	"	I	"	A	"	"	"

Players:

A = Evans,A. 6/0/0
B = Evans,L. 4/0/0
C = Emmerson,G. 42/5/13
D = Farquharson,T. 38/5/0
E = Galbraith,J. 39/5/0
F = Hardy,W. 8/2/0
G = Harris,F. 40/5/2
H = Holt,S. 2/0/0
I = Jenkins,E. 6/0/0
J = John,E. 1/0/0
K = Jones,L. 34/3/5
L = Keating,A. 33/5/23
M = McCambridge,J. 37/5/29
N = McGrath,J. 13/0/0
O = McJennett,G. 1/0/0
P = McNally,O. 6/0/0
Q = O'Neill,H. 10/2/4
R = Morris,E.L. 11/0/0
S = Robbins,W. 34/5/24
T = Roberts,W. 41/5/0
U = Ronan,P. 26/5/1
V = Smith,J. 29/3/0

City's first season in 3rd Division (South) is a 'golden' one - - but leaky defence prevents promotion . . City romp to highest League victory (9-2 v. Thames) - - Robbins scores five . . . . . McCambridge sets new record - 26 League goals in season. 8-0 F.A.Cup victory versus Enfield - another record ! . . . But attendances dip as low as 2,000.

Other Matches

F.A.Cup

	Date	Opposition	Res	Attend.	Goalscorers	1	2	3	4	5	6	7	8	9	10	11
1st	28 Nov	ENFIELD	8-0	7000	Keating 3 O'Neill 2 Emmerson 2 Harris	D	V	T	G	E	U	C	L	Q	M	S
2nd	12 Dec	CLAPTON ORIENT	4-0	10500	McCambrdge Keating Emmerson o.g.(Broadbent)	"	"	"	"	"	"	"	"	"	"	"
3rd	9 Jan	Bradford (P.A.)	0-3	18343		"	"	"	"	"	"	"	"	M	K	"

Welsh Cup

	Date	Opposition	Res	Attend.	Goalscorers	1	2	3	4	5	6	7	8	9	10	11
5th	8 Feb	Llanelly	5-3	5000	Robbins 3 McCambridge 2	"	T	F	"	"	"	"	"	K	M	"
6th	2 Mar	Chester	1-2	5000	Emmerson	"	"	"	"	"	"	"	"	"	"	"

Friendlies

	Date	Opposition	Res		Goalscorers
	21 Apr	Abergavenny Thursday	5-0		Jones 3 Keating McCambridge

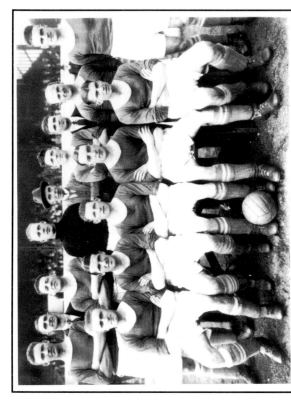

(Back) F. Harris, J. Kneeshaw, J. Smith, L. Evans, F. Stewart (Manager), W. Roberts, J. McGrath, W. Hardy, J. Galbraith.
G. Emmerson, O. McNally, J. McCambridge, H. O'Neil, W. Robbins.

1932-33

Football League – Division 3 South

Secretary/Manager: Fred Stewart **P:**42 **W:**12 **D:**7 **L:**23 **69-99** **Pts:**31 **Pos:**19th.

546

	Date	Opposition	Res	Attend.	Goalscorers	1	2	3	4	5	6	7	8	9	10	11
1.	27 Aug	Reading	2-4	7000	McCambridge Cribb	I	*V	X	E	J	Y	D	*M	S	P	*C
2.	29	BOURNEMOUTH & B.A.	3-0	12000	Keating Cribb Jones	"	"	"	K	"	E	"	Q	"	"	"
3.	3 Sep	NORWICH CITY	4-2	10000	McCambridge 2 Emmerson Cribb	"	"	"	"	"	"	"	M	"	"	"
4.	7	Bournemouth	2-3	8000	McCambridge 2	"	"	"	"	"	"	"	"	"	"	"
5.	10	Brighton & H.A.	0-1	7790		"	"	"	"	"	"	"	*O	"	M	"
6.	17	BRISTOL ROVERS	4-3	6218	McCambridge 2 Cribb Keating	"	"	"	"	"	"	"	Q	"	"	"
7.	24	Aldershot	0-1	4000		"	"	"	"	"	"	"	"	"	"	"
8.	1 Oct	Q.P.RANGERS	2-5	10000	Jones 2	"	"	"	"	"	"	"	"	"	P	"
9.	8	Southend United	2-2	5000	Keating McCambridge	"	O	T	"	"	"	"	"	"	M	"
10.	15	CRYSTAL PALACE	1-1	7144	McCambridge	"	"	X	"	"	P	"	"	"	"	"
11.	22	NEWPORT COUNTY	1-3	12000	McCambridge	"	"	"	"	"	"	"	"	"	"	"
12.	29	Luton Town	1-8	14000	McCambridge	"	T	W	"	"	E	"	M	"	P	"
13.	5 Nov	EXETER CITY	1-3	4000	Emmerson	F	"	O	"	"	"	"	"	"	"	"
14.	12	Torquay United	1-4	5000	Cribb	I	V	"	"	"	"	"	"	"	"	"
15.	19	BRENTFORD	2-1	6000	Jones Cribb	"	T	"	"	"	*G	"	"	"	"	"
16.	3 Dec	BRISTOL CITY	1-1	6000	Jones	"	*Z	"	"	"	E	"	*N	"	"	*B
17.	17	CLAPTON ORIENT	6-1	4433	McCamb.2 Hill Harris Jones Cribb	"	V	"	"	"	"	"	M	"	"	C
18.	24	Swindon Town	2-6	7500	McCambridge 2	"	Z	"	"	"	"	"	"	"	"	"
19.	26	GILLINGHAM	1-0	13000	Jones	"	V	Z	"	"	"	"	"	"	"	B
20.	27	Gillingham	1-1	12000	Jones	"	"	"	"	"	"	*a	"	"	"	"
21.	31	READING	0-1	7000		"	"	"	"	"	O	D	"	"	"	"
22.	7 Jan	Norwich City	1-3	9454	Jones	"	"	"	"	"	"	a	"	"	"	C
23.	14	Coventry City	0-5	9000		"	"	"	"	"	"	D	*U	"	"	"
24.	21	BRIGHTON & H.A.	1-2	4185	McCambridge	"	"	"	Y	"	"	"	*R	"	"	"
25.	28	Bristol Rovers	0-0	7000		"	Z	O	"	"	S	U	"	M	"	"
26.	4 Feb	ALDERSHOT	2-1	4000	Maidment Henderson	"	"	"	K	"	*H	D	"	*L	S	P
27.	11	Q.P.Rangers	1-5	5130	Maidment	"	"	"	"	"	P	"	"	"	"	C
28.	18	SOUTHEND UNITED	2-0	5000	Jones	A	"	"	"	"	S	"	"	"	P	B
29.	25	Crystal Palace	1-4	5805	Maidment	A	"	"	"	"	"	"	"	S	"	"
30.	4 Mar	Newport County	2-4	9000	Emmerson Maidment	I	V	Z	"	"	O	"	"	"	S	P
31.	11	LUTON TOWN	3-2	6000	Maidment Jones Cribb	"	"	"	"	"	"	D	"	L	P	C
32.	18	Exeter City	0-1	9000		"	"	"	"	"	"	"	"	"	"	"
33.	25	TORQUAY UNITED	2-1	7000	Henderson 2	"	"	"	"	"	"	"	"	"	S	P
34.	1 Apr	Brentford	3-7	12000	Henderson 3	"	"	"	"	"	"	"	"	"	"	"
35.	8	COVENTRY CITY	2-2	6000	McCambridge Henderson	"	"	"	"	"	"	"	P	"	"	C
36.	10	Northampton Town	0-2	5000		"	"	"	"	"	"	"	R	"	P	P
37.	14	WATFORD	1-1	10000	Jones	"	"	"	"	"	"	"	"	"	"	"
38.	15	Bristol City	1-3	6520	Russell	"	"	"	"	"	"	"	"	"	"	"
39.	17	Watford	1-2	8000	Jones	I	Z	V	R	"	"	U	M	"	"	"
40.	22	NORTHAMPTON TOWN	6-0	7000	Henderson 5 Cribb	"	"	O	K	"	P	D	R	"	"	C
41.	29	Clapton Orient	0-3	3739		"	"	"	"	"	"	"	"	"	"	"
42.	6 May	SWINDON TOWN	3-0	9000	Cribb 2 Maidment	"	"	"	"	"	"	"	"	"	"	"

Players:

A = Adams,R.   3/1/0
B = Collins,J.   7/1/0
C = Cribb,S.   26/4/11
D = Emmerson,G.   38/6/3
E = Evans,A.   15/0/0
F = Evans,L.   1/0/0
G = Evans,R.   1/0/0
H = Evans,S.   1/0/0
I = Farquharson,I.   38/5/0
J = Galbraith,J.   39/5/0
K = Harris,F.   35/5/2
L = Henderson,J.   16/2/16
M = Hill,F.   21/2/1
N = Horton,R.   1/0/0
O = Jenkins,E.   35/6/0
P = Jones,L.   37/6/16
Q = Keating,A.   7/0/4
R = Maidment,T.   18/4/8
S = McCambridge,J.   41/6/17
T = Morris,E.   4/2/0
U = Paget,W.   3/0/0
V = Pollard,R.   31/4/0
W = Richards,L.   1/0/0
X = Roberts,W.   10/0/0
Y = Ronan,P.   4/3/0
Z = Russell,G.   26/4/1
a = Tennant,J.   2/0/0

Billy Hardy-with City since 1911 leaves to coach Bradford P.A. - George Latham moves on to coach Chester.... The slump continues - re-election bid only just avoided.... League defeats include 1-8 at Luton, 2-6 at Swindon and 3-7 at Brentford.... Fred Stewart resigns at end of season.

Other Matches

F.A.Cup

	Date	Opposition	Res	Attend.	Goalscorers	1	2	3	4	5	6	7	8	9	10	11
1st	26 Nov	BRISTOL ROVERS	1-1	11000	Harris	I	T	O	K	J	Y	D	M	S	P	C
1st Rep.	30	Bristol Rovers	1-4	9000	McCambridge	"	"	"	"	"	"	"	"	"	"	"

Welsh Cup

	Date	Opposition	Res	Attend.	Goalscorers	1	2	3	4	5	6	7	8	9	10	11
7th	22 Feb	TRANMERE ROVERS	4-2	4000	Jones 2 Henderson 2	A	V	Z	S	O	"	"	R	L	"	B
8th	9 Mar	Swansea Town	1-1	3000	Maidment	I	"	"	K	J	"	"	"	S	"	C
8th Rep.	15	SWANSEA TOWN	2-1	5000	Maidment Jones	"	"	"	"	O	"	"	"	"	"	"
S/Final	5 Apr	Chester	1-2	10000	Henderson	"	"	"	"	"	"	"	"	L	"	S

Friendlies

	Date	Opposition	Res	Attend.	Goalscorers
	3 May	TORQUAY UNITED	3-3		McCambridge 2 Henderson

The line-up from the programme for the first League match of the season.

1933-34

Football League – Division 3 South

Secretary/Manager: Bartley Wilson. (Ben Watts-Jones from March 1934)

P:42　W:9　D:6　L:27　57-105　Pts:24　Pos:22nd (re-elect.)

588		Date	Opposition	Res	Attend.	Goalscorers	1	2	3	4	5	6	7	8	9	10	11
1.		26 Aug	Watford	2-1	11500	Hutchinson 2	H	*D	a	R	J	N	*S	*Y	K	O	*M
2.		28	READING	2-0	16000	Henderson 2 (1 pen)	.	.	.	.	.	.	.	.	.	.	.
3.		2 Sep	CHARLTON ATHLETIC	1-1	18000	Postin	.	.	.	.	.	.	.	.	.	.	.
4.		6	Reading	1-3	10000	Maidment	.	.	.	.	.	*F	.	L	.	.	*X
5.		9	Bournemouth	3-1	8000	Henderson 2 Postin	.	.	.	.	.	N	.	Y	.	.	.
6.		16	TORQUAY UNITED	0-1	18000		.	.	.	.	.	.	.	.	.	.	.
7.		23	EXETER CITY	2-1	14000	Marcroft Hutchinson	.	.	.	.	.	.	.	W	.	.	M
8.		30	Gillingham	2-6	7000	Henderson Hutchinson	.	.	.	.	.	.	.	.	.	.	.
9.		7 Oct	CRYSTAL PALACE	4-0	9022	Postin2 Jones Henderson	A	.	.	.	.	.	.	Y	L	.	K
10.		14	Bristol Rovers	1-3	10000	Marcroft	.	.	.	.	.	*T	.	.	.	.	.
11.		21	Q.P. Rangers	0-4	14000		H	*C	.	T	.	N	.	R	Y	.	L
12.		28	NEWPORT COUNTY	1-1	17000	Jones	A	D	.	.	.	.	.	.	.	.	M
13.		4 Nov	Norwich City	0-2	10500		.	.	.	.	.	.	.	.	.	.	.
14.		11	BRISTOL CITY	1-5	8000	Galbraith	.	.	.	.	.	.	.	L	.	.	.
15.		18	Clapton Orient	2-4	8402	Henderson Hill	H	.	.	R	.	.	.	Y	K	.	L
16.		2 Dec	Brighton & H.A.	0-4	5012		A	.	.	.	.	F	.	L	*b	E	X
17.		16	Luton Town	1-3	7000	West	.	.	.	.	.	.	.	O	.	.	M
18.		23	NORTHAMPTON TOWN	1-3	3000	Curtis (pen)	.	.	N	.	.	*B	.	.	.	.	.
19.		25	Coventry City	1-4	27589	Maidment	H	.	a	.	F	.	.	L	N	.	.
20.		26	COVENTRY CITY	3-3	12000	Postin Curtis o.g.(Brisley)	.	.	.	B	J	F	.	R	Y	O	E
21.		30	WATFORD	4-1	6000	Rogers Jones Curtis Postin	.	.	.	.	.	.	*Z	.	.	.	.
22.		6 Jan	Charlton Athletic	0-2	11500		.	.	.	N	*V	.	S	W	.	.	.
23.		17	SWINDON TOWN	0-1	3000		.	.	.	.	.	.	.	R	L	.	.
24.		20	BOURNEMOUTH	4-2	5000	Henderson 2 West Curtis	.	.	.	.	.	.	b	Y	K	E	M
25.		27	Torquay United	1-3	4000	Marshalsey	.	.	.	.	J	.	.	.	.	.	.
26.	3 Feb		Exeter City	0-4	6000		.	.	.	*U	.	.	Z	.	P	.	.
27.		10	GILLINGHAM	1-3	6000	Postin	.	.	.	.	N	.	Y	Y	.	.	.
28.		17	Crystal Palace	2-3	5805	Henderson Curtis	.	.	*G	*Q	.	.	S	R	.	O	.
29.		24	BRISTOL ROVERS	1-5	8000	Postin	.	.	.	.	.	U	.	Y	.	.	.
30.	3 Mar		Q.P. RANGERS	3-1	7000	Henderson 2 Curtis	.	.	a	N	*V	.	Y	*P	.	Q	E
31.		10	Newport County	2-2	9000	Postin 2	.	.	.	.	.	.	.	.	.	.	.
32.		17	NORWICH CITY	0-2	9000		.	.	.	.	.	.	.	.	.	.	M
33.		24	Bristol City	0-3	6500		.	.	.	J	.	.	.	.	.	.	.
34.		30	SOUTHEND UNITED	1-1	5154	Postin	.	.	N	.	.	.	.	.	.	.	.
35.		31	CLAPTON ORIENT	1-2	5154	Postin	.	.	.	.	.	.	R	Y	.	.	.
36.	2 Apr		Southend United	1-1	9000	Postin	.	.	.	.	.	.	T	.	P	.	.
37.		7	Swindon Town	3-6	7000	Keating 2 Lewis	.	.	.	.	.	.	.	.	.	K	.
38.		14	BRIGHTON & H.A.	1-4	4237	Keating	.	.	.	.	.	*I	R	.	.	Q	K
39.		21	Aldershot	3-1	4000	Keating 3	.	G	.	.	.	F	T	.	.	Y	M
40.		25	ALDERSHOT	1-2	2000	Perks	.	.	.	.	.	Q	.	K	.	.	X
41.		28	LUTON TOWN	0-4	3000		.	.	.	.	.	.	S	.	.	.	E
42.	5 May		Northampton Town	0-2	5000		.	.	.	.	.	.	b	.	.	.	X

Players:

A = Adams,R.　8/1/0
B = Adlam,L.　4/0/0
C = Bartlett,J.　1/0/0
D = Calder,R.　37/4/1
E = Curtis,E.　17/3/7
F = Duthie,J.　13/4/0
G = Durkan,J.　6/0/0
H = Farquharson,T.　34/4/0
I = Friend,H.　3/0/0
J = Galbraith,J.　35/4/1
K = Henderson,J.　28/5/13
L = Hill,F.　8/3/2
M = Hutchinson,A.　23/3/4
N = Jenkins,E.　33/3/0
O = Jones,L.　22/3/3
P = Keating,R.　13/0/6
Q = Lewis,E.　14/1/1
R = Maidment,T.　26/2/2
S = Marcroft,E.　22/3/2
T = Marshalsey,W.　7/1/1
U = Molloy,P.　9/0/0
V = Mort,E.　13/0/0
W = Paget,W.　3/0/0
X = Perks,H.　7/0/1
Y = Postin,E.　34/4/13
Z = Rogers,T.　2/1/1
a = Russell,G.　30/5/0
b = West,J.　6/0/2

City's worst ever season!!

Successful League re-election after finishing bottom ... leaky defence concedes over 100 goals ..... Former Director Ben Watts-Jones takes over as manager in March from temporary manager and founder-member Bartley Wilson.

Other Matches

F.A.Cup

	Date	Opposition	Res	Attend.	Goalscorers	1	2	3	4	5	6	7	8	9	10	11
1st	25 Nov	ALDERSHOT	0-0	12000		H	a	D	R	J	N	S	Y	K	O	L
1st Rep.	29	Aldershot	1-3	6000	Hill	A	"	"	"	"	F	"	L	"	"	M

Welsh Cup

	Date	Opposition	Res	Attend.	Goalscorers	1	2	3	4	5	6	7	8	9	10	11
6th	14 Feb	BRISTOL CITY	2-2	1500	Henderson Curtis	H	D	a	Q	N	"	"	Y	"	E	"
6th Rep.	26	Bristol City	0-1	900		"	"	N	N	J	"	L	"	"	"	"

Division 3 (South) Cup

	Date	Opposition	Res	Attend.	Goalscorers	1	2	3	4	5	6	7	8	9	10	11
1st	1 Jan	ALDERSHOT	0-1	3000		"	"	"	T	"	"	Z	K	Y	O	E

Friendlies

11 Oct	JACK HYLTON'S X1	10-6	Henderson 6 Jones 3 Paget
9 Dec	BATH CITY	5-4	Curtis 2 (1 pen) West 2 Maidment
13 Jan	NEWPORT COUNTY	2-2	Hill Paget
18 Apr	GLAMORGAN C.C. X1	5-4	Postin 2 Keating Jenkins Henderson
3 May	Oakdale X1	5-1	Henderson 3 Postin 2

(Back) L. Adlam, R. Calder, T. Farquharson, G. Russell, E. Jenkins, E. Postin.
(Front) E. Marcroft, T. Maidment, L. Jones, E. Curtis, J. Duthie, A. Hutchinson.

1934-35

Football League – Division 3 South

Secretary/Manager: Ben Watts-Jones

P:42 W:13 D:9 L:20 62-82 Pts:34 Pos:19th

630

#	Date	Opposition	Res	Attend.	Goalscorers	1	2	3	4	5	6	7	8	9	10	11
1.	25 Aug	CHARLTON ATHLETIC	2-1	20000	Keating Riley	E	*B	*D	*M	*C	G	*H	*Z	O	*X	*L
2.	27	LUTON TOWN	1-0	24000	Griffiths,P.	"	"	"	"	"	"	"	"	"	"	"
3.	1 Sep	Crystal Palace	1-6	9648	Everest	"	"	"	"	"	"	"	*a	"	"	"
4.	3	Luton Town	0-4	9000		"	*P	"	B	"	"	"	"	"	*S	X
5.	8	Q.P. RANGERS	2-1	15000	Riley Keating	"	"	"	"	"	"	K	"	"	X	*N
6.	10	SOUTHEND UNITED	2-0	14000	Riley Keating	"	"	"	"	"	"	H	"	"	"	"
7.	15	Torquay United	2-5	5000	Hill Lewis,W.	"	"	"	"	"	"	"	S	"	"	"
8.	22	SWINDON TOWN	1-3	7000	Griffiths,P.	"	"	"	M	"	*F	"	"	"	"	K
9.	29	Aldershot	0-2	5000		*Q	"	"	"	"	"	"	"	"	"	L
10.	6 Oct	BOURNEMOUTH	2-1	6000	Riley Bassett	"	"	"	B	"	G	H	"	"	L	"
11.	13	BRIGHTON & H.A.	0-0	8959		"	"	"	"	"	"	"	"	"	"	N
12.	20	Watford	3-1	7000	Hill Vaughan 2	"	"	"	U	"	T	*W	Z	"	K	L
13.	27	NEWPORT COUNTY	3-4	14000	Hill Keating Vaughan	"	"	"	"	"	"	"	"	"	"	"
14.	3 Nov	Reading	1-1	8000	Keating	"	"	"	"	"	"	"	"	"	"	"
15.	10	NORTHAMPTON TOWN	2-2	10000	Riley Hill	"	M	"	"	"	"	"	"	"	"	X
16.	17	Millwall	2-2	15000	Pugh Keating	"	P	"	M	"	*V	"	"	"	S	"
17.	1 Dec	Clapton Orient	1-0	8145	Whitlow	"	"	"	"	"	"	"	K	a	"	L
18.	8	GILLINGHAM	0-2	9000		"	"	"	"	"	"	"	"	"	"	"
19.	15	Exeter City	1-2	3000	Pugh	"	"	"	G	"	"	"	X	O	"	N
20.	22	BRISTOL CITY	3-3	6000	Riley Bassett Keating	"	"	"	"	"	"	"	"	"	"	"
21.	26	Southend United	1-2	11000	Galbraith	"	"	"	"	"	"	"	"	"	"	"
22.	29	Charlton Athletic	1-3	12000	Keating	"	"	"	"	"	M	"	"	"	"	"
23.	5 Jan	CRYSTAL PALACE	2-0	17641	o.g. (Owens) Pugh	"	*I	"	M	"	V	"	Z	"	"	"
24.	16	COVENTRY CITY	2-4	8000	Keating 2	"	P	"	"	"	T	"	"	"	X	"
25.	19	Q.P. Rangers	2-2	5000	Hill Pugh	"	"	"	G	"	"	"	K	"	"	"
26.	26	TORQUAY UNITED	1-1	6000	Hill	"	"	"	T	"	V	"	"	"	"	"
27.	2 Feb	Swindon Town	1-2	6000	Everest (pen)	"	"	"	M	"	T	"	"	"	S	"
28.	9	ALDERSHOT	1-1	10000	Hill	"	"	"	"	U	"	"	Z	"	X	K
29.	16	Bournemouth	1-3	4000	Everest (Pen)	"	"	"	"	C	"	"	K	X	S	H
30.	23	Brighton & H.A.	1-3	5828	Pugh	"	"	"	"	U	"	"	"	"	"	N
31.	2 Mar	WATFORD	2-1	12000	Riley Lewis,W.	"	"	"	"	"	"	"	"	"	"	"
32.	9	Newport County	0-4	9000		"	"	"	I	"	"	"	"	"	"	"
33.	16	READING	1-1	10000	Griffiths,S.	"	"	"	"	"	V	"	"	"	"	*J
34.	23	Northampton Town	0-3	3500		"	"	"	"	"	M	"	"	a	X	T
35.	30	MILLWALL	3-1	7000	Lewis,W. 2 Attley	"	"	"	M	"	N	"	S	O	*A	X
36.	6 Apr	Coventry City	0-2	8000		"	M	"	X	"	"	"	K	"	S	H
37.	13	CLAPTON ORIENT	3-0	7453	Keating Lewis,W. Attley	E	"	"	"	"	"	"	S	"	A	"
38.	19	BRISTOL ROVERS	4-1	15000	Keating 2 Pugh Hill	"	"	"	"	"	"	"	"	"	"	K
39.	20	Gillingham	0-1	5000		"	"	"	"	"	"	"	*R	"	"	H
40.	22	Bristol Rovers	2-3	12000	Keating 2	"	"	"	"	"	G	"	Z	"	K	*Y
41.	27	EXETER CITY	5-0	6000	Keating 4 Attley	"	"	"	M	C	"	"	S	"	A	K
42.	4 May	Bristol City	0-4	4000		"	"	"	"	"	V	"	R	"	"	"

Players:

A = Attley,L. 6/0/0
B = Bland,W. 8/0/0
C = Bassett,W. 39/4/2
D = Everest,J. 42/5/4
E = Farquharson,T. 14/0/0
F = Fursland,S. 2/0/0
G = Galbraith,J. 15/1/1
H = Griffiths,P.M. 13/3/2
I = Granville,A. 5/1/0
J = Griffiths,S. 1/0/1
K = Hill,F. 23/4/7
L = Jackson,W. 12/1/0
M = Jennings,W. 26/3/0
N = Jones,D. 20/3/0
O = Keating,R. 34/2/20
P = Lane,E. 30/4/0
Q = Leckie,J. 28/5/0
R = Lewis,D.B. 2/0/0
S = Lewis,W.L. 24/4/7
T = Molloy,P. 14/2/0
U = Mort,E. 7/1/0
V = Moore,W. 11/1/0
W = Pugh,R. 31/4/7
X = Riley,H. 35/4/9
Y = Taylor,S. 1/0/0
Z = Vaughan,T. 12/2/4
a = Whitlow,F. 7/2/0

City have 8 debutants in opening game of season . . . Keating's goals keep City off bottom of League . . . Goalkeeper Farquharson (record appearance holder) bows out after 4-0 defeat at Bristol City -- exit the last link with greatest team of '20's. Cardiff born Reg Pugh becomes one of the youngest players to represent the Club.

Other Matches

F.A.Cup

	Date	Opposition	Res	Attend.	Goalscorers	1	2	3	4	5	6	7	8	9	10	11
1st	24 Nov	READING	1–2	16739	Lewis,W.	Q	P	D	N	C	V	Z	W	O	S	X

Welsh Cup

	Date	Opposition	Res	Attend.	Goalscorers	1	2	3	4	5	6	7	8	9	10	11
6th	13 Feb	NEWPORT COUNTY	3–2	2000	Riley 2 Lewis,W.	"	"	"	"	"	T	W	K	S	X	H
7th	27 Mar	CHESTER	2–2	2000	o.g. (Burke) Everest	"	"	"	I	"	N	"	"	"	"	"
7th Rep.	10 Apr	Chester	0–3	5000		"	M	"	X	"	"	"	O	"	K	"

Division 3 (South) Cup

	Date	Opposition	Res	Attend.	Goalscorers	1	2	3	4	5	6	7	8	9	10	11
1st	17 Oct	Crystal Palace	1–3		Vaughan	"	P	"	T	"	U	G	L	Z	a	N

Friendlies

	Date	Opposition	Res	Goalscorers
†	3 Nov	Pontypridd District X1	3–0	Vaughan Keating Mallory
	12 Jan	GILLINGHAM	1–1	Riley
	20 Mar	Dutch National X1	1–2	Pugh
	15 Apr	Cwmbran & District	3–0	Whitlow 2 Griffiths,P.
	22	GLAMORGAN C.C. X1	5–5	Vaughan 2 Rees Hill Lewis
	29	ABERDEEN	1–2	Pugh
Benefit	2 May	Barry Town	1–0	o.g. (Jones)

† Gresford Disaster Fund

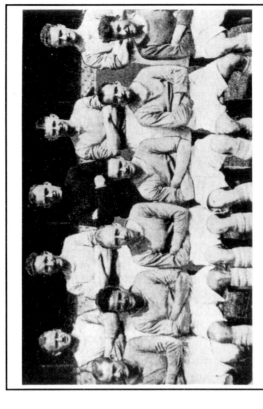

(Back) W. Bland, W. Jennings, T. Farquharson, J. Everest, J. Galbraith.
(Front) W. Bassett, P. Griffiths, F. Whitlow, R. Keating, H. Riley, W. Jackson.

1935-36

Football League – Division 3 South. Secretary/Manager: Ben Watts-Jones
P:42 W:13 D:10 L:19 60-73 Pts:36 Pos:20th

672	Date	Opposition	Res	Attend.	Goalscorers	1	2	3	4	5	6	7	8	9	10	11
1.	31 Aug	Crystal Palace	2-3	16694	Riley Hill	N	*J	F	*Y	B	*H	S	*V	M	U	I
2.	2 Sep	BRISTOL ROVERS	0-0	18000		"	"	"	"	"	"	"	"	*E	"	"
3.	7	READING	2-3	20000	o.g.(Done) Roper	"	"	"	"	"	"	"	"	M	A	"
4.	11	Bristol Rovers	1-1	11000	Pugh	"	B	"	"	P	"	"	"	"	"	"
5.	14	Newport County	0-0	15000		"	"	"	"	"	"	"	"	"	*D	"
6.	16	CLAPTON ORIENT	4-1	7239	Roper Riley Hill 2	"	"	"	"	"	"	"	"	I	U	*W
7.	21	Gillingham	0-3	5000		"	"	"	"	"	Y	"	"	"	"	"
8.	28	BOURNEMOUTH	1-1	12000	Smith	"	"	"	H	"	"	"	"	M	"	"
9.	5 Oct	Luton Town	2-2	12000	Diamond 2	"	"	"	"	"	"	"	"	E	"	I
10.	12	NOTTS. COUNTY	3-2	12000	Hill Diamond o.g(Williams)	"	"	"	"	"	"	"	"	"	I	W
11.	19	COVENTRY CITY	1-0	10000	Roberts	"	"	"	"	"	"	"	"	"	"	"
12.	26	Swindon Town	1-2	9000	Pugh	"	"	"	"	"	"	"	"	"	"	"
13.	2 Nov	ALDERSHOT	0-1	8000		"	"	"	"	"	"	"	-	"	U	"
14.	9	Exeter City	0-2	5000		*C	"	"	"	"	"	"	"	"	O	"
15.	16	MILLWALL	3-1	8000	Roberts 2 Diamond	"	K	"	"	"	"	"	"	"	U	"
16.	23	Bristol City	2-0	9308	Diamond Roberts	"	"	"	"	"	"	"	"	"	"	"
17.	7 Dec	Q.P. Rangers	1-5	4000	Diamond	"	B	J	"	"	"	"	V	"	"	I
18.	25	Southend United	1-3	6000	Everest	"	G	F	"	"	"	"	M	"	A	"
19.	26	SOUTHEND UNITED	1-1	10000	Diamond	N	K	J	"	K	"	"	"	"	U	"
20.	28	CRYSTAL PALACE	1-1	7411	Diamond	C	G	"	*R	B	"	"	U	"	O	"
21.	4 Jan	Reading	0-1	8000	Keating	"	"	"	"	"	H	"	"	"	"	I
22.	11	Torquay United	1-2	6000	Keating	*T	"	"	V	"	"	"	"	"	"	*X
23.	15	WATFORD	0-2	4000		"	"	"	"	"	"	"	"	"	A	"
24.	18	NEWPORT COUNTY	2-0	14000	Smith Riley	"	"	"	H	B	Y	"	U	*Z	O	"
25.	25	GILLINGHAM	4-0	8000	Williams 2 Riley Roberts	"	"	"	"	"	"	"	M	"	U	W
26.	1 Feb	Bournemouth	4-4	8000	Keating 2 Williams Pugh	"	"	"	"	K	"	"	U	"	M	"
27.	8	LUTON TOWN	2-3	14000	Williams 2	"	"	"	"	B	"	"	"	"	"	X
28.	15	Notts. County	0-2	5000		N	"	"	Y	"	"	"	M	"	U	W
29.	22	Coventry City	1-5	10000		"	"	F	"	"	H	"	"	"	V	F
30.	29	EXETER CITY	5-2	5000	Lewis Pugh Smith Diamond Williams	"	"	"	"	"	Y	"	"	"	O	E
31.	7 Mar	Brighton & H.A.	0-1	8198		"	"	"	"	"	"	"	"	"	A	"
32.	14	SWINDON TOWN	2-1	10000	Keating 2	C	"	"	Y	B	H	"	U	"	O	X
33.	18	BRIGHTON & H.A.	1-0	4268	Williams	"	"	"	"	"	"	"	M	"	U	W
34.	21	Millwall	4-2	13000	Keating 3 Williams	"	"	"	V	H	Y	"	"	"	*L	"
35.	28	BRISTOL CITY	1-0	7000	Keating	"	"	"	"	"	"	"	U	"	U	"
36.	4 Apr	Watford	0-4	5000		"	"	"	"	"	"	"	"	"	"	"
37.	10	NORTHAMPTON TOWN	0-0	12000		"	"	"	H	B	H	"	M	"	U	W
38.	11	Q.P.RANGERS	3-2	10000	Riley 2 Pugh	"	J	"	V	"	"	"	D	"	V	F
39.	13	Northampton Town	0-2	5000		"	"	"	"	"	H	"	"	"	O	E
40.	18	Aldershot	1-1	4000	Williams	"	"	"	"	H	Y	"	"	"	A	"
41.	25	TORQUAY UNITED	1-2	6000	Pugh	"	G	"	"	"	"	"	"	"	O	U
42.	2 May	Clapton Orient	1-2	5460	Hill	"	"	"	"	"	"	"	"	*Q	U	I

Players:

A = Attley,L. 6/0/0
B = Bassett,W. 25/2/0
C = Deighton,L. 18/1/0
D = Davis,A. 6/0/0
E = Diamond,J. 18/3/10
F = Everest ,J. 31/3/2
G = Granville,A. 21/1/0
H = Godfrey,C. 42/3/0
I = Hill F. 15/1/5
J = Hearty,H. 18/1/0
K = Jennings,W. 4/2/0
L = Jones,G. 1/0/0
M = Keating,R. 23/3/11
N = Leckie,J. 18/2/0
O = LewisW. 9/1/1
P = Mort,E. 20/2/0
Q = McKenzie,J. 1/0/0
R = McDonagh,C. 2/0/0
S = Pugh,R. 42/4/9
T = Poland,G. 6/1/0
U = Riley,H. 26/3/6
V = Roper,H. 27/2/2
W = Roberts 22/2/5
X = Redwood,D. 6/0/0
Y = Smith,H. 36/4/3
Z = Williams,D. 18/2/9

Reg. Pugh ever present in another disappointing season - - City resist overtures for the talented teenager. . Just seven years after winning F.A.Cup, ailing Bluebirds dumped out of competition - - by non-League Dartford at Ninian Park !

Other Matches

F.A.Cup

	Date	Opposition	Res	Attend.	Goalscorers
1st	30 Nov	DARTFORD	0-3	9000	

	1	2	3	4	5	6	7	8	9	10	11
	C	K	F	H	P	Y	S	I	E	U	W

Welsh Cup

	Date	Opposition	Res	Attend.	Goalscorers
6th	29 Jan	BRISTOL CITY	2-1	6000	Pugh Keating
7th		BYE			
8th	12 Mar	Rhyl	1-2	7000	Pugh

	1	2	3	4	5	6	7	8	9	10	11
	T	G	J	Y	B	H	"	M	N	"	"
	"	"	"	"	"	"	"	"	"	"	"
	"	"	F	V	H	Y	"	"	"	O	E

Division 3 (South) Cup

	Date	Opposition	Res	Attend.	Goalscorers
1st	30 Sep	Crystal Palace	1-2	8000	Diamond

	1	2	3	4	5	6	7	8	9	10	11
	N	B	"	K	P	"	"	V	E	U	M

Friendlies

	Date	Opposition	Res	Attend.	Goalscorers
	14 Dec	CORINTHIANS	2-3		Williams 2
	25 Apr	ABERDEEN	1-1		Riley

The first home game of the season.

1936-37
Football League – Division 3 South.
Secretary/Manager: Ben Watts-Jones (Bill Jennings from April 1937)

P:42 W:14 D:7 L:21 54-87 Pts:35 Pos:18th

714	Date	Opposition	Res	Attend.	Goalscorers	1	2	3	4	5	6	7	8	9	10	11
1.	29 Aug	Walsall	0-1	8000		*G	I	*Z	*O	A	H	Q	*a	*W	*S	*P
2.	31	CLAPTON ORIENT	2-1	16698	Pugh Smith,C.	"	"	"	"	"	"	"	S	"	a	*d
3.	5 Sep	LUTON TOWN	3-0	20000	Smith,C. 2 Pugh	"	"	"	"	"	"	"	"	"	"	P
4.	10	Clapton Orient	1-0	5471	Pugh	"	"	"	"	"	"	"	"	"	"	"
5.	12	Newport County	3-2	16807	Ovenstone Talbot Smith,C.	"	"	"	"	"	"	"	"	"	"	"
6.	14	BRISTOL CITY	3-1	24100	Pugh Pinxton Talbot	"	"	"	"	"	"	"	"	"	"	"
7.	19	Crystal Palace	2-2	18348	Smith,C. Pugh	"	"	"	X	"	"	"	"	"	"	"
8.	26	EXETER CITY	3-1	25000	Ovenstone Talbot Smith,C.	"	"	"	O	"	"	"	"	"	"	"
9.	28	SOUTHEND UNITED	1-1	30000	Pinxton	"	"	"	"	"	"	"	"	"	"	"
10.	3 Oct	Reading	0-3	13000		"	"	"	"	"	"	"	"	"	"	"
11.	10	Q.P. RANGERS	2-0	25000	Talbot Williams	"	"	"	"	"	"	"	"	c	"	"
12.	24	Watford	0-2	12000		"	"	"	"	"	"	"	"	"	"	"
13.	31	BRIGHTON & H.A.	1-2	17805	Granville (Pen)	"	"	"	"	"	X	"	*e	W	"	"
14.	7 Nov	Bournemouth	2-0	9000	Talbot Walton	"	"	"	"	"	H	"	S	e	"	"
15.	14	NORTHAMPTON TOWN	2-1	18000	Pugh Walton	"	"	"	"	"	"	"	"	"	"	"
16.	21	Bristol Rovers	1-5	12211	Talbot	"	"	"	"	"	"	"	"	"	"	"
17.	5 Dec	Swindon Town	2-4	10500	Prescott Smith,C.	"	*F	"	"	"	"	"	D	W	e	*T
18.	19	Gillingham	0-0	9000		R	I	*E	"	"	"	"	a	d	"	"
19.	25	Torquay United	0-1	7000		"	"	"	"	"	*K	"	"	*L	"	"
20.	26	WALSALL	2-2	35000	Walton Menaliphy	"	"	*b	"	"	"	"	"	"	"	P
21.	28	TORQUAY UNITED	0-2	12000	Prescott	"	F	E	"	*Y	H	"	"	"	"	U
22.	2 Jan	Luton Town	1-8	12000		"	*N	*M	"	"	"	"	"	"	"	T
23.	9	NEWPORT COUNTY	0-1	28000		"	I	N	"	H	X	"	S	"	"	"
24.	23	CRYSTAL PALACE	1-1	9415	Talbot	"	"	"	"	"	"	d	"	"	a	e
25.	3 Feb	Exeter City	1-3	6000	Pinxton	"	"	"	"	"	"	Q	"	"	e	U
26.	6	READING	1-1	12000	Walton	"	M	"	"	X	K	"	"	e	a	"
27.	13	Q.P. Rangers	0-6	11000		"	"	"	D	Y	V	L	"	W	"	e
28.	20	Southend United	1-8	7000	Smith,C.	G	"	"	O	b	K	Q	e	"	"	U
29.	27	WATFORD	2-2	7000	Granville(pen) Walton	R	I	"	"	Y	X	"	"	J	"	"
30.	6 Mar	Brighton & H.A.	2-7	10632	McKenzie Granville(pen)	"	"	"	K	"	H	"	"	"	"	"
31.	13	BOURNEMOUTH	2-1	8000	McKenzie 2	G	"	"	O	A	"	"	e	"	"	T
32.	20	Northampton Town	0-2	6000		"	F	"	"	H	V	"	"	"	L	"
33.	26	Notts. County	0-4	18000		R	"	"	"	"	H	"	S	e	e	"
34.	27	BRISTOL ROVERS	3-1	9400	McKenzie Pugh Granville(pen)	"	I	"	"	"	X	"	J	W	"	e
35.	29	NOTTS. COUNTY	0-2	22000		"	"	"	"	"	"	"	"	"	"	U
36.	3 Apr	Millwall	1-3	20000	Granville (pen)	"	"	"	O	A	H	"	e	F	J	T
37.	10	SWINDON TOWN	1-2	10000	Walton	"	"	"	"	"	"	"	"	L	"	P
38.	12	MILLWALL	0-1	10000		"	"	F	"	H	X	"	"	"	"	"
39.	17	Aldershot	1-0	5000	Melaniphy	G	"	"	"	"	H	"	S	"	L	"
40.	19	ALDERSHOT	4-1	8000	Walton Melaniphy 2 Ovenstone	"	"	"	"	"	"	"	J	"	e	"
41.	24	GILLINGHAM	2-0	10000	Melaniphy Ovenstone	"	Y	"	"	"	X	"	"	"	"	U
42.	1 May	Bristol Rovers	1-2	3527	o.g. (Hick)	"	"	"	"	"	"	T	"	*B	"	*C

Players:

- A = Bassett,W. 20/4/0
- B = Brown,A. 1/0/0
- C = Campbell,H. 1/0/0
- D = Davis,A. 2/1/0
- E = Esler,J. 3/0/0
- F = Ford,L. 10/2/0
- G = Fielding,W. 24/2/0
- H = Godfrey,C. 37/4/0
- I = Granville,A. 32/3/6
- J = McKenzie,J. 13/1/4
- K = Main,W 5/1/0
- L = Melaniphy,E. 15/1/5
- M = MacAulay,R. 4/0/0
- N = Mellor,J. 16/2/0
- O = Nicholson,G. 39/4/0
- P = Ovenstone,D. 21/1/4
- Q = Pugh,R. 39/5/8
- R = Poland,G. 18/2/0
- S = Pinxton,A. 20/4/3
- T = Prescott,J. 11/2/4
- U = Redwood,D. 7/0/0
- V = Roper,H. 4/0/0
- W = Smith,C. 15/1/7
- X = Smith,H. 15/0/0
- Y = Smith,J. 7/1/0
- Z = Scott,W. 17/3/0
- a = Talbot,F. 29/4/8
- b = Turner,C. 2/0/0
- c = Williams,D 2/0/1
- d = Welsby,A. 3/1/0
- e = Walton,G. 30/5/10
- f = Deighton,L. 0/1/0

New influx of experienced players, but City still struggle…public show support with average crowds of over 17,000……Chief Coach - - Bill Jennings - - takes over from Watts - - Jones in April…
Bad fire damage to main Stand after attempted theft of gate money from Grimsby F.A. Cup-tie.

Other Matches

F.A.Cup

	Date	Opposition	Res	Attend.	Goalscorers	1	2	3	4	5	6	7	8	9	10	11
1st	28 Nov	SOUTHALL	3–1	14000	Walton Talbot Pugh	G	I	Z	O	A	H	Q	a	e	S	T
2nd	12 Dec	SWINDON TOWN	2–1	16000	Granville Prescott	R	"	"	"	"	"	"	D	"	a	"
3rd	16 Jan	GRIMSBY TOWN	1–3	36245	Melaniphy	"	"	N	"	"	"	"	S	L	"	e

Welsh Cup

	Date	Opposition	Res	Attend.		1	2	3	4	5	6	7	8	9	10	11
6th	10 Mar	Barry Town	1–3	5000	Walton	f	F	"	Y	X	H	"	"	J	e	d

	Date	Opposition	Res	Attend.		1	2	3	4	5	6	7	8	9	10	11
1st	28 Oct	EXETER CITY	0–1	3000		G	"	Z	O	B	K	"	"	e	a	P

Friendlies

	Date	Opposition	Res			
†	29 Apr	C.CITY PAST/PRESENT	1–1	Melaniphy

† Len Davies' Benefit Match.

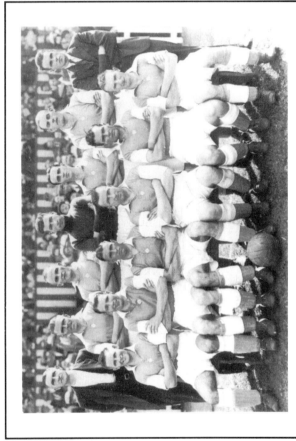

(Back) J. Kneeshaw, G. Nicholson, A. Granville, W. Fielding, W. Scott, W. Bassett, H. Smith.
(Front) R. Pugh, C. Godfrey, C. Smith, A. Pinxton, D. Ovenstone.

1937-38

Football League – Division 3 South

Secretary/Manager: Bill Jennings

P:42 W:15 D:12 L:15 67-54 Pts:42 Pos:10th

756		Date	Opposition	Res	Attend.	Goalscorers	1	2	3	4	5	6	7	8	9	10	11
1.		28 Aug	Clapton Orient	1-1	14548	Collins	*L	J	O	*R	A	I	U	Y	*D	W	X
2.		30	TORQUAY UNITED	5-2	22000	Collins 3 Walton Turner	"	"	"	"	"	"	"	"	"	"	*
3.		4 Sep	SOUTHEND UNITED	5-0	23000	Talbot2 Walton Granville(pen) Turner	"	"	"	"	"	"	"	"	"	"	"
4.		8	Torquay United	1-0	8000	Collins	"	"	"	"	"	"	"	"	"	"	"
5.		11	Q.P.Rangers	1-2	16000	Turner	"	"	"	"	"	"	"	"	"	"	"
6.		13	NORTHAMPTON TOWN	4-1	19830	Godfrey Collins 2 Turner	"	V	"	"	"	"	"	"	"	"	"
7.		18	BRIGHTON & H.A.	4-1	28027	Walton Collins 2 Turner	"	J	"	"	"	"	N	"	"	"	"
8.		25	Bournemouth	0-3	10000		"	"	"	"	"	"	U	"	"	"	"
9.		2 Oct	NOTTS. COUNTY	2-2	35000	Turner 2	"	"	"	"	"	"	"	"	"	"	"
10.		9	WALSALL	3-1	20000	Collins Pugh Turner	"	O	"	"	"	"	"	"	"	"	"
11.		16	Newport County	1-1	24278	Talbot	"	H	"	"	"	"	"	"	"	"	"
12.		23	BRISTOL CITY	0-0	16844		"	J	"	"	"	"	"	"	"	"	"
13.		30	Watford	0-4	10000		"	"	V	"	Q	"	"	"	"	"	"
14.		6 Nov	GILLINGHAM	4-0	14000	Turner Collins Walton Talbot	"	"	H	"	I	S	"	"	"	"	"
15.		13	Exeter City	1-2	10000	Collins	"	"	"	"	Q	I	"	"	"	"	"
16.		20	SWINDON TOWN	2-2	15000	Collins McCaughey	"	"	"	"	"	S	"	"	"	"	"
17.		4 Dec	MILLWALL	3-2	16000	Pugh McCaughey Walton	"	"	*B	"	A	"	"	"	"	"	"
18.		18	CRYSTAL PALACE	4-2	18374	Turner2(1 pen) Collins Talbot	"	I	H	"	"	"	"	"	"	"	"
19.		25	Mansfield Town	0-3	6000		"	"	"	"	"	"	"	"	"	"	"
20.		27	MANSFIELD TOWN	4-1	43000	Pugh Collins Turner2(1 pen)	"	"	"	"	"	"	"	"	"	"	"
21.		1 Jan	CLAPTON ORIENT	2-0	19580	Melaniphy 2	"	J	"	"	*Z	"	"	"	N	"	"
22.		12	Aldershot	1-1	2000		"	I	V	"	A	"	"	"	D	"	"
23.		15	Southend United	1-3	6000	Turner	"	"	"	"	"	"	"	"	"	"	"
24.		22	Q.P.RANGERS	2-2	30000	Walton Turner	"	J	H	"	"	"	T	M	"	"	"
25.		29	Brighton & H.A.	1-2	9802	Collins	"	"	"	S	"	"	P	N	"	"	"
26.		5 Feb	BOURNEMOUTH	3-0	18000	Walton Melaniphy Collins	"	"	B	R	"	"	U	M	"	R	"
27.		12	Notts. County	0-2	14000		"	"	"	"	"	S	T	W	"	N	"
28.		19	Walsall	0-1	5000		"	"	H	"	I	"	*G	E	"	"	"
29.		26	NEWPORT COUNTY	3-1	25000	Turner2 (1 pen) Pugh	"	J	"	"	A	"	*P	Y	"	Y	"
30.		5 Mar	Bristol City	1-0	38066	Collins	"	"	"	"	"	"	U	"	"	W	"
31.		12	WATFORD	1-1	32000	McCaughey	"	"	B	"	"	"	"	M	"	"	"
32.		19	Gillingham	0-1	6000		"	"	"	"	"	"	T	"	"	"	"
33.		26	EXETER CITY	1-1	10000	Collins	"	"	"	"	"	"	P	N	"	"	"
34.		2 Apr	Swindon Town	0-2	8000		"	"	V	Z	"	"	U	M	"	"	"
35.		9	ALDERSHOT	0-1	7000		"	"	"	R	"	"	"	W	"	"	"
36.		15	BRISTOL ROVERS	1-1	10000	Collins	"	"	"	"	"	"	"	"	"	C	*K
37.		16	Millwall	0-1	26000		"	"	H	"	"	I	"	T	M	W	"
38.		18	Bristol Rovers	1-2	10000	Prescot	"	"	"	"	"	"	"	M	D	"	"
39.		23	READING	4-1	8000	Turner 2 Collins 2	"	H	B	"	Z	"	"	"	"	"	T
40.		30	Crystal Palace	0-1	9018		"	"	"	"	A	S	"	"	"	"	X
41.		4 May	Reading	0-0	4000		"	"	"	"	"	"	"	"	T	"	"
42.		7	Northampton Town	0-0	5000		"	"	"	"	"	"	"	"	"	"	*F

Players:

A = Bassett,W.   35/4/0
B = Blenkinsop,E. 10/2/0
C = Brown,A.   1/1/0
D = Collins,J.   39/7/27
E = Davies,A.   1/0/0
F = Evans,T.   1/0/0
G = Finlay,J.   1/1/0
H = Ford,L.   19/3/0
I = Godfrey,C.   25/5/1
J = Granville,A. 30/5/1
K = Harrison,J.   1/0/0
L = Jones,R.   42/7/0
M = McKenzie,J.   9/0/0
N = Melaniphy,E. 5/1/3
O = Mellor,J.   12/2/0
P = Mitchell,J.   2/0/0
Q = Mort,E.   3/1/0
R = McCaughey,C. 41/7/4
S = Nicholson,E. 25/6/0
T = Prescott,J.   5/0/1
U = Pugh,R.   36/6/4
V = Smith,J.   8/0/0
W = Talbot,F.   38/5/5
X = Turner,A.   40/7/21
Y = Walton,E.   30/7/7
Z = Williams,T.   3/0/0

Bob Jones (goalkeeper) Jimmy Collins (centre-forward) & Bert Turner signed- big improvement Attendances grow appreciably.. City lose only one home game.. Ernie Blenkinsop signs (former England International) as player coach but plays only 10 games.

Other Matches

F.A.Cup

	Date	Opposition	Res	Attend.	Goalscorers	1	2	3	4	5	6	7	8	9	10	11
1st	27 Nov	Northampton Town	2-1	14000	Collins 2	L	J	H	R	A	S	U	Y	D	W	X
2nd	11 Dec	BRISTOL CITY	1-1	25472	Turner	"	"	B	"	"	"	"	"	"	"	"
2nd Rep	15	Bristol City	2-0	23050	Collins 2	"	I	H	"	"	"	"	"	"	"	"
3rd	8 Jan	Charlton Athletic	0-5	34637		"	"	O	"	"	"	"	"	"	"	"

Welsh Cup

	Date	Opposition	Res	Attend.	Goalscorers	1	2	3	4	5	6	7	8	9	10	11
6th	16 Feb	CHELTENHAM TOWN	0-1	5000		"	J	B	"	I	"	G	"	"	N	"

Division 3 (South) Cup

	Date	Opposition	Res	Attend.	Goalscorers	1	2	3	4	5	6	7	8	9	10	11
1st	27 Sep	Northampton Town	1-0	3869	Turner	"	"	O	"	Q	I	U	"	"	C	"
2nd	10 Nov	Bristol City	1-2	2130	Collins	"	"	H	"	"	S	"	"	"	W	"

Friendlies

	Date	Opposition	Res	Goalscorers
	6 Oct	Racing Club de Lens	3-1	Walton Collins Talbot
†	4 Nov	Aston Villa	3-0	Pugh 2 Collins
	27 Apr	HIBERNIAN	3-2	Collins 2 Talbot

† Yeovil Challenge Cup

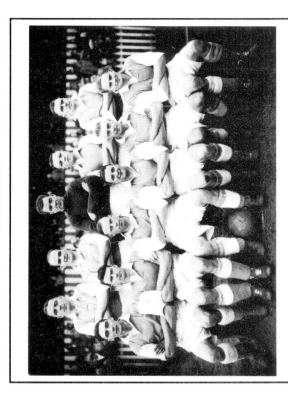

(Back) C. McCaughey, A. Granville, R. Jones, L. Ford, E. Nicholson,
(Front) J. Mitchell, A. Davis, J. Collins, E. walton, A. Turner, T. Williams.

1938-39

Secretary/Manager: Bill Jennings (Cyril Spiers from May 1939)

Football League – Division 3 South. P:42 W:15 D:11 L:16 61-65 Pts:41 Pos:13th

798		Date	Opposition	Res	Attend.	Goalscorers	1	2	3	4	5	6	7	8	9	10	11
1.		27 Aug	EXETER CITY	1-2	30000	Turner	N	L	*O	*F	*C	T	U	b	E	Z	a
2.		31	Mansfield Town	2-2	8000	Collins 2	"	"	"	"	"	"	*W	"	"	"	* Y
3.		3 Sep	Newport County	0-3	18802		"	C	"	"	D	"	"	"	"	"	"
4.		5	WALSALL	2-1	15000	Collins 2	"	"	"	"	"	"	U	W	"	"	a
5.		10	Ipswich Town	2-1	16000	Rickards Prescott	"	"	"	R	"	"	"	"	"	"	V
6.		17	READING	0-1	15000		"	"	"	"	"	"	"	"	"	b	"
7.		24	Bristol Rovers	1-1	10000	Talbot	"	"	"	"	"	"	"	"	"	Z	"
8.		1 Oct	BRIGHTON & H.A.	4-1	17393	Prescott Collins2 Rickards	"	"	"	"	"	"	"	"	"	"	"
9.		8	Bournemouth	0-0	7000		"	"	"	"	"	"	"	"	"	"	"
10.		15	CLAPTON ORIENT	1-2	16317	Talbot	"	K	"	"	"	"	W	Z	"	*M	"
11.		22	Northampton Town	1-2	10000	Prescott	"	"	"	"	"	"	"	"	"	"	"
12.		29	SWINDON TOWN	2-1	12000	Rickards Collins	"	"	"	"	"	"	"	"	"	"	"
13.		5 Nov	Port Vale	1-1	12500	Collins	"	C	"	"	"	"	"	"	"	"	"
14.		12	WATFORD	5-3	10000	Collins 3 McCaughey Hill	"	"	"	"	"	"	"	"	"	"	"
15.		19	Crystal Palace	0-2	17898		J	"	"	"	"	"	"	"	"	"	P
16.		3 Dec	Aldershot	1-1	6000	Collins	"	"	"	"	"	"	V	"	"	Y	*H
17.		17	Torquay United	3-1	3500	Talbot 2 Collins	"	"	"	F	"	"	P	b	"	Z	Y
18.		24	Exeter City	1-1	6000	Egan	"	"	"	"	"	"	*X	"	"	*I	"
19.		26	Q.P.RANGERS	1-0	28000	Collins	"	L	"	R	"	"	"	"	"	"	"
20.		27	Q.P.Rangers	0-5	12000		"	"	"	"	"	"	"	"	"	"	"
21		31	NEWPORT COUNTY	1-2	39113	Smith	"	C	"	"	"	Q	"	"	"	"	"
22.		11 Jan	BRISTOL CITY	2-1	9000	Smith Walton	"	"	"	"	"	T	U	"	"	Z	"
23.		14	IPSWICH TOWN	2-1	14000	o.g. (Parry) Collins	"	"	"	"	"	F	"	"	"	"	I
24.		28	BRISTOL ROVERS	0-2	12000		"	"	"	"	"	T	"	"	"	"	Y
25.		1 Feb	Reading	0-0	4000		"	"	"	F	"	"	"	"	"	I	P
26.		4	Brighton & H.A.	2-1	9770	Egan Collins	"	L	"	"	"	"	P	b	E	"	"
27.		11	BOURNEMOUTH	5-0	12000	Egan 2 Rickards Walton McKenzie	"	"	"	"	"	"	P	*G	"	"	V
28.		18	Clapton Orient	1-1	9035	Egan	N	"	K	"	C	R	X	M	E	Z	"
29.		25	NORTHAMPTON	2-0	9000	Rickards McCaughey	J	"	O	c	"	T	b	S	"	M	"
30.		4 Mar	Swindon Town	1-4	9000	Egan	"	L	"	F	"	"	*B	"	"	"	Y
31.		11	PORT VALE	2-4	10000	Egan Talbot	"	C	"	"	D	"	P	Z	E	Z	"
32.		18	Watford	0-1	6000		"	L	"	"	"	T	B	"	"	Z	I
33.		25	CRYSTAL PALACE	0-1	11910		"	"	"	"	"	"	b	*G	E	M	P
34.		1 Apr	Bristol City	1-1	8720	Egan	"	"	"	"	C	"	P	b	"	I	V
35.		7	Southend United	0-2	10000		N	J	"	"	"	R	X	M	E	Z	"
36.		8	ALDERSHOT	2-4	8000	Prescott Egan	J	"	O	c	"	T	b	S	"	M	"
37.		10	SOUTHEND UNITED	1-0	8000	Pugh	"	"	K	"	F	c	U	"	E	M	"
38.		15	Notts. County	1-1	7000	McKenzie	"	"	"	"	D	R	"	Z	P	M	"
39.		17	NOTTS. COUNTY	4-1	5000	Talbot 2 Anderson Pugh	"	C	"	"	"	"	"	*A	E	Z	M
40.		22	TORQUAY UNITED	3-1	6000	Collins Talbot Hill	N	"	"	"	"	T	"	P	"	"	"
41.		29	MANSFIELD TOWN	0-0	6000		J	"	"	R	c	"	"	b	"	"	"
42.		6 May	Walsall	3-6	5000	Collins Talbot Hill	"	"	"	F	C	R	"	"	"	"	"

Players:

A = Anderson,R.S. 1/0/1
B = Baker,W. 3/2/0
C = Ballsom,W.G. 34/13/0
D = Bassett,W. 34/8/0
E = Collins,J. 36/11/21
F = Corkhill,W. 23/8/0
G = Court,H. 1/0/0
H = Davies,W.J. 1/0/0
I = Egan,H. 17/5/14
J = Fielding,W. 26/13/0
K = Ford,L. 5/1/0
L = Granville,A. 10/3/1
M = Hill ,C. 14/3/3
N = Jones,R. 16/1/0
O = Kelso,J. 41/14/0
P = McKenzie,J. 12/5/4
Q = Main,W. 1/1/0
R = McCaughey,C. 25/9/3
S = Mitchell,J. 1/1/0
T = Nicholson,G. 34/10/0
U = Pugh,R. 18/6/3
V = Prescott,J. 17/4/4
W = Rickards,T. 20/6/10
X = Rhodes,A. 5/0/0
Y = Smith,R. 11/7/2
Z = Talbot,L. 37/12/12
a = Turner,A. 2/0/1
b = Walton,E. 24/7/3
c = Williams,T. 3/3/0

Inconsistancy and lack of support for free-scoring Jimmy Collins keep City in mid-table . . . F.A.Cup victory over 1st Division Charlton, and replay with Newcastle . . . Defeat in Welsh Cup Final to South Liverpool . . . . Cyril Spiers replaces Bill Jennings as secretary-manager at end of season.

Other Matches

F.A.Cup

	Date	Opposition	Res	Attend.	Goalscorers	1	2	3	4	5	6	7	8	9	10	11
1st	26 Nov	Cheltenham Town	1-1	8000	Prescott	J	C	O	R	D	T	W	Z	E	Y	V
1st Rep	3	CHELTENHAM TOWN	1-0	8940	Prescott	"	"	"	"	"	"	"	"	"	"	"
2nd	10 Dec	CREWE ALEXANDRA	1-0	19000	Talbot	"	"	"	"	"	"	P	b	"	Z	Y
3rd	7 Jan	CHARLTON ATHLETIC	1-0	22780	Walton	"	"	"	"	"	"	U	"	"	"	"
4th	21	NEWCASTLE UNITED	0-0	42060		"	"	"	"	"	"	"	"	"	"	"
4th Rep	25	Newcastle United	1-4	44649	Pugh	"	"	"	"	"	"	"	"	"	"	"

Welsh Cup

	Date	Opposition	Res	Attend.	Goalscorers	1	2	3	4	5	6	7	8	9	10	11
5th	8 Feb	SWANSEA TOWN	2-2	4000	Mackenzie McCaughey	"	"	"	F	c	R	b	W	"	I	P
5th Rep	23	Swansea Town	4-1	1500	Egan 2 Rickards 2	"	L	"	"	C	"	B	"	I	Z	Y
6th	8 Mar	NEWPORT COUNTY	5-1	6000	Egan 3 Rickards Mackenzie	"	C	"	"	D	T	"	"	"	"	P
S/final	30	Oswestry	1-1	3000	Granville	"	L	"	"	C	R	b	"	"	"	V
S/fin Rep	13 Apr	Oswestry	2-2	3000	Talbot Collins	"	K	"	"	c	T	U	Z	E	I	"
S/fin Rep2	26	Oswestry	2-1	5000	Talbot Collins	"	L	"	"	D	"	"	P	"	Z	M
Final	4 May	South Liverpool	1-2	5000	Collins	"	"	"	"	c	"	"	b	"	"	"

Division 3 (South) Cup

	Date	Opposition	Res	Attend.	Goalscorers	1	2	3	4	5	6	7	8	9	10	11
1st	16 Nov	Bristol City	0-6	670		N	L	"	C	Q	S	Z	"	"	M	P

Jubilee Benevolent Fund

	Date	Opposition	Res	Attend.	Goalscorers	1	2	3	4	5	6	7	8	9	10	11
	20 Aug	Swansea Town	3-3	6000	o.g.(Simmons) Collins 2	"	"	"	R	D	F	U	b	"	Z	a

Friendlies

	Date	Opposition	Res	Goalscorers
†	2 May	FULHAM	2-3	Wooller Hill

† Billy Hardy Benefit Match

August 1938 - Secretary/manager Bill Jennings welcomes the new signings:
G. Gunn, W. Ballsom, W. Corkhill, J. Kelso, R. Smith and T. Rickards.

1939-40

Secretary/Manager: Cyril Spiers

Football League – Division 3 South.

P:3 W:2 D:0 L:1 5-5 Pts:4 Pos: -

-	Date	Opposition	Res	Attend.	Goalscorers	1	2	3	4	5	6	7	8	9	10	11
1.	26 Aug	Norwich City	2-1	14000	Collins Pugh	F	A	*K	*E	*B	*D	J	*G	C	*I	*H
2.	30	Swindon Town	1-0	10000	Collins	"	"	"	"	"	"	"	"	"	"	"
3.	2 Sep	NOTTS. COUNTY	2-4	20000	Collins 2	"	"	"	"	"	"	"	"	"	"	"

OUTBREAK OF WORLD WAR 2 – FOOTBALL LEAGUE FIXTURES SUSPENDED.

Other Matches:

Welsh Cup

5th	16 Dec	Ebbw Vale	4-0	2000	Court Pugh 3	L	M	N	O	B	P	J	Q	G	R	S
6th	2 Mar	NEWPORT COUNTY	1-1	3000	Owen	"	"	"	"	"	G	"	R	b	W	X
6th Rep	18	Newport County	0-5	800		"	"	"	Y	"	"	"	"	Z	"	G

Football League Jubilee Fund – Friendly Match.

	19 Aug	SWANSEA TOWN	1-1	9000	Marshall	F	K	N	E	B	D	J	G	C	a	H

The day before the War started.

PLAYERS: (Total appearances/total goals scored – all matches. Guest players registered with Club shown in brackets, or if Club unknown shown *)

(Players who appeared in post-declaration of War matches and/or pre-declaration games) (Additional players who played in post-declaration of War games only)

A = Ballsom,W.	23/0	J = Pugh,R.	24/6	S = Sabin,G.	12/3	Anderson,R. 2/1
B = Booth,W.	27/0	K = Sykes,E.	3/0	T = Wilkinson,R. *	15/0	Baker,W. 8/0
C = Collins,J.	12/7	L = Poland,G.	2/0	U = Granville,A.	27/0	Britton,C. (Everton) 1/0
D = Cringan,J.	3/0	M = Ford,L.	4/0	V = Clark,T. *	9/0	Cumner,R. * 2/0
E = Corkhill,W.	4/1	N = Kelso,J.	2/0	W = Jones,B.(Arsenal)	10/0	Forse,T. (Local Am.) 1/0
F = Fielding,W.	3/0	O = Cope,J. *	10/0	X = Tucker	1/0	Griffiths,W.(Local Am.) 1/0
G = Marshall,E.	30/6	P = Hill,C.	1/0	Y = Green	1/0	Hogg,G. (Local Am.) 5/0
H = Myers,J.	3/0	Q = Court,H.	12/6	Z = Boulter,L.(Brentf'd)	2/3	Lewis,A. (Plymouth) 1/0
I = Phillips		R = James,W.	20/4	a = Egan,H.	4/3	McPhillips,L. 3/0
		b = Owen,W.	2/1			Pugh,J. 1/0

Meades,R.	1/3	Reid,C.	9/0
Mitchell,W.	1/1	Rooney,J. *	5/0
Moore,J. (Local Am.)	5/3	Scott,W.	2/0
Morrelli	1/0	Smith,J. *	1/0
Morris,T.	3/1	Steggles,J. (Local Am.)	4/0
Nicholson,W. (Aberd'n)	1/0	Tobin,R. (Local Am.)	3/3
Parker,G. *	5/0	Williams,T.	2/0
Pritchard,F. *	3/0	Wood,T.	1/0
Prosser,C.	2/0	Woodward,L. (Wolves)	1/0

1939-40

South-West League (Wartime)
P:28 W:6 D:9 L:13 45-63 Pts:25 Pos:7th

	Date	Opposition	Res	Attend.	Goalscorers
1.	21 Oct	Bristol City	1-1	6545	Corkhill
2.	28	SWANSEA TOWN	2-2	5000	Court Sabin
3.	4 Nov	PLYMOUTH ARGYLE	1-0	4000	Court
4.	11	Swindon Town	2-2	4161	Collins Marshall
5.	18	BRISTOL ROVERS	0-0	2000	
6.	25	Newport County	1-3	2228	Marshall
7.	2 Dec	TORQUAY UNITED	2-2	1500	Anderson Court
8.	9	BRISTOL CITY	7-3	1195	Marshall 3 Court 2 Sabin 2 Egan
9.	16	Swansea Town	0-4	2500	
10.	23	Plymouth Argyle	2-6	2671	Egan o.g.
11.	30	SWINDON TOWN	1-1	3000	James
12.	6 Jan	Bristol Rovers	0-7	1012	
13.	13	NEWPORT COUNTY	1-0	4000	Court
14.	20	Torquay United	0-5	1200	
15.	10 Feb	PLYMOUTH ARGYLE	0-0	2000	
16.	24	BRISTOL ROVERS	1-1	3000	Pugh
17.	9 Mar	TORQUAY UNITED	1-1	3000	Pugh
18.	16	BRISTOL CITY	3-2	4000	Boulton 2 Pugh
19.	22	Bristol City	2-3	3343	Owen Pugh
20.	23	Swansea Town	0-1	3000	
21.	30	Plymouth Argyle	1-4	3541	Morris
22.	6 Apr	SWINDON TOWN	1-1	3000	Marshall
23.	20	Swindon Town	2-2	1665	Collins 2
24.	11 May	Torquay United	4-2	1137	James Marshall Moore Parker
25.	13	NEWPORT COUNTY	4-1	3000	Parker Tobin Pugh Moore
26.	18	SWANSEA TOWN	2-2	2000	James Tobin
27.	25	Newport County	1-4	600	Baker
28.	1 Jun	Bristol Rovers	3-3	1210	James Meads 2

Other Matches

Cup

Date	Opposition	Res	Attend.	Goalscorers
13 Apr	READING	1-1	3000	Mitchell
17	Reading	0-5	2750	

Friendlies

Date	Opposition	Res	Attend.	Goalscorers
13 Sep	ARSENAL	3-4	5000	Sabin Collins Court
16	NEWPORT COUNTY	2-0	7000	Egan Collins
23	SWANSEA TOWN	1-1	5000	Collins
30	Swansea Town	1-4	3000	Collins
7 Oct	PLYMOUTH ARGYLE	1-1	5000	Collins
14	SWINDON TOWN	3-1	3000	Pugh Collins 2
14	Bristol Rovers	2-1	2000	Mitchell Egan
25 Dec	Bath City	3-1	7500	James Egan Pugh
26	WOLVERHAMPTON W.	2-5	12500	Sabin Court
6 Jan	BIRMINGHAM CITY	4-5	4000	Jones,B. 2 Anderson Griffiths
25 Mar	WEST BROM.ALBION	1-1	8000	Pugh

● **CARDIFF CITY'S** playing staff face the camera in early August 1939, but a month later, War caused football to be abandoned for the duration....

BACK (from left) – Billy Baker, Arthur Granville, Jimmy Myers, Bill Fielding, John Anderson, John Court, Jimmy Kelso, Cyril Prosser. MIDDLE (from left) – George Sabin, Bill Corkhill, George Gunn, George Ballson, Bill Booth, Ernie Marshall, Jim Cringan, Ernie Sykes, John Pugh, John Smith (trainer). FRONT (from left) – Jimmy Collins, Billy James, Frank Smallman, Cyril Spiers (Secretary/Manager), Laurie McPhillips, Reg Pugh, Harry Egan.

1940-41

Football League (Wartime) - South
P:24 W:12 D:5 L:7 75-50 Pos:5th (Based on goal average)

	Date	Opposition	Res	Attend.	Goalscorers
1.	31 Aug	Reading	0-2	2861	
2.	7 Sep	READING	2-2	3000	James Moore
3.	14	BIRMINGHAM CITY	5-2	2175	Moore 3 James Parker
4.	21	Birmingham City	2-3	3500	Pugh James
5.	28	BRISTOL CITY	2-2	3500	James Wrigglesworth
6.	5 Oct	Bristol City	0-1	1546	
7.	12	Coventry City	2-5	2700	Parker 2
8.	19	COVENTRY CITY	2-2	3000	James Hollyman
9.	26	SWANSEA TOWN	8-0	4000	James 3 Moore 3 Parker 2
10.	9 Nov	Southampton	3-1	2000	Moore 2 Parker
11.	16	SOUTHAMPTON	1-1	1500	Moore
12.	23	Bristol City	1-4	2500	James
13.	30	BRISTOL CITY	5-1	2000	James 2 Moore Scott Wood
14.	7 Dec	Stoke City	1-5	1800	Steggles
15.	14	STOKE CITY	4-0	1000	Morris James 3
16.	21	Bournemouth & B.A.	5-2	800	Moore 2 James Baker Parker
17.	25	Swansea Town	3-1	3000	Moore James
18.	28	BOURNEMOUTH & B.A.	1-3	4000	Jones,T.
19.	11 Jan	BRISTOL CITY	5-2	2000	Moore 2 James 2 Joy
20.	25	Swansea Town	3-2	1500	Moore 2 James
21.	8 Feb	Bristol City	7-4	1500	Moore 4 Parker Pugh Williams
22.	17 May	WEST BROM. ALBION	4-4	3009	Parker 2 James 2
23.	24	PORTSMOUTH	4-1	2723	o.g.(Walker) Moore 2 Parker
24.	31	WOLVERHAMPTON W.	5-1	4204	James 2 Moore T.Jones Parker

Other Matches

League Cup

	Date	Opposition	Res	Attend.	Goalscorers
1st/1 Leg	15 Feb	SWANSEA TOWN	3-2	4000	Moore Parker James
1st/2 Leg	29	SWANSEA TOWN	6-2	4000	Moore 3 Parker 2 James
2nd/1 Leg	8 Mar	Reading	1-0	5000	James
2nd/2 Leg	15	READING	4-1	10000	James 2 Baker Moore
3rd	22	Tottenham 'Spur	3-3	5000	Moore 2 Barnes
3rd Replay	29	TOTTENHAM 'SPUR	2-3	21000	James Parker

Western Regional League

	Date	Opposition	Res	Attend.	Goalscorers
	5 Apr	Bath City	1-2	1500	James
	12	LOVELL'S ATHLETIC	3-2	2500	James 2 Parker
	14	Aberaman	2-2	750	Moore Parker
	19	Lovell's Athletic	1-2	2000	Moore
	26	BATH CITY	5-2	1700	James 3 Moore 2
Lge.Cup Fin.	3 Jun	LOVELL'S ATHLETIC	1-6		Hollyman

Both Regional League matches versus Bristol City were postponed.

Friendlies

	Opposition	Res	Attend.	Goalscorers
2 Nov	ARMY X1	18-1	1000	James 7 Scott 5 Parker 2 Moore 2 Allen Pugh
26 Dec	Regional X1	1-3	1200	Jones,T.
10 May	CHELSEA	1-2	4000	Tobin

Players: (All Competitions)

Allen,J.	2/0	Forse,T. (Local Am.)	1/0	James,W.	29/29	Parker,L.	30/16	Scott,W.	3/1
Baker,W.	22/8	Glass,F.	1/0	Jones,H.	13/0	Phillips,R.	2/0	Smith,C.	1/0
Barry,P. *	1/0	Goddard,W. (Wolves)	3/0	Jones,E.	1/0	Pritchard,F.	27/0	Springthorpe,T.	14/1
Burns,J. *	10/1	Granville,A.	19/0	Joy,H.	3/1	Pritchard,G.	1/0	Steggles,J.	14/1
Butler,S.	1/0	Griffiths,K.	1/0	Meades,R.	1/0	Pugh,J.	29/2	Stittall,A.	1/0
Charlesworth,S.(Grimsby)	1/0	Hall,F.	2/0	Moore,J.	30/32	Pugh,R.	11/0	Tobin,R.	26/1
Court,H.	1/0	Hart,P.	1/0	Morgan,G.	1/0	Reid,C.	1/0	Williams,J.	1/1
Dodge,J.	1/0	Hollyman,K.	5/2	Morris,A. *	2/2	Rooney,J. (Wolves)	2/0	Wood,T.	25/1
								Wrigglesworth,W.	2/1

1941-42

Football League (Wartime) – South

P:15 W:9 D:5 L:1 43-28 Pts:19 Pos:3rd (Based on goal average)

	Date	Opposition	Res	Attend.	Goalscorers
1.	30 Aug	West Brom. Albion	3-6	4462	Moore James 2
2.	6 Sep	WEST BROM. ALBION	1-1	4647	Moore
3.	27	SOUTHAMPTON	5-3	3930	Parker 2 Moore Hollyman James
4.	4 Oct	Southampton	3-1	2000	Moore Parker 2
5.	11	Wolverhampton W.	3-0	4612	Lewis Moore Perry
6.	18	WOLVERHAMPTON W.	2-0	3217	James Parker
7.	25	BOURNEMOUTH & B.A.	0-2	2500	
8.	1 Nov	Bournemouth & B.A.	2-3	3000	Moore James
9.	8	LUTON TOWN	6-1	2500	James 3 Moore 2 Dare
10.	15	Luton Town	0-2	2300	
11.	22	SWANSEA TOWN	1-0	2000	Parker
12.	29	Swansea Town	1-4	2500	Parker
13.	6 Dec	BRISTOL CITY	8-2	3000	Parker 3 Weir 3 Thomas Steggles
14.	13	Bristol City	6-2	4000	Parker Dare Weir 2 Wood 2
15.	25	SWANSEA TOWN	2-1	3750	Moore Parker

Other Matches

League War Cup – Qualifying Competition

Date	Opposition	Res	Attend.	Goalscorers
27 Dec	Southampton	5-2	2500	Parker 3 Morris Butler
3 Jan	SOUTHAMPTON	9-1	5000	Parker 5 Moore 2 Morgan Wood
10	Swansea Town	1-1	4000	Moore
17	SWANSEA TOWN	1-1	5000	Parker
24	Bristol City	3-8	3312	Moore 3
31	BRISTOL CITY	0-2	6000	
7 Feb	Bournemouth & B.A.	1-2	2000	Parker
14	BOURNEMOUTH & B.A.	6-1	5300	Parker 3 Moore 2 Wood
21	Swansea Town	5-1	5000	Wright 3 Parker Moore
28	SWANSEA TOWN	8-1	7000	Wood 2 Weir 3 Parker 2 Moore

League War Cup – Competition Proper

	Date	Opposition	Res	Attend.	Goalscorers
1st/1 Leg	4 Apr	SOUTHAMPTON	3-1	5000	Moore 2 Fenton
1st/2 Leg	6	Southampton	1-1	3600	Moore
2nd/1 Leg	11	WEST BROM. ALBION	1-1	10781	Lewis
2nd/2 Leg	18	West Brom. Albion	2-3	10198	Shelley 2

League

Date	Opposition	Res	Attend.	Goalscorers
14 Mar	LUTON TOWN	2-0	5000	Fenton 2
21	SWANSEA TOWN	4-1	4320	Wright Lewis Moore 2
25 Apr	NORTHAMPTON TOWN	0-1	3460	
2 May	Northampton Town	1-6	2271	Moore
25	SWANSEA TOWN	4-1	3720	Moore 3 Griffiths
30	LUTON TOWN	2-4	2695	Hollyman 2

Friendlies

Date	Opposition	Res	Attend.	Goalscorers
13 Sep	CZECH ARMY	0-0	1100	
7 Mar	ROYAL AIR FORCE	3-3	1000	Hollyman o.g.(Morgan) Pugh

Players (All Competitions)

Baker,W.	2/0	Gristock,F.	1/0	Marshall,E.	8/0	Parr,J. (Lincoln C.)	1/1	Sherwood,A.	2/0
Butler,S.	3/1	Hargreaves,J.	1/0	Macaulay,J. (Chelsea)	1/0	Paul,R. (Swansea T.)	1/0	Steggles,J.	9/1
Carey,J. (Man.Utd.)	1/0	Hollyman,K.	34/3	McKenzie,J. (Notts C.)	1/0	Phillips,J.	34/0	Stittall,A.	2/0
Carter,H. (Sunderland)	1/0	Hustwick,D.	1/0	McLoughlin,K.	3/0	Pressdee,H.	1/0	Stuart,D.	1/0
Chilton,A. (Man.Utd.)	3/0	James,W.	7/8	Mitten,C. (Man.Utd.)	1/0	Pritchard,G.	1/0	Thomas,R.	1/1
Clarke,A. (Lovell's Ath.)	1/0	Jones,E. (Swindon)	1/0	Moore,J.	35/27	Pugh,J.	34/0	Tobin,R.	6/0
Dare,R.	14/2	Jones,H.	22/0	Morgan,G.	2/1	Sabin,G.	2/0	Tomkins,A. (Spurs)	1/0
Dunstan,R.	1/0	Jones,J.	2/0	Morris,T.	11/1	Sargeant,G.	1/0	Weir,A. (Hibernian)	11/5
Fenton,B. (Millwall)	5/3	Lewis,I. (Sheff.Wed.)	5/1	Owen,I.	3/0	Shelley,A. (Lovell's Ath.)	1/2	Whatley,W.	1/0
Griffiths,J.	14/1	Lewis,W.	11/2	Parker,L.	25/27	Sheppard,S.	1/0	Wood,T.	18/8
Griffiths,W.	20/0							Wright,G.	10/0

1942-43

(War) League West
P:18 W:8 D:3 L:7 41-45 Pts:19 Pos:3rd

	Date	Opposition	Res	Attend.	Goalscorers
1.	29 Aug	Bath City	0-3	2000	
2.	5 Sep	BATH CITY	2-0	2563	Moore Clarke
3.	12	Bristol City	1-9	2743	Clarke
4.	19	BRISTOL CITY	0-0	2500	
5.	26	LOVELL'S ATHLETIC	4-8	2800	Moore McAulay Griffiths Pugh
6.	3 Oct	Lovell's Athletic	3-1	3100	Clarke Moore McAulay
7.	10	Swansea Town	4-2	1200	Clarke 2 Griffiths,K. 2
8.	17	SWANSEA TOWN	5-0	2500	Wright Clarke 2 Moore Parker
9.	24	Aberaman	5-2	500	Wright 2 Clarke 2 Moore
10.	31	ABERAMAN	5-1	3000	Gracott 2 Clarke 2 Moore
11.	7 Nov	Lovell's Athletic	1-1	3000	Moore
12.	14	LOVELL'S ATHLETIC	0-1	3500	
13.	21	ABERAMAN	1-1	2500	Moore
14.	28	Aberaman	4-2	720	Morgan Clarke 3
15.	5 Dec	BRISTOL CITY	4-3	3000	Griffiths Morgan 3
16.	12	Bristol City	0-5	1800	
17.	19	BATH CITY	1-3	1000	Morgan
18.	25	Swansea Town	1-3	2426	Clarke

Other Matches

(Wartime) League North Cup – Qualifying Competition

Date	Opposition	Res	Attend.	Goalscorers
26 Dec	SWANSEA TOWN	2-2	5000	Griffiths,K. Wright
2 Jan	Bath City	1-2	2700	Moore
9	ABERAMAN	0-1	2000	
16	Aberaman	1-3	640	o.g.(Handford)
23	Lovell's Athletic	0-4	5000	
30	LOVELL'S ATHLETIC	1-4	1800	Moore
6 Feb	BRISTOL CITY	0-3	3000	
13	Bristol City	1-1	3000	Clarke
20	Swansea Town	2-1	2000	Clarke Daly
27	BATH CITY	2-5	3000	Parker Daly
6 Mar	SWANSEA TOWN	2-0	2000	Sparshott 2
13	Swansea Town	1-1	2000	Moore
20	LOVELL'S ATHLETIC	2-5	3000	Nairn 2

League Cup West

Date	Opposition	Res	Attend.	Goalscorers
10 Apr	ABERAMAN	2-3	2500	Clarke 2 Evans
17	Bath City	3-4	1500	Willicombe Clarke 2
24	SWANSEA TOWN	2-5	2500	Murphy Moore

Friendlies

Date	Opposition	Res	Attend.	Goalscorers
27 Mar	ROYAL AIR FORCE X1	1-3	5000	Jones,J.
3 Apr	WESTERN COMMAND	5-4	2500	Clarke 2 Ferrier 2 McDonald
26	Royal Air Force X1	3-1	1000	Sherwood Rees 2

Players (All Competitions)

Artus,K. *	1/0	Dare,R.	1/0
Bewley,R.	1/0	Davies,D.	1/0
Bird,F.	10/0	Devonshire,K.	2/0
Bradshaw,G. (Bury)	2/0	Downs,R.	1/0
Chedgzoy,S. (Swansea)	2/0	Drury,S.	1/0
Clarke,A. (Lovell's Ath.)	1/0	Edwards,W.	9/0
Clarke,R.	28/18	Facherell *	1/0
Collis,R.	3/0	Ferrier *	1/0
Conway,G.	7/0	Ford,L.	5/0
Corbett,W. (Doncaster)	1/0	Foxall	3/0
Courtier,L. *	1/0	Fursland,S. (Stoke)	1/0
Daly,J.	2/2	Gilchrist,M.	1/0
Gilthrow	1/0	Lester,L.	2/0
Gregory,F.	1/0	Lewis,W.	1/0
Griffiths,K.	2/0	Macaulay,J. (Chelsea)	3/2
Griffiths,W.	1/0	Mackay,R. *	1/0
Gristock,F.	1/0	McDonald,J.(Bournem'th)	2/0
Grocott,T.	1/0	McLoughlin,K.	6/0
Hollyman,K.	1/0	Mitchell,J.	1/0
Hustwick,D.	1/0	Moore,J.	32/13
Jenkins,F.	5/0	Morgan,C.	9/5
Jones,A.	3/0	Morgan,D.	1/0
Jones,J.	1/0	Murphy,J. (Hibernian)	2/1
Kinsey,N.	1/0	Nairn,J. (Swansea)	1/2
Orphan,I.	3/0	Stitfall,A.	2/0
Palfrey,V. (Nottm.F.)	1/0	Stitfall,R.	2/0
Parker,L.	23/4	Tame,A.	1/0
Phillips,J.	6/0	Thomas,W.	1/0
Pugh,J.	9/1	Turner,H. (Charlton)	2/0
Rees,N.	2/0	Turner,M.	1/0
Richards,T.	1/0	Vrapehart,W.	2/0
Sergeant,G.	1/0	Welsh,M.	3/0
Shankley,W. (Preston)	1/0	Williams,A.	1/0
Sherwood,A.	32/0	Willicombe,W.	2/1
Sneddon,W.	1/0	Wood,T.	1/0
Sparshott,G.	2/2	Wright,G.	25/2

1943-44

(Wartime) League West
P:28 W:11 D:1 L:6 45-28 Pts:23 Pos:2nd

	Date	Opposition	Res	Attend.	Goalscorers
1.	28 Aug	LOVELL'S ATHLETIC	1-2	3500	Griffiths,K.
2.	4 Sep	Lovell's Athletic	1-3	4000	Moore
3.	11	BRISTOL CITY	4-1	3000	Steggles 2 Williams Sherwood
4.	18	Bristol City	1-2	3310	Raybould
5.	25	Bath City	7-2	3500	Court Williams Clarke2 Moore2 Raybould
6.	2 Oct	BATH CITY	1-3	4000	Moore
7.	9	ABERAMAN	3-2	3000	Moore 2 Williams
8.	16	Aberaman	2-1	450	Wood Clarke
9.	23	SWANSEA TOWN	5-0	4500	Williams 3 Moore Clarke
10.	30	Swansea Town	3-1	2000	Moore 2 Raybould
11.	6 Nov	BRISTOL CITY	1-0	3000	Sherwood
12.	13	Bristol City	1-1	4000	Wood
13.	20	BATH CITY	3-1	3500	Clarke Williams 2
14.	27	Bath City	1-2	2300	Williams
15.	4 Dec	SWANSEA TOWN	1-0	2500	Clarke
16.	11	Swansea Town	4-2	1000	Raybould 2 Williams Moore
17.	18	Lovell's Athletic	1-4	2760	Raybould
18.	25	LOVELL'S ATHLETIC	5-1	3000	Moore 2 Williams 2 Clarke

Other Matches

(War) League North Cup – Qualifying Competition

Date	Opposition	Res	Attend.	Goalscorers
27 Dec	Bath City	2-3	6000	Clarke Steggles
1 Jan	BATH CITY	1-2	4000	Sherwood
8	SWANSEA TOWN	7-1	2500	Moore 3 Sherwood Wood Rees Carless
15	Swansea Town	2-1	1200	Rees Wood
22	Aberaman	2-1	800	Rees Carless
29	ABERAMAN	4-1	3000	Raybould Williams 2 Rees
5 Feb	BRISTOL CITY	2-0	5000	Moore Rees
12	Bristol City	0-2	4000	
19	LOVELL'S ATHLETIC	2-0	6000	Wood o.g.(Low)
26	Lovell's Athletic	1-2	7000	Rees

(War) League North Cup – Competition Proper

	Date	Opposition	Res	Attend.	Goalscorers
1st/1 Leg	4 Mar	Lovell's Athletic	0-2	6000	
1st/2 Leg	11	LOVELL'S ATHLETIC	1-0	10000	Rees

(War) League North – Second Competition

Date	Opposition	Res	Attend.	Goalscorers
18 Mar	ABERAMAN	6-0	2000	Gibson Moore 2 Rees 2 Clarke
25	Aberaman	5-0	1000	Rees 2 Clarke Carless Gibson
1 Apr	BRISTOL CITY	6-0	1000	Clarke o.g.(Preece) Rees2 Carless
8	Bristol City	2-1	2000	Rees Dare
10	LOVELL'S ATHLETIC	1-1	3000	Moore
15	Lovell's Athletic	0-2	3000	
22	Swansea Town	4-2	4000	Gibson 3 Lester
29	SWANSEA TOWN	3-1	2000	Rees 2 Carless

League West – Cup

	Date	Opposition	Res	Attend.	Goalscorers
Fin./1 Leg	6 May	Bath City	2-4	5000	Gibson Clarke
Fin./2 Leg	13 May	BATH CITY	0-0	8000	

Players (All Competitions)

Bufton,T.	1/0	Griffiths,W.	23/0	McLoughlin,K.	2/0	Richards,T.	1/0
Carless,E.	15/5	James,K.	1/0	Moore,J.	39/20	Rowlands,V.	1/0
Chew,J. (Luton)	13/0	Jones,A.	22/0	Parker,L.	1/0	Sherwood,A.	38/4
Clarke,R.	28/12	Jones,J.	3/0	Parker,W. (Bradford C.)	1/0	Smith,A.	5/0
Court,H.	2/1	Kinsey,N.	1/0	Phillips,J.	2/0	Stansfield,F.	39/0
Davies,D.	2/0	Lester,L.	3/1	Pugh,J.	15/0	Steggles,J.	4/3
Day,G.	1/0	Lever,A.	39/0	Raybould,M.	29/7	Williams,W.	31/14
Gibson,C.	9/7	McIntosh,A.	7/0	Rees,W.	19/16	Wood,T.	28/4
Griffiths,K.	2/1					Wright,G.	2/0

1944-45

(War) League West
P:18 W:12 D:3 L:3 54-24 Pts:27 Pos:1st

	Date	Opposition	Res	Attend.	Goalscorers
1.	26 Aug	BRISTOL CITY	4-1	6000	Rees 3 Wood
2.	2 Sep	Bristol City	0-3	3930	
3.	9	BATH CITY	2-1	8000	Wood Rees
4.	16	Bath City	2-2	3000	Rees Wood
5.	23	ABERAMAN	8-2	3500	Rees 3 Moore 2 Wood 2
6.	30	Aberaman	6-0	700	Rees Moore Wood 2 Clarke 2
7.	7 Oct	LOVELL'S ATHLETIC	1-1	9500	Moore
8.	14	Lovell's Athletic	1-1	5500	Moore
9.	21	SWANSEA Town	3-2	7000	Wood Clarke Moore
10.	28	Swansea Town	4-0	5000	Clarke 2 Wood Rees
11.	4 Nov	Aberaman	3-0	800	Wood Rees 2
12.	11	ABERAMAN	3-0	4000	Wood 2 Moore
13.	18	Bath City	2-4	3000	Rees Raybould
14.	25	BATH CITY	6-2	6000	Wood 2 Clarke 2 Rees 2
15.	2 Dec	Swansea Town	3-1	3500	Wood Moore,B. Moore,R.
16.	9	SWANSEA TOWN	3-1	4000	Clarke Wood Rees
17.	16	Lovell's Athletic	3-2	4800	Clarke Moore Rees
18.	23	LOVELL'S ATHLETIC	0-1	2500	

Other Matches

(War) League North Cup – Qualifying Competition

Date	Opposition	Res	Attend.	Goalscorers
25 Dec	SWANSEA TOWN	3-1	4000	Lever Clarke Wood
30	Swansea Town	3-1	4500	Clarke Rees Wood
6 Jan	Lovell's Athletic	0-1	7000	
13	LOVELL'S ATHLETIC	3-0	8000	Moore Rees 2
20	BATH CITY	4-2	3600	Gibson Clarke Rees 2
3 Feb	Aberaman	5-2	1000	Rees 4 Gibson
10	ABERAMAN	0-0	3500	
17	BRISTOL CITY	4-2	11500	Gibson Lester Moore 2
24	Bristol City	0-1	11657	
3 Mar	Bath City	4-1	3000	Clarke Gibson Rees 2

(War) League North Cup – Competition Proper

	Date	Opposition	Res	Attend.	Goalscorers
1st/1 Leg	24 Mar	LOVELL'S ATHLETIC	1-0	12000	Rees
1st/2 Leg	31	Lovell's Athletic	0-0	10000	
2nd/1 Leg	7 Apr	Bristol City †	2-1	20714	Carless Lester
2nd/2 Leg	14	BRISTOL CITY	2-2	23161	Hollyman Rees
3rd/1 Leg	21	Wolverhampton W.	0-3	30000	
3rd/2 Leg	28	WOLVERHAMPTON W.	2-1	35000	Hollyman Carless

† After extra time: Match completed after record 3hrs. 22 mins.

(War) League West – Cup

Date	Opposition	Res	Attend.	Goalscorers
10 Mar	Swansea Town	0-1	4000	
17	SWANSEA TOWN	6-2	10000	Gibson Rees 4 Lester
2 Apr	BRISTOL CITY	3-2	14000	Carless 2 Gibson
12 May	LOVELL'S ATHLETIC	0-4	5000	

Frendlies

Date	Opposition	Res	Attend.	Goalscorers
19 May	Plymouth Argyle	2-1	2000	Carless Griffiths
21	LEAGUE WEST X1	4-4	3000	Pembrey 2 Jones,E. 2
26	PLYMOUTH ARGYLE	2-2	3000	Carless Rees

Players (All Competitions)

Allen,B.(Swansea)	1/0	Day,G.	2/0
Booth,W.	1/0	Evans,L.	1/0
Brain,H. (A.Villa)	4/1	Forse,T. *	1/0
Brooks,H. (Aldershot)	1/0	Foxey (Bristol C.)	1/0
Cain,G. *	1/0	Gibson,C.	1/0
Canning,D.	8/4	Giffiths,K.	2/0
Carless,E.	37/15	Griffiths,W.	33/12
Clarke,R.	1/0	Hill,C.	2/1
Crisp,G. (Nottm.F.)	1/0	Hollyman,K.	20/0
Davies,D.			
Jones,A.	2/0	Pollard,J.	1/0
Lester,L.	37/3	Raybould,M.	4/1
Lever,A.	39/1	Rees,W.	39/33
Lewis,L. (Swansea)	1/0	Rowlands,V.	7/0
Lewis,T.	37/0	Sherwood,A.	38/0
McLoughlin,K.	1/0	Smith,A.	35/0
Moore,J.	2/0	Stansfield,F.	38/0
Moore,R.	1/0	Steggles,J.	1/0
Phillips,J.	3/2	Tennant,D.	2/0
		Wood,T.	23/18

1945-46

Football League Third Division South – South Division
P:20 W:13 D:2 L:5 69-31 Pts:28 Pos:2nd

	Date	Opposition	Res	Attend.	Goalscorers
1.	25 Aug	BOURNEMOUTH & B.A.	9-3	10000	Rees 4 Clarke 2 Gibson Carless
2.	1 Sep	Bournemouth & B.A.	5-1	7000	Rees Clarke 3 Wood
3.	8	TORQUAY UNITED	6-0	12000	Clarke Wood Carless Rees 2 Gibson
4.	12	Crystal Palace	0-3	5000	
5.	15	Torquay United	7-0	2200	o.g.(Spencer) Lester Rees 3 Clarke 2
6.	22	ALDERSHOT	4-1	16000	Rees 2 Carless Wood
7.	29	Aldershot	5-1	4000	Rees Moore Clarke Carless Hollyman
8.	6 Oct	Bristol City	2-3	18711	Moore Rees
9.	13	BRISTOL CITY	2-4	28000	Rees Clarke
10.	20	BRIGHTON & H.A.	4-0	22000	Clarke Rees 2 o.g.(Reece)
11.	27	Brighton & H.A.	3-2	8500	Moore Gibson Clarke
12.	3 Nov	Exeter City	2-3	6341	Gibson Clarke
13.	10	EXETER CITY	0-0	18000	
14.	1 Dec	Swindon Town	2-1	11876	Wood o.g.(Kelso)
15.	8	SWINDON TOWN	3-0	6000	Lever Clarke Wood
16.	15	READING	2-1	8000	Wood 2
17.	22	Reading	1-3	5295	Rees
18.	25	Bristol Rovers	2-2	8000	?
19.	26	BRISTOL ROVERS	4-2	18000	Allen Hollyman Clarke 2
20.	29	CRYSTAL PALACE	6-2	25000	Wright 2 Allen 2 Hollyman 2

F.A.Cup

	Date	Opposition	Res	Attend.	Goalscorers
3rd	5 Jan	WEST BROM. ALBION	1-1	33,000	Allen
3/R.	9	West Brom. Albion	0-4	18,025	

Other Matches

Third Division South Cup – South Div.: Qualifying Competition

	Date	Opposition	Res	Attend.	Goalscorers
	12 Jan	Watford	7-1	7800	Clarke 2 Wright 2 Allen 2 Tennant
	19	WATFORD	0-2	14000	
	26	Exeter City	1-2	8000	Haddon
	2 Feb	EXETER CITY	5-1	15000	Rees 2 Wright Lever Clarke
	9	Torquay United	0-1	4000	
	16	TORQUAY UNITED	3-0	14700	Allen Rees 2
	23	Bristol Rovers	0-1	11200	
	2 Mar	BRISTOL ROVERS	3-0	18000	Richards 3
	9	Bristol City	2-3	17375	Hollyman Allen
	16	BRISTOL CITY	3-2	19000	Hill 2 Allen
	23	Swindon Town	2-3	11779	Rees Moore
	30	SWINDON TOWN	2-0	19500	Allen 2
	6 Apr	Reading	2-3	11000	Clarke Richards
	13	READING	5-2	21500	Richards 2 Rees Clarke Gibson
	20	Crystal Palace	3-0	17500	Clarke
	27	CRYSTAL PALACE	1-1	29000	Allen o.g.(Hudghill) Rees

Friendlies

	Date	Opposition	Res	Attend.	Goalscorers
	14 Aug	SWANSEA TOWN	4-3	2000	Carless 2 Rees 2
	18	LEAGUE WEST X1	2-0	1000	Rees Gibson
	17 Nov	MOSCOW DYNAMO	1-10	31000	Moore
†	10 Apr	Combined BAOR X1	1-1	15000	Rees
	27	NOTTS. COUNTY	5-1	7000	Clarke 2 Rees 2 Richards

† Played in Brunswick

Players (All Competitions. * denotes retained for 1946/47 season)

A = Allen,B.	*	18/12	I = Haddon,H.	*
B = Baker,W.	*	5/0	J = Hill,C.	
C = Canning,D.	*	9/0	K = Hollyman,K.	*
D = Carless,E.		11/4	L = Jones,R.	
E = Clarke,R.	*	36/24	M = Lester,L.	*
F = Foulkes,W.		5/0	N = Lever,A.	*
G = Gibson, C.	*	25/6	O = Lewis,W.	
H = Griffiths,W.		1/0	P = Marshall,E.	*

Q = McLoughlin,K.		2/1	Y = Smith,A.	*	17/0
R = Moore,J.		2/1	Z = Stansfield,F.	*	32/0
T = Phillips,J.		32/6	a = Tennant,D.	*	1/1
e = Raybould,M.		1/0	b = Tobin,R.		3/0
= Rees,W.	*	19/1	c = Wager,L.		1/0
Z = Richards,S.	*	26/2	d = Wood,T.	*	24/7
A = Rowlands,T.		1/0	e = Wright,G.	*	11/5
U = Sherwood,A.	*	2/0			

1946-47

Football League – Division 3 South Secretary/Manager: Billy McCandless

P:42 W:30 D:6 L:6 93-30 Pts:66 Pos:1st (Prom.)

840		Date	Opposition	Res	Attend.	Goalscorers	1	2	3	4	5	6	7	8	9	10	11
1.		31 Aug	Norwich City	1-2	21725	Richards	M	*I	*Q	*G	*R	*K	*E	*N	*O	*A	*D
2.		4 Sep	Swindon Town	2-3	14354	Allen Richards	"	"	"	"	"	"	"	"	"	"	"
3.		7	NOTTS. COUNTY	2-1	35000	James Gibson	*C	"	"	"	"	"	"	*H	"	"	"
4.		9	BOURNEMOUTH	2-0	20000	Allen James	"	"	"	"	"	"	"	N	H	"	"
5.		14	Northampton Town	2-0	7000	Allen 2	"	"	"	"	"	*U	"	"	"	"	"
6.		18	Bournemouth	0-2	8226		"	"	"	"	"	B	"	*F	"	"	"
7.		21	ALDERSHOT	2-1	27000	Baker Clarke	"	"	"	"	"	"	"	A	"	U	"
8.		23	SWINDON TOWN	5-0	25000	Richards Allen Gibson 3	"	"	"	"	"	"	"	N	O	A	"
9.		28	Brighton & H.A.	4-0	13193	Rees Richards 2 Allen	"	"	"	"	"	"	"	"	"	"	"
10.		5 Oct	EXETER CITY	5-0	37000	Allen Richards 2 Baker Clarke	"	"	"	"	"	"	"	"	"	"	"
11.		12	Port Vale	4-0	10000	Richards 2 Clarke Rees	"	"	"	"	"	"	"	"	"	"	"
12.		19	Q.P.RANGERS	2-2	48000	Clarke Richards	"	"	*L	"	"	"	"	"	"	"	"
13.		26	Southend United	2-0	14000	Gibson Rees	"	"	Q	"	"	"	"	"	"	"	"
14.		2 Nov	BRISTOL ROVERS	4-0	35000	Richards 2 Allen Rees	"	"	"	"	"	"	"	"	"	"	"
15.		9	Mansfield Town	3-1	8000	Richards Rees 2	"	"	"	"	"	"	"	"	"	"	"
16.		16	TORQUAY UNITED	1-0	38000	Rees	"	"	"	"	"	"	"	"	"	"	"
17.		23	Crystal Palace	2-1	25275	Richards 2	"	"	"	"	"	"	"	"	"	"	"
18.		7 Dec	Walsall	3-2	16386	Allen 2 Rees	"	"	"	*T	"	"	"	"	"	"	J
19.		21	Ipswich Town	1-0	12288	Gibson	"	"	"	"	"	"	J	"	"	"	D
20.		25	Leyton Orient	1-0	12947	Rees	"	"	"	"	"	"	"	"	"	"	"
21.		28	NORWICH CITY	6-1	36285	Richards 3 Rees Allen Clarke	"	"	"	G	"	"	E	"	"	"	"
22.		4 Jan	Notts. County	1-1	25000	Allen	"	"	"	"	"	"	"	"	"	"	"
23.		18	NORTHAMPTON TOWN	6-2	30000	Allen 3 Rees 2 Richards	"	"	"	"	"	"	"	"	"	"	"
24.		22	READING	3-0	30000	Richards 2 Clarke	"	L	"	"	"	"	"	"	"	"	"
25.		25	Aldershot	1-0	7500	Richards	"	I	"	T	R	"	"	"	O	"	"
26.		1 Feb	BRIGHTON & H.A.	4-0	20533	Richards 2 Rees Clarke	"	"	"	"	"	"	"	G	N	"	"
27.		1 Mar	SOUTHEND UNITED	3-1	33000	Allen Clarke 2	"	"	"	G	"	"	"	"	J	"	"
28.		8	Bristol Rovers	0-1	30417		"	"	"	"	"	"	E	"	"	"	"
29.		15	MANSFIELD TOWN	5-0	10000	Hollyman Gibson Richards2 Clarke	"	"	"	"	"	"	"	A	O	F	"
30.		22	Torquay United	0-0	10000		"	"	"	"	"	"	"	"	"	"	"
31.		29	CRYSTAL PALACE	0-0	24214		"	"	"	"	"	"	J	E	A	"	"
32.		4 Apr	Bristol City	1-2	32273	Rees	"	"	"	"	"	"	E	N	O	A	"
33.		5	Reading	0-0	21522		"	"	"	"	"	"	"	"	"	"	"
34.		7	BRISTOL CITY	1-1	51626	Richards	"	"	"	"	"	"	"	"	"	"	"
35.		12	WALSALL	3-0	37000	Hill 2 Gibson	"	"	"	"	"	"	"	"	"	"	"
36.		19	Watford	0-2	18937		"	"	"	"	"	"	"	"	"	"	"
37.		26	IPSWICH TOWN	3-2	35000	Gibson Richards Allen	"	"	"	"	"	"	"	"	H	"	"
38.		3 May	WATFORD	1-0	33000	Richards	"	"	"	"	"	"	"	"	O	"	"
39.		10	PORT VALE	1-0	37000	Richards	"	"	"	"	"	"	"	"	N	A	"
40.		17	Exeter City	2-0	20000	Gibson Rees	"	"	"	T	"	"	"	"	"	"	"
41.		24	Q.P.Rangers	3-2	25000	Wardle Ross 2	"	"	"	"	"	"	"	"	"	*P	*S
42.		7 Jun	LEYTON ORIENT	1-0	24572	Rees	"	"	"	"	"	"	"	"	"	"	"

Players:

A = Allen,B. 39/1/17
B = Baker,W. 38/2/2
C = Canning,D. 40/1/0
D = Clarke,R. 39/2/10
E = Gibson,C. 38/2/10
F = Hill,C. 5/2/0
G = Hollyman,K. 36/2/1
H = James,W. 6/1/3
I = Lever,A. 42/2/0
J = Lewis,W. 7/1/0
K = Marshall,E. 1/0/0
L = Phillips,J. 2/0/0
M = Poland,G. 2/0/0
N = Rees,W. 35/2/17
O = Richards,S. 34/1/30
P = Ross,W. 3/0/2
Q = Sherwood,A. 41/2/0
R = Stansfield,F. 41/1/0
S = Wardle,G. 2/0/1
T = Williams,G. 7/1/0
U = Wood,T. 2/0/0
V = Griffiths,W. 0/1/0

'Local Heroes' - - City's brilliant 3rd Division (South) Champions nearly all recruited from local football during War... Stan Richards sets new Club record with 30 goals as the Bluebirds score their highest number of League goals... 51,626 see home game v. Bristol City - - an all - time record for 3rd. South - - spectator falls through Grangetown roof, and survives!

Other Matches

F.A. Cup

	Date	Opposition	Res	Attend.	Goalscorers	1	2	3	4	5	6	7	8	9	10	11
3rd	11 Jan	Brentford	0-1	32894		C	I	Q	G	R	B	E	N	O	A	D

Welsh Cup

	Date	Opposition	Res	Attend.	Goalscorers	1	2	3	4	5	6	7	8	9	10	11
5th	6 Feb	Merthyr Tydfil	2-4	3000	Rees James	V	"	"	"	T	"	"	"	H	J	"

Friendlies

	Date	Opposition	Res	Attend.	Goalscorers
	30 Nov	CHESTER	2-2	12000	Clarke 2
†	14 Jun	W.Hughes International X1	1-0	12000	Wardle

† At Llanelly.

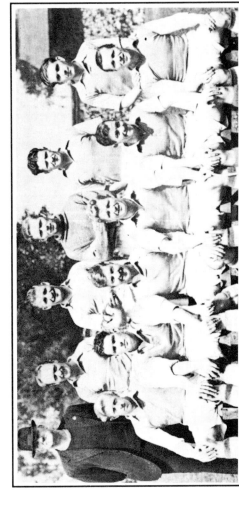

● The Cardiff City line-up in May 1947 at Queen's Park Rangers six weeks after the side's 3-0 home win over Walsall which helped maintain the Club's lead at the top of Division 3 (South). BACK (from left): Bob Allison (Trainer), Billy Baker, Stan Richards, Danny Canning, Glyn Williams, Bernard Ross. FRONT (from left): Colin Gibson, Billy Rees, Arthur Lever, Fred Stansfield (Captain), Alf Sherwood, George Wardle.

1947-48

Secretary/Manager: Billy McCandless (Cyril Spiers from 3.12.47)

Football League – Division 2

P:42 **W:**18 **D:**11 **L:**13 **61-58 Pts:**47 **Pos:**5th

882		Date	Opposition	Res	Attend.	Goalscorers	1	2	3	4	5	6	7	8	9	10	11
1.		23 Aug	CHESTERFIELD	0-0	38000		E	J	R	H	S	C	F	O	P	A	W
2.		25	DONCASTER ROVERS	3-0	47000	Wardle 2 Richards	"	"	"	"	"	"	*L	"	"	*D	"
3.		30	Millwall	1-0	28557	Wardle	"	"	"	"	"	"	K	Q	O	"	"
4.		4 Sep	Doncaster Rovers	2-2	22000	Wardle Blair	"	"	"	"	"	"	F	"	"	"	"
5.		6	TOTTENHAM HOTSPUR	0-3	48894		"	"	"	"	"	"	K	A	"	"	"
6.		8	SOUTHAMPTON	5-1	40000	o.g.(Webber) Rees Moore2 Richards	"	"	"	Y	"	"	W	O	P	"	*M
7.		13	Sheffield Wed.	1-2	36298		"	"	"	"	"	"	"	"	"	"	"
8.		17	Southampton	2-2	16000	McBennett 2	"	"	"	H	"	"	L	"	"	"	W
9.		20	PLYMOUTH ARGYLE	3-0	35000	Blair Lever Rees	"	"	"	"	"	"	"	"	"	"	"
10.		27	BRADFORD (P.A.)	1-0	39796	Rees	"	"	"	"	"	"	"	"	"	"	"
11.		4 Oct	Nottingham Forest	2-1	30500	Gibson 2	"	"	"	"	"	"	F	"	"	"	"
12.		11	LUTON TOWN	1-0	38000	Rees	"	"	"	"	"	"	"	"	"	"	"
13.		18	Brentford	0-0	34000		"	"	*T	"	"	"	"	"	"	"	"
14.		25	Leicester City	1-2	36940	o.g. (Frame)	"	"	R	"	"	"	"	"	"	"	"
15.		1 Nov	LEEDS UNITED	0-0	36851		"	"	"	"	"	Y	"	"	"	"	"
16.		8	Fulham	1-4	40000	Gibson	"	"	"	"	"	"	"	"	"	"	"
17.		15	COVENTRY CITY	1-1	38000	Richards	"	"	"	"	"	*X	"	Q	P	"	"
18.		22	Newcastle United	1-4	57940	Lever	"	"	"	"	"	C	"	O	"	W	D
19.		29	BIRMINGHAM CITY	2-0	42000	Richards 2	"	"	"	"	S	"	"	"	"	"	"
20.		6 Dec	West Brom. Albion	3-2	38914	Blair 2 Gibson	"	"	T	"	"	"	"	"	"	"	"
21.		13	BARNSLEY	1-0	35000	Wardle	"	"	R	"	"	"	"	"	"	"	"
22.		20	Chesterfield	2-2	20000	Stitfall Blair	"	"	"	"	"	"	"	*V	"	"	"
23.		26	BURY	2-2	45000	Wardle Gibson	"	"	"	"	"	"	"	O	T	"	"
24.		1 Jan	Bury	2-1	13000	Rees Richards	"	"	"	"	"	"	"	"	P	"	"
25.		3	MILLWALL	6-0	35000	Rees2 Blair Gibson Richards2	"	"	"	"	"	"	"	"	"	"	"
26.		17	Tottenham Hotspur	1-2	57386	Rees	"	T	"	Y	J	"	"	D	O	"	M
27.		31	SHEFFIELD WED.	2-1	33147	Richards Rees	"	J	"	"	S	"	"	O	P	T	D
28.		7 Feb	Plymouth Argyle	0-3	25043		"	"	"	H	"	"	"	"	*I	W	"
29.		14	Bradford (P.A.)	1-0	14756	Hullett	"	"	"	"	"	"	"	"	"	"	"
30.		21	NOTTINGHAM FOREST	4-1	29500	Hullett 2 Wardle 2	"	"	"	Y	"	"	"	"	"	T	W
31.		28	Luton Town	1-1	24000	Hullett	"	"	"	"	"	"	"	"	"	"	"
32.		6 Mar	BRENTFORD	1-0	40500	Hullett	"	"	"	"	"	"	"	"	"	"	"
33.		13	LEICESTER CITY	3-0	40000	Hullett 2 Wardle	"	"	"	T	"	"	"	"	"	W	D
34.		20	Leeds United	0-4	34276		"	"	"	"	"	"	"	"	"	"	"
35.		26	WEST HAM UNITED	0-3	35000		"	"	"	"	"	"	"	"	"	"	"
36.		27	FULHAM	0-0	35000		"	"	"	"	"	"	"	W	O	"	"
37.		29	West Ham United	2-4	30000	Hullett Wardle	"	"	"	"	"	"	W	*N	*I	"	"
38.		3 Apr	Coventry City	0-1	26000		"	R	T	Y	"	J	F	O	P	"	"
39.		10	NEWCASTLE UNITED	1-1	50000	Lever	"	"	"	"	"	"	"	"	"	D	*U
40.		17	Birmingham City	0-2	53000		"	"	"	"	"	"	"	"	I	"	W
41.		24	WEST BROM. ALBION	0-5	25032		E	"	"	"	J	C	"	"	"	V	D
42.		1 May	Barnsley	2-1	14000	Rees Moore	*B	"	J	"	S	T	"	"	"	N	M

Players:

A = Allen,B. 2/0/0
B = Ashton,R. 1/0/0
C = Baker,W. 35/2/0
D = Blair,D. 37/2/6
E = Canning,D. 40/2/0
F = Gibson,C. 33/1/6
G = Griffiths,W. 1/0/0
H = Hollyman,K. 25/2/0
I = Hullett,W. 13/0/8
J = Lever,A. 42/2/3
K = Lewis,W. 2/0/0
L = McBennett,S. 4/0/2
M = Moore,B. 4/2/3
N = Parker,R. 2/0/0
O = Rees,W. 38/1/12
P = Richards,S. 23/1/9
Q = Ross,W. 6/0/0
R = Sherwood,A. 39/1/0
S = Stansfield,F. 40/2/0
T = Stitfall,R. 20/1/1
U = Sullivan,D. 1/0/0
V = Tobin,R. 2/1/0
W = Wardle,G. 36/1/10
X = Watson,W. 1/0/0
Y = Williams,G. 15/0/0
Z = Foulkes,W. 0/1/0
a = James,W. 0/1/0

Over 47000 see City beat Doncaster Rovers -- 3rd Div. (North) Champs. Dougie Blair -- son of Jimmy, begins City career ... Late season form prevents Bluebirds from promotion challenge ... Ron Stitfall begins long career with Club .... Billy McCandless resigns -- Cyril Spiers rejoins City from Norwich.

Other Matches

F.A.Cup

	Date	Opposition	Res	Attend.	Goalscorers	1	2	3	4	5	6	7	8	9	10	11
3rd	10 Jan	SHEFFIELD WED.	1-2	48000	Rees	E	J	R	H	S	C	F	O	P	W	D

Welsh Cup

	Date	Opposition	Res	Attend.	Goalscorers	1	2	3	4	5	6	7	8	9	10	11
5th	15 Jan	Lovell's Athletic	1-2	5000	Moore	"	T	J	"	"	"	Z	a	M	V	"

Friendlies

	Date	Opposition	Res		Goalscorers
	19 Apr	CARDIFF COR. (Past/Pres.)	2-1		Rees Blair
	3 May	Bristol Rovers	5-1		Ross Parker 2 Hollyman 2

1947 .... BACK (from left): Bob Allison (trainer), Doug Blair, Bill Baker, Dan Canning, Billy Rees, Colin Gibson, George Wardle. FRONT (from left): Ken Hollyman, Alf Sherwood, Fred Stansfield (captain), Arthur Lever, Ron Stitfall.

1948-49

Football League – Division 2.

Secretary/Manager: Cyril Spiers

P:42 **W:**19 **D:**13 **L:**10 **62**-**47** **Pts:**51 **Pos:**4th

924	Date	Opposition	Res	Attend.	Goalscorers	1	2	3	4	5	6	7	8	9	10	11
1.	21 Aug	Bradford (P.A.)	0-3	15049		*K	L	T	I	U	B	*F	X	R	A	D
2.	23	LUTON TOWN	3-3	40000	Hollyman Hullett Moore	"	"	"	"	"	"	X	R	J	"	N
3.	28	SOUTHAMPTON	2-1	43000	Hullett 2	"	"	"	"	"	"	"	"	"	"	Y
4.	30	Luton Town	0-3	20000		"	"	"	"	"	"	"	"	"	"	"
5.	4 Sep	Barnsley	1-1	18500	Sullivan	"	"	"	"	"	"	"	"	"	"	"
6.	9	Q.P.Rangers	0-0	27000		"	"	"	b	"	D	"	"	"	Z	"
7.	11	GRIMSBY TOWN	3-0	33000	Hollyman Rees o.g.(Moody)	"	"	"	B	"	"	"	"	"	R	Y
8.	13	Q.P.RANGERS	3-0	37000	Rees 2 Hullett	"	"	"	"	"	"	"	"	"	"	"
9.	18	Nottingham Forest	0-0	20000		"	"	"	"	"	"	"	"	"	"	"
10.	25	FULHAM	2-1	39000	Hullett 2	"	"	"	"	"	"	"	"	"	"	"
11.	2 Oct	Plymouth Argyle	1-0	29346	Hollyman	"	"	"	"	"	"	"	"	"	"	"
12.	9	TOTTENHAM HOTSPUR	0-1	56018		"	"	"	"	"	"	"	"	"	"	Y
13.	16	West Ham United	1-3	30000	Lever	"	"	"	b	"	"	"	"	"	"	*Q
14.	30	West Brom. Albion	0-2	46036		"	"	"	B	"	"	"	*C	R	*V	N
15.	6 Nov	CHESTERFIELD	3-4	36000	Rees Blair Stansfield	"	"	"	X	"	"	"	"	"	"	X
16.	13	Lincoln City	0-0	13630		"	"	"	"	"	"	I	"	J	"	*P
17.	20	SHEFFIELD WED.	1-1	32000	Stevenson	"	"	"	B	"	"	X	I	C	"	*W
18.	27	Coventry City	1-0	22000	Stevenson	"	"	"	"	"	"	I	C	*G	"	Y
19.	4 Dec	LEEDS UNITED	2-1	31973	Allen Stevenson	"	"	"	"	"	"	"	A	R	"	"
20.	11	Leicester City	2-2	24139	Rees Gorin	"	"	"	"	"	"	G	"	"	"	"
21.	18	BRADFORD (P.A.)	6-1	28002	Edwards Allen Stevenson2 Lever Holl'n	"	"	"	"	"	"	I	"	"	"	*E
22.	25	Brentford	1-1	22687	Allen	"	"	"	"	"	"	"	"	"	"	"
23.	27	BRENTFORD	2-0	50000	Allen Stevenson	"	"	"	"	"	"	"	"	"	"	"
24.	1 Jan	Southampton	0-2	20937		"	"	"	"	"	"	"	"	"	"	"
25.	15	BARNSLEY	0-3	30000		"	"	"	"	"	"	"	"	"	C	"
26.	22	Grimsby Town	2-2	16000	Rees Montgomery	*O	"	"	"	*M	"	"	"	"	V	"
27.	5 Feb	NOTTINGHAM FOREST	1-0	31000	Rees	K	"	"	"	"	"	*H	V	"	D	"
28.	19	Fulham	0-4	36000		"	"	"	"	"	"	B	"	"	"	"
29.	26	PLYMOUTH ARGYLE	1-0	28500	Hollyman	"	"	"	"	*S	M	R	D	"	V	"
30.	5 Mar	Tottenham Hotspur	1-0	51183	Hollyman	"	"	"	I	M	b	B	"	C	"	"
31.	12	WEST HAM UNITED	4-0	28000	Hollyman Stevenson 2 Best	X	"	"	"	"	"	B	"	"	"	"
32.	19	Bury	3-0	15900	Blair Best Edwards	"	"	"	"	"	"	"	"	"	"	"
33.	26	WEST BROM. ALBION	2-2	55177	Blair Best	"	"	"	"	"	"	"	"	"	"	"
34.	2 Apr	Chesterfield	2-0	14000	Best Edwards	"	"	"	"	"	"	"	"	"	"	"
35.	4	BURY	2-1	33000	Blair Best	"	"	"	"	"	"	"	"	"	"	"
36.	9	LINCOLN CITY	3-1	33000	Stevenson 2 Edwards	"	"	"	"	"	"	"	"	"	"	"
37.	15	Blackburn Rovers	1-2	23400	Edwards	"	"	"	"	"	"	"	*a	"	"	"
38.	16	Sheffield Wed.	1-1	32374	Best	"	"	"	"	"	"	"	D	"	"	"
39.	18	BLACKBURN ROVERS	1-0	33325	o.g.	"	"	"	b	"	D	"	a	"	"	"
40.	23	COVENTRY CITY	3-0	27000	Edwards Stevenson 2	O	"	"	"	"	"	"	"	"	"	"
41.	30	Leeds United	0-0	19945		"	"	"	"	"	"	"	"	"	"	"
42.	7 May	LEICESTER CITY	1-1	35000	Baker	"	"	"	"	"	"	"	R	"	"	"

Players:

A = Allen,B. — 17/5/5
B = Baker,W. — 36/5/1
C = Best,T. — 19/3/7
D = Blair,D. — 34/3/4
E = Edwards,G. — 23/5/7
F = Gilchrist,A. — 1/0/0
G = Gorin,E. — 2/2/2
H = Hogg,G. — 1/1/0
I = Hollyman,K. — 37/6/10
J = Hullett,W. — 13/0/7
K = Joslin,P. — 38/4/0
L = Lever,A. — 30/5/2
M = Montgomery,S. — 17/4/1
N = Moore,B. — 2/0/1
O = Morris,E. — 4/2/0
P = Nibloe,J. — 1/0/0
Q = Price,C. — 1/0/0
R = Rees,W. — 28/4/7
S = Rowland,A. — 1/1/1
T = Sherwood,A. — 42/3/0
U = Stansfield,F. — 25/2/1
V = Stevenson,E. — 27/5/14
W = Stitfall,A. — 3/1/0
X = Stitfall,R. — 28/2/0
Y = Sullivan,D. — 11/0/1
Z = Wardle,G. — 2/1/1
a = Williams,R. — 3/0/0
b = Williams,G. — 15/2/0
c = Pembrey,G. — 0/1/0

A season spent on promotion fringe. Spiers rings the changes ... Broken leg finishes Fred Stansfield's career. City sign Montgomery and Rowland (both centre-halves) ... Midnight dash secures signing of George Edwards (Welsh winger) ... Cup-tie at Aston Villa watched by 70,718. ... Accusations of 'arranging' season's last League game!

Other Matches

F.A.Cup

	Date	Opposition	Res	Attend.	Goalscorers	1	2	3	4	5	6	7	8	9	10	11
3rd	8 Jan	Oldham Athletic	3-2	28991	Hollyman 2 Allen	K	L	T	B	U	D	I	A	R	V	E
4th	29 Feb	Aston Villa	2-1	70718	Hollyman Rees	"	"	X	"	M	H	"	"	"	"	"
5th	12	Derby County	1-2	35000	Stevenson	"	"	T	"	"	D	"	"	"	"	"

Welsh Cup

	Date	Opposition	Res	Attend.	Goalscorers	1	2	3	4	5	6	7	8	9	10	11
6th	12 Jan	TROEDYRHIW	3-1	500	Gorin Wardle Best	O	"	"	"	U	"	"	G	C	Z	c
7th	3 Mar	Milford United	2-1	7500	Rowland Edwards	K	"	S	"	M	b	B	A	"	V	E
Semi-final	7 Apr	Merthyr Tydfil	1-3	22000	Stevenson	O	X	W	"	"	"	G	"	R	"	"

Friendlies

Date	Opposition	Res	Attend.	Goalscorers
25 Apr	CARDIFF CORRIES.SELECT	1-1	12000	Stevenson
2 May	BRISTOL CITY	1-0	8000	Baker

(Back) Pearce (Asst. Trainer), Lever, Sherwood, Joslin, Allison (Trainer), Stevenson, Moore, Pembrey
(Front) Hullett, Best, Stansfield, Hollyman, Stitfall, Baker.

1949-50

Football League – Division 2.

Secretary/Manager: Cyril Spiers

P:42 W:16 D:10 L:16 41-44 Pts:42 Pos:10th

966	Date	Opposition	Res	Attend.	Goalscorers	1	2	3	4	5	6	7	8	9	10	11
1.	20 Aug	Blackburn Rovers	0-1	28000		I	J	R	Z	Q	C	H	Y	B	S	D
2.	22	SHEFFIELD WED.	1-0	37913	Stevenson	"	"	"	"	"	A	"	C	"	"	"
3.	27	SWANSEA TOWN	1-0	57510	Best	"	"	"	"	M	"	"	"	"	"	"
4.	29	Sheffield Wed.	1-1	32873	Stevenson	"	"	"	"	"	"	"	*E	"	"	"
5.	3 Sep	TOTTENHAM HOTSPUR	0-1	42649		"	"	"	"	"	"	Y	Y	"	"	"
6.	5	HULL CITY	2-0	40254	Best 2	"	"	"	"	"	"	"	C	"	C	"
7.	10	Bury	2-2	17000	Best, Williams,R.	"	"	"	"	"	"	"	H	"	"	"
8.	17	LEICESTER CITY	2-4	35000	Best, Edwards	"	"	"	"	"	"	"	"	"	"	"
9.	24	Bradford (P.A.)	3-3	13187	Edwards Stitfall,R. 2	N	"	"	H	"	"	"	S	U	"	"
10.	1 Oct	CHESTERFIELD	2-0	32000	Blair Stevenson	I	"	"	"	"	"	"	"	"	"	"
11.	8	Leeds United	0-2	25523		"	"	"	"	Q	"	"	"	"	"	"
12.	22	Coventry City	1-2	20000	Blair	"	"	"	"	M	"	"	"	"	"	"
13.	29	LUTON TOWN	0-0	25000		"	"	U	Z	"	R	"	H	C	A	"
14.	5 Nov	Barnsley	0-1	18000		"	R	"	"	"	C	"	*X	F	S	"
15.	12	WEST HAM UNITED	0-1	21000		"	"	"	"	"	"	"	"	"	"	*K
16.	19	Sheffield United	0-2	25000		"	"	"	"	"	A	"	H	B	"	C
17.	26	GRIMSBY TOWN	1-0	24000	Stitfall,R.	"	J	R	"	"	C	H	Y	U	"	D
18.	3 Dec	Q.P.Rangers	1-0	12000	Stitfall,R.	"	"	"	"	"	"	"	"	"	"	"
19.	10	PRESTON NORTH END	3-2	22000	Stitfall,R. Edwards 2	"	"	"	A	"	"	"	"	"	"	"
20.	17	BLACKBURN ROVERS	2-1	19000	Edwards Stitfall,R.	"	"	"	"	"	"	T	"	"	"	"
21.	24	Swansea Town	1-5	30000	Stitfall,R.	"	"	"	"	"	"	H	"	"	"	"
22.	26	Plymouth Argyle	0-0	30000		"	"	"	"	"	Z	"	"	"	C	"
23.	27	PLYMOUTH ARGYLE	1-0	33000	Evans	"	"	"	"	"	"	E	"	"	"	*P
24.	31	Tottenham Hotspur	0-2	59789		"	"	"	"	"	"	H	S	"	"	V
25.	14 Jan	BURY	1-0	27000	Williams,R.	"	"	"	"	"	"	K	Y	"	E	D
26.	21	Leicester City	0-1	24500		*W	"	"	"	"	"	*L	E	"	C	"
27.	4 Feb	BRADFORD (P.A.)	1-2	25164	Evans	I	"	"	"	"	"	H	"	"	"	"
28.	18	Chesterfield	1-0	15000	Evans	"	U	"	"	"	"	J	"	C	S	"
29.	25	LEEDS UNITED	1-0	28423	Evans	"	"	"	"	"	"	H	S	E	C	"
30.	4 Mar	Southampton	1-3	23000	Evans	"	"	"	"	"	"	"	"	"	"	"
31.	11	COVENTRY CITY	1-0	25000	Edwards	"	"	"	"	"	H	*G	V	J	E	"
32.	18	Luton Town	0-0	15000		"	"	"	"	"	"	"	*O	E	C	"
33.	25	BARNSLEY	3-0	20000	o.g.(Pallister) Evans Grant	W	"	"	"	"	"	"	E	J	"	"
34.	1 Apr	Grimsby Town	0-0	15600		W	"	"	"	"	"	"	"	"	"	"
35.	7	Brentford	0-1	24633		"	"	"	"	"	"	"	"	"	"	"
36.	8	Q.P.RANGERS	4-0	21500	Sherwood Evans 2 Lever	"	"	"	"	"	Z	"	"	C	S	"
37.	10	BRENTFORD	0-0	16200		"	"	"	"	"	"	"	"	"	C	"
38.	15	West Ham United	1-0	14500	Lever	"	"	"	H	"	"	J	"	E	C	"
39.	17	SOUTHAMPTON	1-1	21000	Edwards	"	"	"	A	"	H	"	"	"	"	"
40.	22	SHEFFIELD UNITED	1-2	35000	Lever	"	"	"	"	"	Z	"	"	"	Y	"
41.	29	Preston North End	0-3	15000		"	"	"	"	Z	H	"	"	"	"	"
42.	6 May	Hull City	1-1	18213	Gorin	"	"	"	"	"	"	"	"	F	"	K

Players:

A = Baker,W.   36/7/1
B = Best,T.   9/0/5
C = Blair,D.   33/6/2
D = Edwards,G.   35/7/10
E = Evans,E.   20/7/12
F = Gorin,E.   4/1/1
G = Grant,W.   12/0/1
H = Hollyman,K.   29/6/0
I = Joslin,P.   31/6/0
J = Lever,A.   37/7/3
K = Lamie,R.   3/0/0
L = May,H.   1/0/0
M = Montgomery,S.   37/7/0
N = Morris,E.   1/0/0
O = McLaren,R.   1/0/0
P = Pembrey,G.   1/0/0
Q = Rowland,A.   3/0/0
R = Sherwood,A.   42/5/2
S = Stevenson,E.   23/1/3
T = Stitfall,A.   3/0/1
U = Stitfall,R.   34/7/6
V = Sullivan,D.   2/0/0
W = Steele,A.   10/0/0
X = Taggart,R.   2/0/0
Y = Williams,R.   26/1/2
Z = Williams,G.   27/6/1
a = Stitfall,B.   0/1/0
b = Devonshire,K.   0/2/0

Lack of goals keep City in mid-table... New record attendance of 57,510 for local 'derby' with Swansea - - In return at The Vetch, City lose 5-1 (their worst defeat by local rivals)...

Other Matches

F.A.Cup

	Date	Opposition	Res	Attend.	Goalscorers	1	2	3	4	5	6	7	8	9	10	11
3rd	7 Jan	WEST BROM. ALBION	2-2	38000	Evans Williams,G.	I	J	R	A	M	Z	H	E	U	C	D
3rd Rep.	11	West Brom. Albion	1-0	37400	Edwards	"	"	"	"	"	"	"	"	"	"	"
4th	28	Charlton Athletic	1-1	46000	Evans	"	"	"	"	"	"	"	"	"	"	"
4th Rep.	1 Feb	CHARLTON ATHLETIC	2-0	37000	Evans 2	"	"	"	"	"	"	"	"	"	"	"
5th	11	Leeds United	1-3	53099	Sherwood (pen)	"	"	"	"	"	"	"	"	"	"	"

Welsh Cup

	Date	Opposition	Res	Attend.	Goalscorers	1	2	3	4	5	6	7	8	9	10	11
6th	18 Jan	EBBW VALE	3-0	2500	Edwards Baker	a	"	b	"	"	"	E	F	"	Y	"
7th	23 Feb	Swansea Town	0-3	11000		I	U	"	H	"	A	J	E	C	S	"

Friendlies

	Date	Opposition	Res	Attend.	Goalscorers
	24 Apr	CARDIFF CORRIES. SELECT.	1-1	6000	Evans
	1 May	BILLY JAMES' SELECT X1	2-4	1200	Evans Wilcox
	10	Bristol City	0-2	8250	
	16	Ulster X1	3-0	8000	Evans Lamie 2
	20	Derry City	2-0	5000	Evans McIlvenny

(Back) Lever, Montgomery, Williams, Stitfall, Rowland
(Front) Hollyman, Stevenson, Sherwood, Baker. (Seated front) Edwards, Williams

1950-51

Football League – Division 2.

Secretary/Manager: Cyril Spiers

P:42 W:17 D:16 L:9 53-45 Pts:50 Pos:3rd

1008	Date	Opposition	Res	Attend.	Goalscorers	1	2	3	4	5	6	7	8	9	10	11
1.	19 Aug	Grimsby Town	0-0	20007		H	T	R	G	N	A	W	*K	*P	D	C
2.	23	Manchester City	1-2	14858	Williams,R.	"	"	"	"	"	B	"	"	"	"	"
3.	26	NOTTS. COUNTY	2-0	37000	Oakley Edwards	"	"	"	"	J	A	"	"	"	"	"
4.	28	MANCHESTER CITY	1-1	32817	Evans,E.	"	"	"	"	X	"	"	D	"	U	"
5.	2 Sep	Preston North End	1-1	27000	Edwards	"	"	"	"	"	"	"	"	"	"	"
6.	4	WEST HAM UNITED	2-1	33000	Evans,E. Blair	"	"	"	"	"	"	I	W	D	B	"
7.	9	BURY	2-2	30000	Lamie Evans,E.	"	"	"	"	"	"	"	"	"	"	"
8.	16	Q.P. Rangers	2-3	19000	Evans,E. 2	"	"	"	"	"	"	"	K	"	"	"
9.	23	CHESTERFIELD	1-0	27000	o.g. (Capel)	"	"	"	"	N	"	W	"	"	U	"
10.	30	Leicester City	1-1	25000	Blair	"	"	"	"	"	"	U	"	"	B	"
11.	7 Oct	Blackburn Rovers	0-2	24000		"	"	"	"	"	"	F	"	"	"	"
12.	14	SOUTHAMPTON	2-2	27000	Blair o.g. (Mullen)	"	"	"	"	"	"	"	W	"	"	K
13.	21	Doncaster Rovers	0-0	26250		O	*Q	T	"	"	"	"	"	"	"	"
14.	28	BRENTFORD	1-1	25000	Blair	"	T	R	"	"	"	"	"	"	"	"
15.	4 Nov	Swansea Town	0-1	26100		"	"	"	K	"	G	W	F	X	"	C
16.	11	HULL CITY	2-1	25007	Williams,R. Blair	H	"	"	"	"	X	F	W	G	"	"
17.	18	Barnsley	0-0	22000		"	"	"	G	"	"	*V	"	F	"	"
18.	25	SHEFFIELD UNITED	2-0	27000	Edwards Williams,R.	"	Q	"	"	"	"	"	"	"	"	"
19.	2 Dec	Luton Town	1-1	13000	Grant	"	"	"	"	"	"	"	"	"	"	"
20.	9	LEEDS UNITED	1-0	23716	Edwards	"	"	"	"	"	"	"	"	"	"	"
21.	16	GRIMSBY TOWN	5-2	15000	Grant 3 Williams,R.2	"	"	"	"	"	"	"	"	"	"	"
22.	23	Notts. County	2-1	15000	Grant o.g.	"	"	"	"	"	"	"	"	"	"	"
23.	25	COVENTRY CITY	2-1	40000	Edwards 2	"	"	X	"	"	A	"	"	"	"	"
24.	26	Coventry City	1-2	33000	Grant	"	"	R	"	"	X	"	"	"	D	"
25.	30	PRESTON NORTH END	0-2	28000		"	"	"	"	"	A	"	"	"	"	"
26.	13 Jan	Bury	2-1	10700	Edwards o.g. (Griffiths)	"	X	"	"	"	"	"	K	"	"	"
27.	20	Q.P.RANGERS	4-2	22000	Grant 2 McLaughlin Tiddy	"	"	"	"	"	"	"	*L	"	B	"
28.	3 Feb	Chesterfield	3-0	13500	Grant 2 Marchant	"	Q	"	"	X	"	"	"	"	"	"
29.	17	LEICESTER CITY	2-2	25000	Marchant Baker	"	S	"	"	N	"	"	"	"	"	"
30.	24	BLACKBURN ROVERS	1-0	32811	Grant	"	X	"	"	"	"	"	"	"	"	"
31.	3 Mar	Southampton	1-1	23000	Edwards	"	"	"	"	"	"	"	W	"	"	"
32.	10	DONCASTER ROVERS	0-0	30000		"	"	"	"	"	"	"	L	"	"	"
33.	17	Brentford	0-4	19900		"	"	"	"	"	"	"	"	"	"	"
34.	23	Birmingham City	0-0	15000		"	"	"	"	"	"	"	"	"	B	"
35.	24	SWANSEA TOWN	1-0	45000	Marchant	"	"	"	"	"	"	"	"	"	K	"
36.	26	BIRMINGHAM CITY	2-1	40000	McLaughlin Grant	"	"	"	"	"	"	"	"	"	"	"
37.	31	Hull City	0-2	20239		"	"	"	"	"	"	"	"	"	"	"
38.	7 Apr	BARNSLEY	1-1	30000	Grant	"	"	"	"	"	"	"	*M	"	B	"
39.	14	Sheffield United	2-1	27000	Tiddy Edwards	"	"	"	"	"	"	"	L	"	K	"
40.	21	LUTON TOWN	2-1	34000	Grant o.g.(Owen)	"	"	"	"	"	"	"	"	"	"	"
41.	28	Leeds United	0-2	14765		"	"	"	"	"	"	"	K	"	E	"
42.	5 May	West Ham United	0-0	18000		"	"	"	"	"	"	"	L	"	B	"

Players:

A = Baker,W. — 31/6/1
B = Blair,D. — 27/4/5
C = Edwards,G. — 39/5/14
D = Evans,E. — 16/1/5
E = Evans,L. — 1/1/4
F = Grant,W. — 32/6/18
G = Hollyman,K. — 42/6/0
H = Joslin,P. — 39/6/0
I = Lamie,R. — 3/0/1
J = Lever,A. — 1/0/0
K = McLaughlin,R. — 21/3/2
L = Marchant,M. — 12/3/6
M = Mills,D. — 1/0/0
N = Montgomery,S. — 34/4/0
O = Morris,E. — 3/0/0
P = Oakley,K. — 5/0/1
Q = Rutter,C. — 10/1/0
R = Sherwood,A. — 40/3/0
S = Stitfall,A. — 1/0/0
T = Stitfall,R. — 17/1/0
U = Sullivan,D. — 5/2/0
V = Tiddy,M. — 26/6/5
W = Williams,R. — 20/0/6
X = Williams,G. — 36/5/0
Y = Wilcox,C. — 0/2/0

City just fail in challenge for promotion . . . Injury sees winger Wilf Grant switch to centre - - prayers for regular goalscorer are answered !
Arthur 'Buller' Lever joins Leicester for large fee . . . .
Mike Tiddy (winger) recruited from Torquay United

Other Matches

F.A.Cup

	Date	Opposition	Res	Attend.	Goalscorers	1	2	3	4	5	6	7	8	9	10	11
3rd	6 Jan	West Ham United	1-2	30000	Grant	H	X	R	G	N	A	V	U	F	D	C

Welsh Cup

	Date	Opposition	Res	Attend.	Goalscorers	1	2	3	4	5	6	7	8	9	10	11
5th	31 Jan	BARRY TOWN	8-0	1500	o.g.(Kelly) Marchant 2 Evans,L. 4 Grant	"	T	X	"	"	"	E	L	"	B	V
6th	7 Mar	Bangor City	7-1	12000	Edwards 3 Tiddy 2 Grant Marchant	"	Y	"	"	U	"	V	"	"	"	C
Semi-final	16 Apr	Wrexham	1-0	5000	Edwards	"	Q	Y	"	N	"	"	"	"	K	"
Final	7 May	Merthyr Tydfil	1-1	18000	Grant	"	X	R	"	"	"	"	K	K	B	"
Final Rep.	17	Merthyr Tydfil	2-3	18000	Edwards Tiddy	"	"	"	"	"	"	"	"	"	"	"

Friendlies

	Date	Opposition	Res	Attend.	Goalscorers
	11 Sep	Barry Town	0-2	2000	
	18 Oct	Torquay United	2-4	4000	Evans,E. Montgomery
	27 Jan	TOTTENHAM HOTSPUR	2-3	8000	Marchant 2
	30 Apr	CARDIFF CORINTH. X1	1-0	10000	Grant
	9 May	EINDHOVEN	2-2	3000	Tiddy Grant
	12	Jersey Saturday League X1	6-1	8000	Edwards 3 Grant Blair Tiddy
	14	Guernsey X1	0-2	4000	

(Back) Stiffall, Morris, Montgomery, Blair, Edwards, G.Williams
(Front) R. Williams, Grant, Sherwood, Hollyman, McLaughlin

1951-52

Football League – Division 2. Secretary/Manager: Cyril Spiers

1050   P:42 W:20 D:11 L:11 72-54 Pts:51 Pos:2nd (Prom.)

#	Date	Opposition	Res	Attend.	Goalscorers	1	2	3	4	5	6	7	8	9	10	11
1.	18 Aug	LEICESTER CITY	4-0	35000	Edwards Grant 2 Williams,R.	*J	O	P	A	R	U	S	T	G	B	D
2.	20	ROTHERHAM UNITED	2-4	32000	Grant 2	"	"	"	"	"	"	"	"	"	"	"
3.	25	Nottingham Forest	3-2	32000	Edwards 2 Williams,R.	"	"	U	H	L	A	"	"	"	"	"
4.	27	Rotherham United	0-2	20000		"	"	"	"	"	"	"	"	"	"	"
5.	1 Sep	BRENTFORD	2-0	30000	Grant 2	"	U	P	"	"	"	"	E	"	"	"
6.	8	Doncaster Rovers	0-1	20000		"	"	"	"	"	"	"	"	"	"	"
7.	12	Leeds United	1-2	12860	Evans,E.	"	"	"	R	"	"	"	T	"	E	"
8.	15	EVERTON	3-1	23923	Grant 2 Evans,E.	"	O	"	A	"	U	"	"	"	"	"
9.	17	SHEFFIELD UNITED	1-1	30000	Grant	"	"	"	"	"	"	"	"	"	"	"
10.	22	Southampton	1-1	22000	Tiddy	"	"	"	"	"	"	"	"	"	"	*M
11.	29	SHEFFIELD WED.	2-1	30352	Grant 2	"	"	"	"	"	"	"	"	"	B	D
12.	6 Oct	COVENTRY CITY	4-1	27000	Grant 2 Edwards Tiddy	"	"	"	"	"	"	"	H	"	T	"
13.	13	West Ham United	1-1	24000	McLaughlin	"	"	"	"	"	"	"	K	"	"	"
14.	27	Barnsley	0-2	11500		"	"	"	"	R	"	"	"	"	"	"
15.	3 Nov	HULL CITY	1-0	23500	Grant	"	"	"	H	L	A	*N	"	"	"	"
16.	10	Blackburn Rovers	1-0	22500	Edwards	"	"	"	"	"	"	S	"	"	"	"
17.	17	Q.P.RANGERS	3-1	23000	Blair 2 Sherwood	"	"	"	"	"	"	"	B	"	"	"
18.	24	Notts. County	1-0	20000	Montgomery	"	"	"	"	"	"	"	"	"	"	"
19.	1 Dec	LUTON TOWN	3-0	27000	Blair 2 Grant	"	"	"	"	"	"	"	"	"	"	"
20.	8	Bury	1-1	7800	Edwards	"	"	"	U	"	"	"	"	"	"	T
21.	15	Leicester City	0-3	26000		J	"	"	"	"	"	"	"	"	"	D
22.	22	NOTTINGHAM FOREST	4-1	19860	Sherwood Blair 2 Grant	"	U	"	A	"	"	"	K	"	T	"
23.	25	Swansea Town	1-1	23000	Tiddy	I	"	"	"	"	K	"	R	"	E	"
24.	26	SWANSEA TOWN	3-0	46000	Baker Grant Tiddy	*I	O	U	"	"	"	"	"	"	"	"
25.	29	Brentford	1-1	28000	Tiddy	"	"	P	U	"	"	"	B	"	B	F
26.	5 Jan	DONCASTER ROVERS	2-1	30000	Sherwood 2	"	"	"	"	"	"	"	"	"	"	"
27.	19	Everton	0-3	49230		J	"	"	A	"	"	"	"	"	"	"
28.	26	SOUTHAMPTON	1-0	25000	Grant	"	"	"	"	"	U	"	"	"	"	T
29.	9 Feb	Sheffield Wed.	2-4	42881	Evans,E. 2	"	"	"	"	"	"	T	B	"	T	D
30.	16	Coventry City	1-2	26500	Sullivan	"	"	"	"	"	K	"	R	"	E	"
31.	1 Mar	WEST HAM UNITED	1-1	32000	Blair	"	Q	"	"	"	"	"	"	"	"	"
32.	12	Sheffield United	1-6	15000	Grant	"	O	U	H	"	A	"	B	"	B	"
33.	15	BARNSLEY	3-0	25000	Chisholm 2 Evans,L.	"	"	P	K	"	U	"	"	"	*C	F
34.	22	Hull City	0-0	27009		"	"	"	"	"	"	"	"	"	"	"
35.	5 Apr	Q.P.Rangers	1-1	17827	Grant	"	Q	"	"	"	A	"	T	"	"	D
36.	11	Birmingham City	2-3	34000	Grant Chisholm	J	O	"	"	"	"	T	"	"	"	"
37.	12	NOTTS. COUNTY	1-0	25000	Chisholm	I	"	"	"	"	"	"	B	"	"	R
38.	14	BIRMINGHAM CITY	3-1	28000	Chisholm 2 Grant	"	U	"	"	"	"	T	"	"	"	D
39.	19	Luton Town	2-2	14800	Sherwood Williams,R.	"	"	"	"	"	"	"	"	"	E	"
40.	21	BLACKBURN ROVERS	3-1	31169	Grant Chisholm Sherwood(pen)	"	U	"	"	"	"	"	"	"	"	"
41.	26	BURY	3-0	40000	Blair 2 Grant	"	"	"	"	"	"	"	"	"	"	"
42.	3 May	LEEDS UNITED	3-1	52000	Grant 2 Chisholm	"	"	"	"	"	"	"	"	"	"	"

Players:

A = Baker,W.	38/2/1	
B = Blair,D.	28/1/8	
C = Chisholm,K.	11/0/8	
D = Edwards,G.	37/4/7	
E = Evans,E.	8/2/6	
F = Evans,L.	2/0/1	
G = Grant,W.	42/3/27	
H = Hollyman,K.	11/1/0	
I = Howells,R.	16/3/0	
J = Hughes,I.	26/1/0	
K = McLaughlin,R.	23/3/1	
L = Montgomery,S.	39/3/1	
M = Norman,G.	1/0/0	
N = Nugent,C.	1/2/0	
O = Rutter,C.	30/4/0	
P = Sherwood,A.	38/2/7	
Q = Stittall,R.	3/1/0	
R = Sullivan,D.	13/3/1	
S = Tiddy,M.	36/2/5	
T = Williams,R.	31/2/3	
U = Williams,G.	30/2/0	
V = Wilcox,C.	0/2/2	
W = Moss,D.	0/1/0	

City return to Division 1 . . . Late surge of home wins takes them to runners-up spot . . . Wilf Grant (ever present) -- top scorer . . . Transfer deadline signing -- Ken Chisholm nets 8 goals in 11 games . . . Phil Joslin's career ends after dash in pre-season trial . . . £15,000 - record fee - paid for goalie Iowerth Hughes. . . . Over 50,000 for final game v. Leeds.

Other Matches

F.A.Cup

	Date	Opposition	Res	Attend.	Goalscorers	1	2	3	4	5	6	7	8	9	10	11
3rd	12 Jan	SWINDON TOWN	1-1	40000	Grant	I	O	V	A	L	K	S	B	G	T	D
3rd Rep.	15	Swindon Town	0-1*	24207		"	"	P	"	"	"	"	E	"	R	"

* After Extra Time.

Welsh Cup

	Date	Opposition	Res	Attend.	Goalscorers	1	2	3	4	5	6	7	8	9	10	11
5th	3 Jan	Milford United	3-1	2500	Wilcox 2 Evans,E.	"	"	Q	U	"	W	N	V	E	"	"
6th	2 Feb	Merthyr Tydfil	1-3	13000	Edwards	J	"	P	H	R	U	"	K	G	T	"

Friendlies

	Date	Opposition	Res	Attend.	Goalscorers
†	29 Oct	Swindon Town	1-1	3374	Evans,L.
†	7 Nov	Headington United	3-1	6000	Nugent Evans,E. 2
†	19	Worcester City	0-2	7000	
	29 Mar	BLACKPOOL	1-4	8000	Grant
	5 May	Norwich City	3-4	10000	Grant Willimas,R. Chisholm
	14	Renfrewshire Select X1	1-1	2000	Williams,R.
	15	Hamilton Academicals	3-0	3000	Chisholm Nugent Tiddy

† Floodlight Friendly match.

● **CYRIL SPIERS** with his April 1952 Cardiff City squad which reached Division One.... **BACK** (from left): Walter Robbins (Trainer/Coach), Roley Williams, Stan Montgomery, Cyril Spiers (Secretary/Manager), Ron Howells, Glyn Williams, Ron Stitfall, Doug Blair. **FRONT** (from left); Mike Tiddy, Ken Chisholm, Bobby McLaughlin, Alf Sherwood (Captain), George Edwards, Wilf Grant, Derrick Sullivan.

1952-53

Football League – Division 1.

Secretary/Manager: Cyril Spiers

P:42 W:14 D:12 L:16 54-46 Pts:40 Pos:12th

1092	Date	Opposition	Res	Attend.	Goalscorers	1	2	3	4	5	6	7	8	9	10	11
1.	23 Aug	Wolverhampton W.	0-1	50000		J	U	O	Q	M	A	S	B	F	C	D
2.	27	Middlesbrough	0-3	42159		"	P	"	L	"	"	*H	"	"	"	"
3.	30	SHEFFIELD WED.	4-0	43478	Hazlett Chisholm 2 Grant	"	"	"	A	"	U	"	"	"	"	"
4.	3 Sep	MIDDLESBROUGH	1-1	51512	Blair	"	"	"	"	"	"	"	"	"	"	"
5.	6	Tottenham Hotspur	1-2	62150	Chisholm	"	"	"	"	"	"	V	"	"	"	"
6.	10	West Brom. Albion	0-1	33000		"	*E	"	"	"	"	"	"	"	"	"
7.	13	BURNLEY	0-0	45100		"	"	"	"	"	"	H	"	"	"	"
8.	17	WEST BROM. ALBION	1-2	35000	Thomas	"	"	"	"	"	"	"	*R	"	"	"
9.	20	Preston North End	3-2	30000	Blair Williams,R. Chisholm	P	"	"	"	"	"	S	V	B	"	"
10.	27	STOKE CITY	2-0	40000	Williams,R. 2	"	"	"	"	"	"	"	"	"	"	"
11.	4 Oct	Manchester City	2-2	35000	Chisholm Tiddy	"	"	"	"	"	"	"	"	"	"	"
12.	11	Charlton Athletic	1-3	32000	Edwards	"	"	"	"	"	"	"	"	F	"	"
13.	25	Derby County	1-1	23500	Chisholm	"	"	"	"	"	"	"	B	*N	"	"
14.	1 Nov	BLACKPOOL	2-2	44000	Northcott Chisholm	"	"	"	"	"	"	"	Q	"	"	"
15.	8	Chelsea	2-0	52132	Edwards Sherwood	"	"	"	"	"	"	"	"	"	"	"
16.	15	MANCHESTER UNITED	1-2	41000	Chisholm	"	"	*K	"	"	B	"	"	"	"	"
17.	22	Portsmouth	2-0	44000	Northcott Grant	"	"	"	"	"	"	"	F	"	"	"
18.	13 Dec	SUNDERLAND	4-1	31500	Grant2 Edwards Chisholm	"	"	O	"	Q	"	"	"	"	"	"
19.	20	WOLVERHAMPTON W.	0-0	26000		"	"	"	"	"	"	"	"	"	"	"
20.	25	Newcastle United	0-3	5000		"	"	"	"	"	"	"	"	"	"	"
21.	27	NEWCASTLE UNITED	0-0	51592		"	"	"	"	M	L	H	"	"	"	"
22.	3 Jan	Sheffield Wed.	0-2	40109		"	"	"	*G	"	B	S	"	"	"	"
23.	17	TOTTENHAM HOTSPUR	0-0	36423		"	"	"	A	"	Q	"	Q	"	"	"
24.	24	Burnley	0-0	28000		"	"	"	"	"	B	"	G	"	"	"
25.	7 feb	PRESTON NORTH END	0-2	32500		"	"	"	G	"	L	"	"	F	B	N
26.	14	Stoke City	0-0	22000		"	"	"	"	"	"	"	Q	"	"	D
27.	21	MANCHESTER UNITED	6-0	24487	Williams,R.Thomas2 Grant2 Edwards	"	"	"	A	"	Q	R	V	"	"	"
28.	28	CHARLTON ATHLETIC	0-1	35000		"	"	"	"	"	"	"	"	"	"	N
29.	7 Mar	Arsenal	1-0	59579	Blair	"	"	"	G	"	"	S	"	"	"	"
30.	11	BOLTON WANDERERS	0-0	32000	Chisholm	"	"	"	"	"	"	"	"	"	C	"
31.	14	DERBY COUNTY	2-0	34000	Northcott Williams,R.	"	O	"	"	"	"	"	"	"	"	"
32.	25	Blackpool	1-0	15000	Northcott	"	Q	"	"	"	A	"	"	"	B	"
33.	28	CHELSEA	3-3	20000	Tiddy 2 Blair	"	E	"	"	"	"	"	"	"	"	R
34.	3 Apr	Liverpool	1-2	52000	Northcott	"	P	O	A	"	Q	"	"	"	"	N
35.	4	Manchester United	4-1	37500	Grant 2 Tiddy Chisholm	"	O	K	"	"	B	"	"	"	C	"
36.	6	LIVERPOOL	4-0	35500	Grant 2 Chisholm 2	"	"	"	"	"	"	"	"	"	"	"
37.	11	PORTSMOUTH	0-1	37000		"	"	"	"	"	"	"	"	"	"	"
38.	18	Bolton Wanderers	1-0	21000	Sherwood	"	"	"	"	"	"	"	"	"	"	B
39.	22	ARSENAL	0-0	57893		"	"	"	"	"	Q	"	"	"	"	"
40.	25	ASTON VILLA	1-2	23779	Grant	"	"	"	G	E	"	"	"	M	B	D
41.	27	Sunderland	2-4	7469	Thomas Tiddy	"	"	O	I	M	B	"	"	"	"	R
42.	29	Aston Villa	0-2	17603		*T	E	"	"	"	"	"	"	N	C	"

Players:

A = Baker,W. 29/2/1
B = Blair,D. 32/1/4
C = Chisholm,K. 13/4/15
D = Edwards,G. 28/1/4
E = Frowen,J. 6/2/0
F = Grant,W. 31/2/11
G = Harrington,A. 10/3/0
H = Hazlett,G. 7/1/2
I = Hollyman,K. 7/0/0
J = Howells,R. 41/3/0
K = Mansell,J. 11/4/0
L = McLaughlin,R. 3/2/0
M = Montgomery,S. 40/4/0
N = Northcott,T. 23/2/9
O = Sherwood,A. 39/2/2
P = Stitfall,R. 27/0/0
Q = Sullivan,D. 20/2/0
R = Thomas,K. 6/0/4
S = Tiddy,M. 32/2/6
T = Vearncombe,G. 1/1/0
U = Williams,G. 14/0/0
V = Williams,R. 21/2/5
W = Nugent,C. 0/4/0

City are a huge attraction in their return to the top flight ... worst ever run of 8 successive matches without scoring -- then put six past Manchester City ! Shock defeat at Halifax in F.A.Cup, but win at League Champions - Arsenal - before 60,000 crowd ... Record league crowd at Ninian Park of 57,893 for midweek return with Gunners ... Local youngsters make their League debuts.

Other Matches

F.A.Cup

	Date	Opposition	Res	Attend.	Goalscorers	1	2	3	4	5	6	7	8	9	10	11
3rd	10 Jan	Halifax Town	1-3	25000	Baker,W.	J	Q	O	A	M	B	W	F	C	K	D

Welsh Cup

	Date	Opposition	Res	Attend.	Goalscorers	1	2	3	4	5	6	7	8	9	10	11
6th	15 Jan	Merthyr Tydfil	5-2	8000	Northcott 2 Chisholm 2 Hazlett	T	E	K	G	"	L	H	V	N	C	W
7th	31	Barry Town	3-2	9000	Northcott 2 Tiddy	J	"	"	L	"	Q	S	G	"	"	"
Semi-final	21 Mar	Rhyl	0-1	10000		"	"	O	G	"	A	"	V	F	"	"

Friendlies

	Date	Opposition	Res	Attend.	Goalscorers
	18 Nov	Cheltenham Town	3-1	5000	Harrington Williams,D. o.g.(Hyde)
	17 Feb	Bristol City	2-0	20000	Thomas,K. 2
	17 Mar	Exeter City	3-0	9000	Chisholm Montgomery Hazlett
	13 Apr	Torquay United	1-4	5000	Edwards
	4 May	Bristol Rovers	1-3	10000	Thomas

The record (League) attendance match.

(Back) Stitfall, Montgomery, Howells, Williams, Sherwood, Baker
(Front) Hazlett, Blair, Grant, Chisholm, Edwards

1953-54

Football League – Division 1.

Secretary/Manager: Cyril Spiers (resigned 10.5.54)

P:24 W:18 D:8 L:16 51-71 Pts:44 Pos:10th

1134	Date	Opposition	Res	Attend.	Goalscorers	1	2	3	4	5	6	7	8	9	10	11
1.	19 Aug	Middlesbrough	0-0	33726		L	V	U	B	N	W	Y	a	J	*S	P
2.	22	ASTON VILLA	2-1	28156	Rainford Thomas,P.	"	"	"	"	"	"	*X	"	"	"	"
3.	26	Huddersfield Town	0-2	30089		"	"	"	K	"	"	"	"	"	"	d
4.	29	Wolverhampton W.	1-3	30000	Grant	"	H	"	b	"	"	a	K	"	D	c
5.	2 Sep	HUDDERSFIELD TOWN	2-1	30000	Grant Chisholm	"	V	M	K	"	B	"	C	"	"	F
6.	5	SUNDERLAND	1-1	43000	Chisholm	"	"	"	"	"	"	"	"	"	"	"
7.	7	Sheffield United	1-0	34385	Edwards	"	"	"	B	"	T	"	"	"	"	"
8.	12	Manchester City	1-1	31915	Edwards	"	"	"	K	"	B	"	"	"	"	"
9.	14	SHEFFIELD UNITED	2-0	30000	Edwards Grant	"	T	"	B	"	K	d	"	"	"	"
10.	19	BOLTON WANDERERS	1-1	36000	Chisholm	"	"	"	K	"	B	"	"	"	"	"
11.	26	ARSENAL	0-3	50000		"	U	"	"	"	"	X	"	O	W	"
12.	3 Oct	Portsmouth	1-1	31500	Sullivan	"	"	"	"	"	"	Y	J	O	D	"
13.	10	Preston North End	2-1	24000	Chisholm 2	Z	V	"	B	"	W	"	O	O	D	"
14.	17	TOTTENHAM HOTSPUR	1-0	41083	Grant	L	"	"	"	"	"	Y	"	J	"	"
15.	24	Burnley	0-3	30000		"	"	"	b	"	"	"	"	*E	"	"
16.	31	CHARLTON ATHLETIC	5-0	25000	Dudley Chisholm 3 Tiddy	"	U	"	B	"	"	Y	"	"	C	"
17.	7 Nov	Newcastle United	0-4	43000		"	"	"	"	"	"	"	"	"	D	"
18.	14	MANCHESTER UNITED	1-6	27000	Chisholm	"	T	"	"	"	"	J	"	"	"	"
19.	21	West Brom. Albion	1-6	39000	Chisholm	"	K	W	"	"	C	Y	E	"	"	"
20.	28	LIVERPOOL	3-1	21000	Grant Chisholm Edwards	"	T	"	K	"	B	"	C	J	"	"
21.	5 Dec	Sheffield Wed.	1-2	28183	Chisholm	"	V	T	B	"	W	"	J	*G	"	"
22.	12	MIDDLESBROUGH	1-0	31776	Ford	"	"	"	"	"	"	"	P	"	"	"
23.	19	Aston Villa	2-1	21226	Northcott 2	"	T	W	"	"	C	"	"	"	O	"
24.	26	Chelsea	0-2	61386		"	"	"	"	V	"	"	"	"	"	"
25.	28	CHELSEA	0-0	38000		"	"	"	"	"	"	"	P	G	I	"
26.	2 Jan	WOLVERHAMPTON W.	1-3	43000	Nugent	"	"	"	"	"	W	X	"	"	O	J
27.	16	Sunderland	0-5	40500		"	H	T	K	"	"	Y	"	"	"	"
28.	23	MANCHESTER CITY	0-3	23000		Z	V	*I	B	"	"	"	K	Q	O	"
29.	6 Feb	Bolton Wanderers	0-3	30000		"	*R	U	"	"	W	"	"	G	I	"
30.	13	Arsenal	1-1	45497	Ford	"	I	"	"	"	"	"	P	"	"	"
31.	27	PRESTON NORTH END	2-1	30000	Grant 2	"	"	"	"	"	"	"	"	"	O	J
32.	3 Mar	PORTSMOUTH	3-2	20000	Nugent Tiddy Grant	"	"	"	"	"	"	"	"	"	"	"
33.	6	Tottenham Hotspur	1-0	45248	Tiddy	"	"	"	"	"	"	"	"	"	J	"
34.	13	BURNLEY	1-0	34000	Sullivan	"	"	"	"	"	"	"	"	"	"	"
35.	20	Charlton Athletic	2-3	21000	Grant Ford	"	"	"	"	"	"	"	"	"	O	F
36.	27	NEWCASTLE UNITED	2-1	27000	Nugent Tiddy	L	V	"	"	"	"	"	"	J	"	"
37.	3 Apr	Manchester United	3-2	23000	Grant 2 Sullivan	"	"	"	"	"	T	"	"	"	W	J
38.	10	WEST BROM. ALBION	2-0	45000	Grant Ford	"	"	"	"	"	W	"	"	G	O	J
39.	16	Blackpool	1-4	25000	Ford	"	"	"	"	"	"	"	"	"	"	"
40.	17	Liverpool	1-0	41000	Northcott	"	"	"	"	"	"	J	"	"	"	F
41.	19	BLACKPOOL	0-1	45000		Z	"	"	K	I	T	Y	O	"	"	J
42.	24	SHEFFIELD WED.	2-2	15777	Sherwood Ford	"	"	"	"	"	*A	P	"	"	W	F

Players:

A = Baker,C.　1/0/0
B = Baker,W.　37/30
C = Blair,D.　13/2/0
D = Chisholm,K.　17/0/12
E = Dudley,F.　4/0/1
F = Edwards,G.　29/3/4
G = Ford,T.　19/4/9
H = Frowen,J.　3/0/0
I = Gale,C.　9/4/0
J = Grant,W.　32/4/15
K = Harrington,A.　14/2/0
L = Howells,R.　31/2/0
M = Mansell,J.　13/0/0
N = Montgomery,S.　40/4/0
O = Northcott,T.　24/4/6
P = Nugent,C.　22/4/5
Q = Oakley,K.　2/1/0
R = Parfitt,H.　1/1/0
S = Rainford,J.　3/1/0
T = Rutter,C.　14/3/0
U = Sherwood,A.　22/3/1
V = Stitfall,R.　22/2/0
W = Sullivan,D.　33/5/3
X = Thomas,P.　5/3/1
Y = Tiddy,M.　26/4/5
Z = Vearncombe,G.　11/4/0
a = Williams,R.　8/0/0
b = Hollyman,K.　2/0/0
c = McLaughlin,R.　1/0/0
d = Thomas,W.　3/0/0
e = Callan,D.　0/2/0
f = Bevan,T.　0/1/0
g = Burder,D.　0/1/1

Welsh International Trevor Ford signed from Sunderland for Club record £30,000 . . . 1-0 win at Anfield ensures Liverpool's relegation . . . Manager Cyril Spiers - the man responsible for re-building the Club - - resigns at end of season.

Other Matches

F.A.Cup

	Date	Opposition	Res	Attend.	Goalscorers	1	2	3	4	5	6	7	8	9	10	11
3rd	9 Jan	PETERBOROUGH UTD.	3-1	34000	Ford 2 Northcott	L	T	W	B	N	C	X	P	G	O	F
4th	30	PORT VALE	0-2	27000		"	"	U	"	I	W	O	J	"	C	"

Welsh Cup

	Date	Opposition	Res	Attend.	Goalscorers	1	2	3	4	5	6	7	8	9	10	11
5th	20 Jan	Barry Town	1-1	2500	Burder	Z	V	T	K	"	f	Y	"	Q	X	g
5th Rep.	10 Feb	BARRY TOWN	4-2	4500	Ford Tiddy Nugent 2	"	I	U	B	N	W	"	P	G	F	X
		No 6th Round !														
7th	20	Merthyr Tydfil	5-3	7000	Grant 3 o.g.(Lowe) Northcott	"	V	R	e	"	"	"	"	J	K	O
Semi-final	24 Mar	Flint	1-2	10500	Northcott	"	I	U	"	"	"	"	"	G	O	J

Friendlies

	Date	Opposition	Res	Attend.	Goalscorers
	6 Oct	Crystal Palace	2-2	6000	Oakley 2
	30 Nov	Southampton	0-2	7000	
	16 Mar	Hereford United	2-0	5500	Grant Tiddy
	27 Apr	Exeter City	3-1	5000	Ford 3
	29	St.Austell	4-2	5500	Northcott Edwards Grant Nugent

CARDIFF CITY, 1953-54

Standing: W. Nugent, D. Sullivan, G. Vearncombe, S. Montgomery, W. Baker, W. Parfitt.
Seated: M. Tiddy, G. Edwards, A. Sherwood, T. Ford, C. Gee.

1954-55

Football League – Division 1.

Secretary/Manager: Trevor Morris

P:42 W:13 D:11 L:18 62-76 Pts:37 Pos:20th

1176

	Date	Opposition	Res	Attend.	Goalscorers	1	2	3	4	5	6	7	8	9	10	11
1.	21 Aug	Burnley	0-1	27000		K	S	R	B	M	U	V	X	E	N	H
2.	25	PRESTON NORTH END	2-5	40000	Tiddy Ford	"	"	"	"	U	I	"	"	"	"	"
3.	28	LEICESTER CITY	2-1	26000	Northcott Ford	W	Q	"	I	F	B	"	"	"	"	D
4.	1 Sep	Preston North End	1-7	28000	Grant	"	"	"	"	"	"	"	"	"	"	"
5.	4	Chelsea	1-1	42000	Tiddy	K	S	"	"	M	"	"	"	H	O	"
6.	8	SHEFFIELD UNITED	1-1	28000	Tiddy	"	"	"	"	"	"	"	H	E	*T	"
7.	11	HUDDERSFIELD TOWN	1-1	21840	Sherwood (pen)	"	"	"	"	G	"	"	U	"	"	N
8.	13	Sheffield United	3-1	20000	Sullivan Ford Stockin	"	"	"	"	M	*L	"	"	"	"	"
9.	18	MANCHESTER CITY	3-0	30000	Sherwood o.g.(Ewing) Stockin	"	"	"	"	"	"	"	"	"	"	O
10.	25	Everton	1-1	54540	Nugent	"	"	"	"	"	"	*C	"	"	"	"
11.	2 Oct	NEWCASTLE UNITED	4-2	37000	Sullivan Stockin Ford 2	"	"	"	"	"	"	V	"	"	N	"
12.	9	Manchester United	2-5	39328	Ford Stockin	"	"	Q	"	"	"	"	"	N	"	"
13.	16	Wolverhampton W.	1-1	40000	Stockin	"	"	"	"	"	"	"	"	E	"	"
14.	23	Charlton Athletic	1-4	26443	Ford	"	Q	R	"	"	"	"	"	"	"	"
15.	30	BOLTON WANDERERS	2-2	32000	o.g.(Wheeler) Nugent	"	S	"	U	"	"	C	N	"	"	"
16.	6 Nov	Tottenham Hotspur	2-0	38805	Stockin 2	"	Q	"	I	"	U	V	"	"	"	"
17.	13	SHEFFIELD	5-3	15998	Nugent 2 Northcott Sullivan Tiddy	"	"	"	"	"	"	"	X	"	N	"
18.	20	Portsmouth	3-1	31300	Northcott 2 Ford	"	"	"	U	"	L	"	"	"	"	"
19.	27	BLACKPOOL	1-2	20000	Montgomery	W	"	"	"	"	"	C	"	M	T	"
20.	4 Dec	Aston Villa	2-0	26500	Ford 2	"	"	"	B	"	"	V	N	"	"	"
21.	11	SUNDERLAND	0-1	32500		K	"	"	I	M	"	"	"	E	"	"
22.	18	BURNLEY	0-3	21000		"	"	"	"	"	B	"	"	"	"	"
23.	25	WEST BROM. ALBION	3-2	30000	Ford 2 Montgomery	"	"	"	"	"	U	*P	X	"	"	"
24.	27	West Brom. Albion	0-1	35000		"	"	"	L	"	I	"	"	S	"	"
25.	1 Jan	Leicester City	1-2	25000	Nutt	"	"	"	"	U	"	"	"	M	"	"
26.	5 Feb	Manchester City	1-4	31922	Ford (pen)	"	S	"	B	"	L	"	"	E	"	N
27.	12	EVERTON	4-3	17108	Ford 2 Stockin 2	"	"	"	I	"	"	C	"	"	"	"
28.	26	MANCHESTER UNITED	3-0	16400	Stockin 2 Nutt	"	Q	"	"	M	U	V	"	"	T	"
29.	5 Mar	Sunderland	1-1	40000	Stockin	"	S	Q	"	"	B	"	"	"	"	"
30.	12	CHARLTON ATHLETIC	4-3	21000	Nutt Ford Williams Northcott	"	Q	S	"	F	U	"	"	"	"	"
31.	19	Bolton Wanderers	0-0	24250		"	"	"	"	"	"	"	O	"	"	"
32.	23	CHELSEA	0-1	20000		"	"	"	"	"	"	"	X	"	"	O
33.	26	TOTTENHAM HOTSPUR	1-2	14461	Ford	"	"	R	"	"	"	"	"	"	"	"
34.	2 Apr	Sheffield Wed.	1-1	20295	Nutt	"	S	"	"	M	"	"	V	"	"	"
35.	8	Arsenal	0-2	39052		"	"	"	"	"	"	"	"	N	N	"
36.	9	ASTON VILLA	0-1	24993		"	"	U	"	F	L	V	X	E	T	P
37.	11	ARSENAL	1-2	36000	Harrington	"	"	R	"	"	U	P	V	"	X	O
38.	16	Blackpool	0-0	22000		"	"	"	"	"	"	V	X	"	T	N
39.	23	PORTSMOUTH	1-1	25000	Williams	"	"	"	"	"	"	"	"	"	"	"
40.	27	Newcastle United	0-3	19240		W	Q	S	"	U	L	"	"	"	"	O
41.	30	WOLVERHAMPTON W.	3-2	32000	Ford 2 Hitchens	"	S	R	"	A	"	"	*J	J	N	"
42.	2 May	Huddersfield Town	0-2	10473		"	Q	"	"	"	"	"	X	"	"	O

Players:

A = Baker,C.   2/0/0
B = Baker,W.   8/2/0
C = Dixon,C.   3/0/0
D = Edwards,G.   4/1/0
E = Ford,T.   35/3/24
F = Frowen,J.   11/0/0
G = Gale,C.   2/0/0
H = Grant,W.   5/0/1
I = Harrington,A.   34/2/1
J = Hitchens,G.   2/1/1
K = Howells,R.   36/4/0
L = Jones,I.   20/3/0
M = Montgomery,S.   24/3/2
N = Northcott,T.   28/3/5
O = Nugent,C.   24/2/5
P = Nutt,G.   16/3/4
Q = Rutter,C.   22/4/0
R = Sherwood,A.   34/2/2
S = Stitfall,R.   27/1/0
T = Stockin,R.   31/4/14
U = Sullivan,D.   36/2/4
V = Tiddy,M.   27/2/5
W = Vearncombe,G.   6/0/0
X = Williams,D.R.   25/1/2
Y = Parfitt,H.   0/1/0

Former secretary Trevor Morris takes over . . . City plunge into relegation waters - - escape by beating the mighty Wolves. in last game - - Gerry Hitchens makes scoring debut in game. . Last link with pre-war days severed - - Baker's last game.

Other Matches

F.A.Cup

	Date	Opposition	Res	Attend.	Goalscorers	1	2	3	4	5	6	7	8	9	10	11
3rd	8 Jan	Arsenal	0-1	51298		K	Q	R	L	M	I	V	O	E	T	N

Welsh Cup

	Date	Opposition	Res	Attend.	Goalscorers	1	2	3	4	5	6	7	8	9	10	11
5th	12 Jan	Pembroke Borough	7-0	4000	Ford 4 Nugent Stockin Tiddy	"	S	Q	B	U	L	"	T	"	O	P
6th	17 Feb	Newport County	3-1	10223	Ford Stockin Sullivan	"	Q	R	I	M	U	P	X	"	T	N
Semi-final	13 Apr	Chester	0-2	7961		"	"	Y	B	"	"	"	N	J	"	D

Friendlies

	Date	Opposition	Res	Attend.	Goalscorers
	29 Jan	FULHAM	1-2	8000	Sullivan

(Back) Stitfall, Nash (Trainer) Grant, Tiddy, Howells, Frowen, Baker, Nugent
(Front) Ford, Sherwood, Derrick, Sullivan, Northcott

1955-56

1218   Secretary/Manager: Trevor Morris

Football League – Division 1.   P:42 W:15 D:9 L:18 55-69 Pts:39 Pos:17th

	Date	Opposition	Res	Attend.	Goalscorers	1	2	3	4	5	6	7	8	9	10	11
1.	20 Aug	SUNDERLAND	3-1	36000	McSeveney 2 Ford	J	S	U	H	W	L	D	*M	E	V	O
2.	23	Arsenal	1-3	31352	Stockin	"	"	W	"	F	"	"	"	"	*	*
3.	27	Aston Villa	0-2	25672		"	"	U	"	W	"	"	"	E	"	"
4.	31	BOLTON WANDERERS	1-0	25000	Harrington	"	*C	"	"	G	W	"	"	"	Q	"
5.	3 Sep	WOLVERHAMPTON W.	1-9	45000	Stockin	"	T	"	"	"	"	"	"	"	V	"
6.	7	Bolton Wanderers	0-4	21310		"	C	"	"	W	L	"	Z	"	Z	"
7.	10	Manchester City	1-3	25000	Williams	"	S	U	"	W	"	"	"	"	M	"
8.	17	SHEFFIELD UNITED	3-2	23500	Harrington Ford Hitchens	"	"	U	"	"	"	"	"	E	"	"
9.	24	HUDDERSFIELD TOWN	1-2	24000	Kirtley	"	"	"	"	"	*B	"	"	"	"	"
10.	1 Oct	Blackpool	1-2	33451	Ford	"	U	T	"	"	S	"	Z	"	V	"
11.	8	Preston North End	2-1	19500	Ford Stockin	"	"	"	S	"	H	*Y	M	"	"	"
12.	15	BURNLEY	2-2	24000	Ford 2	"	"	"	"	"	"	"	"	"	"	"
13.	22	West Brom. Albion	1-2	26000	Kirtley	"	C	U	"	F	"	"	"	"	V	"
14.	29	MANCHESTER UNITED	0-1	27759		"	U	T	"	W	"	"	"	E	"	"
15.	5 Nov	Tottenham Hotspur	1-1	34368	Walsh	"	"	"	"	F	W	"	"	"	"	"
16.	12	EVERTON	3-1	22439	Walsh McSeveney 2	"	S	"	H	"	"	"	"	"	"	"
17.	19	Newcastle United	0-4	35600		"	"	"	"	"	"	"	"	"	"	"
18.	26	BIRMINGHAM CITY	2-1	24000	Kirtley Dixon	"	U	"	"	W	A	"	"	"	O	D
19.	3 Dec	Luton Town	0-3	22000		"	"	"	"	"	"	"	"	"	V	O
20.	10	CHARLTON ATHLETIC	3-1	23000	O'Halloran 3	"	"	"	"	*N	"	"	"	"	*R	"
21.	17	Sunderland	1-1	30000	o.g.(Hedley)	"	"	"	"	"	"	"	"	"	"	"
22.	24	ASTON VILLA	1-0	21789	Hitchens	"	C	"	"	"	"	"	"	"	"	"
23.	26	CHELSEA	1-1	30000	Sherwood	"	"	"	"	"	"	"	"	"	"	"
24.	27	Chelsea	1-2	36740	Hitchens	X	U	"	"	"	"	M	"	E	"	P
25.	31	Wolverhampton W.	2-0	37000	Hitchens Ford	"	"	W	"	"	"	Y	M	"	"	O
26.	14 Jan	MANCHESTER CITY	4-1	33240	Hitchens 2 McSeveney Ford	"	"	T	"	"	"	"	"	"	"	"
27.	21	Sheffield United	1-2	23000	Sherwood	"	"	W	"	"	"	"	"	"	"	"
28.	4 Feb	Huddersfield Town	2-1	12500	Hitchens Ford	"	"	"	"	"	"	"	"	"	"	"
29.	11	BLACKPOOL	1-0	37000	Ford	"	"	"	"	"	"	"	"	"	"	"
30.	18	PRESTON NORTH END	3-1	25000	Hitchens Kirtley Ford	"	"	"	"	"	"	"	"	"	"	"
31.	25	Burnley	2-0	18549	Hitchens 2	"	"	"	"	"	"	"	"	"	"	"
32.	7 Mar	NEWCASTLE UNITED	1-1	32000	Baker	"	S	U	W	"	"	"	"	"	"	"
33.	10	Manchester United	1-1	44693	Hitchens	"	U	W	H	"	"	"	"	"	"	"
34.	24	Everton	0-2	29959		"	"	"	"	"	"	"	V	"	"	"
35.	30	Portsmouth	1-1	26443	Ford	"	"	"	"	"	"	"	M	"	"	"
36.	31	WEST BROM. ALBION	1-3	32000	Hitchens	"	"	"	R	"	"	D	V	"	"	"
37.	2 Apr	PORTSMOUTH	2-3	27000	McSeveney Ford	"	"	"	H	"	"	"	M	"	"	"
38.	7	Birmingham City	1-2	37000	Hitchens	"	C	"	"	"	"	Y	"	"	"	"
39.	14	LUTON TOWN	2-0	22000	Hitchens Walsh	"	U	T	"	"	W	"	"	"	"	"
40.	21	Charlton Athletic	0-0	17500		"	"	W	"	"	A	"	I	"	K	"
41.	23	TOTTENHAM HOTSPUR	0-0	19684		"	"	"	"	"	"	"	"	"	I	"
42.	28	ARSENAL	1-2	24000	Hitchens	"	"	"	"	"	"	"	M	"	"	"

Players:

A = Baker,C.   24/7/2
B = Callan,D.   1/0/0
C = Davies,R.   6/2/0
D = Dixon,C.   12/2/1
E = Ford,T.   27/7/22
F = Frowen,J.   5/2/0
G = Gale,C.   2/0/0
H = Harrington,A.   38/5/2
I = Hitchens,G.   36/7/28
J = Howells,R.   27/3/0
K = Jones,B.   2/0/0
L = Jones,I.   6/0/0
M = Kirtley,H.   38/7/4
N = Malloy,D.   23/5/0
O = McSeveney,J.   41/7/10
P = Nugent,C.   1/1/0
Q = Nutt,G.   1/0/0
R = O'Halloran,N.   6/0/3
S = Rutter,C   16/0/0
T = Sherwood,A.   20/3/2
U = Stitfall,R.   36/6/0
V = Stockin,R.   14/0/3
W = Sullivan,D.   32/2/0
X = Veamcombe,G.   15/4/0
Y = Walsh,B.   30/4/5
Z = Williams,D.R.   3/0/1

Wolves win 9-1 at Ninian Park - - equals record Division 1 away score. Win return at Molineux ! Malloy signs from Dundee for £17,000 . . . . Part - timer, O'Halloran becomes only City player to score hat-trick on debut . . . . Tiddy and Nutt go to Arsenal in exchange for Walsh and £20,000 . . . . 37,000 see Welsh Cup v. Swansea .

Other Matches

F.A.Cup

	Date	Opposition	Res	Attend.	Goalscorers	1	2	3	4	5	6	7	8	9	10	11
3rd	7 Jan	Leeds United	2-1	40000	Hitchens McSeveney	J	U	T	H	N	A	Y	M	E	I	O
4th	28	West Ham United	1-2	35500	Ford	"	"	"	"	"	"	"	"	"	"	"

Welsh Cup

	Date	Opposition	Res	Attend.	Goalscorers	1	2	3	4	5	6	7	8	9	10	11
5th	1 Feb	Pembroke Borough	2-2	5000	Ford Hitchens	"	C	U	W	"	"	D	"	"	"	"
5th Replay	8	PEMBROKE BOROUGH	9-0	4549	Ford 4 Hitchens 3 Baker McSeveney	X	U	T	"	"	"	"	"	"	"	"
6th	29	WREXHAM	5-3	5300	Hitchens 3 Ford McSeveney	"	C	W	H	F	"	Y	"	"	"	"
Semi-final	17 Mar	Oswestry	7-0	11418	Ford 2 Hitchens 5	"	U	"	"	"	"	P	"	"	"	"
Final	30 Apr	SWANSEA TOWN	3-2	37000	Walsh 2 McSeveney	"	"	"	"	N	"	Y	"	"	"	"

Friendlies

	Date	Opposition	Res
	7 Nov	Watford	
	10 May	Bristol Rovers	0-1

Record home League defeat (1-9)!

Back Row (Left to Right):
Kirtley, Tiddy, Frowen, Howells, Harrington, Jones
Front Row:
Davies, Stockin, Rutter, McSeveney, Hitchens

1956-57

Football League – Division 1

Secretary/Manager: Trevor Morris

P:42 W:10 D:9 L:23 53-88 Pts:29 Pos:21st (Rel.)

1260	Date	Opposition	Res	Attend.	Goalscorers	1	2	3	4	5	6	7	8	9	10	11
1.	18 Aug	Arsenal	0-0	51069		V	Q	R	G	L	A	W	M	D	H	N
2.	22	NEWCASTLE UNITED	5-2	42000	McSeveney Ford 2 Nugent 2	"	"	"	"	"	T	"	"	"	"	"
3.	25	BURNLEY	3-3	30769	McSeveney Hitchens Ford	"	"	"	"	"	"	"	"	"	"	"
4.	29	Newcastle United	0-1	35000		"	R	T	"	"	A	"	"	"	"	"
5.	1 Sep	Preston North End	0-6	22102		"	B	"	"	"	"	"	"	"	"	"
6.	5	SHEFFIELD WED	2-1	12983	Hitchens McSeveney	"	"	R	L	E	T	"	"	"	"	"
7.	8	CHELSEA	1-1	26000	o.g.(Armstrong)	"	"	"	"	"	"	"	"	"	"	"
8.	12	Sheffield Wed.	3-5	38721	McSeveney 2 (1 pen) Walsh	"	"	"	"	"	"	"	"	"	"	"
9.	15	Bolton Wanderers	0-2	28313		"	"	"	G	L	"	C	"	"	"	"
10.	22	Birmingham City	1-2	39931		"	"	"	"	"	"	D	"	H	O	"
11.	29	WEST BROM. ALBION	0-0	22500	O'Halloran	"	"	"	"	"	"	W	H	D	"	"
12.	6 Oct	LEEDS UNITED	4-1	38333	Hitchens 2 Ford McSeveney	"	"	"	"	"	"	"	*P	"	H	M
13.	13	Tottenham Hotspur	0-5	52429		"	"	"	"	"	"	"	"	"	"	"
14.	27	Wolverhampton W.	1-3	34935	Hitchens	"	"	"	"	"	A	"	M	O	"	N
15.	3 Nov	MANCHESTER CITY	1-1	22000	Reynolds	"	R	T	"	"	"	"	P	D	"	M
16.	10	Charlton Athletic	2-0	17642	Hitchens Reynolds	"	"	"	"	"	"	"	"	H	M	N
17.	17	SUNDERLAND	1-0	20000	Nugent	"	E	R	"	"	T	"	"	"	"	"
18.	24	Luton Town	0-3	13654		"	"	"	"	"	"	"	"	"	"	"
19.	1 Dec	EVERTON	1-0	15600	McSeveney	"	"	"	"	"	"	"	"	O	N	M
20.	8	Blackpool	0-3	16623	Walsh	"	"	"	"	"	"	"	M	H	S	N
21.	15	ARSENAL	2-3	18000	Hitchens 2	G	"	"	A	"	"	"	P	"	"	"
22.	22	Burnley	2-6	10118	Hitchens 2	"	"	"	"	"	"	"	"	"	"	"
23.	26	Manchester United	1-3	28607	Malloy (pen)	"	"	"	"	"	A	"	"	"	"	"
24.	29	PRESTON NORTH END	2-3	40000	Stockin McSeveney	"	R	T	G	"	"	C	"	"	"	"
25.	12 Jan	Chelsea	2-1	28828	McSeveney Hitchens	"	Q	R	A	"	T	W	M	"	"	"
26.	19	BOLTON WANDERERS	2-0	15000	Hitchens Walsh	"	"	"	"	"	"	"	"	"	"	"
27.	2 Feb	BIRMINGHAM CITY	1-2	18000	McSeveney	"	B	"	"	"	"	"	"	"	"	"
28.	9	West Brom. Albion	2-1	22790	Hitchens Baker	I	"	"	"	"	"	"	P	"	"	*F
29.	16	Leeds United	0-3	21695		"	"	"	"	"	"	"	"	"	"	"
30.	23	WOLVERHAMPTON W.	2-2	14000	Hitchens Baker	"	"	"	"	"	"	C	"	"	"	M
31.	9 Mar	BLACKPOOL	3-4	17000	Hitchens 2 McSeveney	"	"	"	"	"	"	"	G	"	K	"
32.	13	Aston Villa	1-4	11834	Hitchens	V	E	"	"	"	"	"	"	"	"	U
33.	16	Manchester City	1-4	26395	McSeveney (pen)	"	Q	"	G	"	A	W	M	"	"	M
34.	23	CHARLTON ATHLETIC	2-3	20000	Baker Hitchens	"	"	"	L	E	"	"	G	"	"	M
35.	30	Sunderland	1-1	40100	Hitchens	"	"	"	G	L	"	C	M	"	S	N
36.	3 Apr	ASTON VILLA	1-0	14820	McSeveney	"	"	"	"	"	"	N	"	"	*J	U
37.	6	LUTON TOWN	0-0	18000		"	"	"	"	"	"	"	"	"	"	"
38.	13	Everton	0-0	24397		"	"	"	"	"	"	"	"	"	"	"
39.	19	Portsmouth	0-1	31223		"	"	"	"	"	"	W	"	"	"	"
40.	20	TOTTENHAM HOTSPUR	0-3	25181		"	B	Q	"	"	"	"	G	"	K	"
41.	22	PORTSMOUTH	0-2	25000		"	"	"	"	"	"	"	S	"	"	"
42.	27	MANCHESTER UNITED	2-3	17708	Hitchens 2	"	Q	R	"	"	"	"	M	"	"	"

Players:

A = Baker,C. 27/5/3
B = Davies,R. 17/2/0
C = Dixon,C. 6/1/0
D = Ford,T. 14/0/4
E = Frowen,J. 9/1/0
F = Godwin,D. 2/1/0
G = Harrington,A. 33/1/0
H = Hitchens,G. 41/5/25
I = Howells,R. 4/2/0
J = Jenkins,B. 4/0/0
K = Jones,B. 7/0/0
L = Malloy,D. 42/4/1
M = McSeveney,J. 34/4/13
N = Nugent,C. 28/2/3
O = O'Halloran,N. 4/0/1
P = Reynolds,B. 14/0/3
Q = Rutter,C. 15/3/0
R = Stitfall,R. 39/5/0
S = Stockin,R. 13/4/3
T = Sullivan,D. 31/5/1
U = Tucker,K. 8/0/0
V = Vearncombe,G. 38/3/0
W = Walsh,B. 32/4/5.
X = Kirtley,H. 0/3/2

1 win in last 14 matches - City relegated ... Trevor Ford is banned 'sine die' by Football League ... Despite relegation, Gerry Hitchens first City player to score over 20 League goals for 30 years.

Other Matches

F.A.Cup

	Date	Opposition	Res	Attend.	Goalscorers	1	2	3	4	5	6	7	8	9	10	11
3rd	5 Jan	Leeds United	2-1	34237	Stockin McSeveney	V	Q	R	A	L	T	W	M	H	S	N
4th	26	BARNSLEY	0-1	32000		"	"	"	"	"	"	"	"	"	"	"

Welsh Cup

	Date	Opposition	Res	Attend.	Goalscorers	1	2	3	4	5	6	7	8	9	10	11
5th	31 Jan	Haverfordwest	3-3	1800	Hitchens 2 Kirtley	"	B	"	"	"	"	"	X	"	"	M
5th replay	6 Feb	HAVERFORDWEST	8-0	3500	Hitchens 2 Walsh 2 Kirtley Stockin Sullivan o.g.(Williams)	I	"	"	E	"	"	"	"	"	"	F
6th	27	CHESTER	0-2	5000		"	Q	G	L	A	C	"	"	"	T	M

Friendlies

	Date	Opposition	Res	Attend.	Goalscorers
	6 Nov	Kidderminster Harriers	1-1		McSeveney

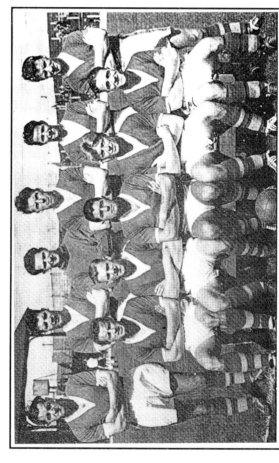

Standing (left to right) R. Stitfall, C. Baker, G. Vearncombe, D. Malloy, A. Harrington, D. Sullivan. Seated (left to right) B. Walsh, C. Nugent, T. Ford, G. Hitchens, J. McSeveney.

1957-58

Football League – Division 2.

Secretary/Manager: Trevor Morris

P:42 W:14 D:9 L:19 63-77 Pts:37 Pos:15th

1302		Date	Opposition	Res	Attend.	Goalscorers	1	2	3	4	5	6	7	8	9	10	11
1.	24 Aug	SWANSEA TOWN	0-0	45000		Y	T	V	F	N	W	*I	*G	H	*Q	X
2.	27	Grimsby Town	1-1	18000	o.g. (Tucker)	"	"	"	"	"	"	"	"	"	"	"
3.	31	Liverpool	0-3	45698		"	"	"	D	"	F	"	"	"	"	"
4.	4 Sep	GRIMSBY TOWN	1-3	16000	Nicholls	"	"	"	F	"	A	"	D	"	"	R
5.	7	MIDDLESBROUGH	0-2	14200		"	"	*P	D	E	"	"	G	"	"	"
6.	11	HUDDERSFIELD TOWN	1-0	10073	Davies	"	V	"	F	N	"	Z	"	D	R	X
7.	14	Leyton Orient	2-4	16852	Davies Nugent	"	"	"	"	"	"	"	"	"	"	"
8.	18	Huddersfield Town	1-1	9821	Reynolds	"	"	"	"	"	"	"	S	H	G	R
9.	21	CHARLTON ATHLETIC	0-3	15000		"	"	"	"	"	D	"	"	"	"	"
10.	28	Doncaster Rovers	1-0	9909	Davies	"	"	"	"	"	W	"	D	"	"	"
11.	5 Oct	ROTHERHAM UNITED	2-2	16000	Walsh Hewitt	"	T	"	"	"	A	"	S	"	"	Q
12.	12	DERBY COUNTY	3-2	15000	Hitchens Hewitt Walsh	"	"	"	A	*C	W	"	"	"	"	"
13.	19	Bristol Rovers	2-0	23292	Hitchens 2	"	V	"	"	"	"	"	"	"	"	R
14.	26	LINCOLN CITY	3-2	14000	Hewitt Nugent Reynolds	"	"	"	"	"	"	"	"	"	"	"
15.	2 Nov	Notts. County	2-5	14911	Reynolds Nicholls	"	T	V	F	"	"	"	"	Q	"	"
16.	4	Stoke City	0-3	12000		"	"	"	"	"	"	"	"	"	"	"
17.	9	IPSWICH TOWN	1-1	16000	Bonson	"	V	P	"	"	"	"	"	N	*B	J
18.	16	Blackburn Rovers	0-4	24700		"	"	"	"	"	A	"	"	B	H	"
19.	23	SHEFFIELD UNITED	0-0	14000		*L	"	"	"	N	"	"	G	"	"	R
20.	30	West Ham United	1-1	24000	Bonson	"	"	"	"	"	*U	"	"	"	"	—
21.	7 Dec	BARNSLEY	7-0	14000	Nugent 3 Hewitt 2 Bonson Hudson	"	"	"	"	"	"	"	R	"	R	"
22.	14	Fulham	0-2	17000		"	"	"	"	"	"	"	S	H	B	"
23.	21	Swansea Town	1-0	23000	Hudson	"	"	"	"	"	A	"	G	B	R	"
24.	26	STOKE CITY	5-2	27000	Hudson Bonson 2 Reynolds Walsh	"	P	"	"	"	"	"	"	"	"	"
25.	28	LIVERPOOL	6-1	30000	Hudson Reynolds 2 Hewitt Bonson 2	Y	V	"	"	"	"	Z	S	"	G	"
26.	11 Jan	Middlesbrough	1-4	23115	Walsh	L	"	"	"	"	"	—	"	"	"	—
27.	18	LEYTON ORIENT	1-1	14000	Hewitt	"	"	"	"	"	*O	"	G	H	R	J
28.	1 Feb	Charlton Athletic	1-3	20556	Nugent	"	"	"	"	"	W	—	"	B	"	"
29.	8	DONCASTER ROVERS	3-1	15000	Walsh Nugent Hewitt	"	P	V	"	"	"	"	"	D	"	"
30.	22	Sheffield United	0-3	19424		"	"	W	"	"	A	Z	"	B	S	R
31.	15 Mar	NOTTS. COUNTY	2-0	11000	Bonson Hewitt	"	V	"	W	"	A	Z	R	"	"	—
32.	22	Ipswich Town	1-3	13469	Bonson	"	P	"	"	"	"	"	"	"	"	"
33.	26	BRISTOL ROVERS	0-2	10000		Y	V	"	"	"	"	—	"	"	G	R
34.	29	BLACKBURN ROVERS	4-3	12000	Hewitt 3 Bonson	L	"	"	"	"	"	—	S	"	R	—
35.	4 Apr	BRISTOL CITY	2-3	15000	Hewitt 2	"	"	"	"	"	*M	Z	G	"	"	J
36.	5	Derby County	2-0	15529	Bonson Jenkins	"	"	"	"	"	"	"	"	"	"	"
37.	7	Bristol City	0-2	25543		"	P	V	"	"	"	"	"	"	"	"
38.	12	WEST HAM UNITED	0-3	19000		"	T	"	"	"	A	Z	"	D	"	"
39.	19	Barnsley	1-1	8861	Hudson	"	"	V	W	"	M	"	R	"	S	—
40.	21	Rotherham United	1-3	7954	Walsh	"	"	W	F	"	A	"	G	B	R	"
41.	26	FULHAM	3-0	10000	Baker Sullivan 2	*K	L	P	A	"	W	"	"	"	"	"
42.	30	Lincoln City	1-3	18000	Nugent	L	"	"	"	"	"	"	"	"	"	"

Players:

A = Baker,C.   23/4/1
B = Bonson,J.   25/5/14
C = Daniel,R.   6/1/0
D = Davies,R.   9/0/3
E = Frowen,J.   1/0/0
F = Harrington,A.   36/4/1
G = Hewitt,R.   35/4/15
H = Hitchens,G.   16/0/3
I = Hudson,C.   28/5/4
J = Jenkins,B.   4/0/1
K = Jones,A.J.   1/0/0
L = Jones,K.   22/5/0
M = McGuckin,G.   4/0/0
N = Malloy,D.   36/5/0
O = Menzies,R.   1/0/0
P = Milne,A.   27/4/0
Q = Nicholls,J.   8/0/2
R = Nugent,C.   31/5/9
S = Reynolds,B.   18/1/6
T = Rutter,C.   10/1/0
U = Scott,R.   3/0/0
V = Stitfall,R.   38/5/0
W = Sullivan,D.   23/1/2
X = Tucker,K.   5/1/0
Y = Vearncombe,G.   19/0/0
Z = Walsh,B.   33/4/7

Despite new signings dreadful start to season . . . Hitchens sold to Villa for £22,500 . . . Barnsley beaten 7-0 - - highest post-war League victory . . . Hudson's goal gives first League win at Swansea . . . League leaders Liverpool beaten 6-1 (5-0 at half-time) ! Third season running, 3rd F.A.Cup win, at Leeds - all 2-1!

Other Matches

F.A.Cup

	Date	Opposition	Res	Attend.	Goalscorers	1	2	3	4	5	6	7	8	9	10	11
3rd	4 Jan	Leeds United	2-1	30000	Harrington Nugent	L	V	P	F	N	A	Z	R	B	G	I
4th	25	LEYTON ORIENT	4-1	35849	o.g. (Bishop) Walsh Bonson 2	"	"	"	"	"	"	"	G	"	R	"
5th	15 Feb	BLACKBURN ROVERS	0-0	37400		"	P	V	"	"	"	"	"	"	"	"
5th Replay	20	Blackburn Rovers	1-2	27000	Hewitt	"	"	"	"	"	"	"	"	"	"	"

Welsh Cup

	Date	Opposition	Res	Attend.	Goalscorers	1	2	3	4	5	6	7	8	9	10	11
5th	29 Jan	HEREFORD UNITED	0-2	4000		"	V	T	C	"	W	I	S	"	"	X

Friendlies

	Date	Opposition	Res	Attend.	Goalscorers
	1 Mar	PORTSMOUTH	1-1	5000	Hewitt

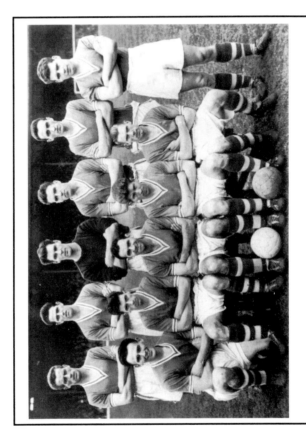

(Back) Walsh, Harrington, Jones, Malloy, Milne, Baker
(Front) Bonson, Reynolds, Stitfall, Hudson, Nugent

1958-59
Football League – Division 2.

Manager: Bill Jones (Permanent from 23.10.58.)
P: 42 **W:** 18 **D:** 7 **L:** 17 **65-65 Pts:** 43 **Pos:** 9th

1344

	Date	Opposition	Res	Attend.	Goalscorers	1	2	3	4	5	6	7	8	9	10	11
1.	23 Aug	BARNSLEY	0-1	23000		J	S	N	E	M	T	W	*K	B	F	G
2.	27	Huddersfield Town	0-3	13266		"	"	"	"	"	"	"	"	R	Q	"
3.	30	Rotherham United	0-1	11500		*P	"	"	"	"	"	"	"	"	"	"
4.	3 Sep	HUDDERSFIELD TOWN	3-2	13078	Baker Walsh Nugent	"	"	"	A	"	"	"	"	"	"	I
5.	6	SHEFFIELD UNITED	3-1	20000	Kelly 2 Reynolds	"	"	"	"	"	"	"	"	"	"	"
6.	8	Bristol Rovers	0-2	20604		"	"	"	"	"	"	"	"	"	"	"
7.	13	Brighton & H.A.	2-2	25009	Hewitt Moore	"	"	"	E	"	A	G	*O	B	F	"
8.	17	BRISTOL ROVERS	2-4	20000	Hudson Moore	"	"	"	"	"	"	"	"	"	Q	"
9.	20	GRIMSBY TOWN	4-1	16086	Hewitt 2 Bonson Jenkins	"	N	T	*C	"	"	W	*U	"	F	"
10.	27	Liverpool	2-1	41866	Bonson Hewitt	"	"	"	"	"	"	"	"	"	"	"
11.	4 Oct	MIDDLESBROUGH	3-2	20560	Jenkins Hewitt Walsh	"	"	"	"	"	"	"	"	"	"	"
12.	11	IPSWICH TOWN	1-2	20357	Tapscott	"	"	"	"	"	"	"	"	"	"	"
13.	25	STOKE CITY	2-1	22000	Stitfall Tapscott	"	"	S	"	"	"	"	"	R	"	"
14.	1 Nov	Derby County	3-1	17532	Reynolds Hewitt(pen) Walsh	"	"	"	"	"	"	"	"	"	"	"
15.	8	LINCOLN CITY	3-0	16000	Hewitt Jenkins Walsh	"	"	"	T	"	"	"	"	"	"	"
16.	15	Fulham	1-2	24000	Walsh	"	E	N	"	"	"	"	"	"	"	"
17.	22	SHEFFIELD WED.	2-2	20195	Jenkins Tapscott	"	N	S	"	"	"	"	"	"	"	"
18.	6 Dec	LEYTON ORIENT	2-1	16000	Hewitt 2	"	"	"	"	"	"	"	"	"	"	"
19.	13	Sunderland	2-0	30097	Tapscott Bonson	"	"	"	"	"	T	"	"	B	"	R
20.	18	Scunthorpe United	0-1	8500		"	"	"	"	"	"	"	"	"	"	"
21.	20	Barnsley	2-3	7731	Hewitt Walsh	"	"	*D	"	"	"	"	"	"	"	"
22.	26	Bristol City	3-2-227266		Bonson 2 Walsh	"	"	S	"	"	"	"	"	"	"	"
23.	27	BRISTOL CITY	1-0	35000	o.g. (Burden)	"	"	"	"	"	"	"	"	"	"	"
24.	3 Jan	ROTHERHAM UNITED	1-0	16000	Reynolds	"	"	"	"	"	"	"	O	"	"	"
25.	31	BRIGHTON & H.A.	3-1	14500	Jenkins Bonson	"	"	"	"	"	"	"	U	*L	"	I
26.	7 Feb	Grimsby Town	1-5	9000	Reynolds	"	"	"	"	"	"	R	"	"	R	G
27.	14	LIVERPOOL	3-0	25000	Tapscott 2 Reynolds	"	"	"	A	"	T	W	"	"	"	"
28.	21	Middlesbrough	1-1	12791	Walsh	"	"	"	A	"	"	"	"	"	"	"
29.	28	Lincoln City	2-4	8736	Reynolds Jenkins	"	E	N	T	"	A	"	"	R	O	I
30.	7 Mar	SWANSEA TOWN	0-1	26000		"	"	"	A	"	T	"	"	L	B	G
31.	14	Stoke City	1-0	11929	Hewitt	"	"	"	"	"	"	"	"	B	F	"
32.	21	DERBY COUNTY	0-0	15000		"	"	"	T	"	A	"	"	L	"	"
33.	28	Ipswich Town	3-3	12040	Tapscott Hewitt Hudson	"	"	"	A	"	T	"	"	B	"	"
34.	30	Charlton Athletic	0-0	14000		"	"	"	"	"	"	"	U	R	"	G
35.	31	CHARLTON ATHLETIC	1-2	15000	Sullivan	"	"	"	T	"	A	"	K	U	T	"
36.	4 Apr	FULHAM	1-2	25000	Walsh	"	"	"	"	"	"	"	"	"	"	"
37.	11	Sheffield Wed.	1-3	23106	Tapscott	"	"	"	"	"	"	"	"	"	"	"
38.	15	Swansea Town	3-1	22000	Kelly 2 o.g.(Nurse)	"	N	S	E	"	"	"	"	U	T	G
39.	18	SCUNTHORPE UNITED	0-2	10000		"	"	"	"	"	"	"	*H	L	F	R
40.	22	Sunderland	2-1	12000	Hewitt Walsh	"	"	"	"	"	"	"	U	"	"	"
41.	25	Leyton Orient	0-3	11465		V	E	N	C	"	"	"	"	B	O	"
42.	27	Sheffield United	1-1	14000	Tapscott	"	"	"	"	"	"	"	"	"	"	"

Players:

A = Baker,C. 39/6/1
B = Bonson,J. 21/5/10
C = Gammon,S. 7/1/0
D = Gray,A. 1/0/0
E = Harrington,A. 20/2/0
F = Hewitt,R. 29/4/17
G = Hudson,C. 17/4/4
H = Hughes,M. 1/0/0
I = Jenkins,B. 19/2/6
J = Jones,K. 2/0/0
K = Kelly,G. 8/1/4
L = Knowles,H. 7/2/4
M = Malloy,D. 42/7/0
N = Milne,A. 42/7/1
O = Moore,G. 5/1/2
P = Nichols,R. 39/4/0
Q = Nugent,C. 6/0/1
R = Reynolds,B. 24/4/8
S = Stitfall,R. 26/6/1
T = Sullivan,D. 35/6/1
U = Tapscott,D. 33/6/13
V = Vearncombe,G. 1/3/0
W = Walsh,B. 39/6/10

Trevor Morris resigns, and moves to Swansea, in summer. Bill Jones acting manager until October...Derek Tapscott signs from Arsenal - - bargain £10,000 Lose in F.A.Cup to 'Giant killers' Norwich ... win Welsh Cup with 2-0 victory over Lovell's Athletic.

Other Matches

F.A.Cup

	Date	Opposition	Res	Attend.	Goalscorers	1	2	3	4	5	6	7	8	9	10	11
3rd	10 Jan	Plymouth Argyle	3-0	36247	Hewitt (pen) Reynolds Bonson	P	N	S	T	M	A	W	U	B	F	R
4th	24	Norwich City	2-3	38000	Hewitt Bonson	"	"	"	"	"	"	"	"	"	"	"

Welsh Cup

					1	2	3	4	5	6	7	8	9	10	11
5th	5 Feb	Gloucester City	1-1	Hewitt (pen)	"	"	"	"	"	"	"	K	"	"	I
5th Replay	11	GLOUCESTER CITY	3-0	Milne Bonson Hudson	V	"	"	A	"	T	G	U	"	R	"
6th	25	RHYL	3-1	Tapscott Reynolds Knowles	P	"	"	E	"	"	W	"	L	"	G
Semi-final	19 Mar	Wrexham	6-0	Knowles 3 Tapscott 2 Hewitt	V	E	N	A	"	"	"	"	"	F	"
Final	30 Apr	Lovell's Athletic	2-0	Bonson Hudson	"	"	N	S	C	A	"	"	B	O	"

Friendlies

	16 May	Braunshell	3-1	Baker Sullivan Bonson
	18	Esbjerg	4-0	

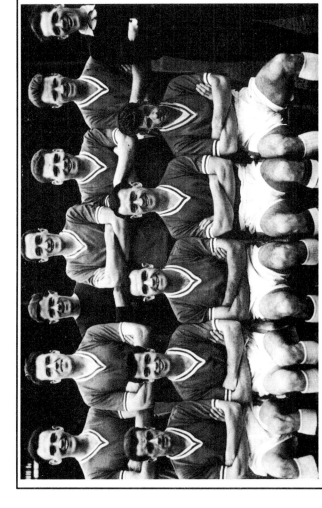

● This was the Cardiff City line-up which played Plymouth Argyle in an F.A. Cup match of January 1959, the only occasion that City and Argyle have met in Cup competition.... BACK (from left): Joe Bonson, Danny Malloy, Ron Nicholls, Alec Milne, Colin Baker, Derrick Sullivan, Wilf Grant (Trainer/Coach). FRONT (from left): Brian Walsh, Derek Tapscott, Ron Stitfall, Ron Hewitt, Brayley Reynolds.

(Pic courtesy Western Mail & Echo Ltd)

1959-60

Football League – Division 2. Manager: Bill Jones

P:42 W:23 D:12 L:7 90-62 Pts:58 Pos:2nd (Prom.)

1386	Date	Opposition	Res	Attend.	Goalscorers	1	2	3	4	5	6	7	8	9	10	11
1.	22 Aug	LIVERPOOL	3-2	32000	Mokone Moore Watkins	S	E	K	Q	J	A	T	R	M	*L	*U
2.	26	MIDDLESBROUGH	2-0	23052	Moore Watkins	"	"	"	"	"	"	"	"	"	"	"
3.	29	Charlton Athletic	1-2	18513	Moore	"	"	"	"	"	"	"	"	"	"	"
4.	2 Sep	Middlesbrough	1-1	29425	Watkins	"	"	"	"	"	"	F	P	"	B	"
5.	5	BRISTOL CITY	4-2	30000	Hudson 2 Watkins Baker	"	E	"	D	"	"	"	"	"	"	"
6.	9	Derby County	2-1	17959	Sullivan 2	"	"	"	"	"	"	"	*C	"	Q	"
7.	12	Scunthorpe United	2-1	10933	Moore Watkins	"	"	"	"	"	"	"	"	"	"	"
8.	16	DERBY COUNTY	2-0	20286	Sullivan Baker	"	"	"	"	"	"	"	"	"	"	"
9.	19	ROTHERHAM UNITED	1-4	28000	Sullivan	"	"	"	"	"	"	"	R	"	"	"
10.	26	Lincoln City	3-2	8402	Sullivan Watkins Harrington	"	"	P	"	"	"	"	C	"	"	"
11.	3 Oct	Hull City	0-0	14933		"	"	"	"	"	"	"	"	"	"	"
12.	10	LEYTON ORIENT	5-1	24000	Moore 2 Tapscott 2 Sullivan	"	"	"	"	"	"	T	R	"	"	"
13.	17	Huddersfield Town	1-0	18367	Tapscott	"	K	"	"	"	"	"	"	I	B	"
14.	24	IPSWICH TOWN	3-2	20233	Baker Tapscott Sullivan	"	E	K	"	"	"	"	"	M	Q	"
15.	31	Bristol Rovers	1-1	27548	Moore	"	"	P	"	"	"	"	"	"	"	"
16.	7 Nov	SWANSEA TOWN	2-1	30000	Sullivan Bonson	"	"	"	"	"	Q	"	"	"	B	"
17.	14	Brighton & H.A.	2-2	16151	Bonson 2	"	"	"	"	"	"	"	"	"	"	"
18.	21	STOKE CITY	4-4	20000	Tapscott Bonson 2 Gammon	"	"	"	"	"	"	"	"	"	"	"
19.	28	Portsmouth	1-1	14018	Walsh	"	"	"	"	"	"	"	"	"	"	"
20.	5 Dec	SUNDERLAND	2-1	20500	Watkins Tapscott	"	"	"	"	"	"	"	"	"	"	"
21.	12	Aston Villa	0-2	54763		"	K	"	Q	"	A	"	"	"	"	"
22.	19	Liverpool	4-0	27291	Tapscott 2 Watkins Bonson	"	"	"	"	"	"	"	"	"	"	"
23.	26	SHEFFIELD UNITED	2-0	30086	Bonson Tapscott	"	"	"	"	"	"	"	"	"	"	"
24.	28	Sheffield United	1-2	18590	Tapscott	"	"	"	"	"	"	"	"	"	"	"
25.	2 Jan	CHARLTON ATHLETIC	5-1	18000	Baker 2 Tapscott Bonson Walsh	"	"	"	"	"	"	"	"	"	"	"
26.	16	Bristol City	3-0	17952	Bonson Moore o.g.(McCall)	"	"	"	"	"	"	"	"	"	"	"
27.	23	SCUNTHORPE UNITED	4-2	15460	Watkins Bonson Tapscott Moore	"	"	"	"	"	"	"	"	"	"	"
28.	30	Plymouth Argyle	1-1	22554	Tapscott	"	"	"	"	"	"	"	"	"	"	"
29.	6 Feb	Rotherham United	2-2	16420	Tapscott 2	"	"	"	"	"	"	"	"	"	"	"
30.	13	LINCOLN CITY	6-2	23600	Bonson 2 Watkins2 Tapscott Walsh	"	"	"	"	"	"	"	"	"	"	"
31.	20	HULL CITY	3-2	27088	Watkins Bonson 2	"	"	"	"	"	"	"	"	"	"	"
32.	27	Leyton Orient	4-3	22918	Tapscott 2 Bonson 2	"	"	"	A	"	*G	"	"	"	"	"
33.	5 Mar	HUDDERSFIELD	2-1	40811	Moore Watkins	"	"	"	G	"	A	"	"	"	"	"
34.	12	Ipswich Town	1-1	18769	Bonson	"	"	"	"	"	"	"	"	"	"	"
35.	19	PORTSMOUTH	1-4	23000	Tapscott	"	"	"	"	"	"	"	"	"	"	"
36.	26	Swansea Town	3-3	26880	Bonson Moore Walsh	"	"	"	"	"	"	"	"	"	"	"
37.	2 Apr	BRIGHTON & H.A.	4-2	15460	Tapscott	N	"	"	D	"	"	"	"	"	"	"
38.	9	Stoke City	1-0	9548	Watkins	"	"	"	"	*O	"	"	"	"	"	"
39.	16	ASTON VILLA	1-0	54769	Moore	"	"	"	"	J	"	"	"	"	Q	"
40.	19	PLYMOUTH ARGYLE	0-1	32686		"	"	"	"	"	"	"	"	"	F	"
41.	23	Sunderland	1-1	20663	Baker	"	E	"	G	"	"	F	"	"	B	"
42.	30	BRISTOL ROVERS	2-2	23000	Moore Watkins	S	"	"	"	"	"	T	"	"	U	H

Players:

- A = Baker,C. 36/5/6
- B = Bonson,J. 26/3/19
- C = Durban,A. 5/1/0
- D = Gammon,S. 21/3/1
- E = Harrington,A. 22/5/1
- F = Hudson,C. 11/2/2
- G = Hole,B. 7/3/0
- H = Jenkins,B. 1/4/3
- I = Knowles,H. 1/1/1
- J = Malloy,D. 41/6/0
- K = Milne,A. 31/3/0
- L = Mokone,S. 3/2/2
- M = Moore,G. 41/5/16
- N = Nicholls,R. 5/1/0
- O = Peck,T. 1/1/0
- P = Stitfall,R. 34/5/0
- Q = Sullivan,D. 30/2/8
- R = Tapscott,D. 35/5/22
- S = Vearncombe,G. 37/6/0
- T = Walsh,B. 33/5/4
- U = Watkins,J. 42/5/16
- V = Monk,A. 0/1/0
- W = Hughes,M. 0/1/0

Goals galore as City stroll back into 1st Division . . . own goal 'specialist', Danny Malloy - only City player to concede two - in opening game ! Almost 55,000 see Villa beaten in Golden Jubilee match . . . Reserves win Welsh Cup tie - fined over £350.

Other Matches

F.A.Cup

	Date	Opposition	Res	Attend.	Goalscorers	1	2	3	4	5	6	7	8	9	10	11
3rd	9 Jan	PORT VALE	0-2	25000		S	K	P	E	J	Q	T	R	M	B	U

Welsh Cup

	Date	Opposition	Res	Attend.	Goalscorers	1	2	3	4	5	6	7	8	9	10	11
5th	20 Jan	LOVELL'S ATHLETIC	5-0	2500	Moore Bonson Watkins Tapscott 2	"	"	"	"	"	"	"	"	"	"	"
6th	2 Feb	Swansea Town	2-1	11000	Knowles o.g.(Woods)	N	V	E	D	O	G	F	W	I	L	H
Semi-final	28 Mar	Bangor City	1-1	7000	Moore	S	K	P	"	J	A	T	R	M	B	U
S/fin.rep.	25 Apr	Bangor City	4-1	2500	Jenkins 2 (1 pen.) Moore Mokone	"	E	"	A	"	G	"	C	"	L	H
Final	2 May	WREXHAM	1-1	11172	Jenkins	"	"	"	"	"	"	"	R	"	U	"
Final rep.	5	Wrexham	0-1	5800		"	"	"	D	"	A	F	"	"	H	U

Friendlies

	Date	Opposition	Res	Attend.	Goalscorers
	30 Sep	LUGANO	1-0	8000	Moore
†	11 May	Sunderland	0-0	3000	

† Played in Berne, Switzerland.

● Cardiff City's first team line-up in December 1959, a couple of months before their 4-3 win at Leyton Orient....
BACK (from left): Joe Bonson, Alec Milne, Graham Vearncombe, Derrick Sullivan, Colin Baker, Ron Stitfall.
FRONT: Brian Walsh, Derek Tapscott, Danny Malloy (captain), Graham Moore, Johnny Watkins.

1960-61

Football League – Division 1.

Manager: Bill Jones
P:42 W:13 D:11 L:18 60-85 Pts:37 Pos:15th

1428	Date	Opposition	Res	Attend.	Goalscorers	1	2	3	4	5	6	7	8	9	10	11
1.	20 Aug	Fulham	2-2	22000	Walsh Moore	V	G	N	F	L	A	W	U	O	*B	Y
2.	24	SHEFFIELD WED.	0-1	31335		"	"	"	"	"	"	"	"	"	*D	"
3.	27	PRESTON NORTH END	2-0	23000	Tapscott 2	"	"	"	"	"	A	"	"	"	B	"
4.	31	Sheffield Wed.	0-2	28493		"	"	"	"	"	"	"	"	"	"	"
5.	3 Sep	Burnley	2-1	20125	Tapscott Watkins	"	"	"	"	"	"	"	"	D	"	"
6.	7	ASTON VILLA	1-1	35000	Tapscott	"	"	"	"	"	"	"	"	"	"	"
7.	10	NOTTINGHAM FOREST	1-3	22500	Tapscott	"	"	"	"	"	"	"	"	O	"	"
8.	12	Aston Villa	1-2	32958	Donnelly	"	"	"	"	"	"	"	"	"	"	"
9.	17	Manchester City	2-4	30932	Tapscott Durban	"	"	*E	S	"	"	"	"	"	C	J
10.	24	ARSENAL	1-0	30000	Tapscott	"	"	"	F	"	"	J	"	"	B	Y
11.	1 Oct	Newcastle United	0-5	17500		"	"	"	"	"	"	"	"	"	"	"
12.	8	Wolverhampton W.	2-2	26000	Hudson Edwards	P	"	"	F	"	I	"	"	E	"	"
13.	15	BOLTON WANDERERS	0-1	18000		"	"	"	"	"	"	"	"	"	"	"
14.	28	LEICESTER CITY	2-1	15000	Donnelly Hogg	V	"	E	"	"	A	W	"	B	S	*H
15.	2 Nov	Tottenham Hotspur	2-3	47605	Donnelly 2	"	"	"	"	"	"	"	I	"	"	"
16.	5	Blackpool	1-6	13457	Tapscott	"	"	"	"	"	"	"	U	D	B	"
17.	12	EVERTON	1-1	19234	Watkins	"	"	R	"	"	"	"	D	U	Y	"
18.	19	Blackburn Rovers	2-2	15100	Tapscott o.g.(McEvoy)	"	"	"	"	"	"	"	"	"	"	"
19.	26	MANCHESTER UNITED	3-0	21000	Hogg 2 Edgeley	"	"	"	"	"	"	"	"	"	"	"
20.	3 Dec	West Ham United	0-2	14000		"	"	"	"	"	"	"	"	"	"	"
21.	10	CHELSEA	2-1	22000	Walsh Baker	"	"	"	"	"	"	"	"	"	"	"
22.	17	FULHAM	2-0	18000	Baker Tapscott	"	"	"	"	"	"	"	"	"	"	"
3.	26	WEST BROM. ALBION	3-1	26000	Baker	*T	"	"	"	"	"	"	O	"	"	"
24.	27	West Brom. Albion	1-1	30131	Tapscott	"	"	"	"	"	"	"	"	"	"	"
25.	31	Preston North End	1-1	11048	Tapscott	"	"	"	"	"	"	"	"	"	"	"
26.	14 Jan	BURNLEY	2-1	25000	Tapscott 2	"	"	"	"	"	"	"	"	"	"	"
27.	21	Nottingham Forest	1-2	19077	Tapscott	"	"	"	"	"	"	H	"	"	B	Y
28.	4 Feb	MANCHESTER CITY	3-3	15478	Moore Tapscott Baker	"	E	"	F	"	"	W	"	"	"	H
29.	11	Arsenal	3-2	33754	Moore Walsh Donnelly	"	"	"	I	"	"	"	"	"	"	"
30.	22	NEWCASTLE UNITED	3-2	25000	Moore 2 Walsh	"	G	"	"	"	"	"	"	"	"	"
31.	25	WOLVERHAMPTON W.	3-2	25000	Walsh Donnelly Tapscott	P	"	"	"	"	"	"	"	"	"	"
32.	4 Mar	Bolton Wanderers	0-3	21815		"	"	"	"	"	"	"	"	"	"	"
33.	11	TOTTENHAM HOTSPUR	3-2	47000	Hogg Walsh Tapscott	"	"	"	"	"	"	"	"	"	"	"
34.	24	BLACKPOOL	0-2	21000		"	"	"	"	"	"	"	"	"	"	"
35.	31	BIRMINGHAM CITY	0-2	18000		V	"	N	"	"	"	"	*X	"	"	*Q
36.	1 Apr	Chelsea	1-6	22697	Durban	"	"	"	A	"	I	"	C	E	X	"
37.	3	Birmingham City	1-2	20047	Moore	"	R	"	I	"	A	U	O	"	C	K
38.	8	BLACKBURN ROVERS	1-1	13000	Edwards	"	"	G	R	"	"	W	"	"	"	H
39.	10	Leicester City	0-3	32042		P	"	N	"	"	"	*M	"	"	B	"
40.	15	Everton	1-5	34382	Ward	T	"	"	"	"	"	"	"	U	X	"
41.	22	WEST HAM UNITED	1-1	11000	Donnelly	V	"	"	"	"	"	W	"	"	B	"
42.	29	Manchester United	3-3	30380	Hogg 2 Tapscott	"	"	"	"	"	"	"	U	O	X	"

Players:

A = Baker,C. 39/9/4
B = Donnelly,P. 26/5/10
C = Durban,A. 4/0/2
D = Edgeley,B. 10/0/1
E = Edwards,T. 14/3/3
F = Gammon,S. 26/5/0
G = Harrington,A. 39/8/0
H = Hogg,D. 26/7/8
I = Hole,B. 19/5/0
J = Hudson,C. 5/2/2
K = Jenkins,B. 1/0/0
L = Malloy,D. 42/9/1
M = McMillan,J. 2/0/0
N = Milne,A. 17/2/0
O = Moore,G. 25/7/11
P = Nicholls,R. 7/3/0
Q = Pickrell,A. 2/0/0
R = Stitfall,R. 20/7/0
S = Sullivan,D. 3/0/0
T = Swan,M. 8/5/0
U = Tapscott,D. 39/8/28
V = Veamcombe,G. 27/1/0
W = Walsh,B. 34/9/10
X = Ward,D. 4/0/1
Y = Watkins,J. 23/3/2
Z = King,P. 0/1/0

Derrick Sullivan after 9 different outfield positions with City leaves Ninian Park ... 'Double' completed over Champions Burnley ... Starlet Steve Gammons breaks leg -- never fully recovers ... First team has to play in Welsh Cup - beat Newtown 16-0!

Other Matches
F.A.Cup

	Date	Opposition	Res	Attend.	Goalscorers	1	2	3	4	5	6	7	8	9	10	11
3rd	7 Jan	MANCHESTER CITY	1-1	25640	Tapscott	T	G	R	F	L	A	W	O	U	Y	H
3rd Rep.	11	Manchester City	0-0*	40000		"	"	"	"	"	"	"	"	"	"	"
3rd 2/R. †	16	Manchester City	0-2	24168		"	"	"	"	"	"	"	"	"	"	"

† Played at Highbury.

Football League Cup

	Date	Opposition	Res	Attend.	Goalscorers	1	2	3	4	5	6	7	8	9	10	11
1st	3 Oct	Middlesbrough	4-3	15695	Walsh Donnelly Hudson Edwards(pen.)	V	"	N	I	"	"	"	U	E	B	J
2nd	24	BURNLEY	0-4	12000		P	"	"	F	"	"	"	Z	"	I	"

Welsh Cup

	Date	Opposition	Res	Attend.	Goalscorers	1	2	3	4	5	6	7	8	9	10	11
5th	28 Jan	KNIGHTON TOWN	16-0	3800	Tapscott 6 Moore 4 Walsh 2 Donnelly 2 Hogg Malloy	T	"	R	"	"	"	"	O	"	B	H
6th	16 Feb	NEWPORT COUNTY	2-1	12192	Hogg(pen.) Moore	"	E	"	I	"	"	"	"	U	"	"
Semi-final	22 Mar	Swansea Town	1-1	10000	Tapscott	P	G	"	"	"	"	"	"	"	"	"
S/Fin. Rep.	28	Swansea Town	0-1	20000		"	"	"	"	"	"	"	"	"	"	"

Friendlies

	Date	Opposition	Res	Attend.	Goalscorers
††	9 Aug	DWS Amsterdam	0-3	5000	
††	11	Zurich Grasshoppers	3-4	7000	Watkins 3
‡	5 Oct	ZURICH GRASSHOPPERS	2-2	15000	Edwards Malloy
	18 Feb	BIEL F.C.	3-0	11000	Moore Baker Donnelly
	27 Mar	VFL OSNABRUCK	1-2	10000	Hogg
	17 May	Shamrock Rovers	2-2	4000	Malloy Walsh
	19	Waterford	5-1	5000	Donnelly Pickrell Walsh Ward 2

†† Pre-season Tour.
‡ First Floodlit home match.

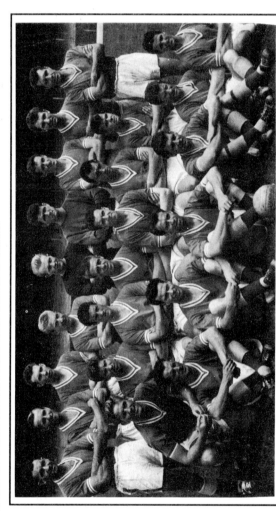

(Back) Stitfall, Edwards, Hole, Hughes, Williams, Swans, Milne, Rankmore, Watkins
(Middle) Moore, Hudson, Edgeley, Knowles, Malloy. (Front) Walsh, Tapscott, Bell, Baker, Sullivan, Harrington.

1961-62
Football League – Division 1. Manager: Bill Jones
P:42 W:9 D:14 L:19 50-81 Pts:32 Pos:21st (Rel.)

#	Date	Opposition	Res	Attend.	Goalscorers	1	2	3	4	5	6	7	8	9	10	11
1.	19 Aug	Blackburn Rovers	0-0	19000		V	G	O	I	*R	A	W	X	*K	P	H
2.	23	SHEFFIELD UNITED	1-1	25000	King,J.	"	"	"	"	"	"	"	"	"	"	"
3.	26	BLACKPOOL	3-2	23000	Ward 2 Hogg	"	"	"	"	"	"	"	"	"	"	"
4.	28	Sheffield United	0-1	19193		"	"	"	"	"	"	"	"	"	"	"
5.	2 Sep	Tottenham Hotspur	2-3	37834	King,J. Ward	"	"	"	"	"	"	U	"	"	"	"
6.	6	CHELSEA	5-2	21349	Ward2 Tapscott Moore og Mortimore	"	"	"	"	"	"	"	"	"	"	Q
7.	9	BOLTON WANDERERS	1-2	22000	Ward	"	"	"	"	"	"	"	"	"	"	Q
8.	16	MANCHESTER UNITED	1-2	29251	Ward	"	"	"	"	"	"	"	"	"	"	C
9.	20	Chelsea	3-2	15804	Donnelly Baker Ward	*J	"	"	"	"	"	"	"	"	D	"
10.	23	Wolverhampton W.	1-1	26000	Harrington	"	"	"	"	"	"	"	"	"	"	"
11.	30	NOTTINGHAM FOREST	2-2	21500	Ward King,J.	"	"	"	"	"	"	"	"	"	"	H
12.	7 Oct	Manchester City	2-1	20143	Hole King,J.	"	"	"	"	"	"	*M	"	"	"	"
13.	18	WEST BROM. ALBION	2-2	17000	Durban Ward	"	"	"	"	"	"	W	X	"	"	M
14.	21	Burnley	1-2	16000	Ward	"	"	"	"	"	"	*L	"	"	"	H
15.	28	ARSENAL	1-1	26000	Pickrell	"	"	"	"	"	"	"	"	"	P	Q
16.	4 Nov	Fulham	1-0	20077	Tapscott	"	"	"	"	"	"	"	U	"	"	"
17.	11	SHEFFIELD	2-1	17987	Tapscott 2	"	"	"	"	"	"	"	"	"	"	"
18.	18	Leicester City	0-3	22000		"	"	"	"	"	"	"	X	"	D	"
19.	25	IPSWICH TOWN	0-3	22823		"	"	"	"	"	"	"	U	"	X	H
20.	2 Dec	Birmingham City	0-3	20000		T	"	"	F	A	I	"	X	E	P	K
21.	9	EVERTON	0-0	15782		J	"	"	I	R	A	"	U	K	"	Q
22.	16	BLACKBURN ROVERS	1-1	14000	Moore	"	"	"	"	"	"	"	"	"	"	"
23.	23	Blackpool	0-3	12000		"	"	"	A	"	F	"	"	"	"	"
24.	26	ASTON VILLA	1-0	16140	Tapscott	"	"	"	"	"	"	"	X	X	"	"
25.	13 Jan	TOTTENHAM HOTSPUR	1-1	33606	King,J. (Pen.)	V	"	"	F	"	A	"	D	K	X	H
26.	20	Bolton Wanderers	1-1	17000	Ward	"	"	"	"	"	"	"	"	"	"	"
27.	3 Feb	Manchester United	0-3	29200		"	"	"	"	"	"	"	X	"	D	"
28.	9	WOLVERHAMPTON W.	2-3	19000	Ward Milne	"	S	"	"	"	"	"	"	*B	"	Q
29.	17	Nottingham Forest	1-2	19500	King,J.	J	G	"	"	"	"	"	"	"	"	*N
30.	24	MANCHESTER CITY	0-0	19650		"	"	"	"	"	"	"	"	"	"	"
31.	3 Mar	West Brom. Albion	1-5	15200	King,P.	V	E	"	"	G	"	"	U	"	D	H
32.	14	BURNLEY	1-1	15000	Charles	"	"	"	"	"	"	"	X	"	K	"
33.	17	Arsenal	1-1	25059	Ward	"	"	"	"	"	"	"	"	"	"	M
34.	23	FULHAM	0-3	18000		"	"	"	"	"	"	"	U	"	D	H
35.	3 Apr	Sheffield Wed.	0-2	18434		"	"	"	G	B	"	"	X	"	X	M
36.	7	LEICESTER CITY	0-4	11000		"	"	"	"	R	"	U	X	B	K	"
37.	14	Ipswich Town	0-1	17693		J	S	"	A	"	"	M	L	"	D	Q
38.	20	West Ham United	1-4	25459	Pickrell	"	"	"	I	"	A	"	"	"	"	"
39.	21	BIRMINGHAM CITY	3-2	8000	Tapscott 3	"	"	"	"	"	"	E	U	"	"	"
40.	23	WEST HAM UNITED	3-0	10000	Ward 2 Tapscott	V	"	"	"	"	"	L	"	X	"	"
41.	28	Everton	3-8	31386	Charles Pickrell 2	"	"	"	"	"	"	"	"	B	"	"
42.	1 May	Aston Villa	2-2	21446	Ward Charles	"	G	"	"	"	"	U	D	"	X	"

Players:

A = Baker,C. — 42/8/1
B = Charles,M. — 12/0/3
C = Donnelly,P. — 4/0/1
D = Durban,A. — 20/2/2
E = Edwards,T. — 7/1/0
F = Gammon,S. — 6/1/0
G = Harrington,A. — 36/7/1
H = Hogg,D. — 15/3/1
I = Hole,B. — 37/7/1
J = John,D. — 21/4/0
K = King,J. — 33/8/10
L = King,P. — 26/6/2
M = McCarthy,D. — 7/2/0
N = McIntosh,A. — 2/1/0
O = Milne,A. — 42/8/1
P = Moore,G. — 14/3/3
Q = Pickrell,A. — 16/2/4
R = Rankmore,F. — 37/6/0
S = Stitfall,R. — 6/1/0
T = Swan,M. — 1/0/0
U = Tapscott,D. — 22/4/9
V = Vearncombe,G. — 20/4/0
W = Walsh,B. — 5/2/0
X = Ward,D. — 31/7/21
Y = Williams,G. — 0/1/0

Danny Malloy leaves in summer following pay dispute . November - City are 7th - but relegated ! Graham Moore sold to Chelsea for £35,000 … Mel Charles signed for £20,000 from Arsenal - but Bluebirds are already on way to 2nd Div. !

Other Matches

F.A.Cup

	Date	Opposition	Res	Attend.	Goalscorers	1	2	3	4	5	6	7	8	9	10	11
3rd	10 Jan	Middlesbrough	0-1	29013		V	G	O	I	R	A	L	U	K	X	Q

Football League Cup

	Date	Opposition	Res	Attend.	Goalscorers	1	2	3	4	5	6	7	8	9	10	11
1st	13 Sep	WREXHAM	2-0	6750	Moore Ward	V	"	"	"	"	"	W	X	K	P	H
2nd	5 Oct	Mansfield Town	1-1	17100	King,J.	J	"	"	"	"	"	"	"	"	D	M
2nd Rep.	23	MANSFIELD TOWN	2-1	4800	King,J. Ward	"	"	"	"	"	"	L	"	"	"	"
3rd	15 Nov	Bournemouth	0-3	12857		"	"	"	"	Y	"	"	U	"	"	Q

Welsh Cup

	Date	Opposition	Res	Attend.	Goalscorers	1	2	3	4	5	6	7	8	9	10	11
5th	24 Jan	NEWPORT COUNTY	4-1	5715	King,P. Durban King,J. 2	V	"	"	F	R	"	"	D	"	X	H
6th	20 Feb	Bristol City	2-0	13579	Ward 2	J	S	"	I	"	"	"	U	"	"	N
Semi-final	20 Mar	Bangor City	0-2	5482		V	E	"	"	G	"	"	X	U	K	M

Friendlies

	Opposition	Res	Attend.	Goalscorers
13 Dec	Racing Club Lensois	4-2	1500	King,P. 2 King,J. Moore
27 Feb	OFFENBACH KICKERS	2-0	3200	Tapscott Charles
7 Mar	RAC. CLUB LENSOIS	2-0	3000	Charles Tapsc

City's last home game in the First Division.

1962-63

Football League – Division 2.

Manager: Bill Jones to 10.9.62 (sacked) George Swindin from Nov. 1962.

P:42　W:18　D:7　L:17　83-73　Pts:43　Pos:10th

1512		Date	Opposition	Res	Attend.	Goalscorers	1	2	3	4	5	6	7	8	9	10	11
1.		18 Aug	NEWCASTLE UNITED	4-4	27673	Hooper Charles Hole 2	K	H	N	I	Q	B	M	E	D	*A	J
2.		22	Norwich City	0-0	25360		"	"	"	"	P	"	"	"	*G	"	*
3.		25	Derby County	2-1	14539	Hooper (pen.) Allchurch	"	"	R	"	Q	"	"	"	"	"	"
4.		29	NORWICH CITY	2-4	26301	Hooper 2	"	"	N	"	"	"	"	"	D	"	"
5.	1 Sep	MIDDLESBROUGH	1-2	19128	o.g. (Neal)	S	*C	"	"	"	"	"	T	G	"	"
6.		4	Swansea Town	1-2	24257	Charles	"	H	R	"	"	"	"	"	D	"	"
7.		8	Huddersfield Town	0-1	17500		"	"	"	"	"	"	"	"	"	"	"
8.		12	GRIMSBY TOWN	5-3	14000	ogDavies Charles2 McIntosh Hooper	"	"	"	H	"	"	"	"	"	"	"
9.		15	SWANSEA TOWN	5-2	24500		K	N	"	I	"	"	"	"	"	"	"
10.		18	Grimsby Town	2-1	9000	Hooper 2	"	H	"	"	"	"	"	"	"	"	"
11.		22	PORTSMOUTH	1-2	22560	Tapscott	"	"	"	"	"	"	"	"	"	"	"
12.		29	Preston North End	6-2	11991	Tapscott Hooper2 Charles2 Durban	S	"	"	"	"	"	"	"	"	E	"
13.	6 Oct	Chelsea	0-6	25239		"	"	"	"	"	"	"	"	"	A	"
14.		13	LUTON TOWN	1-0	15887	Hooper	U	"	"	"	"	"	"	"	"	E	"
15.		27	SCUNTHORPE UNITED	4-0	12000	McIntosh Allchurch 2 Tapscott	"	R	F	H	D	"	"	E	T	A	"
16.		31	Southampton	5-3	16716	Hole Allchurch 2 McIntosh Durban	"	"	"	"	"	"	"	"	"	"	I
17.	3 Nov	Bury	0-1	9915		"	"	"	"	Q	"	"	"	"	"	J
18.		10	ROTHERHAM UNITED	4-1	14300	Hooper 2 Durban 2	"	H	"	D	"	"	"	T	D	"	"
19.		17	Charlton Athletic	4-2	11100	Tapscott 3 Hooper	"	"	"	I	"	"	"	"	"	"	"
20.		24	STOKE CITY	1-1	21900	McIntosh	"	"	"	"	D	"	"	"	"	"	"
21.	1 Dec	Sunderland	1-2	37603	Allchurch	"	"	"	"	"	"	"	"	"	"	"
22.		8	LEEDS UNITED	0-0	11700		"	"	"	*V	Q	"	D	T	D	"	"
23.		15	Newcastle United	1-2	27600	Hooper	"	"	"	"	D	"	M	E	T	"	"
24.		22	DERBY COUNTY	1-0	12946	Hooper	"	"	"	V	"	"	"	"	"	"	"
25.		26	Plymouth Argyle	2-4	18602	Durban 2	"	R	"	H	Q	V	"	T	G	"	"
26.	23 Feb	CHELSEA	1-0	16344	Harrington	"	H	"	B	"	"	"	"	D	"	"
27.	9 Mar	SOUTHAMPTON	3-1	12400	Allchurch Tapscott McIntosh	"	"	"	"	"	"	"	T	"	"	"
28.		15	Scunthorpe United	2-2	7884	Allchurch 2	"	"	"	"	"	"	"	E	"	"	"
29.		23	BURY	3-1	16200	o.g.(Eastham) Hooper Charles	"	"	"	"	"	"	"	"	"	"	"
30.		29	Rotherham United	1-2	8964	McIntosh	"	"	"	"	"	"	"	"	"	"	"
31.	6 Apr	CHARLTON ATHLETIC	1-2	12666	Hole	"	"	"	"	"	"	"	"	"	"	"
32.		13	Stoke City	0-1	30419		K	"	R	"	"	"	"	"	"	E	"
33.		15	WALSALL	2-2	11500	Edwards Tapscott	"	R	F	"	P	"	M	E	T	L	"
34.		16	Walsall	1-2	10381	King	"	"	"	V	"	"	"	T	G	"	"
35.		20	SUNDERLAND	5-2	12397	Tapscott Hooper2 McIntosh Charles	"	H	"	"	Q	B	"	"	D	"	"
36.		24	Luton Town	3-2	7234	Hooper 3	"	"	R	"	"	"	"	"	"	"	"
37.		27	Leeds United	0-3	19752		"	"	F	"	"	"	"	"	"	"	"
38.	1 May	PLYMOUTH ARGYLE	2-1	9650	Allchurch Hole	"	"	P	"	"	"	"	A	"	A	"
39.		4	Portsmouth	0-2	10588		"	"	"	"	D	"	"	"	T	"	"
40.		6	PRESTON NORTH END	1-1	8389	Charles	"	"	"	"	Q	I	"	T	D	A	"
41.		11	Middlesbrough	2-3	9423	McIntosh 2	"	"	"	"	*O	"	"	E	T	"	"
42.		18	HUDDERSFIELD	3-0	8943	King 2 Tapscott	"	"	"	"	Q	"	"	A	"	J	L

Players:

A = Allchurch,I.　35/4/14
B = Baker,C.　35/4/0
C = Brack,A.　1/0/0
D = Charles,M.　32/4/12
E = Durban,A.　23/4/10
F = Edwards,T.　22/3/1
G = Frazer,G.　4/0/0
H = Harrington,A.　39/5/1
I = Hole,B.　37/5/6
J = Hooper,P.　41/5/24
K = John,D.　18/0/0
L = King,P.　3/0/3
M = McIntosh,A.　41/5/9
N = Milne,A.　5/0/0
O = Murray,D.　1/0/0
P = Peck,T.　8/0/0
Q = Rankmore,F.　30/7/0
R = Stitfall,R.　17/1/0
S = Swan,M.　6/1/0
T = Tapscott,D.　34/4/12
U = Vearncombe,G.　18/3/0
V = Williams,G.　13/0/0

Ivor Allchurch & Peter Hooper - new signings have great season - but City's poor start prevents promotion. Manager Jones and coach Grant sacked in September . . . Stitfall and Curtis take temporary charge . . . 6-2 - Record away win (at Preston). George Swindin new manager . . . 17 year old Don Murray makes debut at Middlesbrough.

Other Matches

F.A.Cup

	Date	Opposition	Res	Attend.	Goalscorers	1	2	3	4	5	6	7	8	9	10	11
3rd	18 Feb	Charlton Athletic	0-1	13448		U	H	F	I	D	B	M	E	T	A	J

Football League Cup

	Date	Opposition	Res	Attend.	Goalscorers	1	2	3	4	5	6	7	8	9	10	11
2nd	26 Sep	READING	5-1	4136	Charles Tapscott Durban 2 Hooper (pen.)	S	"	N	"	Q	"	"	T	D	E	"
3rd	23 Oct	Bristol Rovers	0-2	12142		U	"	"	"	"	"	"	E	"	A	"

Welsh Cup

	Date	Opposition	Res	Attend.	Goalscorers	1	2	3	4	5	6	7	8	9	10	11
5th	26 Mar	ABERGAVENNY TH.	7-1	2200	Allchurch2 Durban 2 Hole Hooper Tapscott	"	"	F	B	"	"	I	"	T	"	"
6th	11 Apr	Swansea Town	0-2	11500		"	R	"	H	"	"	"	T	D	"	"

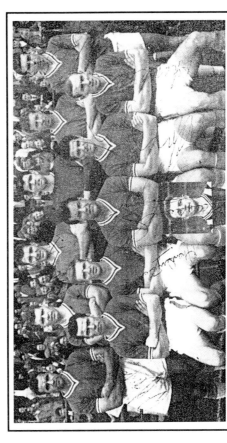

Standing: R. Stitfall, C. Baker, F. Rankmore, M. Swan, P. Hooper, B. Hole
Seated: D. Tapscott, A. Durban, M. Charles, A. Harrington, A. McIntosh.
Inset: Ivor Allchurch

1963-64

Football League – Division 2.

Manager: George Swindin
P: 42 **W:** 14 **D:** 10 **L:** 18 **56-81** **Pts:** 38 **Pos:** 15th

1554	Date	Opposition	Res	Attend.	Goalscorers	1	2	3	4	5	6	7	8	9	10	11
1.	24 Aug	NORWICH CITY	3-1	22078	King Charles,J. Allchurch	X	F	U	D	*C	Z	O	J	T	A	L
2.	28	MANCHESTER CITY	2-2	25352	Allchurch Charles,J.	"	"	"	Z	"	J	"	D	"	"	"
3.	30	Scunthorpe United	2-1	8115	Williams Tapscott	K	"	"	"	Q	"	"	V	"	"	"
4.	4 Sep	Manchester City	0-4	22138		"	"	"	"	"	"	"	D	Z	"	"
5.	7	PORTSMOUTH	1-2	18000	Charles,J.	"	"	"	T	"	"	"	D	"	"	"
6.	11	BURY	2-1	16081	Allchurch 2	X	"	*W	Z	C	"	"	V	D	"	"
7.	13	Rotherham United	0-1	11380		"	"	"	"	Q	"	"	T	"	"	"
8.	17	Bury	1-4	11918	Allchurch	"	"	"	"	"	"	"	"	"	"	V
9.	21	LEEDS UNITED	0-0	16200		K	"	"	"	"	"	O	C	C	"	L
10.	28	Sunderland	3-3	37287	Allchurch 3	"	"	*S	"	"	"	"	V	"	"	"
11.	2 Oct	GRIMSBY TOWN	0-0	13700		"	"	"	B	"	T	"	T	D	"	*N
12.	5	NORTHAMPTON TOWN	1-0	10340	Charles,M.	"	U	"	"	"	"	L	L	"	"	"
13.	19	SWANSEA TOWN	1-1	22000	Scott (pen)	"	B	U	J	C	"	"	"	"	"	"
14.	26	Charlton Athletic	2-5	26534	McIntosh Charles,J.	"	F	W	B	"	"	"	*I	C	"	"
15.	2 Nov	MIDDLESBROUGH	1-1	13600	Charles,J.	"	"	S	"	Q	"	"	J	I	"	O
16.	9	Newcastle United	4-0	38534	King 2 Allchurch Charles,J	"	"	"	"	"	"	"	I	C	"	"
17.	16	HUDDERSFIELD TOWN	2-1	14700	McIntosh Baker	X	"	"	"	C	"	"	V	I	"	"
18.	23	Derby County	1-2	11852	Charles,J.	"	"	"	"	Q	"	"	I	C	"	"
19.	30	PLYMOUTH ARGYLE	3-1	12000	Charles,J.2 Allchurch	"	"	"	"	"	"	"	"	"	"	"
20.	7 Dec	Southampton	2-3	17861	Charles,J. Halliday	"	"	"	"	"	"	F	"	"	"	"
21.	14	Norwich City	1-5	14890	Halliday	"	U	"	J	"	"	L	V	"	"	"
22.	26	PRESTON NORTH END	0-4	18869		"	F	"	"	"	Z	"	I	"	"	"
23.	28	Preston North End	0-4	19458		K	P	F	Z	"	B	V	"	"	J	"
24.	11 Jan	Portsmouth	0-5	12046		"	"	S	"	D	*Y	F	"	"	*E	A
25.	17	ROTHERHAM UNITED	2-1	9600	Charles,M. Scott (pen)	X	F	P	"	C	T	*M	V	D	A	L
26.	1 Feb	Leeds United	1-1	28039	Charles,M.	K	"	"	"	"	"	"	"	"	"	J
27.	8	SUNDERLAND	0-2	15880		"	"	R	"	"	"	M	"	D	"	G
28.	15	Northampton Town	1-2	11831	Charles,M.	"	"	P	"	"	"	"	J	"	"	"
29.	22	LEYTON ORIENT	2-1	8100	Scott (pen) Charles,M.	"	R	F	"	Q	"	"	"	"	"	L
30.	29	Huddersfield Town	1-2	10801	Scott	"	"	"	"	C	"	"	T	"	"	V
31.	7 Mar	CHARLTON ATHLETIC	1-1	8118	Allchurch Charles,M.	"	"	"	"	"	"	"	L	"	"	"
32.	20	NEWCASTLE UNITED	2-2	9200	King Lewis	"	"	S	T	"	"	*G	L	I	"	M
33.	27	Swindon Town	2-1	22096	Charles,M.	"	"	"	"	"	"	M	"	D	"	G
34.	28	Swansea Town	0-3	19000	Charles,M. King	"	"	"	"	"	"	"	"	"	"	"
35.	30	SWINDON TOWN	1-0	8400	Farrell 2 King	"	"	"	"	Q	"	"	J	"	"	"
36.	4 Apr	DERBY COUNTY	2-1	8300	King	"	R	"	"	C	"	"	"	"	"	"
37.	8	SCUNTHORPE UNITED	3-1	9880		"	"	"	"	"	"	"	"	"	"	"
38.	11	Plymouth Argyle	1-1	14091		"	"	"	"	"	Z	"	"	"	"	"
39.	13	Leyton Orient	0-4	7278	Scott (pen) Charles,M.	"	"	"	H	Q	T	"	"	"	"	L
40.	15	Grimsby Town	2-0	8643	o.g.(Knapp) Williams	X	"	"	"	C	J	"	Z	"	"	"
41.	18	SOUTHAMPTON	2-4	10966	Allchurch	"	"	"	T	R	"	M	T	Z	"	"
42.	24	Middlesbrough	1-3	8472		K	B	"	"	"	"	"	Z	D	"	"

Players:

A = Allchurch,I. 41/11/14
B = Baker,C. 12/5/1
C = Charles,J. 33/9/11
D = Charles,M. 26/9/15
E = Coldrick,G. 1/0/0
F = Edwards,T. 30/4/0
G = Farrell,G. 8/1/2
H = Gammon,S. 2/0/0
I = Halliday,T. 12/0/2
J = Hole,B. 30/9/1
K = John,D. 28/8/0
L = King,P. 34/10/12
M = Lewis,B. 16/6/4
N = Mallory,R. 3/1/0
O = McIntosh,A. 21/3/2
P = Milne,A. 5/1/0
Q = Murray,D. 20/5/0
R = Peck,T. 15/4/0
S = Rodrigues,P. 22/6/0
T = Scott,R. 36/7/5
U = Stitfall,R. 8/1/0
V = Tapscott,D. 15/4/4
W = Upton,J. 5/2/0
X = Vearncombe,G. 14/3/0
Y = Watkins,P. 1/1/0
Z = Williams,G. 24/8/2
a = Brack,A. 0/1/0
b = Burns,A. 0/1/0

City sign John Charles from Roma for £25,000 .. The Gentle Giant on debut - scores from 75 yards! Bluebirds ravaged by injuries in early season .. Welsh Cup won - first entry to Europe. Manager Swindin sacked after refusal to resign at season's end

Other Matches

F.A.Cup

	Date	Opposition	Res	Attend.	Goalscorers	1	2	3	4	5	6	7	8	9	10	11
3rd	4 Jan	LEEDS UNITED	0-1	14000		K	F	S	Z	D	B	O	A	C	J	L

Football League Cup

	Date	Opposition	Res	Attend.	Goalscorers	1	2	3	4	5	6	7	8	9	10	11
2nd	25 Sep	WREXHAM	2-2	4688	Tapscott 2	"	"	W	Q	Q	J	"	V	Z	A	"
2nd Replay	7 Oct	Wrexham	1-1	11299	King	"	U	S	B	Q	T	"	L	D	"	N
2nd 2nd R.	21	Wrexham	0-3	8885		"	B	W	Y	"	J	b	"	T	"	a

Welsh Cup

	Date	Opposition	Res	Attend.	Goalscorers	1	2	3	4	5	6	7	8	9	10	11
5th	25 Jan	Ebbw Vale	6-1	4000	King 2 Lewis 2 Charles,M.2	X	F	P	Z	C	T	M	V	D	"	L
6th	19 Feb	CHESTER	3-1	3120	Hole Charles,M. Tapscott	K	R	S	"	"	"	"	J	"	"	V
Semi-final	11 Mar	Newport County	2-2	5200	Allchurch Charles,M.	"	"	F	"	"	J	L	T	"	"	"
S/final Rep.	25	NEWPORT COUNTY	1-0	8400	Charles,M.	"	"	S	"	"	"	M	"	"	"	L
Final	22 Apr	Bangor City	0-2	10000		"	"	"	T	"	"	"	L	"	"	G
Final 2/leg	29	BANGOR CITY	3-1	6000	Lewis Allchurch Charles,M.	X	B	"	Z	Q	"	"	D	C	"	L
Final Rep.	4 May	Bangor City	2-0	10014	King 2	"	"	"	"	"	"	"	"	"	"	"

Friendlies

	Date	Opposition	Res	Attend.	Goalscorers
	14 Aug	Bath City	1-1	3000	Scott
	4 Nov	Worcester City	2-2	4600	Tapscott 2
	7 May	Juventus	3-3	40000	Charles,M. Charles,J. Allchurch
	10	Roma	1-4	25000	Lewis
	14	Latina	3-4	12000	

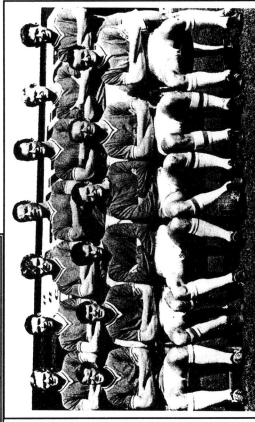

● Three of Welsh football's best known Internationals were in Cardiff City's squad during the 1963-64 season when City and Northampton met in the Second Division for the first time. This was the first team line-up in April 1964 – BACK (from left): Gareth Williams, Barrie Hole, Don Murray, John Charles, Mel Charles, Trevor Peck, Steve Gammon. FRONT (from left): Dick Scott, Greg Farrell, Dilwyn John, Graham Vearncombe, Ivor Allchurch, Peter Rodrigues.

1964-65

Football League – Division 2.

Manager: Jimmy Scoular
P: 42 **W:** 13 **D:** 14 **L:** 15 **64-57** **Pts:** 40 **Pos:** 13th

1596	Date	Opposition	Res	Attend.	Goalscorers	1	2	3	4	5	6	7	8	9	10	11
1.	22 Aug	IPSWICH TOWN	0-0	17057		*Y	V	S	H	C	L	G	P	D	A	Q
2.	26	PRESTON NORTH END	3-3	16200	Allchurch 2 Lewis	"	"	"	"	"	"	Q	"	"	"	*O
3.	29	Plymouth Argyle	1-3	14367	Hole (pen)	"	"	"	"	"	"	"	"	"	"	"
4.	31	Preston North End	1-1	23285	Allchurch	"	"	U	Z	"	"	P	D	I	"	"
5.	5 Sep	BOLTON WANDERERS	1-3	14100	Allchurch	"	"	"	"	"	"	"	W	"	"	"
6.	12	Middlesbrough	0-0	22770		"	"	"	"	"	"	"	D	"	"	"
7.	16	HUDDERSFIELD TOWN	1-1	9525	Hole (pen)	"	"	"	"	"	"	"	"	"	"	G
8.	19	NEWCASTLE UNITED	1-1	12016	Allchurch	"	"	"	"	"	"	"	*R	E	"	"
9.	26	Northampton Town	0-1	12278		"	"	"	"	"	"	"	"	"	"	"
10.	29	Huddersfield Town	1-3	5640	Allchurch	"	"	"	"	"	"	"	"	X	"	O
11.	6 Oct	Rotherham United	1-3	12304	Ellis	"	"	"	"	T	"	"	X	*F	"	Q
12.	10	DERBY COUNTY	2-1	7500	King Tapscott	"	"	"	"	"	"	"	D	"	"	"
13.	17	Swindon Town	3-3	15737	Hole (pen) Charles,M.	"	"	"	"	"	"	G	X	"	D	"
14.	24	PORTSMOUTH	1-0	7500	Tapscott	"	"	"	"	"	"	"	P	X	"	"
15.	31	Manchester City	0-2	13146		"	"	"	"	"	"	"	"	"	F	"
16.	7 Nov	CHARLTON ATHLETIC	2-1	9835	Tapscott Ellis	"	J	V	"	"	"	"	"	"	"	"
17.	14	Leyton Orient	3-1	6348	Ellis 2 Lewis	"	"	"	"	"	"	"	"	"	"	"
18.	21	BURY	4-0	10077	Tapscott 2 Ellis Lewis	M	"	"	"	"	"	"	"	"	"	"
19.	28	Crystal Palace	0-0	18188		"	"	"	"	"	"	"	"	"	"	"
20.	5 Dec	NORWICH CITY	1-3	10400	o.g. (Mullett)	Y	"	"	"	"	"	"	"	"	"	"
21.	12	Ipswich Town	1-1	10010	Ellis	"	"	"	C	"	"	X	Z	F	P	"
22.	19	PLYMOUTH ARGYLE	4-0	9877	Tapscott 2 o.g.(Neale) Rodrigue	"	"	"	Z	"	"	G	X	"	"	"
23.	26	Swansea Town	2-3	18000	Ellis 2	"	"	"	C	"	"	"	H	"	"	"
24.	15 Jan	MIDDLESBROUGH	6-1	9500	King,P.3 Tapscott 2 Williams	"	"	"	"	"	"	"	Z	X	"	"
25.	23	Newcastle United	0-2	37500		"	"	"	Z	"	"	"	P	"	F	"
26.	6 Feb	NORTHAMPTON TOWN	0-2	8100		"	"	"	"	"	"	"	"	C	X	"
27.	13	Southampton	1-1	14740	Allchurch	"	U	"	C	"	"	"	Z	F	A	P
28.	20	Derby County	0-1	10894		"	"	"	Z	"	"	"	P	"	"	*N
29.	27	SWINDON TOWN	2-0	9363	Ellis Hole	"	"	"	C	E	"	"	Z	"	"	P
30.	6 Mar	Norwich City	1-2	18515	Allchurch	"	"	"	"	T	"	"	"	"	"	"
31.	12	MANCHESTER CITY	2-2	9094	Allchurch King,P.	"	"	"	"	"	"	"	"	"	"	Q
32.	22	Charlton Athletic	2-2	7710	Williams 2	"	V	*K	"	"	"	"	"	"	"	"
33.	24	SOUTHAMPTON	2-2	9788	Williams Charles,J.	"	"	"	"	"	"	"	"	"	"	"
34.	27	LEYTON ORIENT	0-2	7777		"	"	"	"	"	"	"	"	"	"	"
35.	3 Apr	Bury	2-1	4292	King,P. Hole	"	"	"	"	"	"	"	"	"	"	"
36.	6	SWANSEA TOWN	5-0	16000	Allchurch 3 Charles,J.2	"	"	"	Z	"	"	"	"	"	"	"
37.	10	CRYSTAL PALACE	0-0	10700		"	"	B	"	"	"	"	"	C	P	"
38.	17	Portsmouth	0-1	12975		"	"	"	"	E	"	"	"	"	"	"
39.	19	COVENTRY CITY	3-1	11300	King Allchurch 2	"	"	"	"	T	"	"	"	"	"	"
40.	20	Coventry City	2-0	23881	Lewis Hole	"	"	"	"	"	"	"	"	"	"	"
41.	24	ROTHERHAM UNITED	3-2	9932	Allchurch Rodrigues King,P.	"	"	"	"	"	"	"	"	"	"	"
42.	28	Bolton Wanderers	0-1	6356		"	U	"	"	"	"	"	G	E	"	"

Players:

- A = Allchurch,I.   27/8/15
- B = Baker,C.   6/3/0
- C = Charles,J.   28/8/4
- D = Charles,M.   8/2/2
- E = Coldrick,G.   3/1/0
- F = Ellis,K.   22/5/11
- G = Farrell,G.   25/10/3
- H = Gammon,S.   4/0/0
- I = Halliday,T.   5/1/0
- J = Harrington,A.   11/6/0
- K = Harris,G.   5/1/0
- L = Hole,B.   42/14/6
- M = John,D.   2/4/0
- N = Johnston,G.   9/3/2
- O = King,G.   6/0/0
- P = King,P.   39/14/16
- Q = Lewis,B.   31/11/5
- R = Lloyd,C.   2/1/0
- S = Milne,A.   3/0/0
- T = Murray,D.   31/12/0
- U = Peck,T.   18/5/0
- V = Rodrigues,P.   41/12/2
- W = Scott,R.   1/0/0
- X = Tapscott,D.   16/8/11
- Y = Wilson,R.   40/10/0
- Z = Williams,G.   38/14/5

Jimmy Scoular appointed manager... First victory - after 12th match! Swansea beaten 5-0 - Allchurch gets hat-trick - helps push Swans into 3rd Division... City reach quarter-finals of European Cup-winners Cup... Welsh Cup won again - another entry into Europe... Player clear-out at end of season... Ron Stitfall's long playing career ends.

Other Matches
F.A.Cup

	Date	Opposition	Res	Attend.	Goalscorers	1	2	3	4	5	6	7	8	9	10	11
3rd	9 Jan	CHARLTON ATHLETIC	1-2	13500	Tapscott	Y	J	V	Z	T	L	G	P	X	F	Q

Football League Cup

	Date	Opposition	Res	Attend.	Goalscorers	1	2	3	4	5	6	7	8	9	10	11
2nd	23 Sep	Southampton	2-3	13076	Lewis King,P.	"	V	U	"	C	"	P	R	"	A	"

Welsh Cup

	Date	Opposition	Res	Attend.	Goalscorers	1	2	3	4	5	6	7	8	9	10	11
5th	26 Jan	Merthyr Tydfil	3-1	6000	King,P.2 Tapscott	"	J	V	"	T	"	G	P	F	F	"
6th	17 Feb	HEREFORD UNITED	3-1	8000	Allchurch Ellis Farrell(pen)	"	U	"	"	"	"	"	D	F	A	P
Semi-final	10 Mar	Swansea Town	1-0	8000	Farrell (pen)	"	"	"	C	"	"	"	Z	"	"	"
Final 1/leg	12 Apr	WREXHAM	5-1	7000	Johnston 2 Allchurch King 2	"	V	B	Z	"	"	N	A	C	P	Q
Final 2/leg	26	Wrexham	0-1	8000		"	K	"	"	"	"	"	"	F	"	"
Final Rep.	5 May	Wrexham	3-0	7840	Allchurch 2 King,P.	"	E	"	"	"	"	"	"	C	"	"

European Cup Winners Cup

	Date	Opposition	Res	Attend.	Goalscorers	1	2	3	4	5	6	7	8	9	10	11
1st/1 leg	9 Sep	Esjberg	0-0	10000		M	V	U	"	C	"	P	D	I	A	G
1st/2nd leg	1 Oct	ESJBERG	1-0	8000	King,P.	"	"	"	"	T	"	G	P	X	"	Q
2nd/1st leg	15 Dec	Sporting Lisbon	2-1	20000	Farrell Tapscott	"	"	J	V	C	"	"	"	Z	P	"
2nd/2nd leg	23	SPORTING LISBON	0-0	25000		"	"	"	C	"	"	"	"	"	"	"
Q/Fin. 1/leg	20 Jan	Real Zaragoza	2-2	35000	Williams King,P.	Y	"	"	"	"	"	"	"	"	"	"
Q/Fin. 2/leg	3 Feb	REAL ZARAGOZA	0-1	38458		"	"	"	"	"	"	"	"	"	"	"

Friendlies

	Date	Opposition	Res	Attend.	Goalscorers
	10 Aug	Newport County	0-1	2000	
	12	NEWPORT COUNTY	3-1	2500	Allchurch Charles,M. Charles,J.

The first ECWC Match to be played at Ninian Park.

1965-66

Football League – Division 2.

Manager: Jimmy Scoular

P:42　W:12　D:10　L:20　71-91　Pts:34　Pos:20th

1638	Date	Opposition	Res	Attend.	Goalscorers	1	2	3	4	5	6	7	8	9	10	11	12
1.	21 Aug	BURY	1-0	13546	Charles	X	T	J	B	F	L	H	W	E	O	Q	U
2.	25	DERBY COUNTY	2-1	17100	Harkin Charles	"	"	B	W	S	"	"	O	"	K	"	P
3.	28	Norwich City	2-3	14500	Johnston (pen) Harkin	"	"	"	"	"	"	"	"	"	"	"	"
4.	1 Sep	Derby County	5-1	10521	Johnston2(1 pen) Charles2 Harkin	"	F	T	"	"	"	"	"	"	"	"	"
5.	4	WOLVERHAMPTON W.	1-4	19700	Johnston (pen)	"	"	"	"	"	"	"	"	"	"	"	"
6.	11	Rotherham United	4-6	8918	Farrell Harkin 2 Johnston	"	J	"	"	"	"	"	"	P	"	"	B
7.	14	Charlton Athletic	2-5	13172	Harkin Johnston	"	"	"	"	"	"	"	"	"	"	"	F
8.	18	MANCHESTER CITY	4-3	11529	Johnston 2 Hole Harkin	N	T	B	F	"	"	O	W	K	P	"	U
9.	25	Bristol City	1-1	15299	Lewis	"	"	"	"	"	"	"	"	W	K	"	E
10.	6 Oct	COVENTRY CITY	1-2	12639	Williams	"	"	"	W	"	"	"	P	"	P	"	U
11.	9	Plymouth Argyle	2-2	10452	Farrell Johnston	"	S	J	"	E	"	H	O	K	"	"	O
12.	16	PORTSMOUTH	1-2	11914	Johnston	X	"	T	*U	S	*M	"	P	*A	K	"	K
13.	23	Bolton Wanderers	1-2	10947	Andrews	"	"	J	"	"	"	"	O	"	P	"	U
14.	30	IPSWICH TOWN	1-0	8444	Farrell	"	"	"	L	"	"	"	"	"	K	P	V
15.	6 Nov	Birmingham City	2-4	10743	Andrews 2	"	"	"	"	F	"	"	"	"	K	P	V
16.	10	CHARLTON ATHLETIC	3-1	8692	Johnston2(pens) Andrews	"	"	"	"	"	"	"	"	"	O	"	U
17.	13	LEYTON ORIENT	3-1-	9168	Johnston Andrews Toshack	"	"	B	"	"	"	"	W	"	"	"	*V
18.	20	Middlesbrough	3-1	11898	Toshack2 Johnston2 (1pen)	"	"	T	"	W	"	"	O	"	*V	"	U
19.	27	HUDDERSFIELD TOWN	0-1	11078		"	"	"	"	"	"	"	"	"	"	"	B
20.	4 Dec	Crystal Palace	0-0	11572		"	"	"	"	"	"	Q	"	"	"	"	Q
21.	11	PRESTON NORTH END	1-3	10922	Johnston	"	"	"	"	"	"	"	"	"	P	Q	B
22.	18	Portsmouth	1-3	8434	Andrews	"	"	"	"	S	"	"	P	"	O	*C	U
23.	27	SOUTHAMPTON	3-5	14897	Harkin Andrews o.g.(Walker)	"	"	"	W	"	L	H	O	"	W	P	K
24.	1 Jan	PLYMOUTH ARGYLE	5-1	9028	Andrews 2 Harkin 2 Hole	*G	"	*I	"	"	M	"	A	"	K	"	B
25.	8	Leyton Orient	1-1	5516	Andrews	"	"	"	"	"	"	"	L	"	"	"	*R
26.	29	Bury	1-1	4677	Johnston	"	"	"	"	"	L	"	O	"	"	"	H
27.	19 Feb	Wolverhampton W.	1-2	24179	Andrews	"	*D	"	"	"	"	"	P	"	P	"	B
28.	26	ROTHERHAM UNITED	0-0	9331		N	"	"	"	"	"	"	"	"	O	"	U
29.	5 Mar	BOLTON WANDERERS	1-1	9122	Farrell	"	"	"	"	"	"	"	"	"	P	Q	"
30.	12	Manchester City	2-2	29642	Toshack Johnston	"	"	"	"	"	"	H	A	V	O	P	M
31.	18	BRISTOL CITY	2-1	13587	King Toshack	N	"	"	"	F	"	"	"	"	"	"	C
32.	26	Coventry City	1-3	20246	Andrews	"	"	D	"	"	"	"	O	A	P	C	F
33.	2 Apr	BIRMINGHAM CITY	1-3	8920	Hole	G	"	"	"	S	"	"	"	"	"	"	"
34.	8	CARLISLE UNITED	1-1	8003	Andrews	"	"	"	"	"	"	"	O	"	P	C	M
35.	9	Ipswich Town	1-2	10395	Toshack	"	F	D	"	"	M	"	L	"	V	P	O
36.	12	Carlisle United	0-2	11252		"	"	I	"	"	"	"	O	"	K	C	M
37.	20	Southampton	2-3	18941	King 2	N	F	D	"	"	L	"	P	"	M	Q	O
38.	23	Huddersfield Town	1-1	19138	King	"	"	"	"	"	"	"	O	"	P	Q	O
39.	30	CRYSTAL PALACE	1-0	9557	King	"	"	"	"	"	"	"	M	"	P	"	I
40.	4 May	MIDDLESBROUGH	5-3	13092	Farrell(pen) Andrews 2 Hole King	"	"	D	"	"	U	"	"	"	"	"	O
41.	7	Preston North End	0-9	10018		"	D	I	F	"	"	"	P	"	L	P	M
42.	10	NORWICH CITY	0-2	6030		"	F	D	U	"	M	"	O	"	P	"	I

Players:

A = Andrews,G.　31/7/20
B = Baker,C.　7/3/0
C = Bird,R.　5/0/0
D = Carver,D.　17/1/0
E = Charles,J.　7/3/4
F = Coldrick,G.　18/5/0
G = Davies,L.　11/5/0
H = Farrell,G.　36/12/5
I = Ferguson,R.　14/2/0
J = Harrington,A.　17/6/0
K = Harkin,T.　19/11/13
L = Hole,B.　40/13/6
M = Houston,D.　16/3/0
N = John,D.　12/2/0
O = Johnston,G.　34/11/24
P = King,P.　35/11/11
Q = Lewis,B.　24/5/3
R = Murphy,P.　0/0/0
S = Murray,D.　32/11/0
T = Rodrigues,P.　22/6/0
U = Summerhayes,D　4/2/0
V = Toshack,J.　7/1/6
W = Williams,G.　35/10/2
X = Wilson,R.　19/6/0
Y = Yorath,D.　0/1/0

Struggle to avoid relegation but plenty of goals... First City sub. is David Summerhayes... Rodrigues sold to Leicester for £40,000...17 year-old George Johnston becomes early scoring sensation - 16 year-old John Toshack scores on substitute debut.. 0-9 defeat at Preston, record post-war defeat.. Alan Harrington's career ended - Colin Baker retires.

Other Matches

F.A.Cup

	Date	Opposition	Res	Attend.	Goalscorers	1	2	3	4	5	6	7	8	9	10	11
3rd	26 Jan	PORT VALE	2-1	18898	King Hole	G	B	I	W	S	L	H	O	P	K	Q
4th	12 Feb	Southport	0-2	14230		"	D	"	"	"	"	"	"	F	"	P

Football League Cup

	Date	Opposition	Res	Attend.	Goalscorers	1	2	3	4	5	6	7	8	9	10	11
2nd	22 Sep	Crewe Alexandra	1-1	5832	Lewis	N	T	B	F	"	"	O	W	K	P	Q
2nd Rep.	29	CREWE ALEXANDRA	3-0	6939	King 2 Harkin	"	"	"	"	"	"	"	P	W	K	H
3rd	13 Oct	PORTSMOUTH	2-0	8803	King Andrews	X	S	T	U	E	"	H	"	A	"	P
4th	3 Nov	READING	5-1	6698	Johnston 3 Harkin 2	"	J	"	L	F	M	"	O	"	"	P
5th	17	IPSWICH	2-1	7748	Andrews Hole	"	"	"	"	W	"	"	"	"	V	"
Semi-Fin/1	20 Dec	West Ham United	2-5	19900	Andrews 2	"	"	"	"	S	"	"	K	"	W	"
Semi-Fin/2	2 Feb	WEST HAM UNITED	1-5	14315	Lewis	G	F	Y	W	"	L	Q	O	"	P	H

Welsh Cup

	Date	Opposition	Res	Attend.	Goalscorers	1	2	3	4	5	6	7	8	9	10	11
5th	4 Jan	Swansea Town	2-2	10000	Andrews King	"	J	B	"	"	"	H	"	"	K	P
5th Replay	8 Feb	SWANSEA TOWN	3-5	9836	Williams Johnston 2	"	F	"	"	"	"	"	"	"	"	"

European Cup Winners Cup

	Date	Opposition	Res	Attend.	Goalscorers	1	2	3	4	5	6	7	8	9	10	11
Prelim 1 Leg	8 Sep	STANDARD LIEGE	1-2	12798	Johnston	X	J	T	"	U	"	"	"	E	"	Q
Prelim 2 Leg	20 Oct	Standard Liege	0-1	30000		"	"	"	"	"	"	"	"	"	"	"

Friendlies

Date	Opposition	Res	Attend.	Goalscorers
7 Aug	Cheltenham Town	3-2	3000	Hole 2 Charles
13	Hereford United	4-2	4000	Harkin 2 Lewis Charles
18	HEREFORD UNITED	8-3	3500	Harkin 2 Johnston 2 Charles 2 Lewis Farrell
26 Sep	Toulon	3-3	20000	Harkin 2 Johnston
27 Apr	Lower Gornal	3-0	2000	

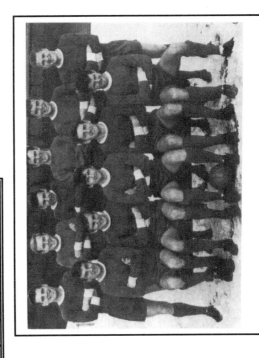

(Back) Baker, Williams, Hole, Davies, Murray, Ferguson
(Front) Farrell, Johnston, King, Harkin, Lewis

1966-67
Football League – Division 2.
Manager: Jimmy Scoular
P: 42 **W:** 12 **D:** 9 **L:** 21 **F:** 61-87 **Pts:** 33 **Pos:** 20th

1680	Date	Opposition	Res	Attend.	Goalscorers	1	2	3	4	5	6	7	8	9	10	11	12
1.	20 Aug	IPSWICH TOWN	0-2	7735		M	E	J	W	S	F	I	Q	A	V	R	N
2.	27	Bristol City	2-1	11911	Toshack (pen) Andrews	"	"	"	F	"	W	"	"	"	"	"	a
3.	31	WOLVERHAMPTON W.	0-3	13951		"	"	"	W	"	F	"	A	Q	"	"	"
4.	3 Sep	CARLISLE UNITED	4-2	7014	Toshack King 2 Andrews	"	"	"	"	"	"	"	Q	A	"	"	N
5.	7	HUDDERSFIELD TOWN	1-1	10743	Andrews	"	"	"	"	"	"	"	A	Q	"	"	"
6.	10	Blackburn Rovers	1-4	12085	Toshack	"	"	"	"	"	"	"	A	Q	"	"	P
7.	17	BOLTON WANDERERS	2-5	7719	Andrews Toshack (pen)	"	"	"	"	"	"	"	A	Q	"	"	N
8.	21	Wolverhampton W.	1-7	19678	Andrews	G	"	"	F	"	*B	"	W	A	Q	"	V
9.	24	Charlton Athletic	0-5	10182		"	"	"	W	"	F	"	N	Q	V	B	P
10.	1 Oct	DERBY COUNTY	1-1	6631	Williams	"	"	*T	"	F	L	R	"	A	Q	"	"
11.	8	HULL CITY	2-4	9602	Lewis Andrews	"	"	"	"	"	U	N	A	"	Q	R	b
12.	15	Plymouth Argyle	1-7	14525	Williams	"	"	"	"	S	*K	"	A	*D	"	"	F
13.	29	Millwall	0-1	12586		Y	F	J	"	"	"	R	"	"	"	"	E
14.	4 Nov	ROTHERHAM UNITED	0-0	6056		"	"	"	"	"	"	"	N	"	"	C	I
15.	12	Preston North End	0-4	11283		"	"	"	"	"	"	Q	"	V	*X	"	*Z
16.	19	BURY	3-0	6038	Toshack 2 Brown	"	"	"	"	"	"	I	N	D	V	"	U
17.	26	Coventry City	2-3	19680	Toshack 2	"	"	"	"	"	"	"	V	"	N	"	Q
18.	3 Dec	NORWICH CITY	2-0	5647	Farrell Coldrick	"	"	"	"	"	"	"	"	"	Q	"	U
19.	10	Birmingham City	2-1	16356	Coldrick Brown	"	"	"	"	"	"	"	"	"	"	"	R
20.	14	NORTHAMPTON TOWN	4-2	8077	Williams 2 Brown 2	"	"	"	"	"	"	"	"	"	"	"	"
21.	17	Ipswich Town	0-0	11617		"	"	"	"	"	"	R	"	"	"	"	U
22.	26	CRYSTAL PALACE	1-2	17158	Williams	"	"	"	"	"	"	I	"	"	"	"	"
23.	27	Crystal Palace	1-3	13553	Toshack	"	"	"	"	"	"	"	"	"	"	"	"
24.	31	BRISTOL CITY	5-1	12460	Brown 2 o.g.(Low) Bird 2	"	"	"	"	"	"	"	"	"	"	"	"
25.	7 Jan	Carlisle United	0-3	10295		"	"	"	U	"	"	"	N	"	"	"	P
26.	14	BLACKBURN ROVERS	1-1	11509	Brown	"	"	"	"	"	"	"	"	"	"	"	R
27.	21	Bolton Wanderers	1-3	8891	Johnston	"	"	"	W	"	"	R	"	"	"	"	U
28.	3 Feb	CHARLTON ATHLETIC	4-1	10971	Bird King Johnston 2	"	"	"	"	"	"	*P	"	"	"	I	"
29.	11	Derby County	1-1	14573	Brown	"	"	"	"	"	"	"	"	"	"	C	"
30.	25	Hull City	0-1	23629		"	"	"	"	"	"	"	"	"	"	"	B
31.	4 Mar	MILLWALL	1-1	11023	King	"	E	"	"	"	"	N	N	V	"	T	P
32.	18	Northampton Town	0-2	11787		"	"	"	"	"	"	*O	*H	D	"	C	T
33.	22	PORTSMOUTH	0-0	11855		"	F	"	"	"	"	"	"	"	"	"	E
34.	25	PLYMOUTH ARGYLE	4-1	11587	Toshack Dean Jones Brow	"	E	"	"	"	"	"	"	"	V	Q	C
35.	27	Portsmouth	2-1	16363	King Williams	"	"	"	"	"	"	"	"	"	Q	C	Z
36.	1 Apr	Rotherham United	1-4	8119	Jones,Barrie	"	"	"	"	"	"	"	Q	"	"	"	T
37.	8	PRESTON NORTH END	4-0	0795	Jones,Barrie King Brown 2	"	F	"	"	"	K	"	Q	H	"	"	b
38.	15	Bury	0-2	6234		"	"	"	"	"	"	"	D	O	"	"	N
39.	22	COVENTRY CITY	1-1	19592	Brown	"	"	"	"	"	"	"	"	H	"	"	Z
40.	29	Norwich City	2-3	14650	Williams Dean	"	"	"	"	"	"	"	V	V	"	"	"
41.	6 May	BIRMINGHAM CITY	3-0	12872	Brown 2 Jones,Barrie	"	"	"	"	"	"	"	V	H	"	"	c
42.	13	Huddersfield Town	1-3	3847	Brown	"	"	"	"	"	"	"	D	"	"	Z	E

Players:

A = Andrews,G. 12/0/6
B = Bell,G. 3/0/0
C = Bird,R. 27/8/4
D = Brown,R. 29/9/18
E = Carver,D. 17/3/0
F = Coldrick,G. 39/10/3
G = Davies,L. 5/0/0
H = Dean,N. 10/2/3
I = Farrell,G. 24/4/2
J = Ferguson,R. 39/11/1
K = Harris,B. 28/9/0
L = Houston,D. 1/0/0
M = John,D. 7/2/0
N = Johnston,G. 14/9/9
O = Jones,Barrie 11/2/4
P = Jones,Bryn 1/1/0
Q = King,P. 40/11/10
R = Lewis,B. 15/5/2
S = Murray,D. 40/11/0
T = Ryder,D. 4/0/0
U = Summerhayes,D. 3/0/0
V = Toshack,J. 22/2/11
W = Williams,G. 40/11/8
X = Winspear,J. 1/0/0
Y = Wilson,R. 30/9/0
Z = Derrett,S. 0/0/0
a = Harkin,T. 0/2/0
b = Baker,C. 0/0/0
c = Phillips,L. 0/0/0

Relegation avoided despite big early season defeats . . Bobby Brown signs for £15,000. . Brian Harris arrives from Everton - debut in 1-7 defeat at Plymouth. Johnston goes to Arsenal for £20,000 . . . Deadline signings Barrie Jones and Norman Dean help City out of trouble.

Other Matches

F.A.Cup

	Date	Opposition	Res	Attend.	Goalscorers	1	2	3	4	5	6	7	8	9	10	11	12
3rd	28 Jan	Barnsley	1-1	21464	Bird	Y	F	J	W	S	K	R	N	D	Q	C	P
3rd Replay	31	BARNSLEY	2-1	21020	Johnston (pen) King	"	"	"	"	"	"	"	"	"	"	"	"
4th	18 Feb	MANCHESTER CITY	1-1	37205	Williams	"	"	"	"	"	"	I	"	"	"	"	B
4th Replay	22	Manchester City	1-3	41616	Johnston (pen)	"	"	"	"	"	"	"	"	"	"	"	"

Football League Cup

	Date	Opposition	Res	Attend.	Goalscorers	1	2	3	4	5	6	7	8	9	10	11	12
1st	24 Aug	BRISTOL ROVERS	1-0	5574	Toshack	M	E	"	"	"	F	N	a	Q	V	R	L
2nd	14 Sep	EXETER CITY	0-1	5384		"	"	"	"	"	"	"	"	"	"	"	C

Welsh Cup

	Date	Opposition	Res	Attend.	Goalscorers	1	2	3	4	5	6	7	8	9	10	11	12
5th	17 Jan	Swansea City	4-0	11816	Lewis Farrell Johnston 2	Y	F	"	"	"	K	R	N	D	Q	I	C
6th	8 Feb	HEREFORD UNITED	6-3	11490	King Johnston2 Coldrick Ferguson Brown	"	"	"	"	"	"	I	"	"	"	C	P
Semi-final	15 Mar	Newport County	2-1	8500	Brown King	"	E	"	"	"	"	P	"	"	"	"	V
Final/1 leg	17 Apr	Wrexham	2-2	11437	Brown King	"	"	"	"	"	"	O	D	H	"	"	Z
Final/2 leg	3 May	WREXHAM	2-1	8299	Dean o.g.(Showell)	"	F	"	"	"	"	"	"	"	"	"	V

Friendlies

	Date	Opposition	Res	Attend.	Goalscorers
	6 Aug	Chelmsford City	5-2	2200	Bell Toshack King 2 Williams
	10	Reading	1-3	1500	Toshack
	13	READING	1-1	2000	Andrews
	17	Lower Gornal	3-1	1200	Farrell Andrews Williams
†	15 Nov	Arsenal	2-4	10000	Johnston 2

† Aberfan Appeal.

(Back) Carver, Murray, Ferguson, Davies, Williams, Coldrick
(Front) Farrell, King, Andrews, Toshack, Bell

1967-68
Football League – Division 2.
Manager: Jimmy Scoular
P:42 W:13 D:12 L:17 60-66 Pts:38 Pos:13th

1722

#	Date	Opposition	Res	Attend.	Goalscorers	1	2	3	4	5	6	7	8	9	10	11	12
1.	19 Aug	PLYMOUTH ARGYLE	1-1	17343	Brown (pen)	V	H	L	E	S	M	N	U	*A	D	O	J
2.	26	Bolton Wanderers	1-1	10469	King	"	"	"	U	"	E	"	D	O	M	C	"
3.	30	CRYSTAL PALACE	4-2	14750	Jones Brown Bird King	"	"	"	"	"	M	"	"	J	O	"	E
4.	2 Sep	Portsmouth	1-3	17308	Brown	"	E	"	"	"	"	"	"	"	O	"	G
5.	5	Charlton Athletic	1-1	8523	Brown	"	"	"	"	"	"	"	"	O	*G	"	T
6.	9	NORWICH CITY	3-1	14863	King Brown(pen) Jones	"	H	"	"	"	"	"	"	T	O	"	E
7.	16	Rotherham United	2-3	5541	King Murray	"	"	"	"	"	"	"	"	O	G	"	T
8.	23	DERBY COUNTY	1-5	15397	Bird (pen)	"	"	"	"	"	"	"	A	T	O	"	G
9.	27	Crystal Palace	1-2	20424	Jones	"	"	"	"	"	"	"	D	O	G	"	T
10.	30	Preston North End	0-3	13735		"	"	"	"	"	"	"	"	"	"	"	Z
11.	7 Oct	IPSWICH TOWN	1-1	11282	Toshack	"	"	E	"	"	"	"	D	T	O	Q	G
12.	14	Bristol City	1-1	15609	Brown	"	"	L	G	"	"	"	"	O	T	C	Y
13.	24	MIDDLESBROUGH	3-0	10461	Toshack 2 King	"	"	"	"	"	"	"	"	O	"	"	E
14.	27	Hull City	2-1	18579	Brown Bird	"	"	"	"	"	"	"	"	"	"	"	"
15.	11 Nov	Blackpool	1-3	11234	Clarke	"	"	E	"	"	"	"	"	"	"	"	K
16.	18	BIRMINGHAM CITY	1-3	13817	Toshack	"	*K	L	"	"	"	"	"	"	"	"	B
17.	25	Carlisle United	3-1	10966	Toshack 2 Bell	"	"	"	"	"	"	"	"	"	"	B	Y
18.	2 Dec	BLACKBURN ROVERS	3-2	9774	King 2 Clarke	"	"	E	"	"	"	"	"	"	"	C	J
19.	5	MILLWALL	2-2	12108	Toshack Brown	"	"	"	"	"	"	"	"	"	"	"	"
20.	9	Huddersfield Town	0-1	8552		"	"	"	"	"	"	"	"	"	"	J	L
21.	16	Plymouth Argyle	0-0	10736		"	H	"	"	"	"	"	"	"	"	B	†
22.	23	BOLTON WANDERERS	1-3	11206	Brown	"	"	"	"	"	"	"	"	"	"	*P	C
23.	26	ASTON VILLA	3-0	18195	Lea 2 Toshack	"	"	"	"	"	"	"	"	"	"	"	B
24.	30	Aston Villa	1-2	17653	Dean	"	K	L	"	"	"	"	J	"	"	"	"
25.	6 Jan	PORTSMOUTH	3-0	14841	Clarke Bird King	*I	"	B	"	"	"	"	P	"	"	C	A
26.	29	ROTHERHAM UNITED	2-2	8766	Bird Phillips	V	H	"	"	*R	K	"	"	"	"	"	*Y
27.	3 Feb	Derby County	4-3	18906	Clark 2 King 2	"	B	L	"	S	"	"	*F	"	"	P	"
28.	10	PRESTON NORTH END	2-0	12800	Clark Toshack	"	K	"	"	"	M	"	"	"	"	"	B
29.	24	Ipswich Town	2-4	15580	Clark Lea	I	"	"	"	"	"	"	F	"	"	"	"
30.	2 Mar	BRISTOL CITY	0-1	15546		"	"	"	"	"	"	"	"	"	"	"	C
31.	9	Middlesbrough	3-2	15582	Toshack Clark Jones	"	"	"	"	"	"	"	"	"	"	"	"
32.	22	HULL CITY	2-3	12039	Clark King	"	H	"	J	"	"	"	"	"	"	"	G
33.	30	Millwall	1-3	7944	Lea	"	"	"	G	"	"	"	"	"	"	"	"
34.	6 Apr	BLACKPOOL	1-3	14439	King	V	"	"	"	*R	"	"	"	"	"	C	K
35.	12	Q.P.Rangers	0-1	23043			"	"	"	S	"	"	J	"	"	P	F
36.	13	Birmingham City	0-0	29044			E	"	"	"	"	"	F	"	"	P	J
37.	16	Q.P.RANGERS	1-0	20035	Toshack		"	"	"	"	"	"	"	"	"	"	X
38.	20	CARLISLE UNITED	1-0	13948	Jones		"	"	"	"	"	"	"	"	"	"	"
39.	27	Blackburn Rovers	1-1	7195	Jones		"	"	"	"	"	"	"	"	"	"	"
40.	4 May	HUDDERSFIELD TOWN	0-0	10669			K	E	"	R	K	"	"	"	"	"	X
41.	8	Norwich City	0-1	11448			E	L	"	S	M	"	G	"	"	"	J
42.	11	CHARLTON ATHLETIC	0-0	8412			"	"	G	"	"	"	J	"	"	"	F

Players:

A = Allan,A. — 2/0/0
B = Bell,G. — 4/0/1
C = Bird,R. — 19/11/9
D = Brown,R. — 21/5/13
E = Carver,D. — 19/5/0
F = Clark,B. — 13/3/6
G = Clarke,M. — 34/14/5
H = Coldrick,G. — 20/8/1
I = Davies,F. — 17/5/0
J = Dean,N. — 9/8/5
K = Derrett,S. — 16/5/0
L = Ferguson,R. — 32/16/0
M = Harris,B. — 39/17/1
N = Jones,Barrie — 42/17/11
O = King,P. — 42/15/18
P = Lea,L. — 20/7/8
Q = Lewis,B. — 1/0/0
R = Morgan,R. — 2/0/1
S = Murray,D. — 40/16/1
T = Toshack,J. — 34/15/17
U = Williams,G. — 11/4/0
V = Wilson,R. — 25/11/0
W = Davies,L. — 0/1/0
X = Jones,Bryn — 0/1/0
Y = Phillips,L. — 0/0/0
Z = Summerhayes,D. — 0/0/0

† No named substitute

Bobby Brown's career ended by injury...Gareth Williams sold to Bolton for £45,000...League delay in Lea registration - results in no sub. at Plymouth...Fred Davies and Brian Clark signed at bargain prices. Leighton Phillips scores in debut with first touch, as sub...City reach semi-finals in Europe...Tour to Australia and New Zealand.

Other Matches

F.A.Cup

	Date	Opposition	Res	Attend.	Goalscorers	1	2	3	4	5	6	7	8	9	10	11	12
3rd	27 Jan	Stoke City	1-4	23563	Jones	I	K	L	G	S	M	N	P	T	O	C	B

Football League Cup

	Date	Opposition	Res	Attend.	Goalscorers	1	2	3	4	5	6	7	8	9	10	11	12
1st	23 Aug	Aldershot	3-2	5133	Brown 2 King	V	H	"	U	"	"	"	D	J	"	"	E
2nd	12 Sep	Burnley	1-2	11631	Coldrick	"	"	"	"	"	"	"	"	"	G	"	T

Welsh Cup

	Date	Opposition	Res	Attend.	Goalscorers	1	2	3	4	5	6	7	8	9	10	11	12
5th	16 Jan	EBBW VALE	8-0	3542	Toshack 3 Bird 3 (1 pen) King Lea	W	"	"	G	"	"	"	P	O	T	"	K
6th	12 Feb	Wrexham	3-1	7671	Jones Lea Bird	I	K	"	"	"	"	"	F	"	"	"	B
Semi-final	27 Mar	Chester	3-0	5488	King Toshack Lea	"	H	"	"	"	"	"	"	"	"	P	J
Final/1 leg	6 May	Hereford United	2-0	5442	Jones King	"	E	"	"	"	"	"	"	G	"	"	-
Final/2 leg	16	HEREFORD UNITED	4-1	6036	Dean Clarke o.g.(Jones) Lea	"	"	"	G	"	"	"	J	O	"	"	F

European Cup

	Date	Opposition	Res	Attend.	Goalscorers	1	2	3	4	5	6	7	8	9	10	11	12
1st/1 Leg	20 Sep	Shamrock Rovers	1-1	21883	King	V	H	"	U	"	"	"	T	O	G	"	W
1st/2 Leg	4 Oct	SHAMROCK ROVERS	2-0	14180	Brown Toshack	"	"	E	"	"	"	"	D	T	O	"	"
2nd/1 Leg	15 Nov	NAC Breda	1-1	10000	King	"	K	L	G	"	"	"	"	"	O	T	"
2nd/2 Leg	29	NAC BREDA	4-1	16411	Brown Jones Toshack Clarke	"	H	"	"	"	"	"	"	"	O	T	"
Q.F./1 Leg	6 Mar	MOSCOW TORPEDO	1-0	30567	Brown,Jones,Barrie	"	K	"	"	"	"	"	X	"	"	"	"
Q.F./2 Leg	19	Moscow Torpedo	0-1	65000		"	"	"	"	"	"	"	J	"	"	"	"
Q.F.Replay	3 Apr	Moscow Torpedo	1-0	33000	Dean	"	H	"	"	"	R	"	"	"	"	"	"
S/F.1 leg	24	SV Hamburg	1-1	64500	Dean	"	E	"	J	S	"	"	"	"	"	P	"
S/F.2 leg	1 May	SV HAMBURG	2-3	43070	Dean Harris	"	"	"	G	"	"	"	G	"	T	"	"

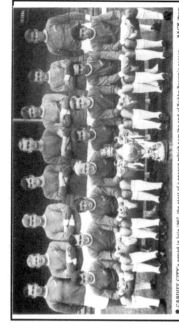

● CARDIFF CITY's squad in July 1967, the start of a season which saw the end of Bobby Brown's career... BACK (from left): Norman Dean, Bobby Ferguson, Don Murray, Lyn Davies, Bob Wilson, John Toshack, Derek Ryder, David Carver. FRONT (from left): Bernard Lewis, Graham Coldrick, Brian Harris, Gareth Williams, Peter King, BOBBY BROWN, Ronnie Bird, David Summerhayes.

Friendlies

	Date	Opposition	Res	Attend.	Goalscorers
	9 Aug	Torquay United	2-1	2000	Allan Brown
	12	Exeter City	4-2	1800	Allan 2 Brown 2
	28 May	New Caledonia	4-1		Clark Bird Dean Toshack
	30	Auckland	3-0		Dean 2 Jones
	1 Jun	Central League X1	2-0		Bird Clark
	3	Southern League X1	2-3		Jones Phillips
	5	New Zealand	3-0		Clark2 King
	9	Victoria	1-1		Clark
	10	Tasmania	5-1		Toshack Bird 2 Clark Coldrick
	15	Northern N.S.W.	2-0		Clarke Clark
	16	New South Wales	1-1		Clarke
	19	Australian X1	6-0		Harris Dean Bird 2 Clark Lea
	23	Queensland	7-2		Bird 2 Clark 2 Lea 2 Toshack
	26	Australian X1	3-1		Clark 2 Lea
	29	South Australia	3-2		Jones Bird Lea
	7 Jul	Western Australia	6-1		King 2 Clark 2 Lea 2

1968-69
Football League – Division 2.

Manager: Jimmy Scoular

P:42 W:20 D:7 L:15 67-54 Pts:47 Pos:5th

1764	Date	Opposition	Res	Attend.	Goalscorers	1	2	3	4	5	6	7	8	9	10	11	12
1.	10 Aug	CRYSTAL PALACE	0-4	16395		H	D	K	*S	R	L	M	E	N	V	C	I
2.	14	CHARLTON ATHLETIC	0-1	12001		"	"	"	*U	"	"	"	"	"	"	"	V
3.	17	Norwich City	1-3	15033	Bird	"	G	D	I	"	"	"	"	"	F	"	V
4.	21	Bury	3-3	7214	Clark Jones Toshack	"	"	B	F	"	"	"	"	"	V	"	J
5.	24	PRESTON NORTH END	1-0	11347	King	"	"	"	"	"	"	"	"	"	"	"	"
6.	28	BIRMINGHAM CITY	4-0	14991	Toshack 2 Bell Clark	"	J	"	"	"	"	"	"	"	"	"	U
7.	31	Portsmouth	3-1	21871	Clark King Toshack	"	"	"	"	"	"	"	"	"	"	"	G
8.	7 Sep	MIDDLESBROUGH	2-0	14244	o.g.(Gates) Clark	"	G	J	"	"	"	"	"	"	"	B	S
9.	14	Huddersfield Town	0-3	7523		"	"	B	"	"	"	"	"	"	"	C	J
10.	21	CARLISLE UNITED	2-1	10826	Clark Jones	"	"	J	U	"	"	"	"	"	"	O	G
11.	28	Bristol City	3-0	21630	King Toshack Jones	"	G	"	"	"	"	"	"	"	"	"	S
12.	5 Oct	ASTON VILLA	1-1	17136	Toshack	"	"	"	"	"	R	"	"	"	"	"	"
13.	8	Birmingham City	0-2	28238		"	"	"	F	"	U	"	"	S	"	"	C
14.	12	Millwall	0-2	13664		"	"	J	U	"	L	"	"	"	"	"	G
15.	19	BOLTON WANDERERS	0-2	12047		"	G	"	"	"	J	"	"	"	"	"	D
16.	26	Hull City	3-3	17027	Toshack 2 Clark	"	D	"	"	"	"	"	"	O	"	"	G
17.	2 Nov	BLACKBURN ROVERS	2-1	11695	Toshack Bird	"	"	K	"	"	"	"	"	"	"	"	S
18.	9	Blackpool	2-1	12085	Toshack 2	"	"	B	"	"	"	"	"	"	"	"	"
19.	16	DERBY COUNTY	1-1	17254	Clark	"	"	"	"	"	"	"	"	"	"	"	"
20.	23	Oxford United	2-0	9756	Clark Toshack	"	"	"	"	"	"	"	"	"	"	"	"
21.	30	SHEFFIELD UNITED	4-1	14271	Bird2 (1pen) Clark Toshack	"	"	B	"	"	"	"	"	"	"	"	G
22.	7 Dec	Fulham	5-1	13191	Clark Jones 2 Toshack Lea	"	"	"	"	"	"	"	"	"	"	"	S
23.	14	MILLWALL	2-0	22424	Toshack Clark	"	"	"	"	"	"	"	"	"	"	"	G
24.	21	Bolton Wanderers	2-1	8726	Lea Jones	"	"	"	"	"	"	"	"	"	"	"	G
25.	26	Aston Villa	0-2	41250		"	"	"	"	"	"	"	"	"	"	"	G
26.	28	HULL CITY	3-0	24863	Clark Bird Toshack	"	"	"	"	"	"	"	"	"	"	"	N
27.	11 Jan	Blackburn Rovers	0-1	12100		"	"	"	"	"	"	"	"	"	"	"	S
28.	25	BRISTOL CITY	3-0	24235	Clark 2 King	"	"	"	"	"	"	"	"	"	"	N	C
29.	1 Feb	Derby County	0-2	34589		"	"	"	"	"	"	"	"	"	"	"	L
30.	8	OXFORD UNITED	5-0	16415	Bird Clark2 Toshack 2	"	"	"	"	"	"	"	"	"	"	C	G
31.	12	BLACKPOOL	1-0	24229	Toshack	"	"	"	"	"	"	"	O	"	"	"	S
32.	1 Mar	Crystal Palace	1-3	19663	Jones	"	"	"	"	"	"	"	E	"	"	*T	C
33.	7	NORWICH CITY	3-1	21415	Toshack King Bird	"	"	"	"	"	"	"	"	"	"	"	"
34.	11	Sheffield United	2-2	14508	Clark Jones	"	"	"	"	"	"	"	"	"	"	C	S
35.	15	Preston North End	1-0	10752	Bird	"	G	"	"	"	"	"	"	N	"	"	"
36.	21	PORTSMOUTH	2-2	21814	Toshack 2	"	"	B	J	"	L	"	"	"	"	T	A
37.	25	FULHAM	0-2	20747		"	"	G	S	"	"	"	"	"	"	"	C
38.	29	Middlesbrough	0-0	24470		"	J	D	U	"	"	"	N	S	"	"	E
39.	4 Apr	Charlton Athletic	1-4	22215	Murray	"	D	B	F	"	J	"	E	"	"	C	"
40.	7	BURY	2-0	13253	Toshack Allan	"	J	D	N	"	L	"	A	O	"	T	T
41.	12	Carlisle United	0-1	5546		"	"	"	"	Q	R	"	"	"	"	"	C
42.	19	HUDDERSFIELD TOWN	0-2	11570		"	"	"	"	R	*P	T	O	M	"	C	E

Players:

A = Allan,A. 2/0/1
B = Bell,G. 32/7/2
C = Bird,R. 27/3/10
D = Carver,D. 30/7/0
E = Clark,B. 37/10/19
F = Clarke,M. 9/1/0
G = Coldrick,G. 9/2/0
H = Davies,F. 42/10/0
I = Dean,N. 1/0/0
J = Derrett,S 34/9/0
K = Ferguson,R. 3/0/0
L = Harris,B. 16/5/0
M = Jones,B. 42/10/11
N = King,P. 26/8/5
O = Lea,L. 24/7/4
P = Lewis,T. 1/0/0
Q = Morgan,R. 2/1/0
R = Murray,D. 42/9/1
S = Phillips,L. 7/0/0
T = Sharp,F. 6/3/0
U = Sutton,M. 29/8/0
V = Toshack,J. 41/10/31

Inconsistancies prevent success in Promotion challenge..Toshack becomes leading 2nd Division scorer..Crowds begin to return to Ninian Park...Over 100,000 spectators watch two F.A. Cup matches with Arsenal...Tour to Mauritius and Zambia.

Other Matches

F.A.Cup

	Date	Opposition	Res	Attend.	Goalscorers	1	2	3	4	5	6	7	8	9	10	11	12
3rd	4 Jan	ARSENAL	0-0	55136		H	D	B	U	R	J	M	E	O	V	C	N
3rd Replay	7	Arsenal	0-2	52681		"	"	"	"	"	"	"	"	"	"	"	"

Football League Cup

	Date	Opposition	Res	Attend.	Goalscorers												
2nd	4 Sep	Carlisle United	0-2	7714		"	G	J	F	"	L	"	"	N	"	U	S

Welsh Cup

	Date	Opposition	Res	Attend.	Goalscorers												
3rd	15 Jan	Aberystwyth Town	3-0	5000	Lea Toshack Jones	"	D	B	U	Q	J	O	"	M	"	N	C
4th	5 Feb	BETHESDA ATHLETIC	6-0	6749	Clark 2 Lea Jones Bell Toshack	"	"	"	"	R	"	M	"	O	"	"	"
Semi-final	19 Mar	Chester	2-0	8404	Toshack 2	"	"	"	"	"	"	"	"	N	"	T	"
Final/1 leg	22 Apr	Swansea City	3-1	10207	Toshack 2 o.g.(Nurse)	"	J	D	N	"	"	T	"	O	"	M	P
Final/2 leg	29	SWANSEA CITY	2-0	12417	Lea Toshack	"	"	"	"	"	"	"	"	"	"	"	C

European Cup

	Date	Opposition	Res	Attend.	Goalscorers												
1st/1 leg	18 Sep	F.C. PORTO	2-2	19202	Toshack Bird	"	"	B	U	"	"	M	"	N	"	C	G
1st/2 leg	2 Oct	F.C. Porto	1-2	55000	Toshack	"	G	"	"	"	J	"	"	"	"	O	S

Friendlies

	Date	Opposition	Res	Attend.	Goalscorers
	10 Dec	Newport County	5-3	3800	Toshack Bell Bird Clark
	25 Apr	Aldershot	0-1	2500	
	18 May	Mauritius	1-0		Sharp
	22	Mauritius	5-0		Allan Jones 3 King
	25	Mauritius	2-2		Clark Allan
	29	Zambia	1-1		Allan
	2 Jun	Zambia	2-1		Allan 2
	5	Zambia	1-1		Allan

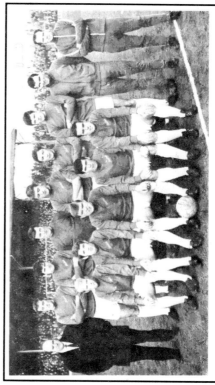

CARDIFF CITY

Standing: J. Scoular (Manager), David Carver, Fred Davies, Brian Clark, Steve Derrett, John Toshack, Graham Coldrick, Lewis Clayton (Trainer).
Seated: Barrie Jones, Leslie Lea, Don Murray, Gary Bell, Ronnie Bird.

1969-70
Football League – Division 2.
Manager: Jimmy Scoular
P:42 W:18 D:13 L:11 61-41 Pts:49 Pos:7th

1806	Date	Opposition	Res	Attend.	Goalscorers	1	2	3	4	5	6	7	8	9	10	11	12
1.	9 Aug	Carlisle United	3-2	10506	Toshack Clark King	G	D	B	R	O	J	K	E	M	S	L	H
2.	13	SWINDON TOWN	2-2	27791	King 2	"	"	"	"	"	"	"	"	"	"	"	P
3.	16	BLACKBURN ROVERS	0-0	19776		"	"	"	"	"	"	"	"	"	"	"	A
4.	19	Swindon Town	1-2	21562	Clark	"	"	"	"	"	"	"	"	"	"	C	H
5.	23	Bristol City	2-0	23237	Clark Bird(pen)	"	"	"	L	"	"	"	"	"	"	"	"
6.	27	MIDDLESBROUGH	1-0	21648	Toshack	"	"	"	R	"	"	"	"	"	"	"	C
7.	30	BOLTON WANDERERS	2-1	21168	King Toshack	"	"	"	"	"	"	"	"	"	"	L	P
8.	6 Sep	Charlton Athletic	0-0	13784		"	"	"	P	"	"	"	"	"	"	"	R
9.	13	LEICESTER CITY	1-1	26978	Toshack	"	"	"	"	"	"	"	"	"	"	"	"
10.	20	Sheffield United	0-1	17296		"	"	F	R	"	"	"	"	P	"	"	C
11.	27	Q.P.RANGERS	4-2	30083	Toshack 3 King	"	"	D	B	"	N	"	"	L	"	Q	F
12.	4 Oct	Blackpool	2-3	18115	Toshack 2	"	"	"	"	"	J	"	"	M	"	L	N
13.	8	Blackburn Rovers	0-1	15062		"	"	"	"	"	"	P	"	"	"	"	"
14.	11	ASTON VILLA	4-0	25896	Toshack 2 Bird 2(1 pen)	"	"	"	"	"	"	L	"	"	"	"	P
15.	18	NORWICH CITY	0-1	23618		"	"	"	"	"	"	"	A	E	"	"	F
16.	25	Birmingham City	1-1	28385	Clark	"	"	"	"	"	"	M	"	A	"	L	H
17.	1 Nov	HULL CITY	6-0	20446	King(pen) Clark2 Toshack2 Sutton	"	"	"	"	"	"	"	E	"	"	"	Q
18.	8	Portsmouth	0-3	17302		"	"	"	"	"	T	"	"	"	"	"	H
19.	15	Oxford United	1-1	11012	Lea	"	"	"	"	"	"	L	"	M	"	A	F
20.	22	PRESTON NORTH END	2-1	22678	Clark King	"	"	"	"	"	"	*T	"	"	"	L	A
21.	6 Dec	WATFORD	3-1	15058	Clark 2 Bird	"	"	"	"	"	"	L	"	J	"	C	"
22.	13	Leicester City	2-1	23590	Clark King	"	"	"	"	"	"	"	"	"	"	"	P
23.	15	Millwall	2-1	9421	King Bird(pen)	"	"	"	"	"	"	"	"	"	"	"	"
24.	20	CHARLTON ATHLETIC	1-0	13926	Clark	"	"	"	"	"	"	"	"	"	"	"	H
25.	29	BRISTOL CITY	1-0	18496	Toshack	"	"	"	"	"	"	"	"	"	"	"	"
26.	10 Jan	SHEFFIELD UNITED	3-0	25136	Clarke 2 Bird	"	"	"	"	"	"	"	"	"	"	"	P
27.	17	Q.P.Rangers	1-2	22033	Toshack	"	"	"	R	"	"	P	"	"	"	L	C
28.	24	Huddersfield Town	0-1	21788		"	"	"	"	"	J	L	"	"	T	C	A
29.	31	BLACKPOOL	2-2	24717	Toshack 2	"	"	"	"	"	"	"	"	"	"	"	M
30.	7 Feb	Aston Villa	1-1	27000	Clark	*I	"	"	"	"	"	M	"	"	S	"	C
31.	14	CARLISLE UNITED	1-1	20143	Woodruff	"	"	"	T	"	J	L	"	M	"	"	H
32.	21	BIRMINGHAM CITY	3-1	21910	King Bird(pen) Clark	"	"	"	"	"	"	"	"	"	"	C	"
33.	28	Norwich City	1-1	12074	Clark	"	"	"	"	"	"	"	"	"	"	"	U
34.	14 Mar	HUDDERSFIELD TOWN	0-1	26004		"	"	"	R	"	T	"	"	J	"	M	C
35.	18	Bolton Wanderers	1-0	10126	Woodruff	"	"	"	"	"	J	"	"	M	T	Q	"
36.	21	Watford	1-2	17152	Clark	"	"	"	"	"	"	T	"	"	"	"	H
37.	25	PORTSMOUTH	2-0	17005	Woodruff Sutton	*I	"	"	"	"	"	"	"	"	S	"	"
38.	28	OXFORD UNITED	0-0	21118		"	"	"	"	"	"	"	S	"	"	"	"
39.	31	Hull City	1-1	13038	Sharp	G	"	"	"	"	"	L	"	"	T	"	S
40.	4 Apr	Middlesbrough	1-2	13829	Clark	"	"	"	"	"	P	"	E	E	M	"	H
41.	15	MILLWALL	0-0	8436		"	"	"	"	"	"	"	"	M	S	M	C
42.	20	Preston North End	2-1	7882	Bird Murray	"	"	"	"	"	"	"	E	"	T	C	Q

Players:
A = Allan,A.   4/3/3
B = Bell,G.   41/13/0
C = Bird,R.   16/6/12
D = Carver,D.   42/14/0
E = Clark,B.   42/14/28
F = Coldrick,G.   1/0/0
G = Davies,F.   40/14/0
H = Derrett,S.   0/2/0
I = Eadie,J.   2/0/0
J = Harris,B.   39/12/0
K = Jones,B.   12/2/0
L = King,P.   40/14/16
M = Lea,L.   31/9/4
N = Lewis,T.   1/1/0
O = Murray,D.   42/14/1
P = Phillips,L.   7/1/0
Q = Sharp,F.   7/2/0
R = Sutton,M.   35/14/3
S = Toshack,J.   39/11/22
T = Woodruff,R.   21/9/5
U = Morgan,R.   0/0/0

Toshack scores after 28 secs. at Carlisle . . . Injury at Blackpool ends career of Barrie Jones . . . Bobby Woodruff bought for £25,000 . . . 7 successive wins puts City on top - later slump prevents promotion . . . City get 7 in European game . . . Clark scores five in Welsh Cup-tie.

Other Matches

F.A.Cup

	Date	Opposition	Res	Attend.	Goalscorers	1	2	3	4	5	6	7	8	9	10	11	12
3rd	3 Jan	York City	1-1	8439	o.g. (Swallow)	G	D	B	R	O	T	L	E	J	S	C	P
3rd Replay	7	YORK CITY	1-1	21623	Toshack	"	"	"	"	"	"	"	"	"	"	"	A
3/2nd R †	15	York City	1-3	7347	King	"	"	"	"	H	T	"	A	"	"	L	F

Football League Cup

	Date	Opposition	Res	Attend.	Goalscorers	1	2	3	4	5	6	7	8	9	10	11	12
2nd	3 Sep	Crystal Palace	1-3	18616	Lea	"	"	"	"	"	J	K	"	M	"	"	P

Welsh Cup

	Date	Opposition	Res	Attend.	Goalscorers	1	2	3	4	5	6	7	8	9	10	11	12
3rd	21 Jan	BARMOUTH & DYFFRYN	6-1	4901	Clark 5 Toshack	"	"	"	"	"	T	L	"	J	"	C	A
4th	4 Feb	WREXHAM	3-0	12332	Clark 2 King	"	"	"	"	"	"	M	"	"	"	L	C
Semi-final	11 Mar	SWANSEA CITY	2-2	18050	Woodruff Toshack	"	"	"	"	"	"	L	"	"	"	M	A
S/Fin. Rep.	2 May	Swansea City	2-0	16000	Bird King	"	"	"	"	"	J	"	T	M	E	C	S
Final/1 leg	8	Chester	1-0	3087	Bird	"	"	"	"	"	"	M	"	E	L	"	"
Final/2 leg	13	CHESTER	4-0	5567	Woodruff Bird Lea Clark	"	"	"	"	"	"	"	"	"	"	"	"

European Cup Winners Cup

	Date	Opposition	Res	Attend.	Goalscorers	1	2	3	4	5	6	7	8	9	10	11	12
1st 1 Leg	17 Sep	Mjondalen I.F.	7-1	8000	Clark 2 Toshack 2 Lea Sutton King	"	H	D	"	"	J	P	E	M	S	L	K
1st 2 Leg	1 Oct	MJONDALEN I.F.	5-1	14753	King 2 Allan 3	"	D	B	"	"	N	K	"	A	"	"	M
2nd 1 Leg	12 Nov	Goztepe Izmir	0-3	24000		"	"	"	"	"	J	M	"	L	"	Q	A
2nd 2 Leg	26	GOZTEPE IZMIR	1-0	17866	Bird	"	"	"	"	"	"	A	"	M	"	L	C+F

Friendlies

	Date	Opposition	Res	Attend.	Goalscorers
	26 July	Bradford Park Avenue	4-0	3000	King Allan Phillips Clark
	31	S.V. WERDER BREMEN	2-2	8846	Clark 2
	2 Aug	Torquay United	0-2	1722	
	27	Newport County	2-2	3000	Clark King
	5 May	Bridgwater X1	0-1	2000	

Left to right
Back row: DAVID CARVER BOBBY WOODRUFF GARY BELL FRED DAVIES
STEVE DERRETT DON MURRAY BRIAN HARRIS
Front row: PETER KING BRIAN CLARK LESLIE LEA JOHN TOSHACK RONNIE BIRD

1970-71
Football League – Division 2.
Manager: Jimmy Scoular
P:42 W:20 D:13 L:9 64-41 Pts:53 Pos:3rd

1848	Date	Opposition	Res	Attend.	Goalscorers	1	2	3	4	5	6	7	8	9	10	11	12
1.	15 Aug	Leicester City	1-0	27578	Clark	*K	C	A	P	J	H	D	*G	Q	S	I	B
2.	22	MILLWALL	2-2	25299	Toshack King	"	"	"	"	"	"	"	"	S	Q	"	M
3.	26	Sheffield Wed.	2-1	16586	Clark Sutton	"	"	"	"	"	"	"	"	"	"	"	"
4.	29	Bristol City	0-1	24920		"	"	"	"	"	"	"	"	"	"	"	B
5.	2 Sep	SHEFFIELD UNITED	1-1	21455	Clark	"	"	"	"	"	"	"	"	"	"	"	"
6.	5	BIRMINGHAM CITY	2-0	22081	Toshack 2	"	"	"	"	"	"	G	D	"	"	"	"
7.	12	Bolton Wanderers	2-0	10777	Gibson Clark	"	"	"	"	"	"	"	"	"	"	"	"
8.	19	NORWICH CITY	1-1	23768	Clark	"	"	"	"	"	"	"	"	"	"	"	"
9.	26	Orient	0-0	11992		"	"	"	"	"	"	"	"	"	"	"	M
10.	3 Oct	MIDDLESBROUGH	3-4	21072	Clark Woodruff King	"	"	"	"	"	"	"	"	"	"	"	B
11.	10	Watford	1-0	16244	Clark	F	"	"	"	"	"	"	"	"	"	"	M
12.	17	LEICESTER CITY	2-2	25968	Gibson (pen) Carver	"	"	"	"	"	"	"	"	"	"	"	B
13.	24	Carlisle United	1-1	10995	Toshack	"	"	"	"	"	"	"	S	M	"	"	D
14.	28	PORTSMOUTH	1-0	18529	Toshack	"	"	"	"	"	"	"	"	"	"	"	"
15.	31	HULL CITY	5-1	21856	Toshack3 Gibson Phillips	"	"	"	"	"	"	"	Q	"	S	"	"
16.	7 Nov	Q.P.Rangers	1-0	14267	Phillips	"	"	"	"	"	"	"	"	"	"	"	"
17.	14	BLACKBURN ROVERS	4-1	18213	King Clark 2 Woodruff	"	"	"	"	"	"	"	D	"	"	"	L
18.	21	Charlton Athletic	1-2	10762	Woodruff	"	"	"	"	"	"	"	"	"	"	"	B
19.	28	LUTON TOWN	0-0	26689		"	"	"	"	"	"	"	"	"	"	"	O
20.	5 Dec	Oxford United	0-1	12206		"	"	"	"	"	E	"	"	S	*O	"	M
21.	12	SUNDERLAND	3-1	15639	o.g.(Pitt) Phillips Gibson	"	"	"	"	"	"	"	S	M	D	"	B
22.	19	Millwall	1-2	8591	Clark	"	"	"	"	"	H	"	"	"	"	"	E
23.	26	SWINDON TOWN	1-1	24813	Sutton	"	"	"	"	"	"	I	D	"	*R	S	I
24.	9 Jan	SHEFFIELD WED.	4-0	21490	Warboys 2 King Bell	"	"	"	"	"	"	I	G	R	M	*N	D
25.	16	Portsmouth	3-1	24747	Murray Warboys 2	"	"	"	"	"	"	"	"	"	"	"	"
26.	6 Feb	OXFORD UNITED	1-0	14875	Parsons,J.	"	"	"	S	"	"	G	"	D	"	"	L
27.	13	Sunderland	4-0	11566	Clark Parsons,J. o.g.(Irwin) Gibson	"	"	"	P	"	"	"	D	I	R	"	"
28.	20	CHARLTON ATHLETIC	1-1	18034	Gibson (pen)	"	"	"	"	"	"	"	*L	"	D	"	S
29.	27	Hull City	1-1	25091	Warboys	"	"	"	"	"	"	"	D	"	R	"	"
30.	6 Mar	CARLISLE UNITED	4-0	22502	Warboys 4	"	"	"	"	"	"	I	G	R	S	"	D
31.	13	Blackburn Rovers	1-1	10562	Clark	"	"	"	"	"	"	"	"	"	"	"	B
32.	20	Q.P.RANGERS	1-0	23133	Warboys	"	"	"	"	"	"	"	G	"	"	B	D
33.	27	Birmingham City	0-2	49025		"	"	"	"	"	"	"	"	"	"	N	"
34.	3 Apr	BRISTOL CITY	1-0	24687	o.g. (Wimshurst)	"	"	"	"	"	"	G	"	"	"	B	H
35.	7	BOLTON WANDERERS	1-0	21305	Clark	"	"	"	"	"	"	I	D	S	R	"	"
36.	10	Swindon Town	2-2	21158	Warboys 2	"	"	"	"	"	"	G	"	"	"	"	S
37.	13	Middlesbrough	1-1	19559	King	"	"	"	"	"	"	"	"	"	"	I	E
38.	17	WATFORD	0-1	26536		"	"	"	"	"	"	"	D	"	R	"	"
39.	24	Norwich City	2-1	15607	Clark Warboys	"	"	"	"	"	E	"	"	M	"	"	S
40.	27	Sheffield United	1-5	42963	Derrett	"	"	"	"	"	"	"	"	"	"	"	"
41.	1 May	ORIENT	1-0	15750	Clark	"	"	"	"	"	"	"	"	"	"	"	"
42.	4	Luton Town	0-3	10784		"	"	"	"	"	"	"	"	"	"	"	"

Players:

A = Bell,G. 42/16/1
B = Bird,R. 3/4/1
C = Carver,D. 42/16/1
D = Clark,B. 33/13/22
E = Derrett,S. 5/1/2
F = Eadie,J. 32/13/0
G = Gibson,I. 40/14/12
H = Harris,B. 25/9/0
I = King,P. 41/15/10
J = Murray,D. 42/16/2
K = Parsons,F. 10/3/0
L = Parsons,J. 1/2/4
M = Phillips,L. 29/12/4
N = Rees,N. 9/5/1
O = Showers,D. 1/0/0
P = Sutton,M. 41/13/3
Q = Toshack,J. 16/5/13
R = Warboys,A. 17/4/13
S = Woodruff,R. 33/15/5
T = Morgan,R. 0/0/0

Toshack joins Liverpool for £110,000 - fans accuse Club of lack of ambition - replacement, Warboys, scores four in Carlisle match . . . Real Madrid beaten by Clark goal . . . Late season defeats by Watford & Sheffield United end hopes of Promotion. Welsh Cup won again.

Other Matches

F.A.Cup

	Date	Opposition	Res	Attend.	Goalscorers	1	2	3	4	5	6	7	8	9	10	11	12
3rd	2 Jan	BRIGHTON & H.A.	1-0	19338	King	F	C	A	P	J	H	G	S	M	D	I	N
4th	23	BRENTFORD	0-2	23395		"	"	"	"	"	"	I	"	R	M	N	D

Football League Cup

	Date	Opposition	Res	Attend.	Goalscorers	1	2	3	4	5	6	7	8	9	10	11	12
2nd	8 Sep	Q.P.Rangers	0-4	15026		K	"	"	"	"	"	G	D	S	Q	I	B

Welsh Cup

	Date	Opposition	Res	Attend.	Goalscorers	1	2	3	4	5	6	7	8	9	10	11	12
3rd	2 Feb	Newport County	1-1	6162	Clark	F	"	"	"	"	"	I	G	D	M	N	L
3rd Replay	10	NEWPORT COUNTY	4-0	10350	Parsons,J. Gibson Murray King	"	"	"	M	"	"	"	L	S	D	B	G
4th	17	BANGOR CITY	5-0	5019	Gibson Clark Rees Parsons,J. King	"	"	"	S	"	M	G	"	I	"	N	T
Semi-final	31 Mar	CHESTER	0-0	5522		"	"	"	P	"	"	"	D	S	R	B	I
S/final Rep	19 Apr	Chester	2-1	7352	Clark Derrett	"	"	"	E	"	"	"	"	R	S	I	P
Final/ 1 leg	10 May	Wrexham	1-0	14008	Woodruff	"	"	"	P	"	"	I	G	"	"	B	D
Final/ 2 leg	12	WREXHAM	3-1	4587	Bird Gibson 2	"	"	"	"	"	"	"	"	D	"	"	H

European Cup Winners Cup

	Date	Opposition	Res	Attend.	Goalscorers	1	2	3	4	5	6	7	8	9	10	11	12
1st 1 Leg	16 Sep	P.O. LARNACA	8-0	12986	Sutton Gibson Woodruff Clark 2 King Toshack 2	K	"	"	"	"	H	G	D	S	Q	I	M
1st 2 Leg	30	P.O. Larnaca	0-0	10000		"	"	"	"	"	"	"	"	"	"	B	G
2nd 1 Leg	21 Oct	F.C. NANTES	5-1	17905	Toshack 2 Gibson King Phillips	F	"	"	"	"	"	"	D	"	"	N	"
2nd 2 Leg	4 Nov	F.C. Nantes	2-1	10000	Toshack Clark	"	"	"	"	"	"	"	Q	M	S	"	D
Q.F. 1 Leg	10 Mar	REAL MADRID	1-0	47500	Clark	"	"	"	"	"	M	I	G	D	"	N	T
Q.F. 2 Leg	24	Real Madrid	0-2	65000		"	"	"	"	"	"	"	"	"	"	"	H

Friendlies

	Date	Opposition	Res	Attend.	Goalscorers
	1 Aug	Torquay United	3-0	2000	Sutton Gibson King
	4	Plymouth Argyle	5-2	4561	Gibson (pen) Toshack King Sutton Lea
	7	A.D.O. THE HAGUE	2-3	10763	King Toshack

● This was Cardiff City's line-up against Oxford United at home in a Second Division match at home on February 6th,1971, a fortnight after Brentford had won 2-0 at Ninian Park in the Fourth Round of the F.A. Cup.... BACK (from left): Brian Harris, Gary Bell, Mel Sutton, Jim Eadie, Dave Carver, Brian Clark, John Parsons (sub.). FRONT (from left): Peter King, Ian Gibson, Don Murray (Captain), Leighton Phillips, Nigel Rees.

1971-72

Football League – Division 2.

Manager: Jimmy Scoular

P:42 W:10 D:14 L:18 56-69 Pts:34 Pos:19th

1890	Date	Opposition	Res	Attend.	Goalscorers	1	2	3	4	5	6	7	8	9	10	11	12
1.	14 Aug	BURNLEY	2-2	23026	Clark 2	F	B	A	U	O	S	H	C	X	W	*G	M
2.	16	Blackpool	0-3	19253		"	"	"	S	"	E	"	"	"	"	S	Q
3.	21	Orient	1-4	7894	o.g. (Mancini)	P	"	"	U	"	*I	"	Q	W	C	S	M
4.	28	HULL CITY	1-1	17136	Warboys	F	"	"	"	"	S	"	C	"	W	G	Q
5.	31	Bristol City	0-2	23450		"	"	"	"	"	"	"	"	"	"	"	M
6.	4 Sep	Watford	2-2	1-233	Parsons,J. Clark	"	"	"	I	"	"	"	"	U	"	"	Q
7.	11	SHEFFIELD WED.	3-2	17195	Warboys 2 Clark	"	*K	"	U	"	"	"	"	X	"	"	"
8.	18	Middlesbrough	0-1	18288		"	"	"	"	"	"	M	"	"	"	H	T
9.	25	SWINDON TOWN	0-1	16292		"	"	"	"	"	"	H	"	"	"	I	G
10.	2 Oct	Preston North End	2-1	13511	King Clark	"	"	"	I	"	"	M	H	C	X	G	W
11.	9	MILLWALL	1-2	17954	Clark	*J	"	"	U	"	"	H	C	X	W	I	G
12.	16	Burnley	0-3	12459		"	"	"	"	"	"	M	"	"	"	H	Q
13.	23	CHARLTON ATHLETIC	6-1	13092	Clark 2Parsons,J2 Gibson(p)o.g Went	"	B	"	"	"	"	H	Q	"	C	T	G
14.	30	Norwich City	1-2	20814	Clark	"	"	"	"	"	"	"	"	"	"	"	"
15.	6 Nov	Q.P.RANGERS	0-0	16914		"	"	"	"	"	"	"	"	"	"	"	W
16.	13	Fulham	3-4	10700	Warboys Clark 2	"	"	"	"	"	"	*V	C	"	W	H	Q
17.	20	SUNDERLAND	1-2	12735	Gibson	"	"	"	X	"	"	"	"	M	"	X	T
18.	27	Carlisle United	1-2	6835	Parson,J.	"	"	"	"	N	"	"	Q	*D	C	"	E
19.	1 Dec	PORTSMOUTH	3-2	10268	Gibson(pen) Clark Woodruff	"	"	"	S	"	E	"	C	"	X	"	T
20.	11	Luton Town	2-2	10606	Phillips Clark	"	"	"	*L	N	"	"	"	M	"	T	X
21.	18	WATFORD	2-0	11113	King Warboys	"	"	"	"	O	"	"	"	X	W	W	V
22.	27	Birmingham City	0-3	40793		"	"	"	U	"	"	M	"	X	"	T	D
23.	1 Jan	MIDDLESBROUGH	1-0	12773	Clark	"	U	B	"	O	N	"	"	M	"	"	U
24.	8	Hull City	0-0	12678		"	B	A	U	"	S	"	"	X	"	"	X
25.	22	Portsmouth	0-2	11039		"	"	"	"	"	"	"	"	"	"	G	E
26.	29	BLACKPOOL	3-4	11719	Clark Warboys Gibson	"	"	"	X	"	"	"	"	M	"	"	M
27.	12 Feb	Charlton Athletic	2-2	7526	Woodruff Clark	"	"	"	*L	N	"	"	"	"	X	T	W
28.	19	NORWICH CITY	0-0	17706		"	"	"	"	O	"	"	"	"	W	W	V
29.	4 Mar	FULHAM	1-0	13140	Clark	"	"	"	U	"	"	"	"	"	"	T	W
30.	11	Millwall	1-1	13649	Warboys	"	"	"	"	"	"	"	"	L	W	M	T
31.	21	OXFORD UNITED	1-1	14499	Clark	"	"	*R	"	"	"	"	"	"	"	"	"
32.	25	Sheffield Wed.	2-2	12910	Warboys Woodruff	"	"	"	"	"	N	"	"	X	"	"	L
33.	29	PRESTON NORTH END	5-2	13394	Clark Warboys 3 King	"	"	"	"	"	S	"	"	"	"	"	"
34.	1 Apr	BIRMINGHAM CITY	0-0	23692		"	"	"	X	"	"	"	"	M	"	G	Q
35.	4	Swindon Town	1-3	15393	Clark	"	"	"	"	"	"	"	"	"	X	T	W
36.	8	Sunderland	1-1	15224	Sutton	"	"	"	"	"	"	"	"	"	W	W	V
37.	12	ORIENT	1-0	16866	Woodruff	"	"	"	"	"	"	"	"	"	"	W	V
38.	15	CARLISLE UNITED	3-1	17734	King Clark Woodruff	"	"	"	"	"	"	"	"	"	"	T	W
39.	22	Oxford United	0-1	8869		"	"	"	"	"	"	"	"	"	"	M	"
40.	26	BRISTOL CITY	2-3	17249	Warboys Woodruff	"	"	"	"	"	"	"	"	"	W	M	G
41.	29	LUTON TOWN	1-1	12587	Warboys	"	"	"	"	"	"	"	"	"	"	"	L
42.	3 May	Q.P.Rangers	0-3	8430		P	"	A	X	"	"	V	"	M	"	T	H

Players:

A = Bell,G. — 30/13/0
B = Carver,D. — 36/11/0
C = Clark,B. — 42/14/27
D = Couch,A. — 3/0/0
E = Derrett,S. — 5/0/0
F = Eadie,J. — 9/4/0
G = Foggon,A. — 9/7/3
H = Gibson,I. — 40/13/5
I = Hoy,R. — 7/1/0
J = Irwin,W. — 31/10/0
K = Jones,K. — 6/4/0
L = Kellock,W. — 5/6/1
M = King,P. — 22/10/5
N = Morgan,R. — 8/2/0
O = Murray,D. — 36/12/1
P = Parsons,F. — 2/0/0
Q = Parsons,J. — 5/0/4
R = Pethard,F. — 11/1/0
S = Phillips,L. — 41/14/1
T = Rees,N. — 10/1/0
U = Sutton,M. — 30/8/1
V = Villars,A. — 6/2/0
W = Warboys,A. — 34/10/15
X = Woodruff,R. — 34/11/9
Y = Rees,B. — 0/1/0
Z = Showers,D. — 0/0/0

City slump - Ninian Park pitch sinks ! 1000's of tons of sand needed . . . Good F.A.Cup run includes two replays with Sunderland and over 50,000 at Cardiff for Leeds match . . . . Penalty shoot-out ends Europe hopes . . Welsh Cup final defeat

Other Matches

F.A. Cup

	Date	Opposition	Res	Attend.	Goalscorers	1	2	3	4	5	6	7	8	9	10	11	12
3rd	15 Jan	Sheffield United	3-1	29342	Murray Woodruff Carver	J	B	A	U	O	S	H	C	X	W	G	T
4th	9 Feb	SUNDERLAND	1-1	26943	King	"	"	"	X	N	"	"	"	M	"	"	V
4th Replay	14	Sunderland	1-1	39348	Clark	"	"	"	L	O	"	"	"	"	X	Y	E
4th/Rep.†	16	Sunderland	3-1	8868	Clark Woodruff Kellock	"	"	"	"	"	"	"	"	"	"	G	W
5th	26	LEEDS UNITED	0-2	50000		"	"	"	"	"	"	"	"	"	"	"	"

† At Maine Road

Football League Cup

	Date	Opposition	Res	Attend.	Goalscorers	1	2	3	4	5	6	7	8	9	10	11	12
2nd	8 Sep	West Ham United	1-1	24420	Foggon	F	K	"	U	"	"	"	"	X	W	"	Q
2nd Replay	22	WEST HAM UNITED	1-2	30109	Clark	"	"	"	"	"	"	"	"	"	"	I	M

Welsh Cup

	Date	Opposition	Res	Attend.	Goalscorers	1	2	3	4	5	6	7	8	9	10	11	12
5th	3 Jan	Swansea City	2-0	14391	Warboys Clark	J	B	"	"	"	"	"	"	M	X	T	D
6th	22 Feb	Llanelli	1-0	6000	Foggon	"	"	"	L	"	"	"	"	X	G	Z
Semi-final	14 Mar	Rhyl	2-1	5000	Clark Warboys	"	"	R	U	"	"	"	"	L	W	M	T
Final/1 Leg	8 May	Wrexham	1-2	6984	Woodruff	"	"	A	L	N	"	V	"	H	"	"	X
Final/2 Leg	12	WREXHAM	1-1	6508	Foggon	"	"	"	"	U	O	"	"	M	"	G	"

European Cup Winners Cup

	Date	Opposition	Res	Attend.	Goalscorers	1	2	3	4	5	6	7	8	9	10	11	12
1st 1 Leg	15 Sep	Dynamo Berlin	1-1	12000	Gibson	F	K	"	"	"	"	M	"	X	"	H	Q
1st 2 Leg	29	DYNAMO BERLIN	1-1*	12676	Clark	"	"	"	"	"	"	"	"	"	"	"	G

* Lost, 4-5 on penalties.

Friendlies

	Date	Opposition	Res	Attend.	Goalscorers
	31 July	Bournemouth	4-3	4000	Clark 2 Parsons,J. Warboys
	4 Aug	F.C. SHALKE 04	5-3	8236	Clark2 Warboys Parsons,J.
	7	Trowbridge Town	0-1	2500	

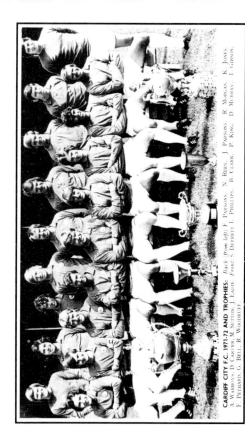

CARDIFF CITY F.C. 1971-72 AND TROPHIES: *Back from left;* F. Parsons, N. Rees, J. Parsons, R. Morgan, K. Jones, A. Warboys, D. Carver, M. Sutton, J. Eadie. *Front:* S. Derrett, L. Phillips, B. Clark, P. King, D. Murray, I. Gibson, F. Pethard, G. Bell, R. Woodruff.

1972-73
Football League – Division 2.

Manager: Jimmy Scoular
P: 42 **W:** 11 **D:** 11 **L:** 20 **F-A:** 43-58 **Pts:** 33 **Pos:** 20th

1932		Date	Opposition	Res	Attend.	Goalscorers	1	2	3	4	5	6	7	8	9	10	11	12
1.	12 Aug		LUTON TOWN	2-1	16364	Bell(pen) Warboys	K	C	B	G	O	*N	H	D	V	c	Z	a
2.	19		Portsmouth	1-3	14067	Showers	"	"	"	"	"	"	"	"	"	"	"	d
3.	26		BLACKPOOL	1-2	12401	Bell(pen)	"	"	"	"	"	"	d	"	"	"	"	a
4.	30		MILLWALL	1-0	10116	Clark	S	U	"	L	"	V	H	"	d	"	a	E
5.	2 Sep		Oxford United	1-2	8082	Rees	"	"	"	"	"	"	"	"	a	d	Y	"
6.	9		ASTON VILLA	0-2	15729		"	"	"	"	R	"	"	"	d	c	Z	Y
7.	16		Carlisle United	0-4	5911		"	C	"	"	O	"	a	"	"	Z	Y	E
8.	19		Nottingham Forest	1-2	6414	Gibson	K	"	"	"	"	"	H	"	E	"	d	Y
9.	23		BRISTOL CITY	1-3	14204	Bell(pen)	"	"	"	"	"	*W	"	"	d	V	* X	"
10.	27		BRIGHTON & H.A.	1-1	9531	Foggon	"	"	"	d	"	"	"	"	V	X	G	L
11.	30		Q.P.Rangers	0-3	11182		"	"	"	"	"	"	"	"	"	"	"	"
12.	7 Oct		Orient	0-0	6284		"	*F	"	V	"	"	"	L	d	G	X	E
13.	14		MIDDLESBROUGH	2-0	10430	Vincent Bell(pen)	"	"	"	"	"	"	Z	T	Z	*b	X	N
14.	21		Burnley	0-3	13140		"	"	"	"	"	"	L	"	"	"	"	Y
15.	28		PRESTON NORTH END	3-0	12208	McCulloch Woodruff 2	"	"	"	"	"	"	"	d	"	"	"	d
16.	4 Nov		Brighton & H.A.	2-2	16387	Murray Kellock	"	"	"	"	"	*Q	"	*P	"	"	a	N
17.	11		NOTTINGHAM FOREST	2-1	12750	McCulloch Woodruff	"	"	"	"	"	"	"	d	d	X	X	Z
18.	18		Huddersfield Town	1-2	5886	Reece	"	"	"	"	"	"	"	P	d	"	"	"
19.	25		FULHAM	3-1	9960	McCulloch 2 Woodruff	"	"	"	"	R	"	"	"	"	G	X	E
20.	9 Dec		SHEFFIELD WED.	4-1	9909	Phillips 2 Woodruff 2	"	"	"	"	"	"	"	"	Z	*b	"	"
21.	16		Hull City	1-1	5875	Kellock	"	"	"	"	"	"	"	"	"	"	"	"
22.	26		Bristol City	0-1	20490		"	"	"	"	"	"	"	"	"	"	X	E
23.	29		PORTSMOUTH	0-2	12382		"	"	"	"	"	*J	"	"	"	"	"	Z
24.	19 Jan		OXFORD UNITED	2-0	7026	McCulloch 2	"	"	"	"	O	W	"	"	I	"	"	E
25.	27		Aston Villa	0-2	25856		"	"	"	"	"	"	"	"	"	"	"	d
26.	10 Feb		CARLISLE UNITED	1-0	7819	McCulloch	"	"	"	"	"	Q	"	"	N	Z	"	"
27.	17		Luton Town	1-1	10442	Woodruff	"	"	"	E	"	"	"	"	d	"	b	"
28.	27		Swindon Town	0-3	9770		"	"	U	N	"	"	b	"	"	"	"	Y
29.	3 Mar		ORIENT	3-1	8463	McCulloch 2 Bell(pen)	"	"	B	M	"	W	"	"	V	V	*A	Z
30.	7		Blackpool	0-1	5303		"	"	"	V	"	"	L	"	Z	b	"	d
31.	10		Middlesbrough	0-2	7686		"	"	"	"	"	"	d	"	"	"	"	e
32.	17		BURNLEY	0-1	11960		"	"	"	"	"	"	U	"	"	"	"	E
33.	24		Preston North End	0-0	6889		"	"	"	"	"	"	X	L	P	"	"	Z
34.	31		Fulham	1-1	6262	McCulloch	"	"	"	E	"	V	L	P	d	E	"	"
35.	7 Apr		SWINDON TOWN	1-1	9438	McCulloch	"	"	"	N	"	Q	"	"	V	b	"	"
36.	14		Sheffield Wed.	0-1	10952		"	"	"	V	"	Q	X	"	V	"	"	I
37.	18		Q.P.RANGERS	0-0	11958		"	"	"	"	"	"	"	"	d	"	"	"
38.	21		HUDDERSFIELD TOWN	4-1	12379	McCulloch 2 Reece 2	"	"	"	"	"	"	"	"	"	"	"	a
39.	23		Sunderland	1-2	27551	Phillips	"	"	"	"	"	"	"	"	"	"	"	U
40.	28		Millwall	1-1	7811	McCulloch	"	"	"	"	"	"	"	"	"	"	"	"
41.	7 May		SUNDERLAND	1-1	22005	McCulloch	"	"	"	"	"	"	"	"	"	"	"	a
42.	9		HULL CITY	0-2	6295	Woodruff	"	"	"	"	"	"	"	b	"	"	"	Z

Players:

A = Anderson,W. 15/3/0
B = Bell,G. 41/11/7
C = Carver,D. 7/2/0
D = Clark,B. 11/2/2
E = Couch,A. 4/2/0
F = Dwyer,P. 31/9/0
G = Foggon,A. 5/2/1
H = Gibson,I. 9/2/1
I = Hoy,R. 7/0/0
J = Impey,J. 1/0/0
K = Irwin,W. 37/11/0
L = Kellock,W. 28/8/4
M = King,P. 1/1/0
N = Lamour,A. 5/3/0
O = Murray,D. 36/9/1
P = McCulloch,A. 26/9/19
Q = Morgan,P. 16/3/0
R = Morgan,R. 6/2/0
S = Parsons,F. 5/0/0
T = Parsons,J. 1/0/0
U = Pethard,F. 6/0/0
V = Phillips,L. 42/11/7
W = Powell,D. 16/4/0
X = Reece,G. 23/5/8
Y = Rees,N. 2/2/1
Z = Showers,D. 16/6/3
a = Villars,A. 5/0/0
b = Vincent,J. 24/8/3
c = Warboys,A. 5/3/0
d = Woodruff,R. 31/4/10
e = Mcinch,J. 0/0/0

Alarming slump - Scoular rings the changes - out go Gibson, Clark and Warboys - in comes Powell and Reece - Vincent costs £40,000 more . . . Dwyer makes debut - Anderson record £60000 fee . . No away wins in League.

Other Matches

F.A. Cup

	Date	Opposition	Res	Attend.	Goalscorers	1	2	3	4	5	6	7	8	9	10	11	12
3rd	13 Jan	Scunthorpe United	3-2	6379	Kellock McCulloch Phillips	K	F	B	V	R	W	L	P	d	b	X	Y
4th	3 Feb	Bolton Wanderers	2-2	24729	Kellock Phillips	"	"	"	"	O	"	"	"	X	"	Y	E
4th Replay	7	BOLTON WANDERERS	1-1	14849	McCulloch	"	"	"	"	"	Q	X	"	L	"	"	"
4th/2 R.†	12	Bolton Wanderers	0-1	6609		"	"	"	"	"	W	L	"	M	Z	b	d

† At The Hawthorns.

Football League Cup

	Date	Opposition	Res	Attend.	Goalscorers	1	2	3	4	5	6	7	8	9	10	11	12
1st	16 Aug	BRISTOL ROVERS	2-2	14540	Bell(pen) Showers	"	C	"	G	"	N	H	D	V	c	Z	"
1st Replay	22	Bristol Rovers	1-3	14550	Clark	"	"	"	"	"	"	"	"	"	"	"	"

Welsh Cup

	Date	Opposition	Res	Attend.	Goalscorers	1	2	3	4	5	6	7	8	9	10	11	12
4th	3 Jan	Aberyswyth Town	7-1	3500	McCulloch 2 Reece 2 Vincent Woodruff 2	"	F	"	V	R	Q	L	P	d	b	X	E
5th	20 Feb	Newport County	3-1	11350	Vincent Phillips Showers	"	"	"	"	O	"	"	"	Z	b	Y	"
Semi-final	21 Mar	Chester	1-0	2158	McCulloch	"	"	"	E	"	V	"	Z	b	A	d	"
Final/1 Leg	4 Apr	Bangor City	0-1	5005		"	"	"	"	"	"	"	"	"	d	"	W
Final/2 Leg	11	BANGOR CITY	5-0	4679	Reece 3 Phillips Bell	"	"	"	N	"	W	X	"	V	b	"	Z

Friendlies

	Date	Opposition	Res	Attend.	Goalscorers
	29 Jul	Plymouth Argyle	1-1	3185	Clark
	2 Aug	Torquay United	2-0	2423	Clark 2
	5	Exeter City	0-1	1900	
	6 Jan	PLYMOUTH ARGYLE	0-3	817	

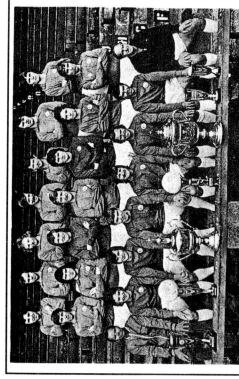

CARDIFF CITY—1972/73. Back row: (left to right): Nigel Rees, Ken Jones, Derek Showers, Ritchie Morgan, Peter King, Alan Warboys, Albert Larmour. Centre: David Carver, Alan Foggon, Frank Parsons, Brian Clark, Bill Irwin, Billy Kellock, Roger Hoy. Front: Lew Clayton (trainer), Freddie Pethard, Leighton Phillips, Don Murray, Ian Gibson, Bobby Woodruff, Gary Bell, Jimmy Scoular

1973-74

Football League – Division 2. Manager: Jimmy Scoular, Frank O'Farrell (from Nov 1973) Jimmy Andrews (from Apr 1974)

P:42 W:10 D:16 L:16 49-62 Pts:36 Pos:17th

1974		Date	Opposition	Res	Attend.	Goalscorers	1	2	3	4	5	6	7	8	9	10	11	12
1.		25 Aug	Carlisle United	1-1	6863	Bell (pen)	J	E	B	*V	P	R	T	U	Z	W	A	I
2.		1 Sep	PORTSMOUTH	1-1	10110	McCulloch	.	.	.	.	.	.	W	N	.	X	.	K
3.		8	Sunderland	1-1	29094	Vincent	.	.	.	.	.	.	.	.	.	.	.	.
4.		12	OXFORD UNITED	5-0	8572	McCulloch3 Villars o.g.(Clarke)	.	.	.	.	.	.	.	.	.	.	.	.
5.		15	FULHAM	0-0	11251		.	.	.	.	.	.	.	.	.	.	K	I
6.		22	Crystal Palace	3-3	17789	o.g.(Blyth) Woodruff Vincent	.	.	.	.	.	.	.	.	.	.	U	K
7.		29	HULL CITY	1-3	10449	Bell	.	.	.	.	.	.	.	.	.	.	.	T
8.		6 Oct	Aston Villa	0-5	24473		.	.	.	.	.	.	T	.	U	Z	K	.
9.		13	BLACKPOOL	1-0	7693	Reece	.	.	.	L	.	.	.	.	.	X	Z	K
10.		20	SHEFFIELD WED.	0-1	7748		.	.	.	V	O	.	.	.	.	.	.	M
11.		24	Oxford United	2-4	6147	Anderson Smith	.	.	.	K	P	.	W	.	T	U	.	U
12.		27	Preston North End	2-2	12050	McCulloch Reece	.	.	.	V	.	.	Z	.	.	X	A	W
13.		3 Nov	WEST BROM. ALBION	0-1	10668		*G	.	.	.	.	.	.	.	.	.	.	.
14.		10	Millwall	0-2	8075		.	.	.	.	.	.	.	.	.	Z	.	I
15.		14	LUTON TOWN	0-0	5839		J	.	.	I	.	.	W	*M	U	.	T	X
16.		17	Middlesbrough	0-3	18034		.	.	.	.	.	.	.	.	.	.	S	.
17.		24	BOLTON WANDERERS	1-0	9606	Reece	.	.	.	S	.	Z	*F	*C	N	W	T	I
18.		1 Dec	Orient	2-1	9564	Woodruff McCulloch	.	.	.	.	.	.	.	N	T	C	W	V
19.		8	NOTTINGHAM FOREST	1-1	10339	Reece	.	.	.	.	.	.	.	.	.	.	R	R
20.		12	Luton Town	0-1	7139		.	.	.	.	.	.	.	.	.	.	.	V
21.		15	BRISTOL CITY	0-1	9388		.	.	.	.	.	.	.	.	.	V	.	A
22.		22	Hull City	1-1	6826	Farrington	.	.	.	.	.	.	.	.	R	C	A	.
23.		26	SWINDON TOWN	2-1	10071	Farrington Murray	.	.	.	.	.	.	.	.	.	.	.	Z
24.		29	SUNDERLAND	4-1	14799	Farrington 3 Anderson	.	.	.	.	.	.	.	.	R	.	.	.
25.		2 Jan	Portsmouth	0-1	20062		.	.	.	I	.	.	.	.	.	.	.	I
26.		12	Fulham	1-0	7413	Farrington	.	.	.	.	.	.	.	.	T	.	.	Z
27.		19	CARLISLE UNITED	2-2	10797	McCulloch Phillips	.	.	.	.	.	W	.	.	R	.	.	T
28.		26	NOTTS. COUNTY	1-0	8454	Phillips	.	.	.	.	.	.	.	.	.	.	.	Y
29.		2 Feb	Bristol City	2-3	24487	Phillips McCulloch	.	.	Q	.	.	R	.	.	.	.	.	.
30.		16	Blackpool	1-2	7410	Farrington	.	.	.	.	.	W	.	.	*Y	.	.	a
31.		23	ASTON VILLA	0-1	12310		.	.	.	S	.	S	.	.	.	Y	T	A
32.		2 Mar	Swindon Town	1-1	5126	Powell	.	.	.	I	.	.	.	.	R	Y	R	T
33.		9	PRESTON NORTH END	2-0	7216	Dwyer Whitham	.	.	.	S	.	W	.	.	.	.	A	T
34.		16	Sheffield Wed.	0-5	13841		.	.	.	.	.	V	.	.	.	U	.	Y
35.		23	MILLWALL	1-3	7662	McCulloch	.	.	.	L	.	W	.	.	.	C	Y	T
36.		30	West Brom. Albion	2-2	10537	Vincent 2 (1 pen)	*H	.	.	*D	.	.	T	X	.	.	A	U
37.		6 Apr	Bolton Wanderers	1-1	14857	Reece	.	.	.	.	O	.	.	.	R	.	.	.
38.		13	MIDDLESBROUGH	3-2	12856	Reece Carlin Vincent	.	.	.	.	.	.	.	.	.	.	.	.
39.		15	Notts. County	1-1	6975	Anderson	.	.	.	.	.	.	.	.	.	.	.	.
40.		20	Nottingham Forest	1-2	11138	Vincent	.	.	.	.	.	.	.	.	.	.	.	.
41.		27	ORIENT	1-1	11640	Reece	.	.	.	.	.	.	.	.	.	.	.	.
42.		30	CRYSTAL PALACE	1-1	26781	Villars	.	.	.	.	.	.	.	.	.	.	.	.

Players:

A = Anderson,W. 27/4/3
B = Bell,G. 29/7/3
C = Carlin,W. 22/2/1
D = Charles,C. 7/2/0
E = Dwyer,P. 42/10/1
F = Farrington,J. 19/15/7
G = Grotier,P. 2/0/0
H = Healey,R. 7/1/0
I = Impey,J. 8/4/2
J = Irwin,W. 33/10/0
K = King,P. 3/2/0
L = Larmour,A. 2/1/0
M = McInch,J. 2/0/0
N = McCulloch,A. 32/7/14
O = Morgan,R. 7/4/0
P = Murray,D. 35/8/2
Q = Pethard,F. 13/4/0
R = Phillips,L. 37/9/3
S = Powell,D. 14/3/0
T = Reece,G. 24/4/10
U = Showers,D. 9/7/2
V = Smith,G. 14/5/1
W = Villars,A. 31/7/3
X = Vincent,J. 17/8/7
Y = Whitham,J. 4/2/1
Z = Woodruff,R. 22/5/3
a = Sayer,P. 0/0/0

George Smith costs £45,000 from Birmingham... Scoular sacked after 9 years ... Frank O'Farrell takes over - pays £62,500 for Farrington ... After less than 6 months O'Farrell leaves! Last gasp point prevents relegation..Peter King quits following long injury.

Other Matches

F.A.Cup

	Date	Opposition	Res	Attend.	Goalscorers	1	2	3	4	5	6	7	8	9	10	11	12
3rd	5 Jan	Birmingham City	2-5	22435	Impey McCulloch	J	E	B	I	P	R	F	N	X	W	A	T

Football League Cup

	Date	Opposition	Res	Attend.	Goalscorers	1	2	3	4	5	6	7	8	9	10	11	12
1st	29 Aug	HEREFORD UNITED	2-0	9821	McCulloch 2	"	"	"	V	"	"	W	"	U	X	"	I
2nd	10 Oct	BURNLEY	2-2	8775	McCulloch Vincent	"	"	"	"	O	"	T	"	"	Z	X	"
2nd Replay	16	Burnley	2-3	12313	Woodruff Bell (pen)	"	"	"	K	"	"	"	"	"	X	Z	S

Welsh Cup

	Date	Opposition	Res	Attend.	Goalscorers	1	2	3	4	5	6	7	8	9	10	11	12
4th	9 Jan	TON PENTRE	1-0	856	Impey	"	"	"	I	P	V	F	C	"	"	W	M
5th	21 Feb	Oswestry	3-1	2500	Reece 2(1 pen) Farrington	"	"	Q	"	"	S	"	N	R	W	T	a
Semi-final	13 Mar	Shrewsbury Town	2-1	1193	Showers Murray	"	"	S	"	W	"	U	C	Y	A
Final/1 Leg	24 Apr	Stourbridge	1-0	5729	Showers	"	L	"	O	"	D	"	V	Y	U	Z	"
Final/2 Leg	6 May	STOURBRIDGE	1-0	4030	Reece	H	E	"	D	O	R	T	W	X	I	A	U

European Cup Winners Cup

	Date	Opposition	Res	Attend.	Goalscorers	1	2	3	4	5	6	7	8	9	10	11	12
1st/1 Leg	19 Sep	SPORTING LISBON	0-0	12000		J	"	B	V	P	"	W	N	Z	X	"	K
1st/2 Leg	3 Oct	Sporting Lisbon	1-2	50000	Villars	"	"	"	Z	"	"	"	"	U	"	K	T

Friendlies

	Date	Opposition	Res	Attend.	Goalscorers
	8 Aug	BIRMINGHAM CITY	1-3	5398	Vincent
	11	TOTTENHAM HOTSPUR	1-3	9418	Reece
	15	Southport	2-1	1000	Reece Dwyer
	18	Tranmere Rovers	2-1	1200	Reece Showers

Back row, from left to right:
GEORGE SMITH, ALBERT LARMOUR, JOHNNY VINCENT, PETER KING, RICHARD MORSE
BILL IRWIN, ROGER HOY, WILLIE ANDERSON, ANDY McCULLOCH, PETER MORGAN

Front row, from left to right:
PHILIP DWYER, RICHIE MORGAN, DAVE POWELL, GARY BELL, DON MURRAY,
FREDDIE PETHARD, BOBBY WOODRUFF, LEIGHTON PHILLIPS, GILBERT REECE

1974-75

Football League – Division 2.
Manager: Jimmy Andrews

P:42 **W:**9 **D:**14 **L:**19 **36-62** **Pts:**32 **Pos:**21st (Rel.)

2016	Date	Opposition	Res	Attend.	Goalscorers	1	2	3	4	5	6	7	8	9	10	11	12
1.	17 Aug	OXFORD UNITED	1-1	10000	Charles	I	E	D	R	P	W	X	V	T	M	A	J
2.	24	Fulham	0-4	8119		"	"	"	"	"	"	"	"	Y	"	"	T
3.	27	York City	0-1	5532		"	"	Q	W	"	R	Y	M	T	M	"	J
4.	31	MANCHESTER UNITED	0-1	22500		"	L	"	"	"	"	M	D	Z	T	"	U
5.	7 Sep	Sheffield Wed.	2-1	9850	Anderson Reece	"	"	"	X	"	"	"	"	V	"	"	"
6.	14	BRISTOL CITY	0-1	8856		"	J	"	"	"	"	"	"	"	"	"	B
7.	21	Portsmouth	2-2	9519	Showers Vincent	"	"	"	"	"	S	F	Y	"	M	D	U
8.	24	Blackpool	0-4	5579		"	E	"	"	"	"	"	"	"	"	"	"
9.	28	HULL CITY	1-2	5672	Reece	"	"	"	"	"	"	A	"	"	T	*U	D
10.	5 Oct	Bristol Rovers	0-1	10410		K	"	"	"	O	"	F	"	"	Y	A	J
11.	12	WEST BROM. ALBION	0-2	6723		"	"	"	"	"	"	"	W	"	"	"	T
12.	16	YORK CITY	3-2	5883	Vincent 2 (1 pen) Reece	"	"	"	*C	"	"	T	"	"	*G	"	Y
13.	19	Bolton Wanderers	1-2	9439	Buchanan	"	"	"	"	"	W	"	"	Y	"	"	"
14.	26	OLDHAM ATHLETIC	3-1	6751	Vincent Buchanan Finnieston	"	"	"	"	"	"	"	"	"	"	"	L
15.	2 Nov	SUNDERLAND	2-0	9883	Finnieston Anderson(pen)	"	"	"	"	"	L	"	W	"	"	"	J
16.	9	Orient	1-1	6412	Dwyer	"	"	"	"	"	"	"	"	"	"	"	"
17.	16	NOTTINGHAM FOREST	2-1	9401	Dwyer Showers	"	"	"	"	"	"	"	"	"	"	"	J
18.	29	SOUTHAMPTON	2-2	10654	Whitham Showers	"	"	"	"	"	"	"	"	"	Z	"	Y
19.	7 Dec	Norwich City	1-1	17685	Reece	"	"	"	"	"	"	"	"	"	G	"	J
20.	11	FULHAM	0-0	8485		"	"	"	"	"	"	"	"	"	"	"	Y
21.	14	Oxford United	0-1	8107		"	"	"	"	"	"	"	"	"	"	"	J
22.	21	NOTTS. COUNTY	0-0	6671		"	"	"	"	"	"	Y	"	"	Z	"	N
23.	26	Bristol City	0-0	12485		"	"	"	"	"	"	T	"	"	"	"	J
24.	28	ASTON VILLA	3-1	11040	Showers Buchanan Whitham	"	"	"	"	"	"	X	"	"	"	"	J
25.	11 Jan	NORWICH CITY	2-1	11637	Reece 2	"	"	"	"	"	"	"	"	"	T	"	Z
26.	25	Millwall	1-5	8101	Reece	"	"	"	"	"	"	"	"	"	"	"	J
27.	1 Feb	ORIENT	0-0	8011		"	"	"	"	"	"	"	"	"	"	"	"
28.	8	Sunderland	1-3	29315	Anderson	"	"	"	"	"	"	Y	"	"	"	"	Z
29.	14	MILLWALL	0-1	6598		"	"	"	W	"	"	X	C	Z	Y	"	X
30.	22	Nottingham forest	0-0	12806		"	"	"	C	"	"	*H	"	V	"	"	U
31.	1 Mar	Manchester United	0-4	43601		"	*B	"	"	"	"	"	Y	"	T	"	M
32.	8	BLACKPOOL	1-1	8134	Reece	"	"	"	"	"	"	W	E	E	D	"	Y
33.	15	Hull City	1-1	5248	Showers	"	"	"	"	"	"	W	T	E	D	"	V
34.	22	SHEFFIELD	0-0	6637		"	"	"	"	E	"	"	D	V	T	"	Y
35.	29	Notts. County	2-0	8105	Dwyer Charles	"	"	"	"	O	"	A	"	"	E	U	"
36.	2 Apr	PORTSMOUTH	1-0	9892	Sayer	"	"	"	"	"	"	"	"	"	"	"	"
37.	5	Oldham Athletic	0-4	10243		"	"	"	"	"	"	"	"	"	"	"	"
38.	9	Aston Villa	0-2	32748		"	"	"	"	"	"	Y	"	Z	"	"	J
39.	12	BRISTOL ROVERS	2-2	13928	Dwyer McClelland	"	"	"	"	"	"	"	M	T	J	Y	N
40.	19	West Brom. Albion	0-2	10182		"	"	"	"	E	O	U	T	V	D	*N	Y
41.	22	Southampton	0-2	14273		"	"	"	E	"	"	"	W	T	Y	A	"
42.	26	BOLTON WANDERERS	1-2	6396	Reece	"	"	"	"	"	"	C	Z	"	"	"	H

Players:

A = Anderson,W. 37/9/3
B = Attley,B. 11/3/0
C = Buchanan,J. 29/6/5
D = Charles,C. 15/2/2
E = Dwyer,P. 37/7/6
F = Farrington,J. 4/1/0
G = Finnieston,S. 9/0/2
H = Giles,D. 3/3/1
I = Healey,R. 9/2/0
J = Impey,J. 4/0/0
K = Irwin,W. 33/7/0
L = Larmour,A. 30/7/1
M = McInch,J. 9/2/1
N = McClelland,J. 1/2/1
O = Morgan,R. 31/4/0
P = Murray,D. 9/3/0
Q = Pethard,F. 41/9/0
R = Phillips,L. 6/1/0
S = Powell,D. 6/2/0
T = Reece,G. 29/6/10
U = Sayer,P. 8/1/1
V = Showers,D. 33/7/8
W = Smith,G. 29/4/0
X = Villars,A. 14/6/0
Y = Vincent,J. 17/2/4
Z = Whitham,J. 8/1/2
a = Pontin,K. 0/2/0

'No money for new players' - Chairman Goldstone tells manager Andrews .. all season struggle ends in relegation . . . Leighton Phillips sold to Villa for £80,000 . . . Farrington and Northampton's Buchanan swop Murray plays last game for City

Other Matches

F.A.Cup

	Date	Opposition	Res	Attend.	Goalscorers	1	2	3	4	5	6	7	8	9	10	11	12
3rd	4 Jan	Leeds United	1-4	31572	Showers	K	E	Q	C	O	L	T	W	V	Z	A	X

Football League Cup

	Date	Opposition	Res	Attend.	Goalscorers	1	2	3	4	5	6	7	8	9	10	11	12
1st	19 Aug	Bristol City	1-2	8813	McInch	"	Q	D	W	P	R	X	V	T	M	"	J

Welsh Cup

	Date	Opposition	Res	Attend.	Goalscorers	1	2	3	4	5	6	7	8	9	10	11	12
4th	14 Jan	HEREFORD UNITED	2-0	3515	Showers Reece	"	E	Q	C	O	L	X	W	V	T	"	Z
5th	19 Feb	OSWESTRY TOWN	4-0	1296	Buchanon Showers Giles o.g.(Morgan)	"	"	"	"	"	"	"	H	"	"	"	U
Semi-final	11 Mar	Newport County	1-0	3808	Dwyer	"	B	"	"	"	"	H	E	T	Y	"	"
Final/1 Leg	5 May	Wrexham	1-2	6862	Buchanan	"	"	"	"	"	a	"	"	"	N	"	X
Final/2 Leg	12	WREXHAM	1-3	5280	Larmour	"	"	"	"	"	"	X	"	V	"	"	T

European Cup Winners Cup

	Date	Opposition	Res	Attend.	Goalscorers	1	2	3	4	5	6	7	8	9	10	11	12
1st/1 Leg	18 Sep	Ferencvaros	0-2	20000		I	Q	D	S	P	"	F	V	X	M	"	J
1st/2 Leg	2 Oct	FERENCVAROS	1-4	4229	Dwyer	"	E	Q	X	"	S	A	W	V	T	Y	F+J

D. Murray, L. Phillips, G. Smith, D. Showers, W. Irwin, F. Pethard, R. Healey, J. Whitham, J. Vincent, J. Impey,
W. Anderson
J. Farrington, D. Powell, P. Dwyer, G. Reece, J. Andrews, G. Bell, R. Morgan, A. Villars, C. Charles

Friendlies

†	31 Jul	ARSENAL	1-2	10327	Whitham
	3 Aug	Aldershot	2-2	1764	Reece Murray
	10	AFC Bournemouth	1-0	2120	Vincent

† Fred Keenor Cup

1975-76

Football League – Division 3.

Manager: Jimmy Andrews
P: 46 **W:** 22 **D:** 13 **L:** 11 **69-48** **Pts:** 57 **Pos:** 2nd (Prom.)

2062	Date	Opposition	Res	Attend.	Goalscorers	1	2	3	4	5	6	7	8	9	10	11	12
1.	16 Aug	Grimsby Town	0-2	6283		M	C	F	D	*I	O	V	*G	S	R	*H	K
2.	23	BURY	1-1	6664	Villars	"	I	"	C	*J	"	"	"	"	*P	"	"
3.	30	Brighton & H.A.	1-0	11353	Villars	"	"	"	"	"	"	"	"	U	"	*K	B
4.	6 Sep	CRYSTAL PALACE	0-1	10479		"	C	"	I	"	"	"	"	"	"	"	S
5.	13	Mansfield Town	4-1	6682	Giles Dwyer Reece 2(1pen)	"	"	"	"	"	"	"	"	S	"	"	U
6.	20	HALIFAX TOWN	0-0	8035		"	"	"	"	Q	"	L	"	"	"	"	Q
7.	22	Port Vale	1-2	5143	Attley	"	"	"	"	J	"	V	"	"	"	"	L
8.	27	Preston North End	1-3	8103		"	"	"	"	"	"	"	"	"	"	"	"
9.	4 Oct	WREXHAM	3-0	7653	Dwyer 2 Evans	"	"	"	"	"	"	D	"	K	"	B	S
10.	11	Rotherham United	0-1	4272		"	"	"	"	"	"	"	K	G	"	"	R
11.	18	SHEFFIELD WED.	2-0	7930	Evans o.g.(Quinn)	"	"	"	"	"	"	"	S	K	"	"	G
12.	22	Aldershot	1-2	3678	Anderson (pen)	"	"	"	"	"	"	"	G	"	"	"	R
13.	25	Chester	1-1	5342	Evans	"	"	"	"	"	"	"	"	"	"	"	B
14.	31	CHESTERFIELD	4-3	7512	Alston 2 Evans Anderson	"	"	"	"	"	"	V	P	"	*A	B	S
15.	4 Nov	WALSALL	0-0	8884		N	R	"	"	"	"	"	"	"	"	"	C
16.	8	Gillingham	2-2	6391	Anderson Evans	"	"	"	"	"	"	"	"	"	"	"	S
17.	15	COLCHESTER UNITED	2-0	6781	Evans Alston	"	I	"	S	"	"	L	"	"	"	"	D
18.	29	SHREWSBURY TOWN	3-0	8002	Anderson Evans Alston	"	"	"	"	"	"	D	"	"	"	"	L
19.	6 Dec	Millwall	3-1	6092	Reece 2 Evans	"	"	"	"	"	"	"	"	"	"	"	C
20.	22	SOUTHEND UNITED	3-1	9342	Evans 2 Alston	"	"	"	"	"	"	"	"	"	"	"	L
21.	26	Swindon Town	0-4	10003		"	"	"	"	"	"	L	"	"	"	"	C
22.	27	PETERBOROUGH UTD.	5-2	16094	Anderson Dwyer2 Evans2	"	"	"	"	"	"	D	"	"	"	"	L
23.	10 Jan	BRIGHTON & H.A.	0-1	17728		"	"	"	"	"	"	"	"	"	"	"	V
24.	17	Halifax Town	1-1	2399	England	"	"	"	V	"	"	"	"	"	"	"	R
25.	20	MANSFIELD TOWN	1-0	10161	Evans	"	"	"	S	"	"	"	"	"	"	"	V
26.	31	ALDERSHOT	1-0	8934	Alston	"	"	"	"	"	"	"	"	"	"	"	T
27.	4 Feb	Hereford United	1-4	12962	Buchanan	"	R	"	V	"	"	"	"	"	"	"	"
28.	7	Walsall	3-2	7109	Alston 2 Dwyer	M	I	"	R	Q	"	"	"	"	"	"	V
29.	14	GILLINGHAM	4-1	11025	Livermore Buchanan Evans Alston	"	"	"	"	"	"	"	"	"	"	T	J
30.	21	Colchester United	2-3	3248	Dwyer Anderson (pen)	"	"	"	"	"	"	L	"	"	"	B	T
31.	25	PORT VALE	2-0	9129	Livermore	"	R	"	"	I	"	D	"	"	"	"	L
32.	28	CHESTER	2-0	10000	Alston Buchanon	"	"	"	"	"	"	D	"	"	"	"	R
33.	6 Mar	Chesterfield	1-1	4095	Alston	"	"	"	*E	"	J	"	"	"	"	"	"
34.	8	Wrexham	1-1	5674	Evans	"	"	"	T	J	O	"	"	"	"	G	U
35.	13	ROTHERHAM UNITED	1-1	11072	Aslton	"	"	"	"	Q	J	"	"	"	"	"	T
36.	17	Sheffield Wed.	3-1	8869	Evans Charles Clark	"	"	"	"	"	"	"	"	"	"	"	"
37.	20	Shrewsbury Town	1-3	7573	Evans	"	"	"	"	I	"	"	"	"	"	"	R
38.	27	MILLWALL	0-0	12511		"	R	"	"	"	"	L	"	"	"	"	T
39.	29	Southend United	2-0	4596	Dwyer Evans	"	"	"	"	J	"	D	"	"	"	"	T
40.	3 Apr	GRIMSBY TOWN	2-1	9645	Evans Buchanan	"	"	R	"	"	O	"	"	"	"	B	G
41.	7	PRESTON NORTH END	1-0	12447	Evans	"	I	"	"	J	"	D	"	"	"	"	T
42.	10	Crystal Palace	1-0	25603	Alston	"	"	"	"	"	"	T	"	"	"	"	"
43.	14	HEREFORD UNITED	2-0	35549	Livermore Campbell	"	"	"	"	"	"	"	"	"	"	"	S
44.	17	SWINDON TOWN	0-0	23438		"	"	"	"	"	"	L	"	"	"	S	G
45.	19	Peterborough Utd.	0-0	6846		"	"	"	"	"	"	"	"	"	"	B	"
46.	4 May	Bury	1-0	7135	Alston	"	"	"	"	"	"	T	"	"	"	"	F

Players:

A = Alston 33/9/20
B = Anderson,A. 28/9/6
C = Attley,W. 14/1/1
D = Buchanan,B. 27/7/5
E = Campbell,A. 14/3/1
F = Charles,C. 39/12/1
G = Clark,B. 19/7/4
H = Durrell,J. 2/1/0
I = Dwyer,P. 45/14/10
J = England,M. 40/8/1
K = Evans,A. 44/13/31
L = Giles,D. 8/4/1
M = Healey,R. 33/8/0
N = Irwin,W. 13/6/0
O = Larmour,A. 39/11/0
P = Livermore,D. 45/13/4
Q = Morgan,R. 10/4/0
R = Pethard,F. 17/10/1
S = Reece,G. 18/5/7
T = Sayer,P. 6/4/0
U = Showers,D. 2/1/0
V = Villars,A. 10/3/2
W = Pontin,K. 0/1/0
X = Morgan,M. 0/0/0

Brian Clark, Mike England and Tony Evans arrive, free transfers Doug Livermore costs £18,000 from Norwich... After Alston's transfer from Luton - form picks up. Late unbeaten run results in promotion.. Nearly 36,000 at Ninian Park for Hereford victory.

Other Matches

F.A. Cup

	Date	Opposition	Res	Attend.	Goalscorers	1	2	3	4	5	6	7	8	9	10	11	12
1st	22 Nov	EXETER CITY	6-2	7538	Alston 3 Reece 2 Evans	N	I	F	S	J	O	D	P	K	A	B	L
2nd	13 Dec	WYCOMBE WANDS.	1-0	11607	Evans	"	"	R	"	"	"	"	"	"	"	"	"
3rd	3 Jan	Orient	1-0	8031	Alston	"	"	F	"	Q	"	V	"	"	"	"	C
4th	24	Southend United	1-2	5812	Evans	"	"	"	R	"	"	D	"	"	"	"	T

Football League Cup

	Date	Opposition	Res	Attend.	Goalscorers	1	2	3	4	5	6	7	8	9	10	11	12
1st/1 Leg	20 Aug	BRISTOL ROVERS	1-2	6688	Reece (pen)	M	"	"	D	J	"	V	G	S	R	H	K
1st/2 Leg	26	Bristol Rovers	1-1	7220	Clark	"	C	"	"	"	"	"	"	"	P	K	D

Welsh Cup

	Date	Opposition	Res	Attend.	Goalscorers	1	2	3	4	5	6	7	8	9	10	11	12
5th	14 Jan	SULLY	5-0	3260	Evans 3 Livermore Buchanan	N	I	"	T	"	"	D	P	S	A	B	X
6th	17 Feb	SWANSEA CITY	1-1	5812	o.g. (Bruton)	M	"	"	R	Q	"	"	"	"	"	"	T
6th Replay	2 Mar	Swansea City	3-0	10056	Clark Alston 2	"	"	"	"	"	J	"	"	"	"	G	"
Semi-Final	23	Chester	0-0	3743		"	R	"	E	W	I	L	"	"	"	"	"
S/Fin. Rep.	1 Apr	CHESTER	1-0	4244	o.g. (Dunleavy)	"	"	"	"	J	"	T	"	"	G	B	D
Fin./1Leg †	29	Hereford United	2-2	6980	Evans 2	"	I	R	"	"	"	L	"	"	A	"	G
Final/2 Leg	18 May	HEREFORD UNITED	3-3	3709	Evans Dwyer 2	"	"	F	L	I	"	T	"	"	U	G	C
Final	19	HEREFORD UNITED	3-2	2648	Pethard Clark Evans	N	"	"	"	"	"	"	"	"	G	B	U

† Match declared void

Friendlies

	Date	Opposition	Res	Attend.	Goalscorers
	26 Jul	BIRMINGHAM CITY	1-4	2081	Clark
	30	BRISTOL CITY	0-1	1700	
	2 Aug	Reading	1-1	1300	Showers
	9	Torquay United	1-1	1000	Clark
	11 May	BRISTOL CITY	1-2	5867	Clark
‡	15	Hereford United	0-2	3500	

‡ Hereford Senior Cup

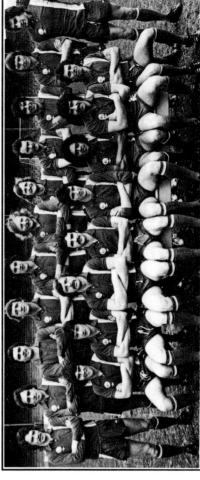

● Cardiff City's squad in May 1976, a few weeks after the 2-0 win over Hereford United seen by 35,549…. BACK (from left): Freddie Pethard, Doug Livermore, Ron Healey, Brian Clark, Keith Pontin, Derek Showers, John Buchanan, Tony Villars, Willie Anderson, Albert Larmour, Phil Dwyer. FRONT (from left): David Giles, Peter Sayer, Richie Morgan, Tony Evans, Adrian Alston, Clive Charles, Alan Campbell, Brian Attley. Absent from picture – Gil Reece, Mike England, Bill Irwin.

1976-77

Football League – Division 2.   Manager: Jimmy Anderson

P:42 W:12 D:10 L:20 56-67 Pts:34 Pos:18th

#	Date	Opposition	Res	Attend.	Goalscorers	1	2	3	4	5	6	7	8	9	10	11	12
1.	21 Aug	Charlton Athletic	2-0	9762	Showers 2	M	Q	F	E	*R	N	S	O	T	A	B	C
2.	25	BRISTOL ROVERS	1-2	12680	Charles (pen)	"	"	"	"	"	"	"	"	"	"	"	D
3.	28	BLACKBURN ROVERS	2-1	11871	Alston Showers	"	"	"	"	"	"	"	"	"	H	"	A
4.	4 Sep	Oldham Athletic	2-3	8503	Evans Livermore	"	"	C	"	"	"	"	"	H	T	"	D
5.	11	NOTTS. COUNTY	2-3	11989	Showers Buchanan	"	"	F	"	P	"	"	"	"	"	"	"
6.	18	Orient	0-3	5743		"	"	"	"	"	"	D	"	"	A	"	S
7.	24	MILLWALL	0-0	10352		"	G	"	D	"	"	S	"	"	"	T	Q
8.	2 Oct	Chelsea	1-2	28409	Charles (pen)	"	C	"	"	"	"	"	"	"	"	B	E
9.	9	BOLTON WANDERERS	3-2	11007	Alston(pen) Buchanan Evans	"	G	"	"	G	"	"	"	"	"	"	"
10.	16	Plymouth Argyle	2-2	14198	Evans Dwyer	"	"	"	"	*U	"	"	"	"	"	"	Q
11.	23	BLACKPOOL	2-2	12178	Evans 2	"	"	Q	"	"	"	"	"	"	"	"	C
12.	30	SHEFFIELD UNITED	0-2	12056		"	"	"	"	"	"	"	"	"	"	"	F
13.	6 Nov	Fulham	2-1	12366	Buchanan Evans	L	"	"	"	"	"	"	"	"	T	"	A
14.	13	SOUTHAMPTON	1-0	15190	Dwyer	"	"	"	"	"	"	"	"	"	"	"	K
15.	20	Luton Town	1-2	8845	Evans	"	"	"	"	"	"	"	"	"	"	"	A
16.	27	NOTTINGHAM FOREST	0-3	12770		"	"	"	"	"	"	"	"	"	"	"	"
17.	4 Dec	Burnley	0-0	8959		"	"	"	"	C	"	*K	"	"	A	E	S
18.	11	HULL CITY	1-1	8310	Buchanan	"	C	"	"	G	"	"	"	"	"	"	"
19.	18	Carlisle United	3-4	5934	Sayer Buchanan Evans	"	"	"	"	"	"	"	"	"	"	"	"
20.	27	HEREFORD UNITED	3-1	14465	Giles Evans 2	"	"	F	"	"	"	"	"	"	T	S	J
21.	1 Jan	FULHAM	3-0	20266	Buchanan Friday 2	"	G	"	"	U	"	"	"	"	*I	"	C
22.	15	Bristol Rovers	1-1	9272	Evans	"	"	C	J	"	"	"	"	"	"	"	B
23.	22	CHARLTON ATHLETIC	1-1	11153	Went	"	"	"	"	"	"	"	"	"	"	"	"
24.	5 Feb	Blackburn Rovers	1-2	9516	Sayer	"	"	"	D	"	"	"	K	T	S	J	E
25.	12	OLDHAM ATHLETIC	3-1	12708	Friday Evans Sayer	"	"	"	"	"	"	D	G	H	I	S	J
26.	19	Notts. County	0-1	9401		"	"	"	"	"	"	N	"	"	"	"	"
27.	2 Mar	ORIENT	0-1	9357		"	"	"	S	"	"	K	"	S	"	J	D
28.	5	Millwall	2-0	9479	Evans 2	"	"	F	"	"	Q	"	"	"	"	"	"
29.	8	Sheffield United	0-3	12907		"	"	"	"	"	"	"	"	"	T	"	"
30.	12	CHELSEA	1-3	20194	Dwyer	"	"	"	J	"	"	"	"	"	"	S	J
31.	26	PLYMOUTH ARGYLE	0-1	9587		"	"	C	E	"	Q	D	"	T	D	D	J
32.	2 Apr	Blackpool	0-1	7531		"	"	"	"	"	"	"	"	H	D	S	K
33.	6	Hereford United	2-2	7670	Sayer 2 (1 pen)	"	"	"	"	"	"	K	"	"	"	"	"
34.	9	WOLVERHAMPTON W.	2-2	15445	Sayer Went	"	"	"	"	"	"	D	K	"	D	"	O
35.	11	Southampton	2-3	22674	Friday Evans	"	"	"	"	"	"	N	G	I	S	J	J
36.	16	LUTON TOWN	4-2	10460	Sayer Friday 2 Dwyer	"	C	Q	"	"	N	"	"	"	I	"	J
37.	23	Nottingham Forest	1-0	20646	Sayer	"	R	C	"	"	Q	"	"	S	T	S	"
38.	26	Wolverhampton W.	1-4	21234	Sayer	"	C	Q	"	"	R	"	"	"	"	"	"
39.	30	BURNLEY	0-1	11064		M	"	"	"	"	"	"	"	"	"	"	"
40.	7 May	Hull City	2-1	3511	Buchanan 2 (1 pen)	L	G	"	"	"	N	O	S	H	I	D	K
41.	10	Bolton Wanderers	1-2	22060	Buchanan (pen)	"	"	"	"	"	"	"	"	"	"	"	"
42.	14	CARLISLE UNITED	1-1	15801	Campbell	"	"	"	"	"	"	"	"	K	"	"	T

Players:

A = Alston,A. 11/7/4
B = Anderson,W. 15/5/0
C = Attley,B. 21/6/0
D = Buchanan,J. 27/10/10
E = Campbell,A. 21/9/1
F = Charles,C. 14/7/2
G = Dwyer,P. 36/9/5
H = Evans,A. 34/13/24
I = Friday,R. 18/4/7
J = Giles,D. 11/6/4
K = Grapes,S. 22/7/1
L = Healey,R. 29/12/0
M = Irwin,W. 13/3/0
N = Lamour,A. 35/15/0
O = Livermore,D. 37/14/1
P = Morgan,R. 3/3/0
Q = Pethard,F. 26/9/1
R = Pontin,K. 7/5/0
S = Sayer,P. 37/11/12
T = Showers,D. 15/4/5
U = Went,P. 30/6/2

Battle against instant relegation. Final game 1-1 draw ensures survival ... Alston, Anderson & Charles join America exodus ... £30,000 paid for Paul Went from Portsmouth ... Robin Friday arrives from Reading ... All three F.A.Cup games on T.V.

Other Matches

F.A. Cup

	Date	Opposition	Res	Attend.	Goalscorers	1	2	3	4	5	6	7	8	9	10	11	12
3rd	8 Jan	TOTTENHAM HOTSPUR	1–0	27868	Sayer	L	G	C	D	U	N	K	O	H	"	J	R
4th	29	WREXHAM	3–2	28953	Giles Sayer Buchanan	"	"	"	"	"	"	"	"	"	S	"	B
5th	26 Feb	EVERTON	1–2	35582	Evans	"	"	"	"	"	"	"	"	"	"	"	T

Football League Cup

	Date	Opposition	Res	Attend.	Goalscorers	1	2	3	4	5	6	7	8	9	10	11	12
1st/1 Leg	14 Aug	BRISTOL ROVERS	2–1	8496	Evans Alston (pen)	"	Q	F	E	R	"	S	"	"	A	B	D
1st/2 Leg	17	Bristol Rovers	4–4	5592	Evans 4	"	"	"	"	"	"	"	"	"	"	"	T
2nd	1 Sep	Q.P. RANGERS	1–3	23618	Evans	M	"	S	"	"	"	O	T	"	"	"	C

Welsh Cup

	Date	Opposition	Res	Attend.	Goalscorers	1	2	3	4	5	6	7	8	9	10	11	12
5th	19 Jan	STOURBRIDGE	2–0	1782	Dwyer Giles	L	G	C	J	U	"	K	O	"	I	S	B
6th	16 Feb	Bangor City	2–0	5000	Giles Grapes	"	"	"	D	"	"	"	"	"	"	"	J
Semi-final	16 Mar	Bridgend Town	2–1	2000	Sayer Evans	"	"	F	J	"	"	"	"	"	S	D	T
Final/1 Leg	16 May	SHREWSBURY TOWN	2–1	2907	Pethard Friday	"	"	Q	E	R	"	"	S	"	I	"	T
Final/2 Leg	18	Shrewsbury Town	0–3	3178		"	"	"	"	"	"	J	S	T	"	"	K

European Cup Winners Cup

	Date	Opposition	Res	Attend.	Goalscorers	1	2	3	4	5	6	7	8	9	10	11	12
Prel. 1/Leg	4 Aug	SERVETTE GENEVA	1–0	10226	Evans	"	Q	F	"	P	"	D	O	H	A	T	J
Prel. 2/Leg	18	Servette Geneva	1–2	21500	Shopwers	"	"	"	"	"	"	S	"	"	"	"	D
1st 1/Leg	15 Sep	DYNAMO TBILISI	1–0	11181	Alston	M	"	"	"	"	"	D	"	"	"	B	T + S
1st 2/Leg	29	Dynamo Tbilisi	0–3	100000		"	"	C	F	G	"	"	"	"	"	"	B + S

Friendlies

	Date	Opposition	Res	Attend.	Goalscorers
	30 Jul	Pwllheli & District	3–1	1200	Evans 2 Alston
	31	Bangor City	0–2	1500	

(Back) Anderson, Evans, Healey, Irwin, Lamour, Buchanan. (Centre) Campbell, Attley, Showers, Dwyer, Giles. (Front) Sayer, Alston, Livemore, Andrews (Manager), Morgan, Charles, Pethard.

1977-78

Football League – Division 2. Manager: Jimmy Anderson P:42 W:13 D:12 L:17 51-71 Pts:38 Pos:19th

2146

#	Date	Opposition	Res	Attend.	Goalscorers	1	2	3	4	5	6	7	8	9	10	11	12
1.	20 Aug	BRISTOL ROVERS	1-1	7603	Went	K	F	A	C	T	M	J	N	*G	R	I	B
2.	27	Blackburn Rovers	0-3	7088		L	"	"	E	"	"	P	*B	*Q	"	"	D
3.	3 Sep	TOTTENHAM HOTSPUR	0-0	8901		"	"	"	"	"	"	*D	C	"	"	"	B
4.	10	Notts. County	1-1	7330	Dwyer	"	"	"	"	"	"	"	"	"	"	"	J
5.	17	MANSFIELD TOWN	1-1	6896	Robson	"	"	"	"	"	P	"	"	G	Q	"	J
6.	24	FULHAM	3-1	8810	Robson Evans 2	"	"	"	"	"	"	"	R	"	"	R	I
7.	1 Oct	Blackpool	0-3	8605		"	"	"	"	"	"	"	N	"	"	C	N
8.	4	Sunderland	1-1	18484	Livermore	"	"	"	"	"	"	"	R	"	"	"	O
9.	8	LUTON TOWN	1-4	8276	Dwyer	"	"	"	"	"	"	"	R	"	"	"	N
10.	15	Orient	1-2	5444	Grapes	"	"	"	"	"	"	J	O	R	A	"	I
11.	22	OLDHAM ATHLETIC	1-0	6910	Went	"	"	O	"	"	"	"	R	Q	"	"	D
12.	29	Brighton & H.A.	0-4	22704		"	A	"	"	"	"	"	"	"	H	"	I
13.	5 Nov	STOKE CITY	2-0	8428	Dwyer Sayer	"	*S	"	"	"	"	I	F	R	Q	J	A
14.	12	Hull City	1-4	5228	Sayer (pen)	"	"	"	"	"	"	"	"	"	"	"	"
15.	19	BURNLEY	2-1	7085	Dwyer Sayer (pen)	"	A	"	"	"	S	"	"	"	"	C	C
16.	26	Crystal Palace	0-2	16139		"	"	"	"	"	D	"	"	"	"	"	P
17.	3 Dec	SHEFFIELD UNITED	1-6	6409	Buchanan	"	"	"	"	"	S	"	"	"	"	"	B
18.	10	Bolton Wanderers	3-6	16090	Robson Sayer Bishop	"	F	"	"	"	P	"	R	Q	"	"	"
19.	17	HULL CITY	0-0	5675		"	"	"	"	"	"	"	"	"	H	"	C
20.	26	Southampton	1-3	21861	Robson	"	"	"	"	"	M	"	I	"	B	"	"
21.	28	MILLWALL	4-1	8253	Bishop Buchanan 2(1 pen) Robson	K	"	"	"	P	"	"	C	"	"	A	J
22.	31	CHARLTON ATHLETIC	1-0	8488	o.g.(Berry)	"	"	"	"	"	"	"	"	*U	"	"	T
23.	2 Jan	Bristol Rovers	2-3	11945	Giles Pontin	"	"	"	"	"	"	J	"	"	"	C	C
24.	14	BLACKBURN ROVERS	1-1	6949	Bishop	"	"	"	"	"	"	"	I	"	Q	"	"
25.	21	Tottenham Hotspur	1-2	29104	Went	L	"	"	"	"	"	"	"	"	T	"	S
26.	28	SUNDERLAND	5-2	8459	Buchanan 2(1 pen) Went 2 Bishop	K	"	"	"	"	"	"	R	"	"	"	R
27.	11 Feb	Mansfield Town	2-2	6538	Bishop Buchanan	"	"	"	"	"	"	"	"	"	"	"	S
28.	25	BLACKPOOL	2-1	7322	Went Grapes	"	"	"	"	"	"	"	I	"	H	"	A
29.	4 Mar	Luton Town	1-3	6095	Buchanan	"	"	"	"	"	"	"	"	"	B	"	S
30.	7	Fulham	0-1	6571		"	S	"	"	"	"	D	F	"	"	"	J
31.	18	Oldham Athletic	1-1	5758	Went	"	"	"	"	"	"	B	I	F	T	"	A
32.	24	BRIGHTON & H.A.	1-0	10222	Buchanan (pen)	"	"	"	"	"	"	J	"	G	"	"	B
33.	25	Millwall	1-1	5948	Bishop	"	"	"	"	"	"	"	"	B	"	"	G
34.	29	SOUTHAMPTON	1-0	11359	Bishop	"	"	"	"	"	"	"	F	"	"	"	I
35.	1 Apr	Stoke City	0-2	14804		"	"	"	"	"	"	"	"	U	"	I	D
36.	4	Charlton Athletic	0-0	8947		"	"	"	"	"	"	"	"	B	"	C	I
37.	8	CRYSTAL PALACE	2-2	9328	Dwyer 2	"	"	"	"	"	"	"	"	"	"	"	G
38.	15	Burnley	2-4	11577	Buchanan Evans	"	"	"	"	"	"	B	"	G	"	"	D
39.	22	BOLTON WANDERERS	1-0	12566	Bishop	"	"	"	"	"	"	J	"	"	"	"	B
40.	29	Sheffield United	1-0	13687	Evans	"	F	"	"	"	"	"	B	"	"	"	S
41.	3 May	NOTTS. COUNTY	2-1	9528	Buchanan Went	"	"	"	"	"	"	"	"	"	"	"	"
42.	9	ORIENT	0-1	8270		"	"	"	"	"	"	"	"	"	"	"	A

Players:

A = Attley,B. 19/8/0
B = Bishop,R. 22/6/10
C = Buchanan,J. 34/8/14
D = Byrne,G. 9/3/0
E = Campbell,A. 41/12/0
F = Dwyer,P. 39/12/7
G = Evans,A. 12/4/4
H = Friday,R. 2/0/0
I = Giles,D. 25/10/4
J = Grapes,S. 25/6/2
K = Healey,R. 22/7/0
L = Irwin,W. 20/5/0
M = Larmour,A. 26/9/0
N = Livermore,D. 2/4/0
O = Pethard,F. 33/6/0
P = Pontin,K. 36/9/1
Q = Robson,K. 21/3/6
R = Sayer,P. 19/8/6
S = Thomas,R. 14/2/0
T = Went,P. 38/8/9
U = Williams,C. 3/0/0
V = Charles,C. 0/2/0

Safety of Grounds Act hits Cardiff - Ninian Park capacity set at only 10,000 for part of season l Covered Grangetown end is dismantled . . . Troubled season - but relegation is avoided . . . Entire playing staff put up for sale - only Sayer is sold - for £100,000 to Brighton . . Orient avoid relegation - City accused of 'helping'

Other Matches

F.A. Cup

	Date	Opposition	Res	Attend.	Goalscorers	1	2	3	4	5	6	7	8	9	10	11	12
3rd	7 Jan	IPSWICH TOWN	0-2	13584		K	F	O	E	P	M	I	R	T	B	A	J

Football League Cup

	Date	Opposition	Res	Attend.	Goalscorers	1	2	3	4	5	6	7	8	9	10	11	12
1st/1 Leg	13 Aug	Torquay United	0-1	3925		"	A	V	"	F	"	C	N	G	R	I	J
1st/2 Leg	17	TORQUAY UNITED	3-2	2509	Dwyer Giles Sayer	"	"	"	"	"	"	J	"	"	"	"	P
1st Replay	24	TORQUAY UNITED	2-1	1711	Sayer (pen) Buchanan	L	"	P	C	T	"	"	E	F	"	"	B
2nd	30	Swindon Town	1-5	8919	Buchanan	"	F	A	E	"	P	D	C	Q	"	"	B

Welsh Cup

	Date	Opposition	Res	Attend.	Goalscorers	1	2	3	4	5	6	7	8	9	10	11	12
5th	21 Dec	Worcester City	2-2	2915	Went (pen) Bishop	"	"	O	"	"	M	I	"	"	B	J	D
5th Replay	11 Jan	WORCESTER CITY	3-0	963	Bishop Robson o.g.(Barton)	K	"	"	"	P	"	J	I	T	"	R	A
6th	1 Mar	KIDDERMINSTER HAR.	1-1	1639	Buchanan	"	"	"	"	"	"	"	"	T	"	C	G
6th Replay	15 Mar	Kidderminster Har.	3-1	3000	Giles 2 Buchanan (pen)	"	S	"	"	"	"	"	F	F	"	"	T
Semi-final	13 Apr	WREXHAM	0-2	8928		"	"	"	"	"	"	A	F	B	T	"	G

European Cup Winners Cup

	Date	Opposition	Res	Attend.	Goalscorers	1	2	3	4	5	6	7	8	9	10	11	12
1st 1/Leg	14 Sep	F.K. AUSTRIA MEMPHIS	0-0	7000		L	A	D	"	T	P	N	R	G	F	I	J
1st 2 Leg	28	F.K. Austria Memphis	0-1	15000		"	O	A	"	"	"	D	C	"	"	R	B+N

Friendlies

	Date	Opposition	Res	Attend.	Goalscorers
	27 Jul	SWINDON TOWN	4-1	1000	Evans 4
	30	Reading	1-4	1180	Went

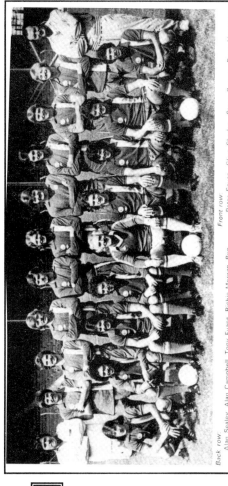

Back row: Alan Sealey, Alan Campbell, Tony Evans, Richie Morgan, Ron Healey, Paul Went, Bill Irwin, Keith Pontin, Albert Larmour, John Buchanan, Ken Whitfield
Front row: Peter Sayer, Clive Charles, Steve Grapes, Doug Livermore, Jimmy Andrews, Phil Dwyer, David Giles, Fred Pethard, Brian Attley

1978-79

Football League – Division 2.

Manager: Jimmy Anderson (Richie Morgan from Dec 1978)

P:42 W:16 D:10 L:16 56-70 Pts:42 Pos:9th

2188	Date	Opposition	Res	Attend.	Goalscorers	1	2	3	4	5	6	7	8	9	10	11	12
1.	19 Aug	PRESTON NORTH END	2-2	7812	Dwyer Went	N	Z	T	G	a	*W	K	*E	I	C	D	F
2.	23	Stoke City	0-2	16005		*H	"	"	"	"	"	"	"	"	"	F	P
3.	26	OLDHAM ATHLETIC	1-3	6929	Buchanan	"	"	"	"	"	"	L	"	"	K	D	A
4.	2 Sep	Bristol Rovers	2-4	6855	Roberts Buchanan (pen)	"	"	"	"	V	"	"	"	"	*M	"	F
5.	9	CAMBRIDGE UNITED	1-0	6154	Buchanan	*B	"	"	"	"	"	"	"	"	C	"	X
6.	16	Luton Town	1-7	7752	Bishop	"	"	"	"	"	"	"	"	*X	"	"	C
7.	23	BLACKBURN ROVERS	2-0	6248	Stevens Bishop	N	I	"	"	"	"	"	D	"	C	*Q	A
8.	30	Wrexham	2-1	11766	Buchanan 2 (1 pen)	"	"	"	"	"	P	"	"	"	"	"	Z
9.	7 Oct	NOTTS. COUNTY	2-3	7974	Buchanan Stevens	"	"	"	"	"	"	"	"	"	"	"	"
10.	14	Orient	2-2	6064	Buchanan Stevens	"	"	W	"	"	"	"	"	"	J	"	T
11.	21	LEICESTER CITY	1-0	8791	Stevens	"	"	"	Z	"	F	"	"	"	"	"	"
12.	28	Newcastle United	0-3	21856		"	"	"	G	"	Z	"	"	"	"	"	C
13.	4 Nov	CHARLTON ATHLLETIC	1-4	7842	Stevens	*U	"	Z	"	"	P	K	"	"	"	"	"
14.	11	Preston North End	1-2	9268	Evans	"	"	"	"	"	"	A	C	"	"	"	D
15.	18	Oldham Athletic	1-2	5356	Bishop	"	"	"	"	"	"	"	"	"	"	D	Q
16.	25	CRYSTAL PALACE	2-2	8739	Evans Dwyer	"	"	"	"	"	"	"	"	J	X	"	T
17.	2 Dec	Millwall	0-2	5381		N	"	"	"	"	"	"	"	"	"	"	"
18.	9	SUNDERLAND	1-1	7178	Evans (pen)	"	"	"	"	"	"	"	X	"	D	*R	"
19.	16	Sheffield United	1-2	14000	Evans (pen)	"	"	"	"	"	"	T	D	"	I	Q	X
20.	23	FULHAM	2-0	5558	Evans Roberts	"	Z	T	"	W	"	A	"	"	"	"	"
21.	27	Brighton & H.A.	0-5	20172		"	"	"	"	"	"	"	X	"	"	"	"
22.	30	Burnley	0-0	9807		"	I	"	"	V	"	"	C	"	Z	"	M
23.	13 Jan	Cambridge United	0-5	5344		"	*O	*Y	G	"	I	L	"	*S	"	D	C
24.	24 Feb	ORIENT	1-0	8256	Buchanan	"	"	"	"	"	"	"	X	X	J	"	C
25.	28	Blackburn Rovers	4-1	7158	Stevens Moore Buchanan Evans	"	A	"	W	"	"	"	"	"	"	"	R
26.	3 Mar	Leicester City	2-1	12820	Dwyer Stevens	"	W	"	"	"	"	"	C	X	S	"	J
27.	10	NEWCASTLE UNITED	2-1	11116	Bishop Stevens	"	O	"	"	"	"	"	"	"	"	"	"
28.	17	Charlton Athletic	1-1	5658	Buchanan (pen)	"	W	"	"	"	"	"	"	"	"	"	L
29.	24	STOKE CITY	1-3	14869	Buchanan (pen)	H	"	"	"	"	"	"	"	J	"	"	"
30.	27	Notts. County	0-1	8211		N	"	"	"	"	"	"	"	"	"	"	Q
31.	31	Crystal Palace	0-2	18672		"	"	"	"	W	Z	C	J	S	X	Q	Z
32.	7 Apr	MILLWALL	2-1	7714	Stevens o.g. (Kitchener)	"	O	"	"	V	I	"	"	"	"	D	R
33.	11	Fulham	2-2	6067	Dwyer o.g. (Money)	"	"	"	"	W	Z	"	"	"	S	"	Q
34.	14	BRIGHTON & H.A.	3-1	12613	Stevens Evans Moore	"	"	"	"	"	"	"	C	X	"	"	"
35.	16	West Ham United	1-1	29058	Bishop	"	"	"	"	"	"	"	"	"	"	"	L
36.	21	SHEFFIELD UNITED	4-0	10592	Stevens Buchanan 3 (1 pen)	"	"	"	"	"	"	"	"	"	"	"	"
37.	25	LUTON TOWN	1-0	10509	Moore Stevens	"	"	"	"	"	Z	"	"	S	"	"	"
38.	28	Sunderland	2-1	36526	Moore Bishop	"	"	"	"	"	I	"	"	"	"	"	"
39.	5 May	BURNLEY	1-1	10270	Sullivan	"	"	"	"	"	I	"	"	"	"	"	"
40.	7	BRISTOL ROVERS	2-0	10185	Stevens Buchanan (pen)	"	"	"	"	"	"	L	"	"	"	"	R
41.	11	WEST HAM UNITED	0-0	13140		"	"	"	"	"	"	"	"	"	"	"	"
42.	14	WREXHAM	1-0	11910	Buchanan	"	"	"	"	"	"	"	"	"	"	"	Q

Players:

- A = Attley,B. 8/2/0
- B = Barber,K. 2/0/0
- C = Bishop,R. 26/4/7
- D = Buchanan,J. 36/4/18
- E = Burns,M. 6/2/0
- F = Byrne,G. 2/0/0
- G = Campbell,A. 40/3/0
- H = Davies,J. 4/0/0
- I = Dwyer,P. 39/5/5
- J = Evans,A. 30/3/8
- K = Giles,D. 4/2/0
- L = Grapes,S. 22/3/1
- M = Harris,G. 1/0/0
- N = Healey,R. 32/5/0
- O = Jones,L. 14/0/0
- P = Larmour,A. 15/3/0
- Q = Lewis,J. 13/3/0
- R = Micallef,C. 1/0/0
- S = Moore,R. 18/0/3
- T = Pethard,F. 14/3/0
- U = Platt,J. 4/0/0
- V = Pontin,K. 27/3/0
- W = Roberts,D. 28/1/2
- X = Stevens,G. 32/2/14
- Y = Sullivan,C. 19/0/1
- Z = Thomas,R. 22/5/0
- a = Went,P. 3/2/1
- b = Sherman,R. 0/0/0

Micky Burns becomes player-coach-but moves to Middlesbrough after 8 games! Dave Roberts signs for £65,000... Manager Anderson sacked - Richie Morgan takes over.. City at bottom of League when 2 months are 'lost' to freeze-up... New record signing Ronnie Moore costs £100,000... Amazing late recovery lifts City to finish a creditable 9th.

Other Matches

F.A.Cup

	Date	Opposition	Res	Attend.	Goalscorers	1	2	3	4	5	6	7	8	9	10	11	12
3rd	9 Jan	Swindon Town	0–3	9983		N	I	W	G	V	P	A	C	J	Z	Q	D

Football League Cup

	Date	Opposition	Res	Attend.	Goalscorers	1	2	3	4	5	6	7	8	9	10	11	12
1st/1 Leg	12 Aug	OXFORD UNITED	1–2	4500	Buchanan	"	N	T	"	I	"	E	K	a	C	D	L
1st/2 Leg	16	Oxford United	1–2	4760	Bishop	"	A	"	"	N	Z	L	E	"	K	"	C

Welsh Cup

	Date	Opposition	Res	Attend.	Goalscorers	1	2	3	4	5	6	7	8	9	10	11	12
5th	17 Jan	MERTHYR TYDFIL	2–1	694	Stevens Evans (pen)	"	I	Z	Q	V	P	"	C	J	X	"	b
6th	12 Feb	Worcester City	2–3	2500	Dwyer Buchanan	"	"	T	L	"	Z	C	D	"	"	Q	R

Friendlies

	Date	Opposition	Res	Attend.	Goalscorers
†	1 Aug	Bristol Rovers	0–1	5095	
†	5	FULHAM	1–0	4149	Dwyer
†	8	Bristol City	0–1	6916	
	21 Feb	Minehead	3–1	700	Stevens 3

† Anglo–Scottish matches.

Cardiff City's 1978-79 line-up: Back row (left to right): Alan Campbell, Paul Went, Keith Pontin, John Davies, Albert Larmour, John Buchanan, Steve Grapes. Front: Gerry Byrne, Rod Thomas, Brian Attley, Phil Dwyer, Jimmy Andrews (manager), Richie Morgan, Ray Bishop, Tony Evans, David Giles.

1979-80

Football League – Division 2.

2230   Manager: Richie Morgan   P:42   W:16   D:8   L:18   41-48   Pts:40   Pos:15th

#	Date	Opposition	Res	Attend.	Goalscorers	1	2	3	4	5	6	7	8	9	10	11	12
1.	18 Aug	Notts. County	1-4	7157	Jones	J	L	T	C	Q	E	A	S	O	*R	B	W
2.	22	Q.P.RANGERS	1-0	11656	Stevens	"	"	"	"	"	"	G	"	"	"	"	N
3.	25	BIRMINGHAM CITY	1-2	11314	Stevens	"	"	"	"	"	"	"	"	"	"	"	"
4.	1 Sep	Wrexham	1-0	9830	Stevens	"	"	"	"	"	"	A	"	"	"	"	I
5.	8	SHREWSBURY TOWN	1-0	8668	Stevens	"	"	"	"	"	U	"	"	"	"	"	F
6.	15	Watford	1-1	13741		"	"	"	"	P	E	"	"	"	"	*F	B
7.	22	CAMBRIDGE UNITED	0-0	8539		"	"	"	"	"	"	F	"	"	"	B	A
8.	29	Bristol Rovers	1-1	8949	Pontlin	"	"	"	"	"	"	"	"	"	"	"	U
9.	6 Oct	LUTON TOWN	2-1	9420	Bishop 2	"	"	"	"	"	"	A	"	"	"	*K	B
10.	9	Q.P.Rangers	0-3	12215		"	"	"	"	"	"	"	"	"	"	"	"
11.	13	Burnley	2-0	6361	Bishop Ronson	"	"	"	"	"	"	"	"	"	"	B	K
12.	20	CHELSEA	1-2	16328	Moore	"	"	"	"	"	"	"	"	"	"	"	"
13.	27	Charlton Athletic	2-3	6870	Bishop Hughes	"	"	"	"	"	"	"	B	"	"	"	"
14.	3 Nov	NOTTS. COUNTY	3-2	8341	Bishop 2 Buchanan	"	U	"	"	"	"	"	"	"	"	M	S
15.	10	Newcastle United	0-1	21243		"	"	"	"	"	"	"	"	"	"	"	"
16.	17	ORIENT	0-0	8119		"	L	"	"	"	U	G	S	"	"	"	B
17.	24	West Ham United	0-3	20292		D	"	"	"	"	"	A	E	"	O	"	S
18.	1 Dec	OLDHAM ATHLETIC	1-0	7061	Bishop	"	E	"	"	"	"	F	A	"	"	"	"
19.	8	Sunderland	1-2	25370	Bishop	"	"	"	"	"	"	"	"	"	"	"	"
20.	15	PRESTON NORTH END	0-2	6419		*H	L	"	"	"	"	A	O	S	"	K	B
21.	21	Leicester City	0-0	12877		"	E	"	"	"	"	M	A	"	R	"	O
22.	26	FULHAM	1-0	8354	Pontlin	"	"	"	"	"	"	"	"	"	"	"	"
23.	29	Birmingham City	1-2	16682	Bishop	"	L	"	"	"	"	N	"	"	"	O	B
24.	1 Jan	Swansea City	1-2	21400	Lewis	"	E	"	"	"	"	"	"	O	"	B	S
25.	12	WREXHAM	1-0	10324	Moore	J	"	"	"	"	"	A	"	"	"	"	"
26.	19	Shrewsbury Town	2-1	6870	Buchanan Moore	"	"	"	"	"	"	B	"	"	G	"	N
27.	2 Feb	WATFORD	1-0	7995	Lewis	"	"	K	"	"	"	"	"	"	R	"	"
28.	9	Cambridge United	0-2	5229		"	G	"	"	"	"	"	"	"	"	"	T
29.	16	BRISTOL ROVERS	0-1	6840	Buchanan	"	"	M	"	"	"	"	"	"	"	S	V
30.	23	BURNLEY	2-1	6358	Pontlin Stevens	"	E	"	"	"	"	"	S	"	"	G	S
31.	1 Mar	Chelsea	0-1	18449		"	"	"	"	"	"	"	"	"	"	"	B
32.	8	CHARLTON ATHLETIC	3-1	6652	Stevens 2 Buchanan	"	"	"	"	"	"	A	"	"	"	"	"
33.	14	Luton Town	2-1	9246	Buchanan Stevens	"	T	"	"	"	"	B	"	"	"	"	N
34.	22	NEWCASTLE UNITED	1-1	9304	Stevens	"	"	"	"	"	"	"	"	"	"	"	"
35.	29	Orient	1-1	4081	Buchanan	"	"	"	"	"	"	"	"	A	"	"	T
36.	7 Apr	SWANSEA CITY	1-0	14677	Ronson	"	"	"	"	"	"	"	"	"	"	"	"
37.	8	LEICESTER CITY	0-1	10291		"	"	"	"	"	"	"	"	"	"	S	V
38.	12	Oldham Athletic	3-0	6339	Buchanan Stevens Micallef	"	T	"	"	"	"	"	"	A	"	G	S
39.	15	Fulham	1-2	4916	Bishop	"	"	"	"	"	"	"	A	S	"	I	T
40.	19	WEST HAM UNITED	0-1	12076		H	G	"	"	"	"	"	N	"	"	"	E
41.	26	Preston North End	0-2	7481		J	"	"	"	"	"	"	A	"	"	"	"
42.	3 May	SUNDERLAND	1-1	19340	Bishop	H	"	"	"	"	"	F	O	"	"	"	N

Players:

A = Bishop,R.   31/4/11
B = Buchanan,J.   26/4/8
C = CampbelDvaiu   42/5/0
D = Davies,J.   3/0/0
E = Dwyer,P.   31/5/0
F = Elliot,M.   6/1/0
G = Grapes,S.   18/1/0
H = Grotier,P.   7/0/0
I = Harris,G.   3/0/0
J = Healey,R.   32/5/0
K = Hughes,W.   7/0/1
L = Jones,L.   17/2/1
M = Lewis,J.   28/3/2
N = Micallef,C.   4/0/1
O = Moore,R.   36/5/3
P = Pontin,K.   37/3/3
Q = Roberts,D.   5/2/0
R = Ronson,W.   41/4/2
S = Stevens,G.   30/3/11
T = Sullivan,C.   28/5/0
U = Thomas,R.   30/3/0
V = Davies,P.   0/0/0
W = Lloyd,K.   0/0/0

New Record fee received of £125,000 for Tony Evans - new record fee paid of £130,000 for Billy Ronson . . . Gary Stevens scores in 5 consecutive games. Lack of goals ensures mid-table finish . . . Buchanan scores 8 goals in friendly at Rhayader.

Other Matches

F.A.Cup

	Date	Opposition	Res	Attend.	Goalscorers	1	2	3	4	5	6	7	8	9	10	11	12
3rd	5 Jan	ARSENAL	0-0	21972		J	E	T	C	P	U	M	A	O	R	B	S
3rd Replay	8	Arsenal	1-2	36582	Buchanan	"	"	"	"	"	"	"	"	"	"	"	"

Football League Cup

	Date	Opposition	Res	Attend.	Goalscorers	1	2	3	4	5	6	7	8	9	10	11	12
2nd/1 Leg	28 Aug	Everton	0-2	18061		"	L	"	"	Q	E	G	S	"	"	"	U
2nd/2 Leg	5 Sep	EVERTON	1-0	9698	Buchanan	"	"	"	"	"	"	A	"	"	"	F	B

Welsh Cup

	Date	Opposition	Res	Attend.	Goalscorers	1	2	3	4	5	6	7	8	9	10	11	12
5th	22 Jan	Newport County	0-2	7709		"	E	"	"	P	U	M	A	"	S	B	G

Back row (from left): John Lewis, Dave Roberts, Keith Pontin, Ronnie Moore, John Davies, Ron Healey, Gary Stevens, Rod Thomas, Alan Campbell, John Buchanan. **Front row:** Brian Harris (assistant manager), Steve Grapes, Billy Ronson, Phil Dwyer (captain), Richie Morgan (manager), Colin Sullivan, Ray Bishop, Linden Jones, Doug Livermore (coach)

Friendlies

Date	Opposition	Res	Attend.	Goalscorers
29 Jul	Saltash United	2-2	600	Moore Stevens
2 Aug	Frederikshaven	2-0	2000	Dwyer Buchanan
4	Brovst	4-0	1700	Stevens 3 Buchanan
6	Thisted	1-1	3000	Ronson
8	Norresundby	5-0	2500	Moore 3 Elliot Stevens
10	WOLVERHAMPTON W.	2-2	7000	Moore Buchanan
31 Oct	Aberystwyth Town	1-0	2000	Thomas
26 Feb	GOTHENBURG	3-2	4500	Lewis Micallef Dwyer (pen)
22 Apr	Rhayader	11-2	800	Buchanan 8 Grapes Moore Lewis
28	Darlaston	1-0	500	

1980-81

Football League – Division 2.

Manager: Richie Morgan

P: 42 **W:** 12 **D:** 12 **L:** 18 **44-60** **Pts:** 36 **Pos:** 19th

2272	Date	Opposition	Res	Attend.	Goalscorers	1	2	3	4	5	6	7	8	9	10	11	12
1.	16 Aug	BLACKBURN ROVERS	1-2	6908	Stevens	I	H	N	E	Q	V	A	P	T	S	B	C
2.	19	Wrexham	1-0	7772	Bishop	"	"	"	"	"	"	"	"	"	"	N	P
3.	23	Oldham Athletic	0-2	5690		"	"	E	C	"	"	"	B	"	"	"	*M
4.	30	ORIENT	4-2	5649	Stevens 2 Dwyer Buchanan	"	"	N	"	"	E	"	*M	"	"	B	V
5.	6 Sep	Newcastle United	1-2	15804	Kitchen	"	"	"	"	"	"	"	"	"	"	"	O
6.	13	BOLTON WANDERERS	1-1	6649	Stevens	"	"	"	"	"	"	"	"	"	"	"	C
7.	20	BRISTOL ROVERS	2-1	6122	Ronson Pontin	"	"	"	*O	"	"	"	"	"	"	"	C
8.	27	Notts. County	2-4	7229	Dwyer Kitchen	"	"	"	"	"	"	P	"	"	"	"	V
9.	4 Oct	WATFORD	1-0	6407	Micallef	"	"	"	"	"	"	"	"	"	"	"	R
10.	7	West Ham United	0-1	20402		"	"	V	K	"	R	"	"	"	"	A	O
11.	11	Sheffield Wed.	0-2	15396		"	"	"	C	"	"	"	"	"	"	N	E
12.	17	CAMBRIDGE UNITED	1-2	4059	o.g. (Smith)	"	"	L	"	"	"	"	"	"	"	"	"
13.	22	Q.P.RANGERS	1-0	4489	Grapes	"	"	N	H	"	E	A	"	B	"	O	T
14.	25	Shrewsbury Town	0-2	4466		"	"	"	"	"	"	"	"	"	"	"	"
15.	31	CHELSEA	0-1	8489		"	"	"	"	"	"	"	"	T	"	B	P
16.	8 Nov	Preston North End	1-3	5458	Kitchen	"	"	"	K	"	"	"	"	"	"	"	"
17.	12	WREXHAM	1-0	4562	Kitchen (pen)	J	"	"	"	"	"	P	"	"	"	"	H
18.	15	Blackburn Rovers	3-2	7854	Kitchen 2 Buchanan	"	"	V	"	"	"	*G	"	"	"	"	A
19.	22	LUTON TOWN	1-0	6064	Buchanan	"	"	"	"	"	"	"	"	"	"	"	N
20.	29	Derby County	1-1	15581	o.g. (Clark)	"	"	"	"	"	"	"	"	"	"	"	"
21.	6 Dec	GRIMSBY TOWN	1-1	6063	Kitchen (pen)	"	"	"	"	"	"	"	"	"	"	"	"
22.	26	Bristol City	0-0	14921		"	"	R	"	"	"	N	"	T	"	"	G
23.	27	SWANSEA CITY	3-3	21239	Stevens Kitchen Buchanan	"	"	N	"	"	"	A	"	"	"	"	"
24.	10 Jan	Luton Town	2-2	9013	Kitchen Giles	"	V	R	"	"	"	G	"	"	"	"	"
25.	17	Orient	2-2	3836	Maddy 2	"	"	"	"	"	O	"	"	"	"	"	P
26.	31	OLDHAM ATHLETIC	0-2	5687		"	"	L	E	"	E	"	"	*D	"	"	K
27.	3 Feb	Q.P.Rangers	0-2	9834		"	"	"	K	"	P	"	"	P	"	"	O
28.	7	Bolton Wanderers	2-4	8115	Buchanan 2	"	"	"	R	"	"	"	"	T	"	"	K
29.	20	NOTTS. COUNTY	0-1	4987		"	"	*F	H	"	V	P	"	"	"	"	G
30.	25	NEWCASTLE UNITED	1-0	4235	Kitchen	I	"	"	"	"	"	N	"	"	"	"	P
31.	28	Bristol Rovers	1-0	7525	Grapes	"	"	"	"	"	"	"	"	"	"	"	"
32.	4 Mar	SHEFFIELD WED.	0-0	7002		"	"	"	"	"	"	"	"	"	"	"	"
33.	7	Watford	2-4	10014	Kitchen Jones	"	"	"	"	"	"	"	"	"	"	"	P
34.	21	Cambridge United	0-2	3790		"	"	E	K	"	"	"	"	"	"	"	"
35.	28	SHREWSBURY TOWN	2-2	5201	Lewis Dwyer	"	"	"	P	"	"	"	"	"	"	"	O
36.	4 Apr	Chelsea	1-0	11569	Stevens	J	"	U	H	"	"	"	"	"	"	"	K
37.	11	PRESTON NORTH END	1-3	4991	Dwyer	"	"	"	"	"	E	"	"	"	"	"	"
38.	18	Swansea City	1-1	19038	Kitchen	"	"	"	"	"	"	"	"	"	"	G	P
39.	20	BRISTOL CITY	2-3	5579	Grapes Kitchen	"	"	"	"	"	"	"	"	"	"	P	G
40.	25	Grimsby Town	1-0	7377	Stevens	"	"	"	"	"	"	"	"	"	"	"	"
41.	2 May	DERBY COUNTY	0-0	7583		"	"	"	"	"	"	"	"	"	"	"	"
42.	6	WEST HAM UNITED	0-0	10558		"	"	"	"	"	"	"	"	"	"	"	V

Players:

A = Bishop,R. 15/5/3
B = Buchanan,J. 34/8/7
C = Campbell,A. 7/3/0
D = Davies,P. 1/0/0
E = Dwyer,P. 32/4/4
F = Gilbert,T. 5/0/0
G = Giles,P. 10/3/1
H = Grapes,S. 27/5/3
I = Grotier,P. 22/5/0
J = Healey,R. 20/3/0
K = Hughes,W. 13/3/1
L = Jones,L. 29/5/1
M = Kitchen,P. 39/6/19
N = Lewis,J. 31/6/2
O = Maddy,P. 7/1/2
P = Micallef,C. 14/2/1
Q = Pontin,K. 41/8/1
R = Roberts,D. 6/2/0
S = Ronson,W. 42/7/1
T = Stevens,G. 38/8/8
U = Sullivan,C. 7/0/0
V = Thomas,R. 20/4/0

> Mediocre season keeps City in lower half of table... Peter Kitchen signed from Fulham for £100,000 - £90,000 received from Rotherham for Moore... Campbell signs for Carlisle... Reserve team not re-elected to Football Combination.

Other Matches

F.A.Cup

	Date	Opposition	Res	Attend.	Goalscorers	1	2	3	4	5	6	7	8	9	10	11	12
3rd	3 Jan	Leicester City	0-3	17527		J	L	N	K	Q	V	G	M	T	S	B	P

Football League Cup

		Opposition	Res	Attend.	Goalscorers	1	2	3	4	5	6	7	8	9	10	11	12
1st/1 Leg	9 Aug	Torquay United	0-0	3441		I	H	"	L	"	R	A	P	"	"	"	K
2nd/2 Leg	13	TORQUAY UNITED	2-2	3149	Bishop Stevens	"	"	E	"	"	"	"	"	"	"	"	"
2nd/1 Leg	22	CHELSEA	1-0	6549	Bishop	"	"	N	C	"	E	"	M	"	"	"	V
2nd/2 Leg	3 Sep	Chelsea	1-1	12959	Kitchen	"	"	"	"	"	"	"	"	"	"	"	"
3rd	23	Barnsley	2-3	13135	Buchanan Lewis	"	"	"	"	"	V	"	"	"	"	"	R

Welsh Cup

	Date	Opposition	Res	Attend.	Goalscorers	1	2	3	4	5	6	7	8	9	10	11	12
5th	3 Dec	CARDIFF CORINTHIANS	6-0	1080	Kitchen 5 Hughes	J	L	V	K	"	E	G	"	"	N	"	A
6th	27 Jan	Wrexham	0-3	4880		"	"	"	"	"	O	"	"	"	S	"	P

Friendlies

		Opposition	Res	Attend.	Goalscorers
†	26 Jul	Hamilton Academicals	1-0	--	Stevens
†	27	Cowdenbeath	1-0	--	Pontin
†	29	Montrose	1-0	--	Buchanan (pen)
	1 Aug	STOKE CITY	3-1	3200	Stevens Buchanan Moore
	4	Evesham	4-0	1000	Stevens 2 Buchanan
	15 Apr	NOTTINGHAM FOREST	1-2	4000	Kitchen

† Matches played behind closed doors.

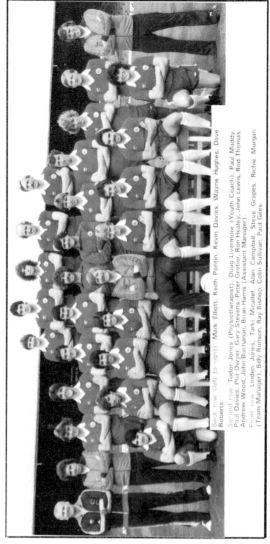

Back row (left to right) Mark Elliott, Keith Pontin, Kevin Davies (Youth Coach), Paul Maddy, Paul Davies, Phil Dwyer, Gary Stevens, Peter Grotier, Ron Healey, John Lewis, Rod Thomas, Andrew Wood, John Buchanan, Brian Harris (Assistant Manager)
Second row: Tudor Jones (Physiotherapist), Doug Livermore (Youth Coach), Wayne Hughes, Dave Roberts
Front row: Linden Jones, Tarki Micallef, Alan Campbell, Steve Grapes, Richie Morgan (Team Manager), Billy Ronson, Ray Bishop, Colin Sullivan, Paul Giles.

1981-82 Football League – Division 2

Manager: Richie Morgan. Graham Williams from Nov 1981. Len Ashurst from Mar 1982.

P: 42 **W:** 12 **D:** 8 **L:** 22 **45-61** **Pts:** 44 † **Pos:** 20th (Rel.)

† 3 points for a win introduced.

2314	Date	Opposition	Res	Attend.	Goalscorers	1	2	3	4	5	6	7	8	9	10	11	12
1.	29 Aug	Oldham Athletic	2-2	4383	Stevens Dwyer	K	N	Z	I	U	E	P	O	Y	V	C	Q
2.	5 Sep	CHELSEA	1-2	8898	Kitchen	"	"	"	"	"	"	"	"	"	"	"	R
3.	12	Rotherham United	0-1	7197		"	"	"	"	"	"	"	"	"	"	"	a
4.	19	BLACKBURN ROVERS	1-3	4253	Ronson	"	"	"	*X	"	"	"	"	"	"	Q	R
5.	22	Luton Town	3-2	9015	Kitchen (pen) Sayer Stevens	"	"	"	"	"	"	"	"	"	"	R	a
6.	26	Barnsley	1-0	12114	Stevens	"	"	"	"	"	"	"	*a	"	"	P	O
7.	3 Oct	NEWCASTLE UNITED	0-4	5764		"	"	"	"	"	"	*B	"	"	"	"	"
8.	10	Sheffield Wed.	1-2	15621	Bennett,D.	"	"	G	b	"	"	"	R	"	M	"	H
9.	17	BOLTON WANDERERS	2-1	3879	Stevens Bennett,D.	J	"	"	Q	"	"	"	"	"	"	"	b
10.	24	SHREWSBURY TOWN	1-1	4357	Stevens	"	I	"	"	"	"	"	"	"	"	"	"
11.	31	Cambridge United	1-2	4041	Micallef	"	"	"	"	"	"	"	"	"	"	"	"
12.	4 Nov	WREXHAM	3-2	4625	Micallef Lewis Stevens	"	N	"	"	*B	"	"	"	"	"	"	a
13.	7	NORWICH CITY	1-0	5704	Bennett,D.	"	"	"	"	"	b	"	"	"	"	"	b
14.	14	Watford	0-0	13907		"	"	"	"	U	B	"	"	"	"	"	"
15.	21	LEICESTER CITY	3-1	6687	Micallef Bennett,D. Stevens	"	"	"	"	"	"	"	R	"	"	"	a
16.	24	Wrexham	1-3	3625	Dwyer	"	"	"	"	"	"	"	"	"	"	"	E
17.	28	Q.P.Rangers	0-2	10225		"	I	"	E	"	"	"	"	"	"	"	a
18.	4 Dec	DERBY COUNTY	1-0	5515	Micallef	K	"	"	Q	"	"	"	Q	"	"	M	Q
19.	28	CHARLTON ATHLETIC	0-1	7887		"	"	E	"	"	"	"	"	"	"	"	I
20.	20 Jan	OLDHAM ATHLETIC	0-1	4097		"	N	G	"	"	M	"	I	"	"	*W	H
21.	30	Blackburn Rovers	0-1	7001		"	"	"	"	"	"	"	Q	"	"	H	F
22.	6 Feb	ROTHERHAM UNITED	1-2	3823	Kitchen	"	*F	"	"	"	"	"	"	E	E	H	O
23.	13	Newcastle United	1-2	15049	Stevens	"	N	"	"	"	B	"	R	Y	O	E	H
24.	17	Chelsea	0-1	9710		"	"	"	U	M	"	"	"	"	A	"	W
25.	20	BARNSLEY	0-0	4503		"	"	"	E	"	"	"	*L	"	"	E	"
26.	27	SHEFFIELD WED.	0-2	5674		"	"	"	"	R	*S	"	"	"	"	M	Q
27.	6 Mar	Bolton Wanderers	0-1	6269		"	"	"	"	"	"	"	"	"	"	"	I
28.	9	Crystal Palace	0-1	6526		"	"	L	F	S	*T	"	R	A	Y	O	"
29.	13	Shrewsbury Town	1-1	4089	Bennett,G.	"	"	"	I	R	S	"	T	Y	O	Q	M
30.	20	CAMBRIDGE UNITED	5-4	3243	Stevens 3 Kitchen 2	"	"	"	"	"	"	"	"	"	O	"	A
31.	27	Norwich City	1-2	12720	Gilbert	"	"	"	U	M	B	"	"	"	M	Q	M
32.	30	GRIMSBY TOWN	2-1	3924	Stevens o.g.(Moore)	"	"	"	"	"	"	"	"	"	B	O	M
33.	3 Apr	WATFORD	2-0	6734	Bennett Micallef	"	"	"	"	M	"	"	R	"	"	Y	W
34.	10	ORIENT	2-1	5689	Bennett Kitchen	"	"	"	"	"	"	"	"	"	"	"	"
35.	13	Charlton Athletic	2-2	4186	Stevens Mullen	"	"	"	"	"	"	"	"	"	"	"	G
36.	17	Leicester City	1-3	13650	Kitchen	"	"	"	"	"	"	"	"	"	"	"	"
37.	24	Q.P.RANGERS	1-2	5979	Micallef	"	"	"	"	"	"	"	"	"	"	"	"
38.	28	Orient	1-1	3125	Maddy	"	"	"	"	M	"	"	"	"	"	"	"
39.	1 May	Derby County	0-0	10111		"	"	"	"	"	"	"	"	"	"	"	G
40.	8	CRYSTAL PALACE	0-1	5762		*D	"	G	R	R	"	"	"	"	"	Y	Q
41.	15	Grimsby Town	1-0	8148	Micallef	K	"	L	"	"	"	"	G	B	Y	A	O
42.	17	LUTON TOWN	2-3	10277	Kitchen Micallef	"	"	"	"	"	"	"	"	"	"	"	"

Players:

A = Bennett,D.	35/7/7	
B = Bennett,G.	19/7/2	
C = Buchanan,J.	3/2/0	
D = Dibble,A.	1/2/0	
E = Dwyer,P.	21/6/3	
F = Francombe,P.	2/0/0	
G = Gilbert,T.	28/3/1	
H = Giles,P.	3/0/0	
I = Grapes,S.	24/7/0	
J = Grotier,P.	9/0/0	
K = Healey,R.	32/8/0	
L = Henderson,M.	11/4/0	
M = Hughes,W.	22/4/0	
N = Jones,L.	36/7/0	
O = Kitchen,P.	25/4/11	
P = Lewis,J.	19/5/2	
Q = Maddy,P.	23/4/2	
R = Micallef,C.	29/8/11	
S = Mullen,J.	12/2/1	
T = Polycarpou,A.	7/2/0	
U = Pontin,K.	40/10/0	
V = Ronson,W.	7/2/1	
W = Sanders,A.	1/0/0	
X = Sayer,P.	4/0/1	
Y = Stevens,G.	38/9/18	
Z = Sullivan,C.	7/2/0	
a = Sugrue,P.	2/2/2	
b = Thomas,R.	2/0/0	
c = Lythgoe,G.	0/2/0	
d = McEwan,S.	0/1/0	

Bennett costs £120,000, Ronson sold for £90,000 ... Managerial changes - Morgan and Williams sacked - Ashurst takes over in March - fails to save City - From 9th in table - 2 points from 12 games dooms City to relegation. Bluebirds Lose to Swansea in Welsh Cup Final.

Other Matches

F.A.Cup

	Date	Opposition	Res	Attend.	Goalscorers	1	2	3	4	5	6	7	8	9	10	11	12
3rd	2 Jan	Manchester City	1-3	31547	Maddy	K	I	E	Q	U	B	A	R	Y	M	P	a

Football League Cup

	Date	Opposition	Res	Attend.	Goalscorers	1	2	3	4	5	6	7	8	9	10	11	12
1st/1 Leg	2 Sep	EXETER CITY	2-1	2688	Stevens 2	"	N	Z	I	"	E	P	O	"	V	C	R
2nd/2 Leg	16 Sep	Exeter City	1-3	4449	Sugrue	"	"	"	"	"	"	"	a	"	"	"	M

Welsh Cup

	Date	Opposition	Res	Attend.	Goalscorers	1	2	3	4	5	6	7	8	9	10	11	12
3rd	6 Dec	Bridgend Town	4-1	1000	Micallef 2 Lewis Sugrue	"	I	E	Q	"	B	a	R	"	M	P	H
4th	15	NEWPORT COUNTY	3-1	3915	Bennett,D. Dwyer Stevens	"	"	"	"	"	"	A	"	"	"	"	a
5th	9 Jan	WREXHAM	4-1	2767	Stevens Kitchen 3	"	N	G	I	"	"	"	"	"	O	E	W
S/Final 1 Leg	8 Apr	Hereford United	0-0	4832		"	"	L	U	"	"	"	T	"	"	R	Q
S/Final 2 Leg	19	HEREFORD UNITED	2-1	3635	Micallef Stevens	"	"	"	"	R	M	I	"	O	A	Y	"
Final 1 Leg	12 May	SWANSEA CITY	0-0	11960		D	"	"	U	"	S	c	G	B	"	"	d
Final 2 Leg	19	Swansea City	1-2	15828	Bennett,G.	"	"	"	"	"	"	"	"	"	d	"	Y

Friendlies

	Date	Opposition	Res	Attend.	Goalscorers
	12 Aug	BIRMINGHAM CITY	0-0	2000	
	15	COVENTRY CITY	1-0	2200	Maddy
	19	WOLVERHAMPTON W.	1-1	2760	Stevens
	24	Oldswinford	1-1	600	Sugrue

Back row (left to right): Jimmy Mullen, Mick Henderson, Wayne Hughes, Gary Stevens, Ron Healey, Gary Bennett, Keith Pontin, P. Kitchen.
Front row: John Lewis, Paul Maddy, Andy Polycarpou, Dave Bennett, Tarki Micallef, Steve Grapes, Linden Jones, Alan Sanders.

1982-83

Football League – Division 3.

Manager: Len Ashurst   **P:**46 **W:**25 **D:**11 **L:**10 **76-50** **Pts:**86 **Pos:**2nd (Prom.)

2360	Date	Opposition	Res	Attend.	Goalscorers	1	2	3	4	5	6	7	8	9	10	11	12
1.	28 Aug	WREXHAM	1-2	5018	Bennett,D.0	*K	M	*C	F	R	Q	A	*U	*G	*J	O	B
2.	5 Sep	Millwall	4-0	5620	Lewis Bennett,D.2 Gibbins	*T	B	"	P	"	"	"	"	"	"	N	F
3.	8	Orient	0-4	2021		"	"	"	"	"	"	"	"	"	"	O	M
4.	11	WIGAN ATHLETIC	3-2	3850	Lewis Bennett,G. Woof	"	"	"	"	"	"	"	"	"	*V	N	"
5.	18	Walsall	2-1	3161	Hemmerman Dwyer	"	M	"	"	F	"	"	"	"	J	"	B
6.	25	SHEFFIELD UNITED	2-0	7147	Bennett,D. Hemmerman	"	"	"	"	"	"	"	"	"	"	"	L
7.	28	EXETER CITY	2-0	4867		"	"	"	"	"	"	"	"	"	"	"	"
8.	2 Oct	Oxford United	2-2	6018	o.g.(Shotton) Mullen	"	"	"	"	"	"	"	"	"	"	"	"
9.	9	A.F.C.Bournemouth	1-3	5818	Hemmerman	"	"	"	*L	"	"	"	"	"	"	"	"
10.	16	GILLINGHAM	1-0	4828	Ingram	"	"	"	"	"	B	"	"	"	"	"	B
11.	19	BRADFORD CITY	1-0	5007	Bennett,G.	"	"	"	"	"	"	"	"	"	"	"	P
12.	23	Huddersfield Town	0-4	6121		"	"	"	"	"	"	"	"	"	"	"	"
13.	30	PORTSMOUTH	1-0	7082	Hemmerman	"	"	"	P	"	"	"	"	"	"	"	U
14.	3 Nov	Reading	2-1	2982	Bennett,G. Dwyer	"	"	"	"	"	"	"	"	"	"	"	"
15.	6	PRESTON NORTH END	3-1	5546	Hemmerman Bennett,D. Ingram	"	"	"	"	"	"	"	"	"	"	"	L
16.	13	Lincoln City	1-2	6585	Bennett,D.	"	"	"	"	"	Q	"	U	"	"	"	"
17.	4 Dec	Doncaster Rovers	2-2	3087	Micallef Hemmerman	E	"	"	"	"	"	*I	"	"	"	"	H
18.	7	CHESTERFIELD	1-1	3813	Hatton	"	"	"	U	"	"	A	G	I	"	"	"
19.	17	Southend United	2-1	3476	Hatton Gibbins	"	"	B	"	"	"	"	"	"	"	"	"
20.	27	NEWPORT COUNTY	3-2	15972	Hatton Hemmerman 2	"	"	Q	"	"	B	"	"	"	H	"	O
21.	28	Plymouth Argyle	2-3	8631	Hatton Bennett,G.	"	"	"	"	"	"	"	"	"	J	"	H
22.	1 Jan	BRISTOL ROVERS	3-1	11050	Hemmerman 2/1 pen) Bennett,G.	"	"	"	"	"	"	H	"	"	"	"	C
23.	3	Brentford	3-1	7602	Gibbins Hemmerman 2	"	"	"	"	"	"	A	"	"	"	"	O
24.	15	Wrexham	0-0	3846		"	"	"	"	"	"	"	"	"	"	"	"
25.	22	WALSALL	3-1	6237	Bennett,G. Hemmerman(p) Bennett,D	"	C	"	"	"	C	"	"	"	"	C	H
26.	29	Exeter City	2-0	4019	Hemmerman Hatton	"	"	"	"	C	"	O	"	"	"	O	O
27.	1 Feb	MILLWALL	3-0	5643	Bennett,G. Bennett,D. Hemmerman	"	"	"	"	F	"	"	"	"	"	N	M
28.	5	Sheffield United	0-2	11641		"	M	"	"	"	"	"	"	"	"	"	O
29.	12	OXFORD UNITED	3-0	6970	Hemmerman(pen) Bennett,D. Hatton	"	"	"	"	"	"	O	"	"	"	C	H
30.	16	Bradford City	2-4	3786	Dwyer Gibbins	"	"	"	"	"	"	"	"	"	"	O	"
31.	19	A.F.C.BOURNEMOUTH	1-1	4878	Gibbins Hemmerman 2(1pen)	*D	"	"	"	"	B	A	"	"	"	N	O
32.	26	Gillingham	3-2	4587		"	"	"	"	"	"	"	"	"	"	"	"
33.	1 Mar	READING	0-0	6173		"	"	"	"	"	"	"	"	N	"	"	I
34.	12	Portsmouth	0-0	24354		*S	"	"	"	"	"	"	"	"	"	"	P
35.	15	HUDDERSFIELD TOWN	1-1	10379	Hatton	"	"	"	"	"	"	"	"	"	"	"	"
36.	19	Preston North End	1-2	4608	Hemmerman	"	"	"	"	"	"	"	"	"	"	"	"
37.	26	LINCOLN CITY	1-0	8021	Bennett,G.	"	"	"	"	"	"	"	"	"	"	P	C
38.	2 Apr	PLYMOUTH ARGYLE	0-0	7226		"	"	"	"	"	"	"	"	"	"	"	H
39.	4	Newport County	0-1	16052		"	"	"	"	"	"	H	"	N	"	"	I
40.	9	DONCASTER ROVERS	3-0	5456	Tong 2 Gibbins	E	"	"	"	"	"	N	"	I	"	"	"
41.	16	Wigan Athletic	0-0	4447		"	"	"	"	"	"	"	"	"	"	"	A
42.	23	SOUTHEND UNITED	4-1	6141	Hatton Lewis 2 Hemmerman	"	"	"	"	C	"	A	"	"	"	"	H
43.	30	Chesterfield	1-0	2799	Bennett,D.	"	"	"	"	"	G	"	H	"	"	"	"
44.	2 May	BRENTFORD	3-1	9112	o.g.(McNichol) Hatton Bennett,D.	"	N	"	"	F	B	"	G	"	"	O	W
45.	7	ORIENT	2-0	11480	Lewis Bennett,D.	"	M	C	"	"	"	"	"	"	"	N	H
46.	14	Bristol Rovers	1-1	10731	Gibbins	"	"	Q	"	"	"	"	"	"	"	"	C

Players:

A = Bennett,D. 40/7/13
B = Bennett,G. 34/5/8
C = Bodin,P. 27/8/0
D = Brown,J. 3/0/0
E = Dibble,A. 20/4/0
F = Dwyer,P. 40/6/3
G = Gibbins,R. 46/8/12
H = Giles,P. 4/0/0
I = Hatton,R. 29/0/9
J = Hemmerman,J. 44/8/26
K = Humphries,S. 1/0/0
L = Ingram,S. 7/1/3
M = Jones,L. 40/8/3
N = Lewis,J. 39/8/5
O = Maddy,P. 5/0/0
P = Micallef,C. 18/5/1
Q = Mullen,J. 39/7/1
R = Pontin,K. 4/1/0
S = Steele,E. 7/0/0
T = Thomas,M. 15/4/0
U = Tong,D. 43/8/3
V = Woof,W. 1/0/1
W = Matthews,W. 0/0/0

Club launches Blue Dragons Rugby League Club ... Summer clearout - in come free transfer, on loan and trial players ... Billy Woof scores late winner in only game for City ... City lose at home to Weymouth in F.A.Cup Geoffrey Ingram reputedly bought for £200,000 - returns to America for same fee 2 months later! After losing at Newport, late run gains promotion.

Other Matches

F.A.Cup

	Date	Opposition	Res	Attend.	Goalscorers	1	2	3	4	5	6	7	8	9	10	11	12
1st	20 Nov	Wokingham Town	1-1	2973	Tong	E	M	C	P	F	Q	A	U	G	J	N	L
1st Replay	23	WOKINGHAM TOWN	3-0	3755	Jones Hemmerman Ingram	"	"	"	L	"	"	"	"	"	"	"	P
2nd	11 Dec	WEYMOUTH	2-3	4446	Gibbins Hemmerman	"	"	"	U	"	"	"	G	B	"	"	H

Milk (formerly Football League) Cup

	Date	Opposition	Res	Attend.	Goalscorers	1	2	3	4	5	6	7	8	9	10	11	12
1st/1 Leg	28 Aug	HEREFORD UNITED	2-1	1808	Bennett,D. Gibbins	T	"	"	B	R	"	"	U	G	"	"	P
2nd/2 Leg	15 Sep	Hereford United	2-1	3301	Gibbins Hemmerman	"	"	"	P	B	"	"	"	"	"	"	F
2nd/1 Leg	5 Oct	Arsenal	1-2	15115	Gibbins	"	"	"	"	F	"	"	"	"	"	"	L
2nd/2 Leg	26	ARSENAL	1-3	11632	Hemmerman	"	"	"	"	"	B	"	"	B	"	"	"

Welsh Cup

	Date	Opposition	Res	Attend.	Goalscorers	1	2	3	4	5	6	7	8	9	10	11	12
3rd	30 Nov	Newport County	0-1	7800		E	"	"	"	"	Q	B	"	"	"	"	H

Friendlies

	Date	Opposition	Res	Attend.	Goalscorers
	10 Aug	Chippenham Town	4-1	700	Hemmerman 2 o.g.(Webb) Micallef
	12	Forest Green Rovers	1-0	500	Gibbins
	14	CHELSEA	1-3	2600	Gibbins
	17	Crewe Alexandra	0-1	650	
	20	SWINDON TOWN	4-1	2100	Pontin Gibbins Bennett,D. Hemmerman
	3 Oct	Chepstow Local X1	4-1	500	Giles Matthews 3
	10 Nov	Maesteg Park	3-2	600	Evans Giles
	11	STOKE CITY	2-2	3000	Hemmerman Evans
	23 May	SOUTHAMPTON	1-3	2800	Townsend

(Back) Gibbins, Dibble, Thomas, Tong. (Middle) Parsons(Equipment), Hemmerman, Pontin, G.Bennett, Maddy, Woodruff(Youth Coach). (Front) Lewis,Micallef,Ashurst(Manager), Mullen,Goodfellow(Coach), D.Bennett,Jones.

1983-84

Football League – Division 2.

Manager: Len Ashurst (Jimmy Goodfellow, Jimmy Mullen [joint] from Mar 1984. Jimmy Goodfellow from May 1984)

P:42 W:15 D:6 L:21 53-66 Pts:51 Pos:15th

2402	Date	Opposition	Res	Attend.	Goalscorers	1	2	3	4	5	6	7	8	9	10	11	12
1.	27 Aug	Charlton Athletic	0-2	4525		F	N	C	G	B	W	*S	I	*E	*U	P	Q
2.	29	MANCHESTER CITY	2-1	8899	Bodin 2	"	"	"	"	"	"	"	"	"	"	"	"
3.	3 Sep	GRIMSBY TOWN	3-1	5135	Owen 2 (1 pen) Crawford	"	"	"	"	"	"	"	"	"	"	"	R
4.	6	Shrewsbury Town	0-1	4406		"	"	"	"	"	"	"	"	"	"	"	"
5.	10	Leeds United	0-1	12336		"	"	"	"	"	"	"	"	"	R	"	Q
6.	17	PORTSMOUTH	0-0	9033		"	"	"	"	"	"	"	"	"	"	"	"
7.	1 Oct	BARNSLEY	0-3	6433		"	*H	"	"	R	"	"	"	*Z	*Y	B	"
8.	8	CARLISLE UNITED	2-0	4596	Owen Vaughan	"	"	"	"	"	"	"	"	"	"	*V	X
9.	15	Chelsea	0-2	15459		"	V	"	"	"	"	"	"	*X	"	H	Q
10.	19	NEWCASTLE UNITED	0-2	9926		"	"	"	"	"	"	"	"	"	"	"	"
11.	31	Fulham	2-0	5929	Bennett Owen	"	"	"	"	"	"	"	"	B	"	"	"
12.	5 Nov	Middlesbrough	0-2	7686		"	"	"	"	"	"	"	"	"	"	"	"
13.	8	Crystal Palace	0-1	5299		"	"	"	*Q	G	"	"	"	"	"	"	X
14.	12	CAMBRIDGE UNITED	5-0	4730	Gibbins2 Vaughan Owen2	"	"	"	"	"	"	"	"	"	"	"	"
15.	19	Oldham Athletic	1-2	3587	Dwyer	"	"	"	G	B	"	"	"	"	"	"	Q
16.	26	HUDDERSFIELD TOWN	3-1	6067	Bodin o.g.(Laws) Owen	"	"	"	"	"	"	"	"	*A	"	"	"
17.	3 Dec	Brighton & H.A.	1-3	9924	Baird	"	"	"	"	"	"	"	"	"	"	"	"
18.	10	BLACKBURN ROVERS	0-1	5200		*T	"	"	"	"	"	"	"	"	"	"	a
19.	17	Sheffield Wed.	2-5	14580	Baird 2	F	"	"	"	"	"	"	"	"	"	Q	"
20.	26	SWANSEA CITY	3-2	14580	Gibbins Vaughan Lee	"	"	"	"	"	"	"	"	"	"	*D	D
21.	26	Derby County	3-2	16054	Baird 2 Dwyer	"	"	"	"	"	"	D	"	"	"	*O	Q
22.	31	Grimsby Town	0-1	7164		"	"	"	"	"	"	"	"	"	"	"	S
23.	21 Jan	Portsmouth	1-1	11938	Lee	"	H	"	"	"	"	S	"	"	"	"	V
24.	31	CHARLTON ATHLETIC	2-1	4522	Owen Bennett	"	"	"	"	"	"	"	"	"	"	"	J
25.	4 Feb	Barnsley	3-2	7107	Baird Owen o.g.(May)	"	"	"	"	"	"	"	"	Y	M	*J	C
26.	11	LEEDS UNITED	0-1	9407		"	"	"	"	"	"	"	"	"	"	A	J
27.	19	FULHAM	0-4	7149		"	"	"	"	"	"	"	"	"	"	O	C
28.	25	Newcastle United	1-3	27909	Vaughan	"	"	"	"	"	"	"	"	"	"	"	"
29.	3 Mar	MIDDLESBROUGH	2-1	4422	Elsey Goldsmith	"	"	*K	"	"	"	"	"	"	H	"	J
30.	10	Cambridge United	2-0	2512	Smith Vaughan	"	"	"	"	V	"	"	"	"	J	"	M
31.	17	SHREWSBURY TOWN	2-0	3870	Vaughan Owen	"	"	"	"	"	"	"	"	"	M	"	J
32.	24	Manchester City	1-2	20140	Owen	"	"	"	"	"	"	"	"	"	"	"	"
33.	31	CHELSEA	3-3	11060	Gibbins Owen(pen) Vaughan	"	"	"	"	"	"	"	"	"	"	"	"
34.	7 Apr	Carlisle United	1-1	4704	Goldsmith	"	"	"	"	"	"	"	"	"	"	"	"
35.	14	OLDHAM ATHLETIC	2-0	4637	Owen (pen) Lee	"	"	"	"	"	"	"	"	"	"	"	"
36.	17	CRYSTAL PALACE	0-2	4901		"	"	"	"	"	"	"	"	"	B	"	"
37.	21	Swansea City	2-3	10275	Smith Owen	"	"	"	"	"	"	"	"	"	M	"	R
38.	23	DERBY COUNTY	1-0	5056	Owen	"	"	B	"	"	"	"	"	"	J	"	"
39.	28	Huddersfield Town	0-4	5599		"	"	"	"	"	"	C	"	"	"	"	C
40.	5 May	BRIGHTON & H.A.	2-2	4366	Lee Vaughan	"	V	K	"	B	"	S	"	"	H	"	"
41.	7	Blackburn Rovers	1-1	3107	Lee	"	C	"	"	V	"	"	"	"	B	"	R
42.	12	SHEFFIELD WED.	0-2	14171		"	V	"	"	B	"	S	"	"	C	"	Q

Players:

A = Baird,I. 12/2/7
B = Bennett,G. 32/7/3
C = Bodin,P. 26/8/3
D = Burke,M. 3/1/0
E = Crawford,A. 6/3/3
F = Dibble,A. 41/6/0
G = Dwyer,P. 42/8/3
H = Elsey,K. 29/4/1
I = Gibbins,R. 42/8/5
J = Goldsmith,M. 3/0/2
K = Grant,D. 12/0/0
L = Heycock,R. 0/1/0
M = Hemmerman,J. 10/0/0
N = Jones,L. 6/1/0
O = Lee,T. 21/1/6
P = Lewis,J. 6/2/0
Q = Matthews,W. 4/4/0
R = Mullen,J. 8/3/0
S = Owen,G. 38/8/19
T = Plumley,G. 1/2/0
U = Rodon,C. 4/2/0
V = Smith,C. 34/4/2
W = Tong,D. 42/8/0
X = Townsend,C. 2/1/1
Y = Vaughan,N. 36/4/10
Z = Walker,P. 2/0/0
a = Evans,P. 0/1/0

Dave Bennett goes to Coventry for £120,000 - Bob Hatton retires - Vaughan and Elsey arrive - Lewis, Jones and Micallef go in multi-deal with Newport ... Free transfer Owen top scorer in mediocre season ... Toshack returns to Ninian Park as Swansea player/manager .. Ashurst resigns - Goodfellow new manager.. Record receipts at last home game.

Other Matches

F.A.Cup

	Date	Opposition	Res	Attend.	Goalscorers	1	2	3	4	5	6	7	8	9	10	11	12
3rd	7 Jan	IPSWICH TOWN	0-3	10188		F	H	C	G	B	W	S	I	a	Y	D	L

Milk Cup

	Date	Opposition	Res	Attend.	Goalscorers	1	2	3	4	5	6	7	8	9	10	11	12
1st/1 Leg	31 Aug	Exeter City	3-2	4005	Dwyer Owen Crawford	"	N	"	"	"	"	"	"	E	U	P	R
1st/2 Leg	13 Sep	EXETER CITY	2-1	2721	Crawford Bennett	"	U	"	"	"	"	"	"	"	R	"	Q
2nd/1 Leg	4 Oct	NORWICH CITY	0-0	4425		"	V	"	"	R	"	"	"	X	E	Q	L
2nd/2 Leg	26	Norwich City	0-3	9887		"	"	"	"	"	"	"	"	L	B	"	X

Welsh Cup

	Date	Opposition	Res	Attend.	Goalscorers	1	2	3	4	5	6	7	8	9	10	11	12
3rd	22 Nov	TAFF'S WELL	5-0	894	Matthews Owen Gibbins Vaughan Townsend	T	"	"	"	B	"	"	"	Q	Y	"	"
4th	18 Jan	MAESTEG PARK	4-0	905	Owen 2 (2 pens.) Baird Lee	"	H	"	"	"	"	"	"	A	"	O	V
5th	7 Feb	HEREFORD UNITED	1-3	2033	Vaughan	F	"	V	"	"	"	"	"	"	"	C	Q

Friendlies

	Date	Opposition	Res	Attend.	Goalscorers
	9 Aug	Wokingham Town	1-2	600	Owen (pen)
	10	Shepton Mallet	2-1	300	Lewis (pen) Crawford
	12	Forest Green Rovers	2-2	400	Gibbins Owen
	13	Bishop's Cleeve	3-1	300	Micallef Heycock Crawford
	15	Cardiff Civil Service	7-5	250	Micallef 2 Owen 2 Mullen Dwyer Crawford
	16	Trowbridge	0-0	400	
	18	Llanelli	2-1	150	McCarthy Tong
	19	BIRMINGHAM CITY	1-2	2000	Rodon
	28 Nov	WOLVERHAMPTON W.	3-5	2500	Vaughan Williams Bennett,D.

(Back) G.Bennett, Roden, Gibbins, Dibble, Plumley, Evans, Dwyer, Bodin.
(Front) Crawford, Matthews, Lewis, Owen, Mullen, Micallef, Jones, Tong.

1984-85

Football League – Division 2.

Manager: Jimmy Goodfellow (Alan Durban from Sep 1984) P:42 W:9 D:8 L:25 47-79 Pts:35 Pos:21st (Rel.)

2444	Date	Opposition	Res	Attend.	Goalscorers	1	2	3	4	5	6	7	8	9	10	11	12
1.	25 Aug	CHARLTON ATHLETIC	0-3	5020		*X	*M	K	C	Y	a	D	J	b	*W	*Z	B
2.	1 Sep	Sheffield United	1-2	12133	Gibbins	"	"	"	"	"	"	"	"	"	"	"	A
3.	8	BRIGHTON & H.A.	2-4	4634	Seasman(pen) Elsey	*U	a	D	"	"	*A	*I	"	"	"	B	*d
4.	12	LEEDS UNITED	2-1	7300	Bodin Dwyer	T	M	K	"	"	a	"	A	D	"	"	J
5.	15	Barnsley	0-2	4692		"	"	"	"	"	"	"	"	"	"	"	"
6.	18	Blackburn Rovers	1-2	5924	Summerfield	"	D	"	"	"	Z	"	J	b	"	"	a
7.	22	MANCHESTER CITY	0-3	6089		"	M	"	"	"	"	"	"	D	"	"	b
8.	29	Middlesbrough	2-3	4266	Seasman Vaughan	"	"	"	"	"	a	"	"	b	"	"	R
9.	6 Oct	PORTSMOUTH	1-2	6201	Elsey	X	"	"	"	"	"	"	"	"	"	D	"
10.	14	Notts. County	2-0	5893	Vaughan 2	"	"	"	"	"	"	"	"	"	B	"	W
11.	20	Fulham	2-3	5358	Smith Elsey	"	"	"	"	"	"	"	"	"	"	"	"
12.	27	GRIMSBY TOWN	2-4	3607	Vaughan 2	"	"	"	"	"	"	"	"	"	D	B	S
13.	3 Nov	Wolverhampton W.	0-3	7537		"	"	"	"	"	"	W	"	"	"	S	R
14.	10	OLDHAM ATHLETIC	2-2	3429	Vaughan 2	"	Y	S	"	K	"	Z	"	"	Z	D	"
15.	17	CARLISLE UNITED	2-1	3005	Vaughan Tong	"	"	"	"	*O	"	*F	"	"	"	"	a
16.	24	Huddersfield Town	1-2	6495	Vaughan	"	*N	"	"	"	"	"	"	"	"	"	Y
17.	1 Dec	BIRMINGHAM CITY	1-2	5057	Elsey	*E	"	"	"	"	"	*R	"	"	"	"	B
18.	9	Crystal Palace	1-1	6004	Gibbins	"	"	"	"	a	O	"	Z	"	J	"	Q
19.	15	WIMBLEDON	1-3	2976	Dwyer	"	Y	"	"	O	J	"	*Q	"	Z	"	P
20.	22	SHEFFIELD UNITED	1-3	3306	Withey	"	N	"	"	"	a	"	J	"	*c	"	R
21.	26	Oxford United	0-4	12237		X	"	"	"	"	"	"	Q	"	"	"	P
22.	29	Leeds United	1-1	11798	Withey	"	D	"	"	*H	"	"	J	J	"	Q	R
23.	1 Jan	SHREWSBURY TOWN	0-0	4609		"	"	"	J	"	"	"	"	"	"	"	N
24.	2	MIDDLESBROUGH	2-1	2564	Meacock 2	T	N	D	"	S	J	"	Q	"	"	*P	R
25.	9	Brighton & H.A.	0-1	7337		"	"	S	"	H	a	P	"	"	"	D	"
26.	16	Oldham Athletic	1-0	3952		"	"	"	"	"	"	F	"	"	F	P	B
27.	23	WOLVERHAMPTON W.	0-0	4694		"	"	"	"	"	"	"	R	"	c	"	J
28.	2 Feb	Grimsby Town	3-6	4585	Mullen(pen) Withey Gibbins	"	"	"	"	"	"	"	Q	"	"	"	"
29.	5	Charlton Athletic	4-1	3930	Mullen(Pen) Withey 2 Dwyer	"	"	"	"	"	"	B	"	J	"	"	"
30.	9	FULHAM	0-2	4399		"	"	"	"	"	D	"	"	"	"	"	b
31.	17	NOTTS. COUNTY	1-4	3631	Gibbins	"	"	"	"	"	"	"	"	"	"	"	"
32.	23	Portsmouth	0-0	13620		"	"	"	"	"	a	P	"	b	"	B	G
33.	30	Manchester City	2-2	20047	Withey Gibbins	"	"	"	"	"	"	"	*V	"	"	*L	F
34.	6 Mar	OXFORD UNITED	0-2	6686		"	"	*G	"	"	"	"	"	"	"	"	Q
35.	9	Shrewsbury Town	0-0	3929		"	"	F	"	"	"	"	"	"	"	"	"
36.	13	BLACKBURN ROVERS	1-2	3240	Vaughan	"	"	B	"	"	"	"	Q	"	"	"	V
37.	20	Carlisle United	1-0	2651	Vaughan	"	"	D	"	"	"	"	"	"	"	"	B
38.	23	BARNSLEY	3-0	3044	Vaughan 2 Ford,M.	"	"	"	"	"	"	B	"	"	"	"	V
39.	27	HUDDERSFIELD TOWN	3-0	3414	Vaughan 2 Meacock	"	"	S	"	"	F	"	"	J	"	"	P
40.	4 Apr	Birmingham City	0-2	15570		"	"	"	"	"	"	"	"	"	"	"	D
41.	6	CRYSTAL PALACE	0-3	5207		"	"	"	"	"	a	"	R	"	c	"	P
42.	11	Wimbledon	1-2	3252	Micallef	"	F	"	"	"	"	D	"	"	b	"	Q

Players:

- A = Bannon,P. — 3/0/0
- B = Bodin,P. — 15/3/1
- C = Dwyer,P. — 31/7/3
- D = Elsey,K. — 30/7/5
- E = Felgate,D. — 4/0/0
- F = Flynn,B. — 22/3/0
- G = Ford,F. — 1/0/0
- H = Ford,M. — 20/2/1
- I = Francis,G. — 7/0/0
- J = Gibbins,R. — 36/7/8
- K = Grant,D. — 13/4/1
- L = Hamilton,D. — 10/0/0
- M = Jones,V. — 11/4/0
- N = King,J. — 23/1/0
- O = Martin,M. — 7/1/0
- P = McLoughli,P.n — 14/0/0
- Q = Meacock,K. — 18/2/3
- R = Micallef,C. — 5/1/2
- S = Mullen,J. — 25/3/2
- T = Plumley,G. — 24/1/0
- U = Rees,M. — 1/0/0
- V = Saunders,D. — 3/0/0
- W = Seasman,J. — 10/4/2
- X = Smelt,L. — 13/6/0
- Y = Smith,C. — 16/4/1
- Z = Summerfield,K — 10/2/1
- a = Tong,D. — 33/6/2
- b = Vaughan,N. — 35/7/18
- c = Withey,G. — 22/2/7
- d = Woods,J. — 0/0/0

Three players sold - no money for replacements! Dreadful start results in Goodfellow's exit - Alan Durban appointed new manager.... Phil Dwyer sets new appearance record - released to Rochdale before end of season.... More players move - but City relegated again ... 0-4 home defeat to Hereford in Welsh Cup... Red Dragons leave Ninian Park.

Other Matches

F.A.Cup

	Date	Opposition	Res	Attend.	Goalscorers	1	2	3	4	5	6	7	8	9	10	11	12
3rd	21 Jan	Gillingham	1–2	5452	Withey	X	D	S	C	H	a	F	J	b	c	Q	R

Milk Cup

	Date	Opposition	Res	Attend.	Goalscorers	1	2	3	4	5	6	7	8	9	10	11	12
1st/1 Leg	29 Aug	Exeter City	0–1	3469		"	M	K	"	Y	"	D	"	"	W	Z	B
1st/2 Leg	4 Sep	EXETER CITY	2–0	2026	Gibbins 2	"	"	"	"	"	"	"	"	"	"	B	d
2nd/1 Leg	25	Watford	1–3	12884	Gibbins	T	"	"	"	"	"	"	"	"	"	"	"
2nd/2 Leg	9 Oct	WATFORD	1–0	4607	Grant	X	"	B	"	K	"	Z	"	"	"	D	R

Welsh Cup

	Date	Opposition	Res	Attend.	Goalscorers	1	2	3	4	5	6	7	8	9	10	11	12
3rd	27 Nov	MERTHYR TYDFIL	5–0	1399	Tong Micallef Vaughan 2 Elsey	"	Y	S	"	O	"	F	"	"	R	D	M
4th	30 Jan	HEREFORD UNITED	0–4	2075		"	N	"	H	J	"	Q	"	"	c	"	R

Back Row (left to right): Karl Elsey, Roger Gibbins, Phil Dwyer, Gary Plumley, Lee Smelt, Colin Smith, David Grant, Paul Bodin. *Front Row (left to right):* Vaughan Jones, David Tong, Jimmy Mullen, Nigel Vaughan, Kevin Summerfield, John Seasman.

Cardiff City
SEASON 1984-85

Friendlies

	Date	Opposition	Res	Attend.	Goalscorers
	27 Jul	Aberystwyth & Dist.Lge.	5–0	300	Tong 2 Vaughan Bodin Irving
	1 Aug	Forest Green Rovers	2–0	400	Kelly Summerfield
	4	Bishop's Cleeve	2–0	250	Irving Woods(pen)
	6	Wokingham Town	1–2	400	Gibbins
	8	Llanelli	4–0	300	Woods 2 (1 pen) Bodin (pen) Elsey
	11	Worcester City	2–2	700	Elsey Seasman
	15	Caerleon	0–1	150	
	18	STOKE CITY	3–0	2000	Summerfield 2 Tong
	3 Dec	ASTON VILLA	3–0	2200	Gibbins Hemmmerman 2
	25 May	SOUTH WALES F.A.X1	2–0	1800	Farrington McLoughlin

1985-86
Football League – Division 3.

Manager: Alan Durban (Jimmy Mullen – temporary – from May 1986)

P:46 W:12 D:9 L:25 53–83 Pts:45 Pos:22nd (Rel.)

2490	Date	Opposition	Res	Attend.	Goalscorers	1	2	3	4	5	6	7	8	9	10	11	12
1.	17 Aug	Notts. County	4-1	3856	McLough. Farrton Vghan Mullen(p)	*X	M	*B	J	I	S	G	*F	*c	d	P	R
2.	24	CHESTERFIELD	0-2	3601		"	"	"	"	"	"	"	"	"	"	"	"
3.	26	Newport County	2-1	5027	Mullen(pen) Vaughan	"	"	"	"	"	"	"	"	"	"	"	"
4.	31	READING	1-3	3539	McLoughlin	"	b	"	"	"	"	"	"	"	"	"	"
5.	7 Sep	York City	1-1	3760	Ford	W	P	"	"	"	"	*L	"	d	Q	*K	"
6.	14	BRISTOL CITY	1-3	4412	Withey	"	"	"	"	"	"	"	"	"	f	"	"
7.	17	BURY	0-0	2011		"	"	"	"	"	"	G	"	"	"	R	Q
8.	21	Blackpool	0-3	3783		"	"	"	"	"	"	"	"	"	"	"	"
9.	28	DERBY COUNTY	0-2	3435		"	"	"	"	*D	"	"	"	"	*e	I	E
10.	1 Oct	Rotherham United	0-3	2906		"	"	"	"	"	"	"	"	*E	"	"	R
11.	5	A.F.C.BOURNEMOUTH	0-1	2156		"	J	"	I	"	"	"	"	f	d	e	"
12.	12	Gillingham	0-2	3367		"	*Z	*N	"	"	"	"	"	c	*O	*K	"
13.	19	WIGAN ATHLETIC	3-1	2020	Marustik Turner Vaughan	X	*V	B	"	"	"	P	d	"	"	"	Q
14.	22	Darlington	1-4	2446	McLoughlin	W	B	P	D	I	"	K	"	"	"	Q	E
15.	26	BOLTON WANDERERS	0-1	2502		X	P	*a	I	M	"	*C	"	"	"	F	G
16.	2 Nov	Brentford	0-3	3934		"	"	"	"	"	"	"	"	"	K	"	F
17.	5	Walsall	3-6	3282		"	M	N	"	a	"	"	"	"	F	"	P
18.	8	DONCASTER ROVERS	0-1	2015		Y	"	"	"	"	"	"	"	"	P	"	G
19.	23	Bristol Rovers	1-2	4563	Mullen(pen)	"	E	K	O	"	"	"	"	f	*U	R	F
20.	30	WOLVERHAMPTON W.	1-1	2453	Curtis	"	N	"	"	"	"	"	"	c	e	E	"
21.	14 Dec	Lincoln City	4-0	2127	Vaughan Turner Mullen(pi) Farrington	"	E	"	L	"	"	"	"	"	"	I	R
22.	20	Chesterfield	4-3	1773	Turner Christie Vaughan Farrington	"	"	"	"	a	"	"	"	"	"	R	"
23.	26	SWANSEA CITY	1-0	9375	Vaughan	"	E	"	O	"	"	F	"	c	"	"	L
24.	28	NEWPORT COUNTY	1-1	7450	Ford	"	"	"	I	*A	"	"	"	"	F	"	e
25.	1 Jan	Plymouth	4-4	8920	Turner Ford Vaughan Mullen(pen)	"	"	"	"	"	"	"	"	"	"	"	"
26.	4	BRENTFORD	1-0	3398	Vaughan	"	"	"	"	"	"	"	"	"	e	"	F
27.	11	Reading	1-1	6784	Ford	"	"	"	"	"	"	C	"	"	"	"	"
28.	18	NOTTS.COUNTY	1-3	2410	Mullen(pen)	"	O	"	O	"	P	"	"	"	F	"	e
29.	25	Bristol City	1-2	7541	Wheeler	"	"	"	I	a	S	R	"	e	"	e	P
30.	31	YORK CITY	1-2	2051	Vaughan Wheeler	"	"	"	"	A	"	P	"	c	F	"	H
31.	4 Feb	DARLINGTON	0-1	2222		X	"	"	O	"	"	"	*H	"	R	I	e
32.	8	Wigan Athletic	0-2	3428		Y	O	"	I	"	"	"	d	*T	"	H	c
33.	22	BLACKPOOL	1-0	2430	Curtis	X	E	"	O	"	"	"	d	c	F	"	d
34.	1 Mar	Derby County	1-2	11014	Vaughan	"	"	"	"	"	"	C	"	H	"	"	c
35.	8	A.F.C.BOURNEMOUTH	1-1	2707	Turner	Y	O	"	d	"	"	"	"	"	"	"	c
36.	15	GILLINGHAM	1-1	2505	Gummer	"	"	"	"	"	"	"	"	H	"	"	d
37.	22	Bolton Wanderers	0-5	4114		"	"	"	O	"	V	C	"	T	F	e	U
38.	25	ROTHERHAM UNITED	2-3	1863	McLoughlin Mullen(pen)	X	"	"	"	"	"	P	"	c	F	e	H
39.	28	PLYMOUTH ARGYLE	1-2	3834	Nardiello	Y	O	"	I	"	"	"	"	c	R	"	e
40.	31	Swansea City	0-2	6643		X	E	"	O	"	"	"	"	*T	"	H	c
41.	5 Apr	WALSALL	1-1	1777	Foley	X	"	"	"	"	"	"	"	c	"	I	d
42.	8	Bury	0-3	1720		Y	O	"	d	"	"	"	"	H	"	"	c
43.	12	Doncaster Rovers	2-0	2051	Nardiello 2	"	E	"	O	"	V	C	"	T	"	"	P
44.	19	BRISTOL ROVERS	2-0	2735	o.g.(Tanner) Vaughan	"	"	"	"	"	S	P	"	"	"	e	H
45.	26	Wolverhampton W.	1-3	3353	Nardiello	"	P	"	"	"	"	e	"	"	c	"	"
46.	3 May	LINCOLN CITY	2-1	1904	Turner 2	X	E	"	"	"	"	"	"	H	"	"	P

Players:

A = Brignull,P. 15/0/0
B = Carver,J. 13/2/0
C = Christie,D. 18/5/2
D = Comer,D. 6/0/0
E = Curtis,W. 23/7/2
F = Farrington,M. 24/3/4
G = Flynn,B. 10/2/2
H = Foley,W. 5/0/1
I = Ford,M. 44/11/4
J = Gibbins,R. 11/2/0
K = Giles,D. 34/8/1
L = Gummer,J. 5/0/1
M = King,J. 7/2/0
N = Leonard,C. 4/3/0
O = Marustik,C. 26/9/2
P = McLoughlin,P. 26/8/4
Q = Meacock,K. 2/1/0
R = Micallef,C. 21/7/0
S = Mullen,J. 44/11/8
T = Nardiello,G. 7/0/4
U = O'Connor,T. 1/0/0
V = Price,A. 2/1/0
W = Rees,M. 9/1/0
X = Sander,C. 13/1/0
Y = Smett,L. 24/9/0
Z = Spring,A. 1/0/0
a = Stevenson,N. 14/1/1
b = Tong,D. 1/0/0
c = Turner,R. 31/7/8
d = Vaughan,N. 42/11/17
e = Wheeler,P. 17/5/2
f = Withey,G. 5/1/1
g = Hemmerman,J. 0/3/2

Continual financial restraints - new inexperienced players recipe for disaster ! Best opening day League result... Swansea declared bankrupt fulfill Xmas fixture at Ninian Park.... Sander saves two penalties in game. Record number of 19 players make debut for Club - fail to prevent further disaster... Durban dismissed after relegation confirmed.

Other Matches

F.A. Cup

	Date	Opposition	Res	Attend.	Goalscorers
1st	16 Nov	Exeter City	1-2	2772	Stevenson

Milk Cup

	Date	Opposition	Res	Attend.	Goalscorers
1st/1 Leg	20 Aug	SWANSEA CITY	2-1	4218	Flynn 2
1st/2 Leg	3 Sep	Swansea City	1-3	4621	Farrington

Welsh Cup

	Date	Opposition	Res	Attend.	Goalscorers
3rd	26 Nov	Caerleon	3-2	500	Vaughan 2 Marustik
4th	8 Jan	MOLD ALEXANDRA	4-1	604	Turner Hemmerman Vaughan 2
5th	11 Mar	BARRY TOWN	0-0	2053	
5th Replay	13	Barry Town	2-0	1750	Hemmerman Giles
S-fin/1 Leg	15 Apr	Wrexham	1-4	1639	Vaughan
S-fin/2 Leg	22	WREXHAM	1-2	1255	Marustik

Freight-Rover Trophy

	Date	Opposition	Res	Attend.	Goalscorers
Prelim.	21 Jan	Newport County	0-1	1863	
Prelim.	28	SWANSEA CITY	0-2	1006	

Friendlies

	Date	Opposition	Res	Attend.	Goalscorers
	26 Jul	Spencer Works	7-0	200	Farrington 5 (2pens.) Vaughan Curtis
	27	Cwmbran	2-2	400	Turner Mullen(pen)
	31	Ebbw Vale	4-1	452	Turner Farrington Withey Flynn
	1 Aug	Merthyr Tydfil	0-1	710	
	4	Parkway Clayton	5-1	227	Micallef Withey Ford Mullen(pen) Tong
	6	Wrexham	2-4	500	Wright 2
	9	Swansea City	0-1	1700	
	12	NEWPORT COUNTY	1-3	1400	Flynn
	24 Sep	Briton Ferry Athletic	5-1	150	Vaughan 2 (1 pen) Farrington 2 Gibbins
	14 Oct	Rhayader Town	9-0	400	Vaughan2 Turner2 Mullen McLoughlin Giles2 Ford

Our current First-Team squad... BACK (from left): Alan Durban (Manager), Carlton Leonard (player/Physio.), vin Meacock, Mel Rees, Rob Turner, Lee Smell, Mark Farrington, Paul McLoughlin, Jimmy Mullen,(Asst. manager), FRONT (from left): Tarki Micallef, Brian Flynn, John Carver, Roger Gibbins, Jake King, Mike Ford, Nigel Vaghan, David Tong, Graham Withey.

1986-87

Football League – Division 4.

Manager: Frank Burrows
P: 46 **W:** 15 **D:** 16 **L:** 15 **48-50 Pts:** 61 **Pos:** 13th

2536	Date	Opposition	Res	Attend.	Goalscorers	1	2	3	4	5	6	7	8	9	10	11	12
1.	23 Aug	Hartlepool United	1-1	2800	Turner	*L	*J	*S	*X	C	*B	G	U	W	V	*R	F
2.	30	ROCHDALE	0-0	3546		"	"	"	"	"	"	"	"	"	*D	"	"
3.	6 Sep	Wolverhampton W.	1-0	5740	Wimbleton (pen)	"	"	"	"	"	"	"	"	"	"	"	U
4.	13	TRANMERE ROVERS	0-2	2868		"	"	"	"	"	"	"	V	"	"	"	"
5.	16	LINCOLN CITY	1-1	2402	Rogers	"	"	"	"	"	"	"	D	"	V	"	"
6.	20	Exeter City	0-0	3066		"	"	"	"	"	"	"	"	"	"	"	P
7.	27	HEREFORD UNITED	4-1	3353	Wheeler Vaughan Wimbleton(p) Curtis	"	"	"	"	"	"	"	"	"	"	"	"
8.	1 Oct	Peterborough Utd.	2-1	2600	Wheeler Vaughan	"	"	"	"	"	"	"	"	"	"	"	"
9.	4	CREWE ALEXANDRA	1-1	3570	Vaughan	"	"	"	"	"	"	"	"	"	"	"	"
10.	11	Wrexham	1-5	2926	Vaughan	"	"	"	"	"	"	M	"	"	"	"	"
11.	17	Colchester United	1-3	3169	Wheeler	Q	"	"	"	"	"	"	"	"	"	"	"
12.	25	SCUNTHORPE UNITED	1-1	2145	Boyle	"	"	F	"	"	"	G	"	"	"	"	"
13.	31	Halifax Town	1-1	1640	Platnauer	"	"	"	"	"	"	*P	"	"	"	M	A
14.	4 Nov	Preston North End	1-0	6614	Ford	"	"	"	"	"	"	"	"	"	"	"	"
15.	8	SOUTHEND UNITED	0-2	3025		"	"	"	"	"	"	"	"	"	"	"	"
16.	22	Stockport County	0-2	1674		"	"	"	"	"	"	"	*E	"	"	"	"
17.	29	CAMBRIDGE UNITED	3-0	2071	Bartlett 2 Wimbleton(pen)	L	G	"	"	"	"	D	*A	R	"	"	P
18.	13 Dec	ALDERSHOT	2-0	2443	Platnauer Vaughan	"	"	"	"	"	"	P	"	*O	"	"	W
19.	19	Burnley	3-1	1702	Vaughan Pike Wimbleton	"	"	"	"	"	"	"	"	"	"	M	R
20.	26	SWANSEA CITY	0-0	11505		"	"	"	"	C	"	"	"	"	"	"	D
21.	28	Northampton Town	1-4	11138	Pike	"	J	"	"	"	"	"	T	"	"	"	"
22.	3 Jan	STOCKPORT COUNTY	1-1	3038	Wheeler	"	G	"	"	"	"	"	D	W	"	"	R
23.	24	WOLVERHAMPTON W.	0-2	3331		Q	"	"	"	"	"	"	W	O	D	"	E
24.	7 Feb	Lincoln City	1-0	1954	Wimbleton (pen)	L	J	"	"	"	"	"	A	"	"	"	V
25.	21	Hereford United	2-0	3969	o.g.(Ceglieski) Horrix	"	M	"	"	J	"	"	S	*I	*T	"	A
26.	24	Tranmere Rovers	1-2	1456	Simmons	"	"	"	"	"	"	"	R	"	"	"	"
27.	28	PETERBOROUGH UTD.	0-1	2620		"	J	"	"	C	"	"	T	"	"	R	"
28.	3 Mar	HALIFAX TOWN	0-0	1784		"	"	"	"	"	"	"	"	"	"	"	D
29.	7	Scunthorpe United	3-1	1935	Kerr Horrix 2	"	"	"	"	"	"	"	W	"	"	"	T
30.	10	Rochdale	0-0	1114		"	"	"	"	"	"	"	"	"	"	"	"
31.	14	COLCHESTER UNITED	0-2	2222		"	"	"	"	"	"	"	"	"	D	M	H
32.	17	Orient	0-2	2401		"	"	"	"	"	"	"	"	"	"	H	S
33.	21	WREXHAM	0-0	1805		Q	"	"	"	S	"	"	A	"	"	"	A
34.	24	ORIENT	1-1	1562	Platnauer	"	"	"	"	"	"	"	"	A	"	V	H
35.	28	Crewe Alexandra	2-1	1762	Wheeler 2	"	"	"	"	H	"	"	"	"	"	"	K
36.	31	EXETER CITY	0-0	1825		"	*N	"	"	C	"	"	"	"	"	H	"
37.	3 Apr	Southend United	0-2	3917		"	J	"	"	"	"	"	"	*K	"	"	V
38.	11	PRESTON NORTH END	1-1	2528	Wimbleton	"	"	"	"	"	"	"	"	"	"	V	A
39.	18	TORQUAY UNITED	3-1	1840	Mardenborough Curtis Wheeler	"	V	"	"	H	"	"	"	"	"	R	"
40.	20	Swansea City	0-2	6653		"	"	"	"	C	"	"	"	"	"	R	R
41.	25	BURNLEY	1-0	2003	Wimbleton (pen)	"	"	"	"	"	"	"	"	"	"	H	A
42.	28	Torquay United	0-1	1365		"	"	"	"	R	"	"	A	"	"	"	W
43.	1 May	Cambridge United	1-2	1563	Gummer	"	"	"	"	"	"	"	"	"	"	"	"
44.	4	NORTHAMPTON TOWN	1-1	2682	Curtis	"	"	"	"	"	"	"	W	"	"	"	A
45.	7	HARTLEPOOL UNITED	4-0	1510	Curtis Gummer Bartlett Wimbleton	"	"	"	"	"	"	"	"	A	"	"	J
46.	9	Aldershot	2-1	3680	Gummer Bartlett	"	"	"	"	"	"	"	"	"	"	"	"

Players:

A = Bartlett,K. 12/7/7
B = Boyle,T. 46/14/3
C = Brignull,P. 34/13/0
D = Curtis,A. 40/7/4
E = Davies,G. 1/1/0
F = Ford,M. 35/12/1
G = Giles,D. 16/6/1
H = Gummer,J. 13/0/3
I = Horrix,D. 9/0/3
J = Kerr,A. 31/9/1
K = Mardenborough,S. 9/0/1
L = Moseley,G. 25/8/0
M = Marustik,C. 17/10/3
N = Perry,J. 1/0/0
O = Pike,C. 6/4/3
P = Platnauer,N. 33/12/5
Q = Rees,M. 21/6/0
R = Rogers,A. 25/6/1
S = Sherlock,S. 14/3/0
T = Simmons,A. 4/0/0
U = Turner,R. 3/2/2
V = Vaughan,N. 31/12/9
W = Wheeler,P. 32/9/10
X = Wimbleton,P. 46/12/11
Y = Curtis,W. 0/1/0
Z = Fry,C. 0/0/0

Parent Company - Kenton Utilities - sell Club ownership to Tony Clemo... Frank Burrows appointed manager... Disappointing home form ensures stay in lower half of table - good F.A. and Littlewood's Cup run (recover from 1-4 to win 5-4 versus Plymouth) keeps season 'alive'... Moseley - first City keeper to be sent off... Last game - record low attendance.

Other Matches

F.A.Cup

	Date	Opposition	Res	Attend.	Goalscorers	1	2	3	4	5	6	7	8	9	10	11	12	14
1st	15 Nov	Ton Pentre	4-1	2700	Wimbleton Marustik 2 Wheeler	Q	J	F	X	C	B	P	D	W	V	M	R	A
2nd	9 Dec	BRENTFORD	2-0	2531	Wimbleton Bartlett	L	G	"	"	"	"	"	A	"	"	"	J	E
3rd	10 Jan	Millwall	0-0	5615		Q	"	"	R	"	"	"	D	"	"	"	X	"
3rd Rep.	20	MILLWALL	2-2	4585	Vaughan Marustik	"	"	"	"	"	"	"	A	O	"	"	"	W
3rd 2/Rep.	26	MILLWALL	1-0	5012	Pike	L	J	"	X	"	"	"	"	"	"	"	J	E
4th	31	Stoke City	1-2	20423	Wimbleton	"	"	"	"	"	"	"	"	"	"	"	E	G

Littlewoods (formerly Milk) Cup

	Date	Opposition	Res	Attend.	Goalscorers	1	2	3	4	5	6	7	8	9	10	11	12	14
1st/1 Leg	26 Aug	PLYMOUTH ARGYLE	5-4	2503	Vaughan 2 Turner Boyle Wheeler	"	"	S	"	"	"	G	U	W	"	R	D	F
1st/2 Leg	2 Sep	Plymouth Argyle	1-0	5829	Giles	"	"	"	"	"	"	"	"	"	D	"	Y	"
3rd †	28 Oct	CHELSEA	2-1	8018	Platnauer	Q	"	"	"	"	"	P	D	"	V	F	H	A
4th	18 Nov	Shrewsbury Town	0-1	4634		"	"	F	"	"	"	"	"	"	"	M	R	"

† Drawn 'away' to Luton Town in 2nd Round. Luton refused to issue tickets to Cardiff supporters, Cardiff awarded tie.

Welsh Cup

	Date	Opposition	Res	Attend.	Goalscorers	1	2	3	4	5	6	7	8	9	10	11	12	14
3rd	25 Nov	TAFF'S WELL	4-0	581	Bartlett 2 Wheeler Boyle	"	"	"	"	Y	"	"	A	"	"	"	"	R
4th	3 Feb	Wrexham	0-1	1915		L	"	"	"	C	"	"	"	O	D	F	"	V

Freight-Rover Trophy

	Date	Opposition	Res	Attend.	Goalscorers	1	2	3	4	5	6	7	8	9	10	11	12	14
Prelim.	2 Dec	WOLVERHAMPTON W.	0-1	1201		"	G	"	"	"	"	W	"	"	R	V	P	E	J
Prelim.	6 Jan	A.F.C.Bournemouth	0-1	1482		"	M	"	"	"	"	P	D	E	"	"	R	W	Z

Friendlies

	Date	Opposition	Res	Attend.	Goalscorers
	30 Jul	Aberystwyth Town	2-3	600	Wheeler Wimbleton
	2 Aug	Newtown	3-1	250	Curtis.A. Wheeler Wimbleton
	6	Cwmbran Town	2-0	300	Wheeler Curtis.A.
	9	Forest Green Rovers	2-2	200	Wimbleton Wheeler
	12	Gloucester City	1-0	500	Turner
	16	NEWPORT COUNTY	1-1	1700	Wheeler
	18	SWINDON TOWN	3-1	1400	Vaughan Wheeler 2

BACK (from left): Chris Marustik, Mike Ford, Andy Kerr, Alan Rogers, Graham Moseley, Mel Rees, Rob Turner, Paul Wheeler, Steve Sherlock, Phil Brignull. FRONT (from left): Nigel Vaughan, Paul Wimbleton, Alan Curtis, Terry Boyle, Wayne Curtis, Jason Gummer, David Giles.

1987-88

Manager: Frank Burrows

Football League – Division 4. P:46 W:23 D:13 L:9 66-41 Pts:85 Pos:2nd (Prom.)

2582	Date	Opposition	Res	Attend.	Goalscorers	1	2	3	4	5	6	7	8	9	10	11	12	14
1.	15 Aug	LEYTON ORIENT	1-1	3357	Gilligan	N	O	G	I	*S	D	E	*R	*H	*M	*K	L	T
2.	22	Bolton Wanderers	0-1	4530		"	"	"	P	"	"	"	"	"	"	"	T	B
3.	29	SWANSEA CITY	1-0	6010	Gilligan	"	L	"	"	"	"	"	"	"	"	"	O	"
4.	1 Sep	Cambridge United	0-0	2079		"	"	"	"	"	"	"	"	"	"	"	"	"
5.	5	WOLVERHAMPTON W.	3-2	2258	McDermott Bartlett Boyle	"	G	P	L	O	"	"	B	"	"	"	R	X
6.	12	Wrexham	0-3	2212		"	"	"	U	*A	"	"	"	"	"	"	"	L
7.	15	DARLINGTON	3-1	2201	Abraham Bartlett 2	"	"	*C	"	"	"	"	"	"	"	"	"	"
8.	19	CARLISLE UNITED	4-2	2659	Gilligan 2 Ford Boyle	"	C	G	"	"	"	"	"	"	"	"	"	A
9.	25	Tranmere Rovers	1-0	2543	Wimbleton	"	"	"	"	P	"	"	"	"	"	"	"	T
10.	29	HALIFAX TOWN	0-0	3666		"	G	P	"	S	"	"	"	"	"	"	"	"
11.	2 Oct	Stockport County	1-0	2332	Bartlett	"	C	G	"	"	"	"	"	"	"	P	"	K
12.	10	HEREFORD UNITED	0-1	4420		"	"	P	"	"	"	"	"	"	"	G	R	"
13.	17	Peterborough United	3-4	3473	Ford 2 McDermott	"	"	"	"	K	"	"	L	"	"	"	B	"
14.	20	TORQUAY UNITED	2-1	3503	Ford Gilligan	*J	"	"	"	"	"	T	"	"	"	"	I	T
15.	24	Scunthorpe United	1-2	2872	Sanderson	"	"	"	"	G	"	"	"	"	"	"	R	S
16.	31	ROCHDALE	1-0	3046	Gilligan	"	"	"	S	"	"	"	"	"	"	K	"	B
17.	4 Nov	Scarborough	1-1	2599	Wimbleton	"	"	"	U	"	"	E	G	"	"	R	K	"
18.	7	EXETER CITY	3-2	3474	Gilligan 2 Boyle	"	"	"	"	K	"	"	"	"	"	"	L	"
19.	21	Newport County	2-1	4022	Wimbleton Platnauer	*Q	"	"	"	"	"	"	"	"	"	B	R	L
20.	28	HARTLEPOOL UNITED	1-1	3232	McDermott	J	"	"	"	G	"	"	K	"	"	"	"	"
21.	12 Dec	Crewe Alexandra	0-0	2010		"	"	"	"	"	"	L	S	"	"	T	"	K
22.	19	BURNLEY	2-1	3401	Gilligan 2	"	"	"	"	S	"	"	G	"	"	"	B	"
23.	26	TRANMERE ROVERS	3-0	5233	Gilligan 2 Wimbleton	"	"	"	"	"	"	E	"	"	"	"	K	R
24.	28	Colchester United	1-2	2599	Kelly	"	"	K	"	K	"	"	"	"	"	K	R	T
25.	1 Jan	Swansea City	2-2	10360	Ford Gilligan	*F	"	"	"	"	"	"	"	"	"	"	T	K	B
26.	16	Carlisle United	0-0	2344		"	"	"	"	"	"	R	"	"	"	B	L	"
27.	30	CAMBRIDGE UNITED	4-0	4012	Wimbleton(p) Bartlett McD'ott Boyle	*W	"	"	"	"	"	"	"	"	"	"	R	K
28.	2 Feb	Darlington	0-0	2332		"	"	"	"	"	"	E	"	"	"	"	K	L
29.	6	Wolverhampton W.	4-1	9072	Gilligan 2 Wimbleton 2	"	"	"	"	"	"	"	"	"	"	"	V	"
30.	13	COLCHESTER UNITED	1-0	5458	Ford	"	"	"	"	"	"	"	"	"	"	"	L	V
31.	20	Leyton Orient	1-4	3523	Bartlett	"	"	"	"	"	"	"	"	"	"	"	"	*"
32.	27	STOCKPORT COUNTY	0-0	4008		Q	"	K	"	"	"	"	"	"	"	*V	R	T
33.	1 Mar	Halifax Town	1-0	1128	Bartlett	"	"	"	"	"	"	"	"	"	"	"	B	L	"
34.	4	PETERBOROUGH UTD.	0-0	4172		W	"	"	"	"	"	R	"	"	"	"	"	"
35.	13	Hereford United	2-1	3210	Gilligan Bartlett	"	"	"	"	"	"	E	"	"	"	"	L	V
36.	16	WREXHAM	1-1	4083	Gilligan	"	"	"	"	"	"	"	"	"	"	"	K	L
37.	26	SCUNTHORPE UNITED	0-1	4527		"	"	P	"	"	"	"	"	"	"	"	V	"
38.	29	Rochdale	2-2	1435	Bartlett o.g.(Bramhall)	"	"	"	"	"	"	"	"	"	"	"	L	V
39.	2 Apr	Exeter City	2-0	2649	Bartlett 2	W	"	"	"	"	"	"	"	"	"	"	"	*"
40.	4	NEWPORT COUNTY	4-0	6536	Stevenson Wimbleton McD'ott Ford	"	"	"	"	"	"	"	"	"	"	"	L	K
41.	9	Torquay United	0-2	3082		"	"	"	"	"	"	"	"	"	"	"	"	"
42.	15	BOLTON WANDERERS	1-0	6705	Gilligan	"	"	"	"	"	"	"	"	"	"	"	"	K
43.	23	SCARBOROUGH	2-0	5751	Curtis McDermott(pen)	"	"	"	"	"	"	"	M	"	K	"	M	T
44.	30	Hartlepool United	1-0	1097	Gilligan	"	"	"	G	"	"	"	"	"	"	"	O	"
45.	2 May	CREWE ALEXANDRA	2-0	10125	Bartlett McDermott	"	"	"	"	"	"	"	"	"	"	"	L	"
46.	7	Burnley	2-1	8525	Curtis Gilligan	"	"	"	"	"	"	"	"	"	"	"	"	"

Players:

- A = Abraham,C. 2/1/1
- B = Bartlett,K. 30/9/14
- C = Bater,P. 40/10/0
- D = Boyle,T. 46/12/4
- E = Curtis,A. 40/12/4
- F = Enderby,S. 4/1/0
- G = Ford,M. 45/13/9
- H = Gilligan,J. 46/13/26
- I = Gummer,J. 1/1/0
- J = Judge,A. 8/2/0
- K = Kelly,M. 28/11/2
- L = Mardenborough,S. 9/2/0
- M = McDermott,B. 45/11/9
- N = Moseley,G. 13/3/0
- O = Perry,J. 3/2/0
- P = Platnauer,N. 38/12/1
- Q = Roberts,J. 8/4/0
- R = Sanderson,P. 8/3/2
- S = Stevenson,N. 35/8/1
- T = Wheeler,P. 6/1/0
- U = Wimbleton,P. 40/8/11
- V = Walsh,I. 1/1/0
- W = Wood,G. 13/3/0
- X = Morgan,J. 0/0/0

£100,000 package deal accepted for Rees move to Watford. . . More free transfers (including Phil Bater and Stevenson) - Gilligan bought for reported £17,500 - scores regularly . . Bater becomes first player to be sent off in debut for City! Mike Ford wears six different numbered shirts during season. . . . 'Double' achieved with Promotion and Welsh Cup win.

Other Matches

F.A.Cup

	Date	Opposition	Res	Attend.	Goalscorers	1	2	3	4	5	6	7	8	9	10	11	12	14
1st	14 Nov	Peterborough United	1-2	3600	Bartlett	Q	C	P	U	K	D	E	G	H	M	B	R	L

Littlewoods Cup

	Date	Opposition	Res	Attend.	Goalscorers	1	2	3	4	5	6	7	8	9	10	11	12	14
1st/1 Leg †	18 Aug	NEWPORT COUNTY	1-2	3383	Curtis Gilligan	N	O	G	L	A	"	"	R	"	"	K	T	B
1st/2 Leg	25	NEWPORT COUNTY	2-2	3550	Gilligan Sanderson	"	"	"	P	S	"	"	"	"	"	"	"	"

† Venue Switched to Ninian Park

Welsh Cup

	Date	Opposition	Res	Attend.	Goalscorers	1	2	3	4	5	6	7	8	9	10	11	12	14
3rd ††	18 Nov	EBBW VALE	0-0	935		Q	C	P	U	G	"	"	K	"	"	B	R	L
3rd Replay	5 Dec	EBBW VALE	1-0	975	Bartlett	J	"	"	"	"	"	"	"	"	"	"	L	R
4th	9 Jan	PORT TALBOT	3-1	1382	Ford 2 Gilligan	F	"	"	"	S	"	"	G	"	"	"	"	K
5th	24 Feb	MERTHYR TYDFIL	3-1	7213	Gilligan Wimbleton 2	Q	"	"	"	"	"	"	"	"	"	"	V	T
S/Fin.1 Leg	19 Apr	CAERNARFON TOWN	2-1	2750	Wimbleton (pen) Kelly	W	"	"	"	"	"	"	"	"	K	B	M	"
S/Fin.2 Leg	27	Caernarfon Town	1-0	3000	McDermott (pen)	"	"	"	"	"	"	"	M	"	"	"	T	L
Final	17 May	Wrexham	2-0	5645	Curtis Gilligan	"	"	"	G	"	"	"	"	"	"	"	L	T

†† Venue switched to Ninian Park.

Freight-Rover Trophy

	Date	Opposition	Res	Attend.	Goalscorers	1	2	3	4	5	6	7	8	9	10	11	12	14
Prelim.	13 Oct	WREXHAM	3-2	1102	Wheeler McDermott Gilligan	N	"	"	I	K	L	T	"	"	M	G	B	R
Prelim.	24 Nov	Walsall	1-3	2420	Gilligan	J	"	"	U	K	D	E	G	"	B	R	L	T
1st	20 Jan	Notts.County	0-2	2704		Q	"	K	"	"	"	"	"	"	M	B	R	"

Friendlies

	Date	Opposition	Res	Attend.	Goalscorers
‡	28 Jul	GILLINGHAM	2-1	–	Gummer (pen) Boyle
	1 Aug	Kings Lynn	2-0	500	Sanderson Bartlett
	3	Great Yarmouth	3-1	400	Boyle Gilligan Wheeler
	4	Lowestoft	1-0	350	Curtis
	6	Watton	7-1	250	Kelly Gummer McDermott Sanderson Vaughan Gilligan 2
	8	Wisbech Town	1-2	600	McDermott

‡ Played behind closed doors.

(Top) Gilligan,Ford,Wheeler,Kelly. (Middle) Mardenborough,Stevenson,Moseley,Roberts,Curtis Platnauer, Bater. (Bottom) Abraham, Gummer, Wimbleton, Boyle, McDermott, Bartlett, Perry.

1988-89
Football League – Division 3

Manager: Frank Burrows
P:46 W:14 D:15 L:17 44-56 Pts:57 Pos:16th

2628	Date	Opposition	Res	Attend.	Goalscorers	1	2	3	4	5	6	7	8	9	10	11	12	14
1.	27 Aug	FULHAM	1-2	6024	Walsh	W	C	O	*L	R	D	E	T	H	M	J	B	Q
2.	3 Sep	Bolton Wanderers	0-4	4831		"	*Q	"	V	"	"	"	"	"	I	"	S	U
3.	10	HUDDERSFIELD TOWN	3-0	3891	Stevenson Walsh 2	"	"	"	"	"	"	L	"	"	"	L	C	"
4.	17	Port Vale	1-6	4280	Gilligan	"	"	"	"	"	"	E	M	"	"	"	U	C
5.	23	Southend United	0-0	3199		"	"	"	"	"	"	L	E	"	C	"	B	M
6.	1 Oct	BRISTOL ROVERS	2-2	5038	Gilligan Bartlett	"	C	"	"	"	"	"	B	"	M	"	U	a
7.	8	READING	1-2	4057	Curtis	"	"	N	*N	"	"	E	"	"	"	L	F	"
8.	15	Chester City	0-0	2796		"	"	"	A	"	"	U	"	"	*K	"	N	A
9.	22	Mansfield Town	2-2	3566	Ketteridge McDermott	"	"	"	Q	"	"	M	"	"	"	"	C	M
10.	29	Blackpool	0-1	3843		"	O	"	J	"	A	V	"	"	"	"	"	B
11.	1 Nov	BURY	3-0	2411	Gilligan Bartlett Ketteridge	"	Q	O	V	"	"	E	K	"	J	"	"	L
12.	5	GILLINGHAM	1-0	3658	Bartlett	"	"	"	"	"	"	"	B	"	K	J	"	U
13.	12	NORTHAMPTON TOWN	1-0	3280	Bartlett	"	"	"	"	A	D	"	"	"	"	L	"	"
14.	25	BRENTFORD	1-0	3405	Gilligan	"	"	"	"	"	"	O	"	"	*S	"	"	U
15.	3 Dec	Preston North End	3-3	4926	Gilligan Bartlett 2	"	"	"	"	"	"	"	"	"	"	"	"	"
16.	17	Bristol City	0-2	7493		"	"	"	"	"	"	"	"	"	I	"	"	"
17.	26	SWANSEA CITY	2-2	10675	Gilligan 2	"	"	R	"	"	"	"	"	"	"	"	a	J
18.	30	WIGAN ATHLETIC	2-2	4621	Bartlett Curtis	"	"	"	"	"	"	"	"	"	J	"	Z	U
19.	2 Jan	Aldershot	1-0	2768	Curtis	"	"	"	"	"	"	"	J	"	B	"	U	S
20.	10	Wolverhampton W.	0-2	14870		"	"	"	"	"	"	"	B	"	J	"	C	U
21.	14	BOLTON WANDERERS	1-0	4212	Bartlett	"	"	"	"	"	C	"	"	"	"	"	U	D
22.	21	Huddersfield Town	0-1	4869		"	"	"	"	"	R	O	"	"	"	"	D	U
23.	28	PORT VALE	3-0	4507	Gilligan 2 Bartlett	"	"	C	"	D	"	"	"	"	"	"	D	N
24.	4 Feb	Bristol Rovers	0-2	5813	Gilligan	"	"	"	"	"	"	"	"	"	"	"	"	"
25.	11	SHEFFIELD UNITED	0-0	5772		"	"	O	"	"	C	"	"	"	"	"	"	a
26.	18	Reading	1-3	4359	Walsh	"	"	"	"	"	A	E	C	"	U	"	J	T
27.	28	Notts.County	0-2	4266		"	"	"	"	"	"	"	"	"	"	"	"	"
28.	4 Mar	MANSFIELD TOWN	0-0	3217		"	"	"	"	"	"	"	J	"	J	"	C	N
29.	11	Gillingham	2-1	2927	Boyle Platnauer	"	"	"	"	"	R	"	N	"	"	"	J	L
30.	18	Fulham	0-2	4261		"	"	"	"	"	"	"	C	"	T	L	T	Y*
31.	21	Chesterfield	0-4	2888		"	"	"	"	"	"	"	"	"	"	"	"	G
32.	25	ALDERSHOT	3-2	3251	Gilligan (pen) Wheeler Curtis	"	"	"	"	"	"	"	"	"	"	"	U	"
33.	27	Swansea City	1-1	9201	Gilligan	"	"	"	"	"	"	"	"	"	T	"	"	"
34.	1 Apr	BRISTOL CITY	1-1	6152	Platnauer	"	"	"	N	"	"	*G	"	"	U	"	E	I
35.	4	WOLVERHAMPTON W.	1-1	7219	Platnauer	"	"	"	V	"	"	E	N	"	"	"	"	"
36.	7	Wigan Athletic	0-1	2083		"	"	"	"	A	"	"	C	"	"	"	U	"
37.	11	Sheffield United	1-0	11618	Abraham	"	"	"	N	"	"	"	"	"	"	"	E	F
38.	15	Bury	0-1	2124		"	C	"	"	"	"	E	V	"	"	"	G	"
39.	18	NOTTS.COUNTY	0-1	3079		"	"	"	"	"	"	"	"	"	"	"	"	"
40.	22	SOUTHEND UNITED	2-0	3268	Abraham Gilligan	"	"	"	"	"	"	"	"	"	G	*F	J	T
41.	29	Northampton Town	0-3	3194		"	O	"	"	"	C	"	"	"	"	J	F	R
42.	1 May	CHESTERFIELD	0-0	3244		"	"	"	"	"	R	"	C	"	"	"	I	U
43.	5	PRESTON NORTH END	0-0	3196		"	"	"	"	"	D	"	"	"	"	F	"	"
44.	9	CHESTER CITY	2-0	3002	Boyle Gilligan	"	C	"	"	"	"	"	"	"	I	"	U	V
45.	13	Brentford	1-1	4865	Gummer	P	S	"	V	"	"	U	"	"	I	L	N	c
46.	16	BLACKPOOL	0-0	3246		W	Q	"	G	"	"	E	C	"	"	L	"	F

Players:

A = Abraham,G. 31/10/2
B = Bartlett,K. 18/14/13
C = Bater,P. 27/7/0
D = Boyle,T. 34/15/3
E = Curtis,A. 34/14/5
F = Fry,C. 5/2/0
G = Gibbins,R. 9/0/0
H = Gilligan,J. 46/17/22
I = Gummer,J. 9/6/1
J = Kelly,M. 24/12/1
K = Ketteridge,S. 6/1/2
L = Lynex,S. 34/11/1
M = McDermott,B. 4/5/1
N = Morgan,J. 13/1/0
O = Platnauer,N. 39/13/3
P = Roberts,J. 1/0/0
Q = Rodgerson,I. 39/13/0
R = Stevenson,N. 31/10/1
S = Tupling,S. 3/1/1
T = Walsh,I. 4/1/4
U = Wheeler,P. 15/1/2
V = Wimbleton,P. 35/15/2
W = Wood,G. 45/17/0
X = Haig,R. 0/0/0
Y = Holmes,M. 0/0/0
Z = Lewis,A. 0/0/0
a = Perry,J. 0/1/0
b = Wile,J. 0/0/0
c = Roberts,Jason 0/0/0

Record £150,000 received for Ford. . £35,000 paid for Hereford's Ian Rodgerson & £7,000 for Newport's Steve Tupling . . . Controversial Ron Jones - managing director/secretary- joins Portsmouth . . . After 11 years, Return to Europe - Gilligan scores hat-trick v. Derry City . . . Financial problems mount - Bartlett sold - Club put up for sale by Chairman Clemo.

Other Matches

F.A.Cup

	Date	Opposition	Res	Attend.	Goalscorers	1	2	3	4	5	6	7	8	9	10	11	12	14
1st	19 Nov	HEREFORD UNITED	3–0	4341	Bartlett Tupling Gilligan	W	Q	O	V	A	D	E	B	H	S	L	C	U
2nd	11 Dec	Enfield	4–1	3604	Wimbleton(pen) Lynex Gilligan	"	"	"	"	"	"	"	"	"	"	"	"	"
3rd	7 Jan	HULL CITY	1–2	7128	Gilligan	"	"	R	"	"	"	"	"	"	"	"	U	S

Littlewoods Cup

	Date	Opposition	Res	Attend.	Goalscorers	1	2	3	4	5	6	7	8	9	10	11	12	14
1st/1 Leg	30 Aug	SWANSEA CITY	0–1	6241		"	"	O	I	R	"	"	"	"	M	J	T	L
2nd/2 Leg	20 Sep	Swansea City	2–0	6987	Wheeler Boyle	"	"	"	V	"	"	L	E	"	I	"	U	C
2nd/1 Leg	28	Q.P.Rangers	0–3	6078		"	"	"	"	"	"	"	"	"	C	"	"	N
2nd/2 Leg	11 Oct	Q.P.RANGERS	1–4	2629	Curtis	"	a	A	N	"	"	E	B	"	U	F	Z	b

Welsh Cup

	Date	Opposition	Res	Attend.	Goalscorers	1	2	3	4	5	6	7	8	9	10	11	12	14
3rd	15 Nov	BATH CITY	3–0	1517	Bartlett 2 Wimbleton	"	Q	O	V	A	"	"	"	"	K	J	C	U
4th	17 Jan	WORCESTER CITY	1–0	1522	Kelly	"	"	C	"	"	R	F	"	"	J	L	"	D
5th	8 Feb	Kidderminster Harriers	1–3	3012	Bartlett	"	"	"	"	"	D	M	O	"	"	"	"	E

European Cup Winners Cup

	Date	Opposition	Res	Attend.	Goalscorers	1	2	3	4	5	6	7	8	9	10	11	12	14
1st/1 Leg	7 Sep	Derry City	0–0	10500		"	C	O	"	"	R	D	E	T	"	J	M	B
1st/2 Leg	5 Oct	DERRY CITY	4–0	6993	McDermott Gilligan 3	"	"	"	"	"	"	"	B	"	M	"	a	N
2nd/1 Leg	26	AARHUS	1–2	6156	Gilligan	"	O	C	"	"	"	M	"	"	J	L	E	Q
2nd/2 Leg	9 Nov	Aarhus	0–4	3700		"	O	O	"	A	"	E	"	"	"	M	L	U

Sherpa Van (formerly Freight Rover) Trophy

	Date	Opposition	Res	Attend.	Goalscorers	1	2	3	4	5	6	7	8	9	10	11	12	14
Prelim.	6 Dec	SWANSEA CITY	2–0	2986	Curtis Gilligan	"	"	"	"	"	"	"	"	"	I	L	C	U
Prelim.	20	Torquay United	1–3	1187	Wimbleton (pen)	"	"	"	"	"	"	"	"	"	"	"	"	J
1st	24 Jan	Bristol Rovers	1–2	4029	Wimbleton	"	"	R	"	"	C	"	"	"	J	"	D	N

Friendlies

	Date	Opposition	Res	Attend.	Goalscorers
	3 Aug	Gloucester City	0–2	700	
	16	Weymouth	3–0	500	Bartlett 2 Wheeler
†	17	WEST HAM UNITED	3–4	4018	Walsh Kelly Curtis
	20	SWINDON TOWN	1–2	1055	Walsh

† Graham Moseley Testimonial.

● Our First Team Squad 1988-89 with the Welsh Cup – BACK (from left): Alan Curtis, Jimmy Gilligan, Steve Tupling, John Roberts, Nigel Stevenson, George Wood, Paul Wheeler, Ian Walsh, Phil Bater. FRONT (from left): Ian Rodgerson, Brian McDermott, Paul Wimbleton, Nicky Platnauer, Terry Boyle (Capt.), Kevin Bartlett, Steve Lynex, Jason Gummer, Mark Kelly.

1989-90
Football League – Division 3.
Manager: Frank Burrows (Len Ashurst from Sept.1989)
P:46 **W:**12 **D:**14 **L:**20 **51-70 Pts:**50 **Pos:**21st (Rel.)

2674	Date	Opposition	Res	Attend.	Goalscorers	1	2	3	4	5	6	7	8	9	10	11	12	14
1.	19 Aug	BOLTON WANDERERS	0-2	4376		Z	U	Q	H	A	S	E	R	I	M	*T	a	G
2.	26	Tranmere Rovers	0-3	5628		"	"	"	"	"	"	"	"	"	"	"	"	"
3.	2 Sep	BRENTFORD	2-2	3499	Gilligan Fry	"	"	*F	Q	"	"	"	"	"	"	"	f	"
4.	9	Mansfield Town	0-1	2766		"	"	"	"	"	"	"	"	"	"	*P	W	"
5.	16	BRISTOL CITY	0-3	5970		"	"	"	"	"	"	"	"	"	"	*W	P	"
6.	23	Wigan Athletic	1-1	2345	Lynex	"	"	"	"	"	"	"	"	"	"	"	"	"
7.	26	NORTHAMPTON TOWN	2-3	2801	Pike Lynex	"	"	"	"	"	"	"	"	"	"	T	W	"
8.	30	Rotherham United	0-4	4998		"	"	"	"	"	H	"	*N	W	"	"	S	"
9.	7 Oct	Huddersfield Town	3-2	5835	Griffith Pike 2(1 pen)	*Y	"	"	*B	"	S	R	*J	N	"	"	Q	"
10.	13	CHESTER CITY	1-1	3675	Barnard	*L	*O	"	"	"	"	"	"	Q	"	G	N	a
11.	17	BRISTOL ROVERS	1-1	6372		"	U	"	"	"	"	Q	"	N	"	T	R	O
12.	21	Blackpool	0-1	3502		"	"	"	"	"	H	"	"	"	"	R	"	f
13.	28	LEYTON ORIENT	1-1	2370	Griffith	"	"	"	"	"	"	R	"	"	"	T	O	V
14.	31	Birmingham City	1-1	7468	Morgan	Y	"	"	"	"	"	"	"	"	"	"	"	G
15.	3 Nov	BURY	3-1	3437	Pike 2 Barnard	L	"	"	"	"	"	"	"	T	"	*D	c	"
16.	11	Fulham	5-2	4030	Pike 2 Griffith 2 Morgan	"	"	"	"	"	"	"	"	"	"	"	G	V
17.	25	PRESTON NORTH END	3-0	3270	Rodgerson Pike Griffith	"	"	"	"	"	"	"	"	"	"	"	"	"
18.	2 Dec	Crewe Alexandra	1-1	3373	Morgan	"	"	"	"	"	"	"	"	"	"	"	"	Q
19.	16	NOTTS. COUNTY	1-3	3610	Pike	Z	"	"	"	"	"	Q	"	"	"	"	R	V
20.	26	Swansea City	1-0	12244	Barnard	L	"	"	"	S	"	R	"	"	"	"	V	K
21.	30	Walsall	2-0	4256	Griffith Pike	"	"	"	"	"	"	"	"	"	O	Q	"	M
22.	13 Jan	TRANMERE ROVERS	0-0	4300		"	"	"	"	A	"	"	"	T	"	"	"	"
23.	20	Bolton Wanderers	1-3	7017	Griffith	"	"	"	"	"	"	"	"	"	S	M	g	K
24.	3 Feb	WIGAN ATHLETIC	1-1	3218	Rodgerson	"	"	"	"	R	"	D	"	"	"	"	"	"
25.	10	Bristol City	0-1	11982		"	"	"	"	"	"	"	"	"	"	"	O	G
26.	17	CREWE ALEXANDRA	0-0	2086		"	"	"	"	"	"	R	"	"	"	"	Q	D
27.	21	Brentford	1-0	5174	Abraham	"	"	"	"	"	"	Q	"	"	D	"	S	G
28.	24	Preston North End	0-4	5716		"	"	"	*X	"	"	S	"	"	Q	"	D	"
29.	2 Mar	SHREWSBURY TOWN	0-1	2751		"	"	"	B	"	"	"	"	"	M	Q	G	D
30.	6	ROTHERHAM UNITED	2-0	2570	Pike Barnard	"	"	"	"	"	"	"	"	"	S	D	A	G
31.	10	Northampton Town	1-1	2574	Pike	"	"	"	"	"	"	"	"	"	"	"	"	Q
32.	13	Shrewsbury Town	0-0	2318		"	"	"	"	"	"	R	"	"	S	*K	X	O
33.	17	HUDDERSFIELD TOWN	1-5	2568	Pike	"	"	"	"	"	"	"	"	"	"	M	G	"
34.	20	Chester City	0-1	1866		"	"	*C	B	"	"	M	"	"	"	D	a	"
35.	24	Bristol Rovers	1-2	4631	Rodgerson	"	"	"	"	"	"	R	"	"	"	"	"	V
36.	27	MANSFIELD TOWN	1-0	2280	Barnard	"	"	F	"	M	"	Q	"	"	"	"	A	G
37.	31	BLACKPOOL	2-2	2850	Gibbins Pike	"	"	"	"	"	"	"	"	"	"	"	"	C
38.	7 Apr	Leyton Orient	1-3	3411	Pike	"	"	"	"	A	"	M	"	"	A	*V	R	D
39.	10	BIRMINGHAM CITY	0-1	3322		"	"	"	"	"	"	"	"	"	"	D	O	C
40.	14	Reading	1-0	3198	Griffith	"	"	"	R	"	"	"	"	"	"	"	Q	G
41.	16	SWANSEA CITY	0-2	8350		"	"	"	"	Q	"	"	"	"	"	G	C	V
42.	21	Notts. County	1-2	5533	Pike (pen)	"	"	"	B	"	"	"	"	"	"	R	G	O
43.	21	WALSALL	3-1	2509	Barnard Pike Griffith	"	"	"	"	D	"	"	"	"	"	Q	"	C
44.	28	FULHAM	3-3	3932	Daniel Barnard Rodgerson	"	"	"	"	"	"	"	"	"	"	G	O	"
45.	1 May	READING	3-2	3375	Barnard Pike(Pen) Griffith	"	"	"	"	C	"	"	"	"	"	D	V	O
46.	5	Bury	0-2	4224		"	"	"	"	D	"	"	"	"	"	C	R	"

Players:

A = Abraham,G. 34/11/4
B = Barnard,L. 35/12/10
C = Blake,N. 3/0/0
D = Chandler,J. 21/7/0
E = Curtis,A. 8/2/0
F = Daniel,R. 43/12/1
G = Fry,C. 3/2/1
H = Gibbins,R. 38/12/1
I = Gilligan,J. 7/2/1
J = Griffith,C. 38/10/12
K = Haig,R. 1/1/0
L = Hansbury,R. 35/7/0
M = Kelly,M. 41/11/2
N = Kevan,D. 6/1/0
O = Lewis,A. 3/1/0
P = Love,I. 1/0/0
Q = Lynex,S. 22/4/3
R = Morgan,J. 29/10/3
S = Perry,J. 36/9/0
T = Pike,C. 41/11/23
U = Rodgerson,I. 45/14/6
V = Scott,M. 1/4/3
W = Sendall,R. 3/0/0
X = Thompson,C. 1/0/0
Y = Ward,G. 2/2/0
Z = Wood,G. 9/5/0
a = Gummer,J. 0/0/0
b = Miethig,M. 0/1/0
c = Powell,C. 0/0/0
d = Roberts,Jason 0/0/0
e = Searle,D. 0/1/0
f = Tupling,S. 0/0/0
g = Youds,E. 0/1/0

Wimbleton, Boyle and Platnauer sold - Ray Daniel bought for £40,000 - 1 victory in first 14 games - worst ever start to season ... Burrows leaves for Portsmouth - Len Ashurst appointed new manager - again ... Burglars get record £50,000 gate from cup-tie - later recovered ... 5-1 at Fulham (best away win for 20 years) - late surge - but relegated.

Other Matches

F.A.Cup

	Date	Opposition	Res	Attend.	Goalscorers	1	2	3	4	5	6	7	8	9	10	11	12	14
1st	18 Nov	HALESOWEN TOWN	1-0	3972	Pike (pen)	Z	U	F	B	A	H	R	J	T	M	D	G	V
2nd	9 Dec	GLOUCESTER CITY	2-2	4531	Scott 2	"	"	"	"	"	"	"	"	V	"	"	Q	K
2nd Replay	12	Gloucester City	1-0	3877	Scott	"	"	"	"	"	"	"	V	T	"	"	"	"
3rd	6 Jan	Q.P.RANGERS	0-0	13834		L	"	"	"	"	"	"	J	"	S	Q	g	M
3rd Replay	10	Q.P.Rangers	0-2	12226		"	"	"	"	"	"	"	"	"	"	M	Q	g

Littlewoods Cup

	Date	Opposition	Res	Attend.	Goalscorers	1	2	3	4	5	6	7	8	9	10	11	12	14
1st/1 Leg	22 Aug	PLYMOUTH ARGYLE	0-3	2620		Z	"	Q	H	"	S	E	R	I	M	T	a	G
1st/2 Leg	29	Plymouth Argyle	2-0	5728	Pike Lynex	"	"	F	Q	"	"	"	"	"	"	"	"	"

Welsh Cup

	Date	Opposition	Res	Attend.	Goalscorers	1	2	3	4	5	6	7	8	9	10	11	12	14
3rd	25 Oct	NEWPORT A.F.C.	1-0	2929	Abraham	L	"	F	B	"	H	G	J	N	"	R	O	V
4th	16 Jan	PORT TALBOT ATH.	4-1	1128	Rodgerson Pike 2 Barnard	"	"	"	"	g	"	D	"	T	S	M	Q	A
5th	6 Feb	ABERYSTWYTH TOWN	2-0	1319	Rodgerson Kelly	"	"	"	"	A	"	"	"	"	"	"	"	R
S/Fin.1 Leg	2 Apr	HEREFORD UNITED	0-3	2393		"	"	"	"	M	"	G	"	"	"	D	A	C
S/Fin.2 Leg	4	Hereford United	3-1	2955	Pike Abraham Griffith	"	"	"	"	A	"	M	"	"	"	V	R	"

Leyland-Daf (Formerly Sherpa Van) Trophy

	Date	Opposition	Res	Attend.	Goalscorers	1	2	3	4	5	6	7	8	9	10	11	12	14
Prelim.	7 Nov	WALSALL	3-5	1487	Griffith Barnard Abraham	Z	"	"	"	"	"	R	"	"	M	D	c	G
Prelim.	19 Dec	Shrewsbury Town	0-4	1058		"	"	e	"	S	O	"	b	V	K	Q	d	C

Friendlies

	Date	Opposition	Res	Attend.	Goalscorers
	26 Jul	Q.P.RANGERS	0-1	1473	
	31	Hamilton Academical	0-0	550	
	2 Aug	Clydebank	1-1	400	Pike
	5	Raith Rovers	2-3	600	Curtis,J. Morgan
	12	BOTAFOGO	0-3	2603	

● **BACK** (from left) – Jimmy Goodfellow, Richard Haig, Gareth Abraham, Morrys Scott, George Wood, Pat O'Hagan, Chris Pike, Roger Gibbins, Jeff Chandler, Leigh Barnard. **FRONT** (from left) – Jon Morgan, Chris Fry, Steve Lynex, Ray Daniel, Tony Clemo, Ian Rodgerson, Len Ashurst, Cohen Griffith, Mark Kelly, Damon Searle, Jason Perry.

1990-91

Football League – Division 4.

Manager: Len Ashurst **P:**46 **W:**18 **D:**15 **L:**16 **43-54** **Pts:**60 **Pos:**13th

2720	Date	Opposition	Res	Attend.	Goalscorers	1	2	3	4	5	6	7	8	9	10	11	12	14
1.	25 Aug	SCARBOROUGH	0-0	3819		J	T	E	C	A	R	*M	I	H	S	*K	D	Z
2.	1 Sep	Hartlepool United	2-0	2800	Griffith Pike	"	"	"	"	"	"	"	"	"	"	"	"	"
3.	8	TORQUAY UNITED	3-3	3656	Griffith Pike 2	"	"	"	"	D	"	"	"	"	"	"	Z	N
4.	15	Lincoln City	0-0	3152		"	"	"	"	"	"	"	"	"	"	"	O	"
5.	18	Aldershot	0-0	2310		"	"	"	"	"	"	"	"	"	*O	"	N	Q
6.	22	STOCKPORT COUNTY	3-3	3608	Griffith Pike Gibbins	"	"	"	"	"	"	O	"	"	S	"	M	N
7.	29	Scunthorpe United	2-0	2573	Pike 2	"	"	"	"	O	"	M	"	"	"	"	D	"
8.	2 Oct	ROCHDALE	0-1	3391		"	"	"	"	"	"	"	"	"	"	"	"	"
9.	5	WREXHAM	1-0	3452	Pike	"	"	"	"	"	"	"	"	"	"	"	"	"
10.	13	York City	2-1	2596	Blake 2	"	"	"	"	N	"	"	"	"	D	"	G	V*
11.	20	Hereford United	1-1	5782	Jones	"	"	"	"	"	"	"	"	"	"	"	"	S
12.	23	DONCASTER UNITED	0-2	3891		"	"	"	"	"	"	"	"	"	"	"	"	G
13.	27	PETERBOROUGH UTD.	1-1	2940	Pike	"	"	"	"	"	"	"	"	D	S	*V	"	Q
14.	3 Nov	Maidstone United	0-3	2010		"	O	V	"	O	"	"	"	H	"	"	D	a*
15.	10	CHESTERFIELD	2-1	2019	Gibbins Pike	"	N	"	"	"	"	"	"	"	"	K	"	W
16.	24	Gillingham	0-4	3793		"	"	"	Q	*B	"	"	"	T	*W	"	G	a
17.	1 Dec	Burnley	0-2	6353		"	"	"	*F	O	"	"	"	H	S	"	Q	W
18.	15	WALSALL	0-2	2017		"	G	"	D	"	"	*X	F	"	"	"	N	Q
19.	21	Northampton Town	0-0	3303		"	D	"	F	"	"	"	I	"	"	"	"	G
20.	26	CARLISLE UNITED	3-1	2281	Pike Taylor 2	"	G	"	D	"	F	"	"	"	"	"	"	M
21.	29	HALIFAX TOWN	1-0	2903	Taylor	"	"	"	"	"	"	"	"	"	"	"	"	"
22.	1 Jan	Darlington	1-4	3151	Griffith	"	M	"	"	"	R	"	"	"	"	"	"	Q
23.	12	HARTLEPOOL UNITED	1-0	2619	Griffith	"	"	"	"	"	"	"	"	"	G	"	"	"
24.	26	LINCOLN CITY	0-1	2513		"	O	"	"	R	M	*U	"	"	S	N	G	K
25.	1 Feb	ALDERSHOT	1-3	1692	Gibbins	"	"	"	"	"	C	"	"	"	G	"	G	C
26.	15	GILLINGHAM	2-0	2170	Gibbins Pike (pen)	"	"	"	"	"	"	"	"	"	G	"	S	Q
27.	19	Scarborough	2-1	1192	Griffith 2	"	"	"	"	"	"	G	"	"	S	K	G	N
28.	23	Chesterfield	0-0	3065		"	"	"	"	"	"	"	"	"	"	"	a	"
29.	26	Stockport County	1-1	3376	Blake	"	"	"	"	"	"	"	"	"	"	"	W	"
30.	1 Mar	BURNLEY	3-0	3591	Heard Pike(pen) Griffith	"	"	"	"	"	"	"	"	"	"	"	N	a
31.	9	Walsall	0-0	3950		"	"	"	"	"	"	"	"	"	"	"	"	"
32.	12	Rochdale	0-0	1569		"	"	"	"	"	"	"	"	"	"	"	"	"
33.	16	SCUNTHORPE UNITED	1-0	2873	Pike (pen)	"	"	"	"	"	"	"	"	"	"	"	*Y	N
34.	19	YORK CITY	2-1	2620	Heard Barnard	"	"	"	"	"	"	"	"	"	"	"	"	"
35.	22	Wrexham	0-1	1787		"	"	"	"	"	"	*Y	"	"	"	"	G	"
36.	30	Carlisle United	2-3	2264	Matthews Blake	"	"	"	"	"	F	*L	"	"	"	"	"	"
37.	1 Apr	NORTHAMPTON TOWN	1-0	4805	o.g. (Campbell)	"	"	"	"	"	"	"	"	"	*P	"	"	"
38.	6	Halifax Town	2-1	1364	Pike Heard	"	"	"	"	"	"	"	"	"	"	"	"	"
39.	10	Torquay United	1-2	3341	Gibbins	"	"	"	F	"	P	"	"	"	S	"	"	C
40.	13	DARLINGTON	0-1	4544		"	"	"	"	N	"	"	"	"	"	"	"	G
41.	17	Blackpool	0-3	4813		"	"	"	"	"	R	"	D	"	"	"	"	"
42.	20	HEREFORD UNITED	0-2	2845		"	"	"	"	R	"	"	I	"	"	"	I	N
43.	27	Doncaster Rovers	1-1	2227	Heath	"	"	"	"	"	N	"	"	"	"	"	N	G D
44.	2 May	BLACKPOOL	1-1	1793	Griffith	"	"	"	"	"	"	"	"	"	"	"	D	a
45.	4	Peterborough Utd.	0-3	6642		"	"	"	"	"	"	"	"	G	"	"	"	c
46.	11	MAIDSTONE UNITED	0-0	2011		"	B	"	M	"	"	"	"	"	"	"	*b	"

Players:

A = Abraham,G. — 2/1/0
B = Baddeley,L. — 2/0/0
C = Barnard,L. — 26/8/1
D = Blake,N. — 33/5/4
E = Daniel,R. — 13/4/0
F = DeMange,K. — 15/0/0
G = Fry,C. — 14/0/0
H = Gibbins,R — 43/9/5
I = Griffith,C. — 43/9/15
J = Hansbury,R. — 46/9/0
K = Heard,P. — 38/7/3
L = Heath,P. — 11/0/1
M = Jones,M. — 19/8/1
N = Lewis,A. — 16/5/0
O = Matthews,N. — 36/7/1
P = McDonald,K. — 8/0/0
Q = Morgan,J. — 1/0/0
R = Perry,J. — 43/9/0
S = Pike,C. — 37/6/16
T = Rodgerson,I. — 14/6/0
U = Russell,K. — 3/0/0
V = Searle,D. — 34/5/0
W = Stephens,L. — 1/1/0
X = Taylor,M. — 6/0/3
Y = Toshack,C. — 1/0/0
Z = Chandler,J. — 0/0/0
a = Summers,C. — 0/0/1
b = Unsworth,J. — 0/0/0
c = Ward,G. — 0/0/0

> After reasonable start bad pre-Xmas run... Greatest humiliation - F.A.Cup replay defeat to non-League Hayes - after scoreless home draw - crowd of only 1,844... Further embarrassment with Welsh Cup defeat to Merthyr! A mediocre League season finishes with a mid-table final position....
> Now at such a low ebb - can the Bluebirds start the haul up again?

Other Matches

F.A.Cup

	Date	Opposition	Res	Attend.	Goalscorers
1st	17 Nov	HAYES	0-0	1844	
1st Rep. †	21	Hayes	0-1	4312	

† At Griffin Park, Brentford.

Rumblelows (formerly Littlewoods) Cup

	Date	Opposition	Res	Attend.	Goalscorers
1st/1 Leg	28 Aug	Mansfield Town	1-1	1091	Griffith
1st/2 Leg	4 Sep	MANSFIELD TOWN	3-0	2539	Griffith 2 Pike
2nd/1 Leg	25	PORTSMOUTH	1-1	4224	Griffith
2nd/2 Leg	9 Oct	Portsmouth	1-3	6174	Griffith

Welsh Cup

	Date	Opposition	Res	Attend.	Goalscorers
3rd	6 Nov	MERTHYR TYDFIL	1-4	3204	Pike (pen)

Leyland-Daf Cup

	Date	Opposition	Res	Attend.	Goalscorers
Prelim.	13 Nov	EXETER CITY	0-1	1024	
Prelim.	11 Dec	Hereford United	1-1	2007	Griffith

Friendlies

	Date	Opposition	Res	Attend.	Goalscorers
	8 Aug	Merthyr Tydfil	2-3	800	Griffiths 2
	11	PORTSMOUTH	1-0	1389	Heard
	15	Cardiff Civil Service	8-1	400	Blake Gibbins Chandler 5 Summers

BACK ROW (L to R) Neil MATTHEWS, Alan LEWIS, Gavin WARD, Roger HANSBURY, Gareth ABRAHAM, Chris PIKE, Nathan BLAKE
CENTRE ROW (L to R) Stephen HOOKINGS, Damon SEARLE, Chris FRY, Jason PERRY, Jon MORGAN, Leigh BARNARD, Mark JONES, Pat HEARD
FRONT ROW (L to R) Jeff CHANDLER, Lee STEPHENS, Chris SUMMERS, Roger GIBBINS, Cohen GRIFFITH, Ian RODGERSON, Ray DANIEL (now Portsmouth)

ADVANCED SUBSCRIBERS

Cardiff City A.F.C.
Rick Wright – Financial Controller
Tony Clemo – Chairman
Lynda Clemo – Director
David Henderson – Director
Jason Warren

Marilyn Bendon
Mike Lambert
G.D. Painter
John Treleven
John Harris
Phillip Hart
R. Shaw
Steven Emms
Geoff Allman
Michael Campbell
George Mason – Liverpool
J. Ringrose
Jonathon Hall
Louis Burgess
Michael Parsons
L.A. Zammit
Alan Davies
David Keats – Thornton Heath
Phil Hollow
Martin Simons – Belgium
Jeff McInery – Barry, S.Glam.
L. Bern – Portsmouth
Geoffrey Wright
Richard Wells.
Geoff Barnes – Dinas Powys.
John Martel
Jon Neale MFC
Stephen Gurner – Pontypridd
Derek Hyde
David Tilsley Evans
Jimmy Nelson – Always remembered.
P.H.Whitehead
John Lewis, Pontypridd Bluebird
R.D.Mackenzie
David "Bluebird" Robins
Vivian Lewis
Andy Dawes–Waters
Matthew Gregory
Garry William Price
Kathy Shea
Eric Bennett
Andrew Charles Williams
John Martin Harvey
Mick Maddiver
Rhys Richard Owen Davies
David Hamer
Lyndon Beaumont
John and Sarah Leck
Simon Dunn
Paul Davis
Chris and Fiona Woods
Paul James White
Andrew Richard Mayer
David Hemmings
Clive Harry
Peter Gutmann
Revd. Martyn Perry – London
Mr. Stephen Perry – Pontypool
Neil Chambers
Glyn Edward Robins
Mark Halligey
James (Spike) Robinson
Ivan Paul Golten
The Blues Brothers – Abergavenny
Terry Grandin – Grandin Roofing Co.
John Motson
Derek Wheatcroft
Frederick John Lee
Roger Paul – Abertillery
W.A. Wood (Supporter since 1968)
Duncan Watt
Rob Jex
Toivo Haidson (Supporter forever)
Terry Frost

Jonathon and Paul Hicks
David Helliwell
Philip Lancey
R.L. Gibbs
K. Gibbs
Mike Rossiter
David Jowett
Alan Hindley
Harry Kay
Mal Barton
Brian Tabner
Mr. H.J.Gibbs
David Rogers 'Wishing And Hoping'
Robin Pearson
Roy Wilkinson
Paul A.S. Taylor
David Lumb
Göran Schönhult (Sweden)
Barry Horsman – Pontlottyn Blast
Trevor Abraham
Chris Evans
Tim Evans
Mr. Paul Marks – Dinas Powys
To my son Jason–Robert G. Owen
Richard Stocken
Michael McConkey
Donald Noble – Dunkeld, Perthshire
Gordon R. Davies
Howard John Sargent
Paul Anthony Reed
Peter Baxter
Waldron H. Leard
Ingemar Stromberg
Jan Buitenga
Richard Lane
Arthur H. Atkins
Hartmut Vilmar
T. Bluff
W.D. Phillips
Graham Spackman
Gunnar Talgo
B.H. Standish
Colin Cameron
Q.C.M. Olsthoorn
Lars–Olaf Wendler
John Allen
Ian Westbrook
Malc Hartley
Tony Ambrosen
A.P.J.M. Otten
Christopher Gunning Xmas 1991
Robert Gunning Xmas 1991
Martin Bodle
Colin Callaghan
Steve Barrett
Robert Jones
Mr.A. (Tony) C. Higginson
Robert Yeo
H.G.W. Davies
William Edward Hand
Raymond Weeks
Derek Evans – Troedyrhiw
Michael Sweeney
Gordon Keith Steffan Webb
Alan & Val Shields
Gary & David Redwood
Stuart Ropke
Gregory Nelson
Gerwyn Griffiths
E.G. Botchet
John Morgan Davies
Richard Grigg
H.C. Fellingham
Ian Golden PSB Fanzine
Gerald Davies
Anthony Barcello
Bernard James O'Connell
Neil Hadley – Whitchurch, Cardiff
Norman Best – Cathays Cardiff
Dai Harris – Cathays Cardiff
Richard Hunt
R.S. Gill

David "Griff" Griffiths
Mike Miggiano
Angelo Miggiano
Richard Cole
Peter Wesley Blackmore
Huw Dainton
Simon Shackson
Helena and Clive Watson
Paul Wozencroft
Mr. John James Cross
Barrie & Shirley Jones
David Willicombe 1974 Bluebirds
David Edward Griffiths, Whitchurch
Tony Evans of Pontypridd
Robert Michell
Peter Richard Hughes
Andrew Humphrey Bluebirds 1969
G.J. Merrick
The Rev. Clifford Warren
Mr. Jack Rideout
Geoffrey Edwards 'Hallfryn' Montgomery
Albert Thomas Wells
Richard Griffiths
Bryen Smith
Reginald George Smith
Mr. M. Singleton
Jan Astrup
Dr Åke Wallström – Sweden
David Maurice Done
Clive, Peter & Richard Mann
D.H.& B.S. Skelton – Lancs. Bluebirds
Christer Svensson
Mr. W.J. Malpas
Nigel Harris – Fan since (aged 6) 1968
Howard Hams of Tonyrefail
Ronald Edwards of Hemel Hempstead
Douglas Lamming
A. & J.A. Waterman
Anthony Jarman
Susan Ball
Nicholas McCarthy
Alec and Gareth Withers
Simon Beaven
Bryan Boyd, Amanda Boyd
David Brown, Armitage, Staffs.
Peter and Ben Overton
Craig Dennis Thomas
David Walters and Family
Stephen Cook (Cwmbran)
Ross and Caroline Thomas
Michael Pollard
Christopher and Geraint Bodman
Mr. H.W. Semark
Leon and Craig Withey
C.C.F.C. Jones
Frederick Hake
Chris Howells
Mr. John Darren Higginson
Cyril James
Alan James
Steve Lyell
Robert Stephen Gatheridge
Roger Isaacs
Matthew Elliot Paterson
Ray Bailey
Owen M. Thomas, Abernant, Aberdare
Mark Walby
Mr. Owen John Leach
Tim Murphy
Gareth Williams, Basildon, Essex
Geraint and Kate Pritchard
Gareth D. Saunders
Catherine and Ian Shaw
K.J. Powell
Phil Stead
Roger O'Brien
Richard Mortimer
Timothy Mortimer
Geoff and Sandra Leat
Alan and Jeff Bretos
Siân Best
James Emlyn Davies